# Matters of Perspective

## Versioned Realities in Cold War WMD Intelligence

Copyright © 2022 Charles E Tuten Jr

## All Rights Reserved

No part or element of this work may be reproduced, distributed, used or transmitted in any form or by any means, including photocopying, scanning by any electronic or mechanical method without prior permission from the author–except quotations in reviews and noncommercial forms permitted by copyright law.

### ISBN 978-1-881625-15-5

Information Cutoff March 2022

All statements of fact, opinion, or analysis expressed are those of the author and do not reflect the official positions or views of the U.S. Government. Nothing in the contents should be construed as asserting or implying U.S. Government authentication of information or endorsement of the author's views.

# Contents

| | |
|---|---|
| Puzzled Intelligence | 7 |
| The View from Torgau | 11 |
| Assessing the Soviet WMD Game-Plan | 15 |
| Precepts | 25 |
| Operational Evolutions | 79 |
| Nuclear Interlude | 107 |
| Elusive Chemical Echelons | 141 |
| US Intelligence Fabricates Another Model | 191 |
| Hypothesis X | 211 |
| The Case of the Hidden Nukes | 228 |
| Postmortem | 278 |
| Appendix | 282 |
| Illustrations | 286 |
| Endnotes | 290 |
| Index | 350 |

*In memoriam*

Albert Z. Conner Jr.

Martin T. Pinkstaff

uncommon intelligence realists

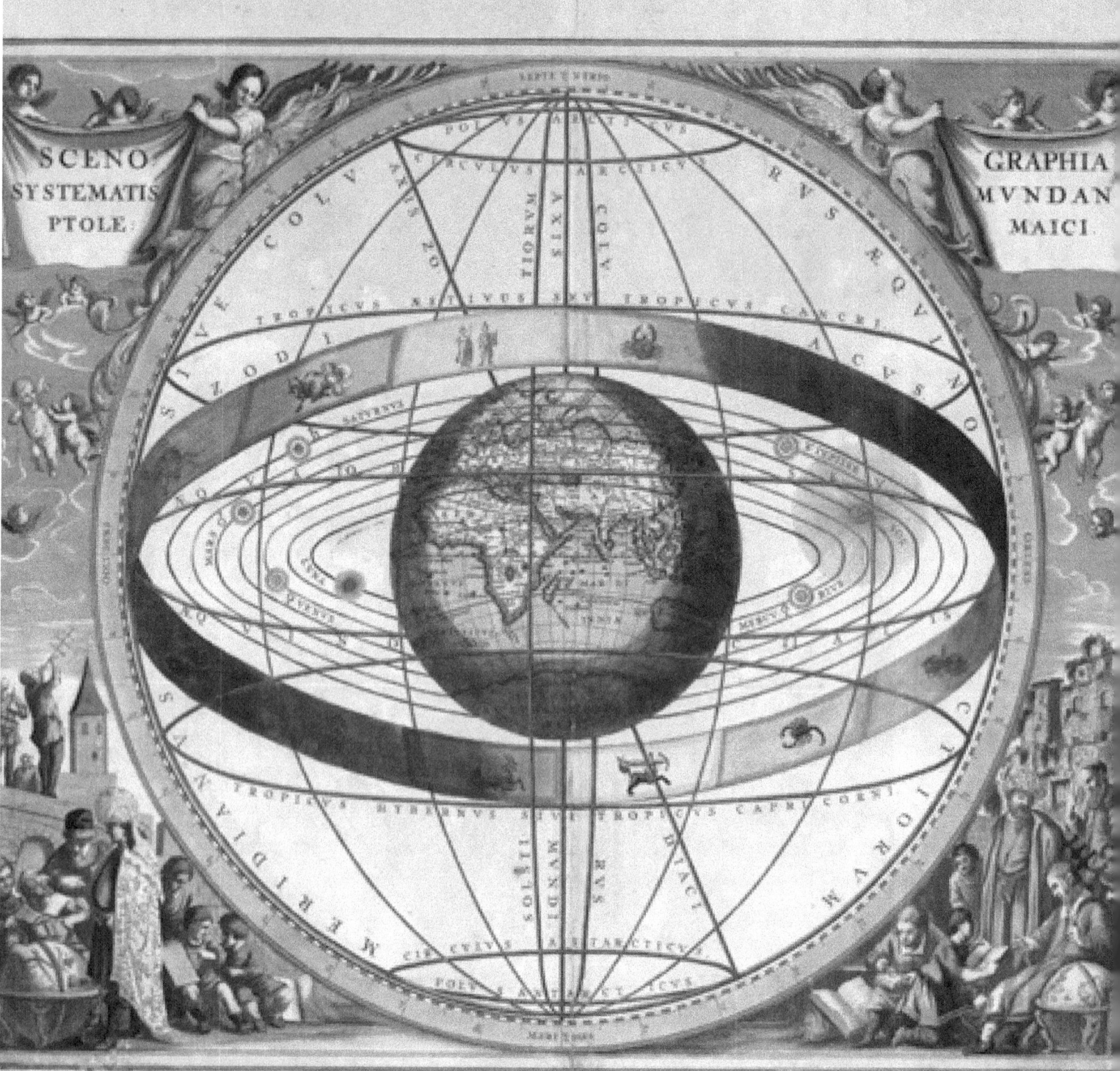

# Puzzled Intelligence

We are all intelligence agents. Everyone is trying to make sense of their environment and the rush of events. While philosophers and psychologists engage in esoteric discourses on the nature of human cognition other callings must tackle more immediate, practical, issues. National security intelligence is only one subset of an array of human enquiry disciplines that have, as a professional objective, the determination of a particular reality. Historians, reporters, scientists, doctors, and detectives are among the discernment vocations that seek out truths in their respectively distinctive fields. Intell functions, as do others in their endeavors, within the constraints and peculiarities of human reasoning which can often act as barriers to achieving an accurate perspective essential to arriving at valid conclusions. Despite variegated substantive coverage the basic problem-solving methodologies used by the diverse professions are surprisingly comparable.

In recent years US intelligence 'insider' accounts have traversed the mandated gauntlet for agency prepublication review. These texts have dealt almost exclusively with paramilitary operations and clandestine action. Despite the enduring popularity of spy novels mole handling is only one of the tools used by the information-collecting colossus that is national intelligence. Covert work is supplemented or, more often, substituted by other human and technical sources. But the penultimate, indeed the only, purpose of all the tools is to deliver information to a relatively small corps of people, the analysts, who must accomplish the assembly work. If their efforts are misdirected or incomplete, successes in the collection channels—information so diligently gathered, often at considerable financial (and sometimes human) cost—might as well be stamped 'return to sender' as made valueless. Some internal- and public-initiated studies have attempted to define and explain the intelligence analytic process. But these have been largely theoretical. Only limited aspects of intelligence analysis in action have appeared in a few publications as well as in commissioned retrospectives on consequential failures such as 9/11 and Iraqi WMD.

Central to this tome is that analytic process; substantially an intelligence study that provides alternative solutions to some key Cold War problems. A nuts-and-bolts approach, in more detail than the general reader may be accustomed, is essential to grasp the complexity and uncertainties of the intelligence environment. There is also an operative assumption in what follows that anyone who would actually peruse the details is capable of thinking through evidence and issues with a minimum of hand-holding. Certain issues during, and since, the Cold War are of such international significance that the repercussions of intelligence done badly can be immediate and devastating. Selected Cold War episodes involving WMD intelligence are examined in depth to demonstrate the results of viewing complex relationships from restricted and skewed perspectives.

Intelligence professionals, scholars, and fans have long been aware (at least in principle) of the detrimental effect that is usually dubbed mindset—a constrictive assortment of beliefs that warp conclusions. This term understates what is a more insidious aspect of intelligence perspective, the penchant to construct alternative realities in the form of Official Models. Any particular model purporting to represent reality incorporates one or more hypotheses encompassing evidence and assumptions. Model-building can aid analyses particularly when dealing with opaque, difficult problems with insubstantial evidence. An official model is both broader and more deep-seated than is mindset; an encapsulated, impervious, artificial construct with a designated collection and arrangement of evidence, connected by approved logical paths. The resultant structure may be remote or entirely dissociated from, and take precedence over, operative reality. Even recognition of what constitutes evidence is obstructed. Carefully conceived models can provide solutions even in situations of fragmentary, inconclusive, and conflicting indications. Poorly constructed models become intellectual straightjackets.

Unfortunately official model-building is an affliction not confined to the field of intelligence. Application is endemic to many other perceptual endeavors—including the customers of intelligence—a 'tribute' to the universal trait of human minds to see only what is wished and, conversely, to ignore an inconvenient reality. For a wide range of issues ideological fantasies, economic self-interest, and the supernatural are among the popular substitutes for a coherent, disciplined, comprehensive thinking-through of complex problems. Ironically the rapid growth and diversification of modern media has served to magnify and reinforce a permanently existent strain of stupid-think, the congenital incapacity to identify, discriminate, evaluate, and relate factual material.

Official models originate and persist due to a variety of factors. Failed models of the intelligence variety usually do not result from any dearth of indications. As the intell handbook states, 'seek and ye shall find.' But looking does not necessarily equate to seeing. Accurate conclusions will never be achieved unless there is a relentless search for, and unified consideration of, all aspects of a given problem—concept, evidence, place, and time among other potential affiliations. The validity of proposed solutions revolves about three kinds of indications—evidence included in an argument (rightly or wrongly); evidence deliberately or negligently discarded; and evidence which is not recognized, as, indicative. Actually the third kind can be most devastating to intelligence assessments. All too often the search is terminated when a seemingly viable answer appears rather then exhausting all possibilities. The fundamental intelligence equation, just as in other disciplines, is question = answer; wrong questions = bad answers. Error is inevitable when no questions are raised concerning obvious anomalies. The roots of defective assessment are myopic perception and lethargic conceptualization rather than insubstantial evidence. The intelligence analyst is a juggler involved in a precarious balancing of information and conclusions, a dynamic rather than a static process, requiring constant alertness for nonconformance. There are rarely any final answers.

Contemporary intelligence reform drives have emphasized the attainment of an analytical rigor, with the application of a body of professional methods to reach and validate conclusions. There is, for example, the competing hypotheses methodology. This entails the conjuring of a range of alternate solutions, then weighting of evidence pro and con to pick a winner with a minimum of negatives. Intelligence has even developed an app to formalize this process. But a gaping hole in this method is what might be called Hypothesis X—the unperceived solution. Available information is often so incomplete, ambiguous, and contradictory that a preferred solution can be affirmed despite what should be obvious flaws, because no other suitable answer is apparent. Only the most disciplined and upright (and in some situations, courageous) intelligence analyst is capable of concluding that all the presented scenarios are erroneous, and that the answer must lie elsewhere.

Prevalent insularity in both the intelligence bureaucracies and their analytic cultures hinder the attainment of perspectives that can simultaneously encompass all three kinds of indications and foster the conception of alternate solutions. Organizational boundaries too often impose limits that only the more adventurous dare to transgress. The cubicles of US intelligence community members tend to be occupied by topically restricted minds—'experts'—only too eager to promote their parochial official model. Connoisseur is a more appropriate label for many of these people, defined in *The Devil's Dictionary* by Ambrose Bierce "a specialist who knows everything about something and nothing about anything else." Unfortunately even the connoisseurs' understanding of their narrowly-defined subject can be seriously flawed. Issue expertise is essential to finding viable answers, but only if approached as an integration of all conceivable relationships—with constant alertness for the inconceivable. The meaning of an activity is rarely self-evident, and even immediately available, apparently related evidence, may be insufficient to find a solution. The answer may lie with less obvious, seemingly unrelated, distant indications. Cubicular organizations and mentalities are incapable of accessing these remote correlations and thereby cross-referencing all indications.

A prevailing theme of the Cold War intelligence issues examined herein is the dogged clinging to solutions that, given wider and better informed perspectives, could not possibly work. Frequently a key causative factor inhered with the incremental approach favored by intelligence, i.e., the extension of prior solutions, building on their presumptions without a thorough re-examination of the problem; as if the incumbents tried to understand the intent and substance of a book by reading only the later chapters, with only a cursory if any scan of preceding material, rather than starting at the preface. Years, even decades, elapsed during the Cold War regarding certain issues which amassed and congealed baseless assumptions and dubious evidence in an official model that even the most experienced connoisseur could not fully clarify. Intelligence hierarchies periodically reinforce this lack of criticality. Some analysts are propelled up the ranks by a singular, apparently standout, accomplishment. But their successors all too often find this new official solution, when reconsidered with more recent or neglected evidence, does not hold up—and any revised perspective is subject to endorsement by the very individual whose career advanced on the basis of the erroneous answer.

This study on mass destruction weapons in the Cold War is not meant to be a hatchet job. The intent is rather to examine the nature of the perceptual challenges that can bite the hardest. The purpose is not solely to highlight intelligence failures thus reinforcing the current public image of US services that cannot get anything right. That image of consistent failure is inaccurate and reflects the critics' poor understanding of the intelligence process. There is also a strange expectation of a standard of absolute rightness that is not also applied to the other enquiry professions. Many Cold War intelligence successes, ironically, may continue obscured by not only the dictates of classification but also the dependent memories of vanishing witnesses.

Note that intelligence herein is effectively defined to encompass not only all the US constituents, the supra-cubicles, but also extend more broadly to allied services. In particular the British so closely collaborated with the US regarding all the issues considered that their viewpoints, whether actively or by default, became largely indistinguishable. Substitute UK for US as desired. This definition is also at variance with the prevailing, simplistic, myth held by outsiders—media, academics, and public—that US intelligence then and now is spelt CIA.

Content is based on my direct involvement with some of the issues, and full access to the (abundant still classified) US intelligence sources and assessments, as well as consideration of post-Cold War material. Conclusions herein draw on more than two decades of hard-won accumulated knowledge. There are some considerations that may be applicable to current WMD issues—perhaps even pointers for a new generation of intelligence analysts. Organizational pathologies, notably the tendency to recurrent dropout of institutional expertise, ensure that there are few left who will have any recollection of these Cold War issues—and lessons learned. The selection of subjects is also aimed at those who might actually still be interested in Cold War verities instead of, yet another, series of historical mythologies and official models.

# The View From Torgau

Torgau is a town in Saxony that has not often intruded onto the German historical scene. *Schloss* Hartenfels, a prominent 15th to 17th centuries palace, presents a fine night-lighted aspect when approaching via the River Elbe bridge. In 1760 Frederick II of Prussia conducted an attack on an Austrian army immediately west of the city gaining the usual victory—at a terrible price in casualties. The Nazi Stalag IV-D prisoner-of-war camp, and a minor Soviet jail, are a less savory legacy. One notable local event, during the terminal phase of World War II, involved the April 1945 initial linkup between the allied US and Soviet armed forces. In a demonstration of the ever-recycling character of history the anniversary has been commemorated in formal style, with the flags of once deadly enemies, German, Russian, and American, raised directly across the Elbe from Hartenfels. Torgau also has a place in the annals of the Cold War that merits an entry in the historical logbook.

Three kilometers southwest of the city, off road number 87 (on the fringe of the 1760 battlefield), are the moldering remains of a former primary munitions depot of the late, unlamented, Group of Soviet Forces, Germany. In 1979 the depot provided a residence for a Soviet Ground Troops *praporshchik* (ensign or warrant officer). Something of a free spirit, in the then reigning Soviet culture this trait implied social deviancy, and a potential security risk. During his tour in the German Democratic Republic he had acquired a personal motorbike. The enmity of his unit commander had been somehow aroused, and this distraction from a spartan military regime confiscated. The former owner unwisely voiced his indignation at this peremptory action. Upon returning from a jaunt to Torgau one May day friends greeted him at the installation gate conveying the warning that a pair of KGB minders awaited at his bunk to have a chat; his response to the effect of 'I'm outta here.' This plucky fellow managed to transit East Germany hopping trains and cross the border into the Federal Republic of Germany.

There he fell into the clutches of those on the lookout for prospective informants. A preliminary screening of the *praporshchik* elicited information that earned him a date with debriefers from the Central Intelligence Agency. His observations would uncover an entirely successful, two-decade-long, Soviet deliberate orchestration of measures that disguised an alternative reality involving the widespread presence of the most dangerous of weapons. The revelation would instigate an intelligence ruckus never formally resolved even at the end of the Cold War. This episode epitomizes an intelligence never-ever land too often crippled by distorted perspectives, dysfunctional organizations, superficial knowledge, historical blindness, and a seemingly boundless capacity for self-delusion. A testimony to how much at risk we are today in a world of loose and expanding WMD proprietorship.

# Assessing The Soviet WMD Game-Plan

Commencing in the 1950s opposing strategists in the NATO and the Warsaw Pact alliances engaged in mutual preparations to carry out a singularly preposterous military notion—that armed forces could survive, let alone conduct organized operations, under the conditions of mass employment of nuclear weapons. Despite growing awareness through the following decades of the inutility of this particular method of mass destruction on European battlefields the nuclear option would be retained through to the informal ending of the Cold War. Regardless of any consideration of the viability of WMD war-fighting concepts the tasks of Western intelligence services encompassed discerning the arming, plans, and intentions of the designated enemy. The long Cold War constituted a unique historical phenomenon, entirely unlike the preceding large-scale, and even concurrent intermittent small, hot wars. Global planned actions, to be implemented by vast military establishments, remained incipient through nearly five decades.

Cold War history, to a considerable extent, exists mainly in the intelligence record and appreciation. Intelligence assessments—often discrepant or conflicted by country, agency, offices within the same agency, and between individuals of particular offices—had the most immediate and direct influence on national policies. But the views, informed or otherwise, of national policymakers intermingled with those of other defense and political actors made the final determinations. Some of these decisions disregarded accurate intelligence judgments while others affirmed misbegotten conclusions.

Some proffered Cold War historical official models depict mistaken intelligence assessments of a USSR and allies in reality merely empty shells with collapse imminent and preordained—the reality of their mass destruction weapons conveniently forgotten. An earlier European empire, the Roman, disintegrated from internal rot as much as external challenge, but historians do not intimate a semblance of power. The time scales of modern events have contracted and accelerated. One strain portrays the massive Soviet deployment in Central Europe functioning, contrary to a Cold War intelligence overwrought portrayal of a mortal threat, merely as jailers; the formidable offensive capability depicted by Western militaries and intelligence services actually a mythic invention sustaining nefarious agendas. This forward based armada would be too preoccupied with containing a restive population and keeping tabs on unreliable national militaries to be any actual threat to the West. Fortunately the accuracy of these particular official models had never been tested.

A retrospective accusation against intelligence is that hardware-based assessments confused capabilities with intent—one academic view considered the focus on the former to be a "dreary assumption" that ignored intentions.[1] The disconnection of capabilities and intent is an abiding fallacy—these elements are in reality inextricably related. Intent without capability is harmless. But when coupled, intent becomes an ignition switch which, from the disarmed setting, can readily be flipped to the on position immediately instigating motion. The centenary of the First World War has recently been marked in various ways by the European participants. There are eerie similarities to the Cold War in the prewar situations decades apart of opposing military establishments with their offensive/defensive plans and preparations featuring mass mobilizations. While there are differing perspectives on responsibility and actual intentions—pinpointing the true aggressor—the ignition spark originated with minor players in a sideshow. The main difference between the two periods is that the later alliances had the prospect of nuclear war to focus minds on the potential outcome of respective actions.

There is at least one significant marker for intent and hurdle to the perspective that national forces of the Warsaw Treaty would have disrupted rather than assisted any Soviet westward march. An accumulation of incontrovertible evidence, collected by Western intelligence during the Cold War and discovered in the archives of the former allies, document Soviet preparations to provide each of the member countries with mass destruction weapons, both nuclear and chemical. National troops equipped with launch means and regularly trained; military staffs studied and practiced; while the Soviets made detailed plans for sustaining massive Warsaw Pact WMD strikes in Europe. In all aspects Soviet operational methods had been duplicated. Both the supporting structure and procedures had been elaborated to deliver WMD munitions to national shooters. Any delusions concerning Central European reliability must have been shared by the Soviets.

Proposed frameworks for evaluating political and military developments during the Cold War include a depiction of events as an ever-rolling cycle of actions and reactions, given impulse by one of the coalitions or an individual member, but not necessarily with any clearly defined progenitor. Armament innovations and operational course changes implemented might have been initiative or a counter-measure, and could alternate responsibility. However even during the Cold War proposals described a more complex set of motivations encompassed internal dynamics as much as external situations on the US side[2] while retrospective wisdom has suggested comparable multiplicity among the Soviets.[3]

Chores of an intelligence service (should have) entailed appraising the developments of the opposing camp while trying to factor in the effects of actions taken by their own side. Net assessment, the two-sided evaluation of capabilities, despite bureaucratic practice to the contrary, is not a separable component but integral to valid intelligence judgments and forecasts. One intelligence rebuttal against accusation of committing the cardinal sin of net assessment defined a convoluted "interactive analysis" to sooth the affronted Defense Department.[4] US and allied intelligence services did not always take care to pinpoint the originator of particular developments and all too frequently ignored close interrelationships. This inability to accurately perceive both Soviet motivation and the nature of their response in the context of US or NATO moves often degraded intelligence conclusions on some strategic and operational issues including WMD.

Reciprocation had been a prevailing Soviet theme throughout the Cold War—one that continues in effect with the Russian successors. A 1981 CIA memorandum[5] regarding their response to the broad military buildup just initiated by the Reagan Administration noted Soviet attempts to communicate to US officials an inevitable response. President L. Brezhnev had stated "the Soviet Union will find a way to react rapidly and effectively to any challenge. We must do so." The memo conveyed the essence of the message delivered by Minister of Defense D. Ustinov "that the USSR would not permit anyone to upset the established equilibrium of strategic-military forces in the world. He vowed that the USSR would give an "effective response" to any and all challenges in the arms race." The Soviets even contemplated a late amendment of their 1981 to 1985 economic plan to accommodate large defense expenditure increases. A 1983 Soviet propaganda piece[6] had been insistent that,

> Throughout the postwar years the Soviet Union has never initiated the development of new types of weapons. In structuring its armed forces it was forced merely to respond to the threats created by the United States and take steps to ensure Soviet security.

Cold War era and post-USSR academics, think-tankers, and historians have produced many weighty studies arguing the intricacies of strategic and theater nuclear strategy. For at least fifteen years, however, a Soviet headsman's axe of mass destruction weapons loomed over Europe double-edged with nuclear and chemical blades. This prospective WMD Operation (my term) had been forged as an overarching structure for theater war in the nuclear age, the unique output of a distinctive Soviet strategic culture. Their blueprint represented the culmination of an extended consideration for a response to the substantial WMD programs, notably those of the US, undertaken by the West in the 1950s. During the second half of the 1950s anonymous Soviet strategists contrived a radical scheme for the employment of mass destruction weapons on the battlefield. By 1959 the Soviets had begun erecting an expansive integrated mechanism. When completed during the following decade, the disposition of complexes had been poised to generate an epochal nuclear-chemical maelstrom that would howl out of the East and make of European civilization a radioactive and toxic ruin. The US and other NATO intelligence services had an extensive assemblage of evidence to track development of this mechanism. But all failed throughout the Cold War to accurately grasp character, scope, and nodes of an existential armament.

Most public studies focus singularly on the nuclear blade, blithely ignorant of the significance of the chemical dimension in Soviet plans for European WMD warfare. A few other investigators have whacked at Soviet chemical warfare, usually with superficial results. Driven by accessible documentary information, the lack of access to the voluminous body of still-classified details is hardly an excuse since National Intelligence Estimates and other appraisals dealing with chemical weapons have been made, partially, available. The most important intelligence sources, in the form of a mass of classified Soviet and Warsaw Pact writings and documents acquired during the course of the Cold War, percolating through the declassification mill. This material can now be supplemented and amplified by documentation found in national military archives. Scholarly treatises have spun elaborate theoretical webs on nuclear issues in a one-sided approach devoid of chemical content. Unfortunately this nuclear/chemical divide had an enfeebled counterpart in the high-walled cubicles installed in the analytical realms of a splintered intelligence otherworld.

Cold War intelligence obtained few solid indications of Soviet intentions in regard to the third WMD element, biological weapons. While acquiring some technical development information, intell had no access to the BW employment plans. The most significant evidence derived from satellite imagery of certain installations within the USSR that displayed characteristics that, when considered in conjunction with the meager take from electronic and human sources, affirmed agent development, production, and potential stockpiling. This minimal information indicated that the Soviets regarded BW as a weapon of strategic effect rather than an option for European battlefields. Soviet-Warsaw Pact military exercises and writings only occasionally featured any BW interest and that mainly in a defensive vein that attributed offensive intent Westward. In striking contrast widespread attention persisted in the same sources to nuclear warfare throughout the Cold War and, for a restricted term, operations with chemical weapons. The relatively slow-acting, and indiscriminate character of, BW would have been poorly matched to the rapid pace of offensive operations envisioned by the Soviet military. A contributor to a recent study on intelligence processes, identified as a retired CIA analyst and RAND think-tanker, nominated the Soviet BW estimate among eight prominent intelligence failures since 1941. Somehow he missed the CW megaflop that had far greater consequences for US policy and military programs—and makes the astoundingly ignorant assertion that there had been "no evidence for a BW program" due to collection deficiencies, despite the definitive imagery and other evidence that had been acquired.[7]

Intelligence assessments drew on a wide variety of sources provided by technical and human means—the 'INTs. The general trend from the 1950s through the 1980s represented a steady up-scaling in the array of information with intelligence value. Acquisition of IMINT (overhead and ground imagery), SIGINT (electronic monitoring), and HUMINT (individual recruits or transients) described an upward curve during the Cold War in variety, scope, frequency, and quality. This restricted access material could be supplemented with information appearing in publications including a considerable body of both originator-classified and open military, political, scientific, and economic-industrial sources in the USSR and Warsaw Pact allies. Information acquired in the 1980s had improved on that from the 1970s–which surpassed that of the 1960s–and rated incomparably better than data available in the 1950s.

Soviet and Warsaw Pact classified information obtained by agents-in-place included technical data, operations manuals, directives, as well as proposals and discussions by senior officers. Intelligence analysts could further their education by reading the highly classified study material issued by the USSR General Staff Military Academy *imeni* K. Ye. Voroshilov. Among many others, Academy Professor General-Colonel I. Glebov helpfully outlined contemporary issues and agreed solutions regarding theater operations and the integrated employment of WMD in the second half of the 1960s in a series of classified articles and lectures. The most sensitive material had to be strictly compartmented, in a special access category, to avoid compromising the sources; nevertheless ultimately betrayed from within the CIA. While joining the CIA in late 1972 and assigned to a Soviet military issues cubicle I did not gain access until 1981—and immediately set to a systematic plunder of this priceless lode. Recent declassification programs have made available a part of the acquired documents; but the CIA continues to squat on a large proportion essential to attaining an accurate version of Cold War reality. I have been attempting to obtain release of indispensable items, via official and not channels, for more than a decade. Requests denial and procrastination have curtailed or precluded treatment herein of key issues. The potential wider and unknowing audience includes not only outsiders but also many of those who worked on Soviet-Warsaw Pact intelligence issues.

Except for the most proficient readers of Russian and other European languages, however, these writings had to be translated. Some errors may have been committed in the first translation, into English; but these manifest trivial compared to the second translation—the rendering of content and meaning into a dialect intelligible to the cleared audience of analysts, their chiefs, and recipients of intelligence products. Too often this restatement mangled actual substance to such an extent—entirely dissociated—that appraisals bore no relation to the source material. US intelligence premises and questioning could be so removed from the reality and details of the Soviet strategic culture that flawed answers became inevitable. Most of those few who made the effort to extensively investigate this vast body of documentation insisted on applying their own, glazed, overlays.

These acquired Soviet classified military writings required more than light reading. Accurate comprehension required a close line-by-line, even word-by-word, scrutiny–essential to alertly consider not only what other authors and documents concurrently presented but also what had been stated before, and afterwards, in similar sources. Critical to full understanding of content, themes, and trends aggregated literature had to be thoroughly explored from the starting date of availability. Less tasking for lazy workers, perusal of only the most recent documentation or only selected items over a more extended period assured a path to wrongheadedness.

The extensive documentary collection built up during the Cold War provided the basis for a cultural transplantation akin to the immersion method employed in foreign language training. Both classified and open, publicly available, politico-military literature provided avenues into a Soviet strategic culture unique in significant aspects. US analysts had been afforded the opportunity to learn not only what, but how, Soviet officers **thought**—both approaches and answers often markedly differed. Soviet solutions to even common technical problems often had no resemblance to the American or Western. Many of their resolutions transpired smarter than ours. Intelligence analysts adopting the methodology of Soviet-think might even be able to resolve issues otherwise lacking in definitive evidence because they could ask questions and attain answers exactly as did the opposition. But a pervasive American monoculture that viewed the world in 'US-think' perceptual windows that ignored or distorted 'them-think' directly afflicted a more than six decades international ascendency littered with costly intelligence and foreign policy disasters.

Intelligence could obtain insights on key issues and follow much of the evolution of Soviet military strategy, especially at the theater level, by reading the same General Staff professional journal, *Voennaya Mysl'* (*Military Thought*), as senior Soviet officers. VM editions appeared at three levels of classification while another unclassified version has been available in recent years. Dissemination came in the form of a monthly restricted edition for lower ranking officers and an aperiodic secret edition down only to the level of Ground Troops division commanders and their other armed forces equivalents. An occasional edition classified top secret had been launched in early 1960 to permit commanders at army-level and above to discuss (and argue) a new nuclear strategy. A tradition of the secret edition of the journal had the reigning Chief of the USSR General Staff drop by to apprise senior officers—and intelligence readers—of current trends and developments. In one of his reviews, a 1970 issue, Marshal of the Soviet Union M. V. Zakharov specified the role of VM in military deliberations.[8]

> The classified edition of the journal should deal with the greatest problems of our military doctrine and of Soviet military science. It must organize and promote a truly free exchange of opinions among the command personnel of our armed forces regarding the principal problems in the development of military theory and practice for the building of our armed forces, especially regarding problems which have been little studied so far and on whose solution depends the further development of the military field as a whole.

Oleg Penkovsky provided US and British intelligence the first of many articles from the classified editions. Delivery would continue even after the loss of Penkovsky via his successors as the CIA and allied services learned how to defeat pervasive Soviet security. Acquisitions expanded to include counterpart journals in Warsaw Pact countries. Unfortunately the Soviet news agent at the CIA, Aldrich Ames (possibly with assistance from other US insiders), eventually cancelled the subscription. Many articles from the restricted version had been, apparently inadvertently, released publicly in the late 1970s. At this writing the CIA has been declassifying the more interesting senior collection. Throughout the Cold War dissemination of these articles continued limited to selected intelligence and other officials. This material will be of considerable value to anyone investigating the accuracy of the US intelligence second translation.

During certain periods of the Cold War individual analysts scattered through offices in the intelligence maze, and among the beltway bandits and research groups, suggested that an accurate understanding of our adversaries might be furthered by a close study of the strategic culture actually presented in these sources. They proposed that intelligence comprehension would be furthered by employing an associated method rather than the version amended in the second translation. When like-minded analysts met up, akin to early Christians in pagan Rome, astonishment registered at encountering others who had undergone intellectual conversion to the same line of enquiry. Secret mutual recognition symbols did not, however, have to be worn to identify co-religionists. More than a few members of this minor sect would be subjected to a bureaucratic crucifixion when they dared to suggest alternatives to official models of particular issues.

Another wellspring exploited signals and imagery tools as well as occasional ground observations to monitor exercises that ranged from tactical unit field training to expansive command-staff practice of Warsaw Pact offensives across Western Europe. Exercise play could be compared with the classified scripts to determine compliance. SIGINT authorities, the US NSA (National Security Agency), Britain's GCHQ (Government Communications Headquarters), Canadian and other NATO services, issued thousands of reports on these exercises varying from glossy multi-volume studies of major events down the hierarchies to preliminary cables from field collection posts. This material offered a database that could be (as I did, along with all other available classified and open source material) in current lingo 'data mined' to create comprehensive behavioral profiles of the Soviets and their allies from strategic to tactical levels.

Unfortunately the massive archive of intelligence firsthand reporting on Soviet-Warsaw Pact exercises is currently locked up and unlikely to become available for an indeterminate period. This lacuna can be substantially compensated from other sources. Material released by the CIA includes not only classified writings in which many of these exercises are referenced and discussed, sometimes in great detail, but also original exercise documents and critiques. Declassified intelligence estimates and reports discuss evidence from exercises that reveal many other details and can be collated to gain a wider perspective. Of considerable significance are those exercise documents surviving in the military archives of the former Warsaw Pact countries. While fragmentary (similarly the electronic acquisitions) representative events are available. Archival materials dating from the 1950s and 1960s are particularly valuable since they cover a stretch when the intelligence take had been weak on scenario details, in contrast to the torrent of the subsequent two decades. Some of these documents afford insights unobtainable by intelligence during the Cold War.

Human and other sources could be similarly collected, organized, and added to the database—by those willing to make the effort. High-level Warsaw Pact defectors revealed aspects of national planning and exercise practice. Signals intercepts provided extensive information concerning armament programs and technical details, military and civil organizations, and procedural matters. Satellite and aircraft imagery surveilled force organization, disposition, and weapons, although the East proved adept at limiting access to forward elements. Open publications provided useful material. A steady stream of lower level emigres and defectors added details, and occasional seminal revelations. This massive trove, an evidential tsunami, opened avenues into hostile planning and preparations. However intelligence did not necessarily utilize this abundance of evidence effectively—or, for many issues, at all. Since the dissolution of the Evil Empire, Central and Eastern European national archives have yielded more official documents that supplement the, still mainly withheld, intelligence holdings, while clarifying—and correcting—intelligence conclusions. However still lacking in both the intelligence and archival acquisitions is the high level political and military documentation of Soviet decision-making that is, in retrospect, attributed greater significance.

Westerners during the Cold War subjected Soviet international goals to wide probing with often sharply varying conclusions based as much on ideological slant as verifiable facts. Soviet strategists implemented the decisions of the national politico-military corporate board—the VGK (Supreme High Command). Western intelligence services had no effective access (even with limited term eavesdropping on leadership limousine telephone calls)[9] to this critical juncture point of the political and military-technical components of Soviet military doctrine. If a Soviet equivalent to the US SIOP (Single Integrated Operational Plan) existed for employing nuclear weapons, neither the US nor any other Western intelligence services had copies. This opacity made for difficulties judging any modifications and shifts in military strategy. The demise of the Cold War Soviet directorship, and the absence of the Western tradition of high-level memoirs, however self-serving, may mean that intentions during any period may never be ascertained.

The GOU (Main Operations Directorate) of the USSR General Staff successfully tucked away from the prying eyes of Western intelligence services elaborated operations plans specifying the strategic actions of the Warsaw Pact armed forces. That these plans had been directly linked to capability-building had been attested by a key CIA source in the Polish armed forces "that operational planning is the main driving force behind Soviet and WP armaments."[10] Indirect indications of content, that often served more to confuse and conflict intelligence assessments, had been provided in the multitude of classified documents and military exercises over several decades. Less ambiguity inhered regarding military objectives. The basic assessment by both intelligence organizations and outsiders that any outbreak of war in Europe, regardless of initiator and motivation, would instigate a decisive and rapid Warsaw Pact offensive with all forces and means, has survived into the post Cold War period.

One of the most telling indications of divergent objectives lay in the scenarios characteristic of NATO and Soviet-Warsaw Pact exercises conducted during the Cold War. NATO notional and live scripts consistently focused on repelling an enemy assault with limited advances to restore preexisting defense lines. While nuclear and conventional strikes on enemy territory had been authorized, extended counterattacks remained politically unacceptable—even strikes in depth could be controversial. In the early 1980s the AFCENT (Allied Forces Central Europe) command prohibited actions that would transgress the eastern border; only preplanned counterattacks to regain lost territory had been acceptable.[11] NATO exercise routines presented inconvenient evidence for the Soviet official model. General-Major A. Slobodenko, who frequently authored articles on NATO, attempted to finesse the apparent defensiveness of the designated enemy in a 1970 VM (S) issue.[12] He noted that US and NATO exercises held from 1965 to 1969 consistently featured defensive action prior to any counteroffensive. "The question automatically arises: have the imperialist states renounced the doctrine of offense in favor of the doctrine of defense?" Slobodenko cited NATO and US official documents in an attempt to prove a negative answer. Engaged in mirror-imaging to such an extent he more than once cited US Army Field Manual 100-5 *Operations* as "*Field Service Regulations*" actually the title of a Soviet counterpart. He considered the defensive emphasis of NATO exercises to be a political ploy to depict the Warsaw Pact as aggressor. Like all ideologues Slobodenko persisted entirely unconscious of the implication of the equations created.

When defensive play had been featured in the many exercises run by the other side actions transpired obviously pro forma and often omitted altogether—at least until the mid 1980s. Essentially all effort pointed toward a massive, decisive (counter)offensive which in larger scale exercises extended to the Pyrenees. After all the compelling historic lessons of two world wars evidenced the implications of any strategic prolongation permitting US reinforcement. The Soviets intended to be the winners of a European armed conflict, conducted at any level or scale or type of weapons employed. The politico-military elite proclaimed a ideological imperative that socialism would win, regardless of the human cost, even if necessary to wage a war to resolution with pitchforks. General-Major N. Smirnov, among many others, stated the Soviet position in his late 1969 VM (S) article[13] on a particular aspect of the beginning of war.

> In conformity with the basic tenets of Soviet military doctrine, our Armed Forces, together with the armies of the other Warsaw Pact countries, will not only repel aggression, but will also engage in decisive offensive operations with the goal of totally destroying the enemy forces.

Their side had detailed knowledge of the NATO reality obtained through an intensive intelligence collection effort. The re-alignment of allies during the 1990s resulted in the discovery of information confirming long-held suspicions that the Soviets and Warsaw Pact comrades had thoroughly penetrated Western ranks. The memoir of an East German intelligence officer outlined the career of agent 'Michelle' at NATO Headquarters from 1967 to 1979 during which she provided, among other material, documents on nuclear contingencies including planning, release procedures, exercises, and US weapons intended for other members.[14] A seemingly unending parade of traitors, in particular, provided details of NATO plans along with comprehensive insights into NATO and US intelligence reporting. Even during the Cold War intelligence had ascertained the situation "...the Pact has substantial and generally accurate knowledge of NATO's organization, force structure, alert procedures and reaction times, equipment, tactics and strategy, and mobilization and reinforcement capabilities."[15]

Exploitation of the soft intelligence target represented by Western countries had been facilitated by their loose practices. A Soviet officer writing in a VM (S) article pointed with pride to the initiative of 8 Guards Army in East Germany just after the end of World War II in obtaining copies of the semi-official *Stars and Stripes* newspaper; they determined the disposition of US forces in Europe—"subsequently confirmed fully by documentary data"—down to regiment level.[16] Soviet open military publications also widely covered activities, events, achievements (and deficiencies) of specific units but identified these only by their five-digit military numeric; our side had the more onerous task to particularize by cross-referencing a variety of other sources, with some success. The Warsaw Pact achieved a, perhaps, historically unprecedented, and potentially war-winning, dual-faceted advantage: knowledge not only of enemy operations plans and WMD preparations but also the content and accuracy of the intelligence assessments that guided NATO strategy. A saving—and simultaneously dangerous—ramification lay in the ideologically-driven Soviet and Warsaw Pact official models, if anything, even more distorted than those of their probable enemies. Providential that the West 'won' a cold war.

European geography fostered a hefty Soviet investment in peripheral strike systems, notably theater-range ballistic missiles. At the apex of deployment in the 1980s the *Pioner* (SS-20 Saber) Western force of thirty mobile regiments (in the nine- and six-launcher complements declared by the Intermediate-Range Nuclear Forces Treaty[17]—to approximate withholds and launch failures) could scatter 729 nuclear warheads (in the tri-warhead configuration) across Europe in the first salvo. When firing 72 SS-20s under the elimination provisions of the INF Treaty all but one, which deviated from the predetermined ballistic path and had to be destroyed, reached the Kamchatka target area; such a demonstrated 98.6 percent reliability would have been the envy of any Western missile design team. Each of the 729 reentry vehicles would detonate with the equivalent of about ten Hiroshima bombs, totaling in all at least 109 megatons. This would amount to an average of 34-ksk (kilotons per square kilometer) for the total land area of thirteen West European NATO members (including Turkey, excluding Iceland). Of course the actual targets along with aim points, and thus effects, would have been unevenly distributed. The remnants of an older theater missile force, submarine-launched missiles, with heavy and medium bomber aviation, even some ICBMs thrown in, would have greatly magnified those effects—and the contribution of missile and aviation strike assets held by the assault forces of the Soviets and their Warsaw Pact allies should not be slighted.

Peculiarly, the initial standard metric for scaling nuclear detonations in terms of conventional high explosive tonnage has endured as an attempt to represent a conditional reality. An early demonstration of the effects of massive explosions had been provided on 6 December 1917 in the harbor of Halifax, Nova Scotia when a ship loaded with 2545 tons of bulk explosive elements suddenly erupted following a collision. This 2.55-kt event killed at least 1650 people outright while destroying 1630, and damaging 12000, buildings in an area of 2.59 square kilometers—or roughly 1-ksk—while 37 survivors had been instantly permanently, and hundreds of others partially, blinded because they had glanced at the source of detonation. These statistics vary somewhat by source but the scale of devastation is manifest.[18]

The effects of such massive nuclear strikes can be gauged by a simulation conducted by the Natural Resources Defense Council calculating that 142.5 megatons delivered in 300 strikes would kill 25 percent of the combined population of all NATO countries—and that 2001 study[19] encompassed the substantially larger geography of North American and new Central European members as well as, presciently, France (President N. Sarkozy re-upped to the NATO military command in March 2009). Another gauge is the combined total yield of about 285 megatons reported by a Russian publication for all of the 715 nuclear tests conducted by the Soviets from 1949 to 1990.[20] This accumulation includes the monster 50 megaton detonation at the northern Novaya Zemlya range in October 1961 as well as 'peaceful nuclear explosions' for civil applications. The US conducted a total 1054 tests up to 1992 but the highest yield amounted to 14.8-mt at the February 1954 Bikini shot.[21]

The Soviets apparently had been working with the same benchmark used in the NRDC study. In a 1964 VM (S) article,[22] the Professor and another general calculated the required level of damage to knock out smaller members of the NATO coalition. The contemporary variant envisioned the exploitation of nuclear strikes conducted by USSR-based strategic systems. Their screenplay involved a territory of around 30000 square kilometers—they must have had Belgium in mind since this is the only member of that size—and with average population densities of 150 to 500 per square kilometer in rural areas and urban of 1000 to 3000. They estimated that only five missile strikes, each with a one megaton warhead (thus achieving a commendable 165-ksk), would be needed to reach the 25th percentile. The generals did note that "strikes against the enemy's military-economic centers naturally will result in colossal casualties among the population." Another article[23] in the same journal two years earlier that reviewed a book dealing with a Soviet tank army advancing through areas of radioactive pollution cited an exercise conducted by the Soviet group in East Germany that calculated an initial massive nuclear strike would contaminate 40000 square kilometers.

By the early 1970s a basic strategic parity had been established as deployments of US and Soviet intercontinental strike systems attained offsetting strengths. Implicit for Europe each coalition leader, now capable of inflicting devastating nuclear strikes on their respective homelands, became highly motivated to restrict the arena of military actions. Intelligence insights into Soviet plans for strategic weapons, limited by poor access to the level of political and military hierarchies occupied by decision-makers, remained largely restricted to assessing the potentials of force structure and weapons characteristics revealed by technical collection means. In contrast a massive trove of information had been acquired that dealt with the employment of the battlefield forces of the Soviets and their Warsaw Pact allies. This material had been often extrapolated in order to better understand strategic nuclear operations. From the 1960s through the 1980s their forward forces and USSR-based reinforcements, increasingly infused with an array of WMD delivery systems, established a solid basis for potential independent nuclear strike operations 'decoupled' from Soviet strategic forces.

The European WMD delivery means could therefore be viewed as a more immediate threat—and dangerous flash point—than the strategic systems that monopolized the deliberations of governments and their intelligence services, politicians, public, and media. As a consequence of this perceptual malapropism, most attention had been directed to assessment and disputation regarding the weapons least likely to be used, the final step in escalation rather than the first. Relative indifference became especially dangerous at the end of the 1960s when the Soviets began to develop a limited nuclear war variant reliant on battlefield systems that excluded the strategic assets based within the USSR. Ironically the diminishment of US and Russian strategic delivery means in the post Cold War era has focused interest and elevated concern regarding 'nonstrategic' nuclear weapons. The current Russian predominance in these weapons, in particular, has brought their continued existence to the European forefront.

Soviet planners assigned top priority to destroying NATO nuclear delivery means and munitions depots, both to limit enemy capability to damage their forces and to create conditions for a successful initiative strike. NATO might want to pursue a similar targeting strategy but, of course, to do so would require precise knowledge of the actual peacetime locations of both shooters and their weapons. An accurate picture of the full nature, extent, and configuration of 'tactical' delivery means would be critical to the NATO defense system. That the US conglomerate and other NATO services failed until the early 1980s to comprehend the full extent of their potential attackers' preparations would be one of the major intelligence fiascoes of the Cold War. Given increasing concern with Russian 'nonstrategic' nuclear armament—apparently knowledge of extent and locations little or no better than the earlier Cold War[24]—establishing the nature of the precedent in order that such failure is not repeated is a current high priority issue.

OF SPECIAL IMPORTANCE

Copy No. ___
Draft ___

D I R E C T I V E

of the Commander-in-Chief of the Combined Armed Forces
of the Warsaw Pact Member States on the Combat Readiness
of the Troops and Naval Forces Allocated to the Combined
Armed Forces

No. _____

Moscow

[Day, Month] 197_

The following are guidelines for the planning and support of the combat readiness of the troops, aviation, and navies allocated to the Combined Armed Forces:

1. In the Combined Armed Forces of the Warsaw Pact member states, four levels of combat readiness are to be established -- CONSTANT, INCREASED, MILITARY THREAT (VOYENNOY OPASNOSTI), and FULL.

a) In CONSTANT COMBAT READINESS, the troops, aviation, and navy engage in everyday planned activity and are in readiness for the fulfillment of combat tasks by constant-readiness large units and units and for the conduct of full mobilization by large units and cadre large units, units, and facilities, reduced-strength and cadre large units, units, and facilities.

Individual large units, units, ships, and subunits are on combat alert (combat duty) according to plans and combat duty rosters.

# Precepts

To arrive at valid assessments of the Soviet WMD game-plan required a thorough intelligence understanding of the fundamental theses—the strategic culture—underlying their military concepts, force planning and preparations. Strategic cultures provide the decisional context, the guidelines and reference points, consciously or not, consulted by political and military elites. Inputs shaping a particular culture range from the geographic to political-ideological dominance. Americans supposedly are a practical, rather than theoretical, oriented people but nevertheless tend to become confused when confronting a culture capable of arriving at solutions that might differ, radically, from their approved formulations. Inadequately-founded perspectives are the direct, inevitable outcome of ignored or distorted them-thought. International policy and intelligence professionals should be cognizant of this perceptual trait, and assimilate appropriate corrections. But historically neither group has won praise for transcending a perspective-distorting empathic disability. All are prone to (mis)translating alien strategic cultural frameworks into a US-think that profoundly alters definitional content.

The following key tenets of the Soviet strategic culture have been elicited from their playbook not the US representation in the second translation; a poured multi-element conceptual foundation essential to grasping the nature and substance of Soviet Cold War WMD activities; and providing the essential structure for successive themes. Comparison with US intelligence products that have become available, and public studies, will reveal more divergence than overlap. The focus is on what the Soviets considered the military-technical, rather than the political, component of State military doctrine, and application mainly to European theaters (also their practice). These precepts have been inherited, and may well be undergoing reactivation, by a resurgent Russia which has a military establishment experiencing increasing attention and resource allocation early in the 21$^{st}$ century.

**Center rules**

The VGK embodied the paramount wartime political-military authority for directing the military establishment. Collegial membership included the Communist Party General Secretary, Minister of Defense, MoD deputies, and others. VGK modules comprised particular types of specialized units, entire field formations, the massive accumulation of war materiel, a significant proportion of mass destruction weapons, even strategic forces—forming a *Rezerv* with the appellation RVGK. These RVGK troops and armament represented a unique politico-military conceptualization that had no Western counterpart—the military expression of the extreme centralization of political power in the Soviet Empire. The VGK held the prerogative in determining the scale and type of mass destruction weapons to be employed, issuing the directives for allocation and distribution from dedicated reservoirs. VGK orders would be implemented through an executive agent, the General Staff of the Armed Forces of the USSR.

Command-staff and control system exercises rarely depicted VGK workings, revealed more often in classified military literature, and best exemplified, even for the Soviets, retrospectively from the experience of the GPW—the Great Patriotic War of 1941 to 1945. For command purposes the VGK (with a *Stavka* or Headquarters coordinator) constituted the Center of military organization as well as war decision-making. However even those at the top realized that the VGK sovereignty did not necessarily have the capability to effectively control the vast geographic sweep of modern multi-theater military actions envisioned by the enforcers of socialist order. Devolution of command would eventually be deemed necessary but the VGK retained the ultimate authority over not only Soviet forces but those of European allies.

The technological advances of the second half of the 20$^{th}$ century—in particular the revolutionary development of nuclear-missile weapons systems that could span not only Eurasia but also reach other continents—had been hailed by the ideologists and military leadership as a means of strategic intervention with instantaneous consequences. From their perspective this armament, for the first time in history, placed in the hands of the Center the means of independently, directly, and quickly determining outcomes through strategic strikes. No longer would a graduated buildup of efforts with a piecemeal distribution of resources over a prolonged period be required to achieve the optimum mass considered essential in the Soviet strategic culture. Among the strategic theorists writing in the 1960s-1970s the amassing of such great power had elicited a sort of Marxist-Leninist nirvana.[25]

> The decisive means of achieving the goals of modern war are rockets and nuclear weapons...This requires maximum centralization of control of the principal nuclear-rocket weapons in the Supreme Command, particularly in the initial period of the war, for here and only here is it possible to decide correctly and most effectively questions concerning the objectives of nuclear strikes, targets for destruction...Only here can the authority be placed for "pressing the button" to activate the principal means of war. The Supreme Command has thus become not only a directing organ of supervision, but also the immediate executor of the principal missions of the armed conflict.

The first generation of surface-surface missiles had been organized as RVGK rocket troops. At the end of the 1950s this array transmuted into an entirely new type of armed service, the Rocket Troops of Strategic Designation (RVSN—SRF to the West, Strategic Rocket Forces). Components defined the world's first military organization with an exclusively offensive mission. This conjoining of ideology, military doctrine and structure, ensured direct control by the Center of the impending widespread deployment of strategic missiles. In a measure of divergent strategic cultures the US just grafted intercontinental missiles onto the Air Force as an adjunct to the prized strategic bomber fleet. But the RVSN also created a massive peripheral strike force that the Center could employ to directly effect European outcomes; culminating with the *Pioner* deployment. A Soviet missile preference had been fixed—and inherited by Russian successors.

The VGK loomed over all considerations of military strategy and operational art. But Western intelligence, in particular the self-imaged US contingent, had such a poor comprehension of the extent of interpenetration by the Center as to distort assessments. Thus a persistent supposition held that all the armed forces of the Soviets and their allies in Central Europe would be committed for a concerted dash westward. But in some exercises—and in classified accounts of exercises obtained by intelligence—individual armies or an entire national front would be withheld in the VGK troop reserve during play of (counter)offensives; even when concurrent reinforcement from the USSR had been depicted. Fronts constituted the highest form of Soviet and allied military field organization, sometimes equated to NATO army groups. The Soviets prioritized direct augmentation of efforts from the VGK *Rezerv* over the re-assignment of deployed assets essential to other regions.

**semicircular authorities**

Soviet planners divvied up global geography (as did their designated US opponent) in order to organize and control deployed military forces; while customizing the details to their unique geo-political situation. Asymmetric importance had been assigned to expansive Western and Eastern Theaters until the mid 1960s when ideological conflict with China began to take on a more ominous cast. Soviet military capability in the Eastern Theater would be significantly augmented during the next two decades. Exercises and writings in the 1970s portrayed wars against either NATO or China, which by the midpoint had become not only concurrent but also attributed coordinated aggression by both enemies.

Each of these two theaters comprised TVD—theater of military action—subdivisions that combined land and water bodies in which wartime strategic missions would be conducted along with solely oceanic TVDs. Delimitation of land TVD in peacetime depended on careful study of characteristics that included political, demographic, economic-industrial, military dispositions, transportation, climate, and terrain.[26] Soviet development of the TVD concept had been evident since at least the 1920s. Boundaries could be subject to modification; apparently sometime after 1975 much of the Near Eastern and Middle Eastern TVDs had been merged into a Southern TVD. This alteration reflected Soviet re-evaluation of that segment of the noose, just as in the preceding Eastern adjustment. In a local war a TVD could become a theater of war. Advance preparation of TVDs in terms of both troop deployments and development of logistics infrastructure consisted a prominent Soviet strategic theme.

Senior officers since at least 1960 had made references in classified writings to the creation of intermediate high commands—GK or *glavkom*—delegated selected responsibilities in respective TVDs. Similar authorities for operational coordination had been organized during the tumultuous events of the 1941 German invasion; on 10 July GK established on three of the five "strategic directions" that had been identified in the prewar period. By June 1942 these commands had been abolished in favor of a system of representatives assigned to operational fronts by the General Staff. Intermittent GK revivals followed in 1942 and, notably, a more durable High Command of Troops in the Far East formed in 1945 to oversee the Manchurian Operation. This remote GK had been re-established in May 1947, in place until April 1953.[27]

Force restructuring in the late 1960s would impel a Soviet reconsideration of the GK in a new form. A Russian biography of the first Cold War Western GK Commander-in-Chief, Marshal N. V. Ogarkov, defined these authorities to be "intended as agencies of operational-strategic command of the armed forces on the theaters of actions."[28] Signs of a GK revival became evident in Warsaw Pact forces exercising by the late 1960s, appraised by intelligence as TVD-oriented. Remote monitoring by intelligence successfully followed at least the outline of high command development, with some details provided by sources that included the CIA liaison to the Polish General Staff, Colonel Ryszard Kuklinski.

Transpiring unremarked by intelligence the Warsaw Pact assault on Czechoslovakia in 1968 had been coordinated by a GK. Russian accounts of Operation Danube indicate that General-Army I. G. Pavlovsky (then Commander-in-Chief of the Soviet Ground Troops) had not been just the 'invasion commander' but actually headed a "*glavnogo komandovaniya*" created on 20 August, the day before Warsaw Pact forces crossed Czech borders. The headquarters set up at Legnica Poland which would later be the location of a peacetime GK. Certain resubordinated GK units included communications, two airborne divisions, air transport, national air defense, and KGB.[29] SIGINT (the predominate source on the Czech event) hazily related Legnica to a theater role, but only in retrospect had there been speculation that a high command had been set up.[30] Nor did intelligence stress this important milestone during the remainder of the Cold War despite intense interest in the Soviet development of TVD authorities.

The GK references in early Soviet classified writings that had been acquired directly linked establishment contingencies to the scale of forces deployed in the TVDs. The relatively sparse force needed to conduct nuclear warfare required a degree and extent of coordination within VGK capabilities without subsidiary assistance. General-Colonel A. Kh. Babadzhanyan in a late 1961 VM (TS) article discussed this nuclear relationship. He rejected the suggestions of other generals that theater commands might be useful, rather that the *Stavka* "will organize strategic coordination" in nuclear conditions in which a limited number of fronts would operate.[31] However, as the prospects of operations conducted with only conventional armament became increasingly likely in the late 1960s and 1970s, the need for a larger force deployment that would require far more complex strategic coordination impelled a re-think. Intelligence assessments of the forthcoming high commands generally failed to recognize the significance of this linkage, not even the character of the upscaling, to enlarged deployment in certain TVDs.

Some two decades of Soviet internal argumentation, largely hidden from Western intelligence, would ensue until a satisfactory arrangement emerged. Information from several sources indicated Soviet consideration of the General Staff Tenth Directorate (responsible for relationships with allies) or the Warsaw Pact Combined Armed Forces staff as the basis for a TVD headquarters. The model for VGK handling of fronts had been the GPW representatives system, executed by the dispatch of what the Soviets termed 'operations groups' to fronts in combat. These OGs composed more than just a few liaison officers but substantial entities supported by dedicated communications. A senior Czech officer stated that in the 1960s an OG would be sent by Warsaw Pact headquarters in wartime to the national front but in exercises Directorate Ten had also established a forward headquarters.[32] Polish information from the mid 1970s asserted that control of deploying national troops would eventually shift to "the High Command of the Combined Armed Forces" even in a prewar situation.[33] But neither of these entities became the basis of the Western GK that eventuated in the 1980s.[34]

Two major issues apparently to be resolved involved whether a *glavkom* represented a wartime expedient or should be pre-established, and what level of assets and responsibilities should be assigned. Studies of the GPW experience with high commands that appeared in the open *Voyenno-Istorichesky Zhurnal* (Military Historical) portended resolution of the issue. A 1979 article by Colonel I. Vyrodov[35] examined the decision to establish an intermediate level to bring VGK authority closer to operations through "coordination of efforts and direction of military actions of major groupings of armed forces in a theater of military actions (TVD) or on a strategic direction." He concluded that the basic reasons for the eventual abolition of the 1941 GKs included their organization during the course of the war rather than in advance as well as the non-allocation of troop and logistics reserves which would have permitted effective operational intervention.

...it became practically impossible for a supreme high command to exercise direction of military operations of major groupings of armed forces without an intermediate echelon and that both an overall system of strategic leadership and its echelons must be set up ahead of time, before the beginning of a war, and their structure must correspond strictly to the character and scope of upcoming military operations.

General-Colonel V. Gurkin in the July 1984 issue reiterated these deficiencies and the key lesson that GK should be set up before the outbreak of war; he diagrammed the staff organization of the Far East headquarters.[36]

Intelligence obtained substantial documentation from national sources in the Warsaw Pact regarding Soviet imposition on their allies of a single, centralized, Supreme High Command and movement toward creating High Commands of Troops in the Western and Southwestern TVDs. Soviet statements in these documents display a familiar justification propensity by highlighting actions of the other side. Proponents for GKs exuded highly complimentary regarding Western arrangements; in a November 1978 meeting of the Pact Political Consultative Committee Marshal V. G. Kulikov (Commander-in-Chief of the Combined Armed Forces of the Warsaw Pact) congratulated NATO on a "well-balanced system" of supreme commander and theater commands. The PCC decided that a draft statute for a new theater command structure should be prepared the next year.[37]

A series of exercises in the early 1970s apparently tested TVD control[38]—but these did not recur until 1977. The General Staff Academy's top secret 1974 textbook *Front Offensive Operations*, while focused on individual front rather than TVD-level coordination, dealt with aspects of VGK interaction that entirely lacked any indication of an intervening authority.[39] Other Academy instructional material in the mid 1970s referenced the possible establishment of TVD commands, but emphasis persisted on VGK direct operational control. General Staff Academy material in a 1977 lecture on a type front operation also gave no indication of an intermediate command[40] nor in an extended course that had only a brief reference to a VGK representative at the Combined Baltic Fleet.[41] The distant reaches of the Soviet Far East became the venue for the first peacetime TVD GK, finalized by the December 1978 arrival of General V. I. Petrov. A reference to this event in a Polish document hinted that the assignment had been presaged in the scenario of the September-October 1978 multi-theater exercise *Tsentr* which depicted China allying with the West on war day 26.[42]

Intelligence had a copy (about 15 months subsequent to the event) of the official Soviet critique, as well as extensive information from direct monitoring, to buttress the assessment that the seminal exercise *Zapad* 1977 premiered screenplay of a Western TVD-level authority with subordinate Warsaw Pact allies.⁴³ Marshal V. G. Kulikov acted as the GK Commander-in-Chief; in his reporting Colonel Kuklinski stressed the unprecedented nature of this *Zapad* in the ongoing rollout of a supreme, and TVD high, command structure.⁴⁴ In March of the following year elements of the Warsaw Pact Combined Armed Forces staff acted concurrently as the directing body for a *Soyuz* exercise and as the High Command in the Southwestern TVD.⁴⁵ Apparently the first full-scale test of a TVD high command played out in the 1978 *Tsentr* exercise, with representation of a staffed GK and command authorities from the Soviet Defense Council down the levels to fronts. Polish documents related the timing of national troops allocation to the Western and Southwestern TVD commanders-in-chief—upon declaration of a new intermediate stage of armed forces combat readiness⁴⁶—this accelerated an earlier 1978 exercise in which subordination took place at the, next, highest stage.⁴⁷ But in that prior scenario there had been an additional shift of control.

> On the same day, the Political Consultative Committee adopted the decision, in view of the threat of the start of war by the West, to grant the General Headquarters [*Stavka*] of the Supreme High Command of the Armed Forces of the USSR the authority to direct the operations of the Combined Armed Forces of the Warsaw Pact member states...

Thus the paramount controller had been revealed.

The 1980 *Statute on the Combined Armed Forces of the Warsaw Pact Member States and Their Command Organs for Wartime* that established the Western and Southwestern TVD commands has also been recovered from national archives and states that a GK would be activated only in the event of war outbreak.⁴⁸ Formal ratification of the *Statute* occurred on 18 March and within a few months the CIA had a copy along with related documents.⁴⁹ These included a 30 April Decision that appointed a certain Marshal of the Soviet Union, Leonid I. Brezhnev, as Supreme Commander-in-Chief of the Combined Armed Forces of the Warsaw Pact. While the *Statute* declared that the two TVD commanders would be "invested with absolute authority" over their subordinates and allocated resources obviously all power flowed from the Soviet VGK authority that came into being on transition to war. Troops and means not allotted to the two GK would be designated RVGK; any leftovers would generously remain national property. The privilege of performing the role of VGK control organ acceded to the USSR General Staff. Polish General Wojciech Jaruzelski would later claim that the role of the Supreme Commander continued to be disputed by the nationals until the dissolution of the Warsaw Pact organization.⁵⁰

These two high commands accomplished Soviet objectives to not only control separate massive strategic operations but also to shackle their allies in the respective directions. A new scheme of force alert, mobilization, and commitment effectively bypassed both allied political and military leaders.

Colonel Kuklinski conveyed to the CIA detailed background and insights from the Polish viewpoint regarding the development of progressively tightened dominance arrangements from the late 1970s to late 1981.⁵¹ He pointed out the Soviet ploys and surprise presentations to their allies of a centralized system that would permit the Soviet VGK and General Staff to commit all national armed forces to a war without consulting political-military leaderships. The forces of the Warsaw Pact had been transformed into automatons, a binding reliability, which would march at the command of the Center. But the Romanians had refused to sign at Nicolae Ceausescu's place and would be the only Pact member to consistently resist Soviet demands.

Information available even in late 1978 enabled a CIA assessor, examining development of the TVD concept, to conclude that the Soviets seemed poised to foist peacetime TVD commands on their allies; noting the likelihood of Warsaw Pact member resistance to ceding a measure of control of national armed forces to these commands—and outright rejection by the Romanians.⁵² But factors beyond those of national reluctance delayed implementation. Early 1980s exercises, particularly *Soyuz* 1981 and *Tsentr* 1982, amounted to final dress rehearsals for the full production. Another CIA study on Soviet control of Warsaw Pact forces conducted by the Office of Soviet Analysis (SOVA), with an information cutoff of 1 August 1983, had examined the background to the 1980 *Statute*.⁵³ Activity included key high level meetings such as that of December 1977 in which Marshal V. G. Kulikov announced the Soviet military consensus that high commands should be created for the purpose of controlling "coalitional operations on strategic axes" (wording per the SOVA paper) in wartime. The last sentence of the study conveyed the SOVA conclusion that "the Soviets have not shown an inclination to activate the High Commands in peacetime." That "inclination" however apparently short-lived since in September 1984 the Soviets established peacetime GK in the Western, Southwestern, and Southern TVDs.

Organization had many similarities to that of their subordinates, including fronts, and the GK assumed nuclear weapons planning responsibility for respective TVD; mid 1980s procedures even delegated individual target number assignment to respective GK.⁵⁴ The 1980 *Statute* had set out the basic composition and responsibilities of the military council as well as the several deputy commanders, staffs, directorates, and departments that comprised a high command.⁵⁵ The Western GK would be manned by about 1600 military and civilian personnel; with Polish slots amounting to…60—despite contributing 22 percent of assets—other nationals viewed their control allowance as similarly disproportionate.⁵⁶ A SOVA 1983 appreciation of nuclear planning attributed a focal shift from the General Staff GOU to the high commands in overseeing subordinate fronts' nuclear strike tasking and timing.⁵⁷ A later SOVA study, citing classified writings, concluded that each GK could order TVD-wide nuclear strikes subsequent to VGK authorization and could confirm/cancel launchings up to ten minutes before execution.[58]

**finding the way without directions**

Vast geographic scaling of the USSR and the multiplicity of potential enemies impelled military doctrine development of conceptual-planning guides that encompassed foreseeable eventualities. Soviet-think stressed definitional schemes regarding all aspects of their recognized categories of strategy, operational art, and tactics. Large-scale strategic actions had to be controlled and organized to conform with the war objectives established by the Center. At the end of the 1950s the debut of strategic and theater nuclear missiles enabled the VGK to directly and immediately accomplish some strategic missions. These missiles, along with strategic aviation, had the potential to accomplish "the content of the entire period of the war" although other armed services would participate and exploit mass nuclear strikes; while there remained the possibility of a more prolonged campaign. Groupings of strategic delivery means and of troops, in particular field organizations known as fronts, would be coordinated according to the specific conditions of TVDs and demarcated missions.[59]

Designated TVDs shaped and tasked military actions in terms of discrete *napravleniya*. This word is often translated as 'axes' or 'sectors' but 'directions' more accurately conveys the full meaning of this unique conceptualization. Unusually both the Russian and English words have the same double meaning of path and control—as in that way, this way. Directions provided a means for coordinating a massive, diverse force and powerful armament operating across expansive terrain in separated groupings. Soviet strategic thought derived from an interior geographic enclosure amidst potential enemies, conceptually established during the civil war struggle against counter-revolutionaries arrayed in a peripheral "ring of fronts" (per the 1960s unclassified opus *Military Strategy*).[60] Despite all the Soviet whining about 'capitalist encirclement' they viewed geographic centrality as facilitating wide maneuver, successively or concurrently, against any objective as a link in a chain.

Missions in a TVD denominated strategic, and constituent operational, directions as integrals of a strategic goal that could decisively influence the course of an armed conflict. A strategic direction could encompass a region of political-military-economic-industrial significance comprising one or several countries, and/or target an important enemy armed forces grouping within a particular strategic region. The end-point of an operational direction could be all, or a part, of one country and/or a divisible portion of an enemy strategic forces grouping.[61] Operational directions might be differentiated from the strategic as the avenues of approach for segmented assault groupings against related objectives of a similar dimension. Operational directions implemented the constrained paths of an offensive that would be prodigious in scaling. Missions fulfillment expressed as directions against concrete objectives; executed by strike groupings of forces and weapons subordinate to particular commands; coordinated and guided by a unified concept and plan; across predefined geography. Minister of Defense Marshal A. A. Grechko stressed the cardinal significance of this unique construct in the 1975 edition of his book *The Armed Forces of the Soviet State*—an open tome subsequently translated and published in the West.[62]

> Speaking of strategy, we distinguish a strategy of waging a war as a whole, its main concept, the chief strategic goal, and a strategy of waging a war on directions to accomplish individual strategic missions and attain particular strategic goals. There is a close dialectical interconnection between them as between a whole and its parts. This connection consists above all of the fact that attainment of the overall strategic goal of war usually is ensured by accomplishing particular strategic missions....
> Further, the tie between war strategy as a whole and war strategy along directions is manifested in their interdependence. War strategy is not constant. It usually changes depending on the military-political situation and on the successes or failures in war, i.e., depending on the winning of particular strategic goals. Changes in war strategy in their turn force us to make certain adjustments in the strategic troop operations along directions and correct particular strategic war goals and methods of attaining them.

The directions schema furnished the pillars for all Soviet military preparations, operational planning, and force deployments—a core precept not simply the ruminations of military theoreticians but rather the blueprint for strategic action and theater operations. Directions prescribed the basis of organization of military actions against European and other external enemies. At the end of the 1950s directions even structured actions of the Ground Troops in conditions of the employment of at least nuclear weapons. The directions might therefore have become defining factors in determining the selection, allocation, and strikes of all appropriate brands of mass destruction weapons.

In a 1967 retrospective on the development of Soviet operational art delivered to the broad audience of officers reached by VM (R) General-Army V. Ivanov examined the advent of nuclear weapons in the 1950s. He differentiated two periods, from 1953 to 1957 in which nuclear means basically modified the operational theory of the GPW and a fundamental rethink that took place from 1957 to 1960.[63]

It was acknowledged that a combination of nuclear strikes and swift actions of troops on the march and according to directions and under the conditions of the absence of solid fronts should be the basis of any capability of defeating the enemy.

Ivanov may have been citing a common authoritative source, or quoted in turn, by the General-Army I. Pavlovsky nearly identical statement in a later 1967 VM (R) article dealing with the Soviet Ground Troops.[64]

The revolution in Soviet military theory that impelled this rethink attributed the causal basis to the widespread introduction of nuclear weapons being implemented in all services and levels. Colonel L. I. Voloshin[65] later viewed the revision as the culmination of an "operation in depth" concept that originated with key theorists in the 1930s, evolved during and immediately after the GPW, and then underwent a nuclear transformation. He strangely attributed to Westerners the elaboration of an offensive on non-continuous frontage "mounted on separate directions" employing highly mobile tank-saturated independent but coordinated formations against "specified territory" exploiting mass nuclear strikes with "linearity" of actions. A directional offensive enabled troop maneuver in wide zones at high rates of advance avoiding obstacles created by areas of massive destruction and contamination. Writing in 1978 Voloshin updated the concept to incorporate factors influencing operations conducted without the use of nuclear weapons but which did not invalidate the WMD version.

These and similar expositions by other officers pinpointed the directions as the basis of an unrivaled Soviet solution for the conduct of theater operations in conditions of widespread nuclear strikes—and a convergence of formulas at the end of the 1950s for the employment of mass destruction weapons on the battlefield. Particular methods investigated during the same timeframe regarded the use of at least nuclear and chemical weapons. Each of these solutions might even have been closely interrelated. Classified writings of the 1960s through the first half of the 1970s, as will be seen, consistently and tightly linked nuclear with chemical weapons in consideration of operational issues. Their WMD Operation presented a super-sized Napoleonic columnar march by independent strike groupings; dispersed and maneuvering on terrain defined by the directions as a nuclear-protective measure; exploiting gaps blasted by nuclear weapons in the NATO defense system; and then advancing at high speed into the depth toward the Channel, Atlantic, and Mediterranean. In the Soviet strategic culture the product of such an epochal contemplation would assuredly be a large-scale implementation.

While theater sub-divisions embodied a familiar approach also adopted by Western strategists, the Soviet concept of directions presented an entirely alien construct. Directions, and their fundamental significance, did not display in the perceptual windows of not only most intelligence specialists but also other observers. Among the diverse Cold War crowd of Western intelligence, defense, and policy apparatchiks, academics, and self-appointed experts, only a relatively small minority perceived this aspect of Soviet military strategy. Fewer still scrutinized details—and a finger-count could be taken of those who recognized the absolute centrality of the directions. A similar disjunctive appreciation related to the Western military categorization of strategy and tactics, between which the Soviets inserted a framework for operational art for which the West had no equivalent.

Delineating the extent and tracing the evolution of the directions during the Cold War entailed tapping a variety of material—no comprehensive directory available for consultation. Sources ranged from classified Soviet and Warsaw Pact documents; military academy lectures in Moscow reported on by the contacts of an attache; Afghan and Bulgarian colonels crossing to our side; subsequent testimony by former alliance officers; along with material found in national archives since the 1990s. The large number of exercises monitored by Western intelligence offered a potential goldmine for identifying and correlating individual directions with operational planning and force lineups. But in practice intelligence reporting on exercises had only limited value.

*Napravleniya* terminology appeared in a variety of contexts during exercises, derivation essential to pinpoint activities involving any attested directions. Collectors and analysts working on exercise data, including those of the US NSA and British GCHQ, had no better grasp of the significance of the Soviet conceptualization than most of the rest of the intelligence community. No systematic effort occurred to identify the directions as depicted in exercises and no retrospective summations as often the case with other issues. Extracting the details from exercise reports mainly had to be accomplished by reading-between-the-lines. In some cases when reporting quoted actual Russian terminology picked up I could tell that unjustified modifications had been made, inserting or deleting words. The fundamental importance of the Soviet construct should have ordained that all exercise analyses regarding theater operations be tied to, and centered on, the framework of both strategic and operational directions.

Consideration of the directions permeated Soviet writings on strategic and operational issues to such an extent that no justification is sustainable for any claimant to familiarity with Soviet strategic culture, whether within or outside intelligence circles, to not recognize the criticality of this structuring for military planning and actions. Unfortunately mainstream intelligence somehow failed the cultural translation. Intelligence vocabulary did not commonly incorporate *napravleniya*. Only in the mid 1980s did the somnambulists in a few intell cubicles, limited to those dealing with Warsaw Pact

DIRECTIONS (CONCEPTUAL)

theater forces, awaken to the significance of the directions when they, belatedly, confronted definitional material—some dating back a decade or more.

Evidently Marshal Grechko's 1975 foundational expression of the significance of the directions had been overly subtle. A full decade ensued before recognition dawned regarding an array of evidence of the second kind. But discussions of the directions had been scattered through classified writings back even to the early 1960s in the material transmitted by Oleg Penkovsky. Particularly crucial evidence had been provided in classified Hungarian studies that broke out the directions, somewhat surprisingly, in the Western TVD as well as their native Southwestern TVD. A document obtained in 1975 which had elicited no intelligence interest whatsoever, considered in conjunction with the 1980 update acquired in 1985, fully delineated the operational directions of the Western TVD. An article from a classified journal, also added to intelligence files in 1985, identified the strategic directions of both TVD along with a partial accounting of Southwestern TVD operational directions.[66]

An uninformed reader of preceding intelligence reporting, both the redacted declassified and fuller classified versions, could not have any sense of the very existence of the Soviet construct. Expansive NIEs on the Warsaw Pact in 1979[67] and 1983[68] (informed to 1 April 1983) contain no trace of the directions. There is no definition or use of the particular Soviet directions in a wide-ranging Defense Intelligence Agency exposition on Warsaw Pact operations in the Western TVD (to 1 January 1984) despite examination of postulated attack routes and terrain characteristics.[69] The earliest declassified intelligence report currently available that actually addresses the directions is a CIA study, evidence cutoff July 1984, which pondered the potential relationship of the Western TVD operational directions to the penetration corridors of the Soviet theater air offensive.[70] In a limited dissemination paper DIA analysts later tendered the bold proposition that the operational directions might be reverse-engineered to establish actual Soviet operations planning and force groupings. Four editions to 1985 (April) of the DoD unclassified series *Soviet Military Power* despite treatment of command structure, TVDs and high commands, lacked any references; only in the 1986 edition did maps of several TVDs depict (inaccurately) strategic and operational "directions" (correctly); maps in subsequent editions improved definition but never matched reality.

In a classified briefing for the House Armed Services Committee on 8 September 1988 (oddly included in a declassified CIA document collection concerning the 1968 Czechoslovakia invasion) the chief of CIA SOVA (Douglas MacEachin) seemingly breathlessly announced, and displayed a map of, "operational axes" approaching the FRG and BENELUX countries. He applied the Soviet names for six of these obtained from the various classified documents. Each "axis" stated to define an operational task for a front of the "first strategic echelon" (which he distinguished from fronts of the "second strategic echelon" in the western USSR) in the Western TVD.[71] MacEachin's secondary translation as "axes" demonstrated at least his, and likely all SOVA cohabitants, shallow grasp of the actual scope of the Soviet conceptualization. Unfortunately those now acquainted did not perceive a need to reexamine prior issues for any sign of this fundamental Soviet tenet—including correlations involving mass destruction weapons—nor did their knowledge seep into the cubicles of other topical kingdoms.

Directions permeated the Soviet strategic culture to such an extent that the concept has persisted into the Russia era. Two colonels writing in a 2005 issue of VM (U) on "Command and Control Problems in Strategic Directions" proposed that the directorates of Russian military districts be reorganized in peacetime as strategic direction commands.[72] Their recommendations became the basis, or reflected ongoing consideration, for action. A *RIA Novosti* item the following January, commenting on an article by Chief of Staff General-Army Y. Baluyevsky, noted that the Russian General Staff had under consideration major military structural changes that included transforming military districts into operational and strategic directions.[73] By 2010 a reorganization being implemented entailed the reduction of the number of military districts from six to four and the creation in each of an operational-strategic command taking the form of a strategic direction. A test of the new Eastern command had been conducted in a June-July 2010 exercise.[74]

Soviet Cold War shorthand expressed the Western Theater directions as Northwestern, Western, and Southwestern; similarly defined prior to the GPW. Identification of specific directions appears to have been permitted only at a minimum classification level of secret. In the full version for the decisive WMD playing field, the Western TVD, the Soviets designated three strategic directions to delineate operations plans; operational objectives of each of these directions, in turn, assigned in two operational directions. All directions tallied an extent, with a maximum force deployment capacity, based on targets, terrain features, and lines of communications. Terrain factors could even determine the type of mass destruction weapon to be employed—nuclear strikes in mountains could create obstacles in the few available passes while non-persistent chemical strikes would have much the same effect on defenders without detritus. Applying persistent chemical agents would deny enemy use of passes with no planned transits. Tactical directions also delimited the operations of lower level formations such as individual ground divisions.

Insights regarding operations planning by the Soviet General Staff could be discerned in remarkable detail even without access to the paperwork. The limited intelligence work attempted using the directions had great potential, but misunderstanding by the analysts, and the total incomprehension of anyone in the West, would probably have only befuddled their audience. Thus intelligence observers could only be nonplussed to find that three high commands permanently established in the mid 1980s might formally designate respective leaders as Commanders-in-Chief on (Strategic) Directions; although the Soviets had not settled on the precise term.[75] The 1983 *Military Encyclopedic Dictionary* defined high commands as strategic organs for troop control "in a strategic direction or a theater of military actions" either led by a commander-in-chief.

## more than one way to skin…NATO

Western intelligence services never did get a complete and accurate picture of particular Warsaw Pact military plans. But this failure could, at least partly, be absolved. The Soviet Union and allies did not pretend to know in advance the exact conditions of any outbreak of war with NATO or leading US member. Their planning and military preparations relied on the preconception of operational variants incorporating a range of potential responses to all foreseeable contingencies and eventualities. This preplanned menu of military actions underlay the building of a massive force lineup that incorporated substantial reserves of assets as well as alternative WMD options. Incertitude regarding the singularities of the next war in Europe impelled the creation of redundancies, caches, and resource hedges seen as essential to meeting unforeseen deviations. But implementation of these measures served also to confirm the Western image of aggressive intentions by a massive establishment exceeding legitimate defense needs. The Warsaw Pact seemed to be not just a deterrent force but one aimed at attaining superiority for a first strike capability.

While acknowledging the possibility of a deterrent intent, the Western perspective had been cogently stated in a 1975 NIE.[76]

However, the size of the Soviet/Pact forces in the forward area, their doctrine of the offensive, and the across-the-board efforts to improve the capabilities of their forces cannot fully be explained in terms of protection against perceived threats from NATO, control of Pact allies, or maintenance of the status quo. Rather, they suggest a desire for more ambitious policy options. At a minimum these would include the goal of clear conventional superiority to support political pressures, as well as to prevail in the event of military action.

A series of interconnected plans differentiated military actions not only by circumstance and direction but also by evolutionary adjustments. Judged only by the NIEs, and some analytical studies, on Warsaw Pact forces that have been partly declassified readers might conclude that the opponent had only one scheme in vogue at any given time. US intelligence persistently cast a restricted menu of 'options' as a flavor-of-the...moment/decade/eternity. Even the full versions of these appraisals fail to convey the complex, multi-faceted nature of theater forces structuring and assignments. Intelligence during successive decades prioritized a limited set of alleged Soviet 'options' with minor permutations; recomposed at different points in the Cold War; lacking any sense of the actual situational basis of Soviet planning. The resultant stereotyped and rigid hierarchy of possibilities not only inaccurately portrayed Soviet intentions but also amplified the military danger.

Each of the Soviet variants would have generated a different Warsaw Pact lineup, objectives, and operational methods. VGK political intent and decisions prescribed the missions implemented by the respective plan. Thus a Czechoslovak defector involved in national forces planning reported that by 1970 six variants existed, each identified by a code word—all offensive— split evenly between nuclear and conventional initiation. Moscow ordered execution of the selected variant. Czech military staffers could rotate plans within twenty-four hours generating a one meter pile of paperwork.[77] An apparent operations plan for one of these variants dated 1964 has been found in Czech archives.[78] A Russian account of the 1968 Operation Danube, offensive goal Czechoslovakia, relates that participating commanders had been handed five instructions packets; informed only on the eve of the invasion which to open and implement.[79] Contents of the other packets doubtless specified actions in case of any NATO interference, even provisions for WMD employment.

Formulated assumptions on the nature of modern war drove operational variants. Outbreak of hostilities could come as a strategic surprise or there might be a threat period. The preliminary international tensions could be indeterminately short or prolonged—which would allow partial or complete pre-combat mobilization and a forward movement of deployment echelons from the USSR. Troops, aviation, and other armed forces might be fully deployed during the period of threat; might begin mobilization-deployment during this period with completion after the onset of war; or deploy only after combat had begun. Local or small-scale conflicts might expand in scope and character. The Warsaw Pact might initiate an offensive; preempt an attack by NATO; or remain on the defensive—and these actions might vary by direction. Operations might be conducted with or without, some or all, of the Soviet fraternal comrades in the Warsaw Pact. Poland and Romania viewed as especially suspect; East Germany and Bulgaria reliable; Czechoslovak dependability essential rather than volunteered; Hungarians useful rather than necessary. Countries in certain directions independent of NATO constituted sub-variants; neutrality could be highly inconvenient during offensive actions. From the mid 1960s regions of potential combat expanded East and then South. The Soviets might face major hostilities not only in Europe but also with China in a potential two-front war.

Basal factors, however, involved the role of mass destruction weapons. The advent of nuclear weapons presented the possibility of a quick outcome but a protracted war could not be ruled out; although rarely discussed in classified writings or depicted in exercise play in any detail. These decisive weapons might be employed on an intercontinental scale; restricted to European theaters (at least at the start of a war); or come in the form of limited rather than mass strikes (again only at the outset). Selection of mass destruction weapons might be nuclear and chemical; solely nuclear; with at least the implication of an independent chemical phase. Bacteriological weapons likely existed somewhere among the variants but Western intelligence services had essentially no access to BW operations planning. WMD initiation might, or might not, be preceded by a interval of combat of unknowable duration with solely conventional arms—this non-nuclear period becoming of mounting significance from the 1970s into the 1980s.

The Soviet General Staff envisaged and developed plan variants practiced by Warsaw Pact theater forces throughout the Cold War. Multi-variant exercising had the side-benefit of confounding Western intelligence services regarding the actual content of the (inaccessible) war plans. Some exercise series obviously focused on a particular variant. Trend lines and turning points could be, carefully, assessed but previous variants could reappear. A pitfall for Cold War historians is reliance on the fragmentary documentation being recovered in former satellite archives. Some scholars attempt to derive definitive appraisals from this limited evidence while the mass of intelligence exercise reporting and a still substantial portion of the snitched Soviet-Warsaw Pact classified material remains out of reach. No one exercise or document is indicative of a tendency, dictum, or 'favored' variant. Multiple variants manifested right to termination of the Warsaw Pact by military establishments preparing to meet all scenarios imposed by the political leadership.

This circumstantial diversity vastly complicated Soviet operational planning. As put in a 1974 classified manual on reconnaissance,[80]

> One of the peculiarities of preparation of the first operation is the fact that it is done beforehand under peacetime conditions in order to ensure the constant readiness of the troops of the border military district (group of forces) to perform combat tasks at any time....Another peculiarity consists in the complexity of preparing an operation in the respect that in one plan it is required to provide for the action of troops and take into consideration the different conditions of the possible entry of the front into war and of the conduct of the operation with conventional means of destruction or with the use of nuclear weapons.

Despite the ingrained attitude of Western political and military establishments that pictured the East as the fount of aggression the opposing perspective sustained a ideological mirror image reflected even in Soviet military planning. A repeated theme—not confined to ideological polemic—attributed an incipient, sudden, NATO attack instigated by the US. This official model persisted despite recurring, highly public, examples of the contentious path to agreement among NATO members on any issue—much less a concerted decision to launch a theater surprise assault. Colonel A. Krasnov in a 1962 VM (S) article compiled a detailed list of indications of a strategic surprise attack "the basis of the military doctrines of the imperialist countries" with appropriate detection mechanisms.[81] Colonel S. Sokolov's 1966 summary of NATO views on initial operations for his fellow officers asserted that "the basic means of unleashing a war in Europe is considered to be a surprise nuclear attack."[82] General-Colonel A. Radziyevsky's 1968 VM (S) discussion of surprise in the outbreak of war chastised some fellow generals for books suggesting a diminishing surprise factor importance or that duration would be limited.[83]

In recent years some among the limited assortment of Cold War aficionados have been hyperventilating a 1983 'war scare' that had been induced among Soviet leaders by the US-NATO exercise Able Archer.[84] A wide-ranging series of notional war gaming and live maneuvers took place in the context of technological challenges being implemented by the Reagan Administration as well as by various US military actions. One of those measures had been the deployment to Europe of missile systems capable of striking the USSR with little warning. This period has been described as a showdown comparable to the nuclear near miss of the 1962 Cuban missile crisis. Whether this characterization amounts to another versioned reality, the beginnings of a persisting historical myth, cannot be here examined in detail. Strangely absent, however, from the varied perspectives applied is the context of Soviet military writings and exercise scenarios which consistently depicted throughout the Cold War aggressive Westerners plotting nuclear war—and accentuating the surprise variant. Quite detailed compilations of warning indicators appeared in these sources. General Staff Academy lectures in 1985 on strategic, and Western TVD operational, reconnaissance strikingly lack any specification of 1983 as a dangerous year and do not reference Able Archer.[85] A 1998 thesis that focused on the SS-20 deployment during this period with an overview of nuclear strategy, drawing on extensive interviews with Soviet officials and some access to classified sources, does not factor the 'war scare' or even mention such an event.[86]

Some Western retrospectives have suggested downgrading or even abandonment of the nuclear variant in the 1980s particularly after the 1987 formal Warsaw Pact adoption of a defense strategy. Yet in March 1988 a Soviet exercise featured a VGK order to execute Variant One upon warning of an enemy nuclear attack, followed by coordinated strategic and theater mass nuclear strikes. In June of the same year a lecture on military doctrine (found in Polish archives) by Marshal S. F. Akhromeyev, Chief of the USSR General Staff, informed Polish senior officers at their General Staff College "In the current situation we accept as an initial premise the possibility of both conventional and nuclear world war. Thus the armed forces need to be equally prepared for both kinds of war."[87] Similarly, scenario for the May 1989 *Vltava* exercise in Czechoslovakia posited NATO nuclear strikes to halt a Warsaw Pact counteroffensive, with immediate Soviet-Czech mass retaliation. But a Czech archive document from that exercise noted that the exchange "allowed the commanders and staff to resurrect somewhat lost practical skills in solving tasks directing the delivery of nuclear strikes...";[88] a study of East German exercise documents found no indications of nuclear play from 1982 to 1987, with resumption in 1988.[89] Exercises in the 1980s did increasingly include nuclear contingency planning without any play of a nuclear strike phase. But the nuclear variant retained validity to The End.

Western intelligence services had to comb through a mass of incoming evidence in order to establish prospective variants and to ascertain Soviet ranking of probabilities. Classified manuals and operational dissertations provided a conceptual-organizational base tested and implemented in command-staff exercises. The Soviet General Staff conducted and coordinated annual programs often variant thematic. There could be a series of separate, localized exercises with a shared background scenario that expanded in scale and complexity. By far the most expansive, *Tsentr* exercises encompassed operations around the periphery of the USSR in all TVD; often the actions of Warsaw Pact members would be depicted without inviting their participation. *Zapad* (West) exercises focused on the main enemy, NATO, in the Western TVD, colleagues occasionally allowed to play along—the 1977 edition involved all members of the Warsaw Pact while in 1981 the Soviets conducted a solo performance. The revival of both exercise series heralds the ambitions of contemporary Russia. The *Soyuz* (Union) command-staff exercises also dealt with large-scale operations in the Western and Southwestern directions but with all, or selected, national forces normally involved; the series had been initiated in the late 1960s as map play then developed into more complex scenarios involving troop participation.[90]

Many other strategic, operational-strategic, operational-tactical, experimental, and tactical exercises conducted varied in scale and purpose. Objectives included testing of command arrangements and communications systems; validation of existing operational variants and development of new or revised versions; weapons technology development and employment evaluations (an intelligence tip-off to impending debutantes); and assessment of proposed changes to organization and operational methods. The action could be confined to map work at a few installations or command bunkers, but might also be accompanied by field excursions. Activity could be local or worldwide in scope. Exercises could be monitored or even controlled by teams from the key General Staff and Frunze military academies. A 1975 Warsaw Pact document provided a concise summation of a myriad of exercise types with procedural advice.[91]

Soviet and Warsaw Pact sources revealed that these exercises simulated features of actual war plans but obviously had to be concealed from uninvited observers. Colonel Kuklinski indicated that when elements of the actual plans had been incorporated distortions accompanied for security purposes. But he also stated that in *Zapad* 1977 Soviet fronts operated in their preassigned directions.[92] Lower level staff and field exercises more closely followed operations plans since they amounted to rehearsals for assigned commanders, staffs, and troop units. Representative units participated live both for real-world tests of prospective schemes as well as role familiarization and skills evaluation.

**ready to roll**

Predicting the nature of the outbreak of war consumed much of the attention of Soviet military theoreticians—well-grounded historic reasons for concern existed. Surprise initiation entailed the greatest danger since strategic nuclear weapons could immediately decide the outcome of a war. But even a conventional attack could disrupt national transition to a war footing. Considered more likely the threat variant, however, surprise outbreak remained a possibility. Documents recovered from Hungarian archives regarding exercising in 1966 implied Warsaw Pact thematic study that year of the surprise-unlimited nuclear variants despite acknowledged US abandonment of a primordial massive retaliation strategy.[93]

Strategic exercising in August 1974 depicted concurrent NATO and Chinese surprise attacks that eliminated the USSR leadership. West forces in *Soyuz* 1983 conducted surprise-conventional assaults throughout western and southwestern Europe;[94] *Zapad* repeated these variants in the next year. Threat periods exercised throughout the Cold War varied in duration either brief—with significant consequences for preparedness—or prolonged along with scenarios depicting complete surprise.

The Initial Period concept assembled war outbreak forecasts. Officers engaged in extensive studies and arguments to reach a definitional consensus—with operational planning implications—that amounted to the start of war until achievement of the first strategic goals[95] (the endpoints of the strategic directions). For the GPW this period had been characterized as the defensive operations conducted by the first strategic echelon of the Soviet Army.[96] But divergent views existed regarding content. In a key 1967 VM (S) article General-Colonel M. Povaly argued that, reviewing the historical background of the Initial Period concept, since the early 1960s "independent significance" had been lost. Not only did the use of strategic nuclear means render meaningless an attainment of immediate goals but also the Soviets now considered that these weapons would not necessarily be employed decisively at the outset of war. A revised periods scheme "being considered" would incorporate new variants involving use of solely conventional weapons and a second, nuclear war with only tactical (battlefield) means. Nevertheless an Initial Period continued to be defined and discussed even into the Russia era.[97] Given the most favorable circumstances VGK politico-military goals for the war could be fulfilled; commencing actions in any event could effect decisive influence on the subsequent course of hostilities.

A Special Period assigned the national economy marked the transition of industry to wartime production carried out with the utmost secrecy. The origin of this codification had been attributed to pre GPW theorist A. A. Svechin who defined a period that extended from war declaration to the beginning of major combat operations.[98] Intelligence noted the first evidence of a postwar formulation in a 1961 top secret civil defense statute; the USSR Council of Ministers had been designated the proclaiming authority.[99] But the Special Period also encompassed both civil and military preparations; upon declaration a network of bio-weapons plants would initiate munitions loading and assembly;[100] troops would "secretly occupy" combat departure positions (supposedly the enemy but the Soviet designation applied);[101] Warsaw Pact navies tasked to shield active merchant and fishing vessels.[102] International observers entirely unaware of the source of this concept puzzled over the July 1990 Fidel Castro declaration of a Cuban Special Period in Peacetime lifted directly from the Soviet lexicon. He placed the Cuban economy on a war footing as a consequence of the termination of cheap oil and trade bargains from the, then collapsing, USSR that had subsidized the regime for decades.

A combat readiness alerting scheme calibrated preparations for the first strategic echelon. Active military units (supposedly) maintained Constant combat readiness, the peacetime routine, to repel any surprise attack. During a threat period of increasing international tension the level of combat readiness would be elevated in stages to Full, from which military operations plans could be executed. This system might be broadly analogous to the US DEFCON arrangement but differed significantly in the particulars.[103] Soviet planners dealt with the danger to the military structure represented by the surprise-unlimited nuclear variants through two basic approaches; by hardening of critical assets; plus removal of units and stocks from their, presumed (correctly) known and targeted, peacetime locations. *Dislokatsiya* (disposition) would be achieved by a coordinated movement on a massive scale, involving most of the armed forces, from permanent stations to preplanned secret reserve areas at specified distances, units from garrisons and materiel from storage facilities. Relocations presented an enormously complex task, unprecedented in war, which might have to be carried out while under nuclear attack.

Dispersal control had been deemed so important a nuclear protective measure that in 1978 the Soviets inserted a new combat readiness stage, Military Threat (variously War Threat or Threat of War), between Increased and Full. *Peredislokatsiya* would take place upon receipt of an implementation alert at the new stage rather than as previously at Full combat readiness during which an array of other tasks would have to be concurrently executed. An indication of the motivation for the new stage had been provided by Marshal V. Kulikov in an August 1977 letter to Polish Minister of National Defense W. Jaruzelski that evaluated lessons from the recently completed *Zapad* exercise.[104] He proclaimed the existing three-stage scheme inadequate to react to "abrupt changes in the military-political situation" in regard to NATO actions. In order to provide for "greater orderliness and flexibility" in the alerting system, without prematurely advancing Warsaw Pact combat readiness, the Soviets recommended the introduction of an intermediate stage that would facilitate responding "more efficiently to the possible actions of the probable enemy in a prewar period."

But the Poles at least did not embrace the Soviet proposal with appropriate comradely enthusiasm. A memo prepared by their General Staff in response to the Kulikov letter[105] pointed out that "a plan for gradual attainment of combat readiness by the Polish Armed Forces" had already been prepared with flexibility in "selective and multistage reaction to enemy activities." These procedures had been implemented subsequent to the Combined Armed Forces Directive No. 001 on combat readiness, dated 27 December 1971, and in effect since 1 January 1972—which had superseded the 18 November 1968 edition of the Directive.[106] While the Soviet recommendation "warrants careful examination" national "specific conditions" dictated "no real need for introducing in the Polish Armed Forces an additional state of readiness" affecting reduced strength, cadre, and newly formed military units. Actually the Poles considered a new intermediate readiness stage "not advisable" and that the same result could be achieved "gradually" over an "extended period" without any structured stage alert. Essentially the proposed readiness stage would jump the process and move all Warsaw Pact forces into a field combat posture in advance of, and without coordination with, any national leaderships' decision.

Despite any Polish qualms a letter from the Chief of the USSR General Staff, Marshal N. V. Ogarkov, to his Polish counterpart, F. Siwicki, stated that one of the objectives of planned early April 1978 staff training would be to test the amended system.[107] The March 1978 edition of exercise *Soyuz*—which focused on, and featured the first GK setup in, the Southwestern TVD—confirmed the need "for more efficient methods of converting the allied armies from peacetime to wartime status" according to Kulikov.[108] The *Lato* exercise that followed in May-June apparently featured the Polish formal incorporation of the new stage. As noted above, the September-October 1978 *Tsentr* exercise featured the next compulsive step taken by the Soviets when national troops had been subordinated to respective high commands at the now effective Military Threat stage. Colonel Kuklinski provided the background to the changes including Soviet imposition of the *Monument* alert signal system that would enable the Soviet VGK control organ, the General Staff, to implement readiness stage elevations without consulting national leaderships. The system would even allow the Soviets to skip intermediate levels and go immediately to Full combat readiness from Constant. In Kuklinski's view this could result in the mobilization of Polish military forces and commitment to a war without formal notification and national concurrence.[109] As in the creation of TVD GK, all Pact members except the Romanians meekly accepted this Soviet abrogation of national sovereignty.

In early 1979 ongoing work to draft a superseding combat readiness directive that would incorporate the new stage and redistribute mandated actions had elicited hopeful Polish comments.[110] By at least March 1979 the CIA had a copy of this or a later version—complete with signature blocks for Pact Commander-in-Chief Marshal V. Kulikov and his Chief of Staff General-Army A. Gribkov—but the Agency failed to comply with a requirement that the preceding 1971 Directive be returned to the Staff of the Combined Armed Forces no later than 1 October.[111] The new Directive specified, with informative details, the measures to be implemented, by type of armed service, at each of the four stages; particularly valuable the comparison afforded by the preceding edition. The Directive locked national forces to a sequence of prescribed actions—and when acquired by intelligence provided an invaluable script for monitoring changes to readiness status by Soviet and Warsaw Pact forces.

Content of these Warsaw Pact readiness directives are suffused with procedural minutia such that the CIA considered too dicey for outsider perusal. The CIA fully denied my request for release. More than six years ensued in the declassification grinder, including January 2012 arrival at the inbox of the final arbiter, ISCAP (Interagency Security Classification Appeals Panel), and their release decision in May 2015—without any substantive redactions. But this appeal only recovered the Directive 1971 edition. The CIA proved more accommodating regarding my subsequent request for the 1979 Directive delivering in less than nine months.

In January 1983 there would be indications of Soviet study regarding yet another, fifth, stage of combat readiness—with an apparent designation Surprise Enemy Attack Using Weapons of Mass Destruction in Progress. Declaration could occur at, and override, any of the other stages. Specified actions included immediate dispersal and sheltering while preparing troop movement (seemingly discrepant in such circumstances).[112] Advancement on implementation remains uncertain; a 1985 General Staff Academy readiness lecture still defines the preceding four stages without any hint at the existence of a fifth;[113] while a CIA report with evidence up to July 1987 also details only four stages.[114]

This combat readiness system applied uniformly to all Warsaw Pact forces; strikingly contrasting with NATO procedures which assigned primary alerting and mobilization control responsibilities to national authorities.[115] Among NATO vulnerabilities in the official critique of the *Zapad* 1977 exercise had been cited "the difference and diversity of the armies in levels of combat preparedness."[116] Colonel Kuklinski's 1981 overview of Warsaw Pact views on NATO strong and weak points considered their opponents to be an "epoch behind" in control arrangements and so inadequate in time-space reaction that within the thirty days of planned NATO mobilization the Pact offensive would already be marching through the Iberian Peninsula.[117] Of particular importance the rapid orchestration of mobilization, deployment, and reinforcement of ready forces when both sides relied heavily on reserves—and the reverse trends from about 1960 saw an increase in the size of the Warsaw Pact active force while that of NATO underwent a substantial decline. Only West Germany expanded the active establishment on a meaningful scale. NATO had become progressively reliant on mobilization of reservists and transatlantic movement of US ground and air forces yet persisted deficient in coordination mechanisms.[118] The Soviets for their part became increasingly confident in the capability of the forward operational echelon to sustain a longer period of combat without support from the second.

Dispersal of troops and weapons constituted an integral component of armed forces strategic deployment, simultaneously protective for movement to departure positions in the TVDs. An extended threat period would permit advance mobilization, dispersal, and marches to establish strike groupings in the operational directions. But the Soviets remained aware that this process could also telegraph a warning to their opponents. Therefore Soviet officers discussed concealed mobilization measures regularly practiced in exercises; the objective would be to both deceive and to forestall enemy action. One variant had ground troops marching directly from permanent garrisons rather than making a pit stop at reserve areas—in the 1960s Czech operation plans this method, as the basis of one of the three variants under both nuclear and conventional conditions, deliberately intended to achieve surprise.[119] Rebasing of aviation—moving aircraft to alternate or combat airfields—could also be a tipoff that would have to be carefully implemented.

A gambit attributed to sneaky NATO entailed conducting military exercises as a cover for attack preparations. Just to determine, in theory of course, whether this could be accomplished, the Soviets and their Warsaw Pact allies practiced this cover variant. During one of the most dangerous periods of the Cold War in Europe, the 1961 Berlin crisis, exercise *Burya* (Storm) had been convened to conceal operational preparations for a Warsaw Pact war deployment. Similarly, exercise *Šumava* (named for the Bohemian forested border region) would be hastily arranged in 1968 to cover grouping of Warsaw Pact forces for intervention in Czechoslovakia. Exercises would be particularly handy in any surprise variant for preemptive assault preparation. The ploy has been considered so effective by Russia that application has not outlived usefulness, witness preliminary use of exercises cover to nibble away at a now independent Ukraine.

## leading the charge

*Fronty* delivered the theater punch by ground and air. The peacetime force structure generated fronts as the culmination of the scheme of staged war readiness measures. Intelligence estimated that each massive, complex aggregation of troops and armament (at least those facing NATO in Central Europe) could amount to as many as 400000 personnel.[120] The 1983 *Military Encyclopedic Dictionary* defined a front as a battlefield command, "tasked with performing operational-strategic missions in one or several operational directions of a continental" TVD.[121] Front complements, strengths, and tasking could vary significantly in each TVD. Thus the 1963 General Staff *Operations* manual noted that "A front offensive zone in northern areas may encompass one or two strategic directions or an entire theater of military actions" while a subordinate army or army corps would usually advance along one constituent operational direction but in rare circumstances occupy a strategic direction.¹²² Eventually some intell connoisseurs did catch on to the significance of these and other such formulations.

Originating in the First World War, fronts assembled Ground Troops and Air Forces conglomerates, the highest command level within a TVD until the interposition of GK. USSR national air defense units might be subordinated and a coastal front would also control naval elements. In the general nuclear war variant fronts exploited the strikes by strategic systems, wading through the resultant radioactive debris. But in a limited nuclear variant aviation and missile delivery means supporting fronts would puncture NATO defenses. In the conventional variant there would basically be a rerun of the GPW—with the important caveat that nuclear weapons could be put into play at any point. Sans USSR strategic systems fronts constituted the determinant actors on the battlefield, the nuclei of strategic operations.

Fronts could be deployed not only by the Soviets but also by the armed forces of their Polish, Czech, Romanian, and Bulgarian allies. Intelligence analyses of communications plans indicated that the sixteen USSR military districts and four Soviet groups of forces in Central Europe could each generate at least one front field command. This work, and a limited selection of other sources, conveyed to intelligence a hazily perceived tiering of echeloned and reserve fronts. Per General-Major I. Anureyev and Colonel B. Khabarov in their 1968 General Staff Academy lecture on automation of troop control "with the onset of war, the districts comprising the first strategic echelon will immediately be reorganized into fronts" while interior MDs would mobilize additional units and materiel resources; predesignated MD elements would in wartime operate as the field command of a front.¹²³ This equation had not altered since the GPW "staffs of the military districts, which were now becoming Front Headquarters" upon mobilization in June 1941.¹²⁴ But a persistent intelligence second translation substantially misconceived what the strata heralded in the ensuing rollout. A range of deployment potentialities afforded the USSR General Staff a flexible suite of operational variants. Unfortunately these plans had not been disseminated to the intelligence reading list. Nevertheless some important evidence—including the second and third kinds—permitted reconstruction of front deployment variations.

One semi-corroborating source had been Vladimir Rezun a.k.a. Viktor Suvorov. He served as a captain in the GRU (Main Intelligence Directorate of the USSR General Staff) until defecting West in 1978. More prosaically known to intelligence as DS-3087 (the DS prefix reserved for defectors) he had been widely debriefed on a broad range of issues, confidently asserting authority. His professed knowledge on so many subjects began to be considered with some skepticism and the initially enthusiastic reception began to wear out. There had been, however, genuinely useful material—but there could be snags differentiating the accurate from uncertain hearsay. Much of this material later went public.¹²⁵ Thus Rezun, presciently, stressed the significance of the "High Commands of the Strategic Directions" even from information dating earlier in the 1970s. He laid out a three-level tiering scheme for the sixteen USSR districts based partly on experience in the intelligence department of the interior Volga MD during 1970-1971. Nine MDs in category one would generate wartime fronts; three districts (along with three Soviet groups in Central Europe) in category two could field fronts, but only after major augmentation; while four MD, including Volga, fell in a third category that would not form fronts (although the Volga headquarters had the capacity to control a front). While the categories basically correlated with other information, in fact that evidence pointed to front deployments quicker in the second and that category three would also convert—but in an ensuing strategic echelon of which Rezun (and intelligence) lacked awareness.

Soviet military strategy emphasized advance preparation of the TVDs as well as the predisposition of armed forces for a rapid buildup of strike groupings. Implementation provided indications, including logistics measures, with presumptive value. By the early 1960s a revolutionary technology had transformed the intelligence capabilities of their prospective enemies. While in earlier times military and other preparations could be largely hidden from prying eyes, the initiation of systematic surveillance by optical imaging satellites disclosed scale and particulars—Soviet preparatory measures imprinted a book open to anyone who might comprehend how to read the glyphs. Integrating the revealed with a varied mass of other sources including SIGINT, exercise scenarios, classified documents, and reporting by human sources provided an opportunity to reverse-engineer Soviet operational variants even when lacking access to the actual plans.

A unique attribute of satellite imagery for intelligence purposes is utility for clusivity analysis. A range of imaged objects may possess features in common, inclusive, and simultaneously exclusive, not found in other objects seemingly even of the same type. The works of the Soviet strategic culture proved to be eminently susceptible to definition through imaged clusivity. An intensive, multi-decade, satellite coverage of the USSR and allies beginning in 1960 (building on limited U-2 aircraft acquisitions from 1956 to 1960)—by imaging systems that improved in resolution and frequency over several generations—accumulated an historically unprecedented holistic database of entire countries across time and geography. As put by one inteller "The photographic record can capture a view of reality with its full information content."¹²⁶ This methodical survey afforded imagery a crucial advantage over the other 'INTs. Electronic watchers and human sources often afforded remarkable—but unevenly successful—penetrations. Large swathes of the adversaries' activities and capabilities remained intelligence lacunae, essentially nonexistent where these means had no access.

But imagery had (and has) limitations and weak points. These deficiencies are accentuated by an objectification propensity transforming this medium into a perceptual versioned reality dissociated from external relationships. Intelligence argument during the Cold War had often been constricted to an identification and cross-comparison of imaged objects that ignored context. An abiding fallacy held by media, academics, and even intelligence professionals is that imaging systems 'see' things. But these are merely electro-mechanical collectors. Nothing is 'seen' until a pair of eyeballs backed by gray matter lock on—and outcomes are determined by substantive knowledge, imagery processing skills, alertness, and that crucial failure point, perspective. The Cold War produced an extensive record of things imaged but not 'seen' with a concomitant lengthy addendum of things 'seen' but which did not actually exist. A definitional certainty is that both of these lists have subsequently acquired numerous additions.

The beginning of satellite near-realtime digital imaging of 'denied areas' on the night of 19-20 January 1977 by system KH-11 mission 5501—along with the subsequent improvements in this medium as well as computer technology—potentially allowed for the fusion of all forms of evidence. Intelligence had a, short, free ride on this system since the Soviets failed to grasp that, despite a higher orbit than they deemed suitable for a photographic reconnaissance system, a revolutionary technology had materialized. A classified lecture prepared for the USSR General Staff Academy admitted "They successfully took advantage of this for a year and a half or two years until our comrades obtained documentation on this Keyhole-11 and sent it here. Then it was learned that this was a brand-new reconnaissance device."[127] The "documentation" undoubtedly the *KH-11 Exploitation Reference Guide*[128] helpfully sold at a bargain price by William Kampiles in early 1978. Subsequent to the end of the Gambit-3 KH-8 high-resolution program in August 1984 (mission 4354) and the global searching Hexagon KH-9 in October 1984 (mission 1219)[129] the KH-11 performed both functions.

While the KH-11 provided immediate results that could not be matched by film-based, delayed return, systems as in many technological advances there would be losses as well as gains. An intelligence crucial requirement for a comprehensive visualization of any Soviet preparations to intervene in the Polish 1980-1981 internal crisis impelled resort to the pending supersession KH-9. Exploiting unusual cloudless conditions over central Europe and the western USSR six overlapping passes during revolutions 1350 through 1393 by mission 1216-4 from 24 to 28 February 1981 blanketed garrisons, airfields, logistics installations, and rail lines from Berlin to east of Moscow and Lake Ladoga south to Budapest. Prevalent snow meant that gatherings and movement could be readily detected by disturbance. A further demonstration took place in the case of the infamous Krasnoyarsk radar—deemed by the US (and later admitted by the USSR) to be a violation of the 1972 Anti-Ballistic Missile Treaty. Construction had been underway for eighteen months when finally detected—via the KH-9.[130] These and other deficiencies motivated the rolling out of the last KH-9 built as mission 1220. But on 18 April 1986 the program terminated when a crack US Air Force team blew up missile and payload on the launch pad.[131] (Oh—no indications of Soviet intervention in Poland had been evident).

The true power of satellite imagery proceeds only when used as a baseplate for a perceptual nexus that incorporates evidence from all the tools available to intelligence whether communications intercepts or media reports or any other fount of knowledge. Modeling by evidential fusion enhances the discovery of functional organization and operational planning; the implementation of military strategy and doctrine; even definition of intent. The advent of digital imaging presented the opportunity to build an integrated database of great analytic utility, perhaps given a catchy name, say, 'google earth.' But an astoundingly large proportion of the intelligence workforce misapprehended the essentiality of relating imagery to other sources. This un-enlightenment extended to the intelligence official audience, other outsiders—and the designers of the imaging satellite constellation. Particularly risky, departed and attendant connoisseurs who focus on imagery as an independent verity. Several representative examples follow herein.

A series of studies I conducted in the early 1980s on theater forces organization, missile and other preparations identified a unique species of warhead-missile-munitions support bases. These could be picked out on satellite imagery as the product of a major construction program that began about 1960 to install nuclear-hardened shelters at selected major Ground Troops conventional ammunition storage facilities. Salient characteristics included colocation of nuclear weapons support elements at what the Soviets categorized as first-class artillery ammunition bases, marked by standard nuclear-hardened warhead storage bunkers; hardened and sometimes legacy soft structures for missile storage that amounted to several multiples of those at army-level missile support bases; and particularized train sets with common numbers of warhead and missile transport railcars. Such rail assets accorded with the Soviet representation of materiel deliveries primarily by rail to field logistics bases of deployed fronts.

Oleg Penkovsky had provided articles from the top secret edition of VM published from 1960 to early 1962 that explicated the beginnings of the front missile support structure—but fully two decades elapsed before the correlating installations that had been erected would be delineated in an intelligence study.[132] In this material senior officer experts laid out a warhead-missile logistics organization, in the original conception, positioned at the top level of the front structure; with separate resupply channels from the Center for warhead and missile reloads; rail rolling stock provided the basis for nearly all onward transport. General-Lieutenant M. Novikov even diagrammed the flow of "special charges" and missiles from a "Front rocket technical base (FRTB)" via specialized units to their launchers (another base supported air defense missiles).[133] General-Colonel G. F. Odintsov followed up on that article with additional details on this FRTB and the support scheme, which had been tested in the 1960 exercise Don, while disagreeing on the front lines of control.[134] The role of the FRTB in the front rear structure had also been discussed by General-Colonel F. Malykhin[135] a key honcho in the logistics organization of the Soviet Armed Forces.

Further modifications to the Soviet scheme could be traced in classified writings and, eventually, in exercises of the components. Many of the documents have now been declassified by the CIA. Operations manuals and course documents of the Military Academy of the General Staff, acquired by intelligence from the early 1970s, provided considerable detail on the logistics context of both front missile-artillery bases as well as the army-level bases that had been subsequently established. The sources prescribed the accumulation of materiel reserves for opening front offensives—sufficient to support forward movement and combat to the full depth of the operation—positioned in the direction of advance.

A massive array of front field bases and rear services units would hold the largest proportion by far of these resources. According to the 1977 Academy lecture on front operations this complex might have 200 or more units and facilities with up to 170000 personnel and 27000 motor vehicles—all established on the basis of, and deployed from, permanent installations during full war mobilization. The lecture also indicated that the proportion of shipments to the bases by rail would be up to 85 percent in the nuclear variant and could be all-rail in conventional conditions.[136] Hardly a recent development, a Soviet history on GPW logistics explained that in the prewar period theater "preparations were made in such a way that at the beginning of the war each front would receive a complete base for troop rear support...."[137] According to a 1969 document of the General Staff Academy on front-army rear services (among many other sources) the front complex echeloned 13 to 14 days of the minimum required materiel reserves for a 20-day first front operation. The balance would be kept on the motor transport assets of subordinate armies and their divisions.[138] This disproportionate allotment reflected the premium the Soviets assigned to maneuverability and rapid advance of relatively lightly-burdened tank and combined-arms armies. The 1977 lecture gave identical echeloned supply days and indicated an extant GPW formula.[139]

Materiel support of an operation at the beginning of war is carried out through the use of the reserves established in peacetime with the troops and at the bases and depots of the armies, military districts, and troop groupings. The amounts of these reserves must fully support the forward movement of troops, their conduct of initial operations to the entire depth, and the establishment of reserves by the end of the operation.

The missile-artillery bases identified from imagery afforded the only possible immediate source for the quantity of ammunition proportioned to the front complex; with the collocated missile elements purposed to deploy as front field missile bases. Unfortunately throughout the 1960s and 1970s the intelligence connoisseurs following nuclear weapons developments rigorously ignored the detailed Soviet documentation that had been acquired on what and how missile support arrangements had been implemented. Imaged correlations persisted unnoticed; connoisseurs in the Warsaw Pact forces analytical shops shared this inability to cross-reference sources and indications. These bases represented placeholders for the fronts that would be generated in the Soviet general war plan. Theater operations specialists never caught on to the value of front bases as markers for the evolving Soviet theater operations variants evident in exercises and classified writings. Yet two more intelligence cubicles remained incapable of recognizing substantial evidence of the second kind.

Positioning of these front missile-artillery bases, on lines of communications accessing the directions, suggested that a fully mobilized Soviet multi-theater strategic deployment provided for up to nineteen fronts arranged in both geographic and mobilization echelons. Identification of the designated 1950s front bases lacked exactitude since nuclear missiles had been introduced into the Ground Troops only at the end of the decade and there had been sparse overhead imagery. Gratitude must be extended to the Soviets for delineation assistance. Three of these bases had been established circa 1965, concurrently with an operational adjustment that had been initiated to magnify forces available for an emergent conventional variant: one each in the Northern-Coastal and Italian Strategic Directions and a reserve front in the Volga region. Additional front bases created in the early 1970s included one base in the Far East, and the second in the Urals region for a reserve front probably oriented towards the Eastern Theater. A readout of the evidence provided by this contingent network of front bases proffered five Soviet forward and reserve fronts to be deployed against the Chinese; while thirteen Soviet echeloned and reserve fronts could be committed against NATO countries, although two of these in the Caucasus could also cooperate with the (nineteenth) Turkestan front in the Southern TVD to contend with neighbors in near eastern directions.

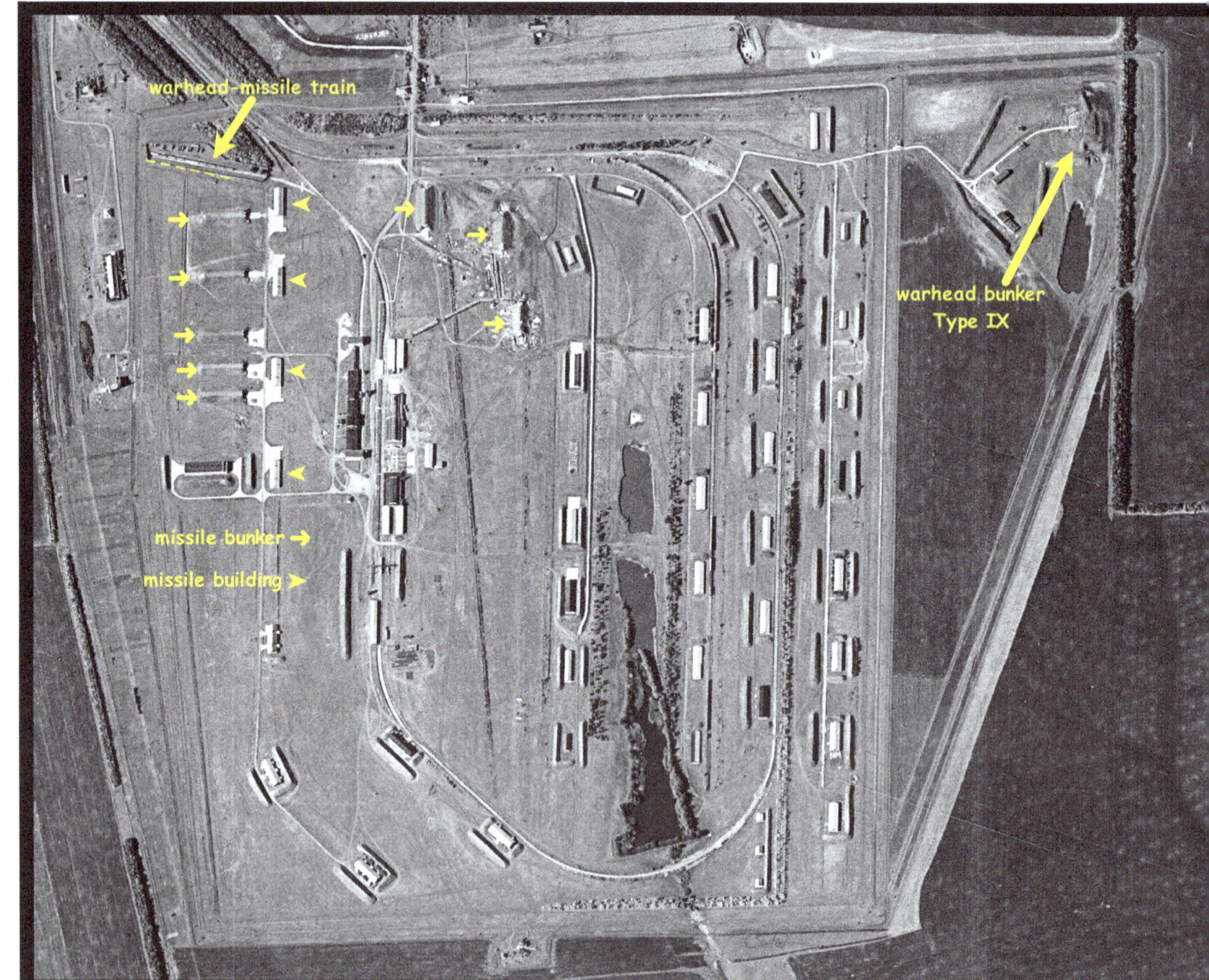

Front Missile-Artillery Base Lozovaya (Lozova)
Ukraine SSR

An inexorable buildup of ammunition stocks at this base would by the end of the 1970s provide about 30 to 40 percent of the requirement for one complete front offensive operation as specified by the USSR General Staff Academy in 1977

Larger scale exercises confirmed intelligence assessments of the scope, if not always the particulars, of the Soviet war plan. A multi-theater-TVD exercise in May 1973[140] fielded at least sixteen Soviet front headquarters, by all four groups of forces in Central Europe along with border and interior military districts. Fronts remained absent from three adjoining districts, probably excluded from this exercise, which would later comprise the Southern TVD. Interior front commands moved toward the TVDs even though these had no apparent subordinates. This exercise may well have marked a Soviet assessment of the full, recently finalized, complement of fronts. In an exercise on a comparable scale, *Tsentr* 1982,[141] Soviet and national fronts had been designated, apparently consecutively in sequence of deployment, up to 23 Front by the time of the Warsaw Pact invasion of Spain. If four of these represented national fronts then the tally of Soviet fronts would have equated to all of the identified front missile-artillery bases. Similar sequential numbering of fronts reached at least 18 and likely 20 in *Tsentr* 1978.[142] Even in the Gorbachev era of good feelings in early 1987 a General Staff exercise designated a military district as 21 Front.

During the GPW by comparison each of the five western border military districts deployed one front at the beginning of the German campaign; with ten operating fronts within six months; peaking at fourteen active fronts (one holding the Far East) in 1943-1944.[143] The need for additional fronts had been partly driven by the expansion of war zone width from 3400-km at the outset to 6000-km by November 1942 as the Germans advanced ever deeper into the USSR. Desperate defensive battles in the first years impelled many trans- and re-formations of fronts in changing operational situations. Thereafter the Soviets deactivated a number of front commands as the counteroffensive frontage contracted (in contrast to a widening zone in any conflict with NATO) and as the fronts up-sized.[144] Three fronts eventually confronted the Japanese during the 1945 Manchurian Operation, a strategic grouping established by the transfer of two front headquarters and substantial reinforcements from the west to augment troops that had remained in the east since the start of the war.[145] While the 1941 fronts had three or four subordinate armies (two in the Southern), by the end of 1944 the less numerous fronts ranged six to nine combined-arms armies each with those on key directions reinforced by one or two tank armies.[146] The strategic operations of January to March 1945 that brought the Soviets into Central Europe orchestrated seven fronts in simultaneous offensives across 1200-km.[147] Front zones averaged about 170-km wide or roughly half the scaling planned for their Cold War counterparts—the wider zone permitted dispersal and maneuver in conditions expected to be, or to become, nuclear. Of course the Soviets fought only in Europe until near the end unlike the two-theater war in prospect during the 1970s-1980s.

Despite an abundance of material to work with, US intelligence had serious difficulties determining the prospective lineup of fronts, particularly following Soviet realignments. In the 1960s and 1970s new national and Soviet fronts would not be identified for several years, even as much as a decade, after they had been created. A crucial intelligence misapprehension regarding the role assigned to Polish forces persisted through the Cold War. Intelligence reporting characterized the 1968 Czech invasion as a gaggle of divisions of different nationalities,[148] with no inkling of the cobbling together of the fronts actually fielded to conduct Operation Danube.[149] Not a great testimony for the ability of intelligence services to accurately inform NATO in a timely manner so that an effective defense could be prepared in the event of a premeditated Warsaw Pact attack.

Nuclear weapons use, or potential transition to a nuclear phase, impelled the Soviets to plan operations of fronts in demarcated zones. NATO reservation of nuclear first use, however controversial, had the militarily immensely significant import of limiting Warsaw Pact forward-loading of an attack deployment during a threat period. To ensure nuclear-protective dispersal and wide maneuver, the operation of a front would be conducted in a wide zone the dimensions of which fluctuated depending on TVD or direction conditions, the scaling of strategic nuclear strikes, and complement. Exercises along with classified writings and documents on zone dimensions could show substantial variations and contradictions, even in the same timeframe, at least partly due to differing views among Soviet officers.

The front offensive zone in the nuclear free-for-all of the first half of the 1960s ranged from 300- to as much as 600-km.[150] The operational adjustment subsequently implemented to increase available forces for conventional conditions reduced the zone. According to the Professor, at the end of the 1960s this amounted to either 200 or 300 to 500, identical for nuclear and conventional warfare.[151] Zones in conventional conditions had to be maintained as in nuclear since a transition could take place at any, unforeseeable, point of an operation. By the mid 1970s, the front offensive zone width seems to have stabilized at 300- to 400-km in the Western TVD, but could be wider in other TVDs.[152] A front defensive zone could be 500-km or more. Divisions served as basis units in these calculations for establishing both front and army zones. In 1960 nuclear conditions each division would have a (proposed) 20-km zone,[153] effective into the early 1970s for both nuclear and conventional variants; then narrowed 15- to 20-km[154] to allow for more troops at the line of scrimmage; which by the mid 1980s ranged 10- to 20-km for both tank and motor rifle divisions.[155] The nuclear variant had impelled a sharp break with prescriptions even in 1959 which had provided for division zones of 6- to 12-km and fronts 250- to

300-km.[156] Thus the number of subordinate divisions deployed on the line determined the overall zones of the parents.

The Soviet General Staff analysis of individual TVD conditions determined the deployment of forward and reinforcing fronts. In turn, opposing intelligence services could have enhanced reverse-engineering of plan variants by considering the directions in conjunction with the norms for front, army, and division zones. Any perusal of the current stock of declassified US intell documents will seek in vain for even the slightest hint of any such approach to estimating Soviet-Warsaw Pact deployment of fronts and the creation of the critical strike groupings through most of the Cold War. But of course only in the mid 1980s did the Soviet codification of operational and strategic directions, that evidence of the second kind, be noticed and attributed any significance. The initial Western TVD width as a straight line from the Baltic Sea to the Austrian border is just over 600-km. Colonel S. Sokolov in his interesting appraisal of NATO forces in a 1966 VM (S) article put this distance as an effective frontage of 700- to 740-km, the offensive zone of the NATO Northern and Central Army Groups against East Germany, Poland, and Czechoslovakia.[157]

To maintain nuclear-protective zones reserve fronts could be committed only during an offensive. Another Soviet calculation had the Western TVD expanding in width from 750-km to 1600-km[158] At zonal specifications this would permit two fronts on the starting line or three tightly constrained with limited first echelons, thus highlighting the imperative for a rapid offensive that would allow reinforcing commitments up to four or five adjacent fronts. This had direct implications for Warsaw Pact capability to quickly break the NATO defense line, which at West German insistence had been pushed forward in the mid 1960s. Much of the NATO force deployment resided within 150-km, highly concentrated in the first 50-km, of the international border. Advancing to the River Rhine would surrender 75 percent of the population and economy of West Germany.[159] The Warsaw Pact plans placed a high premium on penetrating this shell, in a nuclear phase by mass strikes, and during operations with only conventional weapons by concentrating forces in narrow breakthrough sectors, with an ensuing rapid offensive into the depth of the Western TVD.

## marshaling the troops

Among the noteworthy characteristics of the Soviet strategic culture resided a proclivity for expansive scaling and insistent definition by numeration. Mass embodied both an ideological principle and a wartime planning objective. But prodigious scaling could also become a snare with international threat perception and domestic economic implications. The theoreticians and planners recognized as unachievable any instantaneous aggregation of forces and means by the Center. In order to attain orders of magnitude the approved solution entailed an orchestrated buildup of efforts by preplanned stages within finite timescales. Notions of swarming and echeloning pervaded all aspects of strategic planning from deployment of troops to the disposition of materiel reserves—and mass destruction weapons.

The Soviets considered mass a crucial prerequisite even for nuclear weapons. A 1950s Revolution in Military Affairs defined in Soviet literature came about not with the introduction of atomic arms into the military services but rather at the end of the decade when fissile material production permitted greatly expanded manufacture of warheads and bombs. Nuclear weapons could thus be deployed on a large scale by all arms. Many Soviet officers pointed out the consequent impact on strategy and operational art in both classified and open writings. They even argued among themselves in early 1960s classified journals as to what constituted 'mass' nuclear strikes. In a 1961 VM (S) article[160] one colonel rejected the contention that exercises prior to 1959 had not used nuclear missiles in a "massed nature" but that even with the few nuclear warheads then available these had been employed widely in conjunction with conventional means in fire preparation for an offensive. He defined a mass nuclear strike as the simultaneous delivery of single and grouped missiles and proposed control and organization improvements to enhance coordinated firings. Officers in a later article[161] offered a key retrospective on the nuclear massing issue and pinpointed the end of the 1950s as the start of a nuclear plenitude for both front nuclear warheads and the delivering missile systems.

Economic, demographic, and geographic factors impose limitations on the size and disposition of national active armed forces; a "detriment to state budget" admitted a prominent theorist.[162] The structure of a multi-theater employment of Soviet forces would be on such a scale that nothing approaching war strength could be maintained in peacetime. A carefully calculated minimum of troops and means, sufficient to repulse the ideologically ordained likely surprise attack by the West, constituted the peacetime establishment. Upon the outbreak of war, units designated for inclusion in fronts, and reinforcing fronts, could be located hundreds or thousands of kilometers from their operational directions. A strategic deployment would have to be implemented that differed even from that envisioned in the 1950s when only limited numbers of nuclear weapons had been available.[163]

> In the modern definition, strategic deployment, as a matter of fact, turns into the process of creating strategic groupings of armed forces for the beginning of the war in agreement with the plan of war and the probable conditions of its unleashing.

Senior officers drew a basic outline in their critique of a 1970 Warsaw Pact exercise.[164]

> Specific ground forces groupings and a portion of the naval and air forces are at a high level of readiness and are on combat alert. However, the available combat-

ready groupings of all branches of the armed forces will undoubtedly be inadequate to conduct total war. Therefore all of them will be reinforced by moving forward additional forces and means and incorporating them into their complement. Furthermore, immediately upon the outbreak of war and during the war it will be necessary to create new operational and strategic groupings in the various theaters of military actions and on the directions.

For the designated enemies, and their intelligence services, the discernible elements would most definitely not be what they would get. Radical, pervasive, and large scale alterations implemented to the structure and the geo-positioning of the Soviet Army as readiness stages elevated and the military, along with the economy, prepared for the titanic struggle forecast by ideology and military strategy.

This humongous restructuring, mobilization, and deployment of armed forces would be a single process with many separate but related elements, orchestrated to execute operations plans-variants in the TVDs. As put by one Soviet general "strategic deployment is the concluding act of peace and the initial act of a war."[165] Soviet planners resolved the discrepancy between structural theory and reality by echeloning forces and means by location as well as their level of readiness (manning and equipment). Full mobilization composed one of the key elements, per *Military Strategy* "As commonly understood, mobilization or mobilization-deployment of the armed forces means their conversion from a peacetime to a wartime footing in accordance with a war plan."[166] Their conception of a mobilization and deployment 'wave train' not some idealization but a practical road map for organization and implementation. Mobilization-deployment constituted a progressive interrelated, linear, event intended to achieve an offensive crescendo—a massive and unrelenting buildup of combat power—in the TVDs. Their conventional variant aimed to replicate the 1944-1945 offensives by manifold fronts, continually reinforced from the VGK reserve, which one Soviet general characterized as a "mighty avalanche" resulting from operations of "mounting scale and intensity" in which the Germans would be rendered incapable of resisting.[167]

Uncertainty regarding war duration engendered Soviet planning for several strategic echelons of active and follow-on forces—the first comprising elements of the armed services designated to conduct the operations, and achieve the objectives, of the Initial Period. Delineated in 1963 by the Chief of the USSR General Staff, Marshal M. V. Zakharov, "The first strategic echelon consists of strategic rocket troops, long range aviation, air defense forces of the country, groups of forces, and border military districts, as well as fleets. These are the forces in constant readiness." With any luck the goal of a war could be attained by this array. But if not sufficient "newly activated contingents will constitute the second strategic echelon of the armed forces."[168] As put by Colonel A. Volkov in his 1966 VM (S) list of measures to be accomplished during one variant period of a war, tasks included "completion of the full mobilization of first strategic echelon troops and mobilization expansion of the second strategic echelon and reserves."[169] Soviet retrospectives attributed the origin of the strategic echelons concept—characterized as "permanent mobilization"—to 1930s military theorist G. S. Isserson.[170] Additional strategic echelons, duplicating the GPW formula, might be mobilized to fight any prolonged war. Identification by intelligence of the waves of mobilization became increasingly more obscured the further back—no armies carried in the orders of battle for central Soviet military districts even though many classified writings dealt with the problems of early mobilization and deployment of interior-based armies.

The first strategic echelon would be further staged in operational echelons that sequenced mobilization over several weeks beginning with those troops and armament in a constant readiness status. This ordering had been laid out in a 1961 VM (TS) article by General-Major Ya. Shchepennikov.[171]

> In speaking of strategic echelons, we mean that the first of these consist of the forces and weapons necessary for achieving the strategic aims of the initial period of a war; it is divided into several (not less than three) operational echelons. The first includes the troops and materiel that are in a full state of readiness for immediate operations, the second is the forces and weapons designated for increasing the efforts of the initial operations with readiness for proceeding to areas of concentration after several days, the third is the forces and weapons to be used only several weeks after the beginning of full mobilization, for the development of the subsequent operations of the initial period of a war.

Intelligence had no direct information as to how this scheme applied to the generation of wartime fronts. But a plenitude of indirect indications existed to enable several approaches to estimating potential deployment of fronts to the TVDs. The Soviet multi-theater requirement for fronts may have been set by the early 1970s and fully tested in the 1973 large scale exercise. Filling out these fronts would have necessitated a much longer period of force development. Soviet classified writings and operations manuals specified the complements of fronts during three decades of evolving theater strategy considerations. These sources, from the early 1960s well into the 1970s frequently stated, with conflicting divergences, that a front deployed in the Western TVD would comprise three or four armies at the outset of a war. Subsequently the allowance stretched up to five armies.

According to "exercises of recent years" per a 1963 VM (S) article complements of fronts varied three or four armies.[172]

But the General Staff operations manual of that year calculated a front zone with four to six armies.[173] A decade later the front operations textbook used by the General Staff Academy cited exercise experience of a Western TVD front comprising three to five armies (including one or two tank armies) but still allowed for a variant of three or four armies.[174] Yet one officer's notes on Academy lectures a year or two later again specified a front composition of three or four armies, one of these a tank army.[175] Even a 1977 Academy lecture on front offensive operations, while giving a three/four/five specification—again only one tank army—indicated that the three- or four-army variant retained validity.[176] The critical variable in these norms had been the subordination of Warsaw Pact armies. Beginning in the early 1960s a national fronts variant had been developed which would absorb these armies; but other variants might still dispense with one or more of these fronts thereby pitching their armies to Soviet-commanded fronts. Even in the 1980s when intelligence consistently projected a three to five armies specification,[177] the 1985 General Staff Academy lecture on the missile-artillery complement of Western TVD fronts calculated on the basis of three to four armies (one tank army).[178]

US intelligence had identified by the mid 1980s a USSR total active 29 armies (six of these designated tank armies) and 11 army corps.[179] Two additional corps based on transformed divisions served as testbeds. Also evident the type and number of units making up the Soviet groups in Hungary and Czechoslovakia indicated that each could form a combined-arms army, a variant depicted in exercises. In Czechoslovakia the army had a coexistent army corps present since 1968 (moved forward from the Carpathian MD). Soviet army corps so frequently recomposed as armies during exercises that each could be regarded as an army-in-being, upgrading presumably dependent on available resources and preparation time. These 42 formations constituted pushpins that the Soviet General Staff could move about, regardless of peacetime location, to establish an initial strategic deployment of fronts. The Soviets treated both fronts and armies as headquarters with prescribed control spans. Armies would be transferred among fronts, and divisions between armies, at the drop of a baton. Also, in the crucial GPW precedent, field headquarters of fronts and armies had often been transferred to and from the VGK reserve, trotted out when arranging new or reconstituted complete formations.

US intelligence tended to assess Soviet reinforcement capabilities and planning with a strange reverence for international and administrative boundaries. While the headquarters of Soviet groups and military districts would be the most likely basis of front field commands, this arrangement did not signify that all or even most of their wartime subordinates inhered coterminous. More than a few connoisseurs spent their intelligence careers fixated on the Soviet group in East Germany as a complete front. But many units the Soviets attributed to the composition of a front absented from East Germany or even Central Europe; and a long trail of evidence substantiated that the armies of the GSFG might not be confined to only one front. Much of the field logistics complex supporting forward fronts would appear only upon their mobilization—in the USSR.

Frequent discussions of operational matters in classified documents had been conditioned on the "arrival" of not only logistics but also combat units according to the mobilization schedule. General-Major V. Yuryev's calculation in a 1966 VM (S) article[180], providing one of many indications, regarded the capability of a front to reconstruct rail lines (then expected to be destroyed by NATO nuclear strikes). The first front railroad brigade would not show up for work until the third day of combat and a second brigade not available until operations day seven or eight (Soviet documents and manuals listing a type front complement included two or three railroad brigades; none deployed in any of the Central Europe groups; all mobilized from the peacetime rail system). He also noted during the course of a front operation receipt of additional divisions and sometimes armies.

Initiation of strategic deployment collated forces and weapons from those already in or near the operational directions as well as by marches of formations and units from locations at varying distances in accordance with the mobilization-deployment schedule. As formulated in the 1977 USSR General Staff Academy lecture "In the first offensive operation, the strike groupings are formed both by using the troops available in the military district (group of forces) in peacetime and by using mobilized contingents and troops arriving from the interior."[181] In exercises and classified writings combat and support units assigned even to a front in East Germany might originate in an interior military district. Geography provided the Soviets an enormous advantage over NATO in that reinforcement could be conducted without spanning an ocean gap; a crucial element of any campaign to forestall US augmentation of NATO in-theater forces. Marches of individual units, armies, and entire fronts prominently featured in Soviet TVD planning, with norms prescribed in manuals, factors discussed in great detail in journals, verified by frequent exercise practice. *Peregruppirovka* (regrouping) represented a priority consideration of Soviet military science.

Even during the heyday of strategic 'massive retaliation' the Soviets proposed to conduct extensive regroupings over long distances in nuclear conditions. One of the eight chapters in the 1963 General Staff operations manual for Ground Troops had been entirely devoted to the problem;[182] detailing front and army regroupings—specifying from the USSR interior to TVDs and between TVDs—despite an expectation of disruption by enemy nuclear (and chemical) attacks. Regrouping of armies held such importance that the General Staff Academy conducted a special six week segment in at least the 1970s, instruction based on the march of an army from the USSR to

East Germany.[183] Difficulties would be ameliorated if the enemy used only conventional weapons, ranged within TVDs, or regroupings initiated prior to the outbreak of war—the official critique of exercise *Zapad* 1977 stressed the necessity of ensuring secrecy of movements during a threat period.[184]

A skewed perspective hampered the intelligence appreciation of the deployment of fronts in the Western TVD. The powerful grouping of Soviet armies, missiles, and aviation packed into East Germany on, apparently the main thrust of the Western TVD the North German Strategic Direction, attained a disproportionate fixation (the GSFG, not TVD directions), and expansive resource allocation, for US and NATO intelligence services. The guiding assumption, lacking access to operations plans, through most of the Cold War persisted that this group would form a single, unitary—**the** type—front in the TVD strategic operation. This conclusion despite arithmetic discrepancies when reconciling the Soviet classified specifications. Limited, uncertain, indications suggested that GSFG subordinates might in fact be subject to sharing—and even some direct evidence of a planned augmentation that would exceed the specified complement for one front.

As early as 1962 Colonels N. Kalayev and A. Tarasov contended in the pages of VM (S) against the prevailing higher level view that part of the complement of a leading front actually emanated from the USSR.[185] They insisted that the second echelon army (or armies) need be present at the outset of a front operation, mainly due to heavy losses in nuclear conditions "the opinion expressed at times in our military literature, for example, in the circles of the Military Academy of the General Staff, that a second echelon of a front will be formed mainly during the operation from among arriving forces, in our view, cannot be considered valid." They cited 1961 front command-staff exercises in May and October (presumably a warm-up for *Burya*) in which a GSFG front second echelon had derived from local armies including an East German army in the May exercise. But their description of the October front operation accounted for only four armies: one tank, two combined-arms, and one unidentified type (most likely combined-arms) that had seized West Berlin. Even though both front echelons had been played from within the ranks of the GSFG, more if one of the October exercise armies originated from the East German contingent, two other armies remained unaccountable. Perhaps the absent armies had been preoccupied with doing their thing in the complements of one or two adjacent fronts.

The GSFG comprised six armies until 1964. In that year a major reorganization deleted 18 Guards Army, redistributing subordinate divisions among the other armies.[186] Six exceeded by at least two or as many as three armies the allowance for an entire front complement according to some early 1960s citations for a 3-4 norm. Five armies still exceeded the lower limit, and only matched the fifth army stretch when firmly established by the 1980s. Unambiguous indications of any multi-front segmentation had been lacking in detected exercising during the Cold War, however, any reflection of such variants would have been well-hidden. Only near The End would US assessments begin to conclude that GSFG flank armies might adhere to one or more adjacent fronts; a 1984 DIA operations modeling placed 2 Guards Tank Army in a Northern Front with the Poles;[187] while a 1985 report allowed that 8 Guards Army might join a Czech-based front.[188] That study had also observed that three of the five GSFG armies had been equipped to a higher standard while the two others closely resembled neighboring Soviet groups. A 1989 NIE permitted one of the armies to be detached but in the context of resubordination to a front moved forward from the USSR prior to outbreak of war.[189] The official model persistently failed to fully comprehend the character of the Soviet creation of forward strike groupings and their augmentation from within the USSR.

Those East German comrades also had role assignments. In the 1960s armament and troop upscaling developed each of the two GDR military districts as a potential corps or combined-arms army. Exercises from the early 1960s variously played either variant; documents from a 1969 exercise depicted two East German armies in a GSFG Central Front.[190] Among the problems in evaluating evidence from Warsaw Pact exercises is that these may only presage operational planning and organizational innovations rather than confirm those already effective. But from 1978 exercises consistently depicted two East German armies; for a total of seven armies in the deployment supposedly comprising a unitary GSFG front—two in excess of the maximum front quota. A milestone of the planned East German role had been provided by the index formation of a Warsaw Pact army, the organic R-300 (SS-1c Scud B) missile brigade. In 1965 the one existing brigade had been subordinated to the northern MD V (5 Army); by 1976 this brigade had been split to form a new missile brigade for the southern MD III (3 Army).[191]

Another GSFG anomaly involved the Soviets' favored tank armies. GRU Captain Rezun had insisted—not just another instance of blowing smoke—that a front would have only one tank army and that since the GSFG had two designated tank armies (and one other that equated) this group would generate more than one front.[192] There had been consistent specification in 1960s-1970s classified material that a Western TVD front would begin operations with one subordinate tank army; a few deviations allotted one or two, likely reflecting potential additions during the course of a front offensive. In a 1961 article General-Colonel P. Koshevoy stated that a front "is usually made up of" one tank army (but gave the front variant of 4-5 total armies)[193]—and might well have been in the know since in the second half of the 1960s he would be the GSFG Commander. The Professor in 1964 also specified one tank army[194] while USSR General Staff Academy lectures in 1976[195] and 1977[196] concurred. But some complicating nuances transpired in frequent reshuffles of the division complements of GSFG armies during more than three decades.

The Soviets faced a particular dilemma in regard to positioning tank armies as the strategies of the opponents evolved during the Cold War. Considered the primary strike force in the nuclear warfare envisioned for the early 1960s, tank armor provided a degree of protection from mass nuclear detonations and the resulting radioactive contamination of vast areas that would have to be crossed during an offensive. The high mobility of tank formations expedited advances through nuclear-created gaps in NATO defenses; with tank army missions specified to the full depth of the planned front offensive. Tank armies keyed front main thrusts although some Soviet officers warned that this association could tip the enemy to identification of the main effort. But even in nuclear conditions some high rankers disputed the operational need for tank armies, favoring a combined-arms army with a strong tank element, eliciting a startling bitter exchange in the early 1960s issues of the top secret edition of VM.

General-Major (Tank Troops) A. Shevchenko, while agreeable to tank divisions, cited both GPW and recent exercises in advocating the elimination of tank armies in favor of combined-arms—these would form the basis of the front strike groupings for which he provided an important definition of the Soviet concept.[197] GPW veteran Marshal (Tank Troops) P. Rotmistrov, defending tanks in contemporary operations, responded as "not scientifically founded" proposals from Shevchenko and others to rely on not only mixed tank-motorized rifle armies but also unified divisions.[198] Rotmistrov's comments on the derelict actions of 5 Guards Combined-Arms Army in the July 1943 Prokhorovka meeting engagement, contrasted with those of 5 Guards Tank Army (failing to mention that he commanded), in turn brought a stinging rebuke from General-Army A. Zhadov (who had led 5 GCAA in this battle); Zhadov still considered the tank army to be viable but noted that a CAA had comparable numbers of tanks and combat power—and that not tank troops but nuclear missiles represented the decisive arm.[199] Soviet infighting must have continued for years afterward regarding TA (which never disappeared) vs. CAA; by 1985 the General Staff Academy declared "military thinking is now coming around to the opinion" that the army types had become similar, meriting a "uniform army"[200] while another lecture noted a trend to uniform divisions.[201]

Tank armies would be postured forward in a front for the nuclear variant, and would therefore have to be located in peacetime or so deployed, to immediately exploit the results of nuclear strikes. But from the mid 1960s the conditions of a front offensive gradually became more likely to be based on conventional arms alone. Tank armies (and tank divisions) employed in the first echelon to conduct a conventional breakthrough would likely be so chewed up in the process by increasingly potent NATO antitank weapons that they would be incapable of any rapid exploitation in depth. A military-scientific conference held at the Frunze Military Academy circa 1969 had warned that the improving NATO capability made imperative that forward use of tank formations "so that by the beginning of nuclear war they will not have sustained serious losses" must be carefully considered.[202] A preference developed that the dirty work of the front breakthroughs be accomplished by combined-arms armies. Arranging the strategic deployment of armies to establish strike groupings in two fundamentally different variants became an increasingly more complex proposition for the Soviet General Staff. The peacetime disposition of the proximate Western assault force, in the GSFG, posed an urgent priority.

Both economically and militarily, swapping unit locations for disparate variants would hardly be possible by moving tank armies and tank divisions about like pieces on a chessboard. The Soviets took up rebalancing as an alternative. Intelligence had relatively good access to the communications arrangements of the GSFG to follow evolving organization and subordination. There had been two designated tank armies from the second half of the 1950s when a major transformation of army structures had been implemented. But in the 1964 reorganization 2 Guards Tank Army had been stripped of two tank divisions, thereby converting to a combined-arms complement that would be maintained to the end of Russian occupation (but still designated 2 GTA); both divisions then resubordinated to 3 Shock Army thereby revamping as a tank army. This army and 1 Guards Tank Army each then had four tank divisions, constituting especially powerful strike groupings (even after 1 GTA lost two tank divisions in the 1980s).[203] Occasional reshuffles of divisions among the armies, and indications of some under dual control, had been detected that pointed to Soviet attempts to solve the variant dilemma. In the 1980s 20 Guards Combined-Arms Army gradually became a third tank army by the expedient of swiping a tank division (90) based at Borne in Poland[204] and converting one subordinate motorized rifle division (14) into a tank division (32)—three TDs plus only one MRD but retaining the CAA designation.[205] There may well have been a deception aspect to all the reshuffles. Intelligence nevertheless managed to ignore this GSFG excess, three tank as well as total armies, beyond the number in a prescribed front, as well as other evidence of the second kind, in persisting to the end of the Cold War assessing this Group as a single unitary front.[206]

Several more gaping holes existed in the intelligence model of the Western TVD. In exercises the Northern Group of Forces based in Poland periodically gave birth to a front, as in May 1973. But the NGF ground complement amounted to all of two divisions, and otherwise (i.e. variants) in exercises these reinforced armies in the GSFG or composed part of a heretofore nonexistent army. Yet the NGF also sported a numbered air army (specification at least one per front) as did the GSFG until the front air army organization disappeared in the 1980s. Yet another hole opened (from 1968) with the Central Group of Forces in Czechoslovakia. The CGF also formed a front in some exercises but did at least have one active corps and the ingredients for an army, still less than the specified minimum front and missing a numbered air army. Given the prevailing rigid, narrow, perspective no one could explain how the Soviets would be able to transform these groups into fronts. Further soiling the official model the, belatedly discovered, Baltic front generated from a district fielding only one active ground army—and a numbered air army. Where or how could these fronts acquire their minimum of three ground armies when the official model also projected unitary Polish and Czech national fronts while confining the armies of the neighboring Belorussian and Carpathian MDs—as well as the GSFG—to their respective unitary front? Intelligence connoisseurs could not account for these ginormous discrepancies and, as can be viewed in the relevant declassified NIEs, just ignored such inconvenient evidential deviations.

By 1978 the CIA had acquired a copy of the official Soviet critique of *Zapad* 1977.[207] Maps and lists attached to the document provided the composition of the three Soviet and two national fronts that had been represented by exercise staffs, as well as the notional Baltic 6 Front. The five staffed fronts had either three or four subordinate ground armies (the Carpathian substituted a corps for one army); organized in accordance with operational directives on the day preceding the imputed attack by the West. GSFG-based 2 Front made do with four armies—but including two TA. The CGF '28' Army acted independently of any front. The NGF '23' Army received RVGK designation as did two other armies; while an East German and one other army served as the TVD High Command reserve. The TVD reserve also held 6 Front; complement included '45' Army which had regrouped from an unspecified location 1500-km distant from a concentration area, originally designated RVGK, and then subordinated to 4 Front (which had regrouped westward from the Belorussian district prior to the outbreak of war). The intelligence official model could not, and did not attempt to, accommodate a Western TVD in which forward or reserve armies—even an entire front—would be withheld under the control of the VGK or GK at the outbreak of war. Only on combat D+8 did 2 Front control five armies and one (East German) corps, but three armies (one tank) had been allocated from the VGK and GK reserves while two original armies (one tank) had been resubordinated to 4 Front. These transfers among fronts are only a sampling of those depicted in the *Zapad* scenario and demonstrate the flexibility of Soviet strike groupings assembly.

Intelligence assessments of the Western TVD lineup, throughout the Cold War, persisted amazingly stereotyped, distorted, and incomplete despite an abundance of evidence of the second kind from exercises and classified writings. Just compare the character of front organization and reworking in the *Zapad* critique with any of the NIEs and reports on Warsaw Pact forces and operations that have been declassified. An early 1980s study on Soviet logistics stocks in East Germany had even concluded that these exceeded the requirements of two fronts.[208] A better informed perspective might have regarded the GDR grouping as a pool of armies intended to supply the complements of several fronts built also from armies arriving from the USSR and those that might be contributed by Pact allies. Only in the second half of the 1980s had the intelligence fixation been modestly altered to allow for other potential rosters.

Other considerations complicate the front census. Soviet fronts could be augmented in the Western and Southwestern TVDs by the more than a dozen armies of the Warsaw Pact allies to meet their quotas, especially in variants that dispensed with national fronts. Soviet fronts in Central Europe could incorporate some or all the armies mobilized by their East German, Polish, and Czech allies—a variant that is the most likely basis for the upper range army complements specified for Western TVD fronts. The Western TVD peacetime dispositions of active armies in the three groups and three border military districts could deploy up to 14 armies (including one CGF and assuming one NGF) while the three allies had seven. The prescribed three-army minimum would enable a Western TVD variant fielding four Soviet and two national fronts while allotting three armies to the VGK-GK reserve; but the five-army variant amounted to only four total fronts plus one reserve army and required deletion of national fronts; while a 3/4/5 army mix deleting one national front would up the front total. Augmenting Soviet fronts could only be accomplished by incorporating national armies and/or acquiring reserve armies from the developing USSR strategic deployment. The long running intelligence estimate of five fronts in the TVD could be met by the mid range of army complements (four apiece)—but nothing then remained for a Baltic front, not to mention a NGF and/or CGF front—and a maxed out complement would subtract one front.

Soviet corps-to-army upgrades presumably corresponded to, and contingent on, the duration of any threat period. In addition not only could the fronts in TVDs other than the Western have fewer armies but these could more likely have subordinate corps. Front war strengths would actually have been adjusted in accordance with operational variants and specific missions in the directions of different TVDs. The 1980 specification for one "coalition front" in the Southwestern TVD amounted to one, two, or three combined-arms armies (the one, Hungarian) plus one or two corps, and no tank armies.[209] Corps inclusive, the 42 active Soviet pushpins could, by the book standard Western TVD, populate exactly fourteen minimal fronts (with no reserves) upon achieving operational readiness, and some of these could be maximized with allied armies. But part of the Soviet active armies-corps contingent might operate independently of fronts or be withheld in the reserves of higher commands as in *Zapad* 1977. Up to five more prospective Soviet fronts remained to be populated. Additional armies and/or corps, with divisions sufficient to meet their respective quotas would have to come from… somewhere. US intelligence largely neglected consideration of these reinforcements while incapable of judging dimensions. Any attempt to do so would have been handicapped by a prevailing perceptual myopia regarding the character of the Soviet mobilization-deployment scheme.

Another approach to determining the number of prospective fronts involved their division complements. The Soviets assigned ground divisions to a variety of preparedness categories—defined by peacetime manning and armament levels, with readiness deadlines—that intelligence attempted to understand and translate, during many years and iterations, to a US definition. Division organizations accorded with four principal brackets. 'A' (А) and 'B' (Б) divisions maintained 60 to 100 percent of personnel and 75 to 100 percent of planned wartime levels of weapons and equipment, but capable of operating within three days. Seventy percent of divisions in two brackets defined as cadre: 'V' (В) divisions with a minimum of 25 percent personnel, 50 percent armed and ready in four to ten days; while 'G' (Г) divisions had has few as one percent personnel and 40 percent armament and would require as much as a month to fill out. The foregoing breakdown is not from intelligence assessments.

The Russian authors of the 2004 book *The Soviet Army During The 'Cold War'*[210] meticulously collected all available information on the order-of-battle of not only the Ground Troops but also the other four armed services. While they did not have access to official sources they could tap a lode of military and topical journals, military memoirs, internet forums, and knowledgeable sources that researchers outside of Russia would find difficult to assemble. Starting from a previous accounting of Soviet forces in the GPW, the book traced the lineage and evolving organization of military units at army- to regiment-level from the end of that war until the dissolution of the USSR. They also profiled the TVDs, groups of forces, and military districts. Their register of active ground armies and corps almost exactly matches the intelligence assessment, differing in a few districts regarding the presence, or corps vs. army status, of some formations. Unfortunately the authors had no data on, or indications of, the fronts lineup. Their work revealed that within the four readiness brackets each division had been assigned a *shtat* (state or establishment, akin to Western table of organization and equipment) amounting to some 25 types for a motorized rifle division and 15 types for a tank division.

Intelligence had detected the Soviet quadripartite bracketing of division readiness during mobilization exercises and in other sources. But mid 1980s CIA studies,[211] incorporated verbatim in NIEs,[212] presented a jumbled mess of division types broadly defined as "ready" or "not ready" dissociated from the actual Soviet brackets schema. The 1982 NIE *The Readiness of Soviet Ground Forces*[213] assigned the 210 divisions then identified into three categories: "most combat-ready" 30 divisions in Central Europe plus ten divisions (including six airborne) in other areas; 42 divisions in western and eastern MDs comprised a [less] "ready" group; with 128 divisions placed in a "not ready" category. Classification basically re-labeled the predecessor scheme that placed divisions in Categories I, II, or III which had been in use from the mid 1960s and persisted in some publications until at least 1984;[214] and comparable to the NATO equivalent.[215] These breakdowns represented a backward entry into the Soviet precept of a first strategic echelon made up of three operational echelons—the conceptual significance of which most of the assessors had little or no awareness.

By 1985 the number of identified divisions had maxed out at 214—51 tank, 142 motorized rifle, 13 "mobilization bases" and 8 airborne—augmented over the prior decade by 33 newly visible divisions—the European comrades added 67 divisions, a dozen accounted to be mobilization bases.[216] The intelligence four-division pickup since 1982 involved the mobilization bases or division major equipment parks that had steadily appeared around the USSR (18 by then, some later upgraded).[217] These 'new' divisions had essentially made a transition from the second strategic echelon to the first. The Russian researchers found evidence for the existence of a late 1980s active ground force of up to 50 tank and 140 motorized rifle divisions (a different approach by individual groups and districts produced a slightly lower number).[218] The somewhat higher intelligence census had mainly been due to those mobilization bases, which fell in the 'G' group that the Russian historians could not fully document. Warsaw Pact national forces had comparable mobilization-expansion plans but based on a far smaller pool of manpower.

Intelligence estimates had no appreciation of the existence, much less scaling, of Soviet planning for the second and any succeeding strategic echelons. But many more divisions would be generated than intelligence could account for, the output of the 'G' group and, preeminently, the second strategic echelon. These divisions, as well as a host of other types of military units, included "second formations" (*vtorogo formirovaniya*) created during full mobilization, based on collocated active units. The intelligence microscope could apprehend only the visible elements comprising the first strategic echelon. Even at this level a complex amoebic like process of replication could be discerned involving unit spin-off duplicates; expansion into a higher level organization; second formations; all drawing on massive armament reserves.[219] The accelerating scope and pace of Soviet buildup of the active Ground Troops complement in the first half of the 1980s had been exemplified by the relocation of twelve second formation divisions to new garrisons in less than two years.[220] By the Western TVD standard these divisions potentially represented two to four complete armies and/or second echelons of six to twelve armies and/or reserve divisions for six to twelve fronts. A subsequent continuous process for the creation of entirely new units would further amplify the armed forces. Western observers often commented on the 'excessive' proportion of officers in the active Soviet armed forces, disregarding their mobilization assignments to the entities that would populate the second strategic echelon.

A 1986 CIA census of twelve reserve armor storage installations estimated that these held some 5000 tanks, representing about nine percent of the Soviet tank fleet in active divisions—a proportion that had not changed for a decade.[221] At the contemporary organization this reserve alone could fill out about 16 tank divisions or 22 motorized rifle divisions or more likely an intermediate number of both types. Given a 50/50 mix of 18 divisions, in accordance with the Western TVD minimums, the reserve tanks would get six armies or two complete fronts. This collection, along with armor reserves collocated with active divisions as well as at installations not pinpointed by intelligence, would then be available for pouring into the fronts, armies, and divisions of the second strategic echelon. The result would be an ever-expanding mass of reinforcing troops. This scheme had produced the major strategic surprise of the 1941 German assault on the USSR.

After destroying the bulk of Soviet divisions identified by their prewar intelligence perplexed Germans encountered a seemingly endless supply of replacements. One Soviet account quotes an entry in the diary of the German General Staff Chief Franz Halder two weeks into the 1941 offensive that of 193 divisions "identified by us" 109 had been totally or largely destroyed[222] (no such entry for that day is in the version published in the West). Within less than six months of the outbreak of the GPW more than 300 divisions or equivalents emerged in the VGK Reserve and had been allocated to reconstituted or new fronts.[223] From July to December 124 rifle divisions had to be removed from the books due to German success but adding 308 divisions created or reformed out of remnants;[224] most of these divisions armed with old or obsolete equipment. At the end of hostilities the Soviet ground component employed 8.491 million personnel and fielded 520 divisions.[225] Pale shadows compared to Cold War divisions in terms of personnel strength and firepower the GPW precedent still provided a yardstick for the extent of prospective Soviet mobilization. Among the critical flaws in the intelligence estimates of Soviet force-generation capability had been the inability to measure, and assess the implications, of the full scope of division mobilization that would reinforce existing and create new armies and fronts in a prolonged conflict. Even the authors of the 2004 book admitted inability to calculate the 'G'+ dimension "...not only foreign, but also Russian military historians cannot accurately count the number of divisions of the Army in a given period."[226]

Another approach to evaluating the prospective deployment of fronts then is by available divisions. Evenly distributing the intell 1972 estimate of 174 Soviet tank and motorized rifle divisions[227] among fronts, at the Western TVD minimums specified by the 1974 General Staff Academy front textbook (three armies, each with five divisions, disregarding four per tank army)[228] would fit out eleven fronts but leave only nine spare divisions for front and higher level reserves. By the mid 1980s the additional 33 Soviet divisions that had been activated or identified equated to eleven minimal armies in accordance with the revised specification of three to five divisions per army,[229] or three minimal fronts plus six leftover divisions. But with the new front requirement for up to two additional armies, each with maximum divisions (5 x 5), only eight fronts could be fulfilled. Per the 1974 General Staff Academy textbook fronts in other TVDs might not have a tank army and could have corps—exercises consistently depicted front complements near the Western minimums. If six potential Soviet fronts in the Western TVD scoffed up the maximum specification of 168 Soviet divisions (each front with three reserve divisions), that would permit the simultaneous fielding of four Soviet minimal fronts in other TVDs—in all still only ten fronts. However these calculations apply the Western TVD norm and do not consider contributions of Warsaw Pact national divisions.

The situation changes significantly when considering Warsaw Pact national divisions in the Western and Southwestern TVDs. Intelligence estimates stressed the Soviet dependence on these divisions which comprised more than half those available in Central Europe.[230] This reservoir could be tapped not only to boost the number of armies but also bring individual Soviet armies up to prescribed complements. Closely monitored exercises by Soviet armies in the GSFG often depicted reinforcement by individual divisions, East German until 1978, or from outside of the GDR. The three Central European allies in the mid 1980s had 38 tank and motorized rifle divisions, nine of these mobilization bases on the Soviet model, exceeding the complements of the seven identified armies at maximum strength.[231] The Polish and Czech national fronts could thereby be generated while East German divisions formed one or two armies, depending on the division contribution to Soviet armies. But if the variant(s) chosen by the Soviet General Staff excluded one or both of these national fronts then the Soviet Western fronts could meet their quotas with national troops while freeing armies and divisions to field more Soviet fronts.

The national armed forces would be major, even decisive, contributors to Warsaw Pact success in the Western TVD, repeatedly stressed by intell assessments. But the Soviets had a strong incentive in a war against encircling enemies to dispense with national fronts in order to incorporate national armies and divisions in Soviet-commanded fronts thereby permitting augmentation of frontal deployments in other TVDs—as well as obviate risky independent national actions. The Chinese elevation to a strategic enemy along with developing threats in Southern directions might well have altered Soviet views on the worthiness of the Warsaw Pact fronts that had been established in the first half of the 1960s.

Yet another approach to estimating the number of fronts in the Soviet strategic deployment plan involves index formations. While the organization of fronts might be customized by TVD, there would also be certain tenants in common. Partial or full lists by type of subordinate appeared in classified documents and could be derived from exercise complements. The indices include aviation and some of the more specialized ground formations.

The aforementioned numbered air armies provides a useful indication, complicated by their formal disestablishment at the end of the 1970s due to subsequent major reorganizations of Soviet military aviation including frontal, strategic, and air defense. That a new front structure for aviation, eliminating the air army, would extend to the allies had been indicated in a 1979 Polish document.[232] Occasional intelligence accountings are scattered through 1960s-1970s declassified publications. Another complicating factor is the sweeping re-numbering of air armies that took place circa mid 1973. This action may have been a consequence of the revision of the strategic deployment plan to incorporate the fronts developed from 1965 to the early 1970s. A persisting turmoil in Soviet aviation organization is reflected in the revival of numbered air armies beginning in 1988. The roster of air armies prior to reorganization would define a first strategic echelon comprising at least fourteen fronts.

Among other classified sources a 1977 General Staff Academy lecture specified that a front complement would include one air army; in the Western TVD this army could have three to five fighter and fighter-bomber divisions and one bomber division.[233] The close tie between air armies and MD/front headquarters had been illustrated in the 1960 military districts merger of the Northern into the Leningrad. The 13 (later 76) Air Army also absorbed 22 Air Army.[234] The 2004 Russian history registered thirteen numbered air armies in districts and groups but missed the NGF 4 (formerly 37) Air Army which had one each subordinate fighter and fighter-bomber division—near to the front specification; the authors not aware that the early 1980s reorganization incorporated most NGF aircraft in the new 4 Operational Air Army VGK. Dribs from declassified intell reports match the Russian accounting, with fourteen numbered air armies prior to reorganization.[235]

Unique to the GSFG 16 (former 24) Air Army organization had two geographically discrete "Fighter Corps" subordinates, the Northern (71) and Southern (61). Their total of five fighter-fighter-bomber divisions constituted the Soviet maximum specification for a front—exceeded when East German aviation divisions affiliated. Each of these corps could potentially be augmented to form the air army of a separate front, particularly if merged with the NGF 4 Air Army or reinforced from the USSR. Never did intelligence contemplation arouse that each corps might in wartime upgrade to, or merge with, separate air armies thus reinforcing other evidence of a GSFG contribution to more than one front. The Southern corps disappeared in 1980 as part of the sweeping reorganization of Soviet air defense forces that included aviation of both the strategic air defense arm and GF-MD air armies.

For the 1980s there are two other markers in the special purpose (*spetsnaz*) and air assault brigades apparently subordinated on the basis of one per front. Both of these brigade types expressed the Soviet stress on penetrating deep into the enemy rear, *spetsnaz* teams, deployed by the front brigade, on reconnaissance and raiding missions; and the troop helicopters of an air assault brigade to vertically bypass defenses. The Russian book identifies fifteen of each type although one *spetsnaz* brigade is attributed to the Navy—not unusual since the evolution of special purpose units is traced from a naval origination. According to the Russians the first special purpose brigades had been formed in ten districts in January 1963 (confirmed in a USSR General Staff Academy lecture)[236]—if so, at least a decade elapsed before intelligence caught on—while air assault brigades dated from 1969, again initially based on naval units.[237] That a front index air assault brigade had shown up in the CGF[238] for example is a tip-off to the actual Soviet plan for the group while also exhibiting army indices; but the Russians do not list a *spetsnaz* brigade with the CGF—while attributing one to the SGF. Intelligence identified both types mainly through imagery and SIGINT over a period of many years. The latest cumulative intelligence count is not currently available due to the few relevant reports declassified including the lack of 1980s ground orders-of-battle. A 1984 NIE does offer a slightly different accounting of sixteen *spetsnaz* brigades, in eleven districts, the GSFG, and "probably" in all four fleets.[239]

These brigades and other potential front index formations can be gamed *ad infinitum*. Consideration of all approaches suggests a Soviet deployment of at least fourteen fronts, and possibly one additional—in the first strategic echelon since only 'visible' ground and air armies, divisions, and indicative brigades can be counted. Any plot of the oncoming array required intelligence comprehension, evaluation, and modeling of all conceivable variants of Soviet and Warsaw Pact actions. The Soviet General Staff would, and Western intelligence should, have considered how active and immediately mobilizable forces could be deployed, simultaneously or not, against enemies in the West, East, or South. Advance preparations, for and in, those five TVDs included the communications structure and logistics bases for the deployment of at least nineteen fronts. Concurrent operations might be necessary only in the most dire military-political situation, permitting a shuffling between TVDs of armies and their subordinate divisions, even complete fronts. But historical prudence and uncertain international conditions would have provided a compelling incentive to initiate generation of all forces on the books to support any variation of an outbreak of general war. The first strategic echelon might be sufficiently sized to meet the objectives set by the political leadership especially since Soviet officers permitted a defensive stance in secondary TVDs. But the full plan encompassed a contingency for at least one more strategic echelon involving entirely new reinforcing fronts with their army and division complements, mobilized simultaneously with the first strategic echelon.

Only the Western TVD positioned fronts in two geographic echelons, the first operational forward in the Warsaw Pact countries, and reinforced from the USSR border and interior military districts. The official critique of exercise *Zapad* 1977,[240] as well as other classified sources, had framed the significance of this arrangement in enabling the Warsaw Pact to seize the strategic initiative.

> This means that the troops of the first operational echelon, aviation, and the fleet must be capable of independently, before the arrival of reserves from the interior, warding off an enemy invasion and inflicting severe damage on his main groupings.

Troop marches and commitment of the fronts of the second operational echelon constituted a most crucial event, that could determine the successful outcome of any campaign against NATO.

> Of decisive importance for the successful conduct of a strategic operation in the Western Theater of Military Actions is the timely movement of operational reserves forward from the interior and their organized commitment to the engagement to build up the efforts of the first echelon.

Verification of the optimum timing of commitment of the fronts, armies, divisions, and specialized units regrouped from the USSR prominently featured in many Warsaw Pact exercises.

This double echelon represented a fundamental departure from the GPW operations of fronts. The Soviet innovation in 1944-1945 of strategic offensives based on groupings of fronts uniformly deployed a single operational echelon, backed only by the individual armies held in the VGK reserve. A rare instance of doubling up took place in the 1943 Kursk battle when the Steppe Front had been positioned behind the Central and Voronezh Fronts to increase defensive depth in anticipation of Hitler's last great Eastern attack.[241] Even the notable Strategic Operation Bagration, initiated in late June 1944 and aimed at the destruction of the German Army Group Center in Belorussia, struck with all six fronts in-line across more than 1000-km.[242] GPW operations tended to grind to a halt when the offensive capacity of the fronts became exhausted. The Soviet objective in the Cold War Western TVD would be a sustained series of concurrent and successive offensives by fronts ensured by a continual buildup of efforts by reinforcing echelons—guaranteed if necessary by the use of mass destruction weapons.

A durable perceptual idiosyncrasy of Cold War intelligence adhered by theater forces connoisseurs, notably in the CIA, referred to this arrangement of fronts in the Western TVD as strategic echelons. Yet another dipstick for the depth of misconception of Soviet military strategy—with deleterious consequences for intelligence assessments. The erudition of the CIA Soviet office chief regarding echelons had been displayed in the 1988 congressional briefing. Available from the early 1970s, a 1967 article by the Professor in VM (S) discussed factors determining "the number and composition of the fronts of the first and second operational echelons."[243] The 1977 lecture prepared for the USSR General Staff Academy made quite clear that[244]

> The place of a front in a strategic operation in a continental TVD is determined by its position in the strategic disposition of troops. With the start of a war, it may advance among the fronts of the first operational echelon, or it may be in the second echelon with the task of commitment to the engagement during the war.

The third stage of exercise *Zapad* 1977 had dealt with the commitment of "second operational echelon fronts" to battle.[245] Elements in the DIA by the 1980s had come to recognize the difference between operational and strategic echelons in their reporting;[246] but evidently stifled by their CIA colleagues who often dominated coordinated estimates. I did not access this particular interface and cannot offer an explanation why—in so far as their reports go—DIA accurately presented theater operational echelons (well, the first two at least).

Despite decades of exposure to military literature those involved in judging the dimensions of the threat facing the West persisted incapable of apprehending the correct definition of a strategic echelon—available in the *Soviet Military Encyclopedia* with the other "c" entries.[247] Numerous other Soviet military articles and documents (many already cited) used and defined the terminology of strategic and operational echelons. This stress on a conceptual mistranslation is not just semantic nitpicking; rather typifying a pervasive, superficial, comprehension of the fundamental precepts of the adversary by even those charged with assessing the character of Warsaw Pact theater offensive planning. Getting the structural details correct is hardly furthered by miscasting the foundation. An analytic culture so deficient in

**VERSIONED REALITY IN...**

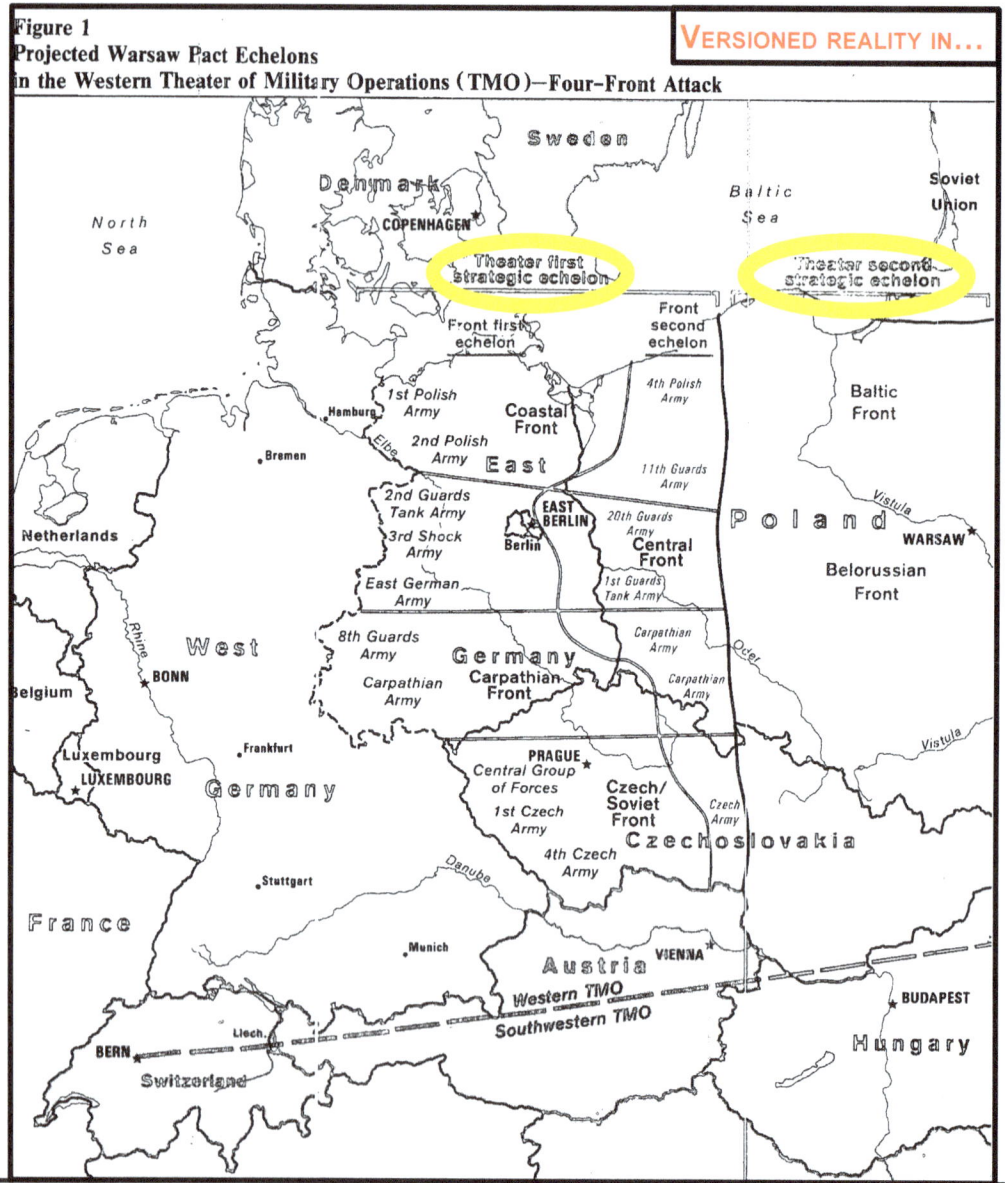

Figure 1
Projected Warsaw Pact Echelons
in the Western Theater of Military Operations (TMO)—Four-Front Attack

1989 CIA REPORT AND NIE DEPICTION OF FOUR FRONTS DEPLOYED IN THE "THEATER FIRST STRATEGIC ECHELON" WITH BACKUP FROM TWO FRONTS IN THE "THEATER SECOND STRATEGIC ECHELON"—FOUR DECADES INTO THE COLD WAR AND MAINSTREAM INTELL DID NOT YET COMPREHEND THE CRUCIAL DISTINCTION BETWEEN SOVIET strategic AND operational ECHELONS (OPPOSITE) ALTERNATIVE PERSPECTIVE OF GERMAN MILITARY HISTORY RESEARCH OFFICE CORRECTLY TRANSLATED ACTUALITY DESPITE FEWER SOURCES
STAFFEL = ECHELON

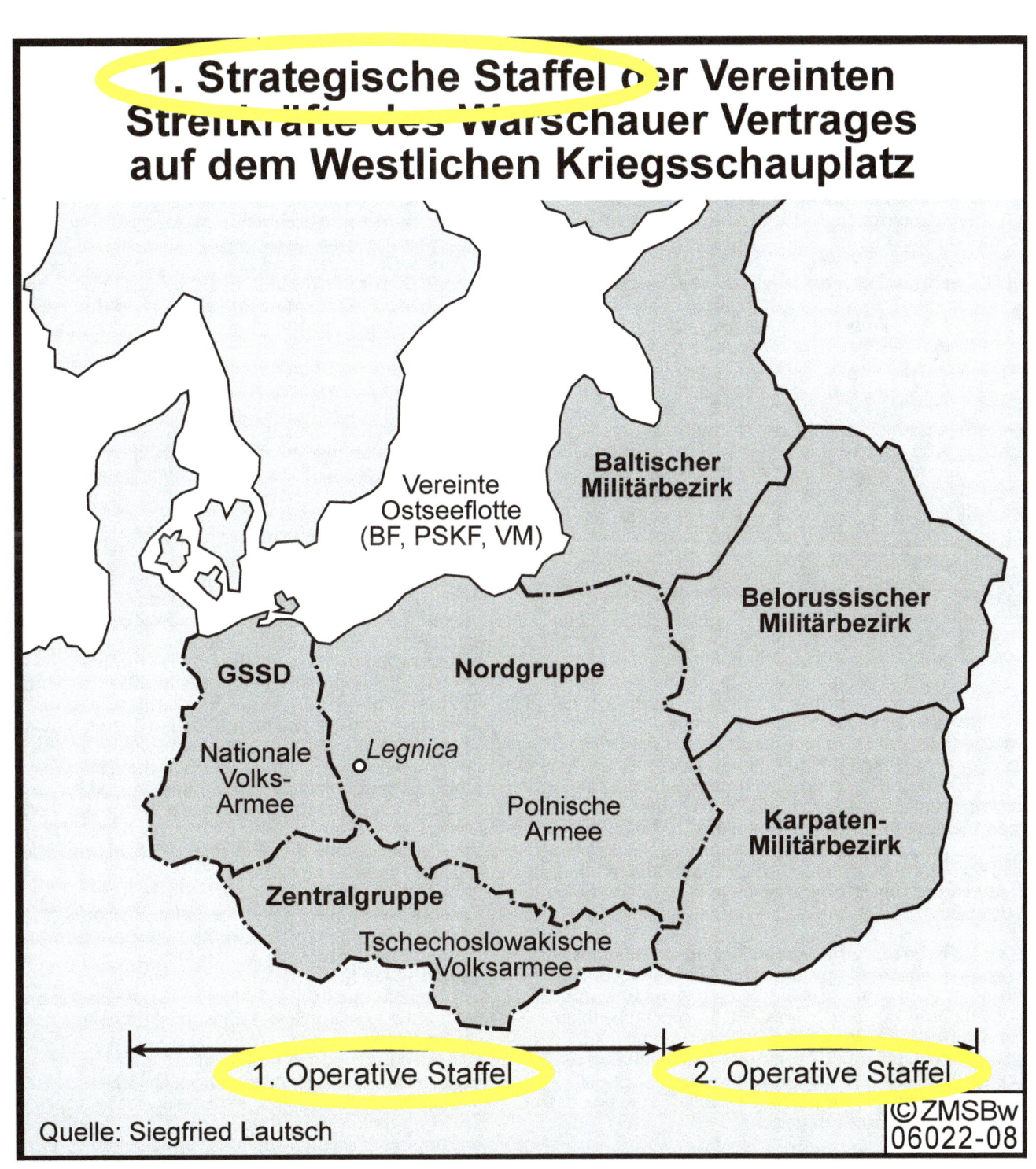

basic reading comprehension is hardly capable of accurately judging complex problems with widely varied evidence. Those details encompassed the Soviet capability to augment the theater punch, both at the outset of combat and in the event of a prolonged war. The intelligence perceptual window (including the DIA folks) lacked cognizance of multiple strategic echelons as defined by the Soviets. Even the significance of the third operational echelon remained invisible. For NATO defenders to successfully shoot down the first waves would be ultimately futile if they were not prepared by their intelligence for the reality and scale of the inevitable oncoming reinforcements.

A 1983 CIA appraisal of the strength of Soviet standing ground forces amounted to 1.8 million; estimating an additional 2.5 million reservists to fully man the maneuver divisions then identified as well as separate combat and support units attained a total 4.3 million.[248] But in the 1990s a key General Staffer, General-Colonel A. A. Danilevich, stated "According to mobilization schedules, the overall size of our forces was supposed to increase four-fold, new formations were supposed to appear. It is because of this capacity that we won the last war."[249] By that multiplier the service that would undergo by far the greatest degree of expansion, the Ground Troops, based on the intelligence appraisal of peacetime strength, would fill out at 7.2 million personnel. The intelligence official strategic deployment model therefore had been oddly incomplete; callously leaving some 2.9 million Soviet citizens without employment—those who would fill out the (invisible to intelligence) second and any succeeding strategic echelons. By May 1945, despite horrendous losses, the full Soviet Armed Forces had mobilized nearly 11.4 million personnel.[250] Thus the intelligence mangled perspective of the mobilization-deployment echelons, persisting through the last three decades of the Cold War, placed the West in the same dangerous situation as the failed German estimate. At a (unlikely) uniform 400000 personnel the fuller mobilization would get at least eighteen fronts; chop 100000 from the average and twenty-four fronts could be fielded. But this intell estimate of a front complement included aviation elements while consideration of non-frontal assignments and the downsized fronts in secondary TVDs would require adjustments that would more than subscribe a projected nineteen fronts—in two strategic echelons.

The Soviets also arranged fronts and armies in echelons with their own pre-calculated optimum timing of the second commitment. Deployment echeloning intertwined with the preplanned mobilization echelons. Thus a second echelon army or armies, and second echelon divisions subordinate to an army, not scheduled to be committed for a set number of days, could be relegated to the next lower mobilization echelon—at differing *shtat*. A VM (S) article[251] spelled out the complexity of readiness situations.

…a combined-arms (tank) army of a border military district may have in a state of constant readiness one or two motorized rifle (tank) divisions, missile large units, air defense units, and also the first echelon of the field headquarters…Different periods of time may be required to bring to readiness the remaining large units [divisions]…[the army first echelon] will immediately begin to advance to the area of forthcoming operations, while the second echelons…will only be starting to deploy and fully mobilize. Thus, the army forces under these circumstances will move forward by echelon at two to three day intervals.

Soviet authors discussed army regrouping zones that could extend 600- to 800-km in depth because first echelon divisions would be on the march while divisions of the second echelon completed mobilization; 800-km the approximate distance from the westernmost USSR to, say, the GDR. They considered all subordinates of first echelon fronts located in Central Europe to be in a status of constant combat readiness; only after many years did intelligence realize that even these units actually did not have full personnel complements. This progression applied to all types of military units. An inspection of a Polish coastal defense flotilla delineated ships in two echelons; the first could attain combat readiness stage Full from Constant in twelve hours and the second eight hours later. Four vessels on combat alert could disperse from port in fifteen minutes.[252]

The 1977 General Staff Academy lecture, among many such formulations, defined a front first TVD offensive achieving two successive tasks—"A second-echelon army of the front usually is committed in order for the front to fulfill a subsequent task, but in individual cases it can be committed also during the fulfillment of the immediate task"—the second task according to the lecture would be accomplished during offensive days seven to fifteen.[253] Thus the second echelon army or armies had nearly a week following initiation of the front assault to mobilize, prepare, and deploy unless tagged for an earlier commitment. The schedule applied to fronts of both first and second operational echelons in the Western TVD and of course the second echelon divisions of individual armies also had specified commitment timings.

In this scheme of multi-level echeloning fronts of the second operational echelon could be maintained at lower peacetime manning levels; respective second echelon armies at less strength than first echelon armies; with differentiated manning among individual army first and second echelon divisions—the reason for so many Soviet division *shtat* conditions. An attack variant at the TVD level could be initiated by first echelons prior to completion of mobilization and regrouping. But mainstream intelligence in at least the US considered any possibility of this 'standing-start' variant so unlikely that scant attention had been allotted. Any systematic interference with regrouping of second echelons would degrade, and might well wreck, the whole scheme. In the 1960s, in particular, NATO defense plans that envisioned a nuclear blockade of these movements forward had been the subject of much discussion in Soviet classified writings. Only in the 1980s would NATO start on developing an interdiction-in-depth capability with new precision conventional armament that might, to a more limited extent, emulate nuclear disruption.

In 1968 the Office of Strategic Research handed in the CIA contribution to the recurring NIE on *General Purpose Forces*. OSR stated that the division Category I-II-III breakdown had been directly and almost entirely based on the 1961 VM Shchepennikov explication of echelonment—with a full quotation.[254] Subsequent CIA assessments into the early 1970s repeated the connection, with quotations, but these soon dropped the important Shchepennikov qualifier that only the "first" strategic echelon had been encompassed; and his definition would soon be entirely omitted. Thus intelligence had still been entirely dependent on the Penkovsky collection for access to classified Soviet military writings. But the 1968 OSR analyst(s) expressed puzzlement. Shchepennikov had indicated three mobilization-deployment echelons, and the open major work *Military Strategy* while listing three strength categories had related initial combat operations to only the first two categories. Other sources, including Czech and Polish, had also depicted initial mobilization in two categories. OSR could not offer an explanation for the Soviet third operational echelon—and none forthcoming from their successors. That the first two correlated with the armies of fronts, and divisions of armies, deploying in successive echelons did not compute. Only in the 1980s would the Soviet concept of echelons be semi-recognized by intell maestros.

When assessing Warsaw Pact reinforcement capability, Cold War intelligence had been curiously inattentive to not only the problem of the Soviet third operational echelon but also constituent 'invisible' armies. Articles in the classified VM and other documents set out deployment of armies originating in at least the interior Volga, Ural, Moscow, and North Caucasus MDs. Only corps had been identified in the North Caucasus, and no entities controlling divisions in Ural or Volga; with one possible Moscow corps. While only three divisions had been identified in the Volga MD, three articles in VM (S)[255] from the early 1960s onward discussed the immediate mobilization and regrouping of a combined-arms army from this district to reinforce a front already engaged in a first offensive operation. Two articles[256] featured movement of a Ural MD army including commitment to a front in combat. Military-scientific work underway in 1961 had included Moscow MD study of an army regrouping zone in the Western TVD; interestingly the same district had been conducting another study on the "large distances" regrouping of a front during the Initial Period.[257]

As early as 1961 a VM (S) article[258] focused on North Caucasus MD exercises of a combined-arms army including one marching within seven days up to 1600-km to reinforce a front already advancing against unstated enemies. That reach could have represented a regrouping to the Southwest TVD beyond Bulgaria but General-Major P. Stepshin also mentions Western TVD conditions and potential nuclear interdiction by NATO—and a distance similar to that of the regrouping of '45' Army in *Zapad* 1977. A conference the next year had as the main topic the 1000-km march from the same district "forward of a combined-arms army from the interior of the country to a theater of military actions for the purpose of reinforcing groupings" to a mountain TVD joining a front[259]—far exceeding the distance to the Caucasus but could have represented a front deep into Turkey. That such regroupings did not go out of style would be indicated in 1985 "There are also operational territorial formations, which include interior military districts which form separate armies at the beginning of a war..." by a General Staff Academy lecture.[260] In the Soviet ordering of the buildup of forces these armies comprised the third operational echelon of the first strategic.

Yet a 1975 *Warsaw Pact Forces* NIE stated that "little evidence" on plans for divisions in the Ural, Volga, or Moscow MDs, as well as the Kiev, had been acquired;[261] some of the cited articles did postdate the NIE but most come from the Penkovsky collection. By the 1980s intelligence, under the persistent output of the secondary translation, had concocted a Soviet "strategic reserve" encompassing a fixed collection of centrally-located military districts: Volga, Ural, Moscow, and Kiev.[262] Somehow active units in these districts would be held back as contingent reinforcements. This misconceived, non-existent, alternative reality thus precluded any appreciation that divisions and armies in these districts would actually complete mobilization and immediately regroup forward to reinforce fronts even in the first operational echelon—and these marches might take place prior to war outbreak. For NATO this augmentation would be a most unpleasant surprise.

Circumstantial evidence suggests that the third operational echelon would not be confined to the interior. One of several instances concerned the Baltic MD in which 11 Guards had been the only army identified through the Cold War. During at least one exercise, *Vesna* 1969, a second army had emanated from this MD. The district had two army missile support bases. One had been installed at a former airfield nuclear storage site near Kedainiai, among the first army-level bases established; the second (Linkaiciai) had been constructed almost two years later from 1964 to 1966. A serviceman in a reserve tank division in the late 1960s had insisted on subordination to an army located in Kaliningrad numbered 18, not 11. The foregoing stray markers are typical of what intelligence had to work with in order to establish a Soviet mobilization-deployment reality. One readout of these tidbits might be that the headquarters of 18 Guards Army, which had disappeared from the GDR in the 1964 GSFG reorganization, had actually been provided new digs in the Baltic MD. Preparations to lead an army of the third operational echelon—among those invisible to intelligence—there proceeding.

Like so much else in Soviet actions the GPW set the precedent for modern conditions. The prewar plan for strategic deployment provided for the creation of five new armies; three of these to be committed to fronts in two of the strategic directions with the other two held in the VGK reserve. Immediately prior to the outbreak of war the forming of two additional armies had been started.[263] These seven armies made up the, as then designated, second strategic echelon contingent mobilized to augment the active armies of the first strategic echelon. When activated the divisions of these reserve armies had not yet been fully manned. Unfortunately for the Soviets the seven new armies constituted the only additional forces envisioned in the second strategic echelon.[264]

> The fact was that the buildup of our armed forces in accordance with the mobilization plans which existed on the eve of the war had already been completed. Further buildup had not been foreseen by any prewar plan, and consequently a reserve of officer personnel and stockpiles of arms and combat equipment for these purposes had not been created.

When finally available, four of the reserve armies became the basis of a recreated Western Front that became the linchpin for the successful defense of Moscow; accomplished by a 'merging' of the retreating first strategic echelon with the newly mobilized second strategic echelon.[265] Despite the self-vaunted precision of Soviet military science German smashing of the first strategic echelon had not been foreseen, necessitating premature commitment of the second strategic echelon, and hasty creation of a third strategic echelon.

Evidence for the Cold War plan of strategic deployment appearing in scattered sources suggests that, unlike the GPW, the second strategic echelon would comprise not only divisions and separate armies but also complete fronts. Vladimir Rezun had insisted that certain military districts would not generate fronts[266] but this variant actually applied only to the first strategic echelon. Classified writings and exercises provided unequivocal evidence that interior MDs would deploy fronts in the second strategic echelon, and that apparently in the interim each of these districts had been tasked to ship at least one army of the third operational echelon. Circumstantial evidence existed that the third operational echelon would comprise new armies appearing even in districts forming fronts of the first strategic echelon such as the Baltic, Belorussian, Kiev, and Far East—in all approximating at least the seven planned before the GPW broke out. No such potential mid term reinforcement had been foreseen by intell.

Many classified VM articles dealt with generalities of the mobilization of armies and even entire fronts from the interior without identifying specific MDs, some indicating a Western TVD destination. In the large scale exercise of May 1973[267] a Volga MD front headquarters had been deployed to the Odessa, and that of the Ural front to the Carpathian MD. While individual armies from these districts might deploy as part of the first strategic echelon these front commands represented the organizing elements of the second strategic echelon to be filled out from the mounting waves of mobilization. Subordinates would come from newly formed units, equipped from reserve armament stocks (including the twelve armor stores) as well as weapons production as industry converted to the preplanned wartime output. In each of these interior MDs, as well as in the North Caucasus, a characteristic front missile-artillery base had already been established. A second front base had been built near Sverdlovsk (Yekaterinburg) in the Ural MD (collocated with the first within the same artillery ammunition base) in the early 1970s, an indicator which pointed to a mission divide between the Western and Eastern Theaters. Subsequent exercises depicted fielding of a front drawn from this district and the Siberian MD (which had no front missile-artillery base) to reinforce the array of forces on the Chinese border.

In the surprise variant only Soviet forces at constant combat readiness and those that could be quickly up-manned would be immediately available for action. The threat variant would permit a progression of implementation dependent on extent of the period. As Soviet officers noted in their classified discussions of strategic deployment under these alternative conditions, a surprise outbreak of war could occur at any moment during a threat period. Of course if the Soviets premeditated a surprise variant in the West, all mobilization-deployment measures could be taken in advance but would have to be conducted with extreme secrecy. Regardless of the chosen or imposed variant, transportation lines throughout the territory of the USSR and allies would be humming with throngs of military commuters on their way to their preassigned workplaces.

During this massive strategic deployment of the armed forces at the outset of a war, active and reserve armies and divisions functioned rather like pieces on a vast chessboard for the General Staff to regroup to achieve different combinations in accordance with the operational variants. And this meant that the forces of the allies would also be arranged to Soviet liking. Many examples of this maneuvering occurred in classified writings and exercises. The two active armies of the Kiev MD could be separately committed to the second echelons of fronts in the Balkan and Italian Strategic Directions; or they could form the first echelon of a Kiev front–the second echelon provided by newly formed or regrouped armies of the third operational echelon; in which case a front of the second strategic echelon would germinate. A Kiev front appeared in exercises of both the Western and Southwestern TVDs to build up the efforts in either of three strategic directions.

Intelligence regarded the three armies in the Belorussian MD as a unitary front; many instances of this variant transpired. But 28 Combined-Arms Army, positioned on the western border, could with 11 Guards Army of the Baltic MD, form the first echelon of a front regrouped to the northern GDR, supplemented with Polish and/or East German armies as well as regrouped Soviet armies. Or, the two armies could be separately committed as the second echelon of a forward front or fronts. In the June 1965 exercise Narew a Polish national front comprising three armies also acquired a second echelon '20' CAA represented by fifteen officers from Belorussia; two other MD armies composed tank persuasions so 28 CAA remained the only available candidate. Exercise scenario depicted this Soviet army arriving late on the fourth day of war at an assembly area along the Narew River (likely the source name for the exercise).[268] Either or both of the two Belorussian active tank armies could regroup to forward fronts or contribute to the first echelon of a front reinforced by new, regrouped, armies from the interior—the Moscow MD appeared to be the source in some exercises. But a few exercises depicted the Moscow MD as a front; potentially incorporating Belorussian armies as well as those regrouped or mobilized in the third operational echelon. Some 1960s documents identified Belorussia as the reserve front[269]—a designation with loaded GPW connotations regarding front nativity.

Commitment of fronts of the second operational echelon would be the crucial event in all variants for a war with NATO—an augmentation essential to the outcome of the first strategic operation—previously noted the official critique of exercise Zapad 1977,[270] had imparted the "decisive importance" for offensive success in the Western TVD of this massive regrouping of complete front massifs spanning hundreds of kilometers across the territory of the Warsaw Pact allies regardless of prospective nuclear obstruction. In a variant dispensing with, or losing, the support of any allies would require immediate compensation. In the nuclear variant the reinforcing fronts would replenish massive losses while in a conventional variant they extended the offensive of forward fronts into the depth of the TVD. The 1974 Front Offensive Operations textbook had declared that fronts of the first operational echelon would have a "decisive influence" in a non-nuclear period.[271]

Exercises in the 1960s, and through most of the 1970s, depicted this commitment as early as the fourth day of a TVD (counter)offensive, and at least by day ten.[272] Zapad 1977 again demarcated an adjustment: two second echelon fronts entered combat on the sixth day, but they had been regrouped 500- to 750-km beginning six days prior to war outbreak. Thereafter, commitment of second operational echelon fronts took place after a more prolonged period, usually 14 to 17 days, even 25 days in major 1978-1979 exercises. *Soyuz* 1987 committed two fronts on D+16; there had been two weeks of training conducted during a threat period prior to war outbreak. Despite depiction of more grueling conventional combat, and NATO improvements in conventional warfare capabilities (particularly against armor) the Soviets apparently expected Warsaw Pact ready force expansion and weapons upgrades to enable sustaining a longer period of first echelon operations without reinforcement.

The intell perspective of the steady state augmentation blueprint persisted entirely dissociated from this Soviet reality. One model emerged in the early 1960s, based on what could then be extracted from exercise scenarios and, most importantly, (mis)perception of the classified documents supplied by Oleg Penkovsky. Revised views held that any offensive against the NATO Central Region (Western TVD) could only take place following reinforcement from the western USSR. This flavor held out until the mid 1970s. Rationales for further model revamping, presenting a new flavor, had then been spelled out in the 1975 edition of the NIE *Warsaw Pact Forces Opposite NATO*.[273] A 1977 CIA-OSR paper[274] reaffirmed the NIE views and surveyed the reasons for both the prior and newly adopted assessments. Of interest is the dissenting comment in the 1975 NIE by the State Department intelligence component which depicted a Soviet view, sourced to the same military writings, that a prior buildup remained essential; an even more distorted second translation. Soviet classified writings of the early 1960s did indeed discuss moves of armies into Central Europe but in a context that intelligence had misconstrued.

The CIA paper based conclusions on 1960s-1970s classified military writings as well as several major exercises since 1969 from which scenario details had been obtained. Issued prior to the 1977 edition of *Zapad*, discussion of evidence, as in the NIE, continued the intell dissociation from the reality of multi-level echelonment. The Soviets did not reference 'preparation' and 'reinforcement' or 'buildup' whether 'prior' or 'post' but rather the arrangement of fronts and their subordinates in echelons. Those 1960s classified writings actually depicted first echelon armies of forward fronts already in combat with second echelon armies, mobilizing in the western districts of the USSR, regrouped and committed within the prescribed timelines (if not nuclear-eradicated). A reserve front, by echeloned armies, then regrouped and committed to the offensive within a similar prejudged timeframe. The crucial impediment, recognized by the Soviets (and considered in more detail later), would be the NATO capability and plan to block advances with mass nuclear strikes. In a favorable variant of increasing tensions, as imputed in the October 1961 *Burya* exercise, all of the fronts could be regrouped forward before the outbreak of war to avoid incineration en route. A later probability, noted in the CIA paper, envisaged a conventional beginning of hostilities that afforded the opportunity to regroup echelons without nuclear interdiction.

The most significant consideration, dominating all estimates from the early 1960s, had been and would be the time required to "assemble" or "prepare" the Warsaw Pact assault force. An imputed critical tradeoff—not evident in Soviet classified documents—insisted that a preemptive or rapid offensive with a limited contingent would have to play against an extended period of full mobilization of a more powerful force incorporating active formations of the USSR western military districts. Particularly in the 1980s intell discussion would center on the time required to integrate and train reservists to a higher combat effectiveness before an attack.

A 1962 NIE had allowed for the possibility of a Warsaw Pact attack without prior buildup but found this variant inconsistent with the Soviet objective of achieving superiority over NATO; estimating that thirty days would be necessary to "prepare" a fifty to sixty division force in East Germany and western Czechoslovakia.[275] By the time of a late 1968 NIE intelligence had just come to the realization that Soviet allies in Poland and Czechoslovakia would field national fronts, providing the Warsaw Pact with potentially five fronts in the Western TVD. The NIE concluded that two weeks would be required to "assemble" this force but at least three weeks to fully mobilize and move forward the Belorussian and Carpathian fronts.[276] An intervening NIE[277] and CIA-DIA study[278] projected as much as four weeks for the 'assembly' and both emphasized the speed vs. power tradeoff; neither of these assessments cognizant of national fronts. A crack in the prior buildup model appeared in the May 1970 product of an intell working group.[279] Most of the members concluded that a minimum of two weeks would be required to "assemble" the main elements of the attackers, and three weeks to fully integrate, but dissenters from the DIA now insisted that forward fronts could initiate an offensive without prior reinforcement from the USSR.

NIE and studies subsequent to the adoption of the no-prior-buildup model in the second half of the 1970s, despite the availability of increasingly granular evidence, essentially adhered to the preparatory theme and the underpinning supposed tradeoff. But a new element calculated not only the extent of preparations but also the amount of warning time that NATO would be afforded. The April 1978 *Warning* NIE[280] based conclusions on, at least in declassified documents, the first use of the stereotyped model of ranked options. The NIE rejected out of hand any possibility of a 'standing-start' attack directly from the peacetime deployment; instead focusing on the probability, and time required, for imputed options involving a Warsaw Pact attack with either two or three forward fronts; with a third option adding the two fronts of the western districts. Considered unlikely an assault with two Soviet fronts, augmented with active GDR and Czech divisions, would require four days to prepare. Three fronts, adding a Polish national, necessitated a minimum eight days, while appending two USSR fronts would require two weeks to prepare and move forward. The NIE asserted that there would be from three to twelve or more days, depending on option, warning of Soviet offensive initiation.

US intelligence assessments of the oncoming wave train persisted so simplistic as to understate the actual scale and timing of a Warsaw Pact offensive. Dissociated perspectives ignored, in particular, the effects of reinforcement of even forward fronts from the interior as well as the complex process of the multi-level echeloned mobilization-deployment. Some intelligence reports that distinguished between "unreinforced" and fully mobilized "reinforced" assaults against NATO proceeded devoid of definitional and explanatory value. A sudden Warsaw Pact assault, a 'standing start', without warning or preparation, had been considered likely only in fringe intelligence and political views during the Cold War. Perversely, the ideological fantasies of the other side somehow managed to attribute such capability and intent to NATO.

Mainstream intelligence views expected that Soviet and Warsaw Pact forces would require a prolonged period to prepare an offensive. Generation of a sort of unaccompanied bums' rush, a singular tsunami, would ensue rather than the ever-amplified wave train of successive reinforcement actually portrayed in Soviet classified writings and exercises. This imputed preparatory delay had increased from a projected several days to two weeks earlier in the Cold War and subsequently two to five weeks (depending on differing assessed front lineups) by the late 1980s. The longer interval reflected a new assumption that about two weeks of post-mobilization refresher and integration training would be required.[281] Glaringly absent from all of these discussions had been consideration or modeling of the actual complexity of multi-level echeloning—national, theater, front, army, division—that might substantially reduce the time required to initiate an offensive.

Perhaps the most succinct statement of the intelligence Cold War official model of Soviet mobilization-deployment in the Western TVD, with limited application of whiteout, occurred in the 1988 CIA briefing to the House Armed Services Committee led by Douglas MacEachin.[282] He claimed "substantial agreement" by the intelligence community as to the main thrust of the presentation. Dissent came within intell and from NATO allies regarding only a few issues—in reality the most crucial. Divergent views held that Soviet war preparations could proceed at a faster pace, and a strategic offensive conducted without full pre-mobilization, than allowed by the official perspective. Peppering the briefing with comments "seen by the Soviets" and "Soviet commanders would prefer" and "we think they would prefer"—the never-ending refrain of more than six decades of institutionalized intelligence dominated by a US-think that has produced such notable surprises as the Korean War, the Cuban missile crisis, 9/11, and other instances—all actions by opponents that intell mavens insisted could not or would never be attempted.

The intelligence official model of Soviet strategic deployment and relentless augmentation, through the course of the Cold War, consistently misconceived some, while disregarding other, key issues. Reviewing 51 other assessments and studies (plus a few 'contributions' to publications) issued from 1962 to 1990—NIEs, coordinated CIA-DIA studies, and individual agency papers regarding warning of war in Europe; Warsaw Pact air and ground forces, their mobilization-readiness and armament, logistics sustainment, reserves; strategy and operational planning; along with gazes into the future—all stress certain themes as fundamental perceptual constituents. Despite the ham-handed efforts of the censors, both the thrust of their conclusions as well as quite detailed discussions of major aspects, have survived.

• multi-level echelonment

Strikingly absent from the documentary record is the establishment as a reference point, much less elaboration or modeling, of both the structure and collective implications of the Soviet formulation for national, theater, front, and army echelons. MacEachin had provided no hint to his audience. NIEs regarding the Warsaw Pact stance opposing NATO not only of the 1960s, but also those billed as comprehensive (re)assessments in 1971,[283] 1979,[284] 1983,[285] and 1985[286] are devoid of any meaningful substantive discussion of the absolutely crucial nature of Soviet echelonment. The 1979 *Estimate* (as in a few other reports) had provided a commitment table for 87 "available" divisions, those forward in Warsaw Pact countries and in the bordering military districts, by M (mobilization directive) plus 24 and 96 hours, eight and fourteen days; a calibration entirely dissociated from the Soviet reality. The accompanying Office of Congressional Affairs Memo that summarized the 1988 briefing had indicated that "There was some detailed discussion of whether we use Soviet planning factors or our own in estimating their combat readiness" with MacEachin obviously preferring the intell second translation. Virtually all reports during nearly three decades had given scarcely any inklings of a perceived echelonment, as in the 1988 Interagency Intelligence Memorandum statement "the Pact would be willing to begin offensive operations with the lead divisions of a front" of the "first strategic echelon" based on (redacted) late 1970s planning material.[287] Even in 1969 a supposition had been noted that "The speed of mobilization of a front apparently is related to the expected timetable for its commitment to battle" in the extensive CIA contribution to a general purpose forces NIE.[288]

In the 1980s there had been at least one cubicle, in the DIA, that deviated from the official model. Presumably their contribution to the 1982 NIM *The Readiness of Soviet Ground Forces*[289] correctly assigned Western TVD fronts in two operational echelons and also distinguished the strategic echelons—but misconceived these as centrally geographic rather than the actual demographic basis. The Executive Summary statement that "the Soviet concept of operational and strategic echelonment is designed to provide for the time-phased introduction of fresh forces into battle to sustain an offensive" is an aberration among the mass of intelligence assessments. An outline of the echeloned commitment of fronts, armies, and divisions by their successive objective days and depths appeared in the detailed text. However, despite extensive availability modeling for Soviet divisions, no attempt had been made to incorporate their echelon concept in the overall conclusions. This is typical of the, ofttimes disjointed, intelligence cut and paste composition of these national opuses.

This DIA group, apparently, had later also recognized the significance of another Soviet precept—operational directions. A series of mid 1980s DIA reports dealt with aspects of echelonment and operations in specific TVDs. The 1985 Western TVD study[290] presented a detailed scenario (i.e. variant) for the Warsaw Pact opening strategic operation that incorporated a basic multi-level echelonment but confined to initial front offensives of the (unspecified) first strategic echelon (the actual version). A review of the more than a dozen other volumes of the DIA series on individual TVD operations would be useful to fully evaluate their attempt at a first translation of Soviet strategy. However my effort to obtain declassification of these studies has proceeded at a glacial pace—the 'D' does not signify a Dynamic enterprise—with uncertainty as to which century they might emerge from the dark side. Regardless of content value, the DIA perceptual model did not qualify for entry into the, supposedly coordinated, national estimates. As previously noted, I cannot explain why their analysis, incorporating evidence of the second kind, had been disregarded.

• trading-off

MacEachin had stressed the Soviet conundrum of conducting a preemptive attack with limited forces, judged not sustainable, versus an extended preparation of a balanced force far superior to NATO. This imputed 'tradeoff' had been an intelligence constant, variously phrased, in appraisals since the 1960s. A 1962 NIE considered that a deliberate surprise or preemptive attack "without prior buildup" could be a possibility but this would be [a variant] inconsistent with "the necessity for numerical superiority" in the theater; the US Air Force had inserted an alternative view that "The Soviets are unlikely to jeopardize achieving strategic surprise in a Soviet-initiated war by undertaking extensive mobilization."[291] A CIA-DIA task force in 1968 found "two basic contingencies" with the opposing goals of rapid action in a crisis versus achieving "the most advantageous balance of forces" prior to the outbreak of a

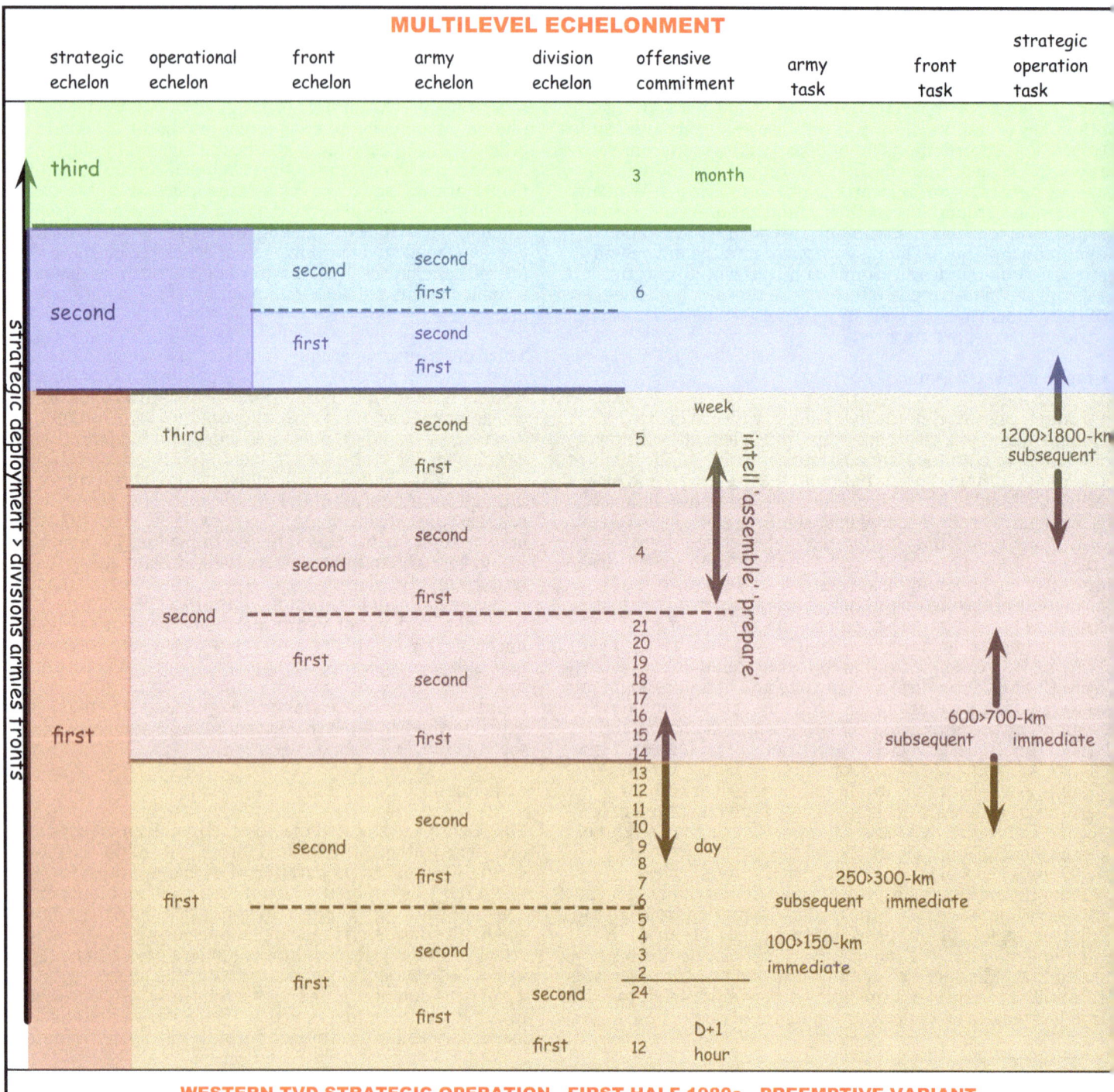

war.[292] The 1974 CIA study of Warsaw Pact mobilization plans contrasted an "availability" dependent on "exigencies of the situation" to "combat effectiveness" that could be attained only by post-mobilization training—among the first intell appraisals to raise the training issue.[293] The 1982 *Readiness* NIE "trade-offs" review proclaimed a distinction between immediate commitment to combat of all divisions whatever their status versus a "deliberate, phased" preparation of a fully trained force.[294] The 1978 *Warning* NIE asserted that the Soviets had the "major dilemma" of a "full combat potential" status "trade off" to achieve a rapid surprise assault that would catch NATO defenses unprepared and that they might be "forced to choose" between "force superiority" and surprise.[295] This "trade off" formulation would be repeated in nearly identical wording in the 1984 edition of the NIE;[296] with continuation of the theme in 1989 of a "highly risky" attack conducted without the training "necessary for minimum offensive proficiency"—subsequent to full mobilization and deployment[297]—that intelligence in the 1980s considered of paramount significance.

In 1987 the CIA had concluded most likely a Soviet-Warsaw Pact buildup to achieve a "decisive advantage in mass" but "We cannot, however, rule out the possibility that during a crisis the Soviets might choose to launch a preemptive attack on NATO without taking time to prepare fully their forces in Central Europe."[298] One of the salient lessons of European warfare—and a proximate causal factor of the First World War—had been the respective perceived necessity of opposing coalitions to deliver their punch before the other side could mobilize to effectively defend or preempt. The Soviet General Staff considered NATO mobilization and overseas reinforcement capability to be a crucial factor in variant determination. The perceived "fatal" weakness of NATO that had been conveyed by Colonel Kuklinski in 1981 would be the Western Europe defensive time-space inadequacy; while mobilized potential might be considerable, Warsaw Pact plans envisioned reaching the Rhine by war day six to eight, marching through Paris by D+15, and by D+30 overrunning the Iberian Peninsula.[299] However by 1985 a lecturer at the Academy had expressed alarm that while the peacetime 40 to 45 NATO divisions or equivalents in the Western TVD could be doubled "we always assumed" only after 30 days of mobilization, scaling up could now be accomplished within ten days.[300] This new reality may have been one of the factors motivating the ongoing Soviet shift to a defense strategy that would be proclaimed by the Warsaw Pact in 1987.

MacEachin had confidently asserted that a minimum of two weeks would be required to prepare forward fronts as well as a Soviet preference for up to thirty days of reservist integration training in "second strategic echelon" fronts. According to the summary memo, in response to a question posed by presiding Representative Les Aspin concerning his estimate of available warning time "Mr. MacEachin responded that the Soviets would certainly not be prepared to launch an attack in less than two weeks" and that intelligence "firmly believe we will identify the process" of a mobilization order after no more than 24 hours—which approximated the time required according to a CIA calculation[301] for GSFG first echelon regiments, of first echelon divisions, of first echelon armies, to occupy their predesignated assault departure positions. A differing expectation at the General Staff Academy in 1977 had first echelons arriving at state borders from their permanent garrisons in three to seven hours or no more than two hours from occupied departure areas.[302]

Intelligence persistence during three decades in espousing the official tradeoff model represented an entirely fallacious dissociation from the Soviet reality. Multi-level echelonment had been conceived as a means to achieve both goals, of immediate and rapid actions simultaneously with progressive buildup of efforts. Assessments that ranged potential Warsaw Pact actions from 'least likely' to 'most likely' had been constructed in a rigid narrow perspective that conflated likelihoods with operational variants, disregarding situational variability—the Soviet perspective. Each outcome represented a variant linked directly to specific strategic situations, i.e. political-military conditions that neither the USSR leadership nor intelligence could foresee. In certain circumstances—say a Warsaw Pact surprise attack—a 'standing start' (or alternatively worded expression) that had been consistently judged likely 'least' could become a 'most' opportune variant. As in many such rankings provided by intelligence, a recipient would be well advised to apply a skeptical 'hour glass' reversal.

- getting sneaky

The insistence by MacEachin in 1988 that two weeks of forward preparations would be necessary to prepare an attack had been, sort of, confirmed by the Soviets—in an exercise shortly after his presentation run by the Western GK a GSFG-based front (along with East German divisions) had been directed to conduct a phased 15-day concealed buildup to achieve war combat readiness. The paramount significance of covert war preparations had not been addressed or even broached by MacEachin to the assembled House members; a paragraph redacted at the top of page 15 of the briefing is the only sufficient text, which from the context is unlikely, that could have referred to concealment; and the blacked-out-less briefing summary memo does not mention this topic as having been covered.

Potential covert military preparations had been a common omission in the 52 intelligence offerings. A 1963 CIA-DIA report[303] mention of "practice of deception" appears to concern evidence regarding the peacetime status of ground divisions rather than war preparations; and the chronological ninth report, a 1966 NIE[304] considered "piecemeal" reinforcement over an extended period to be one method of maintaining "secrecy" but did not find the issue worthy of further discussion. Only the major event of 1968, the Czechoslovakia intervention, finally disturbed the intell slumberers. Number 16 in order, the December 1968 Warsaw Pact forces NIE,[305] in attempting the usual preparations timeline considered the "covert preparatory phases of mobilization" that had probably been initiated in mid July; that a future mobilization would involve both covert, during a tension period, and overt phases; that Soviet writings expected that any overt phase would be detected by NATO; and that the Czech crisis demonstrated the value of timely scheduled exercises.

But the 1975 Warsaw Pact NIE[306] (27th) despite referring to a likely "attempt initially to conceal or disguise their preparations" has no other treatment, with insufficient whiteout application to mask such discussion, in a report classified top secret. Further one of the most comprehensive Warsaw Pact NIEs, of 1979 again top secret,[307] (32d) in wide-ranging coverage of theater planning has no reference to the implications of covertness in getting ready in either the Summary or full Estimate; while a more curtailed 1981 NIE[308] in this series, also top secret, has nothing to offer. The only intelligence report of the 1960s-1970s to have a meaningful appraisal of the covert factor is the 29th, a CIA-OSR 1977 study of the Soviet operational conception for the Western TVD.[309] Therein are discussions of "concealed mobilization" but nothing on how this might be accomplished; the value of an initial covert mobilization to avoid transmitting any warning noise to the West; citation of a early 1960s Soviet article on the advantages of a "concealed, advance buildup" to seize the strategic initiative; and indications in exercise *Lato* 1971 of a precombat covert mobilization in a Polish military district. The DIA element which had been so leading in factoring echelons apparently did not extend attention to covertness. Their extensive 1984 scenario for a Western TVD war[310] has nothing to say regarding this topic. A related 1985 study of readiness in the TVD posited a month-long preparation conducted in a "heavily concealed fashion" with exercise cover but has no consideration beyond this basic statement.[311]

Comparison of the 1978,[312] 1984,[313] and 1989[314] editions of the, piquantly titled, *Warning of War* NIE-NIM series reveals a uniform overweening aplomb in the capability of intelligence to detect theater attack preparations in a timely manner and disregard of clearly expressed deceptive intent. The 1978 edition reassuringly informed that "we judge that Pact security, concealment, and deception would not significantly degrade our ability to interpret quickly the sum of identified activities as preparations for war" with some discussion of indications but nothing specifically on covert mobilization (unless in redacted sections). The NIE somehow considered a "covert buildup" to be a "danger"...**for the Soviets**—because their Warsaw Pact allies might spill the beans to the West. The 1984 edition has sectional treatment of concealment and deception with an itemized listing of potential actions; but remained "confident" regarding intell capability to detect the presumed massive scale of preparations necessary for a TVD offensive—no consideration of the limited first slice of an echeloned buildup anywhere in the NIE even when detailing attack "options"—while not factoring covert measures into warning times available for each option. The NIE did stress the ensuing difficulty of attaining consensus among the assessors as well as convincing those actually responsible for reactive decisions. The warning time reduction in Warsaw Pact deployment of a control structure posed by establishment of peacetime high commands received a mention—implemented four months subsequent to the information cutoff. The finale NIE in the series has no covertness discussion at all (and no redacts) in the Key Judgements. Similarly "confident" a 1987 CIA assessment of war transition among the Soviet groups of forces allowed only for potential hidden forward reinforcement during the semiannual troop rotation.[315] This supreme confidence had been the refrain in some of the few reports that actually considered the subject.

Particularly striking all this reporting lacked urgency, prioritization, and detailed consideration of a concealed, partial or full, mobilization by the Warsaw Pact. A covert mobilization potentiated not just theoretical but featured significantly in some exercises with stress in classified writings. In all, ten of the 52 intelligence pronouncements regarding Soviet and Warsaw Pact force structure, operational planning, and readiness published during nearly three decades actually refer in any way to concealment. Many of these merely contain drop allusions lacking further substantive elaboration. Nevertheless the reports laid out attack "options" with both projected preparation and warning hours, days, and weeks that demonstrate no factoring of concealment in the calculations. Yet covert preparation would be a variant posing the greatest danger to the West, seemingly requiring a pervasive, top priority, examination by intelligence. A 1970 National Security Council memo stressed the implications of intelligence misjudgment "NATO's failure promptly to detect and react to initiation Pact mobilization would place NATO in a much more vulnerable position…a lag in mobilization could be a disaster for NATO…."[316] Timing of a Warsaw Pact offensive constituted a crucial factor for NATO; even in the early 1980s a minimum 48 hours of warning essential for AFCENT (Allied Forces Central) to initiate mobilization.[317]

The fundamental intell conclusion that any attack from the East would have context, in whatever form, of a distinct European crisis whether localized or broad-based, may not be challengeable. Soviet leadership in the Cold War, at least after Khrushchev, had been eminently cautious. Seemingly unlikely that L. Brezhnev would have gone to the office one day and announced 'ok guys let's roll' to his colleagues. Only installation of a Hitleresque regime might have elevated the preemptive surprise assault up the variant scale. But covert preparations had been a prominent theme in Soviet military writings with specific exercise practice. The nub of the intelligence official model inhered a presumed, mind bogglingly misplaced, overweeningly confidence, in Western capability to detect offensive preparations in the face of a clearly stated intent to conceal a mobilization-deployment by numerous techniques.

The 1971 *Combined Armed Forces Directive on Combat Readiness* requirement that "Troops are brought to increased combat readiness without the declaration of a combat alert"[318] had been repeated in the 1979 edition;[319] thus this first stage of war preparations would not be announced by a signal that might be detected in the West—but there would be formal combat alerts elevating to Military Threat and Full. The later Directive had other sneaky provisions. Troops could depart permanent garrisons "without bringing them up to prescribed wartime strength" from stage Constant within three hours, or Increased in a maximum allowed 2.5 hours; full mobilization would have required from six to twelve hours. Among other Soviet classified material the 1963 General Staff operations manual had pointed out the advantage of covertly initiating an offensive directly from garrisons rather than after dispersal to departure or concentration areas—this variant would be practiced in exercise *Soyuz* 1983.[320] Achieving surprise in actions "implied attack from garrison without preliminary mobilization" according to a Czech senior officer.[321] The 1979 *Directive* also specified that front and naval aviation preparation of "concealed airfields" would take place only at stage Military Threat.

A military conference pondering a front operation at the start of war concluded that full readiness would only be achieved during a threat period; when absent the front would launch an attack from peacetime status, reinforced during combat. Considered during the early 1960s, this nuclear variant plan depicted a "first offensive operation being conducted by troops in limited strength."[322] Apparently a priority in the Southern Group, a few years later considerable work under way examined methods for initiating a front offensive directly from garrison locations; "the most characteristic method of actions at the beginning of a war" in the western groups and military districts. Missile troops had deployment priority "under the guise of exercises" a convenient method.[323]

The 1962 edition of *Military Strategy*[324] held that a "concealed mobilization" had a modern application but would be conducted "somewhat differently" (how not specified) than in previous times. Practical experience would be developed in exercises until The End. The Polish front in Narew 1965 initiated "covert mobilization" in attaining Full combat readiness—three days prior to outbreak of war.[325] A 1970 war game had stressed that any eventuating threat period "must be exploited to the maximum to carry out secret full troop mobilization and deployment."[326] The Polish 3 Western Front in *Lato* 1974 "within the framework of secret mobilization" of its "first operational echelon" had been conducted prior to the declaration of the Full level[327]—multi-level echelonment in action. During *Shchit/Tarcza* 1976 the Warsaw Pact initiated the Increased stage ten to twelve days, and "secret mobilization expansion and operational deployment of troops" two days, prior to war start—and one front attained "without declaration of a combat alert" stage Full.[328] These exercises had been conducted prior to the insertion of stage Military Threat. Eastern forces during *Zapad* 1977 had initiated a "secret mobilization and deployment" six days prior to the asserted surprise attack from the West.[329]

Particular importance during the Cold War had been assigned by the Soviets—and presently by their successors—to exercise masking. This ploy had been used with great success in preparing the 1968 invasion of Czechoslovakia. The 1984 *Warning* NIE expressed "considerable confidence" that intelligence, based on decades of experience monitoring Warsaw Pact exercises, could distinguish between routine play and larger-scale departures indicative of offensive preparations; in particular due to a trend in command-staff exercises diminishing representative troop field deployments[330]—innately unmindful of likely first echelons prioritization. The 1979 *Combat Readiness Directive*[331] had given explicit instructions under stage Full.

> In order to covertly build up the forces in theaters of military actions and convert the Combined Armed Forces to a wartime status in a more systematic manner, the covert, full mobilization of troops and naval forces can be carried out under the guise of exercises and assemblies by special order of the Commander-in-Chief of the Combined Armed Forces according to a complete schedule set up in advance or according to a selective procedure.

The *Directive* advised using "the pretext of preparing for exercises" by lower strength and training units to implement actions, and for all troops and naval forces to attain, the Increased stage. Exercise *Shchit/Tarcza* 1988 featured the Polish Armed Forces "brought up to wartime strength under the guise of an exercise" with the added veneer "work on behalf of the economy" as well as many troops attaining stage Full in permanent locations.[332]

Contrary to the assertion of the 1983 'war scare' proponents that this had been the most dangerous Cold War confrontation in Europe, a very real teetering on the precipice of a full-scale war had actually taken place in 1961 over Berlin. The *Burya* exercise held from 28 September into the first two weeks of October had been nothing less than a masked strategic deployment by all of the Warsaw Pact for a preemptive Western strategic operation—a mobilized, forward regrouped, assault on Western Europe that, given the strategies then adopted by the sides, would have inevitably started with, or soon involved, mass nuclear exchanges. Oleg Penkovsky, during a meeting with stewards in Paris on 20 September,[333] had warned that the Pact would be brought to "a state of combat readiness" keyed to actions involving East Germany "what Khrushchev wants to do is to backstop with actual large-scale military preparations camouflaged as manoeuvres" the signing of a peace treaty.

> Khrushchev, our General Staff and the GRU know perfectly well that secret preparations in modern times are not possible due to intelligence techniques, But under the guise of manoeuvres, concerning which he will insist that they are only manoeuvres, their extent and duration can easily be extended.

Penkovsky reported that "Eighth Mechanized Army" (then actually or later designated 8 Tank Army) would be moved to the GDR from the Carpathian MD but he had been misinformed as to the number of armies already in the GSFG.

According to an article in the top secret edition of VM the next year,[334] anticipating a hostile Western response to the impending German peace treaty...

> our Government was obliged to undertake a number of grave measures to reinforce the security of the USSR and to heighten the combat readiness of the armed forces. This found concrete expression in the temporary retention in the army of some contingents due for discharge in the autumn of 1961, in a partial call-up for service from the reserve, in the reinforcement of troops of the border military districts (groups of forces), in the conduct of maneuvers participated in by all arms of troops, including troops of the countries participating in the Warsaw Pact, and in the resumption of experimental nuclear explosions.

The last item 'no accident' as the Soviets would say that nuclear tests last conducted in November 1958 resumed in earnest at the proving grounds on 1 September 1961; 26 conducted during that month, 23 in October—culminating at the end of the month with the 50-mt Tsar bomb event—but only ten in November and a halt until February 1962.[335] They had conveyed seemingly unmistakable notice of atomic consequences for any Western reaction.

Reservists had been moved forward to fill support units;[336] a Soviet "mechanized army" had been detected deploying from the Carpathian MD—thus confirming Penkovsky's information—through southern Poland, into Czechoslovakia.[337] Post Cold War information indicates that repositioning of even strategic forces may have taken place, involving the planned transfer of at least one additional R-12 missile regiment to East Germany.[338] We currently lack evidence regarding other strategic and theater level measures likely implemented that fall. Intell in 1961 had been incapable of distinguishing proaction from simulation, as later demonstrated in the Czech invasion, even though the *Burya* scenario had been assessed at the time to portray a preemptive assault involving widespread frontal nuclear strikes. Even more stunningly the 1984 NIE *Warning of War in Europe* would assert that "The Intelligence Community has never observed the Soviet Union or Warsaw Pact making preparations of the magnitude and duration necessary to go to war with NATO."[339] The devastating irony is that this, profoundly inept, statement is accurate—intelligence in 1961 and thereafter never "observed" that a European armed conflict had been imminent .

Events in 1961 had progressed in exactly the situation of rising tension which intell considered the most likely context for Warsaw Pact war preparations. Successful large-scale military surprises have been conducted throughout history into modern times. Even the vaunted Israeli intelligence had been caught napping by the 1973 Egyptian assault across the Suez Canal. The dilemma for any intended victim would be the conflicting, ambiguous, and fragmentary signs deliberately projected by the aggressor. Historically, dissenters in the ranks who pointed to the trend of specific actions have been ignored or shoved aside (a worse fate awaited them in Stalin's delusional realm during 1941). The Soviets abided keenly aware of the necessary avoidance of signaling actions and would certainly attempt to actively manage Western judgments. Distinguishing actual intentions from realistic practice would a particularly exquisite intelligence problem during larger scale exercises. The other side had similar concerns that increasingly complex NATO exercises in the 1980s had been "marked by enormous scales and are becoming more and more difficult to distinguish from the deployment of armed forces for aggression" according to a lecture prepared for the General Staff Academy.[340]

The perceptually crippling element in all of these intell assessments consisted in the actuality of multi-level echelonment. Warning had been predicated on detection of large-scale preparations throughout the peacetime disposition of armed forces. This fixation had created the preconditions for military disaster in the West. In order to carry out a surprise or preemptive campaign the Soviets and their allies would have to conceal activities only in the first echelons of the first echelons of their strike groupings—limited preparations much easier to conceal even if the exercise ploy had not been adopted. Buildup of efforts would be implemented subsequent to D+1. Intelligence had projected as "most likely" in both the 1978 and 1984 *Warning of War* NIEs the "gradual buildup" "option" conducted over weeks and even months—which afforded the Soviets ample opportunity to implement covert mobilization and preparation measures—in particular, through the exercise gambit. A flawed CIA analysis in particular (as in the 1983 sequential report 38)[341] stressed the essentiality of post mobilization training to attain full combat potential that could actually be accomplished following initial hostilities in echelons the Soviets did not plan to commit for weeks afterwards. In the event of a surprise/preemptive variant imperative the Warsaw Pact would have struck regardless of their state of mobilization and proficiency to forestall NATO counteraction.

- obsoleteness

Another occasional intelligence theme, appearing in a dozen reports, had been the finger-shaking at the Soviets and allies for their reliance on superseded and hand-me-down arms for equipping the back-echelons. The 1987 CIA study on Western TVD readiness pointed to a lack of hardware "homogeneity" with data on selected weapons age mix;[342] while a 1985 DIA report on the same topic implied that "combat potential" in later echelons would be progressively lessened.[343] In 1965 a *Capabilities* NIE[344] had asserted that the main factor limiting mobilization potential would be the lack of modern arms to equip newly created units. Some connoisseurs apparently expected Soviet deep reserves would be committed armed with crossbows and catapults.

A 1984 joint CIA-DIA-Army Assessment[345] had been more nuanced but focused solely on active ground units (i.e visible components of the first strategic echelon). The scaling of Ground Troops deployment amounted such that new armaments had been fielded by the Soviets even as the preceding generation had not yet filled the ranks; compounded by a growing disparity with and among the Warsaw Pact members. An equipment database project had revealed that 1960s vintage items still abounded. Noting "regional variations" that seemed to indicate tailoring by terrain and enemy—in the first translation, that arming might take place in accordance to TVD and direction characteristics sufficient to match levels held by specific opponents—the study relegated to a footnote the observation that all world armed forces had partly aged hardware inventories. A constant refrain in NATO relations had been the futile push for increased expenditures on conventional arms upgrades. Left unsaid by this and other intell reports would be the unprecedented lethal intensity of battles in the Western and some other TVDs. As put by an outside observer in the day, "...the T-34 [will] be the best tank on the battlefield if all the T-64s, and Challengers, and Abrams and Leopards are destroyed..."[346]

The effective precedent, as in all Soviet contemplations, had been GPW experience. From late June to mid August 1941 a series of decisions had been reached to create 156 new rifle divisions, with admittedly low quality ("combat potential"), through measures that included "the issuance to the troops of obsolete models" of arms and equipment.[347] These divisions comprised a third strategic echelon, which ultimately halted the German advance and, when re-equipped with the output of relocated factories (and rarely mentioned foreign deliveries), drove into Central Europe. Vladimir Rezun had stressed the significance of these reinforcements armed with aged hardware for Soviet victories and that these still routinely stashed reserves endured for another generation of troops.[348] Deployment of additional strategic echelons, and their initially 'obsolescent' armament, had not been factored by intell which of course remained blissfully unaware of the nature or existence of this potentially decisive augmentation.

- the war in the air

While a ground offensive might be massive in the scale of first and succeeding echelons the Soviets could not so readily gin up the modern aircraft essential to the complementary theater air offensive. A detailed mid 1980s CIA review[349] of the evolving Air Operation and the recently originated Air Defense Operation had been dubious concerning the Warsaw Pact capability to achieve air supremacy at the outset of nuclear or conventional variants. Assessing the results of aviation reorganizations and operational planning, calculations indicated that their losses would be so high as to cripple the air campaign. Soviet ongoing improvements to guidance systems of front missiles, however, might change the equation by permitting mass conventional strikes for "airfield pin-down" and suppression of air defense systems in a surprise strike. The Soviets may have shared this appreciation. The probability that aircraft of fronts could traverse 100-km of NATO air defenses had been judged in 1985 by the General Staff Academy to be no greater than two percent at high and medium altitudes; low altitude penetrations substantially improved the odds but would still be no more than forty percent. The Academy expected a heavy toll would be exacted by the NATO array of some 70 surface-air missile battalions along with aircraft defenders and other assets in the Western TVD.[350]

No doubt the Soviets intended to strive for air supremacy but complete success would not actually be a prerequisite in the strategic operation—objectives could be also achieved by disrupting or preventing NATO air support to ground pounders. Heavy reliance in tank killing resided with the aerialists. The US Army in particular had no experience in operating without effective close air support. In appraising NATO views Marshal (Aviation) P. Kutakhov concluded[351] "It is considered that the ground forces require the winning of air superiority far more than do the air forces" in the conventional variant—and that failure might require resort to nuclear weapons. The World War II Ardennes 'Battle of the Bulge' disaster featured a German massed attack spearheaded by the few reserve *panzer* divisions; favored by weather precluding effective air support; that caught the Americans by surprise and drove deep into their defenses. Only after a full week of desperate combat in December 1944 did the sky open for Allied air strikes that decimated the attackers and doomed the offensive. Fundamental to the eventual German defeat the *Luftwaffe* had limited capability and, most significantly, Hitler shot the bolt—there could be no ground augmentation from an exhausted reserve. But a comparable Soviet strategic operation would be characterized by a continuous buildup of efforts with a seemingly endless commitment of operational and strategic echelons.

- conning the system

Ironically a potentially significant factor restraining any preemptive or quick assault by at least Soviet fronts would have been leadership awareness that the machinery of strategic deployment might not roll out with quite the precision depicted by their military theoreticians. Much anecdotal evidence of gaming combat readiness norms and other forms of cheating pointed to systemic flaws. Vladimir Rezun had recounted how a commission inspecting his regiment had been handled.[352] The allies had similar problems. Officers of a Hungarian unit told of a 'unannounced' mobilization for exercise Danube 1983 in which some reservists, because word had apparently leaked, showed up drunk and disheveled; the first readiness measure a visit to the military barber. However most personnel had arrived within seven to nine hours, beating the "final limit" of ten hours.[353] A 1982 CIA assessment[354] of Ground Troops readiness evaluations considered examples of upward reporting scams and the potential weak points—especially in lower *shtat* grades—but did not conclude that these incapacitated Warsaw Pact troops. An NIE that year pointed out similar deficiencies while noting that in preparation for the 1968 Czech invasion one USSR *oblast* had assembled 10000 reservists within six hours; detailed comparisons made between Soviet and US readiness reporting determined, astoundingly, only the Soviet system had shortcomings.[355] Such readiness chicanery unknown to Western militaries? Soviet mass scaling might well have compensated for the weak points but that proposition would never, fortunately, undergo a wide-ranging test.

- sustainability

The vast quantity of materiel, and the logistics handlers, required for front operations also arranged by echelons. Intell connoisseurs, however, tend to like to keep things as simple as possible, favoring compact solutions; much easier than dealing with the complexities of reality. That the pervasiveness of echelons in Soviet planning might signify that missiles, ammunition, other stocks, and both combat and support units might be placed backward to multiple locations did not constitute a prominent element in force assessments; especially analytically debilitating to conclusions regarding the location and numeration of WMD reserves. Early Cold War intelligence estimates, in particular, held that lower level Soviet ground units including divisions had limited capability due to lack of the considerable logistics support characteristic of Western forces—the Soviet reverse assessment pictured large, cumbersome divisions unsuited to modern maneuver warfare. In fact substantial support had been built into the Soviet structure but layered higher up the organizational, and mobilization, ladder, largely invisible to intelligence.

The absence in Central Europe of many unit types assigned in the front index could be accounted for by mobilization-deployment of these components from USSR places of origin not necessarily confined to border MDs. Limited information acquired concerning Soviet logistics planning indicated that support complexes of the Center would be deployed as variegated, but on a far greater scale, as those of individual fronts. A lopsided system placed massive reserves at the top of the chute which would continually push the lower echelons to replace respective expenditures. The 1989 NIE[356] on Warsaw Pact forces asserted that ammunition stocks in the Western TVD would suffice for at most 45 days in conditions of intense conventional operations, requiring outside resupply or to "adjust war plans"—as if the Center had not been accumulating reserves in massive quantities for more than a decade at bases and arsenals of interior districts for any such contingency.

The major concern of Soviet logistics planners during the Cold War regarded, contrary to some intelligence estimates, not that engaged combat units would run out of supplies but rather that they would outrun their supporters. Measures and organizational reforms undertaken over decades sought to increase the mobility of the front rear in order to match the pace of the fighters. The planning basis for the accumulation of materiel stocks in peacetime started with the 90 days expected for conversion of the national economy to wartime production.[357] This coincided with GPW experience, the forced evacuation of industry before the German onslaught had been equated to the conditions of nuclear war.

The essential thrust of Soviet classified writings and exercises throughout the Cold War entailed the projection of a more rapid, and greater scaled, buildup of offensive effort widely at variance to that expected by most analysts in at least US intelligence services. From at least 1978 through 1984 assessments laid out a dissociated version of Soviet initial attack "options" involving 2/3/5 fronts. Only in 1989 would intell add a sixth Soviet Baltic Front (the 1988 MacEachin presentment discussed six fronts but a Soviet-Polish rather than Baltic in origin) to the lineup[358]—but still focused on the five-front variant when second kind evidence actually pointed to the Baltic creation fully two decades earlier. The intell butchered perspective of Soviet military strategy had critical ramifications. One or the other side persisted heinously wrong in respective calculations. Erroneous intelligence assessments and forecasts had set the stage for a Western military catastrophe of historic proportions. The strategic reality is that ALL of these fronts would be advancing simultaneously—in a concerted assault—and not two or three or five but six fronts of the Western TVD first strategic echelon. This massive echeloned onslaught would develop concurrent with mobilization-deployment and regrouping of divisions, armies, and fronts of the second strategic echelon in a concatenated buildup of forces and means to steamroller the NATO defense system.

Providential that the West 'won' a cold war.

## going all the way

The Soviet concept of the *strategicheskya operatsiya* subsumed all of the elements of a military campaign. One of the forms of strategic action, General Staff sources defined the strategic operation as a flurry of strategic and frontal strikes in a continental TVD under a unified strategic concept, goal, and leadership.[359] Ground and aviation forces, with naval elements as appropriate, organized in fronts and armies would be orchestrated into a massive and continuously augmented blow (likely magnified by strategic strikes in the nuclear variant) against predefined strategic and operational objectives approached by the directions. Per the Academy "The front conducts offensive operations within the context of a strategic operation in a theater of military actions;"[360] objectives, in turn, established on the basis of the war goal—a decisive defeat of the NATO member states. Essential to the war-winning imperative would be a rapid offensive into the depth of the TVDs to exploit a forecast critical NATO weakness—the ponderous collective political-military decision-making process—to ensure that enemy reactions lagged a rapidly developing battlefield situation.

High-speed attacks would also enable attrition of NATO delivery means to enhance prospects, and limit any damaging response, during the inevitable nuclear exchange; hinder mobilization-deployment of opponents; and outrace overseas reinforcement. Key indices of capabilities and variant success included rates of advance, measured in average kilometers per 24 hour periods. The conventional variant retarded rates but had the advantage of permitting a buildup of forces to ensure victory in the event of unforeseen plan failures. In the late 1970s and early 1980s conventional warfare had increasingly (or more realistically) been depicted as prolonged and difficult, especially considering likely US reinforcements, and given NATO weapons technological innovation. Political winds of change would even by 1987 result in the coincident emergence of a defensive variant, a change of emphasis to the counteroffensive as a strategy rather than an ideological fiction.

A forecasting grid of mathematical precision overlay each TVD in order to develop parameter sets for operational variants stemming from exercise experience, research, and modeling. The averaged and ranged indices presented in Soviet classified documents read rather like the projections of a capitalist business plan with confident assumption of results both quantifiable and datable. Operational indices marked the pace and success of individual front operations, a derivative of the GPW experience of offensive fadeout against a deeply-echeloned German defense system. Optimum front complement and logistics dictated a cycle of advance/replenishment measured by the depth of a series of tasks, duplicated at army level. This scheme of successive front and army missions had been introduced during the GPW strategic offensive.[361] Soviet military planners assessing strengths, weaknesses, and developments among NATO defenders assigned coefficients of relative capabilities as if competitors in a targeted market; potential consumers of (WMD) product lines circumstantially detailed.

The Soviets defined these tasks with a Georgian architectural-like balance. In carrying out the Western TVD initial strategic operation, fronts in the theater first operational echelon would each conduct a first offensive operation over twelve to fifteen days in two cycles, delimited in specified depths by immediate (250- to 300-km or more, requiring six or seven days) and subsequent (a further 350- to 400-km and six to eight days) tasks—thereby accomplishing the immediate task of the strategic operation—at which line a front or fronts of the second operational echelon would be committed to attain the subsequent task of the strategic operation. Since by 1985 this General Staff Academy explication[362] considered the likely depth of a first front operation to be no more than 700-km, at least a second complete operation of the fronts would be necessary to fulfill the subsequent task of the TVD first strategic operation. This lecture justified such arbitrary assignments because "The decision for the first operation is made in peacetime" requiring essential and complex planning to support operations on a massive scale. Subordinate armies in each of these front offensives would in turn also conduct two offensive cycles to fulfill a front immediate task, repeated for the front subsequent task. Thus a first echelon army commander faced the theoretical prospect of as many as eight successive offensive cycles in the initial strategic operation, assuming sufficient personnel and equipment endured the sequence—the purpose for the wave of succeeding echelons which would augment or replace laggards. The Soviets in any case anticipated a NATO defense collapse.

Fronts and armies would be assigned immediate and subsequent objectives, often designated by river or urban lines, during preparation of the offensive plan. Amendment of the intervals and full depth of the front offensive occurred several times during the Cold War, calculations based on results from exercising operational variants, along with theoretical and practical research—and especially revision of the timing and scale of an inevitable resort to nuclear weapons. Soviet historical reviews indicate the initial appearance of limited numbers of nuclear weapons in the early 1950s set off an enthusiastic expectation of an offensive at high rates to a great depth, which contracted substantially until the end of the 1950s when nuclear availability soared, as did the indices once again.[363] The General Staff Academy 1974 textbook thus stated that "present day views" prophesied an initial front offensive in the Western TVD that would reach 600- to 800-km, determined by the depth of a NATO army group disposition (400- to 500-km) plus those of main national forces.[364] Academy lectures and lessons from 1977 reiterated that depth range.[365] The depth of the immediate task of the front equalled that necessary to disrupt enemy operational stability and create conditions for an offensive at high rates of advance, while the subsequent task shattered deep reserves.

The Southwestern TVD depth of 600- to 800-km could be spanned by one front operation in each of the two strategic directions, and objectives might be achieved in a single offensive operation of fronts. But the depth of the Western TVD reached 1200- to 2000-km[366] (1000- to 1200-km[367] in the Northern-Coastal Strategic Direction), which would necessitate multiple front operations. A second strategic operation would finish off the pesky Brits, and emulate the Moorish conquest of the Iberian Peninsula. Complexity of operations against the main NATO enemies required sequenced offensive operations of fronts, preferably without pause. By the second half of the 1960s development had been initiated on a modernized version of the GPW concept of a strategic offensive conducted as a coordinated advance of several fronts. This version would be tested and elaborated in several large scale theater exercises in the following two decades.

Minimal information could be derived from Soviet classified writings and exercises concerning the nature of any additional or extended strategic operation. Yet French, Spanish, and Portuguese ports would be critical for entry of US reinforcements upon overrun of the Channel ports. Lack of discussion as well as exercise study seems to reflect Soviet uncertainty and wariness regarding advance planning in detail the character of post-nuclear exchange warfare; notably absent any indication of war termination variants. Soviet large scale exercises did not take place as isolated, occasional, events. The USSR General Staff planned and directed a systematic, unceasing schedule of exercises that could span European and Asian theaters or be limited to particular TVDs and military districts. In the 1980s a series of exercises alternately verified the operations of at least eighteen Soviet fronts based on different groups and districts—generation of fourteen from the first strategic echelon as well as four and possibly a nineteenth front of the second strategic echelon. A transition under way would task the staffing and communications structures of newly established peacetime TVD high commands.

Actuality of Soviet theater military planning and objectives is evinced in the roll call of exercise practice. The following summarizations are gathered from a wide variety of sources, including primary documents acquired by intelligence and those found in the military archives of retired Warsaw Pact member states;[368] declassified intell assessments as well as studies issued post Cold War by several organizations and individuals;[369] and my contemporary perusal of the take from monitoring of these exercises currently sequestered from public cognizance. Only sources of particular interest are cited. Focused consideration of developments in European TVDs, highlighting alterations to planned strategic actions against the NATO alliance, receives more detailed treatment in Operational Evolutions.

• Western Theater of Military Actions

The Western TVD constituted, to NATO and US intelligence, the most dangerous borderlands and therefore for decades the center of attention for increasingly complex studies and operational modeling. By the mid 1980s accumulated evidence from exercises and classified writings supported comprehensive assessments in NIE as well as departmental studies that did not always coincide with each other or with the supposedly coordinated versions. The DIA in particular, with a perspective more narrowly tailored to the requirements of military commands and NATO, produced dense evaluations of the Western[370] and other TVDs. Certain exercises over a period of decades provided informative snapshots of Soviet plans mingled within these appraisals of forces and operations in the various TVDs.

The October 1961 Warsaw Pact operational-strategic command-staff exercise *Burya* (Storm also the codename for a massive theater nuclear strike) had been conducted as the Berlin crisis moved toward another confrontation involving the proposed Soviet-East German peace treaty. The scenario strategic operation had the, unique for the Cold War, potential of development into the real McCoy. Intelligence collected much information as the exercise unfolded but archive materials reveal a somewhat different slant, in particular frontal roles for the Pact allies that had been misjudged.[371] Intelligence evaluated *Burya* as an unprecedented event, the first large scale exercise ever detected involving all Warsaw Pact armed forces; archival documents support this conclusion of a first exercise "as a coalition."[372] Both sources agreed that the Pact acted preemptively in attacking simultaneously with a full strategic-front mass nuclear strike (variously reported three minutes prior to or five following enemy launch) upon the imputed detection of NATO intents. Intelligence identified some of the five fronts depicted but had only a hazy notion of others—notably entirely missing that the northernmost front had been a Polish command. Scenario depicted full Pact mobilization during a period of tension and regrouping of two second echelon fronts prior to war outbreak; a 1962 Soviet review stated that "movement of large groupings of troops from the interior of the country in the initial period of war was worked out to the fullest extent."[373] Exercise play terminated on the D+10 capture of Paris and Pact troops at the Channel.

The *Zapad* exercise conducted in October 1969 is an early example of the new form of strategic operation for which there are some details available. A document found in Czech archives summarized the operational scenario.[374] Monitoring at the time lacked details; however some exercise documents obtained but not yet declassified may have pertained to this exercise.[375] Conducted under the threat-conventional-national fronts inclusive variants and confined to initial operations in the Western TVD, the scenario depicted a counteroffensive by three forward fronts (one under Polish command) augmented, apparently on the fourth day, by the Reserve and Western Fronts; fronts and their designations identical in the documents made available to intelligence. This exercise conformed to a lineup—evident in *Burya* 1961— that had been discovered only the previous year by US intelligence. Summation by Marshal A. A. Grechko emphasized the superiority of his side in the number of divisions in depth up to 500-km from the border of the Germanys, a marked advantage in combat without nuclear weapons. Grechko faulted the imputed NATO attack for failing to resort to an early employment of nuclear weapons to redress their inferiority! Scenario information provided in the documents did not address the NATO motivation for launching an offensive against manifestly superior Warsaw Pact forces.

The *Zapad* May-June 1977 operational-strategic exercise of the Warsaw Pact States marked an exceptional event of the 1970s; indeed according to the Soviet Chief of the General Staff Marshal N. V. Ogarkov official report, the most important Combined Armed Forces training in fifteen years[376]— presumably referring to the October 1961 *Burya* exercise. The Soviets derived important conclusions regarding not only TVD high commands but also nuclear strike planning. Ogarkov considered the balance of forces in the TVD to be coequal even with only forty percent of Pact troops in three fronts directly confronting NATO—thus the second operational echelon would be vital to a sustained offensive. Available to intelligence had been not only extensive SIGINT reporting but also, among several reports provided by the CIA favorite Pole, the official Soviet critique; while documents found in Czech and East German archives again provide useful details. Ogarkov identified this *Zapad* as one of "special importance" in gaining experience in the conduct of the new form of strategic offensive—"...based on one of the possible variations of joint military action of the Warsaw Pact member states..."[377] As in *Burya,* two fronts of the second operational echelon regrouped forward prior to the start of combat. Direct monitoring at the time detected a 6 Front without details but the official critique confirmed the Baltic MD basis—existence had only recently been perceived. Mutual covert mobilizations notably featured, with NATO use of the exercise cover stratagem. Unlike 1969 a major theme involved an exchange of mass nuclear strikes, the culminating point of the exercise, while depicting the most prolonged period of conventional combat ever observed to that date. The exercise apparently terminated with a post-nuclear situation assessment. Intelligence observers at the time had been impressed by the scale and realism of this exercise. Seemingly amounting to a full-up rehearsal for a war in Europe; the CIA Polish informant stated that the main purpose of the exercise had been to "test selected elements of the war plans" for the Western TVD.[378]

One of the most complete scenarios for the strategic operation in the Western TVD followed in *Tsentr* 1978, held in September-October. A Soviet training directive conjoined this exercise with the preceding *Zapad* as of "critical importance"[379]—a continuation of the Western TVD strategic operation expanded to the multitheater level. Combat during 65 days, coordinated for the first time by a fully staffed *glavkom*, depicted the threat-escalation-national fronts variants. The nuclear phase did not begin until after 27 days of conventional combat (the lengthiest in any known exercise during the Cold War that featured nuclear strikes play), taking the form of a theater-wide strike by strategic and frontal means. A Polish summarization of the exercise[380] reported that NATO limited nuclear strikes preceded by four hours a massive Warsaw Pact response. At least four, and possibly two or three additional, fronts had been committed to achieve objectives in the TVD. France—usually only an incidental participant in prior Warsaw Pact exercises since withdrawing in 1966 from the NATO military structure—here received the full treatment, overrun along with the Benelux countries to the Atlantic coast. By D+51 Pact fronts had advanced within 100-km of the Spanish border according to the Polish summary. The French during this timeframe had reorganized and augmented their ground formations to back up NATO deployments in the FRG, while activating Pluton nuclear missile regiments.[381] Planning—the most extensive yet observed for operations against Spain and the UK—for the succeeding strategic operation occurred during a pause at the English Channel; perhaps necessary to wait out the high level of radioactivity from the mass strategic nuclear strikes before completing this European tour in the British Isles.

The *Tsentr* exercise of June 1982 covered even greater territory than the 1978 running; depicting operations involving at least thirteen (of the 23 numbered) fronts in not only the Western but also the Southwestern and Southern TVDs. A memo located in East German archives[382] provides some details not in the intelligence take, including a background scenario of war initiated by the Chinese in the Eastern Theater, with the support of Japan and Korea (presumably South) no less. Their incursions deep into the USSR had been instigated by the US and NATO to divert Soviet troops in preparation for a surprise attack in the West. Other scenario inputs by the Soviet General Staff seemed to posit a complex situation involving the expanding local wars variant. Mass nuclear strike planning and execution again represented a significant constituent; the exercise focal point the strategic operation in the Western TVD.[383] Variants played included a prolonged conventional phase, and limited combat use of national fronts. Among the seven fronts appearing in the TVD, the Czech, uncommonly, featured as part of the second operational echelon; with the Polish held in reserve—they had presumably fallen out of favor due to the 1980-1981 internal crisis. Salient combat actions included drops of airborne divisions at the River Rhine and Copenhagen (frequent Soviet exercise events) and to capture Paris. The TVD strategic operation persisted all the way to the Atlantic and Mediterranean coasts of France, positioned again for an invasion of the Iberian Peninsula with the commitment of an eighth front, and into northern Italy. Probably due to an earlier nuclear exchange only about three weeks transpired to reach the Pyrenees.

A 'classic' performance of a strategic operation in the Western TVD—incorporating definitional elements—took place during exercise *Soyuz* 1983 in May-June. Scenario followed the surprise-conventional-national fronts inclusive variants. Documents from East German, unusually numerous,[384] and Czech archives[385] again contribute elements unavailable to intelligence. Although extensive nuclear planning occurred, with NATO projected to use nuclear weapons when forward defenses shattered, nuclear strikes did not feature in the scenario. Quite propitious since, according to one document, the Westerners planned to use more than 5000 nuclear weapons, including some 2800 in the first strike. The Warsaw Pact forces executed their (counter)offensive in the variant direct from permanent garrisons rather than from alert dispersal positions—thus enhancing concealment of the initial assault echelon. The Pact offensive committed six fronts to reach France by D+13 or D+15 (quicker with any nuclear assist), then plow across to the Spanish border after 30 or 35 days; thereby achieving the further goals of both second front offensive operations and the TVD strategic operation. An East German document with the text of a presentation by their defense minister confirmed the intelligence conclusion of a six-front assault, with two second echelon fronts committed within France to strike a knockout blow.

The Western TVD strategic operation played in the June-July 1984 *Zapad* also comprised six fronts—but all under Soviet command—indicative of an ongoing exploration since the early 1980s of exclusive control replicating that prior to the early 1960s.[386] All three groups of forces in Central Europe and the three bordering MDs fielded front headquarters. A consistent pattern is evident in which the NGF and the CGF formed fronts with their hosts' national fronts remaining in the theater reserve or not established; fragmentary evidence precludes confirming this substitution variant as an absolute. Two earlier editions of *Zapad*, in 1983 and 1981, had also been confined to Soviet participants. *Zapad* 1977 had been the last to include the Warsaw Pact allies in front roles.[387] Such a variant avoided the more prolonged assembly of the national fronts, and coordination with their individual leaderships—handy for any planned Soviet surprise, preemptive offensive minimizing the likelihood that a warning might reach the West. *Zapad* 1984 scenario depicted, despite play of combat readiness elevation in a deteriorating situation, a surprise conventional attack by NATO forces using a new generation of precision weapons. But four of the fronts generated, or regrouped forward from the western USSR, prior to the onset of combat. This fortuitous preparation somehow allowed the Soviets to launch their counteroffensive within a matter of hours. Mutual nuclear strikes may not have been initiated until after sixteen days of conventional warfare. Many segments conducted had subsidiary live field representations. A role for Marshal D. F. Ustinov, the Defense Minister, as Director marked the significance of the exercise; with no indication of a Western GK active participation.

In September 1987 complementary *Soyuz* and *Tsentr* exercises duplicated the expansion from the Western to multiple TVDs West to East of a decade earlier. But these exercises conducted operations in modes that reflected shifting political winds, a fundamental reorientation of Soviet strategy to the defense; much greater emphasis placed on the imputed massive NATO attack. In *Soyuz* the Western TVD variant evident since the 1960s of three fronts, including Polish and Czech commanded, defended a NATO attack for sixteen days before reinforcement by two or three fronts of the second operational echelon; a counteroffensive then initiated plunged deep into the territory of NATO countries. Despite the recent Warsaw Pact official adoption of the strategic defense, some of the East's offensive élan had been retained. Marshal N. V. Ogarkov oversaw the action at his Western GK post. *Tsentr*, which started eight days later, conspicuously focused strategic coordination in all four peacetime high commands. Also of note in both exercises, while contingency planning had been conducted, no executions of mass nuclear strikes occurred although in *Tsentr* this may have been because no offensive campaign had been played out.

• Northwestern Theater of Military Actions

The strategic and frontal complements of the Northwestern TVD deployed on the right flank of the Western TVD. This theater abutted Finland, Norway, and extended into the Baltic Sea. Contrary to the neat depictions of maps in intelligence publications no finite boundary existed with the Western TVD. Rather jurisdictions overlapped in the Baltic republics of the USSR, on water, and in Denmark;[388] similarly both TVDs shared the Northern-Coastal Strategic Direction bridging the Baltic Sea. This segmentation placed the Baltic MD within two TVDs, reflected in Soviet exercises that depicted operational duality. A listing of subordinate districts in a Russian appreciation of the first Commander-in-Chief of the Western GK, Marshal Ogarkov, excludes the Baltic MD.[389] Scattered evidence tends to support the Russian authors of the 2004 book who, also defining a Western GK minus this MD, subordinate to the Center.[390]

Unlike all the other TVDs which covered several groups and/or districts, only one front based on the Leningrad MD appeared in any individual exercise scenario. There had been two districts in this region, reflecting GPW operations with two fronts, until 1960 when the Northern had been incorporated into the Leningrad which embraced the Karelian ASSR.[391] Ground and aviation units from other districts often reinforced this Leningrad front. Because of this solo front performance a TVD peacetime high command had not been prioritized nor depicted in exercises; and further delayed by an apparent dispute regarding leadership. Two and a half months prior to *Zapad* 1984 an exercise had depicted the Northern Front under direct VGK control defending against a NATO conventional attack—aided by the Finns—extending from north Norway to south Finland. An exchange of mass nuclear strikes accompanied the launch of a Soviet counteroffensive after nearly three weeks of combat. In *Tsentr* 1978 elements of the Polish front that had been transported to Norway after seizing Jutland would converge with an unidentified front attacking from the north.[392]

Less frequently the front in this TVD bore the designation Karelian—as did one of the two GPW fronts that confronted the Finns—or Coastal (*Primorsk*—sometimes translated as Maritime). Such variations in naming a particular front also occurred in other TVDs. The basis of alternating designations had been explained by General-Army S. M. Shtemenko in his history of the General Staff in the GPW "This was not just a matter of changing labels. These designations reflected to some extent the fluctuations in our assessment of the situation and what we thought the enemy were most likely to do…"[393] Operational variations appeared even in this strategically restricted land TVD.[394] Thus in 1986 exercises, in August the front had been designated Karelian and in September, Northern. Reasons for this differentiation continue to be uncertain, possibly reflecting a northward vs. central focus of operations, but in both variants combat might take place across much of Finland with depiction of NATO-Finn collaboration. Yet in September 1982 this front carried the appellation Coastal. The Coastal Front had been evident since at least the end of the 1970s; a direct indication of a variant in the Baltic littoral and suggestive of Soviet exploration of augmentation by MD elements in the Northern-Coastal Strategic Direction. Despite the alternating front designations only one front missile-artillery base supported the Leningrad MD at Kotovo.

Regardless of official neutrality the unfortunate circumstances of geography destined that Finland would inevitably become a NATO-Warsaw Pact battleground. Strikingly absent from the record of both exercises and classified military writings that other neutral state in the Northwestern TVD—Sweden.[395]

Although the Soviets had certainly been aware of Swedish contacts, even military collusion, with NATO no offensive operational depiction evinced in the sources. In a 2002 Swedish interview Poland's senior officer Wojciech Jaruzelski stated that he had attended every Warsaw Pact meeting from 1965; Sweden had never been broached as a specific problem in any discussion, neutrality "accepted as something obvious and natural."[396] The USSR General Staff must certainly have had a Swedish variant but apparently politically forbidden to rehearse operations or even discuss any aspects thereof in classified forums. That there likely existed such a contingency may be indicated by mid 1980s information on the Soviet worldwide nuclear target multi-digit numbering scheme which incorporated country codes—573 designating Sweden (239 their eastern neighbor).[397]

• Southwestern Theater of Military Actions

Exercises during the 1980s played out the operations of three Soviet fronts of the first strategic echelon, based on the Southern Group of Forces plus the Odessa and Kiev MDs. Three months prior to *Zapad* 1984 the week-long *Soyuz* exercise had encompassed both of the strategic directions in the Southwestern TVD. The exercise staff also assumed the role of the High Command of Forces in the TVD which had not yet been formally established. This theater uniquely featured a divergence of strategic objectives across 3000-km. While the Far Eastern TVD covered a greater geographic expanse (5000-km and more than twice the depth),[398] widely separated strategic directions converged against the main opponent fostering a unified plan. But the Strategic Directions Italian and Balkan faced quite dissimilar enemies and situations. In this *Soyuz*, following a lengthy threat period and mobilization, a NATO attack forced the Warsaw Pact forces back some 100-km in two weeks of combat. The TVD-wide strategic operation launched only on D+18. While extensive nuclear contingency planning occurred, involving strategic delivery forces, no strikes transpired.

The Soviet-Hungarian 5 Front, reinforced by an army re-subordinated from the Carpathian MD 4 Front of the second operational echelon, counterattacked through Austria in the Alpine Operational Direction. The players apparently had no interest in the Italians during this *Soyuz*. Not only major combat and logistics elements for this forward front situated in the Carpathian district but also the front missile-artillery base at either Shepetovka (Tsvitokha) or Kalinovka (Kalynivka) in the same MD. Like Finland the neutral Austrians had selected an unfortunate geographic location on the borders of both NATO and Warsaw Pact member states. Czech intelligence considered that their military capabilities "do not represent any important factor" while Austrian significance "lies above all in its geographic location" in the plans of the opposing coalitions.[399] Exercises as well as classified writings presumed that NATO would violate Austrian territory to gain an operational advantage or even that the Austrians would voluntarily join the enemy.

A 1980 article in a classified Hungarian military journal[400] had a detailed discussion "taking into consideration the Austrian defense concepts" of the conduct of opening tactical assaults. One Hungarian army, in the first echelon of the Soviet-led front emanating from Hungary in the Italian Strategic Direction, appeared in a map plot advancing in the North Italian Operational Direction across southern Austria just north of the Yugoslav border toward Klagenfurt. Nothing in the article hinted at any attack on Hungary by Austrian troops or NATO contingents in Austria. The Hungarian army then entered Italy and advanced southwest toward the Venice objective, establishing a coastal defense along the Adriatic shore. A 1984 article of the same journal[401] surveyed in great detail potential tank crossing points on the River Mur between Graz and Leibnitz. Location sketches and hydrological data reflected a diligent collection effort. The Hungarian major expressed some concern regarding radioactive contamination of the crossing line that might eventuate from nuclear strikes in the Graz basin. Seemingly preordained, in a hot war one or both sides would enter Austria regardless of a local decision.

Three fronts, one under Soviet command, deployed in the Balkan Strategic Direction during *Soyuz* 1984. The Odessa MD 2 Front committed from the usual second operational echelon variant augmenting the Bulgarian 1 Front. Romanians (still permitted to play along with the brethren) apparently formed 3 Front. Their participation had been encouraged by the regrouping of the Odessa front along the Black Sea coast through Romania to the left of 1 Front in the Bosporus-Dardanelles Operational Direction. The exercise matched Romanians against Greeks in the Ionian Operational Direction. The critique of a 1970 exercise had also depicted a Romanian role, as 3 Southern Front, but without their actual participation or any detailed operational play; Greece had been tasked to the Bulgarian 1 Southern Front. Commentary highlighted the importance of the straits zone as "not only the "key" to Western Turkey, but also the last obstacle on the way to the Mediterranean Sea."[402] The Odessa front missile-artillery base actually situated beyond district borders at Bogdanovka (Bohdanivka) in the Kiev MD. The Southwestern TVD, as the Northwestern, included a prominent intervening neutral state, Yugoslavia. Although assigned the Adriatic Operational Direction, Yugoslavia presented a touchy political case comparable to Sweden, and any existing planned variant also did not feature in Soviet exercises and classified writings. Slight evidence indicated that the Bulgarian and possibly Romanian militaries would be more proactive in regard to Yugoslavia.

These fronts would be backed by the Soviet champion switch hitter the Kiev MD. When deployed as a front mainly committed in the Southwestern TVD, most often to the Balkans Strategic Direction. The Kiev front did not make an appearance during *Soyuz* 1984. In a December 1986 exercise the Kiev 3 Front regrouped through Romania to assault Greece, however, in other 1970s-1980s exercises the Turks did not escape the attention of the Kiev-ers. Occasional scenarios portrayed actions against the Italians as in a December 1984 exercise. *Tsentr* 1982 presented a sharp deviation. The Kiev 14 Front joined the Western TVD strategic operation apparently replacing the Polish 18 Front which had been held in GK reserve. The Kiev Front could then fulfill what the Soviets termed the subsequent objective of the strategic operation by accelerating the Warsaw Pact advance into southern France and Spain. But the two active armies in the district had been frequently shared out as second echelons or reinforcements to other fronts in both the Southwestern and Western TVDs. In that distribution variant the abundant demographic resources and reserve formations of Ukraine SSR might then be tapped to mobilize a front of the second strategic echelon. Thus the front missile-artillery base near Lozovaya (Lozova) might also alternatively support a front of the first strategic echelon (employing the MD two active armies in the front first echelon) or second strategic echelon (requiring mobilized subordinates).

• Southern Theater of Military Actions

Potential objectives of a Soviet strategic operation in the Southern TVD included Iran as well as neighboring Turkey and Afghanistan.[403] Exercise play in or adjacent to the Southern TVD during the 1980s depicted operations by three Soviet fronts of the first strategic echelon, generated from districts Transcaucasus, Turkestan, and Central Asian—and one front of the second strategic echelon. More than a year after *Zapad*, in June 1985, the Southern High Command of Forces had been sufficiently organized to participate in an exercise but the General Staff still acted as overseer. Soviet exercises in the 1980s typically designated the fronts played in accordance with the respective TVD, in this region 1-2-3 Southern Fronts; with a focus on the Transcaucasus 1 Southern Front. As usually depicted in 1970s-1980s exercises, the subordinate armies of this front carried out a divided offensive in the Operational Directions North Turkish and Western Iranian. In these exercises the Transcaucasus front would often advance up to 850-km to a line established in the middle of Turkey, meeting the Warsaw Pact eastward offensive in the Bosporus-Dardanelles Operational Direction. In a January-February 1981 exercise planning became evident for subsequent operations by two armies against Israel.

Pursuing an offensive into Iran during the June 1985 exercise 1 Southern Front coordinated with the Turkestan MD 2 Southern Front. In 1980s exercises elements of the Transcaucasus front sometimes converged on Tehran with the Turkestan front. Even 40 Army took time off from a busy schedule chasing Afghan *mujahedin* to participate in the

Iranian offensive on the Turkestan front left flank. In a notable variant during *Tsentr* 1982 the Turkestan 2 Southern Front conducted an offensive not only against Iran but also planned to advance through Afghanistan and Pakistan, toward China in coordination with the Central Asian MD front. The Iran objective of the Turkestan front can be traced back into the early 1960s, including discussions by Soviet officers in VM (S). General-Lieutenant L. Baukov's 1965 article[404] dealt with problems of a conventional offensive by the Turkestan front against Iran. He cited a February 1965 exercise in which the front offensive depth, ranging 750- to 960-km, experienced major disparities in unit rates of advance due to the varied terrain. Baukov, like other officers, expected that nuclear weapons at some point would used against the Iranians. In the 1970s and 1980s a missile-artillery base at Mary probably supported this front.

Exercises involving the North Caucasus MD provided among the most substantial evidence for Soviet deployment of a front of the second strategic echelon. The missile-artillery base west of Mozdok held reserves for a Caucasus front by at least 1960 when the base received, prioritized along with three other front bases (one in each of the westernmost TVDs), the first type of warhead bunker assigned to the Ground Troops. But in 1961 work had been initiated on a new front missile-artillery base within the Transcaucasus district near Sitalchay, off the rail mainline in what is now Azerbaijan, 60-km northwest of Baku. In the framework of the front base model such activity indicated an ongoing re-echelonment; that the Sitalchay base would now support a Transcaucasus front of the first strategic echelon while Mozdok had been re-purposed for the mobilization of a North Caucasus front in the second.

North Caucasus MD augmentation of first strategic echelon fronts had been mainly conducted by an early regrouping of active divisions and corps and/or by forming at least one army of the third operational echelon as had been laid out in classified writings. Mobilization of the second strategic echelon front as depicted in several exercises required two to four weeks, drawing on resources up to army scale from other districts. A 1979 NIE, besides erroneously ascribing the Caucasus fronts to the Southwestern TVD, had all of the then identified six divisions in a North Caucasus front without any hint of differentiated echelons.[405] A 1982 CIA assessment of the, now nine known, divisions of this MD assigned these to three readiness [*shtat*] categories, and insisted that a minimum of one month of preparation would be necessary to enable the North Caucasus front—but also had nothing to offer in regard to leveled echelonment.[406] In the June 1985 exercise the district formed 3 Southern Front and committed in Iran with the TVD strategic operation already under way; a March 1983 General Staff exercise committed the North Caucasus 3 Southern Front in Iran to reinforce the second front offensive operation of the engaged Transcaucasus 1 Southern Front only after two weeks conduct of the first front offensive; while in 1988 requiring more than a month of preparatory measures to deploy the front.

The Central Asian MD faced the People's Republic of China from a gap between the Southern and Far Eastern TVDs. There had been some evidence for a Southeastern TVD covering the region but both Cold War and later Russian information does not fully validate existence. While the front generated from this district had been clearly tasked in the Chinese directions there had been conflicting evidence regarding which of the two TVDs expropriated this MD. Intelligence ultimately chose the Southern TVD.[407] However from some indications, particularly the Russian 2004 book testimony, apparently this front, like those of the Baltic and Leningrad MDs, operated independently under the direct supervision of Moscow. The front complement, supported by the missile-artillery base at Arys, comprised two corps of which one upgraded to a combined-arms army by the early 1980s. Exercises frequently depicted reinforcements arriving from interior MDs.

• Far Eastern Theater of Military Actions

Intelligence collection and assessments ordered the Far Eastern TVD immediately after NATO.[408] Eastern autonomy had been in prospect since at least the end of 1978 as indicated by the arrival of General V. I. Petrov and other senior officers. Earlier that year L. Brezhnev and his defense minister D. Ustinov had toured the Far East—one district commander had pointed out to them the value of a high command for this region—by August 1979 construction of a GK command center had been initiated.[409] The Petrov debut marked another step in the steady Soviet upgrading of the military posture on the Chinese border that had been under way since the late 1960s. TVD exercises from the late 1970s into the 1980s played the operations of at least four fronts, numbered 1 through 4, extending from northwestern Mongolia to Vladivostok—evenly divided between the first and second strategic echelons. The *Vostok* (East) series, direct counterparts to *Zapad* exercises, presented the most complex runnings of operations in the theater. As in the West, hostilities with the Chinese usually depicted as initially defensive; but retaliation would have decisive results.

Amazingly the persistent intelligence strategic echelons syndrome extended East as well as West; indicated by a 1985 *Multitheater* NIE that assessed the alleged view from the Center.[410]

> We do not believe they would attempt an attack with Beijing as its objective with fewer than 100 divisions. This would require the movement of an additional 50 Soviet divisions to the Far East. Many of them would have to come from the force opposite NATO, a move that Moscow would almost certainly be unwilling to make.

This debilitated perspective entirely ignored the actuality of the Soviet strategic echelons that had been implemented during the past decade in the form of logistics structural and forces development. Intell could measure ground and air active deployments but, as in the West, a shallow comprehension of strategic arrangements blacked out what the Soviets had been about. Abundant evidence of the second kind pointed to at least one and likely two fronts that would emerge from an Eastern second strategic echelon. A key lesson of the GPW Manchurian Operation, in a strategic situation of potential concurrent theater wars, would be to avoid at all costs the large scale regroupings from the European offensive that had been necessary to establish the strike groupings executing the Japanese campaign. Reinforcement from within the Eastern Theater represented a solution that obviated regroupings from other TVDs. Unfortunately the Soviet classified writings that had been acquired reflected a Western fixation with only limited, oblique, discussion of the Eastern Theater; evidence for their plans depended largely on satellite observation and exercise monitoring.

The 1985 NIE, along with a contemporaneous NIE that focused on the East (updating a 1981 edition),[411] laid out the accumulated evidence of preparations for addressing the China problem. In a spring 1980 exercise directed by the Far Eastern GK a front based on the Far East MD conducted a prolonged counteroffensive, in two successive front offensive operations, penetrating up to 950-km into the People's Republic. Early but limited use of nuclear weapons by the sides featured prominently. A March-April 1985 exercise directed by the General Staff involved at least two fronts including the Transbaikal MD—designated 2 Eastern Front as usually the case in the 1980s—conducting operations to restore the state border; the front missile-artillery base located to the east of Ulan-Ude. A broad definition of USSR borders permitted the inclusion of Mongolia. But the exercise focused on the regrouping of 3 Eastern Front to a position west of 2 Eastern Front in northwestern Mongolia to repulse the Chinese 1 Xinjiang Front. This third front had emerged from the second strategic echelon, mobilized jointly from the Siberian and Ural MDs. Neither of these districts had active armies (a situation identical to the North Caucasus MD); only one corps had been identified by intelligence. Yet the 1985 exercise attributed three or four ground armies to the front complement. In a comparable July 1979 exercise a front, comprising two armies from the Siberian and one army from the Ural, had regrouped to the same general area in Mongolia. Additional evidence of the multi-district character of this front resided in the absence of any front missile-artillery base in the Siberian district. But two such bases had been collocated to the northeast of Sverdlovsk (Yekaterinburg) in the Ural MD, the original oriented West with the second developed onward from 1971 probably facing East.

The following year a GK exercise of the Far East MD 1 Eastern Front focused on the defense of the Maritime region. This front had been consistently designated the First in 1980s exercises, reflecting the importance of a dangerously isolated extremity of the USSR. The missile-artillery base north of Zavitinsk stocked front war reserves of warheads, missiles, and by the mid 1980s substantially more than 100000 tonnes of artillery ammunition. The district active ground troops complement then amounted to four armies and one corps matched only by the Soviet group in East Germany. But solid indications existed for a larger array planned for this area. Hardly unprecedented since the 1945 Manchurian Operation against the Japanese occupiers of China deployed 1 and 2 Far Eastern Fronts alongside the Transbaikal Front.[412]

In the early 1970s a second front missile-artillery base had been developed off the north shore of Lake Bolon, containing an unusually disproportionate fourteen missile storage bunkers and an ammunition reserve increasing to 80000 or more tonnes. In addition by the early 1980s a far more ambitious military expansion gained steam built around 'mobilization centers'—clusters of ammunition, fuels, and quartermaster stores—supporting both active and reserve divisions, corps and/or armies. These logistics centers pointed to a prospective force more than double the number of active armies and corps filling out fronts of both first and second strategic echelons. Several of the complexes had been positioned 200- to 300-km from the Chinese border in order to afford additional spatial protection and reaction time. A comparable support structure had been concurrently installed in the Transbaikal district to support the regrouped Siberian-Ural front as well the local troops. In all 23 mobilization centers had been created to sustain in-district mobilization and regrouping from other regions. The extent, character, and objectives of these particular Soviet measures went unrecognized by intelligence until I laid out this reality in a 1988 study. The 1980s exercises that numbered Eastern fronts up to four may have indicated the appearance of the Far East MD fourth front especially when, as in 1985, the Siberian-Ural front ranked Third in order.

• Heartland

While tapped to provide armies of the third operational echelon, districts Volga, Ural, and Moscow would also each deploy at least one front in the second strategic echelon. Intelligence monitoring of exercises conducted in these districts, due to more limited access, tended to collect fragmentary information rather than broad scenarios. Items included the identifications of particular opponents and notional or active unit operations. Hardened front missile-artillery bases had been established in the early to mid 1960s in the Volga MD at Kedrovka near Sverdlovsk (base one) and at Syzran in the Ural MD. During operational-strategic exercises in 1973-1974 the front headquarters of the second strategic

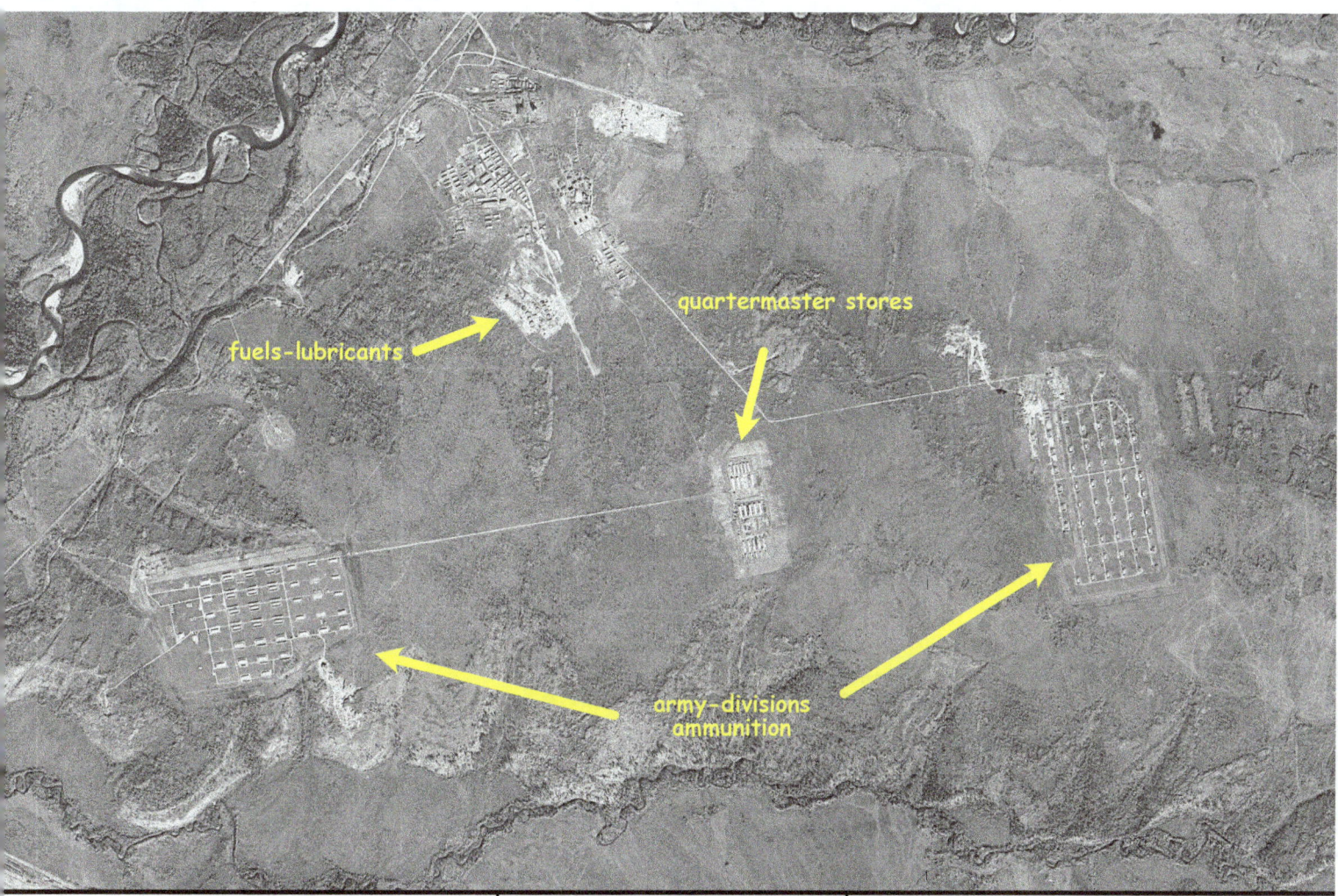

**MOBILIZATION CENTER 1980**
CHEGDOMYN FAR EAST MD

echelon that had been deployed by these MDs had moved westward. Except for the Ural signup with the Siberian to the joint MDs front (Kedrovka base two) oriented to Chinese operations, similar dual fronts deployment would not be detected until the *Tsentr* exercise of 1987 but again lacking in details.

In exercises the Moscow MD had served mainly as a source for reinforcements including individual divisions and specialized units but deployment of an army of the third operational echelon had been periodically depicted. As early as 1961 staff work on the regrouping of front troops during the initial period had been conducted—drawing criticism for not being completed—while a study of 1000-km marches of an army had been finished.[413] One of the earliest hardened front missile-artillery bases, at Karachev in the west of the district, may actually have supported the front originating in Belorussia. By the 1980s the steadily increasing Soviet need for additional feedstock for the conventional war machine apparently turned to the Moscow district for a front of the second strategic echelon. In a May 1984 exercise the deputy chief of the USSR General Staff acted in the role of a Moscow front commander, combating the FRG III, and US V and VII, Corps, specific enemies also featured in other scenarios; this exercising of a front role for the district apparently exceptional, eliciting a comment in a General Staff Academy instruction bloc.[414] By then ten divisions had been identified in this MD[415] (three minimal armies)—but only one active corps. Contemporaneously and subsequently no conclusive evidence has surfaced regarding a Moscow front deployment whether largely by the district or as a cross-border front with another MD such as Volga similar to the Ural-Siberian front exemplar.

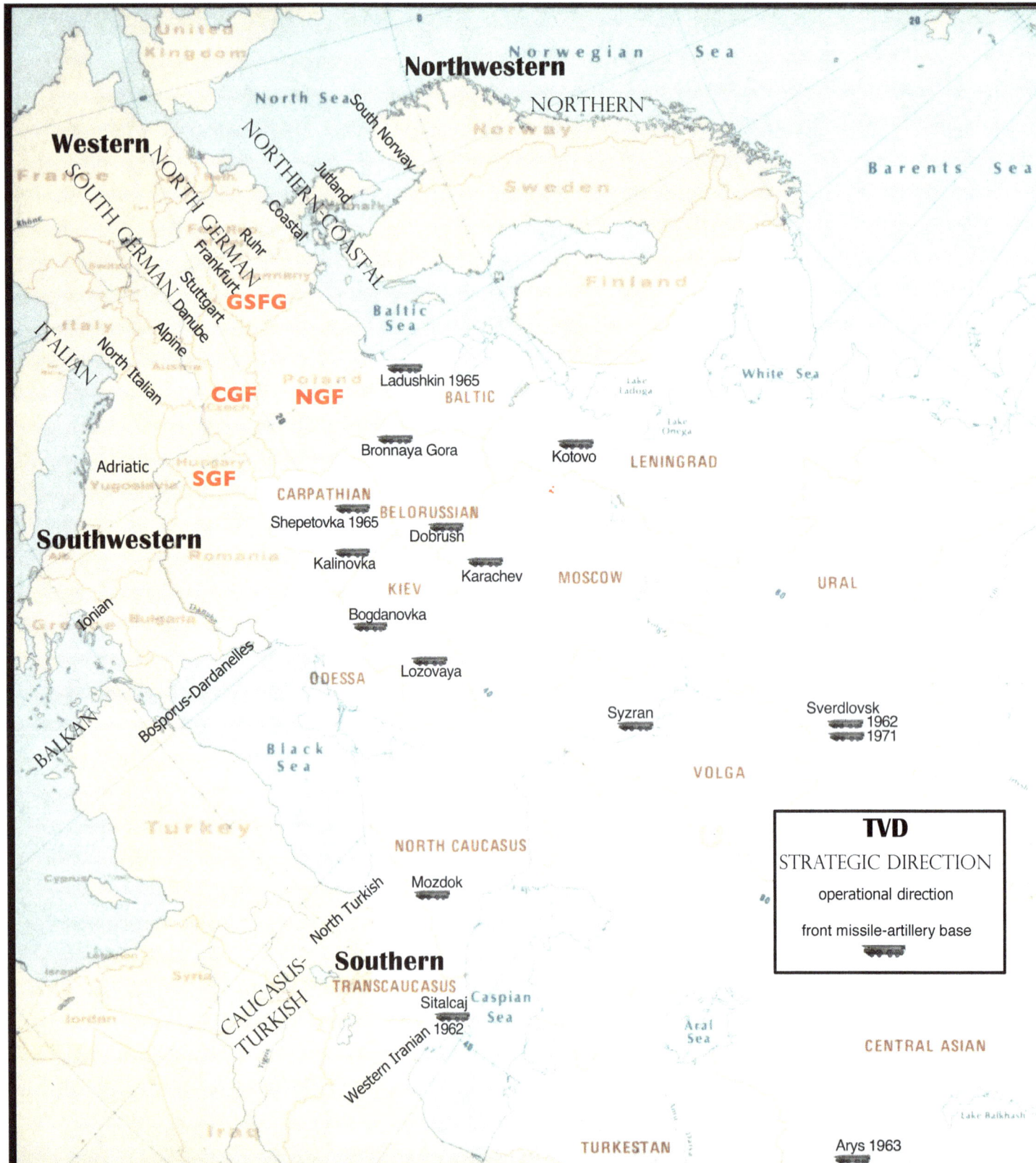

# Operational Evolutions

Opposing NATO and Warsaw Pact coalitions faced off on the European stage like a clumsy dance pair—with a distinctly hostile embrace. Evolving perceptions of the nature of any military conflict, and of the threat posed by the actions of the partner, eventuated a series of key decisions and adjustments. These turning points had both initiative and reactive components. Arguably, Western decisions on the role of mass destruction weapons largely impelled Soviet-Warsaw Pact operational alterations, in particular, as Massive Retaliation gave way to a Flexible Response implemented over several years. Decisions can be formulated relatively quickly–or more to the NATO strategic style–with agonizing deliberation. But force development is a slow, expensive process that may not even be completed at the time of the next adjustment. The massive array to the East altered course gradually, after thorough consideration and testing of revised variants. Western intelligence assessed motivation for adjustments to be ensuring the success of decisive strategic offensive operations; perception of the details less assured.

Intelligence identification of the complement of the oncoming Warsaw Pact wave train tended to lag, sometimes by as much as a decade, their opponents' operational adjustments and forces restructuring. Alertness for any indications of strategic deployment initiation, generation of fronts, and variant selection would be vital for timely warning—critically important given a likely Eastern concealed mobilization, use of exercise cover, as well as other deceptive measures. The intelligence-assessed requirement for several weeks of preparations might pass undetected. Fortunately NATO did not have the unpleasant experience of discovering the inaccuracy of intelligence appraisals of the offensive lineup at any given time. Among the more notable US intelligence mis-estimates:

- Although cognizant of Soviet enhancement of the role of, and armament modernization under way in, European forces that had been increasingly evident through the early 1960s there would be no recognition, until at least seven years subsequent to Soviet authorization, of concurrent creation of fronts under national command. Analysts had been jolted into awareness mainly by a number of Czech senior officer defectors during and after 1968 who had detailed knowledge of their front position in Soviet plans; subsequently perceived that two border military districts of the USSR could each generate a front. Virtually all of the indicative evidence had been available to Cold War intelligence with recent information only filling in some details.

- Once defined, a unitary Polish front would be persistently accorded an independent role along the Baltic coast. Recognition came only in the late 1970s that a contingent Soviet replacement might be available, despite specific evidence that a new Soviet front had been established more than a decade earlier. There never would be an accurate differentiation of Soviet factoring and Polish tasks. Post Cold War evidence tends to confirm that the intelligence confusion concerning operations in the Northern-Coastal Strategic Direction marked the success of an orchestrated Soviet strategic deception.
Surprise: NORTHAG!

- Intelligence failed to identify, for at least ten years following creation, the Soviet-Hungarian front designated for offensive operations through Austria and Italy in the Italian Strategic Direction. Not fully realized even upon recognition the principle targets of this front, the causative factor, comprised the US and NATO corps deployed in the southern FRG. There had been some specific evidence of the second kind to this effect available to Cold War intelligence. However key information regarding the 1960s initiation of this adjustment became available only during the 1990s in Czech and Hungarian archives.
Surprise: CENTAG!

- The difficulty intelligence observers had in detecting deployment of fronts is epitomized by the contemporary and retrospective failure to discern that the Warsaw Pact armies and divisions assembled for the August 1968 Czech invasion had been organized into three Soviet-commanded fronts. The next, and last, mobilization of a Soviet front during the Cold War, in 1986, would be more accurately appraised—objective to contain the Chernobyl nuclear disaster.

- Intelligence perception of an apparent Soviet retreat from the offensive imperative in the second half of the 1980s became so entangled with political dogma regarding the actuality of Gorbachev revisionism that both, genuine, developments would be unjustifiably dismissed as fraudulent.

Providential that the West 'won' a cold war.

**wmd propulsion**

The Warsaw Pact operational lineup during the 1950s had been a mystery for Western intelligence then and has not yet been clarified in the post-USSR period. The specter of a massive conventional force carried over from World War II confronted NATO planners. Troop deployments in the Western TVD had solidified into a substantial array of forward Soviet and national allies (formalized in the 1955 Warsaw Treaty Organization) backed by far greater reinforcement potential in the USSR. But in contrast to what would follow, (counter)offensive reliance had been bestowed on the forces of the successive echelons based in the western, augmented from interior, military districts. Forward Soviet fronts would incorporate national units, had no priority in equipment modernization, and envisaged to absorb the brunt of, apparently defensive, action until reinforcements arrived to propel a decisive offensive to the English Channel and Atlantic Ocean.

A 1989 disclosure of an early variant, the November 1946 plan for the then designated Group of Soviet Occupation Troops in Germany, affords an introduction to TVD strategy.[416] A defensive stance by a "blocking army" would shift to a counteroffensive, in concert with RVGK formations, "to launch a crushing blow" in the border zone; "secondary troops" to mobilize by D+7 and regroup to predesignated concentration areas by D+10 to D+20 to build up the offensive. Soviet armies in the GDR deployed four rifle regiments on the border as a cover force but the forward edge of a main defense zone had been positioned 50- to 150-km further back. Troops would be ready for combat in 90 minutes if warned in advance or three hours if caught by surprise.

Even in 1957 the task of the Group continued to be subordinated to USSR formations. MoD G. K. Zhukov attempted[417] to assuage senior officers in Germany concerning the lack of priority for equipping the Group with the most recent armament; that their weapons would be "adequate for the tasks assigned" and offering the lame excuse of overly attentive Western intelligence. But he emphasized that the second echelon "will have the responsibility for offensive action" moving up to their concentration areas within 46 hours (a CIA correction that four to six hours had been meant is not credible)—based on march rates achieved in the 1956 invasion of Hungary (if so a decided acceleration of the claimed 1946 timelines). Zhukov also stressed that deployments would be preemptive, upon detection of any Western military preparations Soviet troops "must beat them to the punch" insisting that the (counter)offensive should reach the Channel by D+2. His narrative decidedly at variance with the depiction of a postwar strategic defense; but intelligence collection against the GSFG even by 1962 found a consistent lack of the latest generation of weapons. Armament identified included some 900 World War II-vintage T-34 tanks despite parallel classified writings that had been discussing a model T-62—no comparison to USSR-based units then possible because high-resolution satellite imagery had only recently begun to blanket the Soviet Empire.[418]

Documents retrieved from Central European archives in recent years have presented mainly the forward perspective, misleading some historians into a sweeping interpretation of a Soviet political as well as military defensive strategy. This perspective misses the significance of follow-on forces as the offensive fulcrum. Much less information is available on organization and employment of these elements during the 1950s. Whatever the actuality of any early Soviet strategic defense doctrine, in the second half of the 1950s the increasing plenitude of nuclear weapons constrained any inclination to countenance defense when strategic means could at the outset of war in Europe decide the outcome. According to a classified retrospective strategic defense had been considered one of the two forms of strategic action even during the first deployments of nuclear weapons in the early 1950s but[419]

> Toward the end of the 1950s, in connection with the rapid development of means of mass destruction, the prevailing theoretical opinion was that a defense on a strategic scale would be wrong. Recognizing strategic defense as one of the types of strategic actions would have meant recognizing defensive strategy on the whole, which, in essence, might lead to a repetition of the mistakes of the last war.

Only in the later 1980s did the Soviets finally validate strategic defense as the basic variant.

That the largest grouping of armies, the GSFG and East German, may have been the basis for more than one wartime front has already been noted. The six Soviet armies then deployed forward in the Western TVD could have formed (the first echelons of) as many as three fronts. Soviet forward fronts would also have incorporated Warsaw Pact national armies and divisions, adding to the surplus. In his early 1962 VM (S) article that dealt specifically with inter-subordinations of Soviet and national forces Colonel P. Grabovsky reviewed the experience of ten Warsaw Pact exercises from 1957 to 1961.[420] He counted 40 instances during the creation of offensive strike groupings of Soviet divisions resubordinated to national armies and 46 reverse assignments of national divisions to Soviet armies. Grabovsky even cited a May 1961 exercise in which a Belorussian army comprised two divisions of the district along with two Polish divisions. But there had been no hint of the existence of national fronts in his extensive discussion of allied cooperation (this article not acquired until 1976).

Another indication of multiple forward Soviet fronts in the 1950s had been provided in an article that appeared in the 1959 issue 49 of the *Information Collection of the Artillery*, a top secret journal.[421] A suggested exercise scenario focused on a R-170 (SS-1b Scud A) missile battalion that had been attached to an army of 1 Western Front at the outbreak of war to repel an imminent attack by Westerners—and all geography related to the Northern-Coastal Strategic Direction. A map in the article placed the front southern bound just north of Berlin with 2 Western Front southward, i.e., the location of most of the GSFG armies and front support elements. Missile strike targets assigned included No. 49 (the port of Hamburg) and No. 48 (Schwerin rail station—the enemy had advanced into the GDR and the Soviets apparently had no qualms about nuking their Germans). The article had no hints as to the nationalities makeup of the two fronts.

Classified Soviet writings of the early 1960s also uniformly and clearly state that second echelon armies for these fronts would be regrouped from the USSR border military districts. Articles depicted forward fronts arranged as a single echelon, powered by mass nuclear strikes, with a strong multi-division reserve. A 1961 article by General-Lieutenant S. Andryushchenko in VM (TS) entitled "The Deployment and Forward Movement of a Combined Arms Army of a Border Military District in the Initial Period of a War"[422] discussed, in great detail, aspects of a 900- to 1000-km regrouping of an army in march periods of three to four days to establish the second echelon of a forward front already in combat. Unusually specific in the discussion of factors hindering the army move, he depicted an enemy attack with the full WMD spectrum—biological, chemical, and nuclear. Under the conditions of unlimited nuclear warfare, depending on the length of, if any, threat period, the authors did not expect second echelon armies of forward fronts to arrive from the USSR before the start of front subsequent missions five to seven days into an offensive.[423]

In the 1950s US-NATO nuclear superiority had been assumed by both sides. Late in 1953 the first US nuclear delivery system arrived in Europe in the form of 280-mm artillery (nuclear rounds not delivered until the spring of 1955 along with bombs, Matador cruise missile and Honest John rocket warheads), followed by short- to intermediate-range ballistic and medium-range cruise missiles.[424] Forward bases for heavy bombers of the Strategic Air Command backed these systems. Massive Retaliation had been pronounced as official US nuclear policy, and formally accepted by the North Atlantic Council in December 1956. NATO had by then adopted a New Look, a convenient substitution of nuclear weapons for the conventional forces that could not possibly be built up to match those beyond the Iron Curtain. Both sides envisioned battlefield nuclear weapons as an enhancement of traditional fire support. But during the 1950s the US Army in an experimental mood developed the Pentomic Division as an organizational-operational solution to the radically altered conditions of nuclear warfare.[425]

Soviet theoreticians retrospectively defined a period from 1953 to 1959 of nuclear adaptation beginning, unspecified, with the lifting of the dead hand of Stalinist orthodoxy. Nuclear weapons employment began in exercise play, operations manuals issued, and studies organized. According to a classified period survey[426] the first exercise to consider battlefield use of nuclear weapons, involving air and ground forces in the Carpathian MD, took place in October 1953. A MoD directive the following month initiated nuclear operations training. Documentation written during 1954 ended the nuclear monopoly of strategic aviation by adding front bomber aviation tasking, and in 1957 front air forces acquired nuclear cruise missiles. Ground Troops missiles introduced in 1954 provided a nuclear capability albeit very limited in scale and range; however conventional warheads remained their main strike mode. Manuals issued in 1954 dealt with ground operations in nuclear conditions by fronts, armies, corps, and even for battalions.[427] But later Soviet writings would characterize 1950s exercise nuclear weapons practice as a kind of super artillery preparation rather than the full exploitation of revolutionary characteristics. Except for bomber and fighter-bomber aviation basing, any forward deployment to Central Europe of nuclear delivery systems remained an unsolvable riddle to Western intelligence.

According to the General Staff Academy 1974 textbook[428] the indices of a front initial operation with nuclear weapons support, during the period 1957 to 1960, ranged an overall offensive depth of 400- to 800-km; conducted at an average 45- to 60-kmd; extending over 9 to 13 days. The textbook indicated that, in comparison to the postwar theories of the pre-nuclear period that ended in 1953, the maximum depth had increased 400-km while the rate of advance had accelerated an additional 10- to 25-kmd; which reduced the duration of even such a deeper offensive by 2-3 days. The main thrust of immediate postwar armament development had been the full motorization of ground formations which resulted in the transformation of the GPW force for any westward strategic offensive. Nine GPW front operations profiled in the textbook had a wide range of parameters. The maximum depth attained 550-km; requiring up to 23 days; with the most rapid tempo at 26-kmd. The textbook noted that the 1945 Manchurian Strategic Operation exceeded these parameters (another source measured the depth attained at 600- to 800-km).[429] That achievement would continue to be a model to be emulated throughout the Cold War. In comparison to the most successful strategic operations against the deeply echeloned German defense of World War II the Soviet military projected that the 1960 nuclear version planned for NATO would basically more than double the rate of advance and almost halve the duration.

## wmd blowout

Soviet theoreticians marked the next key adjustment point at 1960. In a 14 January 1960 address to the Supreme Soviet Premier Khrushchev had pronounced a revised strategy reliant on nuclear rockets rather than large armed forces. The Soviet strategic culture assigned great significance to such public enunciations of what contemporaries considered course changes. A previous, comparable, signal regarding the role of mass destruction weapons had been delivered by Minister of Defense Marshal G. K. Zhukov in 1956. Among other open and classified statements the importance of the 1960 pivot point had been faithfully reiterated in a 1963 VM (S) article by the Chief of the USSR General Staff Marshal M. V. Zakharov.[430]

> When studying modern military science we must be guided by what was said by N. S. Khrushchev in his report at the 4th Session of the Supreme Soviet of the USSR in 1960, where the nature of a future war and the methods of waging it were defined, the role of the branches of the armed forces in achieving the goals of

war were shown, and the paths toward further development were indicated. The report set forth the basic premises of our military doctrine.

Other senior officers quickly expressed their interpretation of the January proclamation by the ideological-political sovereign. In the very first issue of the top secret version of VM General-Lieutenant V. Baskakov gave his version of the marching orders to include a definition, with the key components, of the new WMD Operation.[431]

> The essence of operations will amount to the following: organizing and delivering nuclear strikes by the forces of rocket troops and aviation for carrying out strategic, operational, or tactical tasks; the employment of chemical and bacteriological weapons; moving divisions, corps, and armies of ground troops forward on selected directions into enemy territory, with the purpose of exploiting the results of nuclear strikes, completing the defeat of the remaining enemy forces not destroyed by nuclear weapons, and the final disruption of his attempts to continue the delivery of nuclear strikes; and organizing the protection of friendly troops from strikes of enemy nuclear weapons.

The delivery of nuclear weapons on a massive scale became a reality with a substantially increased and diversified inventory and the deployment of theater-range missile systems as well as widespread nuclear missile introduction into fronts, armies, and divisions. This distribution marked the beginning of the true Revolution in Military Affairs rather than the earlier technological advent of nuclear weapons. General Staff officers in 1990s interviews[432] depicted an attitude of "nuclear euphoria" from 1960 to 1965 in which preemptive strategic strikes against the US would be accompanied by a nuclear pulse delivered throughout Europe. The role of fronts became the exploitation of mass strikes by strategic missiles in the depth of the Western TVD; while front delivery systems blasted deep fissures in the depth of the enemy defense rather than merely providing fire preparation for tactical breakthrough. One general characterized the role of ground formations as a "broom" to sweep aside enemy survivors of this nuclear eradication.[433]

MoD Marshal R. Ya. Malinovsky continued to push the nuclear vision for Europe in the first 1962 issue of the General Staff journal—an article focused on the importance of highly mobile, and survivable, tank armies in nuclear warfare.[434]

> Apparently, first of all, the enemy troop grouping deployed in the theater will be subjected to massed nuclear/rocket strikes. During this the front and army nuclear/rocket weapons will deliver a strike over the entire depth of the enemy operational troop formation. The rocket troops of strategic designation will deliver an incomparably more powerful strike against the strategic objectives in the depth of the theater. ... We do not have a completely clear concept of what will happen as a result of such a strike. Some say that complete devastation will result and will be difficult to overcome; others say that there will not be such devastation and that considerable life and resistance will remain. Apparently both have to be taken into consideration, but mainly we must consider the huge destruction which nuclear/rocket weapons are capable of inflicting and also all the consequences that arise from them.

Senior officers in the new VM edition had argued alternative approaches to nuclear warfare. A Big Bang school emphasized mass strategic nuclear strikes that would require, in the estimation of General-Colonel A. Gastilovich in early 1960, a TVD single operational echelon of two fronts (and these also in one echelon with a reserve of additional divisions) for mop-up purposes. Each front, with 15 to 20 ground and 2-3 airborne divisions and organized in two or three armies (six armies then in the Soviet GDR group), would advance across a frontage of 600- to 700-km in the Western TVD.[435] General-Colonel G. I. Khetagurov, among others, rejected the nuclear-rockets-solve-all approach, insisting "one must proceed from the necessity of deploying a front not in the TVD, but **on each** of the strategic directions..." (emphasis in original).[436] If intelligence analysts had been aware of the Soviet concept of directions, this statement would have broadcast the intention to create a three-front forward echelon in the Western TVD.

Even between June and July 1960 exercises monitored in the GSFG played wider zones of advance and nuclear strikes in operational rather than tactical depth. Frontal thrusts could now be directed at strong, rather than weak, areas in the enemy formation thus undermining the entire defense system. The General Staff Academy 1974 textbook attributed 1961 indices of a front nuclear offensive in a 450-km zone; at 70-kmd requiring 14 or 15 days to attain a planned depth of 1000-km.[437] Mass strikes with nuclear weapons accelerated rates of advance. The senior Soviet officers writing on nuclear warfare in the classified editions of VM in 1960-1961 stated that the Defense Minister had set a 100-kmd objective as an average rate for first front offensives—specified in his 1961 operational training directive. As one general pointed out, this pace approached the normative, unopposed, troop daily road march distance.[438] General-Lieutenant M. Lugovtsev in a late 1962 VM (S) article objected to this rate-of-advance guideline "the research conducted on this question was one-sided and mostly theoretical, without practical verification during troop exercises, especially during regimental and divisional troop exercises"—and he a tanker.[439] But Lugovtsev represented the only dissenting viewpoint on this issue in the early classified material obtained by US intelligence. Exercise experience and research studies apparently would soon demonstrate that such an offensive tempo would be unattainable. All of these developments took place in the context of NATO-US declarations that any attack would be met with a massive strategic-theater nuclear retaliation.

Nuclear reliance, however, had ramifications for weapons and lineup. A high-speed advance in nuclear conditions depended on expensive armor-saturated formations to traverse contaminated areas; with heavy losses anticipated from NATO nuclear strikes. Operations dependent on reinforcement from the USSR became problematic with the projection of large areas of contamination and destruction. Soviet officers viewed NATO nuclear systems as capable of interfering with regroupings from even the western military districts as well as the interior by creating barriers, inflicting heavy losses on troop movements, and destroying vital axial rail lines. The Colonel I. Milevsky 1961 VM (S) article assessing the NATO FALLEX 1960 maneuvers imputed that one main task had been "…to **interdict the regrouping of troops, especially their transfer from the depths of the operational and strategic reserves**…" (original emphasis). He noted that NATO would establish nuclear barriers at (named) rivers and forests.[440] According to another VM (S) article a command-staff exercise held in 1961 posited a nuclear barrier created by 68 Western ground bursts on the line of the rivers Oder and Niesse extending into the Sudeten Mountains, creating a radioactive region 700-km wide and 200-km deep "which drastically complicated the movement of two fronts."[441] Officers in 1961[442] and 1962[443] disagreed on the effects of WMD strikes against a combined-arms army regrouping from, respectively, the interior North Caucasus and Volga MDs.

The projected nuclear barrier line had a significant impact on Soviet plans for advancing fronts, armies, and divisions into the Western TVD at the outset of war as mobilization progressively completed. An early indication of this concern had been the expansive October 1961 operational-strategic exercise *Burya*. Intelligence knowledge of the scenario derived from real time monitoring and scattered discussions in the Soviet classified press but much of the latter material was acquired long after the event. Additional material has been discovered in national archives. The unprecedented (at least detected) feature of this exercise had been the pre-combat regrouping of armies and fronts from the USSR, all taking place as the Berlin crisis intensified—the prelude to a hot war—a variant occasionally repeated in later years. Of course any premeditated Soviet decision to attack first would have been implemented in a similar fashion to preclude nuclear interdiction—taking appropriate measures, such as convenient field exercises, to cloak troop mobilization and regrouping.

Although intelligence had no direct access to the Soviet operational solutions to these critical problems, the general outline and trends should have been evident. One (hypothesis X) solution to the conditions of all-out nuclear warfare—that would necessitate replacing inevitable heavy casualties and alleviate the difficulty of advancing USSR-based forces, while constructing a powerful forward attack echelon—would be the creation of Warsaw Pact national fronts armed with their own mass destruction weapons. Western intelligence became aware of the creation of national-commanded fronts only in the later 1960s. The essentiality of a more prominent role for Pact forces in the conditions of theater nuclear operations that had been depicted in Soviet writings of the early 1960s, and some exercises, eventuated unremarked.

Prior to 1968 intelligence had only a vague notion of the organization of fronts in the Western TVD. Earlier estimates could only broadly numerate the Soviet and national divisions that might be 'assembled' into an attack force and later, as evidence accumulated, began to consider the potential armies to which the divisions might be subordinated. An evolving mid 1960s perspective initially depicted a "striking force" of three fronts that would combine Soviet divisions of the forward groups and border military districts (correct for misinformed reasons) while adding Pact divisions that might be organized as subordinate national armies. This assemblage would be backed by a "theater reserve" of Soviet and national divisions. Assessments posited that eighteen divisions moved from the western USSR would be incorporated in the twelve to fifteen armies that would make up the three fronts.[444] A refined model projected fourteen armies, including four to six national, in the three fronts with four or five "theater reserve" armies deployed to western Poland and Czechoslovakia.[445] Only in late 1966 did an expanded perspective consider that border districts "would provide the basis for the creation of additional fronts."[446] But there had still been no recognition that part of the USSR contingent might constitute the integral second echelon, whether "strategic" or otherwise, of the TVD strategic operation.

NIE 12-65 *Eastern Europe and the Warsaw Pact*, issued in August 1965, stated that the prevailing view of national divisions subordinate only to Soviet armies had been chucked—but the new assessment had all national armies in Soviet fronts.[447] This conclusion assimilated a late 1964 CIA appraisal of changes underway in Warsaw Pact forces that surmised that as many as nine armies could be formed by six Central and Eastern European members.[448] More than a year later another NIE concluded that the three northern Warsaw Pact countries could field as many as six armies—but national fronts still truant in this particular official model, not even the Bulgarians in the Southwest TVD.[449] An expanding contribution of national forces, with new armament and as a significant proportion of a potential Warsaw Pact offensive, had been recognized;[450] but not the critically important assignment of operational commands and independent missions in the Western TVD. Preliminary findings issued in January 1968 by a joint CIA-DIA group established to assess Soviet reinforcement capability also lacked cognizance of national fronts even though again postulating three forward fronts—arbitrarily designated North, Central, and South—amalgamating armies of bordering Soviet MDs; they remained blissfully unaware that border districts would also generate fronts.[451]

The perceptual redirection brought about by the arrival of General-Major Jan Sejna would be evident within a few months. Only in a June 1968 CIA paper *Warsaw Pact War Plan For Central Region Of Europe* would the discovery of the national fronts that had been created seven plus years earlier be announced by the Office of Strategic Research.[452] Their conclusion had been based on information sourced primarily to a Czech defector as well as reconsideration of exercise and other evidence; they even recognized a Soviet concept of echelons at all levels up to theater (strategic/operational not yet prescribed). A retrospective perception, with Sejna assistance, discerned that the Carpathian MD had deployed as a front in the 1961 *Burya* exercise and that the Belorussian MD also might have a front option. This re-assessment manifested the inception of the Western TVD national-Soviet five-front official model that would endure through the Cold War. But work under way since at least 1965 on two new Soviet western fronts transpired unnoticed.

While exercises monitoring provided some indications of national fronts, US intelligence had been shocked into awareness of a different arrangement only upon the defection of Jan Sejna. He provided detailed information on plans for the Czech Southwest Front along with some insights into the overall Soviet scheme. More Czech defectors soon followed as well as Polish sources—an exercise critique acquired by January 1967 (discussed below) had reflected a Polish national front. Post Cold War documents from the countries concerned, and interviews with senior officers, revealed that the Czech front had been established during 1960-1961, as indicated by the defectors.[453] The Soviets had been slower to accept a national front in Poland. Polish officers had been suggesting such a promotion since the 1950s. Soviet hesitation regarding assigning Poles an operational-strategic mission dated back to the GPW when the creation of a Polish front in 1944 had been aborted. Apparent permission granted by 1961,[454] Polish archival documents outlined the role of their troops as the Coastal Front during the *Burya* exercise. A Polish general who participated in *Burya* at the Zossen-Wünsdorf exercise center (and GSFG headquarters) has stated that the task assigned to this national front occurred as an afterthought, that initially a Soviet front of unknown provenance had been depicted in the same direction.[455] Contemporary US signals intelligence reporting on, and analyses of, *Burya* had failed to recognize the participation of any national fronts.

The resulting lineup permitted the forward commitment of one, largely up to specs, front in each of the three strategic directions of the Northwestern-Western TVDs for the surprise-unlimited nuclear outbreak variants. These fronts would no longer have to depend on the problematic regrouping of armies from the USSR to create their second echelons but draw instead on national mobilization. The unitary Polish front (reinforced by a Soviet army and/or East German corps) in the Northern-Coastal; a Soviet GSFG-East German front in the North German; and the Czechs operating with a reserve of Soviet divisions in the South German Strategic Direction. Unfortunately many years would elapse before anyone in US intelligence knew that strategic directions existed much less their significance. In this Five-Front Official Model that became popular from the late 1960s a front based mainly on the Belorussian district—with the one active army of the Baltic MD joining either this front or the Polish—would regroup to augment the forward fronts. A Carpathian MD-based front would advance in the direction of the Czech front.

## deferring inevitability

Indications of an operational retuning became evident by 1963, revision motivation a direct reaction to the US-NATO adoption of a Flexible Response to any Warsaw Pact attack. The Kennedy administration and chief defense planner Robert McNamera had arrived at the conclusion that the unlimited nuclear variant had become infeasible. Soviet commentators, as in the unclassified 1960s magnum opus *Military Strategy*,[456] placed the genesis of the revised policy during late 1959 to 1961. They attributed the change of heart to US realization of the growing vulnerability of the homeland to a rapidly expanding Soviet intercontinental missile strike capability—but insisted that the intent of the revamped concept aimed at gaining time in order to enhance the orchestration of a surprise nuclear attack on the East.[457] McNamera proselytizing during 1962 in the US and in Europe promoted a "controlled and flexible nuclear response"[458] which initiated an extended campaign of transatlantic negotiations. Culmination ensued in the second half of 1967 with NATO official ratification of an escalatory strategy. The new approach diversified nuclear deterrence regarding timing and scale of nuclear weapons employment, while retaining the option of first use; as if one coalition could dictate the nature and scale of a major European war.

Official body endorsements of the new strategy during 1967 culminated in the December NATO formal acceptance, and options definition in the Military Committee 14/3 paper of January 1968.[459] The internal discussions of a US nuclear initiative, the usual NATO mode, had to balance divergent political as well as military views. Influential voices, especially French, had objected to a strategy that would, at the outset at least, disconnect the fates of Europe and the US by confining warfare to Europe. But the French lost their vote by withdrawing from the NATO military structure in 1966. A 'graduated deterrence' theme would guide NATO strategy through the remainder of the Cold War; endeavoring to instill 'ambiguity' in a controlled escalation from conventional, to limited nuclear, and supposedly to full nuclear arms employment if the Soviets had not understood the 'signals' transmitted. An opening conventional phase had been inserted that would also alter the force structure and operations planning of the Warsaw Pact.

For the West a conventional start to hostilities avoided immediate incineration but both opportunities and dilemmas arose in the new escalation variant for the Soviets and their allies. A period of non-nuclear warfare would permit a systematic effort to degrade NATO-US nuclear means to lessen the impact of the eventual, inevitable, mass nuclear exchange (of course their opponents had the same opportunity). Superior Warsaw Pact forces could be aggregated in order to shatter NATO defenses with the overriding advantage, critical to the Soviet style of war-fighting, of the absence of nuclear interdiction. The unhindered proceeding of an echeloned mobilization-deployment schedule even in the surprise or short-threat variants, the regrouping marches of second and third operational echelons both during any threat period and after the start of combat. Also of great significance, this nuclear immunity extended to the critical, massive, USSR interior mobilization-deployment scheme for fronts of the second strategic echelon as well as reinforcing armies, divisions, and specialized support units could be rolled out without hindrance during a finite, unpredictable, interval.

Planned Warsaw Pact force deployments and buildup of operational efforts could be completed while still retaining the WMD prerogative. But the nuclear variant would now be postponed, matchless firepower unavailable to directly break NATO defenses. During the previous years Warsaw Pact forces had been equipped and trained for nuclear warfare. One of the Czech defectors reported to intelligence that the national front had been caught ill-prepared for the conventional adjustment, in particular due to a limited artillery and close air support capability. To maintain high rates of advance deemed critical to victory in the Western TVD an operational course change would again be necessary. An offensive would have to be conducted under the constant threat of NATO nuclear strikes and, in the Soviet view, inevitably escalate to unlimited nuclear warfare.

The ensuing revival of conventional warfare capability took place along multiple channels, with an increasing momentum, yet would require more than a decade to implement. General Staff planners reached into the GPW grab bag to pull out battle-tried solutions for adaptation to modern conditions. A renewed emphasis on conventional fire support by aviation and artillery resulted in resource allocations to develop and field a new generation of armament. The GPW model of overwhelming force also initiated a search for reinforcements and methods adaptable to operations conducted for an uncertain period without mass destruction weapons.

Theater-wide massed aviation conventional strikes would be a means to achieve superiority in TVDs by degrading NATO nuclear systems and supporting front offensives. This Air Operation impelled a renewed attention to aviation, especially that assigned to fronts, producing an armada of modernized aircraft as well as upper level reorganizations. N. S. Khrushchev's promotion of rocket development in the late 1950s had denigrated the role of aviation of all types. New missile regiments and divisions had even been formed on the basis of existing long range aircraft units. A few authors in VM (S) articles during 1966-1967 had begun addressing the need for aviation mass strikes involving the joint participation of more than one front as well as Long Range Aviation. General-Major (Aviation) G. Yarotsky in a 1968 article[460] apparently gave one of the earliest full expositions on the features of the Air Operation—which would be conducted in a "non-nuclear period" reflecting an ongoing Soviet conceptual reformulation.

Renewed emphasis on artillery–both tube and rocket–followed another channel augmenting offensive and defensive firepower. Development entailed technical innovation on new models, in profusion, as well as the eventual introduction of self-propulsion. As always in the Soviet strategic culture, the mass equation arose. General-Majors (Artillery) I. Konoplev and V. Kuznetsov in a 1965 VM (S) article[461] considered artillery and other fire support issues for the new conventional variant. They noted that the nuclear front had 2500 to 2800 guns and mortars while the GPW conventional front (actually smaller in size) possessed 6000 to 13000. The introduction of surface-surface missiles represented a new factor but the authors considered these means unsuitable for conventional operations if only due to the essentiality of standby readiness for nuclear strikes (employment of chemical warheads would require "an entirely different" role assessment but CW "without simultaneous use of nuclear means is highly problematical"). Aviation had a role in direct support of engaged troops but had certain limitations. Their basic conclusion nominated artillery the primary tactical fire means, requiring "a vast quantity" in particular to destroy the enemy nuclear means located in tactical depth.

The base calculation to penetrate NATO defenses, as in the GPW, conformed to the formula artillery pieces = organic + reinforcement. Thus intelligence began to observe not only an increased quantity of pieces in division and army artillery units but also the reformation of RVGK artillery divisions and brigades. RVGK battalions would be allotted to ground armies and divisions in breakthrough sectors to achieve the high densities so beloved by Soviet artillerists. A much greater amount of conventional ammunition would also be required. Even in 1969 the Chief of the USSR General Staff compared the 15.4 TNT tonnes of a division salvo to that of 2.3 during the GPW.[462] But Zakharov then still expected an early resort to nuclear means. A 1981 CIA broad survey of *The Development of Soviet Military Power* since 1965[463] calculated that the weight of a three minute artillery barrage by a Soviet motorized rifle division had increased from about 60 to 140 tonnes—a late GPW initial barrage by a rifle division had been less than 2 tonnes[464]—and this amount did not account for RVGK artillery reinforcement in breakthrough sectors. NATO defenders would now be confronted with the unpleasant prospect of either nuclear incineration or a more prolonged artillery hell-on-earth.

Another GPW revival to augment ground combat power involved an expanded form of the 'grouping of fronts' in a strategic operation. While prewar Soviet views anticipated a prolonged campaign waged by individual fronts in sequential offensives, the early experience of the German war pointed to the potential of a coordinated simultaneous offensive of two or three fronts aiming at decisive results. Implementation of such a concept had scarcely been possible during the strategic defensive battles of 1941 to 1943. Counteroffensives by several fronts at Moscow and Stalingrad failed to develop beyond the immediate battle area. But the crucial July 1943 Kursk operation, a deliberate defense involving the joint efforts of three fronts, provided the Soviets both a model and the opportunity to seize the initiative with multi-front offensives. The strategic operations that followed unified the actions of several fronts across a wide zone to 'crack' the German defense, advance in considerable depth, capture key areas, and take out their allies.[465]

> The strategic offensive operation of a front group during the Great Patriotic War comprised an aggregate of interlinked operations of front formations, operations and combat actions of formations and combined units, long-range bomber aviation, and National Air Defense Troops, and on coastal directions—naval forces, conducted according to a unified plan for the purpose of achieving a strategic objective.

But unlike the Cold War version each strategic operation had been confined to one or two strategic directions rather than encompassing an entire theater. Focused on narrow sectors with massed tanks and artillery, penetration of tactical defenses had been exploited by committing mobile troops into separated breaches to advance into operational depth, and often, converging to encircle and destroy enemy groupings.

Nuclear weapons radically altered power ratios and obviated, indeed required, a lesser concentration of offensive forces. Opposing views found expression in 1961 top secret VM articles. While General-Colonel N. O. Pavlovsky raised the possibility that the first offensive might be conducted by a group of fronts,[466] General-Colonel A. Kh. Babadzhanyan dismissed this variant in a detailed consideration.[467] Babadzhanyan, while not completely rejecting such a front grouping, pointed out the now predominant role of nuclear missiles. "Consequently, the troops of one front will now operate, as a rule, on each of the strategic or important operational directions. It is our view that under these conditions the combining of several fronts into a group is not advisable..." which he also linked to the difficulty of coordinating across directions. The more limited number of fronts in a nuclear war also rendered "inadvisable" creation of TVD high commands. The Babadzhanyan model attained, briefly, official status: the 1963 USSR General Staff manual *Ground Troops Operations* held that "A front operation is conducted on one or more operations directions of a theater of military actions either independently or in cooperation with an adjoining front (fronts)" with no indication of a grouping of fronts variant.[468]

But the NATO back off from nuclear reliance impelled a Soviet revisit to the GPW variant. Discussion of the front grouping method of strategic action had been newly inserted into the second, 1963, edition of *Military Strategy*. Grouping references had not appeared in the text of the first edition that, according to the publication statement, had been composed in March 1962 and sent to press in May. The Chief of the USSR General Staff, Marshal M. V. Zakharov, in a 1966 VM (S) article attributed "great significance" to a February 1963 military science conference of the armed forces which had as a major topic "a strategic operation in a theater of military actions" which may have marked the kickoff of an operational revision.[469] In a June 1978 Warsaw Pact chiefs of staff conference General S. F. Romanov is quoted in an archive document that the modern strategic operation "has been elaborated and analyzed for more than 15 years" which would also date the genesis circa 1963.[470]

A remarkable glimpse of the ongoing transformation appeared in the pages of VM (S) in the mid 1960s. Issue 72 of 1964 featured an exposition by the Professor and another general[471] on stretching the first offensive operation of a front in the Western TVD not just to the normative 1000-km (which would later actually be curtailed by 200-km or more) but to the outer bounds of 2000- to 2500-km. Discussion addressed only the nuclear variant entailing mass strikes in depth by strategic means (their prospects for poor Belgium already noted) and those of the fronts (glumly admitting that missiles did not range beyond 250-km even if bomber aviation could extend to 800-km). They had doubts regarding two prevailing views: that successive operations by forward fronts would sweep the TVD; or that fronts regrouping from the interior of the USSR to develop the strategic operation would arrive in any condition to augment efforts. A variety of issues had to be overcome but the generals insisted that the existing makeup of a front would suffice to enable a 2000-km advance without any radical alteration. Providing a front with 500 or more nuclear warheads would expedite progress. Successive operations would be conducted only by subordinate first echelon armies; while the front second echelon could provide sufficient horsepower to span the TVD without further augmentation.

Five issues later in 1966 appeared a belated but direct response to this article by Colonel A. Volkov.[472] Not otherwise identified, for someone of his rank to dispute a pair of generals indicates considerable stature or hubris. Volkov concurred with the nuclear scenario presented but picked on several aspects for disagreement. TVD scaling actually not so expansive since by excluding seas and remoter areas the practical depth might be reduced to a more manageable 1500-km or less; a front did not have to seize everything, only key territory. But his main quarrel lay with the generals' contention that advancement of reserve fronts from the USSR to build up efforts would be incompatible with the modern strategic operation, offering an alternative template.

> In a strategic operation conducted in the Western Theater of Military Actions, several front formations, forming two operational echelons, usually can participate as the grouping of armed forces. In this case the operations of the ground forces take the form of simultaneous and successive operations of several fronts....
> 
> The fronts of the first operational echelon, which are assigned to offensives on the most important directions of the theater, begin their operations immediately at the start of the war (at the time of, or immediately following, the initial nuclear strike by strategic means). The front formations of the second operational echelon, which at the start of the war are a considerable distance from the troops of the first echelon, will move to the areas of combat operations over a period of several days and then enter the engagement and conduct their own offensive operations, as a rule on new directions....
> 
> Thus, in considering questions of offensive operations throughout the entire depth of a theater, we should not be guided by only one variant, as is recommended by the authors of the article, in which all tasks of the ground forces will be accomplished by one echelon.

That the Professor got the message, discarding the 'single echelon' variant, would be confirmed in issue 82 the following year.[473] His statement regarding fronts disposed in two operational echelons is quoted in the earlier distinguishing of the strategic and operational varieties—which the intell connoisseurs had failed to grasp.

The three articles by Glebov and Volkov had apparently been acquired separately during 1974 and 1975. Nowhere in mid 1970s or later intelligence material does there appear even the slightest hint that the crucial significance of this interchange had been absorbed. Transformation of the operational paradigm of the Western TVD had been under way entirely without recognition. This evidence of the second kind would be reflected not only in the nature of the strategic operation but also the lineup and composition of the fronts that would execute the revised concept. The intelligence failure proceeded as a direct consequence of the perceptual mangling of Soviet operational-strategic formulations in which analysts persisted unwitting of the, correct, definition and apportionment of echelons; thereby crippling subsequent analyses of the implemented reality of operational adjustments.

Development of the modernized front grouping method would in turn lead to reconsideration of TVD GK to coordinate the amplified operational intricacy. Marshal N. V. Ogarkov observed in the official critique of *Zapad* 1977 that "A modern strategic operation in a theater of military actions is larger in scale and considerably more complex than the operation of a group of fronts in the last war" underlining a major exercise task to explore the creation of TVD high commands.[474] The non-establishment of a *glavkom* in the Northwestern TVD directly reflected the more limited forces deployed in those strategic and operational directions; however, in 1985 evidence surfaced that a peacetime GK might be established, delayed by an apparent intramural squabble whether the commander-in-chief would be from the Navy or the Ground Troops.[475] Ogarkov would later reiterate the distinction between the operations of one front; a grouping of fronts; and "a more modern, perfected and large-scale form—the operation in a theater of military actions."[476]

The flanks of the Western TVD strategic operation represented conventional weak points. A judgment that the Warsaw Pact national fronts in these strategic directions had to be supplemented or replaced to achieve a greater combat power in the strike groupings created during an initial strategic deployment had been indicated, by 1965, in the formation of two new Soviet fronts. US intelligence, well into the 1960s, had not only missed the appearance of national fronts but also the subsequent increasing signs of additions to the frontal lineup in both the Western and Southwestern TVDs. The intelligence discovery of the existence of Czech and Polish fronts, announced in the June 1968 CIA-OSR Memorandum, had resulted in the launch of a new flavor—the durable five-front official model.

One of the most complete initial layouts of the five-front flavor-of-the-decade...plus, available in declassified material, is the 1970 final report of an interagency working group *The Warsaw Pact Threat to NATO*.[477] The group concluded that the Warsaw Pact "basic plan" comprised three forward fronts (GSFG-East German flanked by national-commanded Polish and Czech-Soviet) reinforced by two fronts from the USSR "second strategic echelon" (subsequently intelligence would define these as Belorussian and Carpathian MDs-based). The 1970 report had noted recent Soviet interest in operations without the use of nuclear weapons but considered Warsaw Pact forces to be structured for only the "short duration combat" of a strategic nuclear war. The constraints of the Soviet directions did not pertain because...no one had any inkling of such a concept. Three weeks would be required to mobilize and prepare this force; although dissenters from the DIA suggested that the forward force could begin an offensive prior to reinforcement—a hint of multi-level echeloned mobilization and deployment although the paper has no awareness of even the most basic constituents of this fundamental precept. All held that the "war plan outlined...with minor variations, is the only one practiced in Warsaw Pact exercises" and that the "main variable" involved the "timing of the onset of hostilities."

A 1977 CIA-OSR paper, which explicated a revised intelligence conclusion regarding the capabilities of "first strategic echelon" fronts, retrospectively summarized this development of a "Five-Front Concept" including the influence of the Sejna information. Even into the next decade this official model governed the intelligence perspective. Among other ground forces readiness appraisals the 1982 NIE[478] and CIA-OSR 1987[479] report again defined a (CIA "first strategic echelon") lineup essentially unaltered since 1970 with unitary Polish and Czech fronts, each incorporating Soviet elements, flanking the Soviet-East German front; with trailing unitary Belorussian and Carpathian fronts; while "forces in the Baltic Military District could serve as a reserve" in the Western TVD. Amazingly the NIE assigned to the GDR-based front all five GSFG armies plus two East German armies and tossed in the NGF as an army/army corps—eight despite the persisting Soviet specification that at the outset of war a maximum five armies comprise any Western TVD front. Even the authors of a 1988 NIE upheld the validity of the three- to five-army definition of a front.[480]

The obstinacy of the five-front official model is such that this perspective has survived well past the semi-official termination of the Cold War. A 2010 publication of the German Military History Research Office in Potsdam presented the viewpoints of several contributors on the operational roles of East German and Polish armed forces.[481] Their conclusions derived from surviving material in the military archives of the two defunct states as well as statements by selected Warsaw Pact officers; much of this material discussed in conferences during preceding years. Relevant Soviet archival material could not be considered because this source remains inaccessible. But the European authors ignored the substantial US intelligence reporting that has been declassified, and most significantly, the massive body of Soviet classified writings that the CIA has been releasing. Their conclusions replicated the US intelligence model established in 1968, adopted by NATO, which endured despite the substantial evidence of the second kind that indicates a Polish subsidiary, even fragmented, participation and a much more significant coastal role for Soviet forces.

## cruising the coast

Peacetime disposition of troops in the Northern-Coastal Strategic Direction, which covered the Baltic region and vitally important straits zone, left a gap in the northern GDR between the coast and the main forces of the GSFG. A 1967 article in VM (S) defined a 200-km wide coastal zone at the departure line.[482] In exercises, variously, an East German corps or army formed by their Military District V, one of the GSFG armies operating separately or a GSFG front 'stretch' to the Baltic, occupied this void. Another front, usually designated Coastal or Northern, then moved forward to fill the slot. Scenario of the 1967 Polish exercise *Lato* depicted an MD V army and a Soviet tank army in the gap until resubordinated to the Polish Coastal Front upon forward regrouping.[483] An East German staff officer involved in MD V operations planning during the 1980s has indicated that 5 Army would screen a 200-km zone from Wittenberge to the Baltic coast; and that in one variant the army had as subordinates the Soviet 94 Guards Motorized Rifle Division and two independent tank regiments from 2 Guards Tank Army.[484]

The Baltic littoral from East Germany into the USSR represented a critically sensitive beachfront and potential strategic vulnerability. This coast formed a wide, exposed, flank to the Western TVD strategic operation open at many points for amphibious landings. The US in particular had experience and adeptness at such assaults—enabling an Inchon-on-Baltic that would pose a mortal threat to the massive Soviet westward advance. The scope of this work precludes exploring the extent, if any, of actual NATO planning to exploit this strategic weak point. The Soviets, East Germans and Poles, however, conducted keenly aware of the opportunity presented to the enemy. Writings and exercises of their militaries exhibited considerable alarm concerning the potential threat of assaults over the Baltic Sea. One Soviet knowledgeable of the area, General-Army K. G. Khetagurov (the basis of his expertise to be shortly explored) warned:[485]

> ...at certain moments of a strategic operation in a theater of military actions, the battle against an enemy amphibious landing can reach such proportions that the command of the anti-landing defense will have to be assumed by the High Command of the war theater, if one has been created, or by the Headquarters of the Supreme High Command.

There appeared, during a certain timeframe, to have been much interest in using chemical weapons to repulse amphibious landings.

Evidence from classified material, including courses at the USSR General Staff Academy, highlighted the variants of Baltic deployment timing, contributors to the screening force, and the complement of the Coastal Front as among the most weighty problems of Soviet military strategy. An army operating solo in this area might sometimes be identified in exercises and classified documents as the Independent Coastal Army. The 1983 *Military Encyclopedic Dictionary* defined an independent army as subordinate, at least during initial deployment, to a theater-level command rather than a front. In exercise *Tarcza/Shchit* (Shield) 1976 an Independent Coastal Army had been tasked to deliver one of three main attacks in the Western TVD;[486] *Soyuz* 1975 depicted an Independent

Coastal Army advancing in the Jutland Operational Direction on the right flank of the Polish Coastal Front.[487] The GPW provided the Soviets with an operational model and experience. In late 1943 to early 1944 an Independent Black Sea Army, formed to replace and on the basis of the North Caucasian Front, operated in a similar coastal role in the Crimea. Cooperating with the Black Sea Fleet, the army drove out the Germans and then assumed sole responsibility for the defense of the Crimean Peninsula.[488]

US and other NATO intelligence services through the Cold War presumed, at least after existence had finally been recognized, that a unitary Polish national front served as the designated filler for the coastal zone behind a Soviet and/or East German screening force. Gestation of a Polish national front extended over a long period. Polish General Jan Drzewiecki testified in a 1997 interview to his participation in a May 1950 TVD command-staff exercise in which a role for Polish armies as a coastal front had been first explored. But he rated the Polish armed forces at that time incapable of forming the structure, and fulfilling the tasks, of a front.[489] The reformist Gomulka regime that assumed political power in 1956 also pressed the Soviets for their very own front as an expression of national sovereignty. But the front variant remained only a notion for years to follow during which Polish forces reorganized and armament modernization commenced. Actual operational planning began about 1961 when the Soviets finally assented to a unitary national front variant. A plan adopted in June 1961 by Poland's Defense Committee provided for 'external' and 'internal' fronts as the organizational basis for the national armed forces; designated peacetime sources for the headquarters of the new Warsaw Pact front included commander and chief of staff.[490]

Seven years would elapse before US intelligence concurrence would be finalized even though direct evidence had been obtained by at least early 1967 from a Polish source. Extracts from the official critique of exercise Narew 1965 detailed the operations of a national Masurian Front comprising armies from Poland's three military districts and one notional Soviet army.[491] The following year more exercise documents obtained on a national Coastal Front dated from 1967 or earlier.[492] The Polish unitary front flavor then endured through the remaining years of the Cold War even though intelligence suspicions would gradually be aroused in the 1980s of perhaps a less prominent role assigned to the Poles than had been supposed. But the official view persisted, as stated in the 1981 CIA military power survey, that "it would be difficult for Soviet units to replace the Poles completely without endangering vital wartime objectives."[493] Even the late 1989 NIE *Warning of War in Europe* still portrayed a first echelon Coastal Front composed of three Polish and one Soviet army despite a substantial accumulation of evidence indicating implausibility.[494] All Western intelligence services overvalued the Polish variant—a 1986 document found in East German archives has their chief of staff denying an FRG assessment that materiel reserves had been pre-stocked for Polish forces on GDR territory.[495] Several authors in the 2010 Military History Office book also followed this model of a Polish front among the fave five.[496] But Soviet ambivalence regarding Polish reliability in carrying out, independently, the main task in a strategic direction had been apparent in major exercise scenarios. The 1980-1981 Poland internal crisis certainly accentuated reservations.

One of the most authoritative and detailed intelligence previews of a Warsaw Pact front operations plan had been provided circa 1981 courtesy of Polish General Staff Colonel Ryszard Kuklinski.[497] Comparable, if less specific, information had been acquired in 1968 regarding the tasks of the Czech front although there had been more indications of the nature of Soviet reinforcement. Yet another Polish Defense Ministry document provided the full wartime front complement with mobilization schedule.[498] This Polish plan for the external front had been prepared in the early 1970s and, with minor revisions, remained in effect although the Soviets indicated proceeding work on a revised plan. The two first echelon armies (numbered 1 and 2) based in the Pomeranian and Silesian MDs would be available by D+3, with commitment to combat within 54 hours of the beginning of mobilization. The full Polish front would be available after eight days upon the creation of a second echelon from the Warsaw MD (4 Army). The front zone extended north from Wittenberge—also specified by the former East German operations officer. The main thrust would be delivered along the Coastal Operational Direction, where the second echelon army would be committed, striking for the French border and North Sea coast. A coordinated ground-air assault and amphibious landings supported by the Combined Baltic Fleet would be conducted in the Jutland Operational Direction. The plan specified in detail front and army offensive immediate and subsequent objective days, lines, and assigned divisions for operations anticipated to last at least ten days against strong NATO resistance. Top Polish officers believed this plan exceeded their capabilities particularly for an offensive on diverging operational directions. They felt that reinforcement by at least one Soviet tank army would be needed to attain the designated objectives. Kuklinski stated that, while front exercises had been conducted along all three strategic directions of the Western TVD, Polish front plans corresponded to only the Northern-Coastal Strategic Direction.

Kuklinski had insisted that any deviation from the coastal role had been solely for the purpose of providing training variety for Polish commanders and staffs.[499] Much of the exercise record supported his contention but important exceptions indicated that other variants existed. Several exercises from the late 1960s to 1987 depicted the unitary Polish front, variously, withheld in the VGK reserve or committed south of Berlin in the North German Strategic Direction; Polish armies divvied out to Soviet fronts; or just unaccountable. The June 1974 running of the Polish-directed *Lato* (Summer)[500] specified an exercise objective requiring the national 3 Western Front to deploy a partial complement in western Poland "ensuring the capability to change over to offensive operations on [either] the northern-coastal or Dresden-Frankfurt axis" well south of Berlin. Plan offensive variants included *Pomorze*, along the Baltic coast, and *Sudety*, newly prepared by the Front commander and staff at the order of the Combined Armed Forces Supreme Commander [North German Strategic-Frankfurt Operational Directions]. The day after declaration of Full combat readiness the Supreme Commander directed implementation of the *Sudety* variant. The codename of the new plan reflected the mountainous-forest conditions of the alternate direction. A map attached to the official exercise critique depicted both variants. The September 1976 *Tarcza/Shchit* scenario, based on "one of the many probable variants on how the war and border engagements may have begun" also committed the Polish Northern Front south of Berlin, with an adjoining Central Front south of the line Leipzig-Jena.[501] The Polish front drifted southward during the May-June 1980 exercise *Wiosna* (Spring)[502] and again during the internal crisis disrupted *Soyuz* 1981. That these exercises had not been aberrational is indicated as early as *Jesien* (Autumn) 1966 when the *Wielkopolski* (Greater Poland) Front advanced via Leipzig toward Bonn [i.e. North German Strategic-Ruhr Operational Directions].[503]

Many exercises and Polish sources indicated mobilization and commitment planning for the Polish front by operation days two to five. Intelligence expressed skepticism, and post Cold War interviews with senior Polish officers agree, that Poland would encounter difficulties meeting the mobilization timelines, and that the Soviet-inspired plan exceeded Polish capabilities. The officers indicated that their conclusions that assigned objectives could not be met with the forces available had been passed to the Soviets, who evinced little concern—seemingly a Polish front variant not high on the list for this strategic direction. In the interviews Wojciech Jaruzelski, who became Poland's General Staff Chief in 1965, confirmed the outline of the plan provided by Kuklinski, as well as the qualms regarding Polish capability to fulfill front objectives assigned by the Soviets.[504] However, another Polish Defense Ministry officer serving during the same period as Kuklinski doubted actual Soviet intentions. While apparent that Polish air- and sea-landing forces would participate in an assault on Denmark, the main Polish responsibility would rather be to protect forces regrouping from bordering Soviet MDs. Certain areas between the GDR border and Weichsel River east of Gdansk had been predesignated for Soviet forces, and in fact used by the Soviets in staging the 1968 Czech invasion. Some Polish officer defectors and emigres also denied any planning or exercising of an early offensive particularly beyond the Elbe. One rear services colonel who served in 2 Army in the first half of the 1960s while cognizant of a Polish front, and exercises in both operational directions, noted that some transportation routes would be co-opted for a Soviet front from the Belorussian MD.

A circa 1981 appreciation, presumably by Kuklinski, specifies 20 axial highway routes that delimit the regrouping zones across Poland for three Soviet fronts.[505] When plotted only small gaps remain north of and between the front zones. Thereby no allowance had been made for the concentration and movement of a unitary Polish national front. At most only widely separated armies could be accommodated, unless the Poles immediately moved into East Germany or only after Soviet transit of the northern zone. Assemblage of a Polish front at the outset could only disrupt an early regrouping of Soviet contingents. The central zone assigned to a front from Belorussia, and the southern zone to the Carpathian-based front, correspond closely to the regrouping zones allotted to the same fronts in exercise *Zapad* 1977 scenario—which may well have been intended to test the viability of, and/or gather practical data to fix, the specified routes—extending in length from 800- to 1200-km the two fronts spanned these zones in marches of three to five days. The Poles deployed, on paper or actually, Troop Movement Control Zones and Groups to coordinate the Soviet regroupings.[506] The appreciation assigned the northern zone for the transit of up to a front from the Baltic MD. Thus as clarified by General-Major Florian Siwicki, Chief of the Polish General Staff, in a review of the 1973 edition of exercise *Jesien* "The territory of the Polish People's Republic is the transit zone and staging area for the conduct of operations by ground formations of the Combined Armed Forces."[507] Poland in the role of a regrouping domain would hardly be anything new in Soviet strategy. During GPW offensives four fronts had crossed Polish territory for the final drive on Germany.

In the *Zapad* 1977 scenario the Polish 1 Front had been committed, probably on D+3, in the coastal directions. The Baltic 6 Front regrouped by D+6/7 to an area near Poznan; where, withheld in the VGK Reserve, 6 Front would be committed to combat only after the nuclear phase commencement on D+9. Kuklinski commented on a "carefully staged" situation inserted by Soviet officers in which the Silesian MD army delayed 4 Front Belorussia in the central regrouping zone, a "possible prelude to Soviet attempts to eliminate this army from the Polish front in wartime" and substitute a multinational front.[508] Less than three weeks following *Zapad* Warsaw Pact commander Marshal V. G. Kulikov directed exercise *Fala/Val* (Wave) clearly intended as a direct followup. A supposedly Polish front comprising only one Polish army operated with two Soviet armies and an Eastern German corps against Denmark [Jutland Operational Direction] with amphibious landings on Baltic islands and southeastern Norway.[509] No planning took place regarding the Coastal Operational Direction. A circa 1981 appreciation, presumably also by Kuklinski, voiced Polish suspicions of a Soviet intended "fragmentation" that would subordinate one

Soviet front regrouping zones 1981

Polish army to a front based on the GSFG with a "Baltic Front (or independent army)" advance to fill the coastal slot.[510]

Cold War era material and subsequent investigations indicate a startling lack of Soviet coordination with and among the Polish and East German comrades supposedly assigned key roles in the Northern-Coastal Strategic Direction. A 1977 Polish General Staff Memorandum, responding to issues raised by the Warsaw Pact commander that included work on air bases, cited a national airfield density (per 1000-km$^2$) of 0.313 as well as the coefficients for operational objectives Belgium, The Netherlands, and the FRG. The Memo then amazingly confessed that "We do not know the situation in the German Democratic Republic."[511] Hardly a basis for planning the operations of a Polish front air army. Research during the last two decades in East German and Polish military archives, along with conferences and interviews involving some of their former senior officers, have led some European historians to question actual Soviet intentions. Documents and discussions have revealed an obvious disconnect between the planning of the two Warsaw Pact militaries to the extent of incompatibility. East Germans knew little of Polish preparations and vice versa while neither had a clue regarding Soviet plans. Yet close inter-working and coordination would have been essential to stage Polish forces in the GDR for operations against NATO in northern Europe. That Soviet mistrust of the two allies had been so great that their actual role in the still unavailable theater operations plans is suspect; and unresolvable from the perspectives of former East German and Polish officers as well as archival material; led the 2010 Military History Office study editor Rüdiger Wenzke to admit that such questions "cannot be currently answered."[512]

In the second half of the 1960s the first generation of high resolution photoreconnaissance satellites enabled an increasingly detailed examination of Soviet and national armed forces including those in the border USSR military districts. A coordinated January 1968 CIA-DIA study of the reinforcement potential of the western MDs, predating intelligence confirmation of the Polish front variant, had concluded that the three armies of the Belorussian exhibited readiness for earlier movement than other MDs—notably 28 Combined-Arms Army deployed on the Polish border.[513] In exercise Narew 1967 the Masurian Front complement included a Belorussian MD "combined arms army command" as '20' Army—thus excluding the other two tank armies.[514] This and later studies also highlighted the readiness of 11 Guards Army—with elements deployed close to the border—in the Baltic MD; an army that frequently appeared in exercises advancing into Poland, often to join the Polish front. Only during the late 1970s did recognition gradually emerge that a contingent Soviet replacement existed. But intelligence totally failed to comprehend that a Soviet front might actually play the lead in the coastal role while the Poles only had bit parts.

The muddied perceptual window affected intelligence comprehension of material presented to senior officers at the USSR General Staff Academy. The Academy had been kind enough to provide the CIA, through an intermediary, an entire 1977 instruction bloc How to Run a Front Offensive Operation in 29 Easy Lessons (or something like that).[515] Using the case study method operations planning for the "Coastal Front [which] will be in the first operational echelon in the strategic operation in the Western" TVD proceeded on Baltic operational directions. Students played the roles of front commander and key staff chiefs including air army commander, intelligence and operations directorates, rocket-artillery troops, as well the commander and staff of the Combined Baltic Fleet, all in great detail. The front offensive zone, repeating that given in the other sources, had an initial width of 200-km, allotting first echelon divisions zones up to 15-km (or 17 to 20 in other lessons), which would expand to 250- to 280-km in the directions of the attack. The front second echelon included '10' Tank Army, a brand that could only derive from the GSFG or Belorussia, with a planned commitment on the fifth or sixth day of the offensive. The Coastal Front had seven days to prepare an offensive which would have permitted at least two of the three specified combined-arms armies in the first echelon to regroup from Poland. How true-to-life the case study is of uncertain practicality; the complement may have been arbitrarily arranged for training purposes—but nothing resembling this coastal zone lineup appeared in intelligence assessments.

The scenario posited by the Academy presented a real head-scratcher for intell readers. Two first echelon fronts, prior to the start of war, depicted in the GDR; the Coastal Front boundary with the Western Front placed well south of Berlin—ten years earlier a map from exercise *Troika* had also shown a front boundary along the same line;[516] army areas and other GSFG assets split although still largely in the Western Front zone; four combined-arms armies and one corps subordinate to the Coastal Front. Nationalities unidentified, lacking any indication of a front command other than Soviet; no study topics related to any form of coordination with Warsaw Pact entities appeared in the lessons, only references to East German and Polish fleet element tasking. No hint of the origin of the CAAs given but the one corps implies that fielded by the northern East German MD V. Of particular interest is the single, front-mandated, tank army; this shows up D+2 at 360+ km from the line of contact, a distance equating to western Poland, confirmed by later regrouping to an area east of Berlin in preparation for commitment to combat by D+6. That geography and timing could only have been satisfied by an active tank army—from Belorussia—not surprising then that (presumably Colonel Kuklinski) later reported that an operations group (liaison) from a tank army in that district had been participating in exercises.[517] This game of armies musical chairs in the Western TVD undermined the perceptions of connoisseurs rigidly fixated on Poland, the GSFG, and the western military districts deploying (only active) formations within prescriptive bounds as defined by intelligence.

Some evidence, including the testimony of senior Polish officers during and after the Cold War, point toward Baltic and Belorussian MDs-sourced fronts operating in the Northern-Coastal Strategic Direction in preference to the Polish external front, even in the first half of the 1960s. Augmentation would be essential to the conventional adjustment, in particular to execute the revived grouping of fronts variant of the Western strategic operation. Development of a new, characteristic, missile-artillery base for a Soviet front began in the fall of 1964 at Ladushkin in the Baltic MD, near the Polish border. But recognition by US intelligence of any addition to the lineup of fronts did not come for a full decade thereafter. An early 1978 NIE, appraising warning implications for NATO, examined attack options involving the usual five fronts including unitary Polish and Czech; still with no cognizance of any recent addition despite exercise indications in prior years.[518] Breaking out from the five-front flavor proved exceedingly difficult; through the 1980s intell exhibited befuddlement pinpointing, appraising the existence and roles, of variant Baltic contingents.

Exercise and other evidence might have been conflicting and ambiguous but Soviet military writings offered unequivocal indications. The classified editions of VM provided important clues but these had been relegated by intelligence to the second kind archives. Notable are the career and writings of General-Colonel (1968 General-Army) G. I. Khetagurov. An ethnic Ossetian who made good in the service of the Soviet Empire, he pursued an ascending path from 1920 signup, somehow surviving the Stalin purges and fighting duty in the GPW, to senior rank. From February 1958 until March 1963 he commanded the NGF and then made a, telling, lateral transfer to the Baltic MD to become commander until 1971. Khetagurov had been held in such high esteem even to a later generation that he merited a separate biographic entry with photo in the *Military Encyclopedic Dictionary*. Five of his articles appeared in VM between 1960 and 1970, two of which dealt in detail with operations of the coastal front in the Western TVD. Two of the articles had been transmitted by Oleg Penkovsky and the other three by new sources from early 1974 to late 1976 (acquisition sometime prior to the dates of the declassified CIA transmittal memos attached to their translations).

The insistence of Khetagurov in a 1960 article, contributing to the ongoing nuclear big bang disputation, that one front should be deployed in each strategic direction of the Western TVD has already been noted. In the same article he called for the inclusion of a second echelon army in the composition of these fronts rather than the reserve of divisions in a single echelon front that others proposed.[519] But his late 1961 VM top secret article[520] dealing with a first front offensive in a coastal direction—when still the NGF commander—provides key evidence that this group would provide the front command element for a coastal front drawn largely from the Soviet border armies—and potentially the GSFG. This NGF lineally descended from 2 Belorussian Front that had captured the region in 1945. According to General J. Drzewiecki in 1997 at least one Polish 1950s plan had assigned the army generated by the Pomeranian MD to a Northern Front based on the Soviet NGF, while the Silesian MD army would be destined for a Central Front of the GSFG.[521] A VM article discussed the 1964 exercising and establishing of a front command post in the NGF that combined missile, aviation, and air defense elements.[522] The NGF would continue to exercise as a front long after the departure of Khetagurov. His decade-long interest in the coastal front suggests that he had been the predesignated commander.

Khetagurov defined this northerly strategic direction in the Western TVD to extend 1000- to 1200-km and assigned an imperative objective that the front seize the Baltic straits area and reach the Atlantic by operation days 9 or 10 before US reserves could arrive; advancing in nuclear conditions while coordinating with the Baltic Fleet. The strike groupings of this coastal front would be formed "with the moving out of forces from the depth" and Khetagurov pointed to the difficulties posed by potential destruction of bridges on the rivers Western Bug, Vistula, and Oder—successive intermediate obstacles for troops regrouping from the Belorussian and Baltic MDs. Mainly tank divisions formed the basis of these strike groupings which could only have come from the GSFG and/or at least one of the tank armies located deep in Belorussia. Addressing a proposal to create control centers he noted that these organs had been worked out in three 1959 NGF front command-staff exercises.[523] His discussion clearly points to a NGF front during at least the late 1950s and into the early 1960s in composition including Soviet armies from one or both of the border districts; likely the Pomeranian MD army; and potentially a contribution of the GSFG northernmost army. Intelligence and archival[524] evidence regarding the 1961 *Burya* exercise point to a Western Front comprising at least Baltic and Belorussian armies deviating southward in order to permit the new Polish Coastal Front to take on the Baltic advance but one or both of the two Soviet border armies may have been redirected into the second echelons of forward front(s).

Khetagurov again discussed a coastal front in the pages of the VM secret edition in 1970—but now he commanded the Baltic MD.[525] He based this consideration of defending against enemy amphibious landings on exercise experience of his MD during the offensive of a front along the coastal direction of the Western TVD. The flank of the attacking front would be exposed for 600-km to enemy landings at three locations on the USSR coast; up to six in Poland and East Germany; and up to seven areas from west of Jutland to Cherbourg. In a 1969 VM (S) article focused on WMD employment and reinforcement during a front offensive Khetagurov refers to commitment of the front second echelon in command-staff exercises and operational games conducted in the Baltic MD during the preceding years of 1966 to 1968—from the standpoint of an assignment he had held since 1963.[526]

Khetagurov had also referred to such Baltic front exercises in a 1967 article on staff training.[527] His discourses point to new tasks at the level of a front for the Baltic MD dating from the mid 1960s. So do at least six other VM (S) articles—acquired by intelligence from early 1973 to late 1976—by district officers dating onward from 1966. The MD chief of staff General-Lieutenant M. Ivanov had authored four of the articles. He specified the Baltic MD in regard to exercises (1965-1966) involving front reconnaissance assets; front command post workings; as well as the front air army;[528] after all 15 (30) Air Army resided in this MD. A 1967 Baltic MD front war game included communications of a front rear command post with the attendant air army command post.[529] Ivanov's 1967 VM spiel on masking communications in a border military district during peacetime cited the experience of a Baltic MD front command-staff exercise featuring an official theme "The Conduct of a Front Offensive Operation on a Coastal Direction."[530] An article he wrote the previous year refers to setting up a front communications center within 30-km of the location of the MD's permanent staff.[531]

Among the most striking aspects of Khetagurov's depictions of the coastal front is that they are devoid of any reference to the existence of, much less coordination with, the countries to be traversed. There are no discussions whatsoever of combined actions with the Polish and East German armed forces; this both before and well after the coastal front mission had supposedly been assigned to the Poles. Warsaw Pact interactions persisted entirely absent in his wide-ranging discourses; as if the troops of the Soviet coastal front would be marching through an extension of the USSR. Warsaw Pact allies also abided conspicuously absent from many of the top secret writings that addressed conditions in the Western TVD. The 1977 General Staff Academy lecture on front offensive operations, which opened with an itemization of a front role in the Western TVD strategic operation, does not so much as hint at any cooperation with the allies. Nor does the Warsaw Pact or members feature in matters covered in the available sections on a multiplicity of topics.[532] The Academy 1974 front operations textbook similarly, except for brief treatment of actions with allied navies, has no Warsaw Pact coverage even in separate chapters on political work and troop control.[533]

The wellspring of Khetagurov's front command group could have been one of the border MDs, the GSFG, or the NGF. The eventual intelligence conclusion based the new front on the Baltic MD headquarters. The earliest available (declassified) documents to assess the existence of a Baltic front are a CIA-OSR study on TVDs (information cutoff December 1978)[534] and the early 1979 NIE on Warsaw Pact forces.[535] But all discussions still focused on the persistent five-front flavor and unitary national fronts—Western TVD command charts in both reports list a Baltic Front. CIA analysts retrospectively considering the evidence had spotted indications in exercises dating back to *Vesna* (Spring) 1969. However a scenario map of this exercise in an early 1977 report[536] only has Baltic "forces...join"—including **two** armies—a front with GSFG and GDR elements on D+4, augmenting the usual forward trio. But the report also notes a February 1975 exercise in which a Baltic front expropriated the Polish slot prior to war outbreak; in the May *Obzor* (Scope) at the outset of combat, even swiping the Northern Front designation. Already noted the appearance of the Baltic 6 Front in the VGK Reserve during *Zapad* 1977; regrouped to western Poland by D+7 to be committed upon initiation of mass nuclear strikes.[537] Some later exercises would designate this MD as the Coastal Front. According to one Russian account of the 1968 Operation Danube, the Central Front formed for the invasion had been based on the Baltic district staff,[538] an excellent opportunity to get some large-scale practical experience.

Front-level exercises in the Baltic and Belorussian MDs during the remainder of the Cold War featured apparent exploration of variant army complements. The NGF continued occasionally still in play as a front. The exercises often focused on the role of one of the armies in the front nominally formed by the MD, as if the objective not play of the front role, but rather that of the particular army within a front. While 11 Guards continued to be the only army identified in the Baltic district, there existed an apparent excess of front-level ground units as well as divisions; including two RVGK artillery divisions, essential reinforcements for conventional breakthroughs. Order of battle assessments in 1975 carried seven tank and motorized rifle divisions,[539] increasing by the early 1980s to eleven, all in varying *shtat*;[540] four of these believed to be subordinate to the one active army. According to a 1985 lecture, during a recent exercise an unspecified number of divisions (coupled with the Kiev MD) had required eight or ten days to mobilize—shockingly exceeding the "stipulated" five days.[541] Total active divisions amounted only a bit shy of the neighboring Belorussian and Carpathian districts, each 13 divisions organized into three active armies, the minimum complement of a front in the Western TVD. Nearly all of the Baltic MD divisions resided at a shorter march distance to East Germany than the divisions of the two other border MD.

Evidence for the second Baltic MD army portrayed in exercise *Vesna* 1969, derived from the imperceptible third operational echelon, has been previously noted. From at least 1979 exercises indicated that even a second echelon army and other elements from the Leningrad MD (which did not border Central Europe) had been candidates for inclusion in a Soviet Baltic front. The Leningrad Coastal Front—a loaded designation—had even been depicted in combat with the Dutch

I Corps. But through the mid 1980s intelligence estimates still assumed a five-front attack that included a unitary Polish front, with only a vague sense of a reinforcing Baltic front somewhere in the pileup.

Selected Kuklinski reports declassified by the CIA in late 2008 provide some scenario details from *Zapad* 1981.[542] This expansive set piece, opposed forces, field and staff exercise rolled out on a scale considered by intelligence monitors as comparable to exercises *Vesna* 1975 and *Dvina* 1980. Although held in Ukraine, field activity and background scenario involved amphibious landings by a full motorized rifle division and naval infantry as well as drops of an airborne division and air assault brigade on a coastal direction (using displaced geography, a frequent Soviet technique). Scenario linked an Independent Coastal Army to 1 Belorussian Front; 2 Baltic Front performed the other major role. This could be read as a Belorussian Coastal Front regrouped to the first operational echelon, with a Baltic second echelon front. Although Polish observers had been present at this exercise, they did not participate.

During the early 1980s an unprecedented number of exercises involved Baltic and Belorussian forces, each acting as a front, swapping first and second echelon roles in the northern directions. Clearly the Soviets had been alarmed at the contemporary indications of Polish unreliability. Initial Period variants of the coastal direction exercised seemed to be portraying as the coastal front, alternatively, either a mainly Belorussian front or a mainly Baltic front, deploying the other front in the second operational echelon; with major subordinates contributed from other USSR military districts. The potentiality of a pre-combat regrouping to the first echelon during a threat period played a key factor in role reversals.

*Tsentr* 1982 scenario had Poland and Romania seeking an exit from the Warsaw Pact, a variant discussed during a meeting by the Soviet and East German defense ministers with the Warsaw Pact commander.[543] Yet a month earlier the Polish-run *Lato* depicted their front committed in the 'normal' Coastal and Jutland Operational Directions. The first echelon front in these directions during *Tsentr* comprised one army (possibly two) from Belorussia, one army from the GSFG, and one Polish army; a second echelon Baltic front then committed in northern France after two weeks of combat,[544] thus propelling the next phase of the TVD strategic operation. Exercise *Zapad* 1984, conducted only with Soviet players, depicted pre-combat regrouping of Soviet fronts in the Northern-Coastal Strategic Direction, minus any Polish front. This exercise had a national fronts exclusion theme since the Czechs, unusually, also did not occupy their customary slot. A number of exercises depicted regrouping of USSR armies located on the border to the northern GDR marching 800-km across Poland in two or three days. The official critique of the 1977 *Zapad* gave an average of 250- to 300-kmd for the regroupings of three fronts.[545] Soviet scenarios had these armies mobilizing and at least the advanced *shtat* first echelon divisions reaching East German departure positions faster than the armies of the Polish front.

The Soviet NGF continued to be a versatile player in exercises. Historically appearing not only as a Soviet front but also deployed in some exercises jointly with the Poles as a front or as an operations group (a distinctive Soviet liaison control organ) attached to a Polish front; even playing an army despite having only two divisions (sufficient of course to form an army first echelon) which would reinforce the Soviet front(s) formed in Germany. The NGF thus had a potential switch-hitting role as a front field headquarters in different variants. Subsequent to the 1965 appearance of the Baltic front, and before the 1968 establishment of the Central Group in Czechoslovakia, the NGF could have headed a Soviet front with subordinate Czech and Soviet armies—from either or both the GSFG and the SGF as will be considered. However the transmutation of the NGF 4 (37) Air Army into a VGK air army in 1980 may signify a curtailed front variant. Subsequently the headquarters domicile at Legnica, Poland manifested plush enough to suit the Western TVD GK which expelled the group staff in 1984.

While during the first half of the 1960s only one front, comprised of armies based in the GSFG and USSR border districts could replace the Poles, from the later 1960s any of four variant fronts—NGF, Baltic, Belorussian, Polish—could join in the Western TVD strategic operation against NATO in the Northern-Coastal Strategic Direction. Alternative variants also committed the Belorussian and Polish fronts in other strategic directions. Some exercises pitted a Moscow MD front against West German, Dutch, Belgian, or US corps. Data obtained from East German archives indicated that the two constituent operational directions rated a total capacity of three to four first echelon armies;[546] enabling a powerful strike grouping of more than one front to be established as the zone expanded during the course of an attack against I FRG-Danish and I Netherlands Corps in this strategic direction; with a potential full front in the TVD or VGK reserve.

A diversion from the Cold War intelligence official model suggests that specific evidence available from the early 1960s onward might rather point to a preferred Soviet, rather than Polish, Coastal Front; and that beginning in 1965 further measures had been taken to augment this variant. A varied assortment of evidence, of the second kind, had been entirely ignored. That a front not under Soviet command would be assigned primary responsibility along a strategic direction represented not just an intelligence misapprehension but a mass delusion that potentially imperiled NATO defenses. Polish front planning at the behest of their Soviet controllers as well as representation in exercises may in fact have been one element of a longstanding, orchestrated, Soviet strategic deception to mislead NATO as to the actual opponent. A 1977

Academy lecture[547] defined *Maskirovka* (literally camouflage—emphasis added) "Strategic camouflage is the array of measures conducted by the General Staff to preserve the combat effectiveness of troops and **achieve surprise in a strategic operation in a TVD**." If this had been the situation and their objective, a quite successful ruse endured for more than two decades. The Jutland and Coastal Operational Directions controlled the only outlet for the Combined Baltic Fleet to the North Sea and ended at ports in The Netherlands and Belgium that NATO considered essential to the overseas reinforcement on which a viable defense depended.

Intelligence had enabled a Soviet 'Schlieffen-Moltke' variant compounded by the mesmerizing focus on the grouping in central-south East Germany. The German ostensible Schlieffen Plan prepared before the First World War had envisioned an offensive strong right wing to sweep along the Baltic-North Seas through Belgium and collapse Allied defenses. But assigned troops had gradually been transferred elsewhere, weakening the onslaught at the outset of war, and the British Expeditionary Force reached France faster than expected. The French then had just sufficient time to reinforce and halt the German advance, settling into the calamitous Western Front stalemate. When President Charles de Gaulle withdrew France from NATO in 1966 the new Baltic front and coastal variant had been presented a golden opportunity; drastically reducing NATO defense depth and removing French reserves to defend breaches; denying French ports to vital British and American reinforcements while restricting these to dangerously exposed Antwerp and Rotterdam. How Khetagurov and the staffers at the Main Operations Directorate must have chortled with delight at the opening presented by this French betrayal of the West—likely there would be no repeat of the 'miracle of the Marne.' The main thrust of the Western TVD strategic operation could now be delivered northward of the Ruhr urban-industrial area where development had been presenting an increasing hindrance to rapid tank and armor advances.

Ironically the overrating of the Polish role had been, and continues to be, shared by the Poles and other European researchers. But even Polish senior officers had their doubts as voiced by the 1970s operations deputy chief and later Deputy Minister of Defense, J. Skalski.[548]

> ...there were conversations of the type that all the plans that they were sending us were a camouflage. Never—I can state this without hesitation—never would they have opened their plans and shown us our role and place. We just suspected that it did not have to do with the Polish Front—that it was camouflage. And that front—no revelation here—was in the Northern-Maritime Direction...

Providential that the West 'won' a cold war.

## armageddon on the Rhine

The peacetime disposition of first operational echelon Soviet armies and supporting assets, mainly in the GDR south of Berlin, divulged the primacy of the North German Strategic Direction. A General Staff Academy 1985 lecture confirmed that the strategic operation would have a "direction of the main thrust" in the Western TVD.[549] Exercise advances by armies of the GSFG, apart from the northernmost 2 Guards Tank, consistently tended west-southwest toward, and south of, the Harz Mountains. The General Staff Academy 1977 specification[550] that the immediate task of a front in the first offensive operation would reach a depth of 250 to 350 or more kilometers amounted to passage just beyond the River Rhine barrier in that direction (other sources and exercises vary about 50-km). The Rhine also figured in exercises and classified documents as the crux for achieving penetrations of NATO defenses; in some exercises until and including *Zapad* 1977, commitment of the TVD second operational echelon; major paradrops of one or two airborne divisions to support crossings—and the precipitation of nuclear strikes which the Soviets keyed, and presumed motivated their opponents, to defense line breakthrough—a milestone projected in the 1977 Academy case study.[551]

> Not having been able to achieve the aims of the operation with conventional means of destruction, and faced with the threat of losing the Ruhr industrial area and the possible capture by East of the strategic line of the Rhine River, the enemy is completing preparations to employ nuclear weapons.

This geographic preference had certainly been the view of General-Major N. I. Reut in 1970.[552] Considering both nuclear and non-nuclear variants, he specified the Ruhr Operational Direction as the "main direction" in which a complete front with fifteen to twenty divisions would be committed. In a conventional war NATO would by D+5 be reinforced to a similar number of divisions of the FRG, Belgium, and The Netherlands plus troops airlifted from the US and UK to their prepositioned heavy weapons. The British apparently did not impress Reut since he omitted UK I Corps from the direction calculation. The tenor of the article held that the operational direction needed a unified plan for all variants which focused on the most difficult; Reut cited Colonel A. Volkov approvingly regarding this matter. He also indicated that the Soviets had now come to the conclusion that the depth of the initial front offensive should be reduced to a 600- to 800-km range—this norm would again be somewhat curtailed in the next decade.

The North and South German Strategic Directions encompassed the crucial territory of any NATO-Warsaw Pact conflict; decisive for outcomes determination. Unfortunately the CIA squat gang has successfully blocked any comprehensive discourse regarding aspects of this Cold War climacteric. There are key documents still withheld including issues from VM (S) and national forces journals; directives and other material disbursed by Headquarters, Warsaw Pact Combined Armed Forces (Chief of Staff General-Army A. I. Gribkov a busy guy); as well as other pertinent remnants. Perforce historical treatment of Soviet strategy considerations and evolution in the Western TVD must be grievously curtailed—along with evaluating the accuracy of intelligence assessments.

Even during the "nuclear euphoria" of the early 1960s the Soviets anticipated widespread use of operational (beyond tactical depth) airborne landings. A front advance in a main direction might be allocated one or two full airborne divisions; dropped 300- to 500-km or more in depth; somehow executed as rapidly as possible subsequent to not only frontal but strategic mass nuclear exchanges.[553] But intelligence calculated at the time,[554] and despite later substantial improvements of lift capability, through the mid 1980s[555] that the movement of one full airborne division would require all the aircraft in the VTA (Military Transport Aviation) arm or two divisions if limited to 'assault elements' only—but the potential contribution of Aeroflot civil aircraft could not be accounted—and the Soviets deployed eight active airborne divisions. Some Soviets agreed as in a 1963 VM (S) critique of the nuclear paradrop that noted a division lift amounted to 600 to 700 aircraft or nearly all VTA assets.[556]

Nevertheless airborne landings would continue to rate highly in a NATO war. A 1968 appreciation in VM (S) reported military academy research conclusions that the drop of up to a division (by 12 to 16 VTA regiments) on D+2/3 during a conventional phase would "determine" the "success" of a first operational echelon front in a "selected direction" but at no more than 200-km deep. The effects of NATO nuclear strikes and air defenses did not factor into many Soviet discussions. A rare instance in VM (S) 1970[557] did examine airlift attrition; pointing to a March 1945 massed UK-US drop at the Rhine that, despite total air superiority, lost more than 31 percent of participating aircraft and gliders; while Soviet research and experience during exercise Dnepr 1967 allowed "permissible losses" to be a maximum 15 percent or 60 aircraft destroyed during the transport of one airborne division—while insisting that the loss must not exceed 20 aircraft—the author then entered a detailed consideration of expedients to minimize losses. An entire section of the General Staff Academy 1977 work *The Front Offensive Operation*[558] dealt with airborne landings; considered valid in both nuclear and conventional war; in a TVD strategic operation employing two or more airborne divisions and even a "stripped down" motor rifle division; with tasks detailed; estimating the single sortie lift of one airborne division to require 400 to 450 AN-12 (Cub) aircraft (4-5 VTA divisions—the MRD needed 800 AN-12); and zonal flight corridors to facilitate suppressing air defenses. The Coastal Front in the 1977 Academy Lessons had projected a D+5 airborne division drop at the Rhine to assist a tank army crossing.[559] In the mid 1980s the Academy still allotted a front operating on the main direction of a TVD strategic operation one or two airborne divisions as well as the same number of air assault brigades.[560]

The US intelligence, at best lagging, at worst distorted, assessments of the Soviet-Warsaw Pact lineup of fronts renders the judgments arrived at during different stages of the Cold War rather problematic. An early 1988 NIE assessment of *Warsaw Pact Forces*[561] excitedly presented the intelligence discovery of a supposedly new preference to deploy a fourth front in the "first strategic echelon" of the Western TVD prior to the start of war. One innovation for this NIE series involved the explicit relating of "operational axes" to Soviet strategic deployment (strategic directions did not factor in the discussion). This edition stated a basic purpose to revise the conclusions of a more comprehensive 1983 Warsaw Pact Forces IIM[562] as well as the 1984 *Warning* NIE.[563] Neither of these assessments had addressed the directions in any form—authors entirely clueless as to the significance of the Soviet precept—despite the Reut identification, in an article acquired by early 1973, of one of these as the main direction of advance by an entire front.

**alpine rambling**

Complementary dilemmas for achieving higher conventional war force ratios confronted the Soviets in the South German Strategic Direction (Western TVD) and the Italian Strategic Direction (Southwestern TVD). Exercise documents and 'operation plans' recovered from Czech and Hungarian archives have now clarified developments in the early to mid 1960s only dimly perceived, and that after the fact, by Western intelligence services. The role of the Czech front had been established by exercises and information from the senior officer defectors. These sources indicated that both before and after the events of 1968 the Czech front had the main responsibility (in the South German Strategic Direction) until the second echelon front from the Carpathian MD showed up after five to ten days (this surprise-offensive variant assumed no Soviet pre-combat regrouping). Operational life expectancy of the Czechs had been projected at 10 to 15 days, with losses reaching 80 percent; the survivors to be assigned to the arriving Soviet front and/or occupy captured West German territory. Some observers pointed to the difficult forested-mountainous terrain as rendering unrealistic any major offensive—but then a similar French appraisal in 1940 had afforded operational surprise to the Germans when they advanced 45 divisions (including seven *panzer*) through the Ardennes.[564]

Strategically 'stuck' with Czechoslovakia there would be no immediately available Soviet screening force (as in the north) until 1968. Czechoslovakia provided a vital barrier against a

NATO flanking move around and behind the powerful Soviet group in East Germany. Exercise *Zapad* 1984, the test of a nationals exclusion variant in which the Poles had been concurrently absent, constituted a rare if not unique instance in which the Czech front had no role—replaced in the first operational echelon by fronts based on the Carpathian MD and the Central Group of Forces in Czechoslovakia. In another uncommon depiction, in the *Tsentr* 1982 scenario, the Czech front may have been committed from a second echelon position, and may even have attacked southward through Austria into Italy rather than toward West Germany.[565] A few exercises indicated a variant with the Belorussian front advancing in the (South German Strategic Direction). Events during 1968 that precipitated the Warsaw Pact invasion must have been a profound shock to Soviet military planners who had regarded the Czechs as one of the most reliable of allies. Nevertheless, defectors and emigres would indicate that the operational variants for the Czech front had not been materially affected and post-invasion exercises would reveal variations mainly in the employment of the newly established CGF.

A 'war plan' (for the South German Strategic Direction) dated 11 October 1964, found in Czech archives[566] (presumably one of the six variants—many Czech and Soviet unit designators listed corresponded to actual order of battle), stipulated that a front comprised of Czech armies with Soviet augmentation would cooperate with a Soviet front in East Germany against the facing NATO forces. A disconcerting post Cold War surprise in this document is that the indicated reinforcements included a reserve of Soviet divisions at army strength regrouped from the Southern Group of Forces (all four divisions actually in Hungary) during operation days three to five. There had been no intelligence indications or suspicions regarding any such role for the SGF as a whole or in part. That this transfer represented an established variant is indicated by a June 1963 exercise document found in Hungarian archives[567] which in a situation report states "the forces of the Southern Army Group had left the territory of this country" by a scenario date; a Southwestern Front made up of at least one Hungarian army and one Romanian army that had entered Hungary apparently remained on the defensive while recovering from a enemy mass nuclear attack. This unforeseen SGF regrouping variant had the Soviets inserting their guys in Czechoslovakia, an army to buttress the Czech front, long before creation of the CGF—replicating the variant Baltic MD 11 Guards Army ensuring of the Polish front. While the 1964 plan orders cooperative action with an 8 Guards Army (the designator of the southernmost GSFG army) of 1 Western Front, no reference appears to coordination with any front to the south; remaining SGF and Hungarian troops would only defend the state border.

The escalation variant required a stronger conventional grouping of fronts, eventuating a reoriented Soviet-Hungarian Balaton or Danube front for offensive operations in the Italian Strategic Direction. This development did not signify an entirely new front but a revision of objectives and complement. A few early 1960s classified VM articles refer to the SGF as a front headquarters with Soviet, Hungarian, and Romanian subordinates.[568] The Hungarian June 1963 exercise document, upon the 'departure' of SGF divisions, identified a Southwestern Front composed of only national armies; depicting measures taken to recover from the nuclear strike with no indication of offensive planning. During 1965 construction of a characteristic front missile-artillery base had been initiated at Shepetovka (Shepetivka) in the Carpathian MD; a front missile-artillery base preexisted at Kalinovka (Kalynivka) in the Carpathian MD that, at least originally, supported district front generation. The Carpathian thereby matched the Belorussian MD where one base near the USSR western border could support a forward front with a second front base positioned well back. The new front base, and a key directional WMD installation of the Center on which work had been simultaneously initiated in the same district, represented among the few indications available to Cold War intelligence of a significant change of mission for Soviet groupings.

Important details of what may have been the first exercising of this new front in June 1965 have only become available with the opening of Hungarian military archives. US intelligence had been unaware of at least the scenario, or even the occurrence, of this exercise. Fragmentary documentation[569] from the archives represents a Southwestern Front formed on the basis of the SGF including an air army staffed by the Group aviation headquarters; 36 Air Army had existed since at least October 1965[570] but the precise creation date is uncertain. The exercise proceeded under the nuclear variant, with mobilization only after the outbreak of war, and an offensive from permanent garrisons. Staffs derived from, and represented, the Hungarian 5 Army and the Soviet 28 Army Corps based in the western Carpathian MD. The four Soviet divisions in Hungary lacked attribution separately or as an army with no particular indications of regrouping to the adjacent Western Front (which had at least one subordinate Czech army). The variant Soviet reinforcement of the Czech front apparently presented such a critical factor that no alteration had been planned even to strengthen the offensive capability of the revamped Hungary-based front.

Documents specify a scenario in which Westerners prepare a surprise attack using the exercise cover method, advancing with nuclear strikes at the outset. The front plan initiated an offensive directly from unit garrisons, prior to full mobilization—there is no reference to any defensive phase—seemingly a preemptive assault. A document reference to the Easterners conducting a secret partial mobilization during a period of tension had been lined out on the original. Two thrusts by the front would, north of the Alps, cooperate with the Western Front flanking to the north in "annihilating the Munich grouping of the enemy" then continue across the Alps into northern Italy, joining a southern thrust against the Italians. A few Austrian brigades along the direction apparently considered a minor nuisance. The prior defensive orientation of Warsaw Pact forces in the region had been jettisoned.

Perchance the operational direction of the northern thrust, the Alpine, had been recently created specifically to accommodate the expanded first echelon; supplementing the existing North Italian and Adriatic Operational Directions in the Italian Strategic Direction. Later information would define the Alpine Operational Direction having a width of 180- to 240-km and a depth of 550-km; with a capacity of only six to eight divisions in the mountainous terrain. Unfortunately the authors of the 1988 Warsaw Pact NIE despite their belated recognition of the significance of operational "axes" continued unaware of these, already disseminated, specifications; much ink expended regarded an advance along the Danube Valley Operational (Direction) supposedly inconsistent with a "Linz approach" (the Alpine Direction) that would be of greater value.[571] The revised lineup would subject the "Munich grouping" of US and FRG corps to the combined attacks of three first echelon fronts—one thrust by a strike grouping of a GSFG-based front; the entire Czech front; and the northern strike grouping of the Soviet-Hungarian front. The Soviets would thus be able to execute one of the conventional attack methods prominent in operational guides, strike groupings converging to encircle the enemy or pin his assemblage against a convenient obstacle—such as the Alps. The second echelon Carpathian-based front could then amplify this onslaught and in some exercises a Kiev MD front joined in for the drive across France.

Unfortunately for the troops of the "Munich grouping" US intelligence only became aware of any offensive threat from the direction of Hungary more than a decade later when the Southwest Front turned up in *Soyuz* 1977. Marshal V. G. Kulikov directed this operational command-staff exercise;[572] achieving a degree of realism by the "actual deployment and relocation of control posts" from front to battalion level.[573] Scenario depicted the front repulsing NATO forces with a counteroffensive into Austria and Italy. An exercise document found in Czech archives supposed a surprise-conventional attack by NATO which included violation of Austrian neutrality as well as information on the task of the Czech Central Front.[574] The Southwest Front lineup basically replicated that of the June 1965 exercise with the main differences that the Soviet army corps played now resided in Czechoslovakia and a Hungarian army corps had joined their combined-arms army; available information does not particularize the disposition of the four Soviet divisions of the SGF.

The January 1979 NIE on Warsaw Pact forces[575] ushered the first intelligence assessments to discover the existence of a front that had been deliberately reconstituted by 1965 for offensive action; yet still failed to recognize that the front immediate objective lay in the southern FRG. An annotated map in the NIE clearly shows a Danube Front advance into Austria and Italy that entirely bypasses West German territory. Awareness of the Alpine Operational Direction might have clarified but of course the NIE authors had no clue regarding the significance and purpose of the Soviet directions—hidden beyond their, and intell contemporaries, perceptual blinders. A Balaton Front would appear in a number of exercises into the 1980s. The June 1980 exercise of the Balaton Front depicted a mainly Soviet '4' Army comprised of SGF divisions, reinforced by divisions from the Kiev MD, driving the length of Italy and crossing to Sicily; the Hungarian '12' Army and '10' Corps capturing Austrian territory from Vienna to Salzburg, then into Italy, halting in the north by D+23; while an army of unidentified provenance in the bordering Morava Front advanced from Czechoslovakia toward Munich, there receiving Hungarian assistance.[576] Scenario required the Balaton Front to modify plans upon detection of Yugoslavian armed forces alerting. In *Soyuz* 1984 the first echelon 5 Front played in a Pact counteroffensive against Austrians, Italians, and West Germans. This *Soyuz*, and other exercises, depicted the Carpathian MD 38 Combined-Arms Army regrouping to establish the front second echelon; a continuing demonstration of the trans-border character of Soviet strategic deployment. At least as early as 1968 Carpathian exercises dealt with issues involved in committing a combined-arms army from a regrouping march into a battle already in progress.[577]

A 1980 article—among the most informative regarding several key issues acquired by intell—of the Hungarian military journal *Honvedelem*[578] deviated from usually staid technical material. General-Major Tibor Toth outlined offensive actions on named strategic and operational directions. Revelation of this Warsaw Pact war plan variant is a unique and amazing occurrence for a secret level publication; but the article had been received only by September 1985. The Soviet and Hungarian complement of the "coalition front" attacking in the Italian Strategic Direction would comprise from one to three combined-arms armies and one or two army corps. The Soviet contribution not specified, at least one of the armies and one corps would obviously be Hungarian. The first echelon Hungarian army would advance in the North Italian Operational Direction; cross the Alps through Austria into the Trieste-Venice region; and by conducting two successive army operations across a depth of 200- to 300-km in ten to fifteen days fulfill the front immediate objective at the Adriatic coast. There defensive positions would be prepared. The more rapid schedule could be achieved in the nuclear variant by drawing on the 50 to 60 nuclear weapons allocated to the army. A highlighted operational innovation involved employment of front and army operational maneuver groups (OMG).

The persistent intelligence difficulty in identifying Soviet and Warsaw Pact fronts and their directions had been exemplified by the failure to 'predict' the 1968 Czech invasion; actually, as

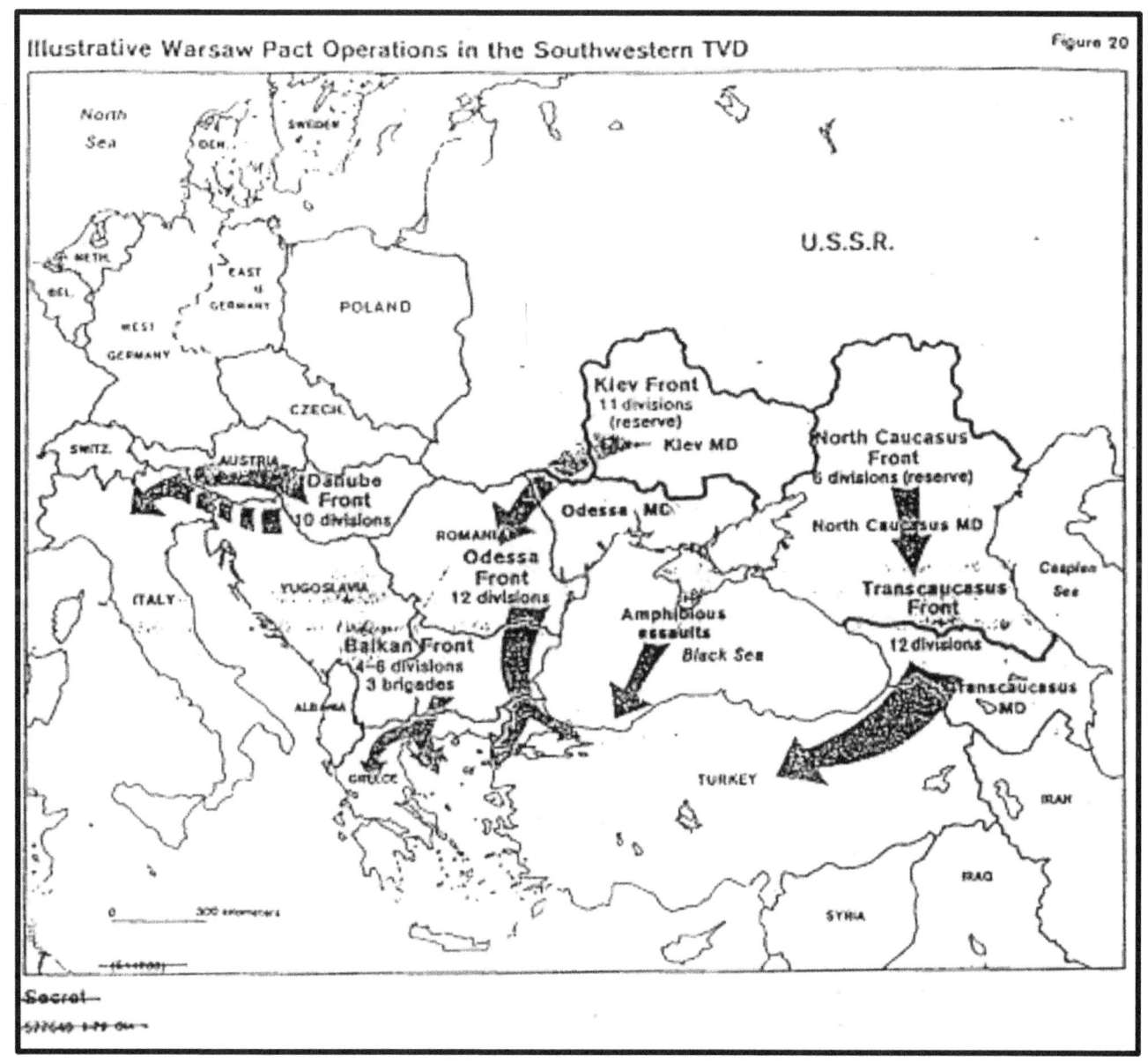

1979 NIE DEPICTED THE DANUBE FRONT ENTIRELY BYPASSING NOT ONLY THE 'MUNICH GROUPING' BUT ALSO THE FEDERAL REPUBLIC

often the case during the Cold War, as much a policy as an intelligence dereliction. Signals intelligence generally tracked the movements of armies and divisions—especially after the fact—but the Soviets successfully obscured the ultimate destination using the exercise cover. But intelligence never did realize that Warsaw Pact invasion forces had been organized as three fronts. Russian accounts have detailed the composition and missions of the Central, Carpathian, and Southern Fronts cobbled together to strike into Czechoslovakia from multiple points.[579] This grouping of fronts for a strategic operation had been precisely the instigation for creating the Operation Danube *glavkom* to coordinate diverse ground and air formations.

The post 1968 deployment of Soviet divisions and other units in Czechoslovakia **exactly** replicated the lineup indicated in the mid 1960s plan and exercises. Three CGF divisions in the western part of the country could form an army and assume the tasks of the army formerly regrouped from the SGF. The forward relocation of 28 Army Corps to Olomouc would enable the execution of a front mission in the Alpine Operational Direction from an advanced position that avoided a time-consuming march from the Carpathian MD. But this repositioning also presented another potential variant. Implementing the well-rehearsed regrouping of SGF divisions to the South German Strategic Direction two first echelon armies (CGF and SGF) would then be available to form a Soviet front that could augment—or replace—the Czech front; reinforced from the Soviet second or third operational echelon. Potential variants included a solely Soviet front or one reinforced with Czech armies and divisions; a national front with substantial Soviet add-ons—or both fronts. By coincidence no doubt the fourth front in the TVD first echelon that had been discovered by the 1988 Warsaw Pact NIE could thereby initially be fulfilled by forward armies rather than by regroupings from a western district. In subsequent exercises by or involving the CGF both army and front roles continued to be major themes. Thus during *Zapad* 1984, in which no Czech front appeared, the CGF played as a first echelon front, while in several exercises in the following years the group still formed an army within a Czech front.

## nonnuclear variant

The contingent of first strategic echelon fronts designated to initiate operations under nuclear conditions during the Initial Period in the strategic directions had, by the late 1960s, been augmented by new fronts in two directions to boost thrusts against NATO when eschewing the ultimate weapon. The renewed emphasis on conventional operations, and consequent resurrection of the grouped fronts variant—as rearranged in the Western TVD operational echelons—would over the next decade lead to adjustments to both the scale and control of nonnuclear warfare. Development of the conventional variant concurrently occasioned a wide-ranging consideration of the nature, scope, and responsibilities of intermediate theater commands. Exercise *Zapad* 1977 represented the pivot point for this nonnuclear variant as well as for strategic coordination in TVDs.

NATO had initially tested a conventional variant to the start of war in 1964 exercises. Intelligence had identified the Warsaw Pact 1965 Narew exercise as the first in which there had been an opening conventional phase,[580] however brief—this conclusion based on the classified critique of the exercise that had been acquired by early 1967.[581] The critique had characterized NATO exercises of 1964 and 1965 as a "radical departure" from the established massive retaliation nuclear strategy. However archive documents point to a more immediate reaction to the NATO strategy revision, in the 1964 *Sputnik* exercise series, and that the Warsaw Pact considered exercise year 1965 as a period of intensified study of combat without nuclear weapons.[582] The 1964 reorganization of the Soviet group in East Germany—redistributing the three divisions of one army to strengthen other forward armies—added to the mounting evidence for nonnuclear prioritization. This particular action-reaction cycle highlights the mutual close monitoring of opposing exercise patterns. Strangely the Soviets insisted that NATO exercises constituted direct indication of intentions, representing actual war plans, even while proclaiming that their own exercises did not signify a strategic offensive strategy. Exercises from the mid 1960s would frequently include an opening conventional phase that did not exceed six combat days prior to nuclear initiation.

The General Staff Academy 1974 textbook[583] indicated that 1966-1967 exercise experience with the incipient conventional phase had reduced the anticipated depth of a front first offensive to 600- to 800-km; in a slightly narrower zone of 350- to 400-km; requiring 9 to 12 days; at an average 60- to 70-kmd. This projection that rates of advance could still reach those of the previous nuclear outset variant reflected the expectation of an early transition to nuclear weapons by the sides. By 1974 further exercising of the conventional variant, while retaining offensive depth, had curtailed the expected average rate of advance to 40- to 60-kmd, prolonging the operation duration by three days. The scenario of *Zapad* 1977 had depicted nuclear exchanges beginning on day nine. Exercises into the 1980s would feature increasingly prolonged conventional battles during offensives across Europe. By the mid 1980s the Academy projected a front initial operation in the Western TVD slightly reduced in depth at 600- to 700-km; markedly slowed at 40- to 50-kmd—but now considered the zippier variant due to the wide extent of nuclear destruction—extending duration range by three days.[584] Conventional weapons in both camps underwent a renaissance in technology, diversification, and force saturation.

Efforts by both sides to enhance conventional capabilities would propel development of a new generation of precision deep strike weapons that would eventually attain what some enthusiasts considered mass destruction equivalence. NATO staffs from late 1979 had begun developing an amendment to Flexible Response with these weapons—while not abandoning the nuclear first-use variant. FOFA or follow-on forces attack sought to enhance flexibility of NATO response options by striking 400-km or more against communications, airfields and other installations, troop and materiel movement choke points and, notably, oncoming troops of the second operational echelon. NATO began to implement this approach in the first half of the 1980s.[585] This innovation confronted the Soviets with a potential obstacle to regrouping fronts and armies on a scale not expected since the nuclear variant of the early 1960s. Renewed emphasis on pre-combat forward deployment became evident in exercises, this confirmed in a regrouping retrospective that appeared in a 2004 article by General-Lieutenant Ye. I. Malashenko in the unclassified edition of VM. The author characterized 1960s, and 1980s, exercises as having similar themes.[586]

> The exercises proved that the best course of action is to move up troops during periods of threat preceding outbreak of hostilities. This precluded big losses and disruption of moving the troops up. Relatively favorable conditions could develop at the start of combat operations with the use of exclusively conventional weapons. The moving of troops from the country's interior over great distances tended to be very problematic in [a] nuclear environment because the enemy with nuclear weapons can employ them on a massive scale thus disrupting the moving of troops and committing them to battle.

Marshal N. V. Ogarkov is quoted, in a *Zapad* archive document evaluating the 1977 exercise, concluding that the Warsaw Pact first echelon complement balanced that of the NATO enemy, despite 60 per cent of the assigned TVD forces still at a distance of 300- to 1200-km.[587] A July 1985 exercise depicted enemy interdiction, using precision weapons strikes and destroying bridges, of a front regrouping from the Carpathian MD, this in the South German Strategic Direction. The capability to move fronts forward prior to the outbreak of hostilities, and without hindrance—critical to the nationals-free variants—had been played out several times in the early 1980s, notably *Tsentr* 1982 and *Zapad* 1984.

The first team lineup had been established by the 1970s but variations in deployment, along with improvements in conventional armament and methods, would be relentlessly pursued. Another GPW spin-off, the OMG, an organizational-operational approach to conventional penetration into the depth of a defense, caused considerable excitement in the 1980s among the NATO and intelligence cognoscenti. Interviews with General Staff officers in the 1990s[588] confirmed that the OMG composed one element of a developing Deep Operation concept—essentially the revival of the 1930s version in a non-WMD format—that renewed confidence in an offensive that could traverse Europe, and reach the Channel, nearly as quickly as the nuclear variant. In their view such a rapid advance could disrupt any NATO organized resort to even limited nuclear weapons employment. The massive SS-20 mobile IRBM force acted as a further deterrent to any NATO nuclear defense variant.

By the mid 1980s the Soviets envisioned that a tank army might function as a front OMG—likely the instigator for rebalancing of 20 Guards Army in the GSFG—with army OMG based on tank and motor rifle divisions. Testing also underway for consideration as front OMG reformed some divisions as corps under the RVGK banner organized in a brigade structure.[589] Acting independently of both first and second echelons a front OMG would conduct "raiding actions" throughout the front zone; key tasks included striking enemy nuclear means and other targets previously assigned in the front initial nuclear strike.[590] But exercising of the OMG method dropped off sharply concurrently with the next major operational adjustment.

### strategic defense variant

An unforeseen opportunity in 1986 for some practical work under nuclear conditions impelled the mobilization of some of the more specialized subordinates of a front. The explosive event at the Chernobyl nuclear power plant on 26 April quickly attracted the unwanted attention of the world especially those downwind. The Kiev MD already had a scheduled exercise underway including deployment of a front command post; which eventually relocated to the Chernobyl area to coordinate military involvement. The Soviet General Staff and even the new peacetime high commands in the Southwestern and Western TVDs took an interest in the action as did the front commands of at least two other MDs. The major military contribution came in the fielding of a truncated version of what Soviet logisticians called a rear front base—the largest complex of depots and rear services units of a front in wartime. The eyes and ears of intelligence closely monitored the unfolding response.

Mobilization-deployment reality played out as reservists filled units and regrouped including two chemical defense brigades from distant MD.[591] Integration of civilian truck fleets took place just as in wartime. Medical bases activated; a contingent from the Leningrad Military Medical Academy showed up for some realistic radiation exposure treatment on a scale that could not have been matched in nuclear war games and modeling. Notable measures involved the mobilization and regrouping of chemical, medical, and civil defense regiments from as distant as Siberia (which required about two weeks) as well as nearby districts just as would have taken place to support a wartime front. Chernobyl must have provided a good workout for the radiation reconnaissance and decontamination units that assembled at the rear front base. Selected combat troops from motorized and tank divisions augmented the reaction force. Even pipeline units mobilized and deployed to pump in water for cleanup operations. Many of these troops suffered serious radiation exposure but still on a scale that would scarcely compare to that of the mass strikes envisioned for the nuclear battlefield.

The disaster at Chernobyl occurred amidst the implementation of a fundamental revision of the Western strategic operation. At the 1987 Warsaw Pact meeting in Berlin an official defensive stance had been proclaimed in the 29 May statement of the Political Consultative Committee, later issued as the document *On The Military Doctrine of the Warsaw Treaty Member States*.[592]

> The combat readiness of the armed forces of the allied states is maintained at a sufficient level so as not to be caught unaware. In the event of an attack, they will give a devastating rebuff to the aggressor.

The USSR foreign ministry in a 1 June briefing would be even more assertive.

> The crux of the Warsaw Pact's military doctrine is as follows: The Warsaw Pact's member states will never, in any circumstances, begin military actions against any state or alliance of states whatsoever, if they themselves are not the object of an armed attack. They will never use nuclear weapons first.

But this pronouncement culminated rather than initiated a significant pivot involving more than the political re-direction instigated by General Secretary M. S. Gorbachev ongoing since 1985. Apparently the proclamation met with some disquiet among Soviet senior officers including the Combined Armed Forces commander, Marshal V. G. Kulikov, who in October stressed that "renunciation of preemptive action would result in certain military-strategic advantages for the aggressor, since he can choose the time to unleash a war, and get his forces and equipment fully ready."[593]

Defense had always been an integral part of Soviet military doctrine but definition and operational content differed substantially from the perspective of the designated opponents. As put in a 1963 VM (S) article by the General Staff Chief, Marshal M. V. Zakharov:[594]

> Our doctrine is offensive. It is based on the premise that the state provides the armed forces with powerful weapons for the accomplishment of its aggressive tasks. Thus conducting a defense on a large operational scale, to say nothing of doing so on a strategic scale, would be unacceptable in a future war.

The Soviet view, consistent through most of the Cold War, insistently portrayed defense as a 'forced' and 'temporary' measure taken in unusual situations, on particular directions, and only by lower-level formations.

Previously not always doctrinal at the end of the 1950s strategic defense had been rejected—defending would be to repeat the great error of the GPW–awaiting an enemy assault (while ignoring valid intelligence indications) rather than preempting. Defense on a strategic scale became no longer tenable under conditions of possible surprise mass nuclear strikes which by then had attained an intercontinental capability. Some Soviet officers argued that defense had no meaning in nuclear conditions while others stipulated defense acceptable as a last resort when few nuclear munitions remained. Not that defense ensued aberrational; through the Cold War exercises rarely caught the Warsaw Pact initiating a clear-cut preemptive attack. Defense against presumptive NATO assaults had been so accomplished that defensive phases, particularly if prolonged, rarely featured in Warsaw Pact exercises, and then only as a background scenario. Most exercise play focused on the usual crushing (counter)offensive.

The revamped Soviet consensus held that a defensive posture might be assumed in secondary TVDs and directions although some argued that defense would be conceivable even in a main TVD. Defense might be a likely method by a ground army but only rarely by a front. All rejected strategic defense as both a military and ideological impossibility. Colonel I. Rachok in a 1968 VM (S) article provided a rare contemporary, comprehensive and definitive, treatment of defense at the outset of a strategic operation.[595] He examined several scenarios in both the "non-nuclear period" and the "period of nuclear actions" involving resort to a defense. In either period a defensive stance might be acceptable on individual directions of a TVD by an army or even a front if weakened by enemy preemptive nuclear strikes or when confronted by superior forces in non-nuclear conditions. Colonel I. Lyutov in a 1970 article which focused on the conventional variant allowed that, although the "basic form" would be an offensive, defensive actions might be necessary by a division, army, even on the scale of a front to be conducted in specified situations.[596]

Archival material assessment points to the 1984 edition of *Tarcza/Shchit*, held in Czechoslovakia, as the first occurrence of a full defensive phase in Warsaw Pact exercises—but subsequent play dealt with an all out offensive; the theme of a senior staff exercise the next year stipulated a defensive strategic deployment.[597] A (retrospective) pinpointing of a Soviet turnabout regarding strategic defense has been provided by Siegfried Lautsch from his position as chief of the East German Military District V operations department from 1983 to 1986.[598] In 1985 the basis for planning the initial combat actions of 5 Army had been altered by Soviet instruction to the defense, with a subsequent counteroffensive—which appears much like the original offensive plan—to be completed by the end of the year. During a meeting held on 3 December 1984 between the visiting Marshal S. F. Akhromeyev with GDR General H. Hoffman the new Chief of the USSR General Staff had provided the Germans with an introduction to the revised scheme.[599] A senior Czech commander provided independent confirmation that work on a new operations plan began in the autumn of 1985.[600]

By 1985 defense on any scale had become a feasibility to the Soviets, the MoD tasking the troops in the training year for "the in-depth comprehensive development, study, and practical assimilation of the methods of preparing and conducting a strategic and operational defense" and as further indicated by the USSR General Staff Academy[601]

> A front defensive operation in a main western theater of military actions will usually be a component of a strategic offensive operation and be conducted in the interests of the main grouping of troops. For the far eastern theaters, a strategic operation at the very outset of a war may begin with defensive actions.

The Academy attributed the reversal to the "growing possibility of a surprise attack" in a situation in which the strategic deployment of troops had not been completed, specifying the new threat of cruise missiles—presumably those recently based in Western Europe. Views on a front "offensive-defensive" first operation receiving discussion in VM articles; citing many examples of front defensive operations during the GPW; while stressing that the modern version had undergone radical changes.

Dispensing with preemptive variants had been reflected in major exercises. By 1986 to the end of the Soviet period a Defensive Strategic Operation, sometimes designating a Front Defensive Operation, had become a new form of strategic action in the Western TVD. The scenario of the 1988 Warsaw Pact command-staff exercise *Tarcza* depicts the GK of the Western TVD ordering the conduct of a Front Defensive Operation.[602] A pivotal revisionary indication came with the near disappearance from exercises of OMGs (an eminently bellicose component of the preceding offensive strategic operation). The OMG concept represented a leading barometer of both offensive planning—and reversal. While the OMG had been prominent in many exercises from at least 1979 until the end of 1986, in the following years performances became a rare event. In 1991 a Soviet general pinpointed the defensive reorientation as the reason for the elimination of the OMG.[603]

The intelligence perspective regarding this apparent new Soviet emphasis on strategic defense became entangled with views on the political actuality of Gorbachev era policy. At the infamous 1988 House briefing Douglas MacEachin had no doubt that the supposed change demonstrated a subterfuge.[604]

> We have heard much of late about the "defensive" nature of Soviet doctrine, Soviet exercises have increasingly portrayed NATO as initiating offensive operations before the Pact is fully ready to go on the offensive…But this is still the strategic offensive; it is merely undertaken under more stressful circumstances…As to the question of what impact Gorbachev has had on our view of these issues, we would say that on the operational strategy [sic] and force posture—not much so far.

That the CIA continued to hew to the line that the Soviets had misrepresented their new defensive military doctrine would be reiterated in a 1989 SOVA Research Paper[605] which concluded that Gorbachev "new thinking" had no military ramifications. In an interesting twist on the intent vs. capability conundrum the author stressed the difficulty of distinguishing armed forces configured for only a counteroffensive rather than a strategic offensive. By 1990 the expressed intell perception shifted to the new reality, attributed to Gorbachev despite substantial evidence that defense as a strategy predated, while emphasizing a contextual "nightmare" of Warsaw Pact collapse and Soviet withdrawals.[606]

A divergent reality had been offered by other observers. In mid 1988 an outside British expert on the Soviet military, Christopher Donnelly differed with intelligence in his book *Red Banner*. Concerning the seeming de-emphasis on the offensive "So far, it appears to me that Soviet statements and proposals on this issue have been consistent and rational, and denote a significant but by no means fundamental change in attitude"—assuming use of only open sources.[607] A 1992 study of Soviet military doctrine plotted thematics in the open VM and VIZ from 1975 to 1989 noting an obvious abrupt soaring in defense consideration beginning in late 1985 along with sharply curtailed offense discussion. Detailing evolution of views in the 1980s, Gorbachev still received credit for the defense modification.[608]

A constant in all variants, however, through to the end of the Cold War, the nuclear edge of the WMD axe hovering over Europe.

# Nuclear Interlude

Nuclear variant intelligence, in a yawning disparity with the other categories of WMD, had a sound basis in evidence occasioning relatively credible reporting. The variety and quantity of sources developed by the US and other Western intelligence services—exercises, classified documents and writings, emigres and defectors—accumulated a vast database of working material. Assessments of trends and many of the details transpired largely realistic, even when viewed with the infinite wisdom of hindsight. Lack of access to the highest politico-military level, however, meant that some vexing issues could not be definitively resolved—notably intentions, the conditions that would impel nuclear initiation, and precise attitudes to limitation of scale. Intelligence could provide no unequivocal answer to the most crucial question of whether US-NATO restricted or 'demonstrative' nuclear strikes would evoke a response in kind or a massive preemptive destruction of Europe and beyond. Available evidence uniformly reflected views and plans asserting the viability of nuclear warfighting. Intelligence had been unaware that nuclear skepticism existed at the highest level of the General Staff—doubts that remained hidden from military subordinates—and post Cold War testimony has revealed discrepant views within the Soviet hierarchy.[609]

The 1960 Revolution proclaimed by Soviet military theoreticians assigned preeminence to nuclear weapons, specifically those delivered by missiles, as an integral of strategic and theater action. When examined in detail, however, expectations for the theater segment appear more like a classic case of military planning based on the last war; employment on European battlefields, on a massive scale, weapons never used in any form of combat, with a degree of destructive effects that defied rational modeling. Technical characteristics exceeded, by an order of magnitude, the conceptual dexterity of military conservatism. The early Big Bangers proposed that a relatively small-scale ground advance would be sufficient to exploit a nuclear spasm. General-Major M. Goryainov while acknowledging "unnecessary to completely destroy everything" considered that the problem of the enemy in the West "is solved" by plastering Europe with a mere hundred 2-mt weapons.[610] Another general in late 1961 supported with detailed nuclear effects calculations his proposal to eliminate the front command in favor of a "nuclear/missile army" striking in coordination with a combined-arms army.[611]

But the Soviet military leaders directing the Revolution represented the generation forged during the GPW. Mesmerized by the expansive formations of that era, their strategic culture remained obsessed with scale, whether in the form of troops, armament—or mass destruction weapons—and they opted for continued reliance on a large, mobilized force. This modern phalanx, albeit employing new methods, would inevitably have widely varying levels of leadership skill and unit training. But the character of postulated operations—a rapid and decisive offensive requiring exquisite coordination in unprecedented conditions—could realistically only have been accomplished by a select, highly proficient force. Ironically the early 1960s Soviet proponents of a relatively small ground force exploiting massive nuclear strikes may have had a, partly, correct solution. A small, highly trained and skillfully led, contingent employing nuclear weapons in limited numbers against carefully selected targets might fracture NATO defenses and develop in depth before the opposition could assess the situation and bring their nukes into play.

Employment of nuclear weapons on a mass, surprise basis inaugurated a capability to decide the course of war at the outset, the consequence an impulse to strike first. Concentration of efforts could now be achieved through nuclear strikes rather than by aggregating troops at selected points for defense breakthrough. Operational prescriptions, however, seemed rather to be built upon, with modification of, principles and experience acquired at great cost during the GPW. There appeared to be such a degree of grafting of old and new that some articles in the unclassified *Military Historical Journal* afforded insights comparable to compartmentalized writings. The GPW constituted a database and fixed point of reference continuously retrieved in both classified and open discussions.

Soviet theoreticians during at least the first decade of the Revolution stressed nuclear weapons as the principle of a military campaign rather than merely a strategic deterrent. Victory on a nuclear battlefield would be possible and the East the winner. Western perspectives and argumentation on the actuality of a Warsaw Pact nuclear warfighting stance received 'assistance' by Soviet denials. Cold War pundits insisted that the public statements seemed aimed more at inhibiting a NATO escalatory strategy than a representation of political views—in particular any limited nuclear variant. Senior Soviet officers in the 1990s interviews confirmed that they believed any acknowledgment of nuclear limitation could induce early NATO use. They equated preparations for nuclear warfighting to deterrence, the Western differentiation unrecognized. According to one general, General Staff Chief N. V. Ogarkov rejected any nuclear limitation since NATO might be more inclined to selected use if they believed the USSR would respond at the same level; other senior officers had been more open to a limited variant.[612] A speech by L. I. Brezhnev at Tula in January 1977 rejected the possibility of victory in a nuclear war, such an option not a reliable instrument of policy since there could be no limitation of scale;[613] a dismissal not evident in the manuals and other literature obtained by intelligence nor in exercise practice.

General Staff officers retrospectively claimed that in the early 1970s studies had been commissioned to evaluate the realities of nuclear warfare. The essential conclusion of this operational modeling that in conditions of large scale nuclear strikes all operations in the European theaters would come to a halt. Some came to believe that theater mass nuclear weapons strikes could not be a plausible method; an assessment not welcomed when presented in 1973 to the Chief of the General Staff V. G. Kulikov (although he understood the findings) and others at the highest political-military level—with dissemination beyond the General Staff prohibited that mass nuclear weapons employment manifested a chimera.[614] Ideologically repugnant and unacceptable that the socialist camp could not prevail even in a general nuclear war, framed in the mid 1960s by a Party military journal, denial of a nuclear victory "...would be not only untrue theoretically but dangerous from a political point of view."[615] Three years later a high-ranker, in the restricted version of VM, flayed fellow Soviets writing in the open press who suggested that nuclear war would be a mutual catastrophe.[616]

> The fundamental line of our party is expressed here with utmost clarity and accuracy: if imperialism commits a crime and plunges mankind into the abyss of nuclear war, it will perish, and not "both sides," not socialism, although the socialist countries, too will face supreme tests and will suffer tremendous sacrifices.

The Central Committee of the CPSU ordered continued development of theater nuclear weapons and war plans integrally featuring application. Despite any doubts among the leaders concerning the realities of nuclear war regardless of scale nuclear play in exercises and discussion in writings persisted. Nevertheless, increased attention began to be given by the General Staff to concepts of nuclear limitation. The political belittling of professional military assessments not a trait confined to communist regimes or even to the Cold War. Western ideologues past (and present) quite capable of comparable strategic behavior, witness the Bush-Cheney-Rumsfeld rejection of discordant views prior to the 2003 Iraq invasion. The careers of the respective message-bearers could even be at risk of early termination.

Nuclear arrows occupied the Soviet quiver until The End and not necessarily as an imposition by NATO. Some scholars maintained in elaborate constructs—official models are not confined to intelligence—that the Soviet military-technical prescription emphasizing nuclear warfare should be strictly dissociated from political intent. Soviet officers wandered about on their own preparing measures not necessarily intended for actual employment. Senior officer retrospectives on at least the Brezhnev era depicted a political-military disjunctive supervision with the latter given considerable freedom to implement nuclear-saturated measures.[617] But if military planning for nuclear operations persisted throughout the Cold War, actions precisely reflected a nuclear variant considered by the leadership as a viable option to be retained for all eventualities. "Soviet military doctrine expresses the views and directives of the Communist Party and the Soviet government on all aspects of the vital activity of the state in wartime" as instructed by the *Officer's Handbook* in expansive treatment on the subordination of strategy to politics.[618] WMD variants continued to be prepared as ordained, or at least sanctioned, by the Supreme High Command.

Several crucial distinctions between Western and Eastern perspectives on the role of nuclear weapons encompassed strike depth, yield—and controllability. Soviet plans emphasized destruction to the full depth of theaters as well as high yield nuclear targeting. Western opponents favored small yields largely against targets in tactical depth. Soviet officers in the 1960s, preeminently missileers, ridiculed NATO for an over-reliance on aviation for longer range nuclear weapons strikes which they considered vulnerable to supposedly impenetrable air defense missiles. But in later years the aviation story line would be revised. Flexible Response supposed an academic-like deliberate selection from a scaleable menu of weapons options. Soviet civil and military commentators pointed to the inevitability of escalation to unlimited nuclear war. An outbreak of war in Europe would entail a mutual striving of opposing coalitions to seek a decisive victory, an ineluctable conclusion from the lessons of history. An offensive at high rates would exploit NATO weaknesses—the ponderous political consultation preceding action and poorly coordinated force alerting—while forestalling European mobilization and transatlantic reinforcement. The logic of such a conflict entailed the employment of whatever weapons would achieve the desired results. General-Colonel P. I. Ivashutin, head of the Soviet Main Intelligence Directorate, characterized the high stakes of a European war which engendered the consideration of all military solutions in a 1964 memo.[619]

> A nuclear strike against the vital centers of a country, against its economy, its system of state administration, its strategic nuclear forces, and other armed forces is the fastest and most reliable way of achieving victory over the aggressor....Nuclear war cannot be long; it will inevitably be short, quick as lightning, because each side would have to use all its might to defeat the enemy in the shortest time. The initial stage of such a war will have the decisive importance ...the stage of most intense massive nuclear strikes.

sounding rather like that of the (now) Warsaw Pact Commander of Combined Armed Forces, Marshal V. G. Kulikov, following exercise *Soyuz* 1983, as quoted in an East German document.[620]

> ...a future war will be carried out relentlessly until the total defeat of the enemy is achieved. This compels us to take into account the entire arsenal of weapons of mass destruction, with the uncontrollable dimensions of strategic actions.

Soviet commanders and staffs engaged in continual practice of nuclear warfare but clearly without expectation of a cakewalk. Classified documents and exercise scenarios depicted Pact military victory despite heavy losses. Soviet theoreticians anticipated the GPW model of forward progress in the midst of appalling casualties during WMD battles. Exercise scenarios sometimes featured an operational pause between nuclear exchanges for reconstitution of forces—the Easterners always seemed to forestall their enemies in resuming combat. Failure to react quickly would mean loss of operational initiative. The Soviet attitude of nuclear 'soldiering on' had been expressed in the 1963 General Staff ground operations manual.[621]

> Even if only a small composite detachment remains of a division, and only small groups of soldiers remain of a regiment or battalion, they must resolutely and boldly fulfill the assigned tasks, bearing in mind that it is no easier for the enemy and that his remaining forces are no greater.

Larger scale exercises of the 1970s to mid 1980s in particular depicted the damaging effects of nuclear exchanges. Exercises of individual fronts, whether in East Germany or in military districts across the USSR to the Far East, commonly depicted loss assessments, units consolidation, and planning by staffs down to division level to recover from mass nuclear strikes in order to resume an advance.

A 1969 General Staff Academy document on rear services, in a section on medical support, indicated that, from exercise experience and research, a front in the nuclear variant could expect to sustain overall troop losses of up to 30 to 35 percent of which 23 percent would be inflicted by nuclear bursts and residual radiation.[622] The 1974 General Staff Academy front operations textbook calculated that losses in the nuclear variant would reach 35 percent overall, compared to a high of 13.5 percent during conventional operations.[623] Similar odds presented in the Academy's 1977 lecture on front operations added a daily troop loss forecast of 2.0 to 2.65 percent in nuclear conditions versus 0.8 to 0.9 percent when using only conventional weapons.[624] Recovered *Zapad* 1977 documents assessed surviving post-exchange Warsaw Pact forces at 36 percent viable but severely limited in capability—their side even lost more divisions than NATO, left in a comparable state[625]—while in the 1984 edition of *Zapad* Soviet planners projected nuclear losses of up to 60 percent versus 27 percent in the conventional variant.

**sharing the load**

The Soviets viewed mass nuclear strikes as an incomparable method for the 'intensification of efforts' deemed crucial to their style of war-fighting. Offensive intensification had been accomplished in the GPW by a mighty pile-on of ground troops. Strategic missiles based in the USSR would strike targets in depth throughout the several TVDs invulnerable to the attrition that would be inflicted on aviation strike elements. Mass nuclear strikes by first echelon fronts supplemented those of the strategic means. But as the Revolution progressed improvements in front capabilities expanded the role of these formations to the point of autonomy. A 'strategic nuclear demarcation line' marked the firebreak between strategic and frontal strikes throughout the Cold War preset by VGK directive in each strategic direction; delineated by the 1977 General Staff Academy lecture on front operations.[626]

> The Supreme High Command can indicate the depth of or demarcation line between the strikes of the strategic and the front nuclear means, as well as areas in the zone of the front in which enemy targets are hit with means of the Supreme High Command.

Also stipulated by the Academy in 1985 among the elements of a front operation plan.[627]

> ...the Strategic Rocket Forces are responsible for the destruction of all targets beyond a certain line, and the front nuclear forces and means are responsible for all the targets up to that line.

Typically defined by a line of cities, the inhabitants of The Hague-Antwerp-Liège-Nancy-Strasbourg-Munich-Innsbruck-Venice remained blissfully unaware that they held such significance in Soviet nuclear plans.

During the early 1960s the Line ranged 300- to 400-km beyond frontiers, contracting to about 250-km in the 1970s—the strike depth of the R-300 (Scud B) missile—with some later indications of a boundary only 100-km into FRG territory.[628] Reapportionment of nuclear strike zones concurrently expanded the territory of Western Europe exposed to higher yield strategic systems while boosting the density of frontal detonations; which would be delivered by an inventory of ground and air delivery systems that steadily increased during these decades. Specific factors involved in the calculation not available to intelligence may have included declining postulated rates of advance during the conventional variant along with reduction in the depth of front first offensive missions—the Line sometimes related to the front immediate objective. NATO had also adopted a Forward Defense posture in 1963 that relocated corps deployments closer to the border. Another potential factor, in the 1980s, entailed insertion between fronts and strategic systems of strike assets reassigned to the TVD high commands. But by the mid 1980s the introduction of new missile systems and modernized aviation had markedly increased the range of frontal strike assets. The General Staff Academy stressed the importance of strategic strikes in preparing the path for advances of the fronts in a 1969 lecture on the role of the Rocket Troops and Artillery arm.[629]

> Under the conditions of general nuclear war, the success of a front (army) offensive operation will be decisively affected by the actions of the strategic nuclear forces (primarily by the actions of the medium-range strategic rocket forces) to defeat the main grouping of enemy troops in the theater of military actions.

A 1970 presentation by the Professor[630] still held to a 300- to 400-km interval from the points of troop combat even though a few years earlier in VM (S)[631] he had cited 1964-1965 General Staff war gaming which set the initial Line at 170- to 250-km from national borders. But a Warsaw Pact classified seminar on the theater strategic operation the same year gave that distance as 200- to 300-km equated to the River Rhine.[632] Seminar material also noted that the Line would be advanced with the progress of the offensive which would have meant a continually rolling demarcation during the conventional variant. In the 1976 Warsaw Pact exercise *Tarcza/Shchit* the Northern Front received Operational Directive No. 001 from the Commander-in-Chief of the Combined Armed Forces designating the Line as Stralsund-Brandenburg-Rosslau (actually GDR territory) beyond which strategic missile and aviation strikes would be conducted if the enemy initiated nuclear war.[633] The 1977 General Staff Academy case study of the Coastal Front operation designated the Line by operational directions: for the Jutland demarcated (based on the indicated place names) 220- to 245-km from the inner German border while along the coast 150- to 175-km distant from front departure positions.[634] These bounds allotted major FRG cities such as Hamburg and Bremen to the area of frontal means while most of Denmark would be hit by strategic systems. During *Soyuz* 1983 positioning of the Line in the FRG had been determined as a boundary between the strike assets subordinate to the TVD GK and those of fronts. Classified writings obtained and exercises monitored during the Cold War provided many, varying, instances of Line designation with subsequent examples in exercise documents found in national military archives.

The NATO transition from Massive Retaliation to Flexible Response offered the possibility of a nuclear variant confined to Europe. General-Colonel Ye. Ivanov had broached as early as 1961, in the top secret edition of VM, an execution of front operations in TVDs sans strategic missiles (he may have excluded these only in front zones).[635] But General-Colonel A. Kh. Babadzhanyan slapped down the proposal in the next issue on the grounds of front systems limitations in range and readiness.[636] Implementation of measures to remedy both deficiencies ensued. Soviet leaders may have looked on approvingly at US efforts to diversify nuclear options. Their sense of vulnerability would be demonstrated in the late 1980s when they agreed, despite being in a position to drive a harder bargain, to eliminate a potent theater missile force in order to rid Europe of US missiles capable of striking the homeland. Both coalition principals could see the advantages of a WMD Thirty Years War in which the combatants trampled only the immediate battlefield.

By the late 1970s a progressive introduction of modernized aircraft, missile launcher complements expansion, and indications of nuclear artillery appearance led the CIA in early 1978 to a revised conclusion regarding the nuclear balance in Central Europe.[637]

> Force improvements carried out to date have increased the flexibility with which the Soviets can employ their tactical nuclear forces and provided them with a capability for conducting theater nuclear war at higher levels of intensity before having to resort to the peripheral strike forces based on Soviet territory.

But the CIA still depicted a Warsaw Pact expectation of escalation whenever the "nuclear threshold" would be crossed.

The appearance by the 1980s of a formalized Strategic Nuclear Forces Operation might imply the severing of USSR-based strike assets from the Western TVD Strategic Operation. The 1985 General Staff Academy lecture on reconnaissance in a TVD strategic operation refers to "the plan for the initial nuclear strike by strategic nuclear forces" for which a separate target recon schedule would be prepared.[638] No conclusive indication has emerged of political allowance, or strategic forces planning, for an autonomous fronts nuclear war variant. Creation of the capability to conduct this variant remained implicit in nuclear systems modernization, range and numbers augmentation. NATO, by adopting Flexible Response, had effectively decoupled even if politically unwelcome to some Europeans. Soviet adoption of any nuclear restriction directly linked to evolving views on limited nuclear warfare and the persistent buildup of frontal striking power. Classified writings and exercise practice of the 1970s-1980s provide substantial evidence that the Soviet General Staff indeed had toyed with nuclear limitation, but whether the political leadership ratified, and strategic forces concurred, remains an open question.

### selecting the victims

The large number of theater targets, many critical and distant, required bringing in the heavy hitters of the RVSN and long range aviation or even naval assets along the coast. The Soviet military imperative of striking targets into the full depth of a TVD motivated the creation of the massive medium- and intermediate-range missile force that so outsized anything in the West. Nuclear attack planning entailed differentiating among strategic and front targets, an enormously complex task; rendered more difficult by NATO target accounting variations among Soviet—and Western—sources, detailed below. The general trend described a sharply upward aggregation of targets; a Soviet mid 1960s numeration of the Western TVD found a minimum 280 which soared to 2300 two decades later. The later estimate determined as many as 1500 worthy of attention at the outset of a nuclear variant—including at least 520 defined as administrative, political, and industrial, i.e. population centers.[639] The Soviets would eventually have to establish prioritized groupings in order to match available strike assets. The top secret 1977 General Staff Academy lecture on front offensives differentiated strategic tasks.[640]

> The strikes of the strategic rocket forces will be delivered mainly against the most important targets in the depth of the theater. Employing them against targets of the enemy grouping directly opposing the front is possible on extremely limited scales, both for considerations of the safety of our own troops and economic feasibility, as well as in view of the mobile nature of the overwhelming majority of these targets.

Exercises and classified documents revealed a specified quota of VGK nuclear strikes allotted to front zones but with a steady downward trend through the 1960s and 1970s.

Apportionment of USSR strategic systems and those of front assets within delivery range evolved during the Cold War. Front missile and aviation capability, expanding in both range and launchers, prorated against a NATO target set determined by Soviet intelligence. One general in the early 1960s reported 140 to 150 targets of interest located in a front zone which at that time could salvo 50 to 70 missiles—more than half left to strategic systems.[641] Some 57 strategic strikes amounting to 3.2 megatons had been planned in the Coastal Front zone during the Warsaw Pact exercise *Lato* 1967.[642] Favoring the zones of three fronts in the Southwestern TVD with 112 strikes by VGK means in a 1970 map game but apparently only 62 delivered in the first nuclear exchanges (the fronts used 425 nuclear weapons).[643] A 1970 Polish summary of the Soviet theater nuclear strike concept, based on course material at the USSR General Staff Academy, projected strategic strikes in "the front" zone west of the strategic demarcation line amounting to 220.5 megatons but the somewhat garbled translation may actually have given the Western Theater/TVD total.[644] A 1970 lecture listed NATO target categories amounting to 621 locations with 558 or ninety percent attacked by strategic systems. In the 1976 *Tarcza/Shchit* exercise 25 strikes of 7.50 megatons by strategic missiles and aviation had been allocated against targets selected by the Northern Front commander.[645]

General-Major P. Altukhov in an early 1966 VM (S) article[646] on nuclear strike calculations cited "scientific research games" conducted by the General Staff Academy in 1964-1965 for a baseline estimate of at least 280 targets in the Western TVD; these targets further broken down by range bands from the national border. Up to 80 or more reposed in the 250- to 500-km band beyond the reach of the most numerous and longest range front missile asset, the R-300. Altukhov pointed out as unattainable the mid 1960s strike complement of a front to engage all of these targets during the initial nuclear strike. The rearward siting of front- and army-subordinate R-300 missile brigades limited engagement of targets to a maximum 250-km into the depth of NATO formations. The R-2 (SS-2 Sibling) nuclear missile had nearly double that range while still in service during the early 1960s but this system had retired. The Academy's 1974 front textbook assumed a maximum front strike range to 400-km with bomber aviation.[647]

The targeting situation would become expansively knotty. A 1977 assessment had 900 reconnaissance objects in a front zone; 400 defined critical; reckoning that in the first offensive up to 70 percent of key targets lay within 15- to 120-km of state borders; and 80 percent could be mobile.[648] By the mid 1980s the Academy projected that the reconnaissance means of one front would have to track 700 to 800 targets, of which 300 would be "most important" against which 500 to 600 nuclear weapons would be applied by the front.[649] But other 1985 Academy material gave a range of 1000 to 1200 targets in a front zone, varying by assigned strategic direction, with the higher number projected by 1990; this estimate had been revised upward from a 600 to 900 range due to the experience of recent exercises. Some 400 to 450 would be key targets and a new term had been introduced "top-priority" for another subset; these could amount to 120 to 150 in each front zone—and had now become the aim points in the front initial nuclear strike.[650] Accounting of the full target deck considered 25 to 30 percent to be offensive nuclear related.[651] Expansion of target sets had been ascribed to NATO developments including deployment of Pershing II and cruise missiles as well as US Army reorganization in the Division 86 concept. For the Soviets a real headache would be the mobile 75 percent of the enlarged target set; crucial not just to detect their location but also track movement until they could be destroyed—and enemy nuclear means had to be detected with a probability of at least 95 percent. Up to 75 percent of the set would be initially positioned between 15 and 200 kilometers from the border, a substantial area that had to be scoured by technical and agent reconnaissance (a front would infiltrate the enemy rear with most of the 240 recon detachments that could be fielded by the subordinate *Spetsnaz* brigade).[652]

The practice of Soviet target analysis is displayed in great detail by the 1977 General Staff Academy lessons.[653] The NATO complement in the zone of the planned Coastal Front first offensive operation, 600-km in depth, amounted to nine corps of several nationalities. According to the Front reconnaissance plan at the start of combat there would be 965 potential targets, projected to increase to 1181 during the operation due to new deployments. Of the larger total 228 had been assessed to be nuclear delivery means—the absolute highest priority category—19 percent. Many of these targets transformed mobile and all removable, even aircraft at airfields and nuclear munitions storage points; the Front analysis concluded that 75 to 80 percent of all targets could be considered mobile. The precombat target situation disposed 700 or more up to 150-km from the state border with the remainder as much as 600- to 800-km in depth. With RVSN strike assets delegated an unspecified number of targets west of the demarcation line, the Combined Baltic Fleet also got in on the nuclear action. Front rocket troops, except the tactical systems, and aviation had the capability to strike targets up to the demarcation line but not to the full depth of the front first operation.

US intelligence and affiliates attempted to reverse-engineer prospective NATO targets. Several studies in the 1980s, based to a considerable extent on data collected from exercises, attempted comprehensive depictions of the scope, systems employed, and targeting during Soviet theater and frontal nuclear attacks. A 1983 assessment[654] derived from 1973 to 1982 exercising mainly by Soviet forces in the GDR attributed about 90 percent of front assignable targets to within 100-km of the line of contact; up to 80 percent mobile. Frontal assets would have responsibility for about a third of the territory of the FRG while strategic missile strikes lately had apparently been shifted beyond the front zone. The report noted target distribution as well as Soviet concerns with locating NATO mobile systems. Difficulty finding the priority targets would be largely mitigated by the massive damage inflicted across a relatively small strike area. A 1985 overview of the nuclear variant[655] delved more into classified writings; some of the reconnaissance target information lifted from the 1977 Academy material; 350 of 1000 targets in a front zone considered key; 80 percent of these mobile. However the CIA depiction did not yet have on hand the data stipulated in the 1985, albeit recently updated, General Staff Academy material.

Other 1980s studies elicited yet more varied statistics. An unclassified study found only 20 high value NATO fixed targets essential to nuclear attack, air defense, control, and reinforcement capability—exclusive of troop units that could disperse from peacetime garrison—within 100-km and 139 others up to 500-km beyond the GDR-FRG border.[656] A 1984 NIE determined that "most primary" NATO targets ranged within 150- to 400-km of the border including about 40 airfields.[657] Likely Western TVD targets, according to a 1987 estimate, amounted to 1900 fixed and mobile within 900-km, most unhardened, including key NATO nuclear and conventional means as well as the military-economic and government-administration structures—750 fixed considered "time urgent" for the Soviets.[658] Only a portion of these targets could be hit by longer range aircraft and a more limited number of missiles available to fronts in the 1960s-1970s but in the 1980s wide introduction of new missile systems substantially enlarged the range envelope. Thus while the strike means available to fronts could inflict irremediable damage on the forward deployed NATO defense forces, only by bringing in the USSR big brothers—such as all those SS-20s—could Western Europe be entirely incapacitated.

Substantial increases in the complements of front missile units implemented in the 1960s-1970s still did not permit simultaneous engagement of all targets, if only because the number of candidates also increased. The 1977 General Staff Academy lecture on front offensives cited the experience of Western TVD exercises in concluding that of the more than 900 targets in the zone of one front subject to reconnaissance 300 would be in the zone of each army (thus three armies in the front first echelon). The 400 of these considered critical included nuclear-capable missiles and artillery; nuclear munitions depots and supply points; airfields; ground divisions, especially tank; certain air defense missiles; as well as their control systems. Per this lecture "The number of launchers in the front has a direct effect on the number of targets hit at one time" and based on calculations, research, and exercises concluded that in one front zone of the Western TVD situated 180 to 200 'must hit' targets. Some of these required strikes by two or more nuclear weapons to achieve the degree of damage required; assuming that 60 percent of the 'must hit' targets would be allotted to missiles and the remainder to front aviation.[659]

Their numeration of a front total missile launcher complement ranged 139 to 160 including 51 to 60 operational-tactical (two front missile brigades plus ranged three or four army missile brigades and division rocket battalions). The 1977 lecture assumed a 12-launcher strength for each of the two front missile brigades and that of army missile brigades, nine. Strangely the Academy 1974 front operations textbook supposed that brigades at both levels had twelve launchers,[660] perhaps only foreshadowing complement increases then under consideration. By the early 1980s the brigade launcher complements had increased by six at front- and three at army-levels so that the 1977 type front would then have 72 to 84 O-T launchers but at the Western TVD maximum five armies there would be 96 O-T launchers. The number of division launchers remained unchanged until a mid 1980s major reorganization; in any case those divisions in the second echelons of armies and in the front reserve might not be able to participate in the nuclear strike for being out of range. General Staff Academy material in 1985 assumed the same front complement as in 1977 of three or four armies (only one a tank army) with 148 to 172 O-T and tactical missile launchers; also noting the ongoing transition to form tactical missile brigades.[661] Yet even in 1983 during exercise *Soyuz* one front planned to strike 132 zonal targets with 198 nuclear missiles but still required a repeat launch.[662] The 1977 lecture, unlike the 1974 front textbook, did not discuss any contribution by the R-900 (SS-12 Scaleboard) to front missile strike assets and range capability; 1985 Academy material also assumed two front-level missile brigades, one R-900 and one equipped with either the R-300 or R-400 (SS-23 Spider).

Intelligence monitors had ringside seats during Warsaw Pact play of nuclear systems employment. They could plot coordinates along with the exercise participants, and determine the identity of the target hit as well as systems and nuclear yields employed. Much more data could be obtained from target practice involving individual missile units, and up to the front level, than available from strategic systems planning. Generally, even though exercise target positions frequently offset, the plots revealed actual NATO installations and units. These data remain locked up for the indeterminate future, however, much of the same material can be viewed in some of the Soviet classified documents which the CIA has been declassifying as well as several analytic pieces dealing with theater nuclear operations. The 1977 General Staff Academy front operation lessons contain quite detailed NATO target type and location specifications. The CIA reviewers have assiduously redacted US nuclear weapons storage sites from the Soviet lists–never mind that their stocks are long gone–so presumably these locations corresponded, if the reviewers actually made that determination.

By the late 1960s at least, forward fronts and armies had been fully equipped with the R-300 while launcher complements had been increased 65 percent. The Soviets deployed KR-500 (SSC-1a Shaddock) cruise missiles early in the 1960s but only (as far as is known) within the USSR. In the late 1970s the number of R-300 launchers had increased another 58 percent while front aviation had been modernized and allotted a bigger slice of the nuclear target pie than in the previous decade. Missiles tended to be assigned fixed, and aviation mobile, targets. NATO planners conscious enough of the threat attempted to keep key assets beyond the range of the nuclear FROG-7 (65-km minus rearward siting distance) but replacement of these unguided rockets ensued with the R-100/120 (SS-21 Scarab) missile. The R-900 missile system had been re-subordinated to the Soviet Ground Troops by 1969,[663] available for ranging TVD targets even from within the USSR. Any requirement for augmentation by strategic systems to engage targets in the front zone had been virtually, if not totally, eliminated. The substantial increase in the number of launchers and ranges made possible the simultaneous engagement of fuller target sets in one salvo, reducing the number of second launches, with less need for strategic systems to meet deficit requirements.

In a 1970 VM (S) article General-Lieutenant L. S. Sapkov made a categorical statement that the "transition to the massive use of nuclear weapons (the first nuclear strike) by front means may be effected both independently and in cooperation with the strategic rocket troops."[664] Some theater exercises in the 1970s depicted mass nuclear strikes in which those of fronts preceded strategic by several hours. A considerable number of front exercises in the groups of forces and military districts featured quite detailed nuclear strikes planning and execution with no evidence of participation by strategic systems. Risks of nuclear expansion would inevitably be compounded when USSR-based systems became involved. Even if confined to TVD targets they posed another step up the escalatory ladder from battlefield systems to a full strategic nuclear exchange involving US intercontinental assets that endangered the USSR motherland. In the 1980s the VGK delegated the new high commands some of nuclear planning role and re-assigned strike assets including air armies and the R-900 which had been moved into Central Europe; thus enabling an intermediate band short of strategic.

As did their prospective enemies, the Soviets collected and analyzed data on potential targets throughout the world. Databasing for computer battle management assigned each target a four digit number within categorized blocks. Strategic and theater services each had customized systems which underwent a complete revamp in the mid 1970s. The 1974 General Staff manual on front reconnaissance outlined the use of this numbering scheme.[665]

> In order to facilitate planning, the targets detected already in peacetime must be numbered and systematized according to the respective categories, kinds, and types, with a description of each target and an assessment of its resistance to different means of destruction. This system of targets must be constantly refined, developed, and added to. It is the basis for the allocation of the detected targets among the forces and means of destruction, and it will facilitate the designation of targets when they are being destroyed.

The multi-digit allocation included target designations by high commands and directions; the General Staff assigned only where no direction existed.[666]

The target sets evident, in exercises at least, clearly aimed counterforce but also obviously Soviet and Warsaw Pact allied nuclear sharpshooters had no concerns regarding who might be in the vicinity. Even open Soviet publications defined targets for strategic systems as 'administrative-political' and 'industrial' which would thereby cover much of the urban territory of Europe. Assignment of front systems to nominally strategic targets in plots of R-300 strikes, sometimes multiple, encompassed West German cities. The Soviets had certainly been aware of the effects of metropolitan strikes from an early date. In a 1961 VM (TS) article General-Major G. Semenov cited a 1960 air defense conference estimate that one 200 kiloton strike in central Riga would kill 109000 people and injure 221000 as well as destroy all major buildings within a 4.5-km radius.[667] The highest yield R-300 warheads of 300 and 500 kilotons would have been eminent city-breakers.

European innocents of the Cold War can now read for themselves what they refused to countenance from Western military and political officials regarding the nature of Soviet plans. Archival documents from the aforementioned June 1965 Soviet-Hungarian exercise depicted 500 kiloton missile strikes on Vicenza, Verona, and Munich with projected results of target "destroyed" or "completely destroyed" (the distinction is not defined). Scenario singled out Vienna for a double whammy of 500 kilotons each (the perfidious Austrians had joined West Germans and French in a surprise nuclear attack).[668] The 57 strategic strikes totaling 3.2 megatons allotted to one front zone in the *Lato* 1967 nuclear contingency plan had been zeroed in on eleven named cities in Belgium, The Netherlands, northern West Germany, and Denmark.[669] During *Soyuz* 1981 a strategic missile hit Glasgow, uncertain the transgression committed by the Scots to deserve such treatment. Exercises involving large scale nuclear weapons employment apparently liberated the imaginations of participants as indicated in the official critique of a Southwestern TVD 1970 war game revealing "a casual approach to the use of those terrible weapons and to the estimate of the situation that will have arisen as a result of the massive use of nuclear strikes by both sides." The critique judged a Hungarian army corps planned missile surface nuclear burst on the Vienna airport "hardly advisable" with no combat aircraft present—and because occupation would eventuate "within several hours."[670] Hungarians do seem to have had a thing about Austrians.

Some discussions strayed from the urban obliteration theme. Two colonels in a 1962 VM (S) article criticized stress in a reviewed book on using nuclear weapons against cities rather than other methods—but their quibble regarded this uneconomic expenditure of resources. Residents of West Germany may not have been reassured at their comment that "calculations made in the course of exercises in the Group of Soviet Forces Germany showed that to destroy only the major cities with a population exceeding 100000 people, assuming that a single nuclear strike will be delivered against them, it would be necessary to expend 64 front missiles in the zone of a single front."[671] Perhaps their concerns would have been alleviated in later years as launcher complements significantly increased from those available in 1962. Even a senior officer of the army Rocket Troops and Artillery arm in 1970 advised "In selecting targets, obviously their position in relation to large population centers also will be taken into consideration in order to lessen the possibility of destroying peaceful inhabitants."[672] The 1974 General Staff Academy textbook, in a rare outburst of Soviet sentimentality, did allow that nuclear strikes on defended urban complexes might be "...undesirable because of the possible destruction of the city and death of civilians..." and suggested that "...it is necessary to take steps to force the enemy, under threat of the use of nuclear weapons, to give up defending the industrial area and surrender it without a battle."[673]

US-NATO and Soviet-Warsaw Pact nuclear targeting regimes differed radically in some aspects. Westerners favored the application of low yields, including sub-kiloton, against their subjects while the East went for substantially higher kilotonnage. Front planners usually employed air bursts, to reduce radiation effects and avoid creating obstacles to rapid advance, at least as observed from the 1970s when intelligence monitoring had substantially improved. A General Staff officer in 1990s interviews stated that practice during the 1960s employed 80 percent ground bursts until the Soviets realized that the resulting mass of radioactive fallout would drift in the prevailing winds back on the shooters.[674] A 1970 VM (S) article[675] confirmed that surface bursts had rarely been dealt with in operational training and exercises, however, the authors attempted to buck this trend by providing detailed calculations and effects data regarding the potential for grouped nuclear strikes at ground level to destroy large enemy targets. With a favorable wind direction these strikes could be as close as 50- to 100-km from their formations (150- to 200-km in adverse winds); to be effective at least 20-kt weapons would have to be used, and research had determined that ground detonations of 100 or more kilotons could be highly effective. They claimed that after 24 hours radiation levels would drop to "harmless" by the time advancing troops reached the strike area. Surface bursts had been rarely observed in exercises during the 1970s-1980s and these strikes in areas where planned movement would not occur. Soviet military literature emphasized the difficulties created for surmounting zones of contamination-destruction. But achieving target destruction criteria with air bursts then required use of much higher yields which would also compensate for relatively inaccurate delivery missiles as well as a recognized location uncertainty factor for some types of targets.

The highest priority targets comprised nuclear delivery means and their suppliers. US-NATO nuclear systems vaulted to the top of the hit list because they not only represented a mortal threat to Soviet forces but also composed the ultimate assurance of Western defense. Air defenses also had priority if only because of the nuclear capability of the Nike Hercules. A 1967 appraisal attributed a third of system missile load with nuclear warheads (12 for each of 24 US batteries in Europe); and, of great significance to the Soviets, usable in a ground targeting mode with greater accuracy than the contemporary Sergeant surface-surface missile.[676] The Soviets recognized—if only by reading NATO documents—that the threat or actuality of a breakthrough of defense lines would inevitably be followed by at least selective use of nuclear weapons. If US-NATO strike capability could be severely degraded or eliminated, effectively nothing remained to halt a Warsaw Pact advance in depth. Some US nuclear stores had been hardened but could be wrecked by strikes of 200 or more kilotons. An apparently increasing concern with destruction assurance may have instigated the 1975 increase in the R-300 top yield from 300- to 500-kt and R-65 from 200 to 300 kilotons. A 1978 exercise document reveals that the Poles had received this data since the 3 Front R-17 (R-300) allocation amounted to forty 500-kt (plus twenty all 10-kt) but the tactical missiles top yield remained at 200-kt.[677] Upping the nuclear kilotonnage reflected a persistent Soviet concern with missile and target location inaccuracy, helping compensate for imprecise coordinates, as well as ensuring the mandated degree of destruction for each target type. Of course this also greatly increased the ksk quotient in the target area.

Soviet officers acknowledged in classified writings the difficulty of detecting targets in a rapidly evolving battlefield environment while still meeting location accuracy norms. Emphasized in 1985 "The effectiveness of the combat actions of front rocket troops and artillery largely depends on the accuracy and timeliness of reconnaissance data on enemy targets to be hit."[678] Particularly for a strike conducted during the conventional variant, both friendly and enemy forces would be on the move, while the strike assets themselves might be redeploying. Conventional means already at work strived to degrade the priority enemy nuclear strike and support elements; and opponents might be having a degree of success in their own targeting efforts despite an extensive set of protective techniques. Frequently expressed doubts concerned the reliability of target acquisition especially in regard to mobile US-NATO nuclear means. Missile launch positions had to be pinpointed and quickly attacked in order to be effectively neutralized. Even as front reconnaissance systems diversified and upgraded with technical advances there remained uncertainty as to actual battlefield performance. According to a 1984 NIE "Accumulated evidence reveals considerable Pact anxiety over the formidable difficulties inherent in locating and destroying NATO nuclear warheads and delivery systems."[679]

Targeting accuracy would have a decisive influence on probability of destruction. One calculation that considered the precision of both missile system and location concluded that a twofold improvement had a nuclear effect multiplier of five to as much as ten (CIA reviewers expurgated the supporting data).[680] General-Major L. Sapkov in a 1966 VM (S) article[681] made detailed calculations that related target coordinate accuracy to missile strike error, yield selection, and number of warheads allotted to achieve the desired reliability of destruction. A derived ratio indicated that the greater the location error, the higher the nuclear yield requirement—doubling the error required twice the yield. The CIA reviewers assigned to declassify this document waxed so perturbed at the good general's reckoning that they redacted two charts and several data points. Their resolute action will no doubt hinder any North Korean, Iranian, or budding jihadist nuclear rocketeers who might not be capable of working out such particulars. The general also stressed the importance of timely reconnaissance information transmission through the front reporting structure. He calculated that NATO missiles such as the Pershing had to be hit within 9 to 18 minutes after detection to achieve a 70 percent degree of destruction reliability or within 3 to 9 minutes for 90 percent—otherwise the missile crews would have skedaddled. Sapkov complained that, all too frequently, target practice in Soviet exercises resulted in strikes against vacated areas, a most "uneconomical expenditure" of socialist resources. Colonel A. Sulim in a 1968 VM (S) article even concluded that 30 to 40 percent of front missile strikes would be on locations unoccupied by the enemy.[682]

Target location accuracy had a direct bearing on nuclear yield selection. Two colonels in another VM (S) 1970 article passed on the accuracy requirements for determining target coordinates, 175 to 200 meters for operational-tactical delivery systems, 100- to 150-m for tactical systems, and as close as 30 meters for artillery conventional fires.[683] Even fifteen years later intelligence still cited their norms.[684] These specifications equated to the Sapkov contribution except for his 50 to 75 meters artillery requirement, and a bit tighter than given in a 1963 article (missiles 150 to 300 and 100 to 200 meters respectively). A 1984 Hungarian consideration of the reconnaissance problem gave similar numbers but interestingly tossed in a 150-m accuracy requirement for strategic missiles;[685] which is quite discrepant with the 1500 meters requirement in 1985 General Staff Academy material[686] (mis-translation may be at work). Slight variations to these norms appeared in other classified writings; 1985 deviation specifications for both R-900 and R-300 systems allowed 150- to 250-m and a reduced tactical missile 80- to 150-m (probably reflecting the more accurate R-100).[687] According to data in a 1970 lecture[688] a 250-m uncertainty required 50-kt to destroy enemy missile launchers while at 1000-m the ante would be upped to one megaton (necessitating a grouped strike). General-Major (Artillery) F. Narkhodzhayev and Colonel V. Daragan had been swimming against the tide when, in that 1963 article, they adduced three objections to the prevailing notion that increased nuclear yields could compensate for target location inaccuracy "this is very uneconomical" plus higher yield warheads might not be available while when expending several missiles against single targets overkill would result.[689]

This dissenting view apparently did not win acceptance. A group of engineer officers in a 1966 article also complained about apparent neglect of meteorological factors that could increase the potential circular error such that the yield of an R-300 would have to be increased two or three times, and the older R-170 by a greater multiplier.[690] The 1970 Gordon-Druganov article detailed Soviet target reconnaissance methods to an extent that should have been of great professional interest to US and NATO nuclear delivery units. Some of the Soviet officers estimated the dwell time of enemy nuclear means and concluded that even if the locations could be determined their own marksmen would not be able to react in sufficient time before the target moved. The 1974 GRU guide to front reconnaissance insisted that data on a detected target must reach the strike planners within fifteen minutes.[691] Gordon and Druganov cited research that 75 to 80 percent of targets designated in the initial nuclear strike plan would relocate at the start of combat actions.[692]

Soviet confidence in the ability of Warsaw Pact forces to find targets had hardly soared even by the 1980s despite a wide array of theater detection assets. A General Staff Academy lecture in 1985[693] ruefully admitted that "at the conference last year the Chief of the General Staff stated that radio and radiotechnical reconnaissance are the only type of reconnaissance that work well" as had also been the case during the 1973 Middle East war. Stipulated basic target detection percentages ranged 70 to 80 in tactical depth (to 150-km); 50 to 55 in the depth of the first front operation (to 700-km); while projecting only a 30 percent rate further to the terminus of the strategic operation (2000-km)—yet insisting that enemy nuclear means required accomplishing at a 90 to 95 rate. But the lecturer confessed "we are not attaining the required target detection rate, particularly for offensive nuclear weapons" even during the favorable conditions of exercises.

Divergent attitudes regarding nuclear engagement spotlighted respective anticipations of the nature of war outbreak in Europe. Warsaw Pact targeting entailed an offensive posture, the high-yield preference indicative of planning use of nuclear weapons only on other people's territory—removing any inhibition. Soviet commanders worked with radically contrastive operational expectations; arranging plans, preparations, and delivery systems to attack the full depth not only of opposing NATO forces in the zones of front strike groupings but also against deep reserves and support systems. Firepower application emphasized neutralization of all potential hindrances to rapid advances in depth of the NATO defense system. Soviet officers in classified writings called for low yield nuclear strikes in tactical depth to protect their troops but high yields would be acceptable on targets at a distance.

NATO plans reflected consideration of the consequences to their own countries. Early missile deployments had dealt with the same requirement as the Soviets to compensate lesser accuracy with higher nuclear yields. By the 1970s these systems began to be considered unusable components of the Flexible Response theory.[694] The West Germans, in particular, as the proximate battleground, made NATO keenly aware of their discomfort with the prospect of high-yield nuclear detonations all around the homeland. According to a 1970 US National Security Council memo nothing resembling the Soviet detailed theater strike plans had been prepared by NATO because the European perspective abided "almost impossible to conceive" of actually executing even a limited nuclear variant that would inflict "intolerable" damage.[695]

## divvying out the goods

The staff of a front initiated nuclear strike planning immediately after generation of the field command group. A VGK, or TVD high command in the 1980s, directive transmitted nuclear weapons allocations for the first front offensives of the strategic operation that became the basis for all subsequent work. Contingency planning ensued preparing and continuously updating during deployment of front elements and throughout any conventional phase. This allocation scheme established early in the Revolution, with modifications, ran until The End. A formalized sequence noted from at least 1960 for two decades apportioned the front allocation, as well as army sub-allocations, by initial strike/immediate task/subsequent task/reserve, the tasks coincident with front mission definition. These categories, each with "tentative" percentages, had been established during several exercises.[696] Exercise *Zapad* 1977 stood out again for a singular revision of the categories as initial strike/repulse/reserve—a unique instance of a nuclear weapons allocation category specifically for the purpose of conducting a defense. Although some exercises, and writings, depicted use of nuclear weapons while on the defensive, the prominent lack of a dedicated defense allocation category demonstrates the Soviet presumption that nuclear weapons would be an offensive instrument. Thereafter the categories, at least by the early 1980s, existed as initial/follow-on/reserve; altered at least partly because of a sharp increase in the proportion of the allocation to be expended in the first salvos.

Collection and analysis of nuclear weapons allocation data became a popular intelligence activity during the last two decades of the Cold War, facilitated by improvements in SIGINT and documents acquisition. Quantification derived largely from data at and below Soviet-Warsaw Pact front level; frequently acquired for missile-artillery allocations; aviation less often; and most rarely, both. Classified writings supplemented this data but with an even greater degree of opportunism and variation. Lower level exercises, in particular, provided much targeting information. TVD totals could in theory be extrapolated from the foregoing, but variations by front mission and nationality, along with degree of second echelon fronts participation, made any reliable estimate problematic. Overall contributions by USSR strategic systems (missile-heavy bomber-SLBM) could in the main only be guesstimated from force structure, systems characteristics, and NATO target inventorying—ours and their categorization. Substantial data is now available from declassified Warsaw Pact documents and has been recovered from archival documents but in a fragmented and episodic form similar to the intelligence monitoring of exercises. This data largely corresponds with, overlaps to some extent, and even supplements the exercises take. Potentially themes, boundaries, and trend lines can be established even without the still classified sources.

Determination of Soviet overall nuclear weapons allocations for initial operations in either the West or East Theaters has little basis in firm evidence. Breakdown by TVD is also hindered by intermittent data but with some indication of scale. In the Southwestern TVD the 1970 war game allocation amounted to 830 nuclear weapons totaling 127 megatons for the first operations of four Warsaw Pact fronts. Three fronts received 613 of these weapons (215 for the Soviet-Hungarian Southwestern plus 129 to the Bulgarian 1 Southern and 278 for the second echelon 2 Southern based on the Odessa MD) while 3 Southern Front in Romania seems to have been disregarded for exercise purposes. USSR strategic systems allotted 112 weapons to the TVD; at least 62 of which delivered in the first nuclear strikes. The remaining 105 weapons may have been assigned to the Black Sea Fleet and supporting naval and long range aviation although 108 are mentioned—frequently the numbers do not add up in these official documents, surprising given the native Soviet math talent.[697]

Profiling the Western TVD, the 1977 *Zapad* operational-strategic exercise numerated an initial nuclear strike by the East of 1129 weapons out of an unspecified kitty allocated to the five staffed fronts (627 for 2 Front in the GDR) and other forces. In this 'meeting' strike the West one-upped their effort with 1130 strikes extending into the western USSR.[698] An expansive CIA study,[699] using the range of evidence available in July 1984, attempted to model the scale of a nuclear strike at the outset of war in the Western TVD (total allocation not attempted); postulating the delivery of up to 2000 nuclear weapons, including 800 aviation, throughout the theater by strategic and naval forces joined by forward fronts—participation of second echelon fronts might add up to 150 strikes. The delivery means of three first echelon Warsaw Pact fronts, composed of both Soviet and national formations, along with those of the Baltic Fleet and 4 Air Army VGK participating with 500 air, 500 missile, and up to 150 artillery warheads—against targets within an assumed demarcation line 100- to 200-km from the border shared by the German states; with up to 1000 strikes assigned beyond the line to strategic missiles and aviation based in the USSR. The study made no attempt at a total megatonnage estimate due to potential widely varying target yields.

Much more data is available from different periods and sources in regard to nuclear operations of individual fronts. Information on nuclear allocations of the 1950s-1960s derived largely from classified discussions by Soviet officers in articles as well as specifications presented in operations manuals. One Soviet survey of the formative nuclear period from 1953 to 1960 provides some front operation allocations.[700] While 30 bombs delivered by medium or heavy bomber aviation would support a front at the beginning of this period by 1956 allocations in a command-staff exercise increased to a, more diversified, total of 44 inclusive of 20 bombs with the addition of missile and artillery-mortar rounds, 12 for each set. By 1957-1958 exercise front allocations had risen sharply, ranging 200 to 285—fifty-five percent missiles—and in 1959 exercises the missile proportion would increase still further to seventy percent. One general in 1961 directly linked the enlarged nuclear allocation to accelerated revision of the Soviet concept of theater operations even over "several months."[701] By 1962 exercise practice provided for two or three nuclear missiles per launcher in a front according to another general.[702] A military science conference held in the Carpathian MD in 1962 assumed that a front would receive 250 or more nuclear weapons for a complete first operation.[703] By 1964 the Professor forecasted a single front requirement for more than 500 weapons.[704] Classified lecture notes dating circa 1970 assigned a type front nuclear capability up to 58 megatons of which 46-mt would be delivered by rocket troops.[705]

Front nuclear allocations in the 1970s-1980s could widely vary but generally described a sharply upward curve. By 1985 the General Staff Academy presumed that each front (at least those Soviet-commanded) in the Western TVD would receive from 800 to 1000 nuclear weapons for the first front operation, half of the allocation expended in a coordinated front mass strike. Subordinate armies would be allotted their piece of the nuclear pie in the front plan; according to the General Staff Academy an army participating on the front main offensive thrust would have 150 to 200 nuclear warheads (missiles and artillery to 152-mm) to blast the way forward.[706] Ground and air armies initiated nuclear targeting on receipt of their sub-allocation as determined by the front commander and staff. Individual army allocations concurrently mushroomed. A 1958 NATO target-based calculation proposed 29 weapons comprising 5 missiles (30-kt R-170 Scud A) plus 15 "heavy rocket" (6 10-kt and 9 15-kt early FROG series) and 9 artillery (10-kt but for systems that would actually never be deployed); all from VGK reserves since an army of the time lacked organic missile units. Fifteen years later a main thrust army would be allocated 100 or more nuclear warheads for, now organic to both army and subordinate divisions, missile—but not artillery—units.[707] Army distributions did not arrive on an even-steven but rather offensive task basis. Allocations in the 1977 Academy front offensive bloc to three first echelon armies amounted to 49-56-62 while one second echelon army received only 34; nuclear artillery again a no-show.[708]

Two major adjustments during three decades of nuclear planning affected the roles of aviation and artillery. The Revolution had downgraded the importance of all aircraft, strategic heavy and medium bombers as well as front aviation, in nuclear tasking in favor of missiles. By the late 1960s the trend had been reversed and in the 1970s front missile troops and aviation realized coequality. Mid-1970s Soviet classified documents indicated air-delivered nuclear weapons might constitute at least half of the total nuclear weapons allocation in the Western TVD first front operation.[709] The transformation of the Soviet Air Forces by the creation of VGK air armies in 1980 'robbed' frontal aviation of much, but not all, of the nuclear mission as well as most light bomber aircraft. The few aviation allocations acquired from exercises in the 1980s pointed to a noticeable drop in front totals, and a commensurate, new, allocation component for VGK air army tasks throughout a TVD.

The aviation proportion of both the front complete, and initial strike, allocations underwent considerable alteration due to aircraft modernization through the 1960s into the 1980s as well as the major reorganizations in the last decade. In 1962 the air army might obtain 30 percent of the front total nuclear allocation.⁷¹⁰ Lecture notes circa 1970 bumped aviation to the next decimal, 30 to 40 percent, of the front initial mass strike.⁷¹¹ The 1977 General Staff Academy lecture on front offensives, based on exercise experience, assumed that 40 to 50 percent of the nuclear allocation for a first operation would go to the air army of a front (Western TVD). An air army of 600 to 800 combat aircraft included 200 to 300 considered nuclear delivery-capable.⁷¹² The nuclear strike plan in the Academy 1977 front operation lessons, with 47 percent apportioned to aviation, complied.⁷¹³ Of the lecture operation amount 50 to 60 percent would be expended in the first mass nuclear strike, which qualified the 53 percent aviation tasking in the lessons.

But during the 1980s the nuclear role of the aviation assigned to fronts had been short-changed. The 1982 running of the *Tsentr* series had featured an unprecedented near-total nuclear monopoly by the missile-artillery means of the GSFG-based 12 Front; apparently aviation had been allotted hardly five percent of the megatonnage; and 4 Operational Air Army VGK had largely absconded with the nuclear air delivery mission. In the March 1984 *Soyuz*, which confined operations to the Southwestern TVD, the strategic operation allocation for 24 Operational Air Army VGK totaled 296 nuclear weapons of which 192 were to be delivered in the TVD initial mass strike. Considering this and other data, the 1985 CIA model⁷¹⁴ assigned 40 percent of all air-delivered weapons in the Western TVD initial nuclear strike, that east of the strategic demarcation line, to 4 Operational Air Army VGK although this calculation included only the aviation of the three forward fronts and the Baltic Sea Fleet—adding that of two second echelon fronts reduced the VGK air army portion to 24 percent. Aviation of the GSFG-GDR front had their initial mass nuclear strike quota reduced to 36 percent.

Sampling exercise information can provide a quantitative measure of the scale of nuclear plans while indicating the wide range of front allocations. As explained by the Professor in a 1969 lecture prepared for the General Staff Academy "we cannot establish any norms (percentages) for the allocation of nuclear warheads…everything will depend on the specific conditions of the situation."⁷¹⁵ Allocation data from the Soviet-Warsaw Pact *Druzhba* (Friendship) 1980 exercise⁷¹⁶ is representative of many others along the trend line except for the lack of any nuclear artillery. Initial offensive allocation for the GSFG-East German 1 Front amounted to 842 nuclear weapons, comprising 587 missile- and 255 air-delivered (30 percent), with a planned initial strike expenditure (46 percent) of 134 missile and 115 aviation munitions. Amounts recovered years apart from even similar fronts operating in the same directions could vary widely with differing variants, target sets, and force composition, as well as for operational experimentation. Incomplete data from thirteen Soviet and Warsaw Pact exercises during late 1973 to 1987 range (disparities due to varying available category totals) front allocations of 210>842; missile-artillery 216>627; and aviation 255>550.

By far the largest quantity observed transpired during an April 1973 exercise.⁷¹⁷ The first offensive allocation for a GSFG front amounted to more than 1500 nuclear weapons, driven skyward by an unusually high aviation component. Official nuclear weapons storage capacity at airfields in Central Europe had recently undergone substantial expansion. The planned initial strike, although only a bit over a fifth of the operation total, amounted to almost 41 megatons—which presumably would have been distributed, unevenly (if in a 350-km front zone forward to the 250-km strategic demarcation line) over an area of perhaps 87500 square kilometers or roundabout 467-ksk. In the actual North German Strategic Direction the detonation area would equal, state-wise, the territory of Hesse, Rhineland-Palatinate, North Rhine-Westphalia, and the southern quarter of Lower Saxony, or, would just fit within the borders of Maine. Fortunately air burst favoritism would have limited neighborhood fallout exposure. The NRDC simulation calculated that strikes of 15 or so megatons would kill a quarter of the population of both Germanys.⁷¹⁸

The artillery nuclear comeback replicated, in a more fundamental way, significant adjustments to the role of frontal aviation during the 1970s-1980s. Nuclear artillery persisted as an unsolvable mystery to intelligence for many years, analysts baffled by the failure of the Soviets to match the high proportion of US-NATO nuclear capability invested in tube artillery. An apparent half-hearted attempt at fielding nuclear-capable heavy artillery had been made by the Soviets during the 1950s in units equipped with 310-mm guns and 420-mm mortars. These pieces eventuated to be unwieldy and poorly adapted to the nuclear concept under development. Artillery entirely lost the nuclear mission in the 1960 adjustment in favor of tactical unguided rockets.⁷¹⁹ For many years thereafter periodic intelligence assessments announced the 'imminent' arrival of Soviet nuclear artillery. However the earliest clear indication of a renewed Soviet interest in a nuclear role for artillery occurred in the identification on satellite imagery beginning in 1973 of the re-formation of heavy artillery units. Tentative associations of artillery with nuclear delivery became evident in exercises by 1974 coincident with discussions in Soviet classified documents of operational employment in the form of "high power" (the appellation signified large caliber not atomic) artillery brigades; these brigades equipped with 203-mm guns and 240-mm mortars.⁷²⁰ A volume of the "Encyclopedia" *Russia's Arms And Technologies* states that nuclear rounds for these pieces had actually been put "in service" during 1970.⁷²¹

From 1976 the new high power artillery brigades regularly appeared in exercises. But these units functioned dual-

**strategic strikes demarcation line**

| operation | weapons (megatons) available {Center delivery} | initial strike | % operation O \| initial strike IS immediate task | subsequent task | reserve |
|---|---|---|---|---|---|
| **Combined Baltic Fleet** 222 (8.22) | 167 {55} | 95/43% O | 90/41% O | 26/12% O | [11/5% O] |
| **Coastal Front** 680 (42.43) | — | 376/55% O (30.54) | 166/24% O (0.878) | 100/15% O (0.725) | 38/6% O (0.593) |
| missile troops 360 (11.42) 53% (27% mt) reload factor R-300 1.6 R-65 1.8 | 289 {71} | 176/47% IS (8.47) 1.0 1.5 | 94/26% O (0.193) | 64/18% O (0.09) | 26/7% O (0.093) |
| aviation 320 (31.01) 47% (73% mt) | — | 200/53% IS (22.92) | 72/23% O (0.685) | 36/11% O (0.635) | 12/4% O (0.5) |
| **total** 902 (50.65) | | 471 = 52% O | 256 = 28% O | 126 = 14% O | 49 = 5% O |

composite initial strike schedule
all air bursts
troop safety line 4–5 km

P front aviation takeoff > P+0:05 front missile strikes known targets
P+0:05 > 0:45 aviation first echelon recon-jam-strike air defenses in flight corridors
P+0:12 > 0:45 aviation strikes known targets—final target recon
P+0:45 > 0:50 tactical missile repeat strikes—final recon and newly detected targets

NUCLEAR STRIKE PLAN 1977 GENERAL STAFF ACADEMY LESSONS (NUCLEAR OUTSET VARIANT)

purposed; artillery of all types undergoing revitalization in support of the conventional variant. The high power brigades also contributed a key reinforcement for achieving massed conventional firepower at breakthrough sectors. As late as 1977 no nuclear tasking appeared in General Staff Academy top secret material. The May 1977 lecture on front offensive operations, despite detailed discussion of artillery employment in conventional strikes, does not even hint at a nuclear role for artillery.[722] Nuclear artillery does not appear in the operation and initial strike data of the 1977 General Staff Academy lessons. Artillery nuclear rounds had appeared in an army nuclear allocation in exercise *Granit* at the end of 1976 but formal allocation to fronts did not actually begin until *Zapad* 1977 which took place after publication of the Academy material.

High power artillery brigades, initially equipped with towed models that would be replaced with modernized self-propelled chassis (2S7 gun and 2S4 mortar), resided in the VGK reserve. Regularly depicted in groups of forces exercises, separate brigades would only be identified within the USSR—components of the echeloned mobilization-deployment. A RVGK artillery division long existed in the GSFG but equipping with nuclear-capable pieces did not occur until the early 1980s. Like all higher level RVGK artillery, full or partial high power brigades would be re-subordinated to reinforce fronts and armies operating in main directions. Exercises frequently depicted one or two high power gun and/or mortar battalions supporting tactical breakthroughs by individual divisions with, for the Soviets, low 2 and 5 kiloton options.[723]

The next phase of Soviet nuclear artillery development involved a smaller caliber. The Russian *Encyclopedia* states that a 152-mm nuclear round had been first accepted "in service" during 1975.[724] This event, and any actual deployment in artillery units, eluded intelligence notice. But an extended, inexplicable, gap between the availability of a particular Soviet weapon and its field appearance often occurred during the Cold War. Only during 1982 did command-staff exercises and field training conducted by Soviet forces in East Germany confirm a nuclear role for the 152-mm gun in both 2S5 self-propelled and towed versions.[725] As with the earlier introduction of high power artillery, US intelligence experts had no ready explanation of the Soviet motivation for a delayed, then expansive, deployment of artillery nuclear capability. Reportedly the Trekhgorny plant produced 17500 nuclear shells from 1968 to 1990; at an annual rate varying 700 to 2000; a ten-year warranty requiring stockpile turnover—the final 1990 output of 2000 ordered extended to the year 2005 when all withdrawn from service.[726] This 1990 inventory of 2000 nuclear shells in the Ground Troops confirmed by a Russian expert and a book published in 2004; with additional 152-mm rounds for coastal defense artillery.[727]

The importance the Soviets assigned to the rupturing of NATO defenses had been demonstrated by exercises in which, unlike missile and aviation strikes in depth, the front initial nuclear strike frequently disbursed the entire operation allocation of nuclear artillery rounds (up to 170 or more in the 1980s). Defeating an increasingly formidable array of NATO antitank weapons in tactical depth which might dent mass Soviet armor penetrations likely motivated expanding artillery nuclear capability. Substantial augmentation of division nuclear support by artillery means eventuated another reorganization beginning in late 1983 and extending over several years—explicitly linked by the Soviets to nuclear artillery. The missile battalions that had been subordinated to divisions since 1960 disappeared and reformed as R-100/120 brigades each with 18 launchers in either two or three battalions. Specified by the General Staff Academy in 1985,[728] a ground army could have a missile brigade equipped with either the R-300 or R-400 and

> ...there can also be a brigade of tactical missiles, that is, divisional missile battalions...This is connected to the advent of nuclear artillery in the division; the purpose is to increase combat readiness and to improve command and control and technical support by making them more centralized.

A ground army then controlled one tactical missile brigade as well as an operational-tactical R-300 brigade with a dozen launchers—several of these actually briefly reequipped with R-400 launchers until arms control spoilsports took them away under the terms of the 1987 INF Treaty. Hints surfaced that the complement of army R-400 brigades would also have been increased to 18 launchers.

**a massing of nukes**

The initial mass nuclear strike represented a decisive moment of the strategic operation in which one or both sides attempted to radically alter the operational and strategic situation. Soviet exercises and documentary expositions conveyed a clear expectation of the ability of Warsaw Pact forces to recover and accelerate a decisive offensive. Execution of a mass nuclear strike involved preparation and planning on a scale and complexity unprecedented in warfare. Orchestration of mass strikes by the fronts might involve preparing the means not only of first echelon armies but also those of second echelon armies that might be in position to participate. Depending on the progress of the strategic operation, even the longer range assets of second echelon fronts could be involved, requiring coordination throughout the TVD. Post-Soviet information indicates that at least one attempt to replicate this theoretical orchestration eventuated in 1978 at the Kapustin Yar missile range. An experimental exercise involving a front established by the Transcaucasus MD carried out a mass strike using 56 missiles of different types.[729]

The Soviet concept of the initial mass nuclear strike at the start of a TVD strategic operation had been codified in the late 1950s and early 1960s in terms expressed in the 1963 VM (S) article by the General Staff Chief Marshal M. V. Zakharov.[730]

> A particularly important factor in the successful conduct of a war is the initial nuclear strike. By this strike we mean the impact of nuclear weapons necessary to ensure the disruption of an enemy nuclear attack, the seizure of the strategic initiative, and the creation of favorable conditions for the successful conduct of military operations by all of the armed forces and the achievement of the goals of the war.

Twenty-two years later this method would still be fashionable.[731]

> The initial nuclear strike is delivered on the order of the Supreme High Command...in coordination with the Strategic Rocket Forces, the Air Armies of the Supreme High Command, and on coastal directions, with the naval forces. The objective of the initial nuclear strike is to inflict major damage on the opposing enemy and to create the conditions for motorized rifle and tank troops to complete the defeat of the enemy with a subsequent offensive.

Soviet discussions on these mass nuclear strikes often took on a surreal quality akin to those who once attempted to calculate how many angels might occupy a pinhead.

One of many delineations of the tasks of the initial strike by front and army means included the 1977 General Staff Academy front operations lecture.[732] Priority objectives included the destruction of enemy operational-tactical and tactical nuclear delivery systems; the infliction of "decisive damage" on his main troop groupings, aviation, and air defense network; and the "incapacitation" of key control posts and rear installations. By the accounting of the lecture, one Western TVD front could, in a single missile launch and sortie of aviation, put from 290 to 385 nuclear weapons on the same number of targets. The Academy 1974 front operations textbook had arrived at a somewhat different numeration—the initial strike nuclear-targets ranged 304 to 436.[733] The Coastal Front in the 1977 Academy lessons had cheerfully complied with a nuclear outset variant initial 376 missile-aviation attack. None of these quantifications, however, had involved any nuclear artillery. Academy 1985 material did incorporate shells in a first mass strike schedule, which amounted to half the thousand nuclear weapons allocated for a front operation; delivered in one or two firings; even nuclear mines purposed to cover potential enemy attack avenues.[734]

Nuclear and Fire Planning Groups at the respective headquarters of fronts and their subordinate armies worked out a precise attack schematic.[735] Elements of the initial nuclear strike plan, according to the 1977 lecture, included objectives and tasks; the desired degree of target destruction; the number and yield of nuclear weapons required; the types of burst; selection of optimum delivery means, whether missile or aviation, with procedures; and target designation using a standard numbering system. The front group comprised the chief of the Rocket and Artillery Troops with officer assistants; the chief of staff or operations chief of the air army and some officers; an operations directorate officer; and the chief of the intelligence directorate with an assistant. The lecture stressed centralization of planning at the front group for an initial mass strike at the outset of combat operations but allowed for a greater role by armies when preparing the strike during an ongoing conventional offensive; liberalization due to the rapid situation and target data changes.[736] Tracing the evolution and the varied Soviet organization solutions from the late 1950s is possible through classified writings and implementation in exercises.

The first mass strike of the nuclear variant—assuming absence of front autonomous actions—would involve coordination of strategic and frontal forces. Soviet senior officers in classified writings stressed measures to reduce the interval between respective strike regimes in which strategic means sustained higher readiness. General-Colonel G. Kariofilli, Chief of Staff of the Ground Troops rocket-artillery arm, perhaps expressing concern that his guys would be late to pile on, in a 1966 VM (S) article discussed measures to reduce response times.[737] He insisted that front strike means should join the strategic mass strike even individually on achieving launch readiness. He proposed moving the strategic strike line closer to national borders so that USSR systems could strike targets in the front zone to compensate for lagging front systems readiness. Kariofilli even suggested a division of responsibilities not limited by the line but rather a strategic-front dialog to divvy up the target list. Exercises indicated that in a mass strike conducted during combat in border areas frontal whacks would be concentrated on main directions and front-army thrusts with allotted strategic strikes further into the front zone and deep in the TVD. Commonly depicted triggering events included Warsaw Pact transition to a counteroffensive; commitment of front and TVD second echelons; with a continual stress on preemption. Initiation during the course of conventional operations would be among the most complex of military actions.

Front commanders faced the problem not only of playing catchup with strategic systems but also a more extended strike sequence; in 1967 requiring missile troops to conduct successive launches, against fixed targets followed by mobile, which prolonged the initial strike for two to three hours. Soviet cognoscenti believed this long interval somehow engendered a reduction in the effectiveness of mass nuclear detonations. General-Major L. Sapkov in 1967 considered that the longer ranges of the recently introduced tactical *Luna M* (FROG-7 unguided rocket) and operational-tactical R-300 would now permit an initial strike of one missile salvo plus one aircraft sortie. But there remained the simmering issue of accurate target location "which continues to be one of our most acute problems" necessitating additional missile salvos.[738]

A first mass nuclear strike would not necessarily be a finale. Exercises frequently played one or more successive mass strikes during a TVD strategic operation. The 1974 General Staff Academy textbook calculated that a front with three or four armies had missile-artillery assets and aircraft sufficient to deliver an initial strike of up to 470 nuclear weapons; in an assortment from 2 to 300 kilotons; to a depth of 400-km; and by using R-900 missiles in siting areas further back to 650-km.[739] But according to the CIA 1983 reading of classified writings[740] a 'typical' late 1970s initial mass strike by any one front in the Western TVD might employ from 300 to 400 nuclear weapons; totaling about 50 megatons; against about 100 targets; in a zone 250- to 400-km wide by 100-km in depth; with delivery means percentages apportioned 40 to aircraft, 35 to missile troops, and artillery 25. Rare Western TVD up-scaling data from *Zapad* 1977 represented a Warsaw Pact mass preemptive strike of about 900 nuclear weapons delivered by three first echelon Soviet and national fronts along with contributions by two fronts of the second operational echelon (their commitment timing and detected NATO nuclear preparations instigated the strike) followed about ten minutes later by more than 500 in the NATO return volley.

An increasingly powerful initial mass strike described one clear trend line through the Cold War. Documents and exercises from the start of the Revolution into the early 1970s consistently indicated the percentage of the operation allocation assigned to the first strike amounted 20 to 30. Later in the 1970s this percentage had increased somewhat to 35 or greater. The Coastal Front initial strike in the 1977 General Staff Academy material reached 55 percent of the operation missile and aviation allocation.[741] Exercise *Tsentr* 1982 apparently marked a sharply upward tilt to a 65 to 75 percent range. Abruptness of this adjustment can be seen in the archive documents.[742] While a *Druzhba* 1980 front missile-aviation initial strike expended 30 percent of the operation allocation, in *Soyuz* 1983 a front disbursed 68 percent of 621 missile-artillery nuclear munitions in the first strike including 91 percent of the allotted artillery nuclear rounds. Widespread introduction of nuclear artillery, with a high proportion used in the mass strike, comprised one element of the upswing. But the increased first strike proportion could also have represented compensation for absent strategic strikes when fronts performed nuclear solos. Exercises in the 1980s, more frequently than in the past, implemented the enlarged strike with complete second salvos by missile units. In the fragmentary data available from 1973 to 1987 initial strikes averaged 31 percent to about 1980 while from 1982 the average jumped to 72 percent. Front missile-artillery first strikes varied 147 to 423, and aviation 63 to 205, but the latter figure insufficiently portrays the VGK air armies cut.

Order of execution of the initial mass nuclear strike followed a prescribed schedule, recovered partially or as a complete timeline in many exercises and classified writings. A representative schedule began with a final target reconnaissance by aircraft and other assets (including *Spetsnaz* teams) followed by the sequential staging of strike means to launch readiness on signal from the higher commands. The mass strike then took place over a period of 70 to 85 minutes after the launch—*pusk*—command. Ten to fifteen minutes might elapse for execution of the first missile-artillery salvo (the calculation allowed for up to ten minutes of shock wave and nuclear cloud). Some target sets aimed at air defense degradation for an ensuing aircraft reconnaissance-strike phase exiting after a further 25 to 35 minutes. Another aerial recon followed up the aviation phase, which often lead to a repeat, full or selected, missile-artillery launch. The elapsed time required for a *Luna M* tactical rocket battalion to relocate and prepare a second salvo amounted to 45 to 60 minutes, while two hours would be necessary for an operational-tactical R-300 refire.[743] These systems 1980s actual or impending replacements likely had brisker performance, however, 1985 General Staff Academy material provided a similar 70 to 90 minutes detailed schedule which incorporated the aviation strike and reconnaissance phases as well as a repeat firing by missiles and artillery.[744]

## up the escalation ladder

Questions of timing and scale of nuclear initiation bedeviled Western intelligence throughout the Cold War. Added to the analytic pot discrepant political judgments of Soviet intentions, their presentments self-serving or that the objective actually manifested nuclear avoidance. Soviet political-military authorities consistently pointed to the inevitability of nuclear escalation, the NATO strategy of nuclear staging operatively delusional. The earliest Soviet dissections of Flexible Response pointed out the far-reaching objectives of a European war that engendered a mutual aspiration to victory impelling a nuclear pistol fast-draw, that escalation would be uncontrollable. A 1981 propaganda treatise, motivated by NATO plans to deploy INF missiles, stressed the unrealism of the limited nuclear war theory "We consider the concept not a bit less dangerous than the threat of all-out nuclear war."[745]

Western commentators delved into respective official models to reach categorical judgments that Soviet statements represented a concerted effort to preclude NATO limited nuclear options or to attribute a conventional favoritism. An alternative perspective is that the Soviets insisted on retention of the WMD prerogative, that their side would decide when to initiate, at what scale to strike, and which WMD to employ—prioritizing not the avoidance of nuclear weapons so much as originating the strike decision. A Czech defector who participated in high level coordination with the Soviets through the 1960s had been convinced that the motivation for nuclear initiation would not be NATO actions but rather strategic-political considerations. He noted a tendency to resort to nuclear weapons in exercises when the national front became 'bogged down' during an attack.[746] The Soviet imperative would be a rapid offensive whether conventional or WMD.

NATO modification of nuclear strategy had been recognized by the opposition well before the official 1967 adoption of Flexible Response. A Czech General Staff intelligence paper dating to the year of conventional study, 1965, found in the national archives, assessed NATO options for limited versus general nuclear war.[747] They concluded that Massive Retaliation had been eased out, but that details of the limited variant had not yet been resolved; phraseology quite similar to NATO Military Committee documents. General-Lieutenant P. Melnikov in a 1966 VM (S) article[748] comprehensively reviewed NATO development of a nuclear war variant that delayed involvement of strategic means. He attributed the start of research on this variant to exercise Green Lion in September 1962, a similar purpose a year later in the South exercise, and more complete consideration during 1964 in FALLEX and other exercises (FALLEX 1964 actually the first NATO exercise with a conventional phase).[749] The Melnikov definition of 'limited' encompassed both solely conventional and non-strategic nuclear strike operations. He expressed great concern that NATO plans to deploy "nuclear land mines" posed serious difficulties as a mainstay of nuclear limitation.

The last (1968) edition of the seminal *Military Strategy* attributed a greater degree of respectability to the Western concept of limited nuclear war, in sharp contrast to belittling comments made in two earlier editions.[750] A 1974 US intelligence study of evolving Soviet concepts for European nuclear war noted that Flexible Response had been tested in a 1964 NATO exercise and that responsive Warsaw Pact exercising took place in the next year.[751] The Czech paper pointed to NATO 1964 exercise use of nuclear weapons to eliminate breaches in defense lines.[752] This is a refrain repeated in subsequent Soviet-Warsaw Pact exercises and writings that consistently related NATO resort to nuclear weapons to breaking up of forward or intermediate defenses.

The Narew exercise in June 1965 depicted a NATO attack with conventional weapons and a Warsaw Pact counteroffensive at the same level; nuclear weapons brought into play only on D+8 when the enemy "under extreme pressure" resorted to localized strikes on one army "This act meant that nuclear war had started" eliciting a front massive nuclear response. The Polish document declared this exercise the first held by the Warsaw Pact in which Polish forces had escalated from conventional to nuclear war.[753] In the *Jesien* 1966 scenario the West initiated strategic nuclear strikes to retain the strategic initiative after 46 hours of a conventional offensive with at least Polish first retaliatory nuclear strikes 80 minutes later.[754] Scenario of the July 1970 Southwestern TVD war game featured three full days of conventional combat and a D+4 unlimited nuclear exchange in at least that TVD. The Polish-directed April 1973 exercise *Kraj* depicted enemy nuclear strikes 25 hours after their conventional attack, escalating to global nuclear war on D+5.[755] The 1976 *Tarcza/Shchit* exercise had opposing sides conducting simultaneous mass strikes as the beginning nuclear act on D+3.[756]

Emplaced nuclear devices (ADM or mine) posed a thorny dilemma for both sides in particular defining whether detonation signified crossing the nuclear threshold, instigating general or only limited nuclear warfare. NATO would be in a 'use it or lose it' situation in that offensive blocking required forward positioning to be of any value; immediately subject to capture at the outset of a Warsaw Pact offensive; yet requiring a US-NATO political release decision which in a conventional variant would be problematic. By at least May 1965 the US had 340 ADM in Western Europe[757] and General-Lieutenant P. Melnikov had noticed plans to add 300 in early 1966 in his detailed treatment of the difficulties both of troop passage and NATO use authorization.[758] According to Colonel (Engineer) Yu. Dorofeyev in a 1968[759] VM (S) article focusing on nuclear minefield reconnaissance and transit, only two prior articles in the journal had dealt with the topic since issue one of 1967 (not acquired or lost by the CIA which cannot locate). The second article reported on results of 1966 war gaming at the Military Engineering Academy dealing with enemy nuclear minefields.[760] The earliest known play of reaction to ADM use came in the 1965 Narew D+8 scenario in which the nuclear exchange did not occur until ten hours after detonation to halt an army advance.[761] ADM would persist as a headache for both sides but would not have been of priority concern to the Warsaw Pact since the West Germans would not countenance prechambering.

According to interviews with Soviet General Staff officers in the 1990s,[762] the years 1976 to 1978 had been characterized by a re-thinking of nuclear inputs according to a *periodizatsiya* framework that projected an intermediate period of limited nuclear strikes between conventional, and general nuclear, warfare. However senior officers of the Strategic Rocket Troops also interviewed emphatically denied the existence of any phase short of all-out nuclear war. They claimed that the highest politico-military authorities never consented to any limitation of nuclear means. Vitaly Katayev, a CPSU Central Committee expert on missile programs, commented that "the military played with this inside their own little box to which they would then pull down the cover…away from exposure to what was really going on." He attended many meetings of the Defense Council which raised the possibility of selected nuclear use "and was always rejected" at both strategic and theater levels. Of course the RVSN officers may have had a "little box" of their own, divorced from that run directly by the USSR General Staff and from the political leadership. But classified writings acquired during the Cold War indicate that the genesis of this "periodization" originated in military treatises a decade earlier.

These conflicting viewpoints point to a sharp divide between theater and strategic forces planning assumptions seemingly acceptable to the political leadership—the senior military officers interviews depicted a Brezhnev period of incompetence and indulgence permitting free play of rival bureaucratic agendas. But US intelligence sources during the Cold War persisted mainly circumscribed to matters in the "little box" under the purview of the General Staff. While strategic exercises could be assessed these did not provide reliable indications of nuclear intentions and scaling envisioned by the political leadership. The NATO command might suppose that a resort to limited or 'demonstration' nuclear strikes would elicit at most a Soviet response in kind when in fact any use of (or indications of preparations to use) nuclear weapons might have resulted in an immediate massive theater systems response. Reiterated—dissenting from a 1985 NIE conclusion of "signs" from the opposition that NATO limited use of nuclear weapons would not elicit a mass response—US Army intelligence regarded as "imprudent" the presumption of anything less than a full nuclear attack.[763]

One early indication of nuclear limitation, albeit only the decoupled variant, appeared in the first 1964 VM (S) issue critique by General-Major M. Cherednichenko[764] of a book published two years earlier by Chief Marshal P. Rotmistrov on the operation of a combined-arms army. Cherednichenko debited the book for considering only the surprise-nuclear variant.

> The surprise unleashing of a worldwide nuclear war is fully probable. It is the most dangerous and extremely complex case of the entry of our armed forces into a war. However, it is not out of the question that a war may first break out in some limited area (a local war) and nuclear weapons will not be employed in it....It may so happen, too, that at the beginning of a war of limited scale only operational-tactical [front] nuclear weapons will be employed. An army conducting an operation in such a war will employ all its forces and means, including nuclear weapons, but strategic nuclear weapons may not participate in the war for some time.

But Cherednichenko's comments are ambiguous, perhaps reflecting only the early stage NATO move toward nuclear flexibility rather than a formal Soviet replication.

The First Deputy Chief (Operations Directorate) of the USSR General Staff, General-Colonel M. Povaly, provided a seminal exposition of evolving Soviet views on nuclear war limitation in the 1967 first issue of VM (S) (number 80).[765] The context a rejection of the official formulation of the Initial Period concept that stressed a decisive opening stage with the employment of the full range of nuclear systems. Povaly reviewed the historical background of the concept, relating content to both changes in weapons technology and views on the commitment of the strategic echelons—yet another usage overlooked by intelligence connoisseurs. He ascribed to MoD Marshal R. Ya. Malinovsky, in comments during a 1965 war game, the redefinition into strategic periods "being considered." At the outset of war a "non-nuclear period" might be possible, which in Europe could last from a few hours to three days, but potential actions included enemy resort to limited use of nuclear weapons. There could also be a "nuclear period" of strategic nuclear actions which could follow or would constitute the only period of a war. This would likely be very short in duration and involve massive destruction in TVDs and in the USSR. There could also be a "concluding period" if the war did not end in the preceding period; this would be fought with conventional and remaining nuclear weapons. To Povaly victory would be achieved in this endgame by the side with the largest quantity of surviving nuclear weapons.

None other than the redoubtable Colonel A. Volkov immediately ratified this tripartite periodization in the next VM (S) issue (number 81) discussing key problems of the "non-nuclear period"—including the strategic echelons—brought about by US-NATO revisionism.[766] Triplication also provided the conceptual basis of Colonel P. Simonok's early 1968 VM (S) (number 83) assessment of NATO views on the nature of the "non-nuclear" period in which "tactical" nuclear weapons might be used prior to escalation to "general nuclear war." He provided a Soviet, or attributed to NATO, the definition of the upper limit of "tactical" weapons at 500-kt.[767] Similarly, in the same issue Captain First Rank N. Vyunenko and an admiral of the reserves discussed the limited use of nuclear weapons in naval operations seemingly as an extension to "non-nuclear" and prior to "general nuclear war" although they did not so strictly define the periods as did other authors.[768] Colonel I. Rachok in issue number 84 again distinguished a "non-nuclear period" and a "period of nuclear actions" lacking any defined interval.[769]

But the Ossetian tiger General-Army G. Khetagurov heralded another revision. Writing in the first VM (S) issue (number 86) for 1969,[770] he delineated a new quadripartite periodization "A front operation can include periods of non-nuclear and limited nuclear operations, the decisive nuclear period and the period of concluding operations." His remarks on the character of front operations in conditions of unlimited nuclear war persisted far more extensive than those addressing a beginning conventional and subsequent limited nuclear variants. Khetagurov proffered the caveat regarding limitation that the goal of nuclear weapons inauguration lay in precipitating a radical change in the battlefield situation "the use of only operational-tactical nuclear means will not enable us to bring effective actions to bear on the enemy simultaneously throughout the entire depth of the front operation." He obviously anticipated a short interval for any limited nuclear period. "The changeover from limited to unlimited use of nuclear weapons will signify the entry of the belligerent sides into general nuclear war."

While earlier articles placed the first, limited, use of nuclear weapons within the "non-nuclear period" and often in more of a NATO context, by 1970 there had been an unambiguous insertion of a fourth period between the non-nuclear and nuclear. In VM (S) issue number 89 General Staffer General-Lieutenant F. Gayvoronsky[771] brought up four ongoing issues including "conduct of operations with limited use of nuclear weapons" which had elicited a "lively discussion" in recent years among the cognoscenti. He pointed to increased Western interest in nuclear restriction and cited the instructions of General Staff Chief Marshal M. Zakharov that the Soviets must also "be flexible."

> It may be that under such conditions we will deliver nuclear strikes against the enemy with operational-tactical means only, while under other conditions part of the strategic nuclear means will be used with them simultaneously. Finally, it is not excluded that we will immediately deliver a general nuclear attack.

Zakharov had, in a 1969 issue 87 rambling article,[772] already affirmed the new period while informing his officers that any war would "proceed in its development through a number of consecutive and closely interrelated periods" or phases and that "we allow for not only a non-nuclear period but also a limited nuclear period." He expected, however, a quick escalation to the "decisive nuclear period" and that there might possibly still be a "concluding period." In his 1970 VM (S) (number 90) article General-Lieutenant L. Sapkov described the enemy concept of limited nuclear strikes and stated outright that this variant had been adopted "selective use"…"new for our forces."[773]

Decoupling, waging a war for at least a short time with only operational-tactical (front) nuclear systems, had thus been adopted in principle by the Soviets but US intelligence lagged, and hesitated, in perceiving change. The CIA Strategic Research Office in 1971-1972 issued two perspectives examining Soviet theater concepts to include any signs of a NATO-like nuclear staging. The May 1971 report concluded that "almost no attention has been given to the concept of gradual escalation through the limited use of nuclear weapons" and that the Soviets considered any limited nuclear response on their part to be an invitation for a NATO mass theater-strategic attack.[774] An October 1972 report assessed Soviet forces—in particular due to the lack of nuclear artillery—as having only slight capability to conduct a nuclear attack at less than a theater scale and that, despite some attention to the flexible response concept, there had been "no evidence that military doctrine and planning have been modified" to permit nuclear use to any extent below theater-level.[775]

Not until early 1974 did the OSR discover a Soviet new interest in limited nuclear war. Acquisition of the Gayvoronsky and Sapkov VM articles before March 1974 (the dates of the translations cover memos), obliquely cited, motivated a rethink.[776] Apparently by 1970 the Soviets had adopted a "more flexible posture" that promoted a tactical forces alternative to reliance on mass strikes by USSR systems; a strategic "withhold" that improvements to frontal assets enabled a "high-intensity" solo performance. Other key articles heretofore cited had not yet been received, circulated separately later in 1974 into 1976. A subsequent OSR theater forces assessment had these articles, as well as better evidence from exercises monitoring, in also pinpointing 1970 as the milestone in the Soviet generation of a limited nuclear war concept.[777]

The General Staff Academy 1974 front offensive textbook[778] acknowledged that NATO had long been working out a limited nuclear variant,

> Nor does Soviet military art in principle rule out the possibility of combat actions with the limited use of nuclear weapons, but at the same time it considers that, in view of the uncompromising nature of a future war, the period of their limited use will hardly be long. It is most likely that the first nuclear strikes in Europe will automatically produce a rapid chain reaction of nuclear escalation and inevitably lead to the unleashing of an all-out nuclear war. Therefore, the Soviet armed forces must be ready to respond to the use of nuclear weapons by the enemy with the use of all types of these weapons on any scale.

MoD Directive 00145 dated 14 November 1978, in reviewing the 1977-1978 training year, had set out a series of tasks for the ensuing 1979-1980 cycle the sixth of which called for commanders and staffs "to work out different variants for going over to the use of nuclear weapons, including their selective use."[779] The instructions bore the signature of the General Staff Chief Marshal N. Ogarkov. But there would be indications in the 1980s that Ogarkov became unenthusiastic, or never embraced, limited nuclear war.

Although the 1974 textbook had separate chapters on conducting a front offensive with nuclear, and with conventional, weapons, a long discussion regarding the 'transition' to nuclear weapons employment occurred at the end of the conventional chapter. This placement underlined the Soviet perspective regarding the overriding significance, and inevitable resort, to nuclear arms in any war with NATO. Until 1977 in *Zapad*, any conventional period elapsed short in duration, with nuclear initiation within two to six days (exactly the same length Soviet classified writings of the time attributed to NATO exercises), and that usually at theater scale.

Escalation to mass exchange continued to be the norm, with no Soviet expectation that a conventional offensive—which they expected to be successful as much as their opponents—could persist without nuclear intervention. From the mid 1960s into the 1980s Warsaw Pact exercises rehearsed, and senior officers discussed in classified writings, several nuclear variants, without indicating any preference, including limited nuclear; selective use by one or both sides; mass exchanges; preemption by one side; retaliation; and rarely by the Warsaw Pact, what some intelligence analysts assessed as initiation. Exercises occasionally portrayed limited nuclear usage by NATO without immediate retaliation, especially when setting off atomic demolition devices. Some exercises ran part or all of the gamut from selective strikes by one or both sides, with or without retaliation, escalation to theater and/or strategic exchanges, or just mass preemption.

Uncertainties continued to dog intelligence assessments. The 1979 major Warsaw Pact-NATO NIE perspective on decoupling insisted "We have found no direct evidence of such a strategy in recent Soviet military writings or information from other human sources" but again pointed to an inherent capability due to continued improvement of frontal attack systems. The NIE reiterated the 1970 adjustment point but drew a direct line to the lack of low yield nuclear artillery, as well as the front missiles high yield preference, in portraying a skeptical Soviet attitude to a NATO-like nuclear escalator. The intelligence inability to predict the Soviet response to NATO selective use remained the critical issue;[780] Soviet preparation of a remedy for the nuclear artillery equation actually in progress. Into the 1980s the CIA continued the denigration that "limited nuclear operations represent only a minor variant in the Soviets' basic plans for war in Europe"[781] while a 1984 NIE found the Soviets to be skeptical regarding any measured nuclear escalation.[782] A 1985 NIE presented an especially detailed intelligence shilly-shally regarding the evidence, classified and open writings as well as exercises, and conflicting scenarios brought about by the lack of topside access.[783] The admonition offered by the US Army interlocutor in another 1985 NIE has already been noted.

Dating of the 1980s tomes indicates the unlikelihood that their authors had a chance to peruse a highly interesting Hungarian contribution, actually in a 1980 article, but which has a transmittal memo stamped 6 September 1985.[784] While focused on their role in the Southwestern TVD, the author obviously had to draw from, or plagiarize, the Soviet prescription in his treatment of strategic and theater nuclear war—to include the variant limited nuclear period "Presumably brief." The intelligence authors should have been aware of exercise *Soyuz* 1981 in which, despite complications from the ongoing Polish internal crisis as described by the CIA liaison,[785] scenario depicted a, particularized, limited nuclear exchange after twelve combat days with at least theater-wide mass nuclear strikes played shortly thereafter.

The 1990s interviews with senior officers elicited comments that Marshal N. V Ogarkov, Chief of the USSR General Staff from 1977 to 1984, had opposed any contemplation of limited nuclear strikes since he held this to the advantage of NATO; nuclear action would more likely disrupt the non-nuclear period if NATO perceived any Soviet restricted predilection; and any use of nuclear weapons must inevitably scale massively. However, the succeeding Chief, Marshal S. F. Akhromeyev, had been more open to limitation.[786] This rejection is awkwardly confirmed in 1985 General Staff Academy material.[787] Ogarkov is cited from a VM article that "he says that to think that there will be a period with limited employment of nuclear weapons is absurd"—but that such a period actually continued under study.
• "we frequently tie ourselves to the views of the probable adversary" and
• "it is truly difficult to predict"

The Soviets conceived (and perhaps intended) the SS-20 missile leviathan to perform as a deterrent and cover for the non-nuclear period of the TVD strategic operation. Forcing a NATO (too) prolonged decision to initiate selected/limited nuclear strikes would permit so deep a Soviet penetration with only conventional weapons that would transform circumstances to game over—while enabling fronts to expedite advances with their nuclear means if necessary without a NATO rejoinder in consideration of the devastation of an SS-20 salvo. The Soviets expressed confidence in detection of NATO nuclear preparations at a very early stage if only by monitoring communications for the release order.[788]

One of the General Staff 1990s interviewees discussed the factors motivating concrete Soviet planning for a limited nuclear variant—and explicitly linked nuclear artillery to evolving views.[789] The delayed introduction, and subsequent expanding role, of nuclear artillery from the second half of the 1970s into the 1980s likely corresponded to both increasing acceptance of views favoring a constricted nuclear phase, and the corresponding prior lack of interest in this variant. Nuclear artillery had no place in the earlier high-yield extravaganza of mass strategic and frontal strikes throughout Europe. At least by the early 1970s intelligence recognized that the absence of artillery nuclear capability precluded a Soviet 'flexible response' exactly matching that of NATO since their lowest level began with tactical missiles—and the warhead yields multi- not sub-kiloton.[790]

Intelligence assessments subsequent to the detection of nuclear shells, especially for 152-mm pieces, did not emphasize a direct linkage to an established Soviet concept of nuclear limitation. Other factors in Soviet selectivity consideration likely included the conclusion derived from the 1970s studies that had been ordered by the General Staff pointing to mutual exhaustion in conditions of mass nuclear exchanges. This

## TIME PERIODS OF A WORLD WAR

depending on the manner of outbreak, the nature of tasks facing the armed forces, weapon types employed, sequence and dimensions of their deployment.

| Time periods | Time spans | Characteristics |
|---|---|---|
| Time period of action with use of conventional means. (optional) | Few days but can also be of a protracted nature. | It can develop: <br><br> - as a result of expanding a local military conflict; <br><br> - as a result of military action spreading to several important theaters. <br><br> Bitter conflict continues for seizing the initiative, assuring the success of military action: <br><br> - destruction of main body of enemy air force and navy; <br><br> - obtaining air superiority; <br><br> - significant reduction of nuclear potential; <br><br> - frustration of enemy efforts to halt the offensive. <br><br> Threat of enemy use of nuclear weapons is constant. <br><br> There are more favorable conditions for mobilization and strategic deployment of armed forces. |
| Time period of action with limited use of nuclear arms. (optional) | Presumably brief. | Crisis situation, developed during action conducted with conventional means, results in conversion to action with nuclear arms. <br><br> Conflict for seizure of initiative <br><br> Nuclear arms launched against specified installations and forces on particular axes or in theaters of operations. <br><br> Essentially tactical and operational-tactical nuclear weapons are deployed. <br><br> Use of nuclear weapons, even in minimal measure, can immediately result in possibility of unlimited usage. |
| Time period of action with [un]limited use of nuclear arms. | | In its course, a few nuclear strikes may be expected. <br><br> First strike of strategic nuclear forces will be decisive. <br><br> Greater part of nuclear ordnance accumulated in peacetime will come into use. <br><br> Effects of mass nuclear strikes: <br><br> - combat capabilities for continuation of planned and organized combat actions very quickly diminish; <br><br> - it is not improbable that in certain theaters and axes there will be no possibility for continuation of military actions for a long period. |
| Time period of following (concluding) military actions. | Can last a long time. | Begins when both sides have already basic stockpiles of nuclear arms and have partially restored combat strength of forces. <br><br> Success of action depends on which remaining forces should be used resolutely, expediently, and without delay. <br><br> Rescue, emergency, restoration operations and reorganization of war production and transport are conducted in the interior of the country. |

factor would have motivated exploration of a smaller scale nuclear phase which both favored and accelerated an offensive continuation. Any influence from the late 1960s of the increasingly important Chinese variant had not been broached in the interviews. This new enemy did not possess anything resembling the NATO wide array of nuclear systems to punish a Soviet strategic operation which could be given substantial impetus in an eastern version by selective nuclear strikes.

Preemption constituted a particularly tricky situation. Exercises so frequently played mutual preemptive attempts, with near-simultaneous mass nuclear exchanges or 'retaliatory-encountering' strikes, that intelligence assessed this scenario as the most likely Soviet theater variant. A major February 1979 exercise identified the VGK as the only authority that could decide on nuclear preemption—too late in this case since the scenario had NATO conducting a surprise full nuclear attack, following mutual detection of strike preparations, that caught Pact units in the midst of deployment. Preemption, however, is also excellent practice for executing the first strike prerogative—one Soviet officer in the 1990s interviews made that equation.[791] The 1977 General Staff Academy lecture on the front offensive stressed "It is of especially great importance to ensure the surprise of the initial nuclear strike."[792] Surprise could hardly be achieved if the opposition struck first. The Czech senior officer in the 1960s stated that top secret operations documents used the term first strike while those of lower classification substituted preemption.[793] Warsaw Pact practice became highly attuned to detection of NATO nuclear indications as a trigger mechanism, but the leadership could choose to broadly define enemy 'preparations.'

While theorists in the West engaged in esoteric discussions of nuclear war strategy the Soviets tended to derive prescriptions from more practical considerations and experience. Given the usual Soviet practice in their strategic culture of deriving even a nuclear apocalypse from prevailing concepts of a previous era, likely the 'retaliatory-encountering' or 'retaliatory-reciprocal' concept had been based on aspects of operational art. Heavy stress placed on ground operations developing into meeting engagements—a collision of opponents during mutual advances—appeared to be mechanically transferred to nuclear war. Also the artillery tactic of counter-preparation, the breaking up of enemy attack measures before they could be put into effect, could have provided the start point for the nuclear version—such a connection made by Colonel V. Savkin in 1972 inclusive of "a limited use of nuclear weapons" although the context of his tract concerned general defense actions.[794] Timely Soviet detection, and correct assessment, of enemy nuclear strike preparations would be crucial to successful preemption.

General Staff publications on front operations in 1974, the Academy textbook[795] and a manual on reconnaissance,[796] are among the more helpful itemized portents of NATO nuclear weapons employment preparation. Indications included deployment of field supply points to issue weapons to nuclear firing units; transfers to allied forces lacking the warheads; and even mass departure of merchant vessels from ports—"...detection of even part of them must serve as the basis for speeding up the preparation of the initial nuclear strike of the front...." Colonel A. Postovalov in a 1970 VM (S) article[797] not only presented a NATO nuclear strike indicator list but also pointed out the value of command detection. The most opportune indication would be the US Presidential authorization transmission which might require one to two hours; while the NATO exercised 15 to 60 minutes transpiring between strike order and execution would not permit processing in sufficient time to preempt. That "the army commander does not have the right independently to take the decision for the initial use of nuclear weapons" would be small comfort.

Academy textbook discussion also emphasized the danger of the enemy getting in the first shot. A sample calculation posited that 350 to 400 nuclear weapons delivered against a front could inflict losses of 35 to 45 percent and destroy 15 to 20 percent of front delivery systems before they could carry out launches. The 1977 Academy presentation[798] calculated damage inflicted by 340 nuclear strikes on a front deploying from permanent garrisons that included up to half of operational-tactical missiles; ten divisions sustaining up to 80 percent casualties (other divisions got off more lightly); 10000 plus square kilometers of destruction; even "the front may lose the ability to accomplish the tasks assigned." This damage assessment came in the context of a premised NATO full spectrum WMD attack entirely lacking in corroboration. Per the 1974 textbook "Considering the serious consequences of a preemptive enemy nuclear strike, the front commander and staff and the commanders and staffs of the armies must take all steps to prevent such a strike." An interesting statement prescribed, while the initial mass nuclear strike would normally be executed on VGK signal, in the event of an enemy surprise attack the front commander could decide to 'preempt' that order. The reconnaissance manual emphasized the complicated situation of spotting nuclear preparations under the dynamic conditions of the non-nuclear period. The complex array of indicators, and high potential for misreading intention of an opponent, would have increased the chances for a cataclysmic nuclear exchange even without a premeditated decision by either side.

Despite any heightened Soviet interest in nuclear limitation all variants continued to be identified in exercise scenarios. Themes of major exercises conducted in 1979 involved the surprise variant with NATO nuclear attacks at the outbreak of war, a flashback to the early 1960s. One depicted NATO unlimited strikes catching the Warsaw Pact short of Full combat readiness. Several major exercises from 1983 to 1987 notably lacked any nuclear phase play although nuclear contingency planning by participants did take place. But even at the end of the 1980s, with the Defensive Operation in vogue, mass nuclear exchanges continued to be exercised.

**allies pitch in**

The nuclear variants would not be a Soviet solo performance but rather executed in a partnership with the Warsaw Pact allies. Convoluted arguments can be alleged regarding Soviet 'intent' to permit nuclear weapons control, handling, and strikes by the national fronts-armies-divisions. Much, unequivocal, evidence had been acquired during the last three decades of the Cold War concerning Soviet planning and preparations to incorporate allied delivery means in theater-wide nuclear (and chemical) strikes. This material has since been emphatically supplemented and confirmed by documents as well as testimony from the former brothers-in-arms. The varied bill of confirming evidence includes front and army staff planning; organization and equipment of firing and logistics units; and realistic nuclear delivery practice by missile units—all with procedures read directly from Soviet guide books. Complementing indications of handover preparations by the Soviet side included, in particular, 'concrete' measures taken in the late 1960s. No confirming evidence had ever been acquired by intelligence during the Cold War of an actual transfer of nuclear weapons from Soviet control. As to retrospective accusation of nuclear proliferation, the Soviets could always point to NATO actions. In 1958 the German *Bundestag* had approved *Bundeswehr* nuclear participation. The US developed a network of custodial storage sites in Germany and other countries to supply both US and NATO delivery units. France and Britain also created independent national nuclear forces aimed eastward.

Warsaw Pact member nuclear weapons allocation planning mirrored the Soviet scheme. Czech and Polish officers had provided intelligence with detailed information on nuclear procedures, corresponding to those of the Soviets, and derived from their manuals and data tables. Archival documents provide additional insights, unique in the case of the 1960s, on nuclear preparations and Soviet supply to Czech, East German, and Polish fronts and armies. US intelligence initially had a much more hazy picture of the nuclear debutantes with little solid information in the 1960s, but filling out in the next two decades. A late 1960 NIE had no doubt that "The Soviets will almost certainly not provide the East European satellites with nuclear weapons."[799] But at least as early as the *Burya* 1961 exercise Czechs and East Germans engaged in nuclear actions even though their forces did not yet possess the depicted delivery systems. Nationals nuclear play subsequently became a common exercise feature even if clearly notional only until the requisite armament had been received and units trained. Czech defectors reported nuclear procedural details and training during the first half of the 1960s involving the R-170 (Scud A) and 3R series (early FROG)—and that supporting missile-technical units had been formed.[800] Nuclear allocations to national fronts ranged well below those of their Soviet colleagues, especially in the aviation category.

The Czech 1964 'war plan' found in archives[801] provided for a 131 nuclear weapons allocation to the Czech Front—the breakdown by front tasks exactly followed the Soviet method. Uncertain is what portion of the allotted 35 aviation bombs may have been delivered by the attached Soviet 57 (subsequent 14) Air Army rebased from the Carpathian MD; or how many of the 96 missiles provided by the two subordinate Soviet missile brigades from the same district (35 RBr actual garrison at Nesterov, 36 RBr later identified in the GDR). These brigades regrouped accompanied by a Soviet nuclear support unit. The plan specified nuclear delivery tasks, however, for Czech missile units. Strategic sharing came in the form of 16 additional bombs carried by the Soviet 184 Heavy Bomber Aviation Regiment (actually based at Bobruysk Airfield in Belorussia). The Czech senior officer reported later 1960s exercise allocations ranging from 150 to 200 (procedures allowed the Czechs to request additional warheads) with aviation nuclear attack sorties still possibly conducted only by Soviet aircraft.

Documents acquired by intelligence as well as those found in national archives provide substantial evidence during the next two decades.
- 1967 *Lato* exercise—Polish Coastal Front, initially comprising three national armies joined later by forward Soviet and East German armies, "received" 246 warheads amounting to about 7 megatons (plus 137 of another WMD variety) rationing a Front initial mass strike 74 nuclear warheads of 2.5-mt.[802]
- 1970 Southwestern TVD exercise—Bulgarian 1 Southern Front allocation 120 nuclear weapons of which 25 to be expended during the initial mass strike with no indication of other nationalities involved.[803]
- 1972—Polish archived 'war plan' allocated their front 258 nuclear weapons of which 53 air-delivered.[804]
- 1976 *Tarcza/Shchit* exercise—Northern Front under Polish command but with armies one Soviet and one Czech as well as two Polish allotted a total 299 nuclear weapons of nearly 10-mt (96 bombs).[805]
- 1980 Southwestern TVD—genuine operation plan for the Hungarian combined-arms army provided 50 to 60 nuclear weapons plus 15 to 20 air-delivered but these may have been Soviet.[806]
- 1981 *Soyuz* exercise—Polish front to employ 250 nuclear weapons of more than 36-mt including 65 bombs—even though their reliability had been deprecated by the ongoing internal crisis.[807]

National military archives provide many other examples reviewed by, among others, the German Military History Research Office.[808] East German armies during exercises into the early 1980s each received 44 to 84 nuclear missiles with indications of aviation nuclear support. National naval forces delivery systems, which at least in the Baltic had only smaller combatants, absented. In the September 1974 *Val*, the first large scale naval exercise of its type conducted by the Warsaw Pact, only the Soviet fleet received a nuclear allocation, leaving out the separate Polish and East German fleets. *Soyuz* 1983 provided the first indication of Czech and Polish nuclear artillery. Nuclear target practice by Czech and East German missile units continued into the second half of the 1980s. The Polish front nuclear allocation in the second half of the 1980s amounted to 213 missiles, 52 bombs, and now 16 artillery rounds—a substantial increase from the 91 missiles and 17 bombs of 1965.

The existence of a fully coordinated scheme to provide nuclear weapons is further substantiated in the official report on a March 1980 high level Polish delegation visit to Moscow led by their General Staff Chief. This "Secret of Special Importance" summary made available to the CIA shortly afterwards,[809] presumably by Colonel Ryszard Kuklinski. In connection to issues regarding operations of the Polish nuclear strike platforms the Soviets updated the delegation.

> The organization of delivery of nuclear warheads remains unchanged—in accordance with accepted provisions of the obligatory operational plan (from Wisla installations). In addition, the Soviet side confirmed the number and yield of the nuclear charges. Recommendations are also in the process of preparation which are supposed to clarify the following recurring problems: system of delivery of special ammunition to missile troops and Air Forces, mating of warheads, command and control, communications, camouflage, and the like.

Western intelligence already had three candidates for "Wisla installations."

Formation and equipping of national missile brigades (front and army) and rocket battalions (division) had been detected in signals intelligence of the early 1960s; in the following decades much additional information would be acquired from unit personnel. Warsaw Pact missile forces actually more successfully denied intelligence imagery access than the Soviets although this may have reflected a lower level of training activity. Penkovsky had provided sketchy information regarding the 1960 beginning of missile deliveries.[810] There is now a copy available of the March 1961 Warsaw Pact Political Consultative Committee plan which envisioned fourteen R-170 brigades to be fielded by 1965;[811] subsequently additional brigades would be formed in East Germany and Bulgaria. According to a Bulgarian officer the first missile brigade had been formed in 1958, and two additional brigades by 1960, but equipment not issued until 1961. Organization and procedures again followed the Soviet manuals. However expense considerations (the Soviets did not provide freebees) accounted among the factors that would cause national missile forces to lag Soviet missile modernization and organization augmentation until The End.

Archive documents relating exercises from 1961 to 1963 indicate notional deployments prior to completion of unit outfitting and training, but intelligence sources detected field training by 1963. An article in the Polish secret version of the Soviet VM detailed field training conducted by a missile brigade during the June 1966 *Rajd* (Raid) exercise directed by the Warsaw MD. After a combat alert and 670-km march to the Drawsko training area the brigade then deployed for "immediate nuclear-missile strikes" with all batteries simulating nuclear firings.[812] Like their Soviet brethren, Warsaw Pact missile crews through the 1980s would be afforded opportunities to conduct field training and live firings, while occupying plush accommodations, at the Kapustin Yar state missile range near the River Volga.

A few Warsaw Pact national missile surprises transpired during the Cold War. Western intelligence services only belatedly discovered in early 1990 that the R-400 (prohibited in the Soviet inventory by the 1987 INF treaty) had been provided to their allies by at least 1985.[813] This missile had been a puzzle to intelligence since deployment began years after the system had been officially declared operational (by our definition). The first unequivocal evidence of forward deployment emerged in September 1987 when a Military Liaison Mission ground team in the GDR photographed a Spider vehicle during a field exercise. This sighting confirmed earlier indications in exercises and other SIGINT sources that certain of the GSFG armies already fielded, or would imminently receive, this system. Within the USSR deployments had been identified from satellite imagery beginning in the spring of 1984 with concurrent exercise indications of a wider kickoff. But only years later did satellite imagery catch Spider missiles at, and vehicles toddling around, the Demen garrison of one of the two East German R-300 brigades. A document from the June 1988 Warsaw Pact exercise *Tarcza* found in Polish archives posits alerting of "9K714 [R-400] missile battalions" at their garrison training areas as part of the background scenario.[814] This exercise centered on a multinational front comprising one each Soviet, Czech, East German, and Polish armies so uncertainty remains which nationality(ties) controlled the "battalions"—Soviet R-400 deployed as brigades and subordinate battalions.

Much less information reached intelligence regarding the nuclear mission of national aviation and archive documents shed no more light. Certainly the Warsaw Pact aviation nuclear assignment, unlike that of missile troops, had been minimal, nowhere near the scale of Soviet aircraft. At least part of the circumstances related to lagging aircraft modernization throughout the Cold War. By implication at least, there must have been reliability concerns as well. The Soviet Special

Service could oversee missile targeting data input, and eyeball launchers orientation. Once nuclear bomb-loaded aircraft took off, and unlocking codes entered, there remained no control over flight azimuth—a nuclear weapon is the pinnacle of 'empowerment.' Careful vetting of selected national pilots would be necessary. Differences in the treatment of missile versus aviation nuclear weapon supply is evident in a secret 1973 document provided by a friendly Pole. The document listed the complete battle order of the Polish national front with designators, locations, and readiness status. While nuclear-missile support units are listed (under the Armament Service category) for the front and each of three ground armies there are no nuclear support units listed among the subordinates of 3 Air Army.[815]

There had been evidence beginning in the mid 1960s for nuclear training involving two fighter-bomber aviation regiments each in the Czech and Polish air forces, focused on a limited number of qualified pilots. By 1978 an exercise document for the air army of Polish 3 Front identified 55 aircraft as "delivery" comprising all 25 SU-20 (export SU-17 Fitter C) of a reconnaissance bomber regiment and all 30 SU-7 (Fitter A) of a fighter-bomber regiment, allocated 70 nuclear weapons with yields of up to 200-kt.[816] The 1973 Polish front mobilization listing[817] carried 7 Bomber-Reconnaissance Brigade, Powidz, and 3 Fighter-Bomber Regiment, Bydgoszcz, an indication of the sometimes close correspondence of exercise material with reality. Exercise play depicted small scale aviation nuclear activity by East Germans, Poles, and Czechs including bombs allocation, air regiment elements on alert or withhold, and strikes. The extent of any Warsaw Pact aviation nuclear role would have been influenced by observed Soviet preparations to rebase their second echelon front aviation into Central Europe at or before war outbreak.

Intelligence evidence of actual Soviet preparations to transfer nuclear weapons to national forces came highly fragmented, limited to the missile arm, and only from the recipient perspective. Even as early as *Burya* 1961 signals intelligence detected exercising of Soviet nuclear supply to Czechs and East Germans. Central European defectors and emigres in the early to mid 1960s gave varying accounts of—and documents recovered from national archives in the 1990s confirm—Soviet "assembly brigades" receiving nuclear warheads from USSR storage sites by helicopter or by rail if time permitted; delivery to Warsaw Pact missile units; and mating to missiles. The Czech October 1964 'war plan' specified two rendezvous near the Soviet border where "special assembly brigades" would be received and which would then be "transferred" to the Czech front.[818] A Bulgarian officer reported being told in the mid 1960s that a nuclear warhead storage site would be constructed near each of three missile brigades. By the late 1970s some exercises had been reflecting delivery by national convoys.

Polish archives have yielded documentation on what seems to have been a key February 1965 test of Soviet nuclear weapons shipments for the natives into at least that country.[819] US and other Western intelligence services had been entirely unaware of this milestone. Directed by General-Army P. I. Batov (Chief of Staff of the Warsaw Pact Combined Armed Forces) the exercise employed multiple avenues to move aviation bombs and missile warheads to western Poland. Four uploaded Soviet SU-7b aircraft flew to an airfield; a vessel transported nuclear weapons across the Baltic to a port; with additional shipments by rail through Brest and by ground transports. Recipients did not include Soviet delivery units. The Soviets assessed the outcome of the test as...a fiasco since delays en route seriously hindered the nuclear readiness of Polish missile troops deployed to a training area. Many senior Polish officers attended the ensuing demonstration. Other documents that have been found specified four Polish missile brigades that would receive nuclear warheads—each of these would eventually be pinpointed by intelligence. Even unlocking instructions and codes for the integrated nuclear weapons security devices had supposedly been passed to the Poles.

Failure to deliver nuclear weapons on a timely basis in this realistic field test may have been one of the factors motivating the Soviets to rectify the situation by moving weapons intended for Warsaw Pact firing units into their respective countries. No one in the West—intelligence services included—would know until after the Cold War that a series of bilateral agreements for in-country storage of at least nuclear weapons had been signed subsequent to this exercise, beginning with the Czechs in December 1965 (to be detailed). These agreements provided for 'concrete' measures to be implemented by each country to store the national allocation. One year subsequent to the exercise in Poland a comparable delivery test occurred in Hungary (again undetected by intell), missile- and air-delivered nuclear weapons, conveyed by the same transport modes (except sea delivery, not available). Upon completion of the exercise, however, the live objects remained in Hungary at a new repository.[820] Henceforward at least the nuclear component of WMD could be transferred to national delivery units within timelines comparable to Soviet forces.

New procedures appeared in the official critique of the September 1976 *Tarcza/Shchit* exercise conducted under the direction of the Polish MoND.[821] Scenario depicted first issue of the 203 nuclear warheads allocated to the Polish-commanded Northern Front delivered to each of the missile-technical units supporting the Front R-300 missile brigade and Polish and Czech army missile brigades along with their R-70 and R-30 divisional rocket battalions. Four identical statements stipulated for Polish front and two army, as well as one Czech army, missile units that a "team for the inspection, assembly, and storage of warheads will arrive at the rendezvous point [Poland location given] within 3 to 5 hours after the declaration of full combat readiness, with the following number of warheads"—exact numbers given by missile system and yields, even differentiated technical readiness conditions. These "teams" (probably an alternate translation for *brigada*) thereby arrived near missile unit deployment areas rather than at the USSR border. Nuclear warhead supply to the Soviet '25' Army however, which had been resubordinated to form the Front second echelon, would be accomplished not by any of these teams but within the USSR prior to regrouping. The Wisla installations apparently did not support Soviet missile delivery units, at least not those transiting Poland. But the 1976 exercise schedule predated the introduction of combat readiness stage Military Threat at which the nuclear warheads would be dispersed, rather than at Full, from permanent storage locations. Earlier arrival at or near missile deployment areas would then be enabled.

A 1978 document provided by the Soviets[822] for another Polish front exercise specified "Nuclear warheads for the front and armies are issued in the established area on written instructions of the USSR Armed Forces General Staff" in a situation where the receiving missile-technical support units had already deployed to reserve areas—accomplished shortly thereafter at Military Threat combat readiness. The document data table for the 3 Front nuclear allocation of 220 weapons indicated that 90 of the front 150 missile warheads, and 36 of the 70 aviation nukes, would be "available in separate missile technical bases of Warsaw Pact countries for Polish Armed Forces" with the remaining 94 "issued from bases of the USSR" in accordance to a given schedule over twelve operations days. In the Czech exercise *Neutron* 1980 an army of 2 Front had even been authorized to mate nuclear warheads to R-300 missiles prior to the outbreak of war.

**conventional complexities**

Deletion, or at least delay, of the unlimited nuclear war variant in the NATO-US strategy of Flexible Response created a wide set of consequences for the conventional-to-nuclear divide. Soviet acceptance of a variant other than general nuclear war in prospect both paralleled and directly reacted to NATO developments. There is no ambiguity regarding the initiator of this particular running of the action-reaction cycle. There had been no apparent Soviet official definition of a dated conventional watershed but rather a process that began gradually and accelerated; open and classified military writings that had provided the basis for this evolution already outlined. By 1985 the General Staff Academy would state "Previously only the initial nuclear strike; now there is an order of the Minister of Defense to plan the first massed strike by conventional weapons"—key components being aviation as well as missiles armed with conventional warheads.[823]

The transformation of 1980s non-nuclear operations exploited a targeting innovation involving the new technology of precision guided weapons. Selected front armament and firing units equipped with homing cluster warheads began to be integrated to carry out specific tasks in the form of reconnaissance-strike (RUK—front and army—against emitting targets) or reconnaissance-fire (ROK—division—against smaller point targets) complexes. According to the Academy in 1985 five types under development incorporated aircraft or missiles and artillery-rocket weapons, even the R-900 for strikes up to 600-km, controlled by new automated systems.[824]

> In our terminology, reconnaissance-strike systems consist of reconnaissance-strike complexes, which are multifunctional complexes that include various weapons and whose function is to hit different types of targets, and reconnaissance-fire complexes, whose function is to hit individual weapons, to hit targets of one type.

The Soviets considered these 'complexes' to be in the same category as NATO systems such as Assault Breaker—and none other than the General Staff Chief N. V. Ogarkov attributed this system a capability to destroy 200 tanks in one hour.[825] Accuracy ensured a first round on-target probability factor of 0.5 and, when lavishly fired, "comparable to the effectiveness of low-yield tactical nuclear weapons"—and now in fact there could be an equivalent "initial massed strike by aviation and the precision-guided weapons systems" during operations using only conventional munitions.[826]

The 1962 *Field Service Regulations* characterization of modern operations referenced the possibility of combat both with and without nuclear (and chemical) weapons.[827] However the 1963 USSR General Staff *Manual On The Conduct Of Operations* volume customized to ground battles, unlike later manuals, had no chapter devoted to combat without mass destruction weapons; conventional weapons consigned mainly to local wars.[828] An early 1964 review of the *Regulations* in VM (S) by Marshal V. I. Chuykov highlighted the indicated conventional variant, in contrast to the lack of treatment in the 1959 edition.[829] According to a recovered archive document, Marshal A. A. Grechko (then Supreme Commander) expressed at a Warsaw Pact seminar in October 1963 the need to practice combat operations without nuclear support.[830] In his early 1966 VM (S) survey of military research in the first half of the 1960s, Marshal M. V. Zakharov critiqued the 1962 and 1963 editions of the seminal open publication *Military Strategy* because "the role and significance of conventional means of destruction in war are underrated."[831] The last edition of that work, actually completed in late 1966, devoted considerably more attention to Western theories of limited nuclear war, and inserted the mea culpa that the preceding editions did not reflect warfare minus nuclear weapons. The ouster of a key nuclear variant proponent, N. S. Khrushchev, from communist party and government leadership posts in October 1964 oddly coincided with the initial exercise scenarios of conventional outbreak—just as the 1953 demise of Stalin swung the nuclear door fully open. That connection openly stated in a 1978 compendium *The Soviet Armed Forces: History of Development*.[832]

> After the October 1964 Central Committee Plenum, certain erroneous views associated with an overevaluation of the potential of the atomic weapon and its influence on the character of war and on the further development of the armed forces were overcome in military science circles.

One of the earliest indications of a non-nuclear deviation came, unusually, from a senior Warsaw Pact official writing in the Soviet VM (S). In a mid 1964 article Imre Gabor, the Hungarian General Staff Operations Directorate Chief, proffered the Marxist-Leninist justification for a conventional adjustment.[833] Gabor rooted a Western change of mood regarding nuclear exclusivity to growing American concern about the vulnerability of the homeland. He noted the universal neglect during the previous 18 years of "classical weapons" (the Soviet editor corrected this phrase to the "more accurately expressed" term "conventional weapons"). But his definition still hedged, differentiating a strategic perspective from operational-tactical considerations. From the strategic vantage point, local or national liberation wars could well be conducted without nuclear weapons and, conceivably, the imperialists could start a world war without nuclear arms. Operations and battles would even more likely be conducted with "classical weapons" but only "on separate directions or in specific periods of a nuclear war" which he attributed to a localized shortage of nuclear weapons—massiness greatly in vogue during the '60s—and limited to army- and division-level combat in secondary TVDs. Gabor anticipated, nevertheless, "far-reaching consequences" for armed forces.

A variety of evidence marks 1964 as the beginning of systematic Soviet contemplation on the nature of a war that would, at least at the outset, not involve nuclear strikes on any scale. The General-Colonel Glebov 1967 VM (S) article had dealt with conclusions on some aspects of front operations derived from a series of war games conducted by the General Staff in 1964-1965 and that the issue of an offensive without nuclear weapons had been explored.[834] General-Colonel F. M. Malykhin offered an early attempt to define the changes to the character of front operations in conventional conditions in a late 1965 issue of VM (S).[835] Pronouncements by Chief of Rear Services Malykhin had attracted a devoted following among US intelligence analysts interested in support issues. His comparable appraisal of nuclear alterations to Soviet views on rear services had been presented in a 1960 VM (TS) article.[836] Malykhin based recommendations on exercises and military science conferences held in 1964 and 1965. Other VM (S) articles from late 1964 and 1965, by Colonels S. Begunov and A. Postovalov with colleagues,[837] attempted to define the "special features" of front offensives begun when neither side employed nuclear weapons. A 1966 book published by the Frunze Military Academy, *Combat Actions of Troops Without the Employment of Means of Mass Destruction*, ranked in VM (S) as the "first serious attempt" to generalize and make recommendations concerning "non-nuclear war."[838]

A long-running intramural clash of views ensued regarding the paperwork commencing front offensives composed in peacetime, manifested in the pages of VM (S). Officers disagreed whether there should be a unified plan for the nuclear variant with provisions for a conventional edition or entirely separate plans for each variant. Colonel A. Postovalov and a colleague in the 1965 article[839] on non-nuclear front operations stated that "no unified opinion" existed yet on conventional procedures. They cited a November 1961 military science conference held at the M. V Frunze Military Academy for establishing the two differing approaches to NW/NNW planning. They voted for separate plans. In 1967 articles the Professor rejected segregation,[840] while General-Lieutenant V. Petrenko in an extended discussion came out for the opposing view "if we are going to have two variants of the decision on the operation, then naturally we must have two operation plans."[841]

Colonel G. Yefimov referred to the Petrenko argument in his 1969 article[842] focused on the planning issue which he indicated continued to be all the rage at military science conferences and exercises. He favored a, sort of, single plan with a non-denominational twist in which there would be a varying number of enemy defense breakthrough sectors that would facilitate use of either NW/NNW variant. Other officers pitched their viewpoints. In an apparent final laying down of the law General-Lieutenant F. Gayvoronsky in 1970[843] cited the authority of the General Staff Chief in rejecting dueling plans "only unified planning—Comrade Zakharov says further— assures continuity in troop operations during abrupt changes in the situation, including during a surprise transition from conventional to nuclear weapons." Consensus had apparently not been attained in a comradely manner. In a 1985 retrospective a General Staff Academy lecturer[844] characterized a process of "many controversies, many discussions, many experimental exercises" which "even reached the point of harsh confrontations" in resolving the issue.

Basic to the perceptual confrontation had been the seemingly greater capabilities inherent to the nuclear variant over conventional reliance. By the 1970s a new reality determined by exercises and operational modeling had emerged; the Soviets even concluded "We have come around to the opinion that the scope of both a nuclear war and a nonnuclear war is the same"[845]—nuclear rates of advance no longer foreseen matching the 1960s proposed high speed pace but by the mid 1980s actually considered to be less than the normative 40- to 50-kmd of conventional operations since expansive destruction and contamination would hinder ground attacks. Asserting that the Americans had come to the same conclusion, another important consideration favoring the integrated planning approach inhered in foreseeing which variant would be activated at the beginning of, and during, the front operation. Nevertheless MoD Order No. 00200 mandated that troop training for conventional actions should not detract from nuclear capability.[846] The outcome of this particular dispute confirms that the Soviet military leadership had not predetermined an exclusively nuclear solution to war in Europe.

General Staff Academy 1985 material had outlined the progression of argumentation that ultimately attained a NW-NNW blend that assigned an undifferentiated offensive objective, zone, and depth.[847]

> This principle of the integration of preparation and conduct of an operation means that a single task is assigned to the troops that is the same with and without the employment of nuclear weapons....
>
> The reason for this principle is the fact that we do not know how an operation will begin, whether it will involve nuclear weapons or a period in which conventional weapons are employed followed by a transition to the employment of nuclear weapons, or how long this period in which conventional weapons are employed will last.

Soviet press discussions of Flexible Response into the 1970s had depicted the strategy as a clever US ploy to prepare a surprise nuclear blow during the conventional phase—a subterfuge for orchestrating a more devastating strike by maximizing available delivery means and their readiness. Renewed NATO-US attention to theater conventional forces had been depicted as a compelled response to the Soviet strategic buildup. Comparable Soviet adjustments apparently would be implemented with internal dissension. Some articles appearing in the restricted VM and other open publications during 1968 to 1972 expressed derision of 'bourgeois fatalism' regarding the effects of nuclear warfare—these weapons should not be "viewed as some kind of mystical force."[848] Ostensibly directed at the West, there may have been more of an inward jab at proposals to move away from nuclear determinism toward the escalation variant.

Until at least 1977 the Soviet documentary view and exercise practice portrayed a conventional interval expected to be brief, and conducted under the constant threat of nuclear insertion. As previously noted, exercises from 1965 into 1977 played conventional openings from two to six days before the launching of nuclear strikes that mirrored the range of conventional days attributed to NATO exercises—this specified by the May 1977 General Staff Academy lecture on front operations[849]—but not to the exclusion of the nuclear outset variant. A Bulgarian officer told intelligence that the national front plan had been revised in 1966, to assume nuclear escalation in several days, approved by the Warsaw Pact command in 1967.

The decisive Warsaw Pact non-nuclear offensive would inevitably trigger NATO escalation, an action often depicted in exercises when defense lines crumbled, an eventuality, ironically, expected by both sides. The 1976 *Tarcza/Shchit* exercise scenario presumed an enemy resort to nuclear weapons when the situation became unfavorable, their first echelon had been broken, and while reserves still existed to exploit nuclear strikes.[850] Absent from the portrayals any variant in which NATO retained possession; neither Soviet writings nor exercises dealt with offensive failure, rather capabilities implied nuclear initiation. A 1985 CIA-SOVA report, however, claimed that these sources did indicate that the Soviets would resort to nuclear weapons in the event of a decisive Warsaw Pact conventional defeat as well as to preempt expected NATO nuclear attack.[851]

Forward deployment of the second operational echelon fronts in conventional conditions not only facilitated the creation of strong strike groupings in accordance with the strategic operation front grouping method but also put into position a more powerful frontal nuclear strike array capable of autonomous action. The main Soviet inhibition against resort to nuclear weapons effectively supplanted once the second echelon fronts arrived at commitment distance as well as when other reinforcements closed the gap. A nuclear conundrum would be created in which NATO defense breakdown might bring about at least limited nuclear escalation by the West, while a successful defense might impel the Warsaw Pact to go nuclear.

Defense breakthrough persisted as a crucial problem. In the nuclear variant the Soviets envisioned attacks from the march into breaches created by mass nuclear strikes against strong defenses. Regression to the GPW conventional model entailed massing troops in breakthrough sectors. But huddling is atomic suicide when conducted against an enemy threatening nuclear initiation at any moment of their choice. The Soviet solution, explained by Colonel B. Samorukov in a 1967 restricted VM article,[852] encompassed retaining the nuclear zones of fronts (300- to 400-km wide) and armies (up to 100-km or more); while concentrating briefly at the division level during attacks at weak points in the defense; and then immediately scattering. Retaining wide zones, just in case, permitted optimum anti-nuclear dispersal and maneuver.

An extended period of ground and aviation conventional armament improvements from the late 1960s reshaped Warsaw Pact forces, especially Soviet. Efforts involved development of more weapon types, larger mobilized forces, and tactical re-orientation. Preparations for a longer period of combat actions included resurrection of artillery as a principal fire means, instigating the development of a diverse range of modernized pieces. Operational prescriptions increased firepower density in tactical breakthroughs made possible by an augmentation of artillery organization. Accumulation of the substantially greater stocks of conventional munitions required appeared in satellite imagery of some 46 USSR central artillery ammunition arsenals and bases (including the front missile-artillery). These stores, largely unchanged since covered on World War II photography by German reconnaissance aircraft, beginning in the early 1970s showed indications of a massive pileup of munitions containers that would continue throughout the Cold War. Soviet planning norms, prior to the observed buildup, specified accumulation of two months reserves for the Western directions (three months in the East) at central stores, with one month assigned to fronts; subsequently full production by munitions plants would be available.[853]

By 1968 the Chief of the Ground Troops missile-artillery arm had called for a (modified) revival of the GPW "artillery offensive"—a massive, integrated, concentration of firepower to break through NATO defenses in conditions of the nonnuclear period.[854] A May 1977 General Staff Academy lecture provided the Soviet formula, derived from exercises and research, for conventional breakthroughs of US and German defenses in the Western TVD.[855] The calculation required, for one kilometer of frontage, indirect fire from 100 to 130 guns, mortars, and multiple rocket launchers along with the direct fire of 15 to 20 guns, tanks main armament, and antitank guided missiles. Three divisions in an army first echelon assigned a breakthrough sector eight to ten kilometers wide would require a minimum of 800 to 1000 indirect fire weapons; but their organic means even with the army artillery brigade and weapons of the army's second echelon division(s) tossed in still left a shortage of 260 to 387 pieces. This gap could be filled only by reinforcement with an entire RVGK artillery division. These specifications accounted for only one army—a Soviet breakthrough would actually be conducted by a front in any one sector using two flanking armies. Such density calculations embodied an offensive stance discussed in many operations guides and articles.

*Zapad* 1977, with nuclear escalation delayed to the ninth day, marked a Soviet attitude adjustment regarding the length and difficulty of a conventional campaign against NATO. The May 1977 General Staff Academy lecture defined this crucial moment in a front operation.[856]

> The transition of troops to the conduct of combat actions with the use of nuclear weapons consists in the delivery of an initial nuclear strike with all the combat-ready means of delivery in the shortest time against the means of nuclear attack and main troop groupings of the enemy, in the disruption or considerable weakening of the nuclear strike of the enemy, and also in the taking of all protective measures against weapons of mass destruction….

The time of the possible transition to the use of nuclear weapons is determined on the basis of an analysis of the operational situation and signs of the immediate preparation of the enemy to employ them. A transition to the use of nuclear weapons is most likely when the troops of a front are accomplishing major operational tasks leading to the achievement of a decisive turning point and development of combat actions and at moments of crisis during the combat actions of the sides.

In *Tsentr* 1978 nuclear initiation did not take place until war D+28 while in *Tsentr* 1982 and *Zapad* 1984 sixteen days of conventional combat transpired. The NATO new FOFA strategy of the 1980s complicated the conventional phase. Intended to raise the nuclear threshold, success might in consequence lower that of the Warsaw Pact. During those years nuclear outbreak and escalation variants continued to be exercised.

Differentiated assignments of delivery means to conventional and nuclear missions created an operational quandary. By the late 1960s development of the theater Air Operation had been well under way, requiring the commitment of substantial frontal aviation assets to mass, multi-wave, conventional attacks. But the nuclear variant loomed. The Soviet solution retained a designated proportion of aircraft on nuclear alert. General-Major M. Kozhevnikov, writing in a 1966 VM (S) article,[857] entered a discussion on the actions of aviation in a war without nuclear weapons; stating as "advisable to divide the air forces into nuclear and non-nuclear echelons." Exercise experience indicated that 60 to 65 percent of Long Range Aviation and 25 to 30 percent of front aviation should be withheld in the "nuclear echelon" but his approach seems to have encompassed entire air regiments. Marshal (Aviation) S. Krasovsky had previously calculated a similar disproportionate withhold of 70 and 30 percent, respectively.[858]

Exercises and other writings on aviation operations indicated planning for more like one squadron of each nuclear-capable air regiment to be held back from large scale conventional strikes. Orders to the Polish '24' Air Army regarding combat alert aviation in exercise *Tarcza/Shchit* 1976 specified that "each fighter-bomber regiment has one flight ready to take on special bombs in suspended position" later identified as SU-7b from three regiments.[859] A 1977 General Staff Academy lesson stipulated that each of the fighter-bomber and bomber aviation regiments in the front air army hold one flight in readiness to use nuclear weapons during conventional operations; the lesson categorized 320 of the front 732 aircraft as nuclear delivery means.[860] A 1979 exercise of the GSFG front featured typical aviation planning of differentiated variants. In the nuclear all 847 aircraft would be sortied while in the conventional variant more than 12 percent of the front aviation complement would be withheld in the nuclear echelon.

But this approach of holding back nuclear-qualified pilots, the best of the lot, would attenuate the conventional blow. In 1967 Colonel A. Volkov again interjected pointing out such weakening but he regarded the massing of aviation as compensatory.[861] Even in a lower classified VM 1967 article Colonel B. Samorukov stressed the disjunct between a requirement for a greater number of aircraft in conventional strikes and diminution by those essential to nuclear readiness.[862] Withdrawals could potentially compromise the success of the conventional Air Operation which must achieve air superiority against strong NATO air forces. Intelligence assessments actually focused on pilot training and qualification, rather than aircraft performance, to calculate nuclear delivery capability. A 1975 Joint Memorandum on Warsaw Pact capabilities graded about 300 Soviet pilots as probably nuclear-qualified despite the 720 aircraft inventoried at that time possessing suitable technical characteristics. There could be 110 additional national nuclear-capable aircraft that might have met the probable criteria except for "uncertainties regarding control and availability of nuclear warheads" which relegated the allies to a possible category.[863] As early as 1961 a comprehensive reverse assessment of NATO-US aviation nuclear capability by Colonel A. Konstantinov used similar criteria including citing a British journal that only a third of flight crews had sufficient nuclear delivery training.[864]

Indications of the scale of the envisioned Air Operation could be viewed in many different sources during the Cold War. Contemporary Soviet judgments had been conveyed to the aforementioned Polish delegation to Moscow in 1980.[865] The main goal aimed to "destroy (weaken) missile-nuclear and aviation groupings of the enemy, and to gain air superiority" in a TVD. The Air Operation constituted a principle method for the conduct of the non-nuclear variant but might also be conducted in a nuclear war. Alternative conditions for the initiation of the Air Operation included "in the event preemptive operations are conducted by our side." Aviation of several fronts as well as air armies subordinate to the TVD High Command comprised assets to be employed, including the aviation complements of second operational echelon fronts that would be rebased forward prior to startup. Six to eight mass aviation strikes would be launched during a period of five days in an area 1000- to 1500-km wide and 1000-km in depth; some 3000 aircraft conducting 20000 to 25000 sorties. According to the 1977 General Staff Academy front operations lecture air reconnaissance flights to identify targets for the initial nuclear mass strike might be conducted as part of the Air Operation.[866]

Soviet attempts to resolve the conflicted missions dilemma culminated during 1980-1981 with the formation of Aviation of the VGK. Aviation regiments and divisions from Central Europe to the Far East redistributed among five VGK air armies. Western and Southwestern TVD tasking assigned to 4 and 24 Operational Air Armies VGK; the SU-24 (Fencer) deep-strike light bomber, the Soviet clone of the US F-111, became the core asset. In mid 1984 each air army had 180 SU-24. Theater backup would be provided by 46 Strategic Air Army VGK while 30 Strategic Air Army VGK aimed at the Chinese; both equipped with a mix of medium and light bombers.[867] These VGK air armies assumed the theater-wide nuclear and conventional burden, leaving remaining aviation to focus on frontal missions. Heavy bombers congregated in 37 Strategic Air Army VGK. These air armies packed a powerful punch. Each operational air army, in a concerted conventional sortie, could deliver 1500 to 2000 tonnes of bombs, 800 air-surface missiles, and 150000 unguided rockets.

Missile troops ultimately enlisted to relieve the air burden posed by the nuclear echelon. Colonel N. Semenov proposed in a 1968 VM (R) article that front missiles supplement aviation with conventional strikes, noting a US company developing conventional solid propellant missiles to strike airfields.[868] His proposal ran against an unfortunate characteristic of Soviet short-range missiles—poor accuracy—not a problem when tossing multi-hundred kiloton warheads, but deleterious to conventional tasks. Tactical R-65 and operational-tactical R-300 did not constitute pinpoint delivery vehicles. Soviet argumentation regarding a conventional role for front missiles had actually been already in progress, at least in the pages of VM (S). Colonel S. Begunov's denial in late 1964 that conventionally-armed missiles represented a viable option had been disputed by Colonels A. Postovalov and K. Kushch-Zharko in their 1965 response. They insisted that "cluster-type" warheads would be substantially more effective than high-explosive versions.[869]

General-Major G. Biryukov and Colonel G. Khoroshilov explored in much greater detail regarding a conventional role for front missile troops in an early 1968 VM (S) article.[870] Their main concern involved the suppression of NATO air defense systems, during operations absent WMD strikes, to clear flight corridors for transport aircraft carrying an airborne division to a drop area up to 200-km behind enemy lines—as many as sixteen aviation regiments would need clear passages. Both tactical rockets (FROG) and R-300 featured in their mathematical modeling of effectiveness, with high explosive warheads of 200 to 800 kilograms combined with warheads containing "napalm-type viscous incendiary mixtures." They calculated that an average of 12 to 16 tactical rockets would be required to neutralize a Hawk firing position and 12 to 17 R-300 for a Nike-Hercules site deployed in greater depth. Effectiveness of the R-300 strikes could be enhanced by use of "active casing" warheads with the expectation that residual liquid propellant would generate large fires. Soviet development of "cluster-type" warheads seemed to be already under way since the authors found these to be "promising."

As late as May 1977 the General Staff Academy lecture on front operations considered aviation to be the principal conventional means for hitting targets beyond artillery range.[871] Nevertheless by the mid 1970s the R-70 version of the FROG would be detected in a conventional role; this system in turn replaced by the more suitable *Tochka* tactical missile fielded in the last half of the 1970s—nickname 'Point' reflecting the faith of the Soviet designers and operators in an accuracy suitable for conventional warheads. Development of a new generation of improved conventional warheads would follow, cassette (cluster or submunition) to enhance area impact; and even the R-300 would be given a chance with a variety of homing (terminal guidance) warheads in the 1980s. The R-400 represented an even better wager, but did not hang around for long.

By 1978 missiles in a conventional role showed up in large numbers during exercises, frequently as part of the front nuclear allocation. Their significance heightened in the 1980s such that an NIE commissioned to assess Warsaw Pact conventional strike capability against NATO airfields had to address the participation of front missiles—the anticipated fielding of the SS-23 (R-400) a particular concern.[872] During the 1983 *Soyuz* one front had fired 132 of on-hand 281 cassette warheads (a fifth R-300) during ten days of conventional combat and a reorder for the expended quantity placed with the Center. Even larger front allocations materialized. An interesting variation for solving the contamination-destruction obstacle problem in another 1983 exercise involved an apparent Soviet initiative or preemptive strike of conventional missiles in the path of a planned advance and nuclear missiles on the flanks. Post Cold War documents found in East German archives indicated that by 1988 planning of massive strikes with missile cassette warheads had also become the norm among national troops.[873] Conventional missiles would be leading elements of the reconnaissance-strike complexes under development as a counter to FOFA precision weapons.

But the nuclear echelon problem resurfaced. Being caught with missiles armed entirely with conventional warheads posed a high risk against an opponent declaring an inclination to nuclear first use. Exercises and other evidence in the mid to late 1980s hinted that the Soviets planned to pre-mate firing unit missiles with conventional warheads and have similarly mated reloads in nuclear support units. The missile-technical units would also keep nuclear warheads nearby for a quick change in the launch units; or accomplish mating and transloading instead of the firing battalion technical subunits which would normally carry out these tasks. To conduct this amended scheme required a re-echeloning of nuclear warheads and re-purposing of nuclear-missile-technical contingents—to be considered. Clearly the Soviets remained confident that they would initiate the nuclear variant or expected to detect NATO nuclear preparations in sufficient time to preempt.

# Elusive Chemical Echelons

US intelligence misapprehensions regarding the mass destruction weapons capabilities and intentions of other countries did not originate post-Cold War in Iraq. The preceding Soviet estimate also lurched erroneous and distorted, a dereliction on a much greater, ominous, scale. Unlike Iraq credible evidence verified the existence of a threat but intelligence pursued a grievously flawed analytic path compounded by uncertain information on extent, nodes, and continuity.

- Electronic monitoring—a nuclear intelligence mainstay—signally failed, throughout the Cold War, to define the dimensions of the Soviet offensive chemical and biological weapons posture; only occasional 'popups' materialized, years apart, amounting to a modest amount of discontinuous evidence entirely inadequate for framing viable conclusions.
- Another power tool satellite imagery persisted systematically, fraudulently, abused.
- WMD issues coped with the usual human witnesses whose credibility ranged from instantly dismissible to those acceptable only if they reinforced preconceptions; structural evidence remained sparse, that pinpointing organizations and channels responsible for toxic chemicals, bacteriological agents, and munitions.
- The only meaningful intelligence derived from the clandestine sources of the CIA Operations Directorate, and foreign partners, mainly in the form of classified material on chemical operational aspects as well as some weapons data.

But those sources did encompass indicative material. The chemical buck in particular stopped at the desks of intelligence connoisseurs whose perceptual myopia effectively blurred the, however limited, evidence of the second and third kinds. US, British, and NATO intelligence services misconstrued the nature of Soviet chemical intentions in the 1960s and early 1970s, and subsequently headlined an offensive threat when the Soviets had actually backpedaled. The inability of Western intelligence to accurately perceive and calibrate Soviet offensive chemical planning and preparations ranks high among the truly miserable performances, and potentially militarily cataclysmic, of modern history. An egregious, comprehensive, failure of strategic intelligence—extending three full decades—has few comparables.

**origins**

Russians confronted a practical experience of battlefield chemical weapons during the First World War, a trauma surpassing that of the Western Front but less dramatized. The new Soviet Union officially acceded to the 1925 Geneva Protocol prohibiting the use of "war gases" and "bacteriological methods" in April 1928—ratification not consummated by the US for a further 47 years. USSR reservations specified that the Protocol would not be binding in relation to non-adherents or transgressors.[874] Signing on did not inhibit collaboration in chemical testing with a resurgent Germany during 1928 to 1933 at the Volsk-Shikhany proving grounds along the River Volga. Editions of the *Provisional Field Regulations of the RKKA* (Worker-Peasant Red Army) issued in 1929[875] and 1936[876] had been notable for the chemical content of offensive and defensive actions. Both works had introductory Protocol affirmations that chemical weapons would be used only if introduced by the "class enemies"—a stipulation reiterated in People's Commissar of Defense Order No. 154 of 21 July 1929[877] that "The chemical weapons indicated in the *Field Service Regulations* will be used by the Red Army only if our enemy uses them first."

A Russian investigator has documented the extensive Soviet-German CW cooperative work that actually began well before that at Volsk-Shikhany.[878] Agreements on joint agent production as well as artillery shell filling, including mustard and phosgene at Chapayevsk, had been set in 1923. Information on these activities had subsequently been publicized in the West. Joint testing had been conducted at the Kuzminki range near Moscow in 1926 and the next year at an aviation site south of Orenburg; which in 1928 shifted to the River Volga proving grounds. Aircraft chemical spray tanks and land mines for terrain contamination attracted particular interest. The Soviets gained knowledge of nearly the full range of German chemical weapons technology although suspicion had been raised concerning reticence on new agents development. Breaking up in 1933 occurred when the Soviets became satisfied that all worthwhile information had been extracted and that proprietary skills developed should no longer be shared. An identical evolution would take place after the world war in regard to missiles, exploiting German work until an independent Soviet program could develop.

The 1936 *Regulations* debuted WMD preemption—striking with artillery and aviation chemical agents to thwart enemy chemical preparations—and likely represented full absorption of collaboration experience. Provisions specified that chemical agents use "is ordered by the commander in chief" in an attack. This edition also featured substantially expanded treatment of chemical defense tasks including the "basic mission" of preserving troop capabilities in the event of **enemy** use of chemical munitions—Cold Warriors would cite the large size of Soviet Chemical Troops as damning evidence of a Soviet offensive intent. Marshal K. Y. Voroshilov laid out the USSR WMD stance, likely also applicable during subsequent decades, in a February 1938 speech.[879]

> Ten years ago or more the Soviet Union signed a convention abolishing the use of poison gas and bacteriological warfare. To that we still adhere, but if our enemies use such methods against us, I tell you that we are prepared—fully prepared—to use them also and to use them against aggressors on their own soil.

The sidelining of chemical weapons during World War II, motivated at least partly by mutual fallacious perceptions of enemy capabilities, would be among the most remarkable non-events of that frenzy of mass killing. Fundamental misconception would also characterize chemical appreciations during the ensuing Cold War. Western intelligence in the late 1940s and through the 1950s had only the murkiest picture of Soviet WMD capabilities, activities, and preparations. Virtually all information derived from interrogations of German and Japanese prisoners returning from the USSR and, notably, German war intelligence all neatly collected in the so-called Hirsch Report. This survey by a German chemical specialist compiled in the early 1950s as *Soviet Chemical Warfare and Biological Warfare Preparations and Capabilities*[880] would continue to be a reference throughout the Cold War.

The first public enunciation since 1938 of the Soviet attitude toward both chemical and biological warfare came in February 1956 at the 20th Congress of the Communist Party. Minister of Defense G. K. Zhukov, in a statement outlining the military doctrine of the Soviet State, declared the expected mass use in modern war of "atomic, thermonuclear, chemical" means, with "bacteriological" thrown in for good measure.[881] There had been earlier indications of interest in chemical weapons during the 1950s but this declaration came from a doctrine *meister*. Such pronouncements from the top leadership tended to be accorded reverential significance in the Soviet strategic culture. The Zhukov proclamation would be the most important exposition on the direction of Soviet military thought until the N. S. Khrushchev speech in January 1960 proclaimed a Revolution in Military Affairs brought about by the mass introduction of nuclear missiles.

Any actual WMD setup may still have been at an early stage barely noticed by the intelligence services of the opposition which in the 1950s had few channels to access any Soviet military developments. A spokesman on military science and technology, professor at the Zhukovsky Military-Air Engineering Academy General-Major G. I. Pokrovsky, noted in a pamphlet published in 1956 that chemical weapons had not been used in World War II nor the Korean conflict and (in translations by Raymond Garthoff)[882]

> ...there were no substantial qualitative advances in their development, this subject has been discussed considerably less in the military press than has, for example, the subject of atomic weapons. Nonetheless, the effectiveness and the variety of chemical warfare are constantly increasing, and, if there were an element of surprise in its use, it could have great significance in combat. As a result, this problem must be borne constantly in the minds of all military commanders and all military specialists.

But in another open publication the next year his attitude had markedly altered.

> Above all, one must take note of chemical weapons...At the present time very effective substances have been created...we have no experience in the employment of these means of mass destruction under conditions of contemporary war. However there is no basis for hoping that in the future such substances will not be employed. On the contrary, chemical weapons may, in the case of mass surprise attacks on the part of an aggressor, find very wide employment.

By associating CW with the surprise factor and mass use Pokrovsky effectively established a direct link to doctrinal alterations regarding nuclear weapons that had been pushed by senior officers since 1954. A 1954 secret manual had asserted "The outcome of a war cannot be determined by atomic weapons alone"[883] but several marshals disagreed. They successfully revised the Stalinist orthodoxy that the USSR would never be defeated in a surprise attack to accept that nuclear weapons employed in a surprise strike could quickly ensure decisive results. During 1955 open articles in military and political journals[884] and in VM (R)[885] had stressed the portentousness of a nuclear surprise. The Marshal Zhukov imprimatur had subsequently defined a WMD triad that would endure through the end of the Cold War.

As usual in the Cold War, evaluation of Soviet intentions and preparations cannot be divorced from those of the designated adversaries. During the 1950s some Western countries, with the US in the lead, had pursued significant chemical and biological armament programs. The potential targets of these WMD arsenals highly likely would accentuate the most threatening variant which, in any case, reinforced their ideological official model. US policy established by National Security Council classified directive 5602/1 in March 1956 provided for use of "chemical and bacteriological weapons in a general war" at the discretion of the President—this modified the retaliatory stance in effect since World War II—signed by D. D. Eisenhower as a measure to bolster development of the full WMD triad.[886] Department of Defense Directive TS-3145.1 dated 6 October 1956 implemented the revision under the heading "Policy" that "the United States must be prepared to use chemical and biological weapons in general war, to the extent that the military effectiveness of the armed forces will be enhanced by their use."[887] An implied preemptive stance had been publicly reaffirmed in the Basic National Security Policy document of 5 August 1959 (officially rescinded in January 1963). US policy pronouncements, classified and public, persisted so muddled and vacillating that even top US defense officials remained uncertain of the operative line at any given time. This is obvious in the memos and studies circa 1969 that have been declassified, when the Nixon administration unilaterally renounced the BW segment, and sought a new position concerning chemical arms.[888]

Both the US and Britain had initiated biological weapons programs during the Second World War. The ever-recurring intelligence-defense-political theme motivating these efforts attributed (substantiated or not) similar intentions to the contemporary designated enemy—Nazi Germany. Development continued in the postwar years, although a UK lateral to their partner in the 1950s transferred responsibilities. US agent tests would be run on an individual to large scale, at proving grounds in Utah, the basis for a significant BW program extending through two decades until abandoned in 1969. Production in Arkansas at the Pine Bluff biological agent plant began in 1954.[889]

US interest had been piqued during the late 1940s concerning the new class of nerve agents developed by the Germans during World War II. The usual studies had been conducted and in June 1950 a recommendation by the Stevenson Committee that the national chemical warfare posture should be improved transmitted to the Secretary of Defense. By November design work on, and in 1951 construction of, plants would be initiated at Muscle Shoals, Alabama and Rocky Mountain Arsenal in Colorado for the multi-step production of the premier nerve agent GB (sarin to the Germans). Plant construction, agent processing, and weaponization (munitions filling) programs ensued. GB agent production ended in 1957 with the planned stockpile level attained. In early 1957 the US had formally selected the persistent nerve agent VX, a more toxic variety originally discovered by the British, as a principal chemical fill, and pursued agent series production. Accomplished by 1961, production would continue until 1967.[890]

Britain also pursued a vigorous chemical armament program on the basis of German leftovers, including sarin pilot production. Exclusive possession in the West of a large stock of German 250-kg bombs, each filled with 190 pounds of agent GA (tabun), provided the basis for extensive CW research. The US had examined tabun but determined to focus on the militarily much more effective agent sarin. The British had access to data from *Luftwaffe* field trials and the Porton establishment continued tabun testing. They finally concluded that, for both strategic and tactical purposes, tabun had little more effectiveness than current phosgene and mustard weapons (production and bomb filling under way during this period). Only in air bursts did the tabun bombs shine but to be useful the German munitions required costly modification with unavailable fuzes. The 1955-1956 Operation Sandcastle disposed of the UK stock of 70697 German tabun bombs by the, now eco-rageously incorrect, method of loading and scuttling three ships in the North Atlantic.[891] By 1957 the British had decided to opt out of the offensive chemical warfare business, at least partly motivated by the nuclear massive retaliation strategy that had emerged as the US-NATO standard.[892] The French, asserting their independence as usual, also worked on CW, outlasting the British.

No information then or now imparted the Soviet perception of these offensive WMD armament programs but the Western chemical buildup could hardly not have contributed to the mid 1950s doctrinal revision. US policymakers approved, and weaponeers developed and deployed, a militarily significant chemical and biological arsenal. They had thereby tossed a largish rock into the Cold War pond. These programs had been pursued oblivious to inevitable strategic ripples—full steam ahead in an intelligence environment unable to accurately gauge the scale and nature of any Soviet counterpoise. An imposing, comprehensive response to the late 1950s US BW-CW programs would be a certainty as had been in regard to the late 1940s US deployment of atomic weapons. Somebody had given a big shove to the action-reaction cycle. US intelligence did not obtain specific information, and continued incapable of providing meaningful assessments, on Soviet chemical and biological programs.

A principal motivation behind the US chemical armament drive had been an unverified assumption. The Soviets had seized both of the German series production plants for nerve agents at Dyhernfurth (tabun—postwar Polish Brzeg Dolny) and Falkenhagen (sarin—near Berlin) so they must perforce be advancing vigorous development programs. Already known from German returnees had been the transfer of equipment from Dyhernfurth to a plant near the city later renamed Volgograd.[893] Less had been learned concerning Falkenhagen although suspicions had been raised about the massive Dzerzhinsk chemical complex, possibly confirmed by Russian information. Apparently no indication of the plants whereabouts would be provided by the Russians in the data exchanges leading to, and under, the 1997 Chemical Weapons Convention.

The sarin and VX output during this period had been filled into a variety of missile warheads, rocket and tube artillery rounds, mines, and for the fly boys, bombs and spray tanks. Late in 1958 the US secretly established a chemical store in West Germany near Kirchheimbolanden, then known as the Rhein Ordnance Depot. Circa 1962 this site held more than 3500 tonnes of sarin and sulfur mustard in artillery and mortar munitions including a small amount in bulk storage. The same US DoD memo[894] that provided that information set forth a proposal to establish three more ground and one aviation chemical storages in the FRG, one naval facility in Italy, and even a massive reserve stock of more than 17000 tonnes at two US-controlled ammunition depots in eastern France (at a time when an American presence still welcome)—these sites to be stocked with the new VX munitions. The planned French accumulation alone represented more than half of the amount of the total US agent stockpile disclosed to the Soviets in a December 1989 bilateral data exchange as well as that declared under the 1997 Chemical Weapons Convention.[895]

FALKENHAGEN
REMAINS OF 500 TONNES PER MONTH GERMAN NERVE AGENT SARIN PRODUCTION PLANT

One of the FRG sites proposed by DoD had been near Clausen. By at least 1974 there would be only one US chemical store in Europe, in West Germany.[896] This depot supported the Army with 155-mm artillery rounds which according to a first-half 1983 inventory totaled 68524 filled with sarin and 27292 with VX as well as a limited number of eight inch shells with the same agents; these rounds amounted to seven percent of all US weaponized toxic agents.[897] The 1974 numeration attributed 440 agent tons, which by the 1983 inventory had somehow dropped to 434.9 tons. During the 1990 removal of the more than 100000 artillery chemical rounds, shipped to Johnson Island, Clausen remained the sole CW deposit.[898] There are doubtless many more aspects of the US BW-CW deployment during the 1950s to 1970s actually implemented that are yet to be disclosed. But while the publics of the US and NATO members may have been ignorant of ongoing programs the main target of this European arsenal highly likely had been fully informed.

Particulars of this offensive chemical armament, by a State that had neglected to ratify the 1925 Geneva Protocol, could scarcely have escaped Soviet attention given the deep intelligence penetration that supplemented public revelations. A late 1961 article by Colonel A. Kuchin in VM (S)[899] that appraised American chemical munitions had been fully cognizant of VX. Kuchin noted agent effectiveness when disseminated by spray tanks and that when delivered by a missile a VX warhead would attain almost nuclear efficiency in causing casualties. He even attributed US work on intercontinental cruise missiles for both chemical and biological attack. Yet one of the most striking aspects of US NIEs and other assessments of Soviet CW preparations at the turn of the 1960s and thereafter lay in the absolute lack of consideration of the measures being developed and implemented by American military compatriots. This one-sided appraisal, as if Soviet measures had no reactive component, just out of the blue, seriously hindered any offensive chemical assessments that might have more accurately pinpointed the nature of their counter-measures.

Regardless of the concurrent state of Soviet WMD work the accelerating momentum of US and other Western weapons deployments can only have reinforced any of their chemical (and biological) armament programs just as US development of atomic weapons had eventually been more than matched. Marxist ideological, and national security imperatives, both demanded that any weapons possessed by an opponent must be equalized. In the Soviet definition equation tended to be defined as quantitative superiority. One of the most persistent of Cold War themes had been the obdurate Soviet insistence on reciprocity. Instances occurred when they formulated political and military actions not as independent decisions but rather as Pavlovian reactions. An equivalence fixed by the late 1950s remained in effect a decade later when enunciated by the Chief of the USSR General Staff, Marshal M. V. Zakharov, in a 1969 VM (S) article.[900]

> Our probable enemies, especially the USA, are continuing to develop and accumulate chemical and bacteriological weapons. Therefore we have no right to lag behind in this field. The Armed Forces of the Soviet Union are prepared to conduct military actions both with the use of conventional means of destruction and with the use of all types of weapons of mass destruction.

Soviet officers received the doctrinal interpretation. All three editions (the last in 1968) of the open tome *Military Strategy* emphasized that "In particular, in a future war one may expect the employment of chemical and bacteriological weapons to whose development great significance is accorded in the Western countries, particularly the United States."[901] This assertion would be repeated in classified documents; Colonel G. Ashin in his 1963 VM (S) article[902] insisted "the experience of troop and command-staff exercises conducted in recent years by the aggressive NATO bloc convinces us that, with the start of a war, the imperialists will employ nuclear, chemical, and bacteriological weapons on a large scale." The message in classified writings on operational issues, which generally avoided ideological tirades, persisted that the US and NATO would employ both chemical and biological as well as nuclear weapons.

A classified 1969 lecture on front-army logistics prepared for the Military Academy of the General Staff by General-Major A. Skovoroda cited exercise experience and calculations as the basis for expecting that a front operating in nuclear conditions would have casualties of 30 to 35 percent—and of this loss 17 percent would be from chemical and 5 percent due to bacteriological weapons. Projected chemical losses amounted to 6 percent higher than the direct nuclear effects although another 12 percent casualties could be expected from radiation.[903] Similar breakdowns appeared in other classified material. Episodic attributions of enemy usage appeared in several documents. Colonel M. Belov, who wrote much on airborne landings, in a 1963 article[904] examined US Army preparations supposedly initiated by 1959 "secret official regulations" to defeat Soviet drops with non-persistent and persistent chemical agents. He warned Soviet sky warriors concerning "the landing of airborne landing forces under conditions in which there is the threat of enemy use of nuclear and chemical attack means."

Some projections of enemy intentions in VM (S) had been even more specific. Lieutenant Colonel I. Rodya asserted in 1969 that the US planned using Army organic "aviation as delivery vehicles for nuclear, chemical and bacteriological weapons" including the UH-1B Iroquois helicopter armed "CBU-191A (E159) with toxic agents."[905] Colonel I. Lyutov in a detailed 1970 look at defense operations in the "non-nuclear period" expected a constant threat of enemy use of nuclear and chemical weapons including "toxic agents with psychogenic and irritant effects" delivered by artillery and aviation.[906] Colonel P. Lyadov, discussing in 1962 an army regrouping, expected enemy chemical strikes even within the USSR.[907] Major I. Grabovoy's 1964 article on WMD defense stressed individual protection "if we assume the possibility of extensive employment of nuclear, chemical and bacteriological weapons (which is most probable under present-day conditions)"—and he detailed the value of Soviet equipment against type chemical agents dissemination.[908] General-Major G. Ostapchuk in 1969 even provided a data table on troop incapacitation from enemy VX and sarin strikes in various protective postures—the companion table on nuclear effects apparently deemed too searing for our delicate feelings so redacted by the CIA reviewers.[909]

Many other articles in issues of VM (S) assumed, or dealt with aspects of, enemy CW-BW employment, notably Colonel P. Simonok (1964);[910] Colonels V. Chagorov and S. Krylov (1965);[911] General-Major A. Listrovoy and General-Major (Medical Service) I. Rogozin (1966);[912] General-Major N. Rumyantsev and colleague (1967);[913] General-Major A. Ovchinnikov and two colonels,[914] General-Major M. Kiryan,[915] Colonel N. Krivopustov[916] (three 1969); and Colonel P. Dubok with others (1970).[917] A similar range of articles, with much less specification, appeared in the VM restricted edition. A 1966 review of a book on NATO military doctrines asserted "it is necessary to consider that American imperialism does not exclude the possibility of conducting so-called 'non-destructive wars,' that is, wars with the use of chemical and biological weapons"—citing a magazine article statement (not verified) that the US DoD had high-priority research underway on this topic—and stressing the "dangerous precedent" represented by US application of toxic chemicals in South Vietnam.[918]

Stress, to a lesser extent than chemical but similar in threat substantiation, had been given on enemy biological warfare preparations. A biophysics specialist G. Frank, a member of the USSR Academy of Sciences, in 1962 provided the readers with a disturbing summary of Western scientific literature on weapons-related work, mainly biological but also some chemical.[919] Colonel (Medical Service) A. Vorobyev in 1964[920] even asserted that "current United States efforts toward the development of biological weapons employing casualty-producing pathogenic microorganisms are given just as much attention as the development of missile/nuclear weapons and other means of armed warfare." In unusually great detail Vorobyev related US BW information, from 1962 field manuals FM 100-5 *Operations* and FM 3-10 on CW-BW employment; types and characteristics of pathogens; strategic and battlefield targets; defoliants use in Vietnam; delivery means and the value of spreading at low altitude; and stability problems. Coverage of large areas through the use of aerosols ensured that "biological weapons can increase the scale of destruction of personnel achieved by employing nuclear or chemical weapons." Fortunately the CIA declassification reviewers prevailed on hiding many technicalities regarding dissemination that might be useful to current WMDers. Vorobyev also examined logistics; weapons flow from plants to US continental and theater depots; storage life limitation; and troop supply to delivery units. He noted that the US planned to provide both biological and chemical weapons through…nuclear supply channels.

However in a quite detailed assessment of the supposed NATO intent to conduct a sudden attack on the East by Colonel S. Sokolov in a 1966 VM (S) article,[921] only two items referred to enemy chemical weapons employment. In his extensive discussion of nuclear strike planning and delivery systems those references strikingly lacked the specification afforded to nuclear matters. An assortment of classified writings, while detailing enemy nuclear operations, lacked any references to their BW-CW planning. There seems to have been a quite uneven education of Soviet officers concerning the actuality of Western chemical and biological intentions.

Many of the Soviet descriptions of the chemical and biological warfare preparations of the prospective enemy had been remarkably similar in tone and in citations of evidence to those in the West who raised a mirrored alarm throughout the Cold War. Unfortunately the Western reflection at least had not been substantiated with as reliable an intelligence validation. Unlike the late 1950s 'bomber gap' and 'missile gap' the intelligence confusion regarding the Cold War 'chemical gap' would never be resolved.

## Soviet WMD operation 1959 to 1974

The few Soviet public chemical warfare comments during the 1950s appeared in the context of a defensive posture but a clear offensive element would eventually dominate Soviet classified material. Documents from a June-July 1956 opposed forces exercise recovered from Hungarian archives posited a nuclear-chemical attack by Westerners and an Easterners counteroffensive with the same weapons.[922] But post-Cold War national archives have yet to reveal substantial material from the mid 1950s and immediately following years that deal with CW. Western intelligence acquired little more evidence from which to derive valid assessments. Available information points to at least increasing Soviet concern and ongoing internal discussions regarding the form of a strategic response to Western WMD armament developments.

The 1957 *Artillery Manual of the Soviet Army* had been acquired by 1961.[923] This detailed technical exposition on artillery firing procedure had no hint of chemical ammunition; the section on "special shells" dealt only with smoke and incendiary rounds. Uncertain, however, is whether the instructions carried a classified label or any access restrictions. Quite detailed discussions of nuclear and conventional fire procedures, target calculations, and suggested exercise scenarios that appeared in 1958 classified material provided by the US-UK agent Oleg Penkovsky also had little of the chemical content of classified documents in the following decade.

Penkovsky passed articles that had appeared in issues 45 and 46 of the *Information Collection of the Artillery*. This journal (*Rocket* soon added to the title) carried the Soviet classification top secret. Unlike the operational and strategic propositions in VM the periodical had been purposed to disseminate specific recent exercise experience and operational-tactical lessons for implementation in the Rocket-Artillery Troops. The editorial preface limited dissemination to ranks upward from commanders of corps artillery, artillery divisions, and engineer brigades—the last designator a cover for short- and medium-range missile units. Articles from an equivalent strategic missile journal published in 1961 also handed over by Penkovsky provided US intelligence with details of procedures for deploying medium-range ballistic missiles and their nuclear warheads. This information would be crucial during October 1962 to understanding the ongoing Soviet basing of MRBM in Cuba. Articles detailed missile operations in such depth as to guide the intelligence assessments of launch readiness that calibrated the US response.

The text of ten 1958 *Artillery* articles had been acquired. Topical content focused on division and army employment of artillery and missiles, with details of nuclear strike calculations including delivery system target and yield assignment; burst types and effects; and various technical factors. Discussion featured a still important conventional strike role for missiles. Two of the articles did have references to enemy use of chemical weapons, with no further elaboration of that aspect, but clearly lacking had been Soviet retaliation in kind.[924] Only one article refers to Soviet chemical munitions fires, by tube artillery—nuclear missile strikes are referenced in the text but minus any hint of chemical warheads for these systems.[925] There is a striking disparity in these articles between the considerable attention to nuclear matters and the almost total lack of CW interest. But there would be an manifest ramping up of a chemical variant the following year. Something had changed. The form of Soviet counter-action had been determined. An expectation of US-NATO use of WMD enunciated by Zhukov and others would by 1959 meet with a concerted chemical response.

Post-USSR information from Russian technicians indicated that attempts to develop an acceptable production process for the nerve agent sarin at the Beketovka plant near Volgograd attained the desired parameters only in 1959. They had been working out a sarin method for several years.[926] The US had also encountered many technical obstacles in the, preceding, sarin program. Russian officials in 1999 confirmed this 1959 start of full sarin output;[927] Soviet munitions filling had only begun two years following the US completion of the entire sarin production run. That statement also claimed that full production of other key nerve agents also lagged behind US work; soman series production did not begin until 1966 and the Soviet formula for VX in 1972. The non-official information confirmed the 1972 full VX production at Novocheboksark but that pilot production at Beketovka had been tasked in 1959 and the first batch available for testing the next year.[928] Thus US production of VX had begun eleven, and ended five, years before the Soviets even got around to full issue of their version. Discussions of these particular agents in Soviet classified writings preceded, sometimes with several years lead time, the actual stated availability. This could represent initial dissemination of weapon characteristics for military planning purposes prior to agent full availability—or Russian fibbing about production runs.

Intelligence during this timeframe had different takes on agent production. A late 1963 NIE "believed" that "limited production of sarin" began in the late 1940s;[929] presumably considered likely that the Falkenhagen plant had been quickly put back into operation in the GDR or USSR. But the 1969 edition of the same NIE series[930] reassessed "quantity production" to "about 1960" overshooting the mark somewhat. However that NIE then dated Soviet VX type production "as early as 1956" thus beating out the US by five years. If the dates stated by the Russians are accurate, this means of course that the USSR, contrary to US intelligence assessments both then and later, could not have had any inventory of munitions with the most potent modern agents before 1960. A Soviet offensive capability with modern chemical weapons, however sizable reserves would become, actually emerged during the 1960s, several years later than the intelligence presumption.

An article in issue 49 for 1959 of the artillery journal dealing with artillery preparation for a counterattack suggested multiple fire strikes with chemical and conventional ammunition, linking this option to a situation of nuclear weapons shortfall—"…advisable to begin with the use of chemical ammunition with quick-acting toxic substances in the first concentration of fire…" and that persistent agents could be used on the flanks of attacking forces in conditions of favorable wind direction.[931] Constituting the earliest expression of an offensive chemical preference in one of the classified documents that US intelligence began to acquire—and appearing in a professional journal purposed to disseminate operational solutions to military commanders—this article marked an explicit integration of chemical warfare into Soviet military operations. Of interest is that another article in the same issue covering only missile usage, while detailing nuclear and conventional warheads, did not discuss Soviet missile chemical warheads even when referencing enemy use of chemical and nuclear weapons.[932] This omission might well have signified that a CW warhead for missiles had not yet been accepted for service—confirmed by later evidence—and also explains the restricted scope of the 1959 MoD publication

*Instructions for the Employment of Chemical Weapons by the Artillery and Rules for Firing with Chemical Shells and Mortar Shells* cited in a 1960 book on artillery[933] (but not acquired).

The extent of Soviet planning and preparations for employment of biological weapons is a greater unknown. A 1990s Russian General Staff Chief quoted in a 2001 *Moscow Times* article claimed that "biological warfare was never an intrinsic part of the Soviet military doctrine, and we did not include biological weapons in our plans."[934] Material acquired by Cold War intelligence, especially indications in classified writings as related earlier, suggested a more prominent role for BW; an obvious expectation of bacteriological weapons as a factor on the battlefield. The absence of extensive discussion in the classified material acquired may reflect the operational-strategic level of content. The secret level 1963 General Staff *Manual on the Conduct of Operations* is one of the most comprehensive sources for the emergent Soviet WMD Operation. The Ground Troops volume informed that "Bacteriological weapons are primarily strategic weapons and their use is determined by decision of the Supreme High Command" but in a world war "In addition to nuclear weapons, chemical and biological means of warfare may be employed..."[935] Limited treatment may also have reflected the backward technical state of biological armament, the lingering impact of Stalinist Lysenkoism—the ideological wholesale destruction of Soviet life sciences. If so, remediation by an intensified effort and resource allocation would be underway by the mid 1970s. Chemical work apparently had not been subjected to interruption.

But the 1963 *Manual* followed the VGK statement with a more specific prescription regarding use in front operations.

> The primary purpose in using bacteriological weapons in ground forces operations is to inflict massive personnel losses on the enemy and also to hinder his troop combat activities and the work of his rear services. These weapons are employed by rocket troops, aviation, artillery, and by covert methods, in combination with other means of destruction, by surprise, massed, and against the most important targets in the enemy's rear. Most effective results are achieved by using biological warfare agents which lead to the rapid spread of disease.

Emphasis thereby had been placed on BW in depth rather than against troops in contact—an obvious complication for the attackers if only because of the slower activation in comparison to other WMD. The mischievous reference to Soviet "covert methods" might be clarified by a later attribution that the "enemy may employ bacteriological means by subversive methods to contaminate water and reserves of food." The 1962 *Field Service Regulations* also references enemy use of disease vectors such as insects and ticks against water and foodstuffs.[936]

Another VM article by Colonel Vorobyev[937] (date inexplicably cut by CIA reviewers but presumably circa 1964 as his previously cited material) attributed NATO a preference also to use BW in the enemy "deep rear in order to wear down troops, wipe out reserves, disorganize the work of the interior of the country, and disrupt the control of industry, transportation, etc." Focusing on technical aspects of "the creation of a biological aerosol (biological cloud)" he noted in particular US attention to pathogenic sabotage methods; American calculations of relative WMD effects finding BW superior for inflicting more expansive territorial losses; and then examined methods to defend against these nefarious attacks. One rare explicit indication of a biological offensive provided by Colonel G. Yeletskikh in a 1966 VM (S) article discussed reconnaissance support of the front initial nuclear strike—which he defined as nuclear-chemical-bacteriological. These WMD would be delivered by at least aviation and cruise missile regiments.[938]

Despite the foregoing and other material no particular urgency regarding BW eventuated among intelligence agencies. The comprehensive 1979 NIE on Warsaw Pact forces[939] devoted all of one paragraph to this WMD, comprising a dozen lines, each in the summary and full estimate volumes. But the authors found room for 34 chemical paragraphs as well as wide consideration of nuclear weapons. The definitive judgment regarding adherence by the Warsaw Pact countries to the 1972 Biological Weapons Convention declared "no evidence that any of them have violated the treaty." The NIE had been issued prior to the intell version of 'breaking news' in the form of the anthrax event involving military object 19 in Sverdlovsk (Ekaterinburg) which would sharpen the focus of BW perspectives.

One of the several biowar installations that had been identified by intelligence presented a forward theater launch point—aimed at the Chinese fraternal comrades. This complex near Mal'ta north of Lake Baikal had been conveniently located 13-km as spores drift from strategic aviation base Belaya. Tagged by a Russian defector at the end of the Cold War as a BW munitions loading plant for at least anthrax,[940] remains can still be viewed in public sources of satellite imagery. The plant may have been under military control as late as 2012 according to a Russian visitor who has posted a nifty photographic tour.[941] In the vicinity is an historically significant Paleolithic site; genetic sequencing of a young boy's remains there revealed that his relations had made a major contribution to the DNA of the first Americans.[942] The discovery imparts a striking contradiction of biological science at work to advance our knowledge of the human chronicle—and perversion for mass murder.

A 1983 Soviet propaganda piece, pointing to the signature affixed to the BW Convention, asserted that "the USSR does not possess any bacteriological (biological) agents or toxins,

Mal'ta 1982
Bio-weapons loading complex

and any equipment and delivery means banned under it."[943] But only with 1990s revelations by program participants did the extent of this blatant lie become clear—that the Soviets had regarded the treaty that they, and the US, had ratified, as a strategic opportunity rather than a constraint. Defectors substantiated a far more persistent and expansive weapons program than any Western intelligence service had suspected. The range of evidence currently available, however, permits an elucidation of the WMD Operation only as to the nuclear and chemical modules.

Other documents available to US intelligence during the early 1960s underlined 1959 as a pivotal year for Soviet consideration and planning for chemical warfare. The 1959 *Field Service Regulations (Division—Corps)*,[944] stamped secret, is especially significant in marking a new integration of chemical with nuclear action. According to the *Regulations* promulgating MoD Order 031 dated 2 March 1959, signed by Defense Minister Marshal R. Malinovsky, this edition superseded that of 1948 along with a 1954 manual on nuclear combat. Both of the cited antecedents had been acquired by the CIA in 1955 from a "usually reliable source"—presumably P. S. Popov, a GRU officer. He had been in contact with the Agency, which officially declares him to have been the first real Soviet mole, from early 1953 and handed over considerable information until his October 1959 arrest. Unfortunately the CIA has managed to lose the nuclear manual, responding to my declassification request with a 'record not found.' Amazingly a request for Popov material met with the same official response—even though a news release on the CIA web site[945] listed categories of information he provided. Evidently there is still a mole in the CIA who is systematically clearing the shelves. All of these publications had been disseminated to defense and intelligence entities; my attempt to access the 1954 nuclear manual from some of these offices met with the usual bewildered responses. Other period intelligence reporting, and low level handbooks acquired, provide some indications of manual contents.

The 1948 *Regulations*[946] are notable for topics not addressed, and as a manifest breakpoint with both the past and future of Soviet military strategy. This edition specifies replacement of the 1936 *Regulations* even though there had been a 1943 issue (an aspect which will also be considered). This first postwar formulation entirely ignored the existence of the atomic weapons that had been introduced but several years would elapse before these would be developed into a form that could be used on battlefields. Assimilating GPW experience with tank and mechanized troops as well as rifle troops (which would be fully motorized over the next decade) and, astoundingly, considerable attention given to the operations of cavalry corps and divisions. There had been thirty extant cavalry divisions at the end of the war.[947] But most significantly the prominent, complete, absence of offensive chemical warfare featured in contemporary Soviet doctrine. Nowhere in the 791 numbered sections of text, even extensive prescriptions for artillery and aviation support in the offense and defense, appeared any hint that the Soviets envisaged a CW variant. Sections 41, 164 to 168, 263, 492, 538, 676, and 746 dealt with the tasks of chemical troops and chemical defense measures. Chemical attacks by the enemy imputed, some of which might be "prolonged" and should be hindered "by the actions of aviation and artillery-mortar fire" met with no indication of a Soviet chemical munitions riposte. In the same situation that had been presented in the 1936 *Regulations* Soviet chemical attacks had been specified. No ideological or military context had been provided for the enemy CW use nor any statement pertaining to the 1925 Geneva Protocol.

Similarly the *Field Service Regulations* for the lower level of regiment and battalion promulgated in April 1953[948] conspicuously lacked any hint of offensive chemical intent, arming, or operational use in 614 numbered sections. An imputed threat of "enemy chemical attack" in sections 59, 78, 84, 85, 137, 153, 372, 409, 576, 603 dealt with tasks of the chemical warfare service including chemical reconnaissance, anti-chemical measures, and negotiation of contaminated areas (as well as combat with flamethrowers and use of smoke), all again without operational context. Notable again the complete absence of nuclear weapons considerations, an indication that Stalinist conformity remained in effect. Fortunately the 1953 *Regulations* still did provide for Soviet cavalry regiments to ride to the rescue of tank and mechanized units.

The 1959 *Regulations*, in a startling revamping of military strategy, waxed replete with prescriptions for employment of chemical with nuclear weapons in offensive and defensive operations. Notably omitted in the received text had been reiteration of statements in the issuing orders for the 1929 and 1936 editions that chemical agents "will be used in the Red Army only if they are first used by our enemies;" manifesting an entirely different formulation.

> Considering that none of the Soviet Government's persistent proposals for the prohibition of atomic weapons and other means of mass destruction has not yet received due recognition, the Soviet Union, proceeding from the requirements of security, has been compelled to train its Armed Forces for operations under conditions of the employment of these weapons. For this reason, the propositions set forth in the *Regulations* take into account the constant threat of the employment of atomic weapons and other means of mass destruction by the enemy. At the same time, the *Regulations* provide general propositions for the use of these weapons by our troops, when the special directive to do so is issued.

About forty repetitions of the phrase "atomic weapons and other means of mass destruction" appeared throughout the text of the 1959 *Regulations*, applied equally to Soviet and enemy forces. However at least twenty-eight occurrences stipulated Soviet chemical and toxic agent offensive actions including a basic definition of usage; target reconnaissance; striking enemy defenses, reserves, and troops at water barriers and other choke points; delivery means; coordination with troop actions; preemptive employment by defending Soviet forces including mountainous, desert, and steppe terrain; and attacking enemy amphibious landings—some twenty-two of these given as "atomic and chemical." No explicit indications of Soviet employment of biological weapons on the battlefield arose despite a few references to protection against enemy bacteriological means. The first known Soviet operations manual since the 1936 edition to specify offensive CW, the 1959 *Regulations* demarcated a decision point in the Soviet attitude to battlefield employment of chemical weapons.

Revisions to Soviet military strategy and operational art at this time had been so frequent and rapid that three years later a superseding edition of the *Field Service Regulations*,[949] signed to press 30 March 1962, had been necessary. This publication largely dispensed with the 'and other means' phraseology, featuring a substantial increase in offensive and defensive tasking particularized as 'chemical.' Both editions stressed the essentiality of sudden, mass employment of chemical weapons. The two editions of the *Regulations*, along with the General Staff 1963 *Manual*, demonstrably indicated that chemical weapons had arrived by the early 1960s not just as armament but also as the basis of theater war—and that the official scripts for the Revolution coupled chemical to nuclear weapons.

The Pokrovsky direct linkage of chemical with mass use and the surprise factor had been a concurrent theme of Soviet writings on nuclear weapons. The implication of developments in Soviet military doctrine during the second half of the 1950s amounted to the casting of a foundation for a nuclear-chemical diarchy, an integration of mass destruction weapons in theater operations. A grandiloquent Tolstoyan streak at the heart of a distinctive Soviet strategic culture ensured that the nature of the response to US initiatives would be a large-scale and sweeping proposition. Still anonymous (to our side) Soviet theorists had codified a WMD Operation along lines that some early writings characterized as a modernization of the Deep Operation of the 1930s. But this version would be propelled by nuclear, chemical, and possibly biological armament; radically magnified in scope, rapidity, and objectives; entailing not only massive destruction among armed forces but also entire European populations. Two decades later US Army counterparts would re-invent the same wheel, integrating theater nuclear-chemical-conventional weapons in the Air-Land Battle concept, an 'innovation' that the Soviets, by then, had discarded.

Soviet military documentation acquired by Western intelligence services provided the main resource for our knowledge regarding the parameters of the WMD Operation. Sources encompassed, among other material, operations manuals stamped top secret; articles in classified journals by mid-grade and senior officers; and exercise summations. A close reading of **all** of these documents, from the late 1940s to the mid 1970s, reveals two distinct 'bumps' in the Soviet attitude to chemical warfare. But to perceive these milestones necessitated reading comprehension of the full course, not tidbits, or just that beginning with the picking up of the chemical ticket. Only in 1984 would an intelligence outlier discover both the 1959 bump-up and the bump-down that took place after 1974. Connoisseurs during the Cold War perceived a straight, dramatically rising, chemical line through the 1950s into the 1980s. The failure to recognize watersheds in the Soviet attitude toward offensive chemical warfare would have an inevitable accompaniment—consequential implementation of the nuclear-chemical diarchy proceeded unperceived. US intelligence would be unable to discern a correlation of the most elementary sort in grasping the import of a radical structural innovation initiated in 1959 that represented the instrumentality of an expansive scheme for employment of mass destruction weapons.

Classified material provided by Penkovsky, and his successors, featured a noteworthy strain of chemical warfare—describing a consistent theme through the 1960s—that alarmed the intelligence readership. Publications classified as low as the secret level dealt with offensive CW with no apparent attempt at security compartmentalizing. Chemical discussions appeared even in tactical journals such as *Voyennye Vestnik* (*Military Herald*). Literature accorded chemical weapons considerable attention but seemingly as a junior partner to nuclear. The earliest manuals and writings had been interpreted by intelligence to indicate that the Soviets viewed chemical weapons as a recompense for a scarcity of battlefield nuclear munitions. Material during the 1960s, however, pointed to the establishment of independent chemical targeting regimes. Area saturation with toxic agents could assist with the location uncertainties inherent in nuclear strike planning although classified documents did not highlight this approach. A new emphasis appeared regarding inflicting casualties as well as impeding enemy troop operations and logistics. The 1963 *Manual* for the Ground Troops[950] had both offensive and defensive chemical tasking, with operational success ensured by "the simultaneous action of nuclear and chemical weapons." Offensive chemical conditions differentiated included amphibious landings; mountainous areas, issuing cautions regarding persistency and flow tendency in ravines and deep valleys; desert toxic agent persistency would be much reduced; while in attacks on cities mainly non-persistent agents would be used both downtown against buildings as well as enemy defenses in the environs.

Besides operational considerations, military-technical weapons information had been scattered throughout this classified material. A 1961 article in issue 54 of the (now) missile-artillery journal "Principles of the Employment of Chemical Rockets"[951] provided intelligence the first reference to agent VR-55 (in Soviet nomenclature VR—*vyazkiy retseptura*—denoted a single agent thickened to enhance persistency) as a warhead massive fill. Russian sources in the 1990s confirmed the suspicion of some intelligence analysts that R-55 equated to the nerve agent soman. The Soviets had developed soman as a principle agent in the mistaken belief that the US had arrived at the same decision—but the 1999 official statement claimed full R-55 production began only in 1966.[952] If correct, the assertion would be yet another indication of Soviet military theory and planning getting ahead of actual capabilities. Discussion in the 1961 article also concerned air-burst height options for R-30 (FROG series unguided rockets) and R-170 systems (thickening reduced agent evaporation while high altitudes expanded the area of surface contamination) and strike norms against specific types of targets e.g. two R-170 against a battalion deployment area of Corporal or Redstone missiles. "In order to achieve surprise, when preparing for an offensive, it is advisable to deliver a chemical rocket strike simultaneously with a nuclear strike"—chemical subsequent to nuclear, with at least 5- to 10-km separation—but independent chemical strikes permissible. Responsibility for centralized planning and employment decisions resided with front and army commanders; reference to authorization by a higher authority absent. Thus by 1961 introduction into service of missile CW warheads had been foreshadowed if not an actuality.

Episodic clandestine reporting had provided intelligence with some informative data on Soviet chemical armament. An early comprehensive listing, circa 1970 under the heading Tabular, from the Czech source of an allied intelligence service provided designators and agent fills for numerous Soviet air- and ground-delivered munitions. A declassification request to the CIA for this and later weapons material met with an amazingly obtuse 'records not located' response. I must therefore have been in an hallucinatory daze during more than two decades of an intelligence career—imagining a series of information reports held in hand that contained data on chemical armament with their designators; fill agent type and weight; contamination persistency and area coverage; and firing rates. These specifications on a wide range of chemical weapons are often discrepant with the composition of the stockpile exhibited at the Shikhany complex in 1987 as well as that declared by Russia under the terms of the 1997 CWC. The rightness and credibility of CIA assessments is dependent on the detection and acquisition of a multitude of relevant evidence; what reliance can be placed on an intelligence organization that cannot find information in particular file systems?

Scattered post-Soviet sources have provided limited details on, in particular, missile chemical warheads. Former Warsaw Pact member archives and Russian documentation, including web sites (content and sites themselves apt to disappear), provide information on early CW warheads not actually available from intelligence sources. Even when integrating the 'not found' data only a partial and timeframe-fragmentary inventory of the full chemical arsenal developed in the Soviet period could be re-created. This later evidence generally points to a more protracted expansion of Soviet chemical armament then had been postulated by US intelligence.

• strategic missiles

US intelligence had been unable to establish during the Cold War whether the Soviets had developed any long range chemical strike capability with warheads for missiles in the strategic category. Subsequently multiple Russian sources have confirmed that at least the R-12 (SS-4 Sandal MRBM) trended CW. A 1999 series on strategic missiles that appeared in a Russian aviation journal revealed the early 1960s *Tuman* (Fog) "cassette type" chemical warhead under design for the R-12[953]— the very missile which on arrival in Cuba touched off a memorable fracas. The term cassette signified a cluster warhead containing submunitions rather a mass liquid fill. A 2005 Russian book by one of the article authors repeated this statement.[954] Other Russian sources indicate the R-12 *Tuman* warhead in service beginning 1963.[955] A prominent Russian researcher has reported the production of V-type agent bulk containers for installing in (unidentified) strategic missile warheads, of 1895.6-kg from 1975 to 1981, and another of 1945-kg during 1982 to 1986.[956] The full extent of Soviet chemical warhead distribution in the MRBM force (R-12 entered service in 1959), or other classes of strategic missiles, is still unknown. Assigned a nominal range of 2000-km, R-12 deployment would have represented a significant, undetected, threat deep into Western territory.

Soviet interest in a long range missile chemical strike capability had also been indicated by the development of the *Tuman*-2 warhead and designation to the *Temp-S* R-900 theater mobile missile, nominal range as indicated by the system designator.[957] The R-900 had been accepted for service in 1966 and had been immediately or soon after placed in the strategic missile inventory. According to another Russian source work on the *Tuman*-2 had been ordered by Decree 178-84 of the USSR Council of Ministers dated 19 February 1962 for the *Temp* first version of this system.[958] Neither of the *Tuman* warheads appeared on the lists of chemical weapons the Soviets began disclosing in 1987 (during the public display at Shikhany) and a decade later under provisions of the Chemical Weapons Convention even though the R-900, and many R-12, missiles continued to be deployed at the end of the 1980s. US intelligence assumed, without hard evidence, that the Scaleboard had a chemical warhead but had no information or suspicions that the Sandal also had this option.

- operational-tactical and cruise missiles

Information on the R-170/R-300 chemical warhead indicates that the initial design had such an excessive weight that airframe structural failure resulted. A solution arrived with the index 8F44G warhead, and further improved in the 8F44G1 design. Fill consisted of 555 kilograms of a V-type agent (R-33).[959] US intelligence had first detected in 1957 what had been assessed as tests of a missile chemical warhead,[960] possibly the troublesome version although to be later discussed a radioactive liquid warhead test series had been conducted that year. However another Russian statement has the 8F44G *Tuman*-3 warhead flight tested in 1963-1964 on the 8K14 (R-300 in service 1962, export version R-17) and not the R-170.[961] But there is evidence from 1960s exercise documents that the Warsaw Pact allies had at least notional access to a R-170 CW warhead; possibly also fielded to those Soviet missile brigades that had not yet converted to the R-300. The 8- prefix is evidence of development work originated in the 1950s; subsequent to the late 1959 creation of a separate strategic missile service the index system had been altered, with 9- designators reserved for Ground Troops armament and 15- for strategic.

The 1961 missile-artillery journal may have prematurely attributed a VR-55 warhead to the R-170. Shikhany 1987 data on the two missile warheads displayed had the 884-mm (R-300) warhead filled with 555-kg of thickened "VX"—presumably VR-33. Neither Shikhany nor CWC inventories had any VR- or R-55 warheads although possibly this agent may have been deleted at some point in favor of (V)R-33. But since R-33 full production supposedly did not begin until 1972 this soman warhead may have been the 8F44G1. Even the 9K714 (SS-23 Spider) deployed in the 1980s had a chemical warhead option, if the Russian edition of Wikipedia has valid information;[962] but no 970-mm warhead had been displayed at Shikhany in 1987 when R-400 transition had become increasingly evident in the SRBM arm; nor is a chemical warhead of that diameter noted in available accounts of the Russian CWC-declared stocks.

Soviet enthusiasm for ground-launched cruise missiles had been at a peak in the late 1950s through at least the late 1960s when development ceased for many years. Subordinated to the air army of the front, the FKR-1 (KR-180, SSC-2a Salish) which had also made the voyage to Cuba, had a delivery accuracy advantage over both aircraft and ballistic missiles. This and other desirable characteristics—as well as deficiencies—for nuclear strikes against certain types of targets had been reviewed in great detail by Colonel P. Plyachenko in a VM (S) 1961 article.[963] He also indicated that the "possibility" of a chemical warhead "is not ruled out" which in the nuclear context of the article, sent to press early in December, points to the lack of a FKR-1 CW option. This absence would be remedied for at least the long range FKR-2 (KR-500) which debuted about the date of the Plyachenko article. Council of Ministers Decree 178-84 dated 19 February 1962 had ordained adaptation of the *Tuman*-1 for the FKR-2 and planned state trials for the third quarter of 1964.[964] Neither of these systems remained operational past the early 1970s.

- tactical missiles

According to Shikhany data the second, 540-mm, warhead contained 216-kg of "VX" also in bulk form. Shikhany did not exhibit cassette warheads despite what must have been a substantial inventory by 1987; but of course strategic missile CW warheads also notably absent. The diameter equates to the index 9K52 *Luna M* system which had been accepted for service in 1964. But a Russian source[965] states that development of the 9N18G chemical warhead for the 9M21G rocket had lagged, available only at the end of 1965. Design work on the chemical warhead for the replacement 9K79 *Tochka* (SS-21 Scarab) guided missile, accepted for service in 1975, had been started by USSR Council of Ministers Decree 788-257 dated 14 September 1970. The Decree specified both 'monoblock' (bulk fill) and cassette versions. The Russian version of Wikipedia[966] detailed *Tochka* cassette warheads each with 65 submunitions, the 9N123G (agent R-33 total 60.5-kg) and the 9N123G2-1 (agent R-55 total 50.5-kg). Warheads for this 650-mm diameter missile had been unaccountably missing from the 1987 exhibit. No 650-mm warheads appear in a Russian semiofficial *Encyclopedia* description of the chemical stockpile declared under the CWC.[967] However one tally had 42 Scarab warheads at the Shchuchye assemblage[968] while another displayed a photo of a canister marked 9N123G.[969]

- tube artillery and rockets

The Tabular data had been among the first extensive representations of Soviet chemical munitions available to the artillery arm. Items exhibited at Shikhany in 1987 encompassed six shells 122-mm, 130-mm, 142-mm and four rockets fired by multiple launchers 122-mm, 140-mm, 240-mm; these all stated variously to be filled with sarin, "VX" and thickened lewisite.[970] Calibers and fills in the Russian *Encyclopedia* are identical.[971] Clandestine data such as Tabular presented a more sizable and variegated array of fuzes, munitions, and agents available in the Soviet chemical armament inventory.

- aviation-delivered

Tabular data had also depicted a wide variety of air munitions. Spray tanks and bombs—KhAB (*khimicheskaya aviatsionnaya bomba*)—furnishing aircraft as mainstays. Interestingly the KhAB designation appeared in the 1958 edition[972] of a military dictionary but not in a 1965 update[973] (both open publications); this a useful if minor indication of the transformed prominence of chemical warfare in Soviet strategy and a new impulse to

| agent | | munition | type | fill |
|---|---|---|---|---|
| R-2 | [?] | **aircraft** | | |
| R-33 | [VX analog] | KhVAP-500 | spray | R-33 or R-55 |
| R-35 | [sarin] | KhAB-250-M-62P | bomb | R-33 or R-55 |
| R-43A | [lewisite] | RBK-250 (submunition OKhAB-5) | bomb | R-55 |
| R-55 | [soman] | **artillery** | | |
| VR-55 | [thick soman] | KhSO | fragmentation | R-35 |
| | | KhS | air burst | R-43A |

RBK-250 DESIGNATED AN AUTOMATIC DISPENSER. AERIAL CW DATA PROVIDED IN THE SHIKHANY DISPLAY AND RUSSIAN *ENCYCLOPEDIA* AGREE, AND AGAIN PRESENT A MORE SIMPLIFIED PORTRAYAL THEN THAT OF THE (IN)VISIBLE CLANDESTINE EVIDENCE.

hide some details. Air munitions prominently featured in a 1966 VM (S) article.[974] Captain First Rank A. Zheludev in "Chemical Weapons for Repulsing an Amphibious Landing" took the prize for agent-dropping. His short but enthusiastic review of, exclusively chemical, munitions that could be employed to kill enemy personnel and contaminate terrain, materiel, and vehicles at various points during preparation and execution of an amphibious operation from staging to hitting the beach. He mentions six toxic agents and five delivery options. Zheludev praised CW as superior to "conventional weapons" for inflicting mass casualties with less expenditure. He preferred reserving nuclear strikes for vessels deployed at a distance from the landing. Zheludev not only specified the most appropriate chemical-delivery means for each phase of an incoming landing but also unkindly recommended hitting the enemy when they retreated. Notable is the listing of R-33 which supposedly did not enter series production until six years later.

An unusual aspect of Soviet chemical armament had been the 'persistent' retention of first generation vesicant (blister) agents mustard and lewisite, employed separately or as mixtures; the US considered both to be obsolete. In 1961 Colonel A. Kuchin nevertheless had asserted that Americans held that "as normal issue" mustard in particular "by no means [has] lost its military significance" due to a skin action property not found in sarin or soman and that protection against gas vapor would be difficult; mustard is also more persistent than sarin.[975] Lewisite had the advantage of reducing liquid freezing points, especially useful as an additive to other agents.

Apparent holdups in the delivery of at least missile chemical armament until the early 1960s may be reflected in classified writings. Conspicuously lacking in the 1960 to early 1962 issues of the VM top secret edition provided by Penkovsky, while replete with nuclear discourses, had been any treatment of chemical warfare. There are only a few references to CW employment and these pertained as much to the enemy as to Soviet forces. The marshals and generals writing within their top level group engaged in widespread contentious, even vituperative, argumentation regarding the operational role of nuclear weapons, but no disputation had been evident regarding the new chemical variant. No one argued the utility, operational aspects, or proposed alternative employment methods of chemical weapons for theater operations against the NATO opponent.

But VM secret edition articles began to interlace more detailed insights into the Soviet concept of chemical warfare.

Colonels A. Postovalov and K. Kushch-Zharko in stating their 1965 views[976] on "Features Of An Offensive Operation When Neither Side Employs Nuclear Weapons" had not only provided a look into early Soviet thinking on the conventional variant but also the positioning of chemical weapons. Their take on unified nuclear-conventional vs. separate front offensive plans clearly favored the latter approach, and they were emphatic that

> The most important component of the operation plan is the establishment of the procedure for changing over from combat actions where only conventional means of destruction are employed to conduct of a nuclear war. For this, the targets for destruction with nuclear and chemical weapons, the procedure for storing nuclear and chemical munitions, the level of combat readiness of rocket troops and aviation for employing them, the

tasks of troops of the first echelon in case of the unleashing of nuclear war, and a number of other things must be defined in the plan and constantly refined during the course of combat actions.

Several authors explicitly defined the initial mass "nuclear" strike of a front to be inclusive…of chemical weapons.

General-Lieutenant V. Petrenko in his 1967 VM (S) article[977] on front offensive operations proposed planning methods "in the event of transition to the use of nuclear and chemical means" and said that "research shows that it is necessary first of all to determine which enemy installations are to be destroyed by nuclear and chemical weapons in the initial nuclear strike"—also among the first to call for a front and army "nuclear planning group" that research at the Frunze Military Academy had found useful. The tasks for this staff should include determining the "sequence for destroying enemy installations with nuclear and chemical weapons." Colonels A. Postovalov (an encore) and L. Pivovar in a 1967 VM (S) article[978] explored the tasks of frontal aviation. Aviation targets for "conventional munitions" to be specified in air army planning but also those "to be struck with means of mass destruction should a nuclear war develop" as well as "the number of aircraft designated solely for the delivery of nuclear and chemical strikes, their readiness level, and the procedure they are to follow when participating in the initial nuclear strike." Their construction pointed to the existence of an aviation chemical, in addition to the nuclear, echelon. The description of the initial nuclear strike by front forces in several contexts involved both chemical and nuclear weapons—and that this mass strike would be delivered on order of the front commander in accordance with VGK directives. General-Lieutenant F. Gayvoronsky in 1970 stressed continual refinement of front missile troops planning during conventional operations including "the targets for destruction in the first massive strike by nuclear and chemical warheads."[979]

Classified discussions also placed chemical weapons in the "nuclear war" distinguished from operations with only conventional arms.

Petrenko had hopped on the conventional bandwagon in his 1967 article which dealt with offensive operations in a "non-nuclear period" to be "unleashed without the use of nuclear and chemical weapons" and in which fronts would be deprived of "the basic means of destruction—nuclear and chemical weapons—which form the basis of the fighting power of modern operational formations." The 1967 article by Colonels Postovalov and Pivovar is entitled "The Transition By Troops From Combat Operations With The Exclusive Use Of Conventional Means Of Destruction To The Use Of Nuclear Weapons"[980] and not only further ratified Soviet acceptance of a conventional variant but also imparted definitions of operational use of chemical weapons. But they firmly adhered to the Soviet line of an inevitable escalation to nuclear war as well as the vital importance of preemption. They discussed coordinating "the moment the transition is made to the use of nuclear and chemical weapons" and many issues for handling this crucial divide between non-use and use of WMD by front aviation and missile-artillery troops. A clear distinction is made between the types of weapons used during a "non-nuclear period" and those introduced for the "nuclear period" while "conventional munitions" are distinguished from chemical; the respective differentiations then applied to both delivery aircraft and missile systems. The authors downgraded the value of missiles in a conventional role due to "the limited effectiveness of such strikes and also to the fact that the use of conventional rockets will lead to decreased readiness to deliver nuclear and chemical strikes" (retracting Postovalov's 1965 view on the value of cassette warheads). Their extensive discussion of nuclear transition provided compelling evidence that Soviet chemical warfare would be initiated in the "nuclear period" rather than integrated with conventional operations.

Colonel A. Kurkov used the same terminology and weapons discrimination in his later article[981] that included a description of the 1967 Dnepr exercise. General-Army G. Khetagurov also expressed definitions and boundaries in an identical manner in his early 1969 article[982] previously noted for coverage of the "limited nuclear" war variant. The theme of the article is the augmentation of front capabilities during a strategic operation in terms of each of delineated periods which also included "non-nuclear" and "nuclear." "The buildup of efforts in operations begun with the unlimited use of nuclear weapons and other means of mass destruction will be achieved primarily by the delivery of massive nuclear and chemical strikes." He distinguished "the use of chemical weapons" from that of "conventional means of destruction" and a short discussion of a "non-nuclear war" fought with "conventional types of weapons" had no hint of chemical weapons employment.

Colonel A. Sulim applied his math talent in a 1968 article[983] to develop a methodology for determining "the number of rockets with nuclear and chemical charges needed by the rocket troops of the Ground Forces for a front offensive operation as part of a strategic operation in a theater of military actions" in great detail. As mentioned earlier in regard to upping nuclear yields, four factors in his numeration included "the possibility of delivering nuclear and chemical strikes against unoccupied areas." A probability calculation table for this factor lists R-30, R-170, R-300 missiles and the KR-500 cruise missile pitted against US missile systems, but he did not specify which or whether all were chemical-capable. All thirteen of the references to chemical warheads or charges in the text coupled with nuclear as in the foregoing quotes. Sulim discussed one scenario of a "preemptive strike from our side" with nuclear and chemical missiles; appearing in a discussion of one of the factors, involving probabilities of front missile losses from several sources, addressing missile support. He assumed as a basis for calculation that in peacetime "rocket-technical units" would hold 60 percent of the front operation missile and warhead allocation—a clear implication that these units held both chemical and nuclear warheads prior to the beginning of war. He further calculated that a front that had seven or eight of these "rocket-technical units" and an allocation "of 300 to 450 rockets with nuclear and chemical charges" would have these units processing an average of three or four missiles each day. Unfortunately, Sulim did not break down by types of warheads. Summarizing he concluded that a coefficient should be applied "when determining the number of rockets with nuclear and chemical charges needed for a front offensive" ranging from 1.5 for tactical rockets (R-30) to as much as 2.5 for KR-500.

A mid 1967 article by two colonels, V. Popov and I. Apanovich,[984] reported preliminary conclusions from a front command-staff war game test of the *Platforma* mobile computer system. Coverage indicated the degree of chemical weapons integration into operational procedures as well as implied targets. The exercise, conducted in the Odessa MD (bordering the Black Sea), dealt with the "Preparation and Conduct of a Front Offensive Operation on a Coastal Direction" in the Southwestern TVD. Thereby the planned front offensive aimed at Turkey and presumably US and NATO forces in the region. The authors went into considerable detail regarding—surprise—deficiencies of the card-fed computer program.

> Problem No. 5. Assessment of the effectiveness of the employment of chemical weapons by rocket troops, artillery, and aviation. The basic shortcoming of this problem is the fact that it deals with only one type of toxic agent—sarin—and does not take account of other types of chemical weapons.

also

> Problem No. 9. Determination of the overall capabilities of a front in the employment of chemical weapons by rocket troops, artillery, and aviation. The program for this problem suffers from the same shortcomings as those in Problem No. 5. There must be constant data put into the computer for calculating the capabilities of aviation in employing all types of chemical warheads and for performing calculations of the total area, measured in hectares, contaminated with toxic agents by rocket troops, aviation, and by tube and rocket artillery.

Problem nine at least related to the Chemical Department, which also handled the forecast of personnel radiation doses from enemy nuclear strikes. They also mentioned other "nuclear and chemical" computer problem areas: allocations by tasks for the front operation, armies and other units; expected results for air army strikes; and the capabilities of a fighter-bomber aviation regiment for destroying enemy targets. As in so many other instances, the intelligence signals operators missed this exercise material.

Other articles scattered over many years examined deficiencies and solutions for existing WMD protection organization; data processing; contamination forecasting and reconnaissance; as well as detailed examinations of post-strike restoration of combat effectiveness. These discourses often dealt with both nuclear and chemical, and less frequently biological, situations—with an obvious presumption of offensive employment of these weapons by one or both sides. Several articles examined civil defense issues all presuming enemy employment of the full WMD triad. Colonel D. Shein argued in a 1962 article[985] that notification of imminent radioactive contamination should be separated from the contemporary unified warning signal for the full WMD spectrum. He had some interesting comments on the differing requirements for nuclear and chemical personal protective gear and shelter preparation. Ye. Zhuravlev in 1967[986] had been more explicit in advocating an alternate definition of WMD "situations" brought about by "the use of nuclear, chemical, and bacteriological weapons by the enemy and by our troops." Colonel A. Novoselov's 1969 examination[987] of methods for replacing the heavy losses of a ground army during the "nuclear period" noted that from "the experience of exercises and games, chemical weapons are less capable than nuclear ones in disrupting troop structure" but that all troops in a chemically-contaminated area would lose their combat effectiveness—and according to his analysis the local forces would also have to take quarantine measures against "enemy bacteriological weapons" as well. The CW content of the referenced "exercises and games" had escaped intelligence notice during external event monitoring.

Surprise in actions is a consistent theme of Soviet operational prescriptions but the unexpected is an absolute prerequisite for successful use of chemical weapons. In chemical combat there could be no distinguishing between preemption, meeting strikes, or retaliation. To achieve surprise against an unprepared and unwarned opponent entailed a premeditated first strike. Any hint of chemical attack would immediately impel the enemy to implement protective measures which, unlike nuclear, could in theory effectively mitigate the potential of toxic agents. As instructed by the 1962 *Regulations*, "Such weapons are used suddenly and in a massed way."[988] Development of a nuclear standoff would impart a geometric magnification of the value of a chemical variant.

One, rare, intelligence glimpse of the scale of integrated chemical-nuclear warfighting envisioned by the Soviets (again thanks to Penkovsky) appeared in the official top secret *Critique of the Front Two-Stage Operational-Rear Area Exercise Conducted in July 1961*.[989] While Warsaw Pact exercise documents providing chemical allocations have been found in national archives, and fragmentary data appeared in some classified documents acquired by intelligence, the July 1961 exercise critique remains the only instance of a Soviet front exercise CW plan. Prepared under the signature of the exercise staff chief and the Director, Marshal V. I. Chuikov (Commander-in-Chief of Ground Troops), the exercise stated objective involved the study of front logistics during the Initial Period, with emphasis on support to missile troops. Marking the significance of this exercise, representative live play involved about 22000 personnel and 7000 vehicles (apparently no one had to walk) including missile launchers and transporters. Scenario depicted a front based on the Carpathian MD in a counteroffensive with two other flanking fronts. The 2 Front first operation received 503 missiles—277 or 55 percent of these with chemical warheads. The allocation breakdown provided for an initial mass strike comprising 24 chemical and 63 nuclear missiles, an average of one apiece for the front complement of ballistic and cruise missile launchers. No discussion appeared on chemical munitions allocation or distribution to aircraft and artillery units. Ten additional nuclear strikes by VGK strategic assets would assist the front.

The critique stipulated missile-technical support units responsibility for both chemical and nuclear warheads, and that 44 chemical and 87 nuclear missiles had been notionally prepared by these units prior to the beginning of the front operation—26 missiles actually assembled during the exercise. Marshal Chuikov noted that the front "chief of the rocket and artillery armament works out plans for the support of troops with rockets with nuclear and chemical charges" but waxed perturbed with that work during the exercise—"incomprehensible" that procedures for delivery of nuclear and chemical missiles had been poorly executed although these "are assigned the decisive role in the destruction of the enemy in a future war." Despite detailed examination of logistics issues nowhere in the text appeared even a hint of a chemical supply channel separated from nuclear.

This exercise had been real-time monitored by Western intelligence, extracting many particulars—with the exception of chemical matters. The critique provided the only source on the chemical play since that aspect had not been discerned by SIGINT agencies, although little more had been obtained on nuclear activity either.

Post-Cold War opening of former Warsaw Pact national archives has revealed additional material and data on chemical operations not available to Western intelligence services. Documents prepared for the aforementioned June 1965 Soviet-Hungarian exercise[990] list a front operation allocation of 149 chemical missiles and 125 missile-aviation nuclear weapons—more chemical than nuclear munitions planned for a complete front initial operation. Actuality of the exercise had been indicated by document references that opposing units-deployments "correspond to reality" and the 20 additive to what intell types called TUDs (true unit designators). A near-equal distribution occurred of chemical and nuclear warheads to the front KR-500 cruise missile battalion, but with at least a 2:1 ratio chemical-to-nuclear warhead assignment to R-170 ballistic missiles and R-30 rockets. Notably the inventory of 45 chemical warheads had been "present at starting position" with the remainder to be supplied during the course of the offensive operation. This implies, on paper at least, elements of the chemical first echelon already present in Hungary. The breakdown also appears to provide the Hungarians, equipped with both the R-170 and the R-30, with a slice of the chemical pie.

Interest in chemical weapons by Soviet forces in Hungary apparently had been long-standing. A 1962 VM (S) article[991] by Colonels A. Andryushchenko and G. Prokopenko concerning group experience in organizing operational training stressed that "in the operational training plan of the Southern Group of Forces, much time is given to the study of the problem of an offensive operation of a front and the employment of nuclear, chemical, and rocket weapons" but complained that some generals and officers lacked a firm understanding of these systems. The original five hours allotted to lecture and seminar "for studying the combat properties of the nuclear and chemical weapons of our own troops" would expand as a remedy "to study nuclear and chemical weapons an additional 12 hours were set aside." Further work on these issues would be conducted during command-staff and troop exercises as well as training sessions. Perhaps by the time of the 1965 exercise the situation had been much improved.

Another Soviet numeration came from Colonel A. Rodin in his 1969 VM (S) article[992] on accumulating missiles for the initial mass strike during the conventional variant. "Accordingly, in carrying out an offensive operation without employing nuclear weapons, it becomes particularly important to determine the time at which action must be initiated to prepare rockets with nuclear and chemical warheads and deliver them to the troops." He proposed a variety of measures to ensure that missile-technical units, interacting with launch units, deployed in a position to maintain a mobile reserve of nuclear and chemical missiles in readiness for conducting the concerted front strike. His calculations at least partly derived from "experience of a series of operational command-staff and research exercises" which, unfortunately, transpired unremarked by signals intelligence monitors. The "rough calculation" for this reserve, based on a front with three armies, ranged 86 to 92 chemical and 168 to 180 nuclear missiles. Operational-tactical (R-300 Scud) and tactical (*Luna* FROG) allocations all calculated in terms of identical launcher sets of two nuclear to one chemical. The variation in the total came from an assumed 11 to 13 divisions in the front first echelon that had organic tactical rocket battalions in strike range. Only the front cruise missile regiment differed with a measly 1.5 airframes per eight launchers. But these numbers related only to the first mass strike—not the complete operation—which at this time would have amounted to about 20 to 30 percent of a front total missile allocation. In comparison to the 1961

Carpathian exercise the size of the initial strike had nearly tripled for a front with the same number of front and army operational-tactical missile brigades and more so for first echelon tactical rocket battalions. The increase came partly because the number of launchers in the three army missile brigades had increased by three each, and rocket battalions from two to three, but also because Rodin assigned his launchers a significantly higher reload factor. Although only an estimate by one officer for argumentation purposes an insight thereby can be obtained as to the scale of offensive chemical plans late in the 1960s.

Documents scattered through the archives of former Warsaw Pact countries complement those acquired during the Cold War concerning the allies involvement in chemical operations. These documents refer to both Soviet and national planning for offensive chemical operations, including logistics, from the early 1960s to the early 1970s. The number of such references to allied forces employing chemical munitions can only hint at the significantly greater scheme of the senior partner. Paperwork acquired on a Polish Coastal Front exercise during or before 1967 provided extensive data breakdowns on an operation allocation of 222 missiles including 30 percent chemical R-300, R-170, and R-30; no aircraft CW enumerated; and the front initial strike exclusively nuclear.[993] The Polish-run *Lato* 1967 exercise allocated a front operation 137 chemical warheads which amounted to 36 percent of the WMD total.[994] A Polish national front 'operation plan' circa 1972 provided for an allocation of 160 chemical and 205 nuclear missiles plus 53 nuclear (only) to aircraft; armies subordinate to this front each allotted 22 to 28 chemical missiles.[995] A graphic of a first nuclear launch during the February 1972 GSFG-East German exercise *Udar* (Strike) depicted planned joint strikes of nuclear and 20 chemical rockets allocated to R-65 (FROG-7).[996] As early as 1962 the East Germans had been depicted in an exercise document with army corps-subordinate R-30 and R-170 allotted chemical as well as nuclear missiles; the inventory of the corps missile-technical unit included both types of warhead.[997] These materials, just as in Soviet sources, consistently couple chemical with nuclear in strike planning and logistics measures.

The archive exercise documents confirm statements by high level defectors during the Cold War concerning planned Soviet provision of chemical weapons to their Warsaw Pact allies. Verifiable evidence that national forces had peacetime stocks may have been lacking, but a clear expectation of supply for wartime operations paralleled the nuclear situation. Czech sources, in particular, provided Western intelligence with detailed chemical munitions data and employment information—as in the Tabular compilation. The Czech officer[998] who participated in front-level exercising reported that Soviet artillery chemical firing tables had been acquired in the first half of the 1960s but only in 1965 did practice begin in planning missile chemical strikes. The officer stated that Czechoslovakia controlled no weapon stocks but delivery could be expected from the Soviets at some point during war preparations. He affirmed that the Czechs did not do bioweapons planning, at least in the early to mid 1960s, and believed that the Soviets reserved BW for strategic objectives.

Signals intelligence, the usual path for monitoring exercises, failed to detect any hint of the chemical content of Soviet and Warsaw Pact exercises. The CIA stressed this conundrum in a July 1971 memo that reviewed these events.[999] Many documents that had been acquired indicated that a third of all allocated tactical warheads would be chemical but "exercise scenarios" depicted an exclusively nuclear initial mass strike. No chemical operations play, no front-army chemical allocation returns, ever derived from SIGINT on exercises during the length of the Cold War. Only limited indications of tactical practice, in a few exercises, sporadically over a period of many years, had been found by this key collection tool. Without the Soviet classified literature being acquired through clandestine channels, the chemical context of these popups would have been an inexplicable mystery to Western intelligence.

The evidence being obtained by Western intelligence regarding extensive offensive chemical planning would eventually lead some to propose the existence of a Soviet-Warsaw Pact variant in which chemical attack preceded nuclear. Offsetting NATO-Warsaw Pact nuclear capabilities positioned chemical warfare as the only variant with a potentially war-winning premium. Massive surprise chemical strikes had effects similar to those of nuclear weapons with the critical advantage of avoiding the wide destruction and long-term radioactive contamination identified by Soviet theorists as major obstacles to rapid penetration and advance into the depth of NATO defenses. Some exercises depicted entire air armies rebasing to West German airfields during an offensive, a maneuver facilitated if not riddled by conventional or nuclear means.

Abortive US attempts to deploy enhanced radiation (neutron) nuclear weapons to Europe during the late 1970s sought to overcome a similar usability issue. The Soviets joined Western Europeans in denouncing any such deployment, albeit with differing motives. Sudden chemical munitions employment would permit the Warsaw Pact to exploit impracticable chemical defensive preparedness, and to paralyze the NATO collective decision-making apparatus. The implications had been recognized by NATO as noted in the Military Committee strategic defense paper 14/3 of January 1968 "…there is a danger that the Soviet leaders might come to believe that their capabilities in these fields [chemical and bacteriological] would give them a significant military advantage."[1000]

Developing and stockpiling the chemical armament that has been highlighted is an eminently defensive measure for any country facing a comparable threat. But other classified documents obtained demonstrated a widespread integration of chemical with other weapons in theater operations and a decidedly offensive bent. Soviet officers frequently referred to the use of CW during a wide variety of operational situations and some explored in considerable depth a number of chemical weapons employment issues throughout the 1960s, extending into the 1970s, in the classified editions of VM. Contrastingly, the restricted edition of VM during the same period dealt mainly with issues of protection against US and NATO chemical means—yielding only ambiguous hints of any Soviet offensive chemical inclination. A sampling of the more interesting items (all from the secret edition unless indicated)—

1960
- while inserting his views into the ongoing nuclear Big Bang dispute, General-Army V. Kurasov did note that "chemical weapons are also employed, mainly against objectives which were not subjected to nuclear strikes, in order to ensure the most complete destruction of the enemy and to preclude the possibility of his counteraction and maneuver"[1001]
- in a more practical vein issues involving the control of an army reinforcing missile and artillery units, most likely based on the experience of exercises in the preceding year, including "the delivery to [tactical rocket] battalions of warheads having nuclear, conventional, and chemical charges" and "centralization of fire control of tube and rocket artillery employing shells with conventional and chemical charges"[1002]

1961
- Colonel Ye. M. Nazarov's work *The Employment of Chemical Weapons in a Front Offensive Operation* would have been of considerable interest—if the piece had been acquired—unfortunately this General Staff Military Academy 1961 dissertation of 213 pages and four diagrams is known only from an abstract that appeared in a 1963 article[1003]
- superiority of chemical over nuclear warheads in mountainous terrain since detonations of the latter in the limited number of passages might block offensive movement[1004]
- calculations of the proportion of missile launchers that could be assigned nuclear vs. chemical missions, especially against enemy nuclear assets, with the consensus that unit complements must be augmented[1005]
- aspects of chemical strikes in depth by missile troops and fighter-bomber aviation (extensive use to be expected during initial meeting engagements) while forces in contact employed tube and rocket artillery[1006]—Marshal S. Varentsov stressed that artillery chemical strikes should only be conducted if surprise could be achieved[1007]
- proposed organizational schemes for controlling joint nuclear-chemical-conventional strikes including a front "fire and chemical center"[1008]
- front fire support for the drop of an airborne division in which missile troops deliver "nuclear strikes and strikes with chemical rockets against objectives and targets in the area of the landing operation and also against the enemy reserves which are closest to this zone" with a distinction between "chemical filler" and "conventional filler"[1009]

1962
- review of work in exercises 1960 to 1962 improving control organization and procedures for missile troops strike readiness centered on the front commander decision "when planning the operation, the commander of the front personally determined the procedure for employing the nuclear and chemical rockets issued to the front" also noting that field-deployed missile-technical units held both nuclear and chemical versions[1010]
- defeating a presumptive NATO mass assault by airborne troops in front rear areas by, alternatively, attacks on a departure airfield by a "bomber aviation regiment with AO-10 and RBK-500 bombs and chemical bombs with persistent toxic agents of the VRK-7 type" or felling the transport aircraft en route before the paras jump or if anyone actually reaches the drop zone a greeting for the survivors by a "fighter-bomber regiment using OKhAB-100 bombs with toxic agent type R-35"—sarin, while VRK-7 designated a thickened mustard-lewisite mixture[1011]
- assigning the task of destroying enemy reserves to front aviation during initial nuclear operations "the air army of the front, employing chemical and conventional means of destruction, can successfully hit the enemy reserves both in concentration areas and on the move"[1012]
- destroying widely dispersed enemy radioelectronic systems (radio stations, guidance systems, radars) "extensive use should be made of toxic chemical agents, especially in his operational depth"[1013]
- detailed discussion of the work of front and army computation and analysis stations [RAST] for assessing the radiation and chemical situations "during massed employment of nuclear and chemical weapons" by both sides based on exercises held by Soviet forces in East Germany and several military districts as well as "the effectiveness of our employment of chemical weapons and of the radiation contamination as a result of our ground nuclear bursts"[1014]

1963
- using the missile troops of a front to defeat enemy amphibious landings with "nuclear and chemical strikes" accomplished in a "recent exercise" taking advantage of CW characteristics "along with nuclear strikes, chemical weapons can also be employed very effectively against a landing force, particularly before the landing when a considerable part of the landing force personnel are situated in the open. At the same time that the chemical weapons are destroying personnel, they will also contaminate the transport means and combat equipment. This will force the enemy to land in means of protection and will contain his maneuvering"[1015]
- disrupting enemy attacks by defense counterpreparation

fires including "rockets primarily with chemical warheads"[1016]
- front bomber aviation support of a tank army offensive with chemical weapons —only fair since the enemy had been attributed a willingness to conduct a massed nuclear and chemical strike against this army[1017]

1964
- recommended relocation procedures for front missile troops during an operation to maximize availability of ready missiles "the role of the front is becoming even greater in the organization of mass chemical strikes by the rocket troops if we consider that the destruction of targets by chemical rockets requires a significantly greater expenditure of rockets than would be used for the destruction of targets with nuclear-armed rockets"–noting that a strike by 12 to 14 R-170 chemical missiles could destroy 30 to 40 percent of Western division personnel[1018]
- examples of computer work in the Leningrad MD included "calculation of the number of conventional and chemical warheads needed to provide for the combat training of the rocket troops and artillery of the district for the training year" an important indication that chemical weapons had been integrated into the training routine of the Ground Troops[1019]
- capabilities of the air army of a front said to "permit it to use up to 50 nuclear warheads with a total yield of over 5000 kilotons in a single sortie. With conventional warheads it is capable of delivering a bomb strike of 250 to 650 tons, and by using chemical weapons, it can destroy enemy personnel in an area of approximately 200 square kilometers"[1020]
- suggested special exercises to address problems in "the control of the rocket troops and aviation when they deliver coordinated strikes with nuclear and chemical warheads" based on the experience of the Kiev MD with many repetitions of the wording "nuclear (chemical)" means and strikes[1021]

1965
- organizing and controlling the missile troops of a reserve front during the march to engagement including "the times the rocket brigades and battalions are to be ready to deliver nuclear strikes, the number of rockets to be issued them with nuclear and chemical warheads and the times they are to be prepared for launch"[1022]
- the character of meeting engagements at the outset of war depicted by General-Lieutenant N. V. Ogarkov—on his way up to Chief of the General Staff "In our view, under modern conditions, lying at the foundation of maneuvering in a meeting engagement must be the employment of nuclear and chemical weapons, the delivery of deep splitting frontal attacks, exploiting breaks in the enemy disposition and gaps formed by nuclear weapons"[1023]
- concern with supporting systems readiness during war waged with only conventional weapons "the procedure for storing nuclear and chemical warheads as well as the degree of combat readiness of operational-tactical and tactical rockets must be such as to ensure the possibility of conducting nuclear strikes against the enemy in the shortest possible time" as well as an explicit statement that a certain type of missile-technical unit prepared and stored both chemical and nuclear warheads in the field[1024]

1966
- a military district use of coded command transmissions for "delivering nuclear, chemical and conventional rockets" in command-staff and special rocket troops exercises[1025]
- the review of the previously referenced Frunze Academy book *Combat Actions of Troops Without the Employment of Means of Mass Destruction* noted a distinction in an army commander decision regarding "the concept of the actions and the tasks of troops in routing the enemy, both with the employment of conventional means and with nuclear and chemical weapons"[1026]

1967
- the estimated requirement for an army counterstrike against the reserves of a NATO corps "complete destruction of this grouping would require 12 to 16 nuclear warheads, 30 to 40 chemically armed rockets" and other means[1027]
- using computers for operational calculations including a scientific research project "for working out problems with regard to planning a front initial nuclear strike and to employing nuclear and chemical weapons during an operation" and in a General Staff Military Academy war game "to establish possible losses on both sides from nuclear and chemical weapons" as well as other data involving use of both of these means[1028]
- conduct of a defense against amphibious assaults with strikes by nuclear and chemical weapons during different phases[1029]
- preferred transfer of command responsibility to an alternate control post created in the rocket-artillery armament service when front or army control posts are disabled because of better qualifications for "preparing and delivering nuclear and chemical strikes"[1030]
- some scenario details of the massive Dnepr exercise of September 1967 overlooked by signals intelligence monitors and Western observers—"the operational directive (order) of the front, the basis of which was a plan of operations involving the use of nuclear and chemical weapons."—both may have been used on the sixth day of the front operation following a "non-nuclear period"[1031]

1968
- pursuing a favorite Soviet pastime of developing numeric models to compare opposing forces, in this case aviation, accounting for factors that included chemical weapons—with separate consideration of "the non-nuclear period of actions" which excluded both "units of fire of the chemical means" as well as the "nuclear echelon"[1032]
- a detailed prescription for defeating NATO resistance to

tank assaults noted that "the great bulk of enemy antitank means will be destroyed at the same time his troop groupings are struck with nuclear and chemical weapons" but just in case the author favored additional measures for neutralizing mobile and area defenses with coupled nuclear and chemical strikes[1033]
- another expression of concern in the same issue with overcoming improving NATO antitank means assumed that "under present-day conditions army and front operations will be conducted with the belligerents widely employing new means of destruction and particularly nuclear, chemical and bacteriological weapons"—an unusual direct assertion of BW employment—but with a hopeful note that better conventional weapons meant that antitank defenses could be defeated "without employing nuclear and chemical weapons"[1034]
- detailed examination of the problem of neutralizing NATO surface-air missiles in transport aviation flight corridors for dropping an airborne division concluded "if, when means of mass destruction are employed, this task is 70 to 80 percent fulfilled by delivering nuclear (chemical) strikes against enemy air defense installations using means of the front and Supreme High Command, then, when conducting combat operations with the employment of only conventional means of destruction, the situation is changed decisively" since missile troops and aviation must be held in readiness to conduct nuclear and chemical strikes[1035]
- the conduct of a tank army meeting engagement under variant conditions stressed "if the enemy actions are to be decisively preempted, the organization of the destruction of the enemy with strikes of nuclear and chemical weapons and with the fire of conventional means must be thorough and timely" and in this long, rambling discourse a continual repetition of "nuclear and chemical" strikes, warheads, weapons[1036]
- the previously cited examination of defense with repeated references to nuclear and chemical strikes "we must consider the principal method for conducting a defensive operation of a front or army during nuclear actions to be the destruction of attacking enemy groupings with nuclear and chemical weapons and with fire from conventional means"[1037]

1969
- detailed conceptualization of a meeting engagement at the outset of war between Soviet and NATO forces distinguished conditions of a "nuclear war" versus "non-nuclear war" and between "chemical and conventional means" in which chemical weapons are employed only in the nuclear variant in contrast to "non-nuclear actions, which by definition employ only conventional means of warfare"[1038]
- the popular meeting engagement further explored in the same issue in the form of a mathematical model which included defeating an advancing enemy reserve of three to four divisions by strikes of 110 to 120 missiles, half of these chemical[1039]
- development of yet another mathematical model—and again in this issue—for staff preparation of a front operation including a diagrammatic representation with separate elements for evaluating "one's own troop groupings in the use of nuclear, chemical, and conventional weapons" and for enemy use of the same weapons[1040]

1970
- concern with the radiation and chemical situation "with massive employment of nuclear and chemical weapons" during through-flights by new Soviet "airborne shock" units transported by helicopters (as in the US airmobile concept) while not specifying the employing side, the importance of providing these units with "chemical weapons" written in emphasis[1041]
- planning the commitment of a combined-arms army to battle in 1969 exercises during a "non-nuclear period" which used only "conventional means of destruction" with a "nuclear war" variant in which "the buildup of strike forces is assured mainly through the use of nuclear and chemical weapons" by missile troops and aviation[1042]

VM (S) particulars cannot be extended since the CIA has not released subsequent issues. Nor can an apparent significant transition phase in the Soviet military consideration of chemical weapons usage be delineated.

By 1973 at least Soviet terminology regarding chemical weapons had altered, indicated by textbooks at high level military academies.[1043] The Military Academy of Armored Troops training text dated 1973 *The Offensive Operation Of A Combined-Arms Army* discusses enemy chemical weapons. But all Soviet references are in the form "hitting the enemy with nuclear and special weapons" with twelve other instances of "special weapons" use by their side. The General Staff Academy 1974 textbook *Front Offensive Operations* even more occurrences of "special weapons" that clearly encompass at least CW. Statements leave no doubt that chemicals are meant.

> Special weapons are used in a front offensive operation to sharply reduce the combat effectiveness of troops and to disrupt the operation of the enemy's control organs and rear services by the mass incapacitation and debilitation of personnel and by the contamination of combat equipment and terrain on enemy territory. They are used by rocket troops, aviation, and artillery on the main axes, by surprise and massed, in combination with other means of destruction and against targets having the greatest density of personnel and the least protection for them.
>
> The principal method of using these weapons is the delivery of massed strikes by rocket troops, aviation, and artillery. Under conditions of the delivery of

nuclear strikes, special weapons are used against troops which are not to be hit with nuclear warheads.

The characteristic combat feature of special weapons is their capability to inflict heavy losses on the enemy not only in the areas of their combat use but also at considerable distances away from them, in the direction of the wind. Therefore, when these weapons are used our own troops must be warned and necessary measures taken to ensure their safety.

and, further on:

Using special warheads, front artillery, in a one-minute fire strike, can neutralize the sheltered personnel of 24 to 25 enemy motorized infantry and artillery battalions and their corresponding subunits.

Notable is the assignment of "special weapons" to the nuclear period in distinction to the nonnuclear; a separate chapter on use of "conventional means" has no hint of Soviet chemical employment.

A perplexing occurrence in the mid 1970s—unnoticed by the assigned connoisseurs— should have transformed the intelligence perspective of the Soviet chemical variant. All instances, not just the explicit discussions cataloged above, to Soviet employment of chemical armament in theater operations vanished. Chemical warfare content disappeared from classified General Staff Academy documents, military writings, and manuals—which constituted the most reliable base of evidence—as completely as in a fundamentalist Christian expurgation of nonconforming views in publications. But nearly a decade would elapse before someone in US intelligence would realize that a major strand had gone missing in the reference material. Perhaps better late than never but in the interval an important US decision had been reached and ultimately implemented, entirely in ignorance of the Soviet retrenchment, regarding chemical arms modernization. The Soviet chemical reality would be further distorted by the intelligence absolute failure to recognize the character of their unique concept for theater operations developed at the end of the 1950s.

Timing of the cutoff can be more closely pinpointed with the assistance of Afghan Colonel Ghulam Dastagir Wardak. During the time when his country rated among 'friends' the Soviet Union afforded an opportunity to further education at the Military Academy of the General Staff. Along with other third world senior officers he attended classes which expounded the Soviet strategic culture, to the inclusion of surprisingly sensitive material. Unfortunately for the Soviets detailed notes from most of the sessions, contravening Academy rules, departed with Colonel Wardak after graduation; and had been made available to US intelligence by 1981. Topical details paralleled, and some elements expanded on, the classified documents obtained via other means. The notes provided holistic coverage of key military issues, representing Soviet conclusions, the school solution, at a particular period—and tipped (a few anyway) analysts to the significance of the directions in Soviet theater war planning. Content has been published in *The Voroshilov Lectures*.[1044]

Colonel Wardak began his two-year course in September 1973 and, after a break in August 1974, graduated in July 1975. The curriculum followed at the Academy taught army-level subjects during the first year and addressed material pertaining to fronts the following academic year; with periodic lectures on strategic issues throughout the course of instruction. The published version of his notes from the first year, covering army operations, contains some 57 textual instances specifying Soviet employment of chemical weapons in the offense and defense. Soviet instructors had apparently been fully aware of the contradiction teaching chemical offense in a manner which Geneva Protocol obligations prohibited. Second year notes on front subjects have just three instances dealing with Soviet chemical weapons employment plus several others on enemy CW usage. Wardak told his intelligence interlocutors that Soviet lecturers on front material that second year had become noticeably guarded concerning anything to do with chemical attacks in striking contrast with their prior volubility. Clearly the Academy lesson plans had been revised by the time, or as, year two got under way not just to downplay but to eliminate all offensive chemical content.

The Polish official critique of the June 1974 *Lato* exercise describes enemy use of chemical weapons but "this fact unfortunately was not reflected in the basic estimates or in specific decisions made by the commanders" perhaps indicating that the participants had ignored this element of the scenario; General-Major F. Siwicki did rail against American disrespect for the Geneva Protocol in Vietnam and binary munitions development.[1045] Additional indications of the disappearance of the CW variant is available in post Cold War material. One key source is documentation found in Polish archives on the March 1975 running of a *Soyuz* exercise involving the Coastal Front.[1046] While not complete, extensive material is available on the overall scenario, progress of operations, nuclear allocations and strikes. Details pertaining to one of the subordinate armies includes nuclear warhead allocation. But there is no indication of chemical weapons allocations or strikes by "Easterners" in notable contrast to the prominence of CW in preceding 1960s and 1970s exercise documents. There are a couple of references to chemical strikes by "Westerners" that lack any operational context. At least one European researcher has discerned a mid 1970s disappearance of Warsaw Pact chemical content in archival documents.[1047]

The chemical offensive did not dematerialize solely from the pages of VM. General Staff Academy instructional material at the top secret level also ceased to deal with offensive chemical warfare by their side. The 1977 front operation lessons block had no Soviet offensive treatment despite many references to enemy CW.[1048] *The Front Offensive Operation* lecture dated May 1977[1049] had no hint of Soviet offensive CW. Both presentments featured detailed treatment of nuclear and conventional offensive variants. The absence of Soviet offensive WMD action contrasts strikingly with the dire proffering of imputed NATO WMD plans in lecture chapter ten on the protection of troops and rear services. In the Western TVD depiction NATO would employ from ten to thirty percent of strategic bombers, carrier and tactical aviation, for chemical strikes. Sarin and VX attacks could inflict up to 60 percent losses in a front. NATO supposedly proposed to deliver biological agents in up to ten percent of missiles and aviation; even "unmanned drifting aerostats" carrying 500-kg of biological compounds would be used. Seemingly the Biological Weapons Convention signed five years earlier had not come to the attention of the Academy professors. A granular depiction of the horrific effects of NATO mass nuclear, chemical, and biological strikes must have sent some Soviet and Warsaw Pact officers fleeing in terror from the lecture hall. This NATO WMD Operation, however, received no response beyond nuclear—as if the chemical variant had become inoperable, whether preemptively or in retaliation, even in situations involving enemy WMD use.

There are disparate indications that the chemical excision might have been one element of a wider set of high level political decisions involving the WMD trio implemented circa 1973-1974. Encompassing the nuclear component, the 1974 General Staff-Main Intelligence Directorate classified manual on reconnaissance in front offensive operations mentions "instructions of the Central Committee of the CPSU that the Soviet Union will not use nuclear weapons first"[1050] a statement repeated with identical wording the next year in a VM (R) article by Colonels Ye. Rybkin and S. Dmitriyev.[1051] These statements point to a 1974 or earlier issuance of a decree from the political leadership instituting new doctrinal guidance for the armed forces involving at least renunciation of nuclear initiation (distinction from preemption uncertain). How direct the connection is not determinable but the 22 June 1973 US-USSR bilateral Agreement on the Prevention of Nuclear War[1052] provided for consultation in any potentially nuclear confrontation; in a 1982 book Marshal N. V. Ogarkov accused the US of threatening a breakout from the Agreement.[1053] What is not yet known is whether the CPSU decree also incorporated decisions on other WMD or that chemical and biological warfare had been addressed in separate directives. But there is other evidence that comparable decisions of some nature regarded each of the WMD. A longer period of deliberation must have preceded all of these decisions.

Another substantial indication of alterations to Soviet WMD preparations at this time involved biological weapons. Only in the 1990s did revelations by defectors from the Soviet BW program reveal a breadth and extent that had not been fully appreciated by Cold War intelligence. Insider program managers Kanatjan Alibekov (Ken Alibek) and Vladimir Pasechnik described a concerted effort to conceal a massive biological warfare research and production complex in the civilian *Biopreparat*, fronted as a benign grouping of industry laboratories. Another set of biological research facilities remained under MoD control until a Central Committee decree in 1986 prepared the way for another reorganization. Alibek has also detailed the mobilization plan for munitions filling at these plants that would be initiated during the Special Period.[1054] A recent comprehensive study of Soviet BW,[1055] while somewhat misreading the intell perspective due to insufficient declassification, drew on the accounts of several eyewitnesses in outlining reorganization of the research and weapons program. Various measures extending from 1971 to 1974 included a 1971 Central Committee-Council of Ministers decree ordaining reorganization of BW (and chemical?) programs; which a 1972 high level meeting amplified in scope; a 25 June 1973 order in turn led to a lateral transfer of responsibility for military biological responsibilities to 15 Main Directorate from the Seventh implemented by a 1 November 1973 MoD decree; and a 24 April 1974 decree setting up *Biopreparat*. By coincidence or not 7 GUMO had been fingered by Penkovsky as the biological-chemical organ of the General Staff, later openly publicized by the CIA.[1056]

Further evidence of a possible chemical-related decree in the same timeframe came from another 1990s refugee Vil S. Mirzayanov. He had been a scientist at the Scientific Research Institute [NII] of Organic Chemistry and Technology for more than two decades. This institute had formerly been designated as NII-42 and had been tracked by intelligence since the re-designation of a Moscow area plant in 1941.[1057] In his 2009 book *State Secrets* Mirzayanov comments regarding the CW program that "in 1974 the Central Committee of CPSU placed this entire complex with all of its scientists, engineers and workers, entirely beyond the bounds of the laws and regulations existing at that time, pretending that it didn't exist" adding "in our country information about scientific research in the area of development of chemical weapons from 1974 up to the current time is a specifically protected state secret."[1058] Unfortunately he provides no further details on the nature of this reorientation. Mirzayanov's statement implies a chemical weapons vanishing act that is strikingly like that concurrently implemented for work on biological. The BW study pointed out the *Biopreparat* coincidence with the Central Committee May 1971 setting up of the *Foliant* cover for developing a new line of nerve agents which had been disclosed by Mirzayanov.[1059] Unlike BW the administrative details have not yet become public. There could well be a connection to the disappearance of chemical weapons in the classified military literature.

The systematizers of Soviet mass destruction had truly acquitted as busy bees in the few years up to the mid 1970s. Another discrete piece of this WMD puzzle, representing perhaps the culmination of the foregoing shakeup and shift of responsibilities, may have been marked by the November 1974 advancement of the military nuclear weapons authority from status as a strategic service component into a MoD main directorate—12 GUMO—to be considered. The full import of these concurrent changes, whether parallel or interrelated, to the Soviet WMD empire cannot be firmly defined at this time. Most of the leading participants have journeyed to the Marxist-Leninist Valhalla. Surviving witnesses may someday come forward but more likely some diligent researcher in Russian archives will discover the relevant decree or decrees that will provide a unifying background.

Two modules of the mass destruction triad had by 1959 been inextricably linked in a new Soviet concept of theater operations. Classified writings, manuals, lectures, and exercise documents uniformly—even after the introduction of the 'non-nuclear period'—denominated the 'nuclear period' for chemical weapons employment. Senior and mid-grade officers defined the initial mass strike as a WMD blitz that integrated at least nuclear and chemical. Documentary material coupled "nuclear and chemical" in a seemingly ordained phraseological unity, this conjunction reiterated as if ocean waves pounding on a beach. Such a linkage and repetition, particularly during the decade of the 1960s, of themselves constituted indications with concrete implications (or perhaps expressions in concrete)—pivotal evidence of the second kind—to all of which the connoisseurs of WMD intelligence remained utterly oblivious.

## begetting the official chemical model

The tenants of US chemical cubicles, along with their UK counterparts, had reacted to the disappearance of offensive chemical warfare in Soviet classified documents with...intell as usual. An aggressive Soviet posture continued to be assessed not only uninterrupted but also on an ever-increasing scale. Nearly a decade would slip away before someone noticed the yawning lacunae in the only consistently persuasive source available to intelligence regarding Soviet CW—as if someone had pried the rocks from the ensembles of the Crown Jewels without alerting, or even catching the attention, of the Tower guardians.

The disappearance of chemical prescriptions in classified manuals and writings relegated intelligence assessments to reliance on a wobbly base of problematic evidence and speculation—all viewed through a constricted perceptual window. Clandestine sources continued testifying to Soviet research into advanced toxic chemical formulations but indications of operational intent, employment planning, and munitions accumulation became limited to irregular occurrences, occasionally in signals intelligence. There had been a few ambiguous—and fewer unambiguous—reflections of chemical weapons practice in a number of Warsaw Pact tactical exercises. The maestros of chemical intelligence, however, creatively compensated for this lack of solid evidence with their own expedients. Overlaying the uncertain mix of prior definitive and sporadic contemporary evidence, disputed assessments persisted among intelligence agencies regarding the role of chemical weapons in Soviet military doctrine. A WMD apartheid accentuated the distortion of analytical perspectives in which the partitions between the chemical and nuclear cubicles in both the CIA and the DIA effected a Berlin wall. The field had been left wide open for intelligence and extramural charlatans to fill in the blanks to suit particular political and institutional biases. Gestation of an official chemical model continued unremittingly.

US intelligence twisted into perceptual knots regarding the 'conventional chemical' model whether in the late 1970s[1060] or 1984.[1061] One pole, headed by the CIA, held Soviet initiation of chemical warfare coterminous with nuclear perceiving a tangible firebreak with the employment of non-nuclear arms. The US Army at the other extreme insisted that the Soviets regarded CW as integral to conventional operations, lacking any separated contingency. The Army had not always adhered to this position. In a December 1964 NIE[1062] nuclear warfare discussion their chief intelligence officer had asserted that CW had been "consistently coupled with tactical nuclear weapons both in writings and in exercises" per a footnoted dissent. The 'conventional chemical' proponents insisted that CW would be employed routinely in the "non-nuclear period" despite the unmistakable drift of classified writings and documents sketching a chemically saturated "nuclear period." Other agencies filled in the interval. All acknowledged at least the possibility of a discrete chemical phase preceding nuclear strikes. Many of the loudest had no access to the compartmented documentary collection and thus remained unaware of the consistent nuclear-chemical diarchy depicted in that material. But even the openly available 1965 military dictionary fixed conventional weapons (number 973 *obychnyye vidy oruzhiya*) as all "weapons with the exception of weapons of mass destruction (i.e. nuclear, chemical, and bacteriological)" while the WMD definition (1036 *oruzhiye massovogo porazheniya*) included "nuclear, chemical and bacteriological weapons."[1063]

Among the inconvenient evidence against the chemical-as-conventional view during the heyday of the chemical variant had been four VM (S) articles by General-Colonel (Artillery) I. Volkotrubenko and Colonel Ye. Yefimov. Published successively in 1965,[1064] 1966,[1065] and 1970 issues 89[1066] and 91[1067] these two officers argued issues of ground systems ammunition supply. While drawing heavily on GPW data and practice the articles contained no references, not so much as hint, of chemical rounds—despite widespread discussions in that journal during the same period that dealt explicitly with chemical weapons.

The DIA and the US Army became particularly assertive in promoting their version of the official chemical model. They built upon the mishmash of mainly human source reporting dating to the Hirsch report—extended with a subsequent chain of information of indeterminate validity—uncompelled to reexamine past assumptions. The chemical connoisseurs pressed onward indiscriminately conflating dubious, ambiguous, insubstantial, and occasionally solid, evidence. Some Army intelligence folks centered their careers on micro-appraising the garrison of a Soviet motorized rifle unit near the city of Kaliningrad because of a serviceman's mid 1970s claim that a regiment conventional ammunition depot held chemical munitions. A few British connoisseurs self-convinced that enclosed conveyors attached to buildings at some ammunition storage facilities signified a chemical indicator, disregarding the functional commonality of conventional munitions bulk assembly, fuzing, and maintenance.

The chemical connoisseurs had mastered the fetish methodology popular in many intelligence cubicles—the arbitrary assignment of governing significance to selected objects regardless of any grounding in specific and/or corroborating evidence. They attributed particular importance to the imposing array of Soviet and Warsaw Pact specialized decontamination trucks and equipment. After all, this fleet loomed prominently visible in overhead imagery and ground photography, and appeared to be inexorably expanding in size. The Soviet decon truck tally had reached 8000 by 1978 as reported by a memorandum on chemical warning indications.[1068] A chemical equation thereby imposed conveniently ignored the missions of the Chemical Troops in the radiological environment of the nuclear warfare that had been, since the mid 1970s, an exclusive theme in the Soviet conception and practice of the WMD battlefield.

The ARS-series vehicle, basically a truck-mounted high capacity tank with an integrated pumping capability, had been a prominent example of the fetish method in action. Every parking slot observed on satellite imagery to be occupied by a decon vehicle tainted that location as a chemical defendant. An *a priori* assumption took hold that these specialized trucks somehow constituted an essential indicator of offensive chemical activity with a resulting impressive pileup of suspects. The wide deployment of Soviet chemical units and their organic vehicles dazzled intelligence, defense, and institutional connoisseurs as well as the ignorant politicians who championed the cause of Soviet chemical threat. The resulting images served to magnify the assumed scale of chemical preparations and intent.

This particular vehicular chemical fetish became so pervasive that similar association extended well beyond the Cold War; diligently applied in the intelligence WMD justification for the Iraq expedition of 2003. Imagery specialists had associated a particular white tank-truck, dubbed the Samarra vehicle from identification at an agent production plant, at certain locations, as a chemical marker. When similar tankers had been observed on imagery in 2002 accompanying convoys at ammunition depots the presumption arose of an indicated renewal of the Iraqi chemical munitions program. Some tankers equalled decon vehicles > therefore the transport activity had to be chemical munitions in nature > therefore chemical warfare preparations advanced > therefore chemical munitions production and stockpiling had been resumed > therefore a preemptive assault against this formidable Iraqi WMD capability must proceed. That final step of course not decided by intelligence. The millennial generation of intelligence connoisseurs had learned nothing from, or had entirely forgotten, the experience of their predecessors.

The US intelligence community unanimously accepted this multipoint linkage despite caveats that there had been minimal reliable evidence concerning the size or disposition of any Iraqi CW stocks—a situation remarkably similar to the Soviet estimate. Their appraisal provided a critical, unnecessary but expedient, rationale for the Bush administration to promote a preconceived solution to an imagined threat. In the words of the 2005 WMD Commission report the overall intelligence chemical conclusion had been "…fundamentally grounded on the single assessment that the Samarra-type trucks seen on imagery were in fact CW-related."[1069] That the celebrity trucks might be fire pumpers escorting munitions movements as a standard measure or even to carry backup fuel supplies, as later suggested, represented inconvenient alternatives to be rejected. An identical, ill-considered, fetish bolstered both the Soviet and Iraqi chemical estimates. But the consequence of the latter misjudgment would be the destruction of many thousands of American, Iraqi, and other, lives.

A chemical tsunami swept through the arenas where the Soviets stood accused of spreading agents and bio-toxic substances. Southeast Asian 'yellow rain' proved to be a bottomless pit of suppositions, conflicting and uncertain evidence, in which an undisputed reality proved impossible to establish. Chemical employment evidence during the Soviet expedition to Afghanistan remained spotty, ambiguous, but often accused. That Afghan rocketeers fired more than a thousand R-300 armed with high explosive warheads during that campaign potentially muddied the pool of evidence. A Russian web page on this system noted,[1070] with apparent glee, that when, as frequently the case, firing near the minimum range of 50-km left up to three tonnes of oxidizer and fuel in propellant tanks. This reserve spectacularly augmented the resulting detonation. Unknowable is what proportion of *mujahedin* reports of 'chemical' incidents had been inspired by such experience. Intelligence assessments did not tend to point out such nonconforming details. The nitric acid-based oxidizer formulated a nasty toxic agent. Soviet threat proponents occasionally trotted out ground photos of missile personnel working around Scuds while wearing full chemical protective gear with the stated or implied implication that chemical warhead mating practice transpired. They conveniently overlooked the reality that the missile crews might be more concerned with oxidizer spillage during airframe fueling.

The DIA helpfully distilled the verdict of intelligence community CW connoisseurs in a 1985 unclassified novella *Soviet Chemical Weapons Threat*.[1071] This publication directly reflected the content and conclusions of a plethora of studies that are still locked up. Soviet readers must have been perplexed at the information and firm judgments, perhaps concluding that this clever American deception aimed to hide what Western intelligence services really 'knew' about Warsaw Pact chemical warfare capabilities. Unfortunately the publication did accurately exhibit the 'known' suppositions. One map displayed nine "chemical weapons depots" within the USSR, symbolized by rail tank cars. Another map provided the general locations of 32 European sites where "chemical munitions are reportedly stored…." The commander of Soviet Chemical Troops apparently referred to this numeration in 1990 when he denied that the USSR had any such externally deployed weapons; General-Colonel S. Petrov labeled as a "pure fabrication" a Western assertion that 30000 tonnes reposed in nine depots of the GSFG (as depicted by the DIA map).[1072] The CGF commander seconded this absence in 1991 that "chemical weapons have never been stored on the Czechoslovak territory."[1073] In reality any itemization of credible intelligence evidence, that which could withstand scrutiny, regarding the presence of chemical weapons in those countries during 49 years of Soviet/Russian occupation amounted to a grand total of…one popup. This item represents a benchmark for the solidity of chemical weapons evidence during the Cold War, among the meager tally of leads acquired by Western intelligence.

In early 1975[1074] a munitions inventory dispatch covering three regiments of the Soviet 105 Fighter-Bomber Aviation Division in East Germany revealed that 497 Fighter-Bomber Aviation Regiment based near Grossenhain held 400 KhAB series. Soviet data provided twelve years later at the Shikhany proving grounds public exhibition of "standard samples" of chemical munitions filled in some details.[1075] Displays informed that the regiment 200 KhAB-250 would have had, variously, an agent fill of 49-kg sarin and/or 45-kg thickened soman (the popular VR-55); while 200 KhAB-100 contained a mustard-lewisite agent mix of 28-kg and/or 39-kg—however 1962 information also had the KhAB-100 fill as R-35 (sarin).[1076] The context of the dispatch acquisition signified the unlikelihood that this airfield deployment constituted a unique example of the presence of the chemical first echelon in Central Europe; especially when considering the emphasis on missile delivery of chemical weapons in Soviet documentary material. But the US and other Western intelligence services did not, in fact, 'know' the whereabouts of any other forward chemical munitions. More than nine years would elapse before similar data emerged regarding another chemical deployment, this time within the USSR, involving an aviation regiment subordinate to the Northern Fleet.

Notably discrepant with the Grossenhain popup had been at least part of a public statement more than a decade later by General Secretary M. Gorbachev. During a speech in Prague on 10 April 1987 he asserted "I can tell you that the Soviet Union has stopped making chemical weapons. As you know, the other Warsaw Treaty countries have never produced such weapons and never had them on their territory. The USSR has no chemical weapons outside its own borders…."[1077] The last element may well have been accurate in 1987 but evidentially not for the preceding deployment of the chemical first echelon. A Soviet Group commander in 1991 admitted that nuclear weapons had been present in his domain but asserted "as for chemical weapons we never kept any…"—but this pertained to Poland.[1078]

Poorly substantiated assessments had not been limited to US intelligence. In a 1986 document found in East German archives their chief of staff 'corrects' an FRG assessment that a plant at Kapen produced chemical agents; in reality an ammunition factory—nor did the GDR possess chemical weapons stocks as accused.[1079] Intelligence appraisals of the Kapen facility had apparently been conflated with use, beginning in the early 1950s and ending in 1962, to dispose of captured German chemicals as well as the World War II function of chemical munitions filling.[1080] When in July 1990 the still extant GDR Government had invited their future countrymen to inspect national installations suspected of chemical storage, nothing more than samples for protective research could be found.[1081] West German military specialists had no further luck when permitted to inspect Soviet installations—the first in August 1990 at a munitions storage depot that did actually have a WMD history.[1082]

A deliberately contorted representation of the missions of the Soviet Chemical Troops embodied the fundamental underpinning of the official chemical model. The "Chemical" designation alone is misleading. The Soviet Army tasked these 'special troops' to conduct multifaceted operations not limited even to those involved in the employment of mass destruction weapons. Chemical Troops of the several armed services had been organized and equipped to support operations in nuclear and biological as well as chemical environments. A large-scale mobilization and deployment of "Chemical" Troops in brigade strength would be implemented to remedy an eminently radiological event at the Chernobyl nuclear power plant in 1986. Specialized units functioned for nuclear burst geo-detection; radiation-chemical reconnaissance and decontamination (using **dual**-purposed vehicles); smoke generation; even combat with flamethrowers and incendiary munitions.

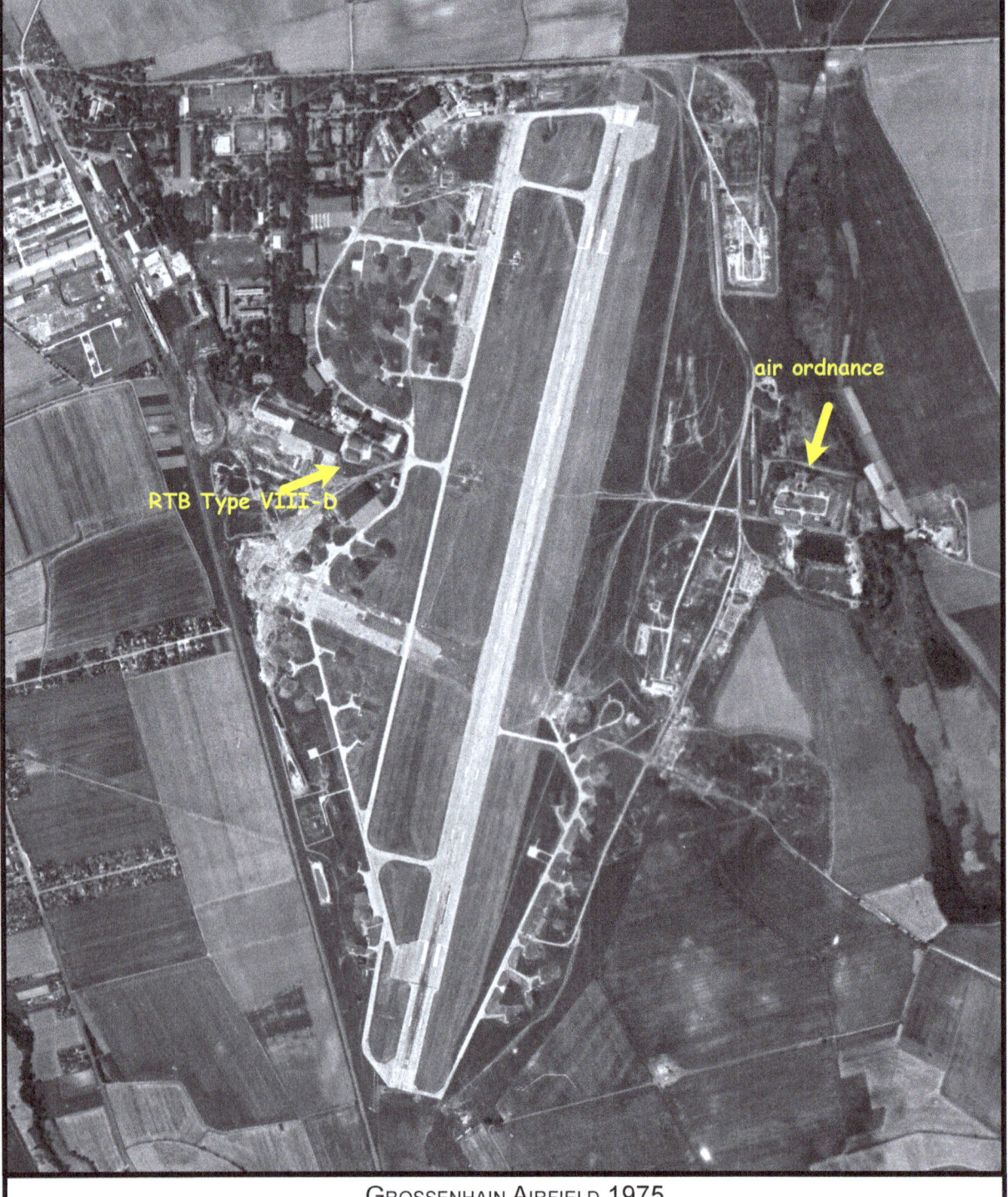

GROSSENHAIN AIRFIELD 1975
KNOWN WEAPONS STORES MARKED—INTELLIGENCE NEVER SURMISED THE LOCATION OF THE CHEMICAL BOMBS

A massive heap of information accumulated over many years from SIGINT, military unit personnel, and documents overwhelmingly specified defensive functions. In particular a densely filled genre of reports—entirely blockaded to date by declassification programs—emanated from Soviet and Warsaw Pact national emigres and some defectors. Personnel serving in many types of chemical service units at levels ranging from platoons in line combat regiments to separate chemical defense brigades provided abundant, if highly variable in usefulness, information. Attendees, including non-bloc students, at the Moscow Timoshenko Military Academy for Chemical Defense informed on faculty organization and subjects. These sources had at best only limited hearsay knowledge of Soviet offensive chemical weapons. A gaping divide existed between the intelligence perceptual depiction of the Chemical Troops ubiquitous role in offensive chemical warfare and the reality of so many unacquainted serving personnel.

SIGINT information on the Chemical Troops revealed only protective functions and exercising, these consistently weighted toward the radiological aspect. Occasionally detected agent use related to small quantities of actual toxic formulas or simulants in the context of defensive training. Some early classified documents had attributed chemical service officers an advisory role to nuclear-chemical strike planning staffs but their dual-faceted work did not involve munitions supply. Specified makeup of the Nuclear Planning Group in the 1977 General Staff Academy front offensive presentation did not include any Chemical Troops officers.[1083] The key 1984 CIA chemical warfare study concluded that front and army Nuclear and Fire Planning Groups (which had undergone a long organizational evolution) had not included respective chemical service chiefs since the mid 1970s.[1084]

Proponents of the official chemical model stressed extensive, and expanding, capabilities of the Chemical Troops organization as definitive evidence of chemical offensive intent. This strident insistence ignored the massive scale of Warsaw Pact nuclear plans and their projections of enemy nuclear-chemical-biological offensive preparations. Chemical connoisseurs persisted blissfully unaware that their governing argument could be flipped; that the defensive tasks of the chemical service, as well as continuous improvements, represented not an offensive accompaniment but directly responded to their perceived existence of a US offensive threat; poised at the end of the 1970s to add a new dimension in the form of the binary weapons program. Soviet and Warsaw Pact military writings, both public and classified, did not cease stressing a US-NATO chemical intent even after the disappearance of their offensive variant. Whichever the direction of argument the actual role of the Chemical Troops in the potentially large-scale nuclear warfare envisioned by the opposing sides rendered the chemical variant mostly a sideshow.

The 1985 DIA publication itemized Chemical Troops missions but somehow overlooked the nuclear warfare role as well as other non-chemical tasking; only chemical offensive responsibilities made the list. The publication had updated a 1983 edition which had an identical set of chemical-only tasks.[1085] The purpose of these unclassified Soviet chemical threat expositions can be judged by a declassified memo from the National Intelligence Officer for General Purpose Forces regarding the convening of a 29 August 1983 meeting to review the DIA workup that preceded the first edition. "This package will be used by the White House in conjunction with Congressional presentations regarding the US chemical weapons modernization program."[1086] This connivance typified a blatant example of an administration ordination, resumption of chemical production in the form of binary munitions, driving intelligence conclusions—and a prostitution of analytic integrity.

Such a politically slanted definition also relied heavily on the mirror-imaging method. The US Chemical Corps participated in chemical agent research, production, and some aspects of logistics. But the balance of the image had been ignored, the transfer of in-theater chemical munitions responsibility to the Ordnance supply channel—the same as that used for nuclear weapons.

The Chemical Troops misappraisal in turn served to undermine estimates of the Soviet chemical agent and filled munitions stockpile. The absolute failure of SIGINT to obtain quantifiable information, and a lack of clandestine sources, regarding dimensions and localization, led to heavy dependence on satellite imagery. Intelligence interest early in the Cold War had been focused on a group of "chemical depots" picked out mainly using overhead coverage within the USSR. The official chemical model promoted these installations as the defining elements of the chemical stockpile, the fount of US, and allied, CW estimates until the receipt of Russian data transmitted under the terms of eventual chemical arms control agreements. These places became the marooned focal points of the official chemical model. The restrictive logic of the determinative association of the Soviet Chemical Troops with offensive CW provided the sole basis for their supposed weapons stockpile. Strangely the much greater body of evidence pointing to the nuclear warfare missions of the Chemical Troops never elicited proposals that components of nuclear weapons might also be stored in the "chemical depots" identified.

But the blessed locations imparted a murky quantification which underwent sharp fluctuations during three decades. US intelligence attempts to size the Soviet chemical stockpile grew increasingly confident during the 1960s, as numerations in NIEs issued in 1963[1087] and 1965[1088] reached apocalyptic levels. By 1968 a NIE on theater forces would state "...the Soviet agent stockpile, which continues to increase, is on the order of

275,000 tons, and production capacity is increasing." The authors supposed that more than half of this amount comprised the latest nerve agents.[1089] However certitude regarding the soundness of the evidence behind such assessments dissipated in the following decade. An early 1969 NIE on chemical weapons repeated the quantum but suggested that the figure "may be high" based on "some recent evidence" while basically adhering to the preceding views.[1090]

Billed as a thorough reassessment of all the evidence available to intelligence, a 1970 CIA Working Paper[1091] (comparable to another, 1984, CIA rethink) reached a divergent conclusion.
> There is little direct evidence bearing on Soviet chemical warfare technology since World War II and no evidence which will permit a confident assessment of CW production, stocks, or military availability.

Nevertheless the author(s) valiantly advanced a detailed methodology for establishing the bounds of the Soviet stockpile of toxic agents and filled munitions (to be examined). Unfortunately the flood of Warsaw Pact classified documents had not yet arrived to more fully inform the perspective. But the meager sources on hand regarding chemical weapons "almost invariably speak of them as being used in conjunction with nuclear" and that toxic chemicals remained "subject to the same restrictions and controls" as that other WMD.

A British delegation that visited Washington in late July 1972 expressed shock at learning that the US State Department INR (Bureau of Intelligence and Research) had concluded that the Soviet chemical agent stockpile amounted to about 25000 tons.[1092] British practice of allied relations during the Cold War regularly conducted such fishing trips, making the rounds of Washington agencies, to catch otherwise unavailable information and glean attitudes not conveyed through official channels. I also hosted such visits, fully aware of their intent, after all we were on the same side. But the British dismissed the INR estimate since quantification derived entirely from war-gaming of the supposed Soviet requirement for thirty days of operations "in our opinion irrelevant" and found disagreement in their meetings at DIA offices.[1093]

The British did note a US general reassessment under way since "Previous estimates, which were substantially higher, had been based on old data from World War II which had been found not to justify the conclusion drawn." No one had any hard evidence, the US had identified "less than 12 installations" that might store filled munitions and bulk agents and had "no information" on the proportions. Regardless the British insisted on upholding recent assessments that the CW stockpile exceeded 200000 tons. Their number had not been established during any independent research but by arbitrarily picking the lowest of US estimates which ranged up to 300000 tons; backed by general considerations that included Soviet industrial capabilities and the size of "CW forces"—they noted that the Germans and other NATO allies subscribed to much higher numbers. The British did state that "We have no evidence that the Soviets hold CW stocks in the forward area" (Central Europe).[1094]

A US coordinated intelligence-defense study dated 11 August 1972 (classified secret) announced "we know that the USSR has chemical weapons stockpiles, but we do not know their size or composition even within very broad limits."[1095] This assessment had been issued in response to a requirement to develop a US position for prospective chemical arms limitation negotiations. By at least 1975, in a NIE on Warsaw Pact forces, no one would even venture an amount in estimate publications.[1096] An early 1979 theater forces NIE concluded "...we do not know the size or the composition of the Soviet stockpile of chemical agents and filled munitions" which in a later paragraph is attributed to "a lack of evidence."[1097] As late as April 1981 a wide ranging survey of Soviet military power prepared by the CIA Office of Strategic Research concluded "we cannot estimate the size of possible stockpiles" of chemical agents (as well as a less than impressive statement regarding BW—"no evidence of a weapon program").[1098]

But the pendulum of this numbers game abruptly swung wide in the opposite direction. US intelligence agencies confidence had so revived that 1984[1099] and 1985[1100] estimates of the chemical stockpile ranged from the CIA nearly 70000 tonnes to at least 300000 tonnes per DIA and the US Army. This new quantification had not been derived from any surge in the evidence—intelligence did not possess hard data in the 1980s any more reliable than the preceding three decades—but impelled by the Reagan Revolution more aggressive Soviet policy. British chemical enthusiasts apparently even considered the DIA figure to be a conservative accounting. *The Times* quoted a numeration surpassing that of the DIA-Army by the UK secretary of state for defence to the House of Commons in February 1982;[1101] an attribution reiterated in a classified memo more than a year later that "The Soviet Union is assessed to have over 300,000 tons of nerve agent, much of this based forward in Eastern Europe, together with the weapons necessary for its delivery."[1102] A 1987 book by British author John Hemsley, *The Soviet Biochemical Threat To NATO*,[1103] closely followed one prevailing line—in the acknowledgements there is a selected roster of the American and British intelligence purveyors of the official chemical model—in stating "large stockpiles of these agents exist and the figure has been calculated well in excess of 300000 tons."

A pivotal analytic distortion underlaying all these guesstimates resided in the positioning within the Soviet military structure of the "chemical depots" anointed by intelligence chemical connoisseurs. Identification depended on markers observed on overhead imagery that in some cases dated back to German World War II cover. These markers included decontamination vehicle collections, supposedly unique railcars, plus an assortment of containers and large tanks in open storage. A

1970 imagery study[1104] had examined 38 storage facilities with favored indicators but noted that one of these, "a "special munitions rail car"...has been identified at several places not related to CW activity." NIEs in 1963[1105] and sixteen years later[1106] still reckoned with "10 major depots" or installations comprising the official group. But only a few of those places pinpointed in the earlier edition endured to the later accounting. At least ten shared all the favored characteristics but the number could be more than doubled if considering SIGINT and HUMINT reporting of other chemical service-affiliated logistics facilities. Selection of the favorites had been an extended, whopping malapropism, a classic exemplar of misapplied image clusivity analysis—magnified in the intelligence perceptual pinhole. Fluctuations in qualified listings over time and by different agency cubicles directly reflected both the paucity of evidence and the poor intelligence comprehension of the Soviet military hierarchy.

The Soviets assigned significant responsibilities for command, training, operational development, arming, and logistics to the several troops—*voyska*—of the armed forces. A widespread network of specialized, troop-dedicated, armaments installations performed support functions. Not exceptionally difficult for US intelligence to identify using satellite imagery, the particular types of equipment at installations spread across the USSR and Central Europe enabled categorization by *voyska*. A hierarchy of central- and military district-subordinate arsenals, bases, and depots constituted a material-technical support organization columnated by *voysk*. This structure included those with combat tasks (such as the Ground Troops rocket-artillery and tank arms) and special troops: communications, engineer—and chemical. These installations performed comparable functions in equipment assembly (at selected central arsenals), repair at bases, and depot storage at all levels, for their respective *voysk*. The arrangement had been implemented just prior to the GPW.[1107]

> The chief of a directorate was made responsible for the training of a certain branch, for its timely supply with materiel, for improvement of its weapons and combat equipment, and for the employment of its cadres.

The "chemical depots" of the official model functioned as chemical service arsenals and bases supporting the Chemical Troops in the same modalities as any other *voysk*. Their branch-customized functions included storage of decontamination vehicles and substances as well as individual protective gear essential for operations in a WMD environment. The mass of equipment stored formed not only a spares pool but also reserves predestined to at least partly outfit the mobilization of the two strategic echelons. But the dissociated reasoning of the tunnel visioneers of intelligence promoted these places into the magazines of the Soviet offensive chemical stockpile. These connoisseurs, ignorantly or willfully, disregarded the position of their "chemical depots" within the logistics system of the Soviet Army. They displayed an appallingly shallow level of knowledge concerning even the most basic aspects of the purposed organization of the USSR armed forces.

Some historical human, and photographic, evidence could reasonably be interpreted to indicate selected installations had been used for bulk storage of captured German chemical agents, as well as GPW-era agents in the Soviet inventory, in cisterns and large tanks. Evidence also indicated that co-located design bureaus worked on new protective equipment, which would involve testing with small amounts of standard agents. Entirely lacking in the take had been evidence for the stockpiling of modern toxic armament, in particular, the nerve agents in production since 1959 along with filled munitions—even if "secret samples" might be present. There had never been a Grossenhain moment involving chemical service installations. Episodic signals intelligence penetration into individual sites organization, operations, and stored items revealed only defensive functions and material—and SIGINT had attained a modicum of success against one arsenal that would be declared as a stockpile location under the 1997 Chemical Weapons Convention.

There had been no effective intelligence attempt to differentiate between levels of "chemical depots" in terms of subordination and function. All got lumped together in one analytic stew. If the connoisseurs had made any effort to widen their field of view, they might have noticed that these facilities had functions in common with the bases of other *voyska*. That these installations came in central and military district varieties and had assembly and maintenance as well as storage responsibilities. Some might have a designated role in the formation of wartime fronts, mobilizing the variety of chemical units and stocking the field bases, while others contributed to those established by the Center. This might have led to better discrimination in their assessments of the purpose of individual installations. But a more fundamental defect inhered within the official chemical model. Intelligence extended historical, probably valid, indications of the connection of "chemical depots" to offensive chemical warfare regardless of a complete lack of evidence for stasis. In particular the official model ignored the alterations implemented after 1959 in Soviet military strategy that conjoined nuclear and chemical warfare–temporally paralleled by a fundamental reshaping of WMD infrastructure.

The exemplar of misbegotten notions underlying agent stock identification and quantification, illustrative of the perennial intelligence problem of truth-in-labeling, lay with the barrel fetish. One of the presumptive indicators used by connoisseurs to pinpoint "chemical depots" had been conferred upon the large quantities of metal containers visible in open storage; equation made to the ton containers used by the US to store toxic agents in liquid form. A core assertion, as stated in the 1985 DIA tome, attributed the nine mapped "... depots contain agents in bulk containers and agent-filled munitions...."[1108] But there had been no basis from information acquired during the Cold War for determining which, if any, storage containers might actually be in use by the Soviets for the official purpose. US intelligence had never obtained any direct evidence from any source since Hirsch days that these blessed drums represented the contemporary Soviet media for bulk chemical agent storage. Yet this very supposition bolstered the graphically depicted sharply rising curve of Soviet offensive chemical capability during the Cold War.

Dissociated thinking on WMD objects had not been limited to our side. Ken Alibek has told of a similar attention to detail by KGB and GRU connoisseurs during a 1991 series of reciprocal visits to former US BW installations. An intelligence briefing held prior to leaving the USSR that included indications evident on satellite imagery highlighted the Pine Bluff, Arkansas facility. The Soviet services assessed this place as a still active component of an aggressive US biological weapons program. A certain spot at this former production plant supposedly had large containers repeatedly exchanged as indicated by color changes. Their fetishists insisted that this phenomenon constituted solid evidence of a high level of biological agent production activity. When a Soviet inspector checked this area, he found...solar panels which when turned to track the sun gave off different coloration.[1109]

Numerology is held in high esteem by intelligence connoisseurs and provided the foundation of many capability estimates. Large quantities, of something, always tend to impress those unaware of the minutiae of a particular issue. An asserted quantity or numeric range often conveniently obscures the inadequacy of the supporting evidence. Thus estimates during the Cold War of the Soviet chemical stockpile had been presented at different times by several actors. One calculation that made a passage through the declassification blockade is the aforementioned 1970 CIA report.[1110] This study reappraised 17 storage sites within the USSR "probable" (two), "possible" (six), and "suspect" (nine); regretfully stating that insufficient evidence precluded rating any site as confirmed. A conscientious CIA declassification team, pursuing the high-minded objective of protecting national security and the American people, redacted all references to study locations—coincidently avoiding embarrassing questions for both US intelligence credibility and Russian treaty declarations. Lacking any evidence of Soviet practice this estimate resorted to the common intelligence blunderbuss method of measuring the floorspace of every structure that might possibly contain bulk agents or filled munitions. The study then developed a blended density formula using, mainly, the differing US Army norms for agent and munitions storage, modified with minimal available Soviet information. Applied to the eight "probable" and "possible" sites the ranged high finding attained 21900 agent tons (19867 tonnes); including all 17 sites the maximum possible storage capacity amounted to 41600 tons (37739 tonnes). Several types of storage tanks observed at one chemical service base (redacted) could hold an estimated additional 6600 tons.

This study had pointed out the crucial flaws in all such quantifications. "A major weakness inherent in any attempt to determine the size of the Soviet chemical stockpile is that the ratio of bulk agent to filled munitions is not known." Another critical unknown reposed with the proportion of the stockpile made up of modern nerve agents rather than obsolete first generation toxic agents. As stated in the study, the total lack of such compositional evidence made for "relatively meaningless" estimates. Some proponents of the official chemical model had asserted that the anointed depots stored modern chemical munitions in massive fill and submunition form along with agents in bulk form. This had actually been the governing intelligence presumption through most of the Cold War. In reality no evidence or imagery indications confirmed the presence of chemical warheads, rockets, shells, or bombs in any of the constituent covered shelters or in open storage. Some solid evidence pointed to installation storage and handling of toxic training grenades and smoke dispensers. But there never had been any plausible information identifying the "chemical depots" as the source of CW delivery munitions. The official chemical model conflated the tasks of Soviet Chemical Troops with those of separate munitions channels. No useful intelligence information had been acquired that pinpointed the Chemical Troops as the supply organ for firing units.

Until about the mid 1980s all numerological endeavors presumed that "chemical depots" stored both bulk agent and filled munitions. Revisionist connoisseurs subsequently modified the schematic on becoming increasingly obvious that no munitions could be stored at these places. The amended official model portrayed stockpiled bulk agent at "chemical depots" transported by fleets of tank railcars and trucks, to somewhere, rendezvousing with munitions from conventional ammunition storage locations. At these unknown locations filling would be accomplished. Despite the DIA 1985 pamphlet assertion of collocated agents and munitions the September 1985 NIE on Warsaw Pact *Trends* opted for the new version. "Sufficient toxic chemical railcars and trucks are held in reserve in and around these depots to permit the rapid transfer of bulk agent to forward locations."[1111] There had been no credible evidence, new or old, attesting to any such Soviet remote filling arrangement. No attempt transpired to reconcile the glaring contradiction between the supposed Soviet capability to immediately massively employ chemical weapons with the expenditure of time and resources—as well as the warning potential for adversaries—necessary to conduct large-scale munitions filling. The 1986 NIE devoted to CW-BW assessment also pushed the new bifurcated model of bulk agent at "chemical depots"—even while admitting "Chemical Troops are protective in nature and are not involved in the technical aspects of the offensive delivery of nuclear or chemical weapons."—and a separate chemical munitions stockpile at conventional ammunition stores.[1112]

The 1970 CIA study had highlighted the preparedness contradiction. If the largest proportion of Soviet toxic agents existed in bulk form, a massive logistics burden would prolong the generation of fireable munitions "a time-consuming process requiring special facilities" that would markedly delay chemical preparations. Based on the US analog some 12000 tons of agent could fill 2.5 million artillery shells; "Using the most efficient CW munitions filling plant in existence in the US, the process would take 13 months." A comparable finding appeared in a detailed 1984 US Air Force study of the US chemical stockpile.[1113] In mid 1983 this amounted to 28581 tons of toxic agents (a five-year reduction from 30500 of which 7200 usable);[1114] 66 percent kept in one-ton bulk containers. Part of the filled munitions stockpile had been for weapons no longer deployed. Of the 6184 agent tons in munitions for active weapons 60 percent received the classification unserviceable. According to the study "most of the unserviceable munitions could be made usable more rapidly than the bulk agents." No Soviet "chemical depots" filling capability had been imagined; no evidence for other planned remote facilities existed; and the field filling stations postulated by some could not possibly operate at a rate approaching that of a dedicated, specialized chemical plant.

Cubicles at intelligence shops that adhered to the same storyline had even worked up incompatible calculations. A 1987 study (information cutoff October 1986) by the Foreign Science and Technology Center *Chemical Warfare Developments—USSR: Soviet Chemical Logistics*[1115] attempted a novel approach determining residual bulk agent capacity; derived from measuring the chemical materiel requirements of the Soviet Ground Troops. The research component for US Army intelligence—the most insistent proponent of a formidable Soviet threat in 'conventional chemical' form—FSTC later disappeared in one of those org chart re-shuffles so beloved of bureaucracies; implemented in the undying hope that conclusions might thereby be made more reliable. The study developed a model for the volume of defined materiel including decontaminants, protective equipment, smoke and flame dispensers. With the stated objective of calculating the remaining storage capacity at official "chemical depots" available for offensive toxic agents, the essence of their finding, substantially (probably deliberately) obscured by complex number crunching...like where? Accentuating the paucity of residual capacities the study had a humongous omission. The FSTC model not only disregarded the aviation component of fronts but also did not venture any estimates of the requirements of the other services—naval, air defense, strategic missile, as well as strategic air forces—while also excluding what some in the West considered to be a massive civil defense program.

This study, unlike the public expositions, acknowledged the full range of tasks assigned to the Chemical Troops; yet faithful to the revised official chemical model that presumed "chemical depots" stored only bulk toxic agents to be poured elsewhere; and filled munitions in conventional ammunition stores. Confessing that "confidence" regarding these and all other underlying assumptions "ranges from moderate to low" the FSTC model developed two separate stockage projections. Requirements for 20 fronts but limited to first echelon armies; and alternatively for 199 divisions at "full readiness" (not defined). The front method consistently derived a lower quantity. Arbitrary presets included elements with dubious validity. The front method prescribed a uniform complement of 2.5 armies (each three divisions) that disregarded the Western TVD-specified three to five armies (up to five divisions apiece); while the division approach entirely ignored the scads created during mobilization of the second strategic echelon—full scaling unmeasurable. Applying the Soviet norm requiring 90 days of wartime operations stocks to be accumulated in peacetime (thus encompassing both strategic echelons) materiel allocation among division, army, front, and "national" (central) echelons accorded with the supply days specified in classified documentation.

Another critical flaw in the model lay with the inability to discriminate which official depots held central reserves versus the substantial materiel flowing to front field bases for initial operations. The study identified 27 chemical-related installations. Requiring a relatively quick two years for my request to declassify this study to be granted by the ISCAP, their adjudication applied whiteout to both the list and map of the accountable "chemical depots" in the report. A measure of the vacuousness of US official declassification is that the DIA Freedom of Information web site posting...disclosed the installation list. Evidently, since the map remained hidden, the DIA considers outsiders incapable of pinpointing these places in the age of commercial satellite imagery. Eleven facilities achieved primary importance definition but "categorizing these depots as national-level, as has previously been done, is difficult because we have little definitive information on the true subordination of these depots." Thus more locations had been added to, or replaced, the nine or ten identified in the studies of the prior decade and a half.

Two "Category A" installations, Kambarka and Gorny (Korneyevka to intelligence), subsequently would be declared storages under the Chemical Weapons Convention. More than two decades of imagery clusivity work had been conducted in such a crude fashion, with poor integration of information from other sources, that intelligence had virtually no inkling of the actual Soviet hierarchy. Chemical connoisseurs persisted unable to assign central, military district, or any other organizational affiliation to the 27 sites. The 1985 DIA booklet had mapped nine primary "chemical depots" (marked by rail tank cars thus among the FSTC A Category) and other groups came up with somewhat different sets. The variations reflected the complete lack of direct evidence for toxic chemical stocks in any form at respectively anointed storage places. The FSTC model allocated 68 averaged supply days of the 90 days total stockpile to eleven "national-level" official depots for replenishing stocks at and below the front level. Sixteen averaged days assumed for front level (plus six days allocated to army bases and divisions) rear and forward bases—by far the largest proportion—actually set up only during the course of a front mobilization-deployment; FSTC made no attempt to discriminate which of the identified peacetime chemical installations might source these bases.

The calculated "national-level" materiel stocks amounted to 499147 tonnes using the front method and 655978 by the division method—plus stocks at front-army-division levels. Even assuming that all of the front portion might be already on hand at respective stores, piles remained that would foster bulging warehouses at identified chemical service facilities. Based on the calculations of this limited scope study, there could hardly be room at the chemical inn for any consequential part of the 300000 tonnes of toxic agent estimated by other Army and DIA chemical experts or even the CIA 70000—and those numerations predated the bulk agent/munitions divorce. These "chemical depots" supposedly held the bulk fill echelon, by far the greatest portion of the chemical stockpile.

A principal task of the Chemical Troops, the reason for all the signature vehicles in storage at official depots and other locations, entailed the outfitting of newly mobilized specialized and combat units—both first and second strategic echelon—that would perform the complex, massive task of battlefield nuclear, chemical, and Soviet-presumed biological, decontamination of personnel, equipment, and terrain. Those vehicles would be charged with a variety of substances such as ammonium bicarbonate, chloramide wash, dichloroethane, carbon tetrachloride, and special foams. Soviet writings on WMD defense indicated that some of these materials required sensitive, and centralized, handling. The FSTC study calculated a most representative requirement (assuming a 50/50 ratio toxic/radiation contamination) for 235416 or 309658 tonnes of decontaminants at "national-level" official depots using the two different methods. Their numeration even provided for 436016 drum equivalents of 250, and 89760 of 100, liter size to hold the lower front model estimate of a selection of liquid decontaminants; exclusive of the quantity held at, wherever these might be, bases and depots generating intra-front stocks.

The FSTC study represented a neat example of the self-entrapment effect of ideological argumentation. One assumption applied considered that the most realistic calculation of the amount of decontaminants stockpiled should be based on a 50/50 chemical/radiological purposing. As explained in the discussion, chemical decontamination required a larger amount of substances then did radiological. Chemical decon agents could, in a pinch, be used as a nuclear remedy but a reverse usage of rad agents would not be feasible. The insistence of the parent US Army intelligence on 'conventional chemical'—an inevitable, selective or massive, chemical attack accompanying conventional operations prior to nuclear introduction—would logically have impelled a higher assumed ratio of chemical decontaminants use, to 75/25. But that presumption would, according to the FSTC calculations, require an additional 106284 or 139985 tonnes of decontaminants at "national-level" depots according to the two force methods—a much greater stockage likely regrading from possibly possible to impossibly possible the likelihood of any space remaining for bulk toxic agents. Accepting the opposing view of no CW use prior to nuclear, updated with the mid 1970s disappearance of the chemical variant in classified documents, the ratio might legitimately have been lowered from 75/25 to 25/75. This would have eliminated 213180 or 280928 decontaminants tonnes and, perhaps, upgraded the argument that toxic agents could be accommodated to probably possible—but back-adding the requirements of the disregarded remainder of the Soviet armed forces would bequeath a residual arid offensive keg-dom.

Where and how did the connoisseurs suppose that the Soviets stored this enormous stock of decon agents? Some of the barrels at the "chemical depots" may well have held toxic agents in particular since Soviet defense training frequently incorporated toxic simulants, insecticides, and even weakened combat agents—a 1975 Warsaw Pact guide to the conduct of exercises stressed the creation of complex WMD conditions including use of toxic agent simulation compounds for terrain contamination training.[1116] Large quantities of smoke agents would also be required according to Soviet practice, widely used during the GPW. An unembellished, Occam's razor-applied, 'solution' prioritizes these other substances. No persuasive evidence had surfaced for an offensive agents alternative. Large tanks had also been identified, based on information not updated since the 1940s-1950s, all parties assigning at least a portion of contents to toxic agents in a liquid state—despite the complete lack of specific corroborating evidence. This intell conclusion turned out to be partly correct, but at only two of the many official depots, in significantly less quantity then presumed, and involving no modern agent types. The unsupported assertion that most drums brimmed with liquefied toxic chemicals rather than decontaminants or other substances constituted the principle factor driving the more stratospheric stockpile estimates.

The eventual Russian declaration under the Chemical Weapons Convention, commencing into force 1997, mortally dented the validity of the barrel fetish. All of the stockpiled nerve agents had been weaponized in aviation, rocket, and artillery munitions, amounting to 81 percent of the announced agent total weight.[1117] The declared bulk nerve agent stocks amounted to zero. The bulk agent stockpile—and no filled munitions—remained confined to only two of the official "chemical depots" and comprised batches that, according to Russian statements, had been last produced in 1946 (lewisite) or 1957 in the case of mustard.[1118] And, this segment resided mainly in steel tanks that had substantially larger capacity then the US standard container. Less than a fifth of the total declared agent weight existed in liquid form, amounting to about 7500 tonnes. The declared stock of almost 6400 tonnes of lewisite at Kambarka had been stored in five buildings, each housing sixteen steel tanks of 80 tonnes capacity—contents present since at least the GPW[1119]—so decrepit that Russians expressed alarm regarding ongoing progressive metallic thinning through corrosion.[1120] The Gorny bulk agent may also have been present since the GPW.[1121] In 1990 General-Colonel S. Petrov claimed that the 10000 agent tonnes advantage over the US held by the Soviets represented stocks "accumulated in the prewar years and during the war. They are obsolete and outdated and are of no value as weapons in the light of current requirements."[1122] The tanks and buildings had been identified by intelligence, incorporated into the quantification, but the DIA and others then went off the charts with their barrels.

The high proportion of toxic agents, and all nerve agents, in filled munitions according to the Russian declaration undermined the atrociously substantiated official chemical model. But this circumstance also signified a colossal intelligence failure regarding Soviet preparedness to wage chemical war. While the US bulk storage of 66 percent of total agent stockpile (prior to the startup of binary munitions production) could not easily or quickly be converted to combat munitions, the Soviet unabridged proportion of filled nerve weapons demonstrably reflected a far more advanced chemical stance. The bombastic proclamations by Western advocates regarding Soviet chemical intentions had actually crucially misapprehended the very real capability of the USSR to quickly inject these weapons into a European war. The Russian declaration also riddled the revised intell model of bulk agent transport from "chemical depots" since all the modern agents in filled munitions must have been stored elsewhere.

The declared bulk agent at two locations reflected a survival of the legacy toxic chemical support system. Residues of bulk lewisite, and munitions mixtures with mustard (long considered obsolete by the US), apparently remained in the Soviet stockpile due to the enhanced agent viscosity at the very low temperatures encountered in much of the USSR landmass. But Russian investigators in the 1990s found that an even larger amount of bulk agent had been transported to Kambarka in the 1940s. During the 1950s and early 1960s an unknown portion of the original stock at several chemical service bases had been systematically eliminated by incineration and burial or dumping at sea; 1200 tonnes of mustard had been destroyed in the early 1960s at the Pokrovka (Chapayevsk) official "chemical depot"—not declared under the 1997 CWC.[1123] The environmental consequences of this haphazard disposal plagues Russia to this day. Intelligence services of several Western countries had described a supposed massive expansion of chemical capability based, first of all, on Kambarka and similar signature places when the Soviets had actually been eliminating much of the existent stockpile of older generation agents.

If the FSTC study findings had been acknowledged, there could hardly be any bulk agent available in the ordained reservoirs to tank-up the official chemical model. The retrospective flaw in the schematic centered on the 81 percent of the CWC-declared agent stockpile already filled in munitions. Skepticism arises that an unknown quantity of liquid agents as well as filled munitions had been made to disappear, as reported by Russian investigators, in a frantic Soviet mass disposal from the late 1980s to early 1990s.[1124] But if there had been a trifling amount of, just first generation, toxic agents in bulk storage at only two "chemical depots" the remote fill model became untenable. The largest proportion of even, at whatever level, the actual Soviet chemical munitions stockpile must have existed in a filled state. And where might the inventory have been held if not at the repositories designated by intelligence?

Conventional ammunition facilities had been the only alternative candidates envisioned by intelligence for prospective storage of chemical weapons. But there had been a comparable scarcity of evidence concerning any presence of such munitions at the hundreds of ammunition stores in the USSR and allied countries. As put by the 1985 *Trends* NIE "little intelligence on the storage of chemical munitions is available" although this did not inhibit the authors from supposing that filled munitions occupied "some depots" within the USSR and "possibly at some" in Central Europe[1125]—a co-storage arrangement reiterated by the more comprehensive 1986 NIE on Soviet CW-BW.[1126] Conventional ammunition storage facilities affiliated with the several armed services at various organizational levels. A multi-decade accumulation of signals and human intelligence evidence on Soviet and Warsaw Pact armament rarely included chemical ammunition references and these, at best, rated as inconclusive. Information provided by these tools on the munitions organizations of several armed services, and occasionally indeterminate references to particular ammunition installations, had been notably lacking in toxic chemicals identification.

Throughout the decades of the Cold War, not so much as a single unambiguous pinpoint of offensive chemical weapons had ever been acquired at an individual ammunition storage facility. There had never been a Grossenhain moment sourced from any intelligence tool. Human intelligence—the multitude of Soviet and Warsaw Pact servicemen emigres and defectors—had produced an abundance of sources familiar with conventional ammunition storage, handling practice, and some

**DIA 1985 REPORT**
DRUM IDENTIFICATION HAD NO BASIS IN EVIDENCE AND ALL OF THE VEHICLE TYPES HAD NON-CHEMICAL ROLES
(OPPOSITE)
SUGGESTED EDITS TO ACCORD WITH REALITY

*Representative of Soviet chemical depots.*

# THE SOVIET CHEMICAL WARFARE ORGANIZATION

The continuing chemical weapons activities include a large well-trained chemical warfare organization directed by the Headquarters Chemical Troops in the Ministry of Defense. This chemical warfare organization is headed by a three-star General and numbers more than 45,000 officers and enlisted men in the ground forces alone. When staffed during a war, the size will double. Their primary responsibilities include the following:

- Technical advisors to the front commanders for chemical weapons and results of their use
- Research and development programs for weapons and protection
- Production and storage of chemical weapons and protective materiel testing and evaluation
- Training of all forces for chemical employment and survival on a contaminated battlefield
- Decontamination and reconnaissance
- Operating the chemical academies (college equivalent)

This corps of specialists also has about 30,000 special vehicles for decontamination and reconnaissance and has developed more than 200 areas for teaching and training all forces on how to protect themselves and clean up following combat where chemical weapons have been used. This training includes the use of actual chemical agents. Also, the

- Nuclear burst geo-location
- Flame weapons employment
- Smokes, obscurants, and incendiaries employment

equipment is bulky and uncomfortable. When worn for an extended period of time in hot weather soldiers become fatigued rather quickly and combat efficiency is lowered. In some cases heat prostration may result. Accordingly, the Soviets have devised norms stipulating desired maximum lengths of time for various temperature ranges for wearing protective suits.

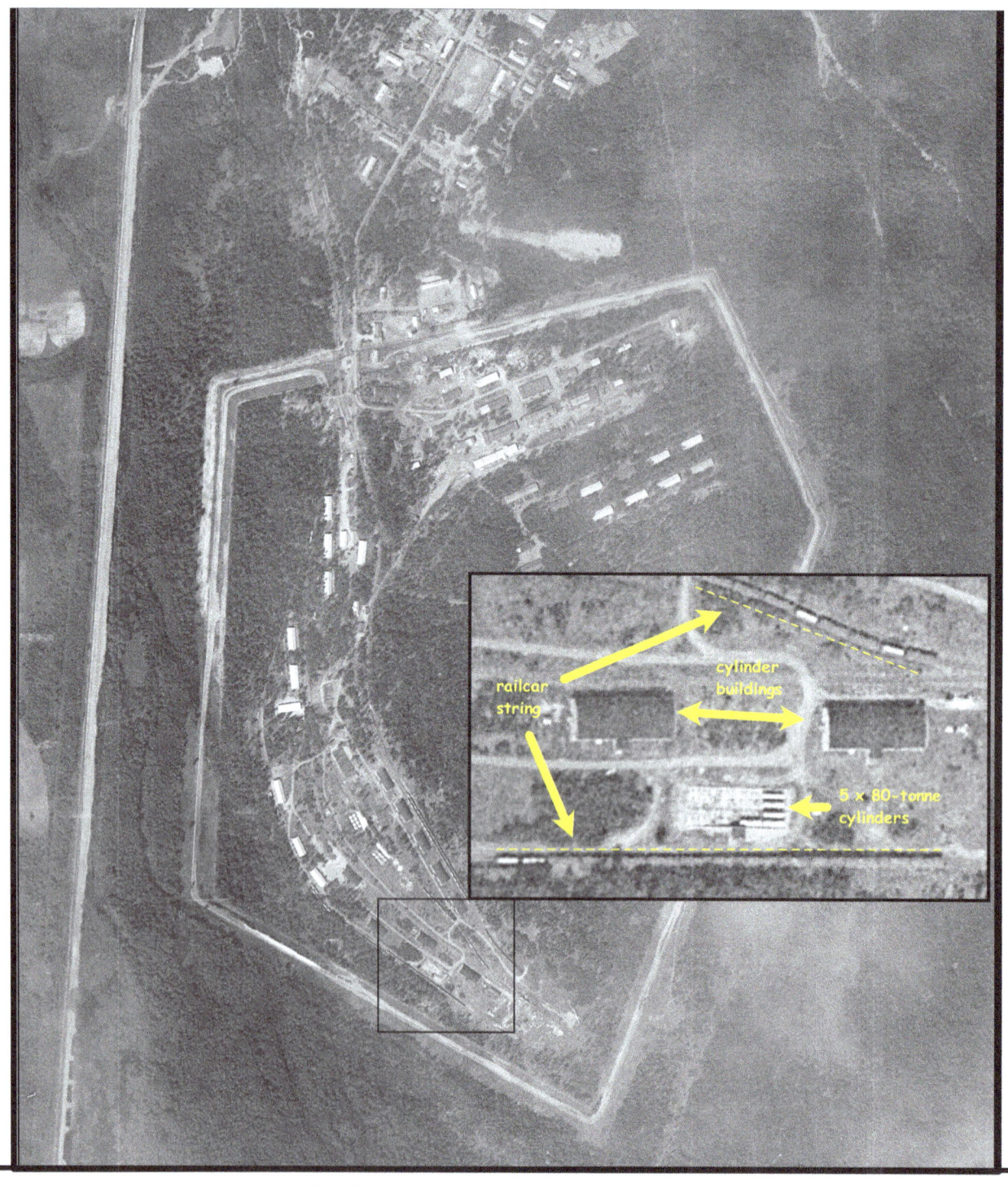

CWC 'CHEMICAL DEPOT' KAMBARKA 1967
FIVE BUILDINGS EACH WITH 16 CYLINDERS HELD DECLARED LEWISITE STOCK—SINCE AT LEAST THE EARLY YEARS OF THE COLD WAR

had higher-level organization experience. An even larger number had served in missile, artillery, and aviation delivery units. But a strikingly small proportion of these sources had professed contact with, or knowledge of, chemical munitions, and the validity of their reporting persisted uniformly suspect.

This lack of SIGINT and HUMINT reporting glaringly challenged the ubiquity of chemical ammunition asserted by some intelligence components. The 'conventional chemical' model did not receive any substantiation from these sources. Reports of the presence of 'chemical' weapons continued always muddied by a divergent Soviet definition of this category. The US armed forces considered munitions such as pyrotechnics and smoke (including toxic varieties) as 'conventional' but the Soviets classed these items, along with flamethrower fuel, and even certain decontaminants, as chemical weapons. German intelligence had encountered the same problem according to the Hirsch Report.[1127]

> ...the term 'Chemical Agent' signifies quite often not only the chemical agents proper, but also all other chemical compounds which find a use in war (e.g., Gunpowder, Explosives, Incendiaries, Decontamination Agents, etc.) even the motor fuels. This is the reason why some information given by reliable and cooperative prisoners of war were quite often erroneous.

The US also excluded 'tear gas' such as CS from the formal chemical weapons definition. This insistence highly convenient given the massive use of CS and other varieties, as well as herbicides, during the Vietnam conflict. Many other nations, not limited to the Communist bloc, considered the application of these agents in Vietnam as waging chemical warfare—an American equivalent to 'yellow rain' but with rather more solid documentation. The consequences of the Vietnamese defoliants deluge remain an environmental problem to this day. In his 1986 explication of the ongoing US binary chemical weapons deployment General-Major A. Kuntsevich linked this Vietnam precursor, with a "first in the world" ecological offensive, as an indistinguishable component of an aggressive US chemical stance.[1128] Even a source pinpointing 'chemical' weapons at a particular location did not necessarily signify the toxic offensive variety. To restate the intelligence situation, during the entire Cold War no unequivocal evidence had ever been acquired regarding the presence of toxic chemical munitions at a particular Soviet or allied conventional ammunition storage facility.

Classified Soviet documents, including those on exercises, confirmed that (at least in the Ground Troops) the rocket-artillery armament service handled chemical warheads. GRAU—Main Rocket-Artillery Directorate—of the MoD, the 800-kg gorilla of the Soviet munitions system, headed this organization. GRAU through designated subordinates also supervised nuclear-missile and conventional ammunition support to operational delivery units—and each of these categories had dedicated storage facilities. There had been no evidence of any departures from the arrangement specified by the 1929 *Field Regulations*.[1129]

> The chemical warfare equipment is supplied to the troop units by order of the chiefs of the chemical warfare service of the corresponding military formations with the exception of chemical artillery shells, chemical aerial bombs and gas hand grenades and rifle grenades, which are issued to the troops by the artillery supply organs.

This setup roughly corresponded with the US Army Ordnance theater supply of special ammunition under the 'complete round' principle. That "chemical depots" stored no filled munitions whatsoever in the Russian Chemical Weapons Convention numeration represented another blow to the credibility of the official model. And, of course, only two of the dozen or so major locations (number and identifications varied every few years and by appraiser) ultimately blessed by intelligence as chemical weapons repositories actually made the Russian declaration listing.

Perceptually confounding the supposition that filled chemical munitions might be stocked at conventional ammunition storage facilities, these places notably lacked the very markers with which the residents of the chemical cubicles had been so enamored. Ammunition stores uniformly absented the decontamination vehicles, "special munitions railcars," as well as bulk tank railcars and containers assigned paramount significance by the official chemical model. A front missile-artillery base in Central Asia presented a unique exception in the presence of a chemical defense vehicle float as well as the signature railcars—which likely represented the collocation of the district chemical service base (no other candidate evident). Even if some decon vehicles had been spotted on imagery at ammunition facilities, no plausible case could be asserted for the presence of chemical munitions since certain types could be equally used by the Soviets as fire pumpers—ditto the infamous Samarra tanker. Hardly consistent as well with the 'conventional chemical' perspective. Hindered by these official fetishisms the chemical connoisseurs ambled on trapped by their own premises.

I personally conducted a systematic investigation over several years of the munition organizations and affiliated storages—all of them—supporting the Warsaw Pact general purpose forces. This clusity analysis examined both current satellite and historical imagery in conjunction with all available classified documents, SIGINT, and HUMINT material. Among the vast array of munitions facilities supporting all the armed services emerged two study groups; within the USSR 224 central- and operational-level (intell-speak non-divisional); in Central and Eastern Europe the Soviets and their allies (excluding Romania) maintained 97 equivalents. Enhanced image clusivity enabled the creation of ammunition models for each of the Soviet armed services. Virtually all individual stores could be categorized by subordination as central, military district or fleet; ground and air army, naval base; even specialized engineer munitions and propellant-high explosive components. Some locations exhibited suspicious anomalies, even fewer serving personnel statements, but no consistent, reliable, indications nor solid non-imagery evidence. If these places had contained any appreciable amount of chemical munitions I, along with generations of intell searchers, had missed unambiguous indications. This circumstance could imply a collective intelligence failure and a Soviet successful coverup—unless the mother lode of chemical munitions actually resided elsewhere in the USSR mass destruction weapons aggregation.

Army specialists had ascribed the apparent lack of offensive chemical planning in Warsaw Pact exercises as an indication of a conventional routine, reinforced by some human sources that supposedly indicated co-storage of chemical and conventional munitions. But others ascribed the failure to distinguish chemical planning in exercises to the essentially identical target sets, procedures, and delivery systems employed in both nuclear and chemical strikes. Of course, in reality, documentary evidence during and after the Cold War confirm that both the Soviets and their allies had played extensively with chemical weapons in exercises during the 1960s into the early 1970s. The signals intelligence collectors mainly responsible for monitoring these exercises had failed to detect CW scenarios—matching their performance in regard to the Soviet munitions organization.

In the first half of the 1960s any distinction between conventional and chemical represented a moot point because nuclear weapons would be employed at the outset. From the beginning of the conventional variant to the disappearance of chemical discussion the interval before mass nuclear strikes measured a few days. Much of the intelligence disputation regarding 'conventional chemical' in the later 1970s to early 1980s had been as dissociated as many other issues because the chemical dropout would only be recognized well after the fact. No answers concerning Soviet plans to initiate chemical warfare could be found in the highly classified documents acquired; no resolution ever achieved; and there remains even today no definitive interpretation of Soviet political-military guidelines.

## chemical excision

Intelligence realization had been unaccountably delayed that the most (uniquely) important evidence regarding Soviet CW had vanished. Only in 1984 did the seemingly obvious dissipation of the Soviet chemical warfare narrative undergo a retrospective. A CIA-SOVA Intelligence Assessment[1130] substantiated the conclusion that an expansive Soviet chemical offensive had become extinct. "An exhaustive examination" of two decades worth of evidence, in particular the "classified military writings from the mid-1950s to the early 1980s" characterized "the most intensive examination of this evidence...ever conducted"—an astounding occurrence, someone had actually conducted a re-read starting from the preface. Note the source; SIGINT, IMINT, HUMINT, and derivatives did not feature among the cited evidence. While commenting that "writings from the 1960s and early-to-mid 1970s placed a much stronger, clearer emphasis on chemical warfare than is seen in subsequent writings" the motivation or factors behind the (undefined) 1960s ramp-up did not receive consideration. Much speculation, however, addressed likely reasons for the pinpointed circa 1975 disappearance of the CW 'emphasis' despite the stated lack of direct evidence regarding the nature and timing of an imputed Soviet decision. Discerning the apparent continued Soviet concern that NATO would use chemicals, the disposal of the prevailing official model regarding the Soviet 'Chemical' Troops furnished an important element of the argument. An appendix devoted to explaining to the unknowing that the multi-various missions of these special troops equated to facilitating operations in a contaminated environment—debunking the notion that they directed a chemical offensive—also noted that evidence increasingly pointed toward the primacy of nuclear reconnaissance and protection.

The CIA revisionism would be accorded a prominent role years later. At the September 1991 US Senate hearings[1131] on the nomination of Robert Gates to be director of central intelligence both he and Douglas MacEachin (yes, again) attempted to demonstrate Gates' independence from political influence. Gates had been accused, notably by his former subordinates, of 'politicizing' analytical conclusions. As exhibit one for the defense the pair cited, and quoted from the key judgments, of this particular SOVA paper that had manifestly contradicted the official chemical threat model. They claimed to have fended off the efforts of CIA higher-ups to abort publication which had occurred simultaneously with the ongoing congressional consideration of funding for US production of binary chemical munitions. Since the report would actually be declassified only in 2012, the legality of their comments in an open session might well be questionable.

The revised perspective would be surprisingly quickly accepted even though MacEachin claimed in 1991 that "every single intelligence agency in the community opposed us." Nevertheless according to the 1984 Special NIE *The Soviet Offensive Chemical Warfare Threat to NATO*[1132] (specifying a necessary revision of views expressed in a 1981 NIE)[1133] "We are...agreed..." that

> Since the mid-1970s, Warsaw Pact writings and plans concerning the use of offensive chemical weapons have decreased. In contrast to the earlier period when detailed allocations of chemical weapons to Pact combat units were featured in Pact writings, we have received very few indications of such allocations in the

past decade despite our access to the same kinds of sources…

Professional writings originating in Soviet military academies have continued to address the application of nuclear, conventional, and, increasingly, improved conventional munitions, but we have not seen references to offensive chemical munitions employment since the mid-1970s…

In sum, we find little evidence during the last decade of Soviet planning and training for the use of chemical weapons against NATO.

But the operative word altered only to "selective" in describing Soviet CW intentions rather than the "massive" (extensive employment throughout the Western TVD) supposition previously in effect. This imputed Soviet distinction would be re-emphasized in the 1986 NIE dealing with CW and BW even with the admission "we do not know how the Soviets define this in relation to CW."[1134] Nothing resembling these chemical use characterizations existed in Soviet military doctrinal or operational elaborations—how could they, since all offensive chemical discussion had ceased. Both terms represented entirely dissociated inventions, yet another intelligence secondary translation that attempted to define a dialectical imponderable. Ironically these two terms derived from that other WMD—nuclear—for which more reliable employment information existed. Yet once again the intelligence connoisseurs had failed to recognize the implication of the cross-connection they had created; while the prevailing divergence of attitudes concerning initiation scenarios persisted among the different intelligence offices.

The situation had been communicated to John Hemsley by his informants "although CBW has always been the subject of the most stringent security measures in the USSR, 1975 represents the cut-off date for any information on Soviet CBW capability, at which point a total and conscious information blackout was applied."[1135] The US and other intelligence services continued, through the remainder of the 1970s and in the 1980s, to acquire classified Soviet and Warsaw Pact documents, including the top secret level. Nuclear weapons employment featured prominently and detailed in the contemplations (as well as in exercises) but the chemical variant did not reappear. Somehow the revisionism of the 1984 NIE would not be reflected in the public representation of the Soviet posture. Not only the DIA 1985 piece but also editions of the DoD *Soviet Military Power* series subsequent to the NIE immediately ignored the CW excision; while the 1981 and 1983 editions barely noticed the chemical issue—each devoting only four paragraphs—the April 1984 edition introduced expansive treatment with sketches, and the assertion that "chemical depots" held both filled munitions and agents bulk storage—to be fair the 1985 edition substantially curtailed coverage and dropped the nifty sketches.

That there might be another explanation for the disappearance of chemical warfare in such important operational material did not occur to the connoisseurs, namely, that Soviet military strategy had been modified. Implicit to the excision, the governing instructions of the USSR political-military leadership had been revised. The chemical variant had been detached from the WMD Operation. A markedly similar disappearance had taken place thirty-one years earlier. Soviet military manuals issued prior to the GPW had treated chemical weapons as an integrated operational method. New *Regulations* issued in 1943,[1136] however, had eliminated the offensive chemical elements—thus apparently implementing a judgment of the Soviet leadership that chemical weapons would not be used during the counteroffensive in progress against Germany. Preambles in 1929 and 1936 regarding chemical initiation disappeared and all, now infrequent, chemical warfare references dealt only with enemy use—exactly as in the post-1974 Soviet classified material. The 1943 *Regulations* repeated the 1936 statement on disrupting enemy chemical attacks but only with non-chemical countermeasures.

Deletion of offensive chemical discussions in the classified literature suggests a comparable judgment regarding the likely nature of a European theater war. Absence did not signify unilateral chemical disarmament or even diminution of capabilities, rather a de-integration of chemical munitions employment from war plans—a conclusion that the chemical blade of the WMD axe had eventuated unusable, unnecessary, or undesirable. There are definite indications, acquired both during and after the Cold War, that at least chemical arms technical advancement continued to be pursued. Operations manuals and other classified materials conveyed the Soviet precepts for waging theater war—both military and ideological bases—and the mandatory instructions for officer education and command execution. If the chemical prescriptions had disappeared, absence meant that the CW variant had ceased to be an active method. In at least operational terms the chemical echelons had been retrograded. The precise point of relocation in Soviet military plans, as with a diving submarine, remains unclear but chemical weapons ceased to be an at the ready component of the WMD Operation.

We still have no inside information as to motivations and process amongst the Soviet leadership in reaching any such conclusion. A number of possibly related events can be tossed out, to fall where they might. The US restatement of a chemical retaliation-only posture by the Nixon administration in 1969[1137] may have finally been accepted as a genuine policy. There had been recent stuttering moves toward chemical arms control talks. A joint communique issued 3 July 1974 culminating the USSR Summit between Richard Nixon and Leonid Brezhnev called for an international agreement eliminating CW as well as a US-Soviet initiative at the Geneva Conference of the Committee on Disarmament to seek an international convention; the Soviets had shortly thereafter provided the US a draft treaty. US officials would later comment that the Soviets seemed "clearly impatient" and "anxious" to prepare the initiative.[1138] But subsequent tortuous negotiations would take many years to bring to fruition. Most significantly, in December of 1974, the Senate had finally ratified US accession to the 1925 Geneva Protocol, Presidentially affirmed the following month. But dropout may as well have been the endpoint of a more prolonged adjustment rather than an abrupt decision; a Soviet 1976 assessment of the US chemical stockpile had already found obsolescent munitions and projected that these weapons would be largely unfit by 1985; binary weapon introduction might change the equation but, at least then, the technology had been considered to have several deficiencies.[1139] However the concurrent masking of a large scale active biological weapons program might indicate a similar redirection for chemical work. The US State Department continues to assert regarding arms control compliance that "Russia's CWC declaration is incomplete with respect to chemical agent and weapons stockpiles" in annual reports.[1140]

Even as the USSR may have been abandoning, or at least back-pocketing, the chemical variant domestic voices sought to revive US chemical capabilities. The Soviet chemical threshold had been raised while that of their opponents would soon be lowered. In a, familiar, narrative a coterie of political, defense, and intelligence zealots rode fallacious intelligence estimates to a misapplied military response. Their persistent efforts would emerge victorious only upon the arrival of the Reagan administration; representing another potential shove to the action-reaction cycle—one that essentially replayed the WMD scenario of the late 1950s which had instigated, or at least substantially reinforced development of, the Soviet WMD Operation. Following the unilateral US abandonment of both chemical and biological weapons ordered by President Nixon the Army deliberately and neglectfully allowed both offensive and defensive chemical capabilities to deteriorate. All chemical agent and munitions production ceased. By 1973 the Army Chemical School had been shuttered. The Chemical Corps underwent a substantial reduction in personnel strength while a merger with the Ordnance Corps received consideration.[1141]

Individuals within the defense and intelligence establishments, urged on by outside specialists, expressed alarm at the downward trend in capabilities. A reversal then accelerated by a startled discovery of the integrated nuclear-chemical protective features of Soviet-supplied equipment captured by Israel during the October 1973 war with Arab states.[1142] Proponents chanted the perceptual mantra of the, disproportionately massive, Soviet Chemical Troops as proof of offensive chemical intent. During the second half of the 1970s efforts centered on funding binary chemical munitions production, which repeatedly failed in Congress,[1143] as well as restoring the Chemical Corps. The Army Chemical School reappeared in Alabama at the end of 1979. Reaganists slowly pushed the binary program against substantial political opposition. The National Security Decision Directive 18 dated 4 January 1982, signed Ronald Reagan, set out policy objectives.[1144]

> Ensure that modernization of short- and long-range chemical weapons systems proceeds so that the United States has a credible and effective deterrent retaliatory capability, and so that the United States can gain negotiating leverage in the area of chemical weapons arms control…

The push for binary weapons funding authorization succeeded in 1985 but Congressional stipulations not met until October 1987. A 1987 schedule, with agents production at Pine Bluff, encompassed the M687 artillery projectile; the XM135 warhead for a new multiple-launcher rocket system; and for VX air delivery the BLU-80B Bigeye bomb.[1145]

The multidimensional buildup of US military capabilities initiated or expedited in the Reagan era allowed the US Army free rein to develop a new Air-Land Battle concept for European theater war. A central tenet featured an integrated nuclear-conventional—and chemical—offensive. War gaming of the concept during 1980-1981 at the US Army Combined Arms Center included Chemical School participation. Doctrinal development culminated in the issuance of the 1982 edition of Field Manual 100-5 *Operations*, revised and reprinted in 1986.[1146] Abortive attempts ensued to deploy binary chemical munitions in Europe. Whatever the Soviet impression of the new Army chemical variant it certainly scared American allies. Even Bernard Rogers, Supreme Allied Commander Europe, a US Army General, hastened to distance service plans from those of NATO in a December 1984 article in which he explicitly broke the chemical connection.[1147] In a dumbfounding irony US chemical initiatives proceeded driven by a long discarded Soviet chemical preference; based on intelligence estimates that had failed to grasp the implications of the mid 1970s changes in the classified military literature; with assumed continuity of Soviet chemical offensive intent.

The 1980s intelligence born-again chemical stockpile quantification did not stem from any surge in the underlying evidence set. Nothing substantial or authoritative had, in fact, been acquired since the no-confidence votes of the previous decade—intelligence had no firmer evidential foundation than in the preceding three decades. The astronomical disparity between the DIA 300000 tonnes and CIA 70000 (less than a quarter of the top range) guesstimates hollered incompatible calculations. The widely differing figures largely came from the CIA unwillingness to fully sign on to the barrel fetish. The yawning gap proclaimed the unreliability of the supporting evidence, faulty assumptions, and the myopic vision of the official chemical model. That perennial intelligence community dissenter, the State Department intelligence office, had access to the same body of evidence as the other agencies, yet footnoted these numerations in the 1984 NIE with the comment "INR does not believe there is sufficient evidence on which to base an estimate of the Soviet bulk agent stockpile, it could be significantly higher or lower than the limits presented here."[1148] This translates to a bureaucratically polite insinuation regarding colleagues full of it. Fifteen years earlier State had a similar response to a sizing estimate.[1149]

Renewed intelligence quantification had been compelled by those seeking modernized US chemical armament. This necessitated that a reluctant Congress be confronted with a formidable, ever-expanding, Soviet capability. Development of the new Army operational concept could be made more palatable, at least in the US. This numerological projection represented classic political intelligence with conclusions driven by a desired solution rather than solid evidence. Disputed indications of Soviet chemical and toxin employment in Afghanistan and Southeast Asia continued to be cited as further proof of Soviet offensive preparations—just as commentators on the other side pointed to US application of chemicals in Vietnam in the form of herbicides and combat using CS 'tear gas' more than a decade earlier. The stockpile numbers game pendulum would swing wide again when the Soviets began to provide their own accounting. By 1994 the IC estimate had dived precipitously with "low-to-moderate confidence" to a 50000 to 70000 tonnes range.[1150] Everyone had just been shooting in the dark, facilitating such extreme adjustments over three decades.

A Soviet campaign against the prospective Reagan chemical modernization in the mid 1980s elicited an opposing numerology, at least in the public presentation. In May 1985 a TASS correspondent reported from Washington in the military *Krasnaya Zvezda* "stockpiles are calculated at 150,000 metric tons of combat toxic agents, and the quantity of munitions at 3 million units" (source not provided) in rejecting US claims of chemical weapons obsolescence. In following months these figures would be cited in other Soviet media including TASS and Moscow TV in which "the calculations of the United States press itself" are attributed (not explaining how the US had gone metric). TASS reports must not have been well coordinated since one report cited "55,000 tonnes of high toxic agents" in storage[1151] while two weeks later the stockpile had somehow grown geometrically to the higher tonnage level. The public claim multiplier of only about five the actual size of the US chemical stockpile did demonstrate somewhat more reliable evidence than did the extreme UK-US six or more times the declared Soviet accumulation.

Binary weapons production gained approval even as all US intelligence organizations "agreed" that Soviet offensive preparations had apparently been scaled down. Strangely, as promotion of the US binary program had begun in the mid 1970s, some intelligence experts 'discovered' that the Soviets had similarly recognized the advantages of the binary technology and had accelerated deployment—mirror imaging is a popular intelligence method, shared by the defense and political sectors. Sporadic evidence of their interest had been acquired but no attempt had been made to differentiate between exploration of the viability of the binary concept and full development. The 1976 Soviet binary appraisal does not appear to have been so enthusiastic; while 1987 Shikhany emphatically stated that "The Soviet Army has no binary weapons...has no binary chemical agents" at the display.[1152]

Some of the best, if conflicting, evidence for a Soviet program would be acquired only in the 1990s from disclosures by Russian scientists. One insider claimed that experimentation with binary agents had begun in 1982 at GSNIIOKhT (State Union Scientific Research Institute for Organic Chemistry and Technology) but only by 1987 did this work near completion;[1153] however another scientist in the *Foliant* program at the GSNIIOKhT Volsk branch until 1994 stated that binary versions of new agents proved not viable.[1154] Binary weapons development did feature in the 6 October 1989 Decree No. 844-186 of the CPSU Central Committee-USSR Council of Ministers; with Lenin and State Prizes awarded in 1991 to researchers.[1155] According to a detailed accounting of prospective *Novichok* series binary agents by Vil Mirzayanov these had been tested no earlier than 1988 and only "experimental quantities" actually ever produced.[1156] If correct, just as in the development of nerve agents in the late 1950s and early 1960s the Soviet program lagged that of the US by several years.

Any Soviet match to the revival of US chemical planning and preparations remained invisible in an intelligence perspective thoroughly perplexed by nearly three decades of misjudgments. The classified Soviet and Warsaw Pact documents still being acquired through the 1980s contained no indications of counteraction-in-kind or revival of the chemical variant. The nature of an, inevitable, Soviet comeback remained a dangerous unknown, replicating the situation during the late 1950s US chemical armament buildup. V. L. Israelyan, who headed the Soviet CW arms control team for nearly a decade, has stated in his memoir *On the Battlefields of the Cold War* that at working meetings with MoD experts their constant refrain had been the necessity of preventing the US binary weapons program. The Reagan administration push for binary production and, in particular, US Congress funding approval "seriously worried" both Soviet military and chemical industry officials.[1157] A General Staff officer in 1990s interviews considered one of the two key developments during the period 1980 to 1985 to be the "need to calculate the effects of chemical use" in Soviet planning.[1158]

As long as the sun continued to rise and set over Europe with equal certainty the Soviets would have reacted to any deployment of additional chemical arms to NATO with reciprocal measures. In their strategic style, demonstrated by practical implementation in several cases, this would have entailed strengthening the chemical first echelon by an order of magnitude. The Reagan administration toxic policies during the first half of the 1980s, if successful in placing binary munitions in Europe, would have inevitably led to Soviet re-positioning or augmentation (depending on the actual extent of forward chemical stocks)—an accumulation of poisons as well as nuclear arms immediately available to magnify the WMD catastrophe of a European armed conflict.

Warsaw Pact intelligence services monitored exercises as intensively as their NATO opponents and would hardly have missed prospective foes 1980s training that practiced both chemical offense and defense. The large scale command post-field exercise Able Archer held in November 1983 stressed the operational transition from conventional-only to integrated chemical-nuclear warfare.[1159] This exercise has been cited as a major source of the supposed Soviet 'war scare' during that period. Such exercise activity included the simulated movement of chemical munitions from storage depots to delivery means as in a WINTEX-CIMEX 1983 scenario briefing "movement of chemical weapons approved" item.[1160] Their intelligence should still have been aware of the official chemical retaliatory stance—reiterated in the US V Corps OPLAN 33001 of 1 January 1981 for which the East Germans had a copy with all attachments and appendices.[1161] Their projection that, in a cute twist on US intelligence debates, NATO "chemical weapons would also be used in conventional warfare for tactical and operational reasons" had been elucidated from analysis of 1988 exercises.[1162]

An uptick in the chemical defense content of Soviet and Warsaw Pact exercises became evident in late 1978 especially in the *Vestnik* (Herald) series. Featured prominently in some 1979 exercises, a major General Staff coordinated series of exercises with a WMD theme begun in June had a common background scenario of a NATO assault with immediate use of strategic and theater nuclear weapons—and chemical. One of the exercises played throughout the Western TVD under the direction of Soviet Chief of Chemical Troops General-Colonel V. K. Pikalov from Legnica (the future GK home). Scenario depicted mass NATO nuclear, and chemical with VX and sarin, strikes and friendly losses. An unusual concurrent exercise by the Soviet nuclear weapons head authority implemented a certain Plan while deploying weapons transport units. The historical failure of signals intelligence to detect exercise chemical scenarios granted the Soviets an opportunity to cloak any renewed offensive work in nominally nuclear-biological-chemical defense exercises such as *Vestnik*.

Scenarios involving chemical weapons into the late 1980s frequently depicted NATO attacks with agents VX and sarin during both nuclear and non-nuclear periods. Hungarian participants disrupted a 1982 operational exercise objecting to a Soviet scenario insertion of NATO chemical strikes which they considered to be a "political" issue. Exercise *Zapad* 1984 notably portrayed NATO employment of chemical weapons on the second day of combat; targeting of both forward and western USSR forces; and consequent heavy losses. But indications of Soviet/Warsaw Pact offensive CW in 1980s exercises remained limited; subject to interpretation; and any seemingly solid occurrences confined to the tactical level. A new element depicted NATO strikes on chemical plants releasing dangerous chemicals such as chlorine and ammonia—a 1989 article in an open publication stressed the threat from conventional weapons to both chemical and nuclear plants with substantial data backup.[1163] The consequences of the 1986 Chernobyl disaster likely furthered this theme.

The 1987 edition of the openly published book *Taktika*, an important tome surveying one of the three components of Soviet military art, suffused with imputed US-NATO chemical-biological preparations (along with nuclear and precision weapons). Text explicitly linked the Air-Land Battle concept with CW "divisions, army corps and tactical aviation utilizing conventional (high precision), chemical and nuclear weapons." But no hint appeared of chemical retaliation, only use of nuclear weapons "to annihilate the enemy's nuclear and chemical attack resources."[1164] A coherent base of intelligence evidence for determining the character and dimensions of any Soviet-Warsaw Pact response to the US offensive chemical buildup, however, continued lacking.

**arms control variant**

US actions in ramping up chemical armament presented a bad rerun of the late 1950s situation—including inaccurate intelligence justification—but this time an alternative became available in the form of the ongoing chemical disarmament negotiations. The only transparent Soviet response to US chemical weapons modernization would be activity in the arms control forum. The 1974 US-USSR communique calling for initiation of chemical arms negotiations had resulted in a limited Geneva session which went nowhere in the face of Soviet resistance to on-site inspection in treaty verification proposals. Bilateral talks got under way in earnest in 1976 and continued until 1980 when the US pulled out.[1165] The bilateral rounds reset in 1984, parallel to work on a chemical weapons treaty under way since 1980 at the United Nations Committee on Disarmament. The second half of the 1980s marked advancement of international efforts to reach agreement on a chemical weapons convention.

Arguably the prospect of a revived US chemical armament capability at the turn of the 1980s forced the Soviets to seriously investigate negotiations as a viable chemical variant as intended by NSD 18. Soviet movement on arms control had been seen by some of the zealots as a clever method to restrain growing US CW capability, probably correctly—to obviate the need to re-integrate chemical weapons into Warsaw Pact operational plans. US chemical proponents had no interest in arms control; intent on modernizing the CW stockpile with supposedly more politically-palatable binary weapons while augmenting the limited proportion still forward deployed in Europe. Soviet accession to a number of arms control treaties can be viewed as a self-interested approach to constrain US innovations so as to avoid the efforts that would be required to (over)balance rather than any political-moral statement. The US chemical arms venture under the Reagan administration represented yet another compelling demonstration of the global danger of intelligence done badly.

The year 1987 eventuated consequential for Soviet WMD including what seems, in retrospect, to have been a coordinated CW campaign. A public exhibition occurred in October of the "standard" array of Soviet chemical munitions attended by an international audience at the Shikhany chemical center. Some attendees commented that the munitions looked rather dated, more 1950s-1960s-ish.[1166] The hosts told visitors, categorically that "beyond minor technical modifications no other types of Soviet chemical weapons exist"[1167] despite the evidence already noted for a wider inventory. In December the first Soviet CW quantification represented the stockpile to "not exceed 50,000 tonnes"[1168]—if at all accurate, signifying that the contemporary DIA and British estimates had been off by only 250000—but 10000 tonnes would evaporate in the subsequent declaration under the ratified chemical treaty.

In another December highlight the signing of the bilateral US-USSR INF Treaty marked Soviet acceptance of declared site inspection and an unprecedented transmittal of formerly highly sensitive armament data. An inexplicable surprise for US intelligence took place in the apparent deactivation during 1987 of what had been assessed to be a national nuclear weapons stockpile site at a location the US called Nyandoma (Soviet Kargopol-2) in a Scandinavian direction. Scores of weapons rail and ground transportation assets departed within a short period. This base had been one of a related group of peculiar installations that had been constructed beginning in 1959 and which in the later 1960s had been the subject of an intense dispute among the US intelligence agencies. Recent Russian information confirms that in 1987 Kargopol-2 had been downgraded and transformed into a nuclear support base for aviation of the Northern Fleet.[1169]

Less scrutiny would be afforded by US intelligence regarding other Soviet actions that may have been under way. A Russian researcher on chemical arms Dr. Lev Fedorov reported in a 1994 paper[1170] when Soviet materials had been more accessible then before or since an interesting conclusion (repeated in similar wording for other publications).

The Soviet Army carried out large-scale transfers of CW from 1987 to 1989 from the bases where they had been stored to seven bases which were subsequently announced. At the same time the arsenals were 'erased' to dimensions that would be comparable with US stockpiles.

US intelligence during the late 1980s had been entirely unaware of any such movements of chemical armament but then no one had a clue regarding "the bases where they had been stored." Statements on chemical weapons by Russian scientists during the 1990s would be considered sufficiently authoritative to be cited even in US intelligence assessments[1171] of the accuracy of the official Russian chemical stockpile declaration as well as their development of new chemical agents (as in the *Novichok* line). Through the 1980s during CW negotiations the Soviets continued in an insistently avoidance mode regarding actual stockpile locations and any inspections thereof.

The chemical transfer represented a plausible finding. By 1987 a similar mass reshuffle under way involved missiles and launchers subject to the INF Treaty.[1172] Notably, in the shorter-range missile force (which had chemical missions), 539 combat missiles in the Non-Deployed category would be compressed from, perhaps twenty or more, echeloned bases (including front missile-artillery and central)—most also configured for storing warheads not covered by the treaty—to the four locations actually declared. An ammunition depot in the Kazakh SSR, with no prior connection to any brand of these systems, became the Balkhash Missile Storage Facility with 138 combat and 47 training missiles limited by the treaty; the depot did not even exist five years earlier and remained under construction. This consolidation gambit had been implemented exactly as, and concurrently in (according to Fedorov) the chemical stockpile. The Soviets in 1989 would initiate another mass scramble beyond the Urals control boundary set by the Conventional Armed Forces in Europe Treaty. Intelligence detected the eastward transfer of tens of thousands of tanks, artillery, armored vehicles, and aircraft accountable and destined for elimination—again anticipating a treaty data exchange.[1173]

During chemical weapons data exchanges in accordance with a bilateral agreement, and under the terms of the Chemical Weapons Convention, the Soviets/Russians owned up to seven stockpile sites. These included only two of the more/less than a dozen "chemical depots" accredited by US and British experts as well as five artillery and aviation ammunition bases not on any list of chemical suspects. The number and interior location of declared storage sites looked quite similar to those unilaterally disclosed by the US in July 1988 at disarmament talks.[1174] There had been absolutely no information during the post-World War II period from any Western intelligence source, whether SIGINT or human, that chemical munitions of any denomination had been or existed present at the five ammunition bases. They had not even appeared in the Hirsch Report.

The declared ammunition sites had not attracted the attention of intelligence chemical connoisseurs since, not only lacking corroborative evidence, satellite imagery since the early 1960s of these places had not revealed any confirmed barrels, special railcars, or other supposed chemical indications to which such significance had been assigned. The blessed decontamination vehicles had been glaringly absent despite the, supposedly preexistent, massive concentration of toxic munitions and agents. A visitor to one base in 1995 had been struck by the lack of even fire-fighting equipment within the exclusion zone; only axes and buckets on hand.[1175] Most of the intelligence "chemical depots" went missing from the Russian CWC declaration; while the long list accumulated during the Cold War of suspected chemical weapons storage sites in Europe and the USSR had been rudely erased.

Despite the intelligence depiction throughout the Cold War of a vigorous and ever-expanding Soviet CW arsenal, the five declared air and ground ammunition bases had an oddly static, remarkably discrepant, history. Either the impressive collection of intelligence evidence for a strong chemical posture had been largely bogus or the Soviets/Russians offered a canny swindle. Most of the storage shelters at the fave five had been present since before the early 1960s as evident in satellite imagery. At least one of the aviation bases had not been altered since German photographic coverage of about 1943, and the original shelters at the other bases obviously dated a similar vintage. The only evident structural changes at the three air munitions declarants related to the infusion of missile systems into the Soviet Air Forces. Several missile storage shelters and bunkers had been built at two bases after the mid 1960s. All three had subsequently been selected, along with other aviation munitions and dedicated missile repositories, for a massive accumulation of ground- and air-launched strategic cruise missiles. Construction of a large number of a new, distinctive, bunker design for this inventory had begun in 1976, with additions into the 1990s.[1176] The ground program had been terminated by the INF Treaty but aircraft versions remained for the successive strategic arms negotiations.

An obvious (except to the chemical cubicles) indication of consolidation transpired at one of the artillery ammunition sites. Chemical artillery shells and missile warheads at the Shchuchye base (13.6 percent share of the declared chemical stockpile)[1177] went into shelters only built starting in late 1986 and largely completed during 1987—or just in time to receive their allocation. In addition construction of a different group of storage shelters (at ground level each would look like a garage with eight stalls) had begun in 1982 within a newly wall-segregated area of the base. At least one shelter of identical design had been built shortly thereafter at another future declarant—Kambarka. By a strange coincidence this 1982 work had occurred immediately subsequent to a Soviet change of course in chemical arms control negotiations.

The Soviets had been persistently skittish about revealing existing chemical munitions storage locations during these negotiations. In June 1982 however, after unabating rejections, in a paper presented by Foreign Minister A. A. Gromyko, the USSR accepted in principle the on-site inspection of declared chemical stocks in order to monitor their destruction.[1178] But this opening came with a snag. The Soviet definition of the new verification format would not be presented until the following year in a plenary statement by Ambassador V. L. Israelyan at a session of the Geneva Committee on Disarmament (from the US State Department transcript translation—emphasis added).[1179]

> After careful study of this question and some realistic proposals made in connection with it, the Soviet Union proposes that in order to ensure reliable verification of the declared stocks, provision should be made for the **creation of store-houses** at the specialized facilities for the destruction of these stocks, the location of which would be declared concurrently with the declaration of the destruction facilities....

Caution must be exercised in drawing straight lines between these dots but a striking echo of the first Soviet inspection proposal is that shelter construction had been initiated at two future CWC storage sites quickly following issuance. There had also been evidence from an intelligence source that from late 1986 work had been under way at several of the declared ammunition bases—including Shchuchye—by a construction authority that specialized in high priority projects.

Those Russian researchers and environmentalists of the 1990s, attempting to uncover the hidden Soviet past and measure decades of damage, found scattered bits of information regarding Soviet chemical armament. Aggregated evidence pointed to a systematic, massive, movement and disposal campaign in the late 1950s and early 1960s involving chemical stocks accumulated before, during WWII, and the decade thereafter (largely the technical developments of the First World War). Agents and munitions destruction proceeded by incineration or burial at installations and removal for dumping at sea. Both "chemical depots" declared under the CWC as well as at least one other not declared (Pokrovka to US intelligence near Chapayevsk) had been heavily involved in this disposal endeavor.[1180] Two of the aviation munitions bases declared by the Russians also appeared in the records. Article III of the CWC exempts declaration of otherwise covered agents buried before 1977 or disposed at sea before 1985—a contingency reportedly inserted at Soviet/Russian insistence[1181]—conveniently avoiding questions regarding this massive chemical hoard. These dates also helpfully provide a timeline

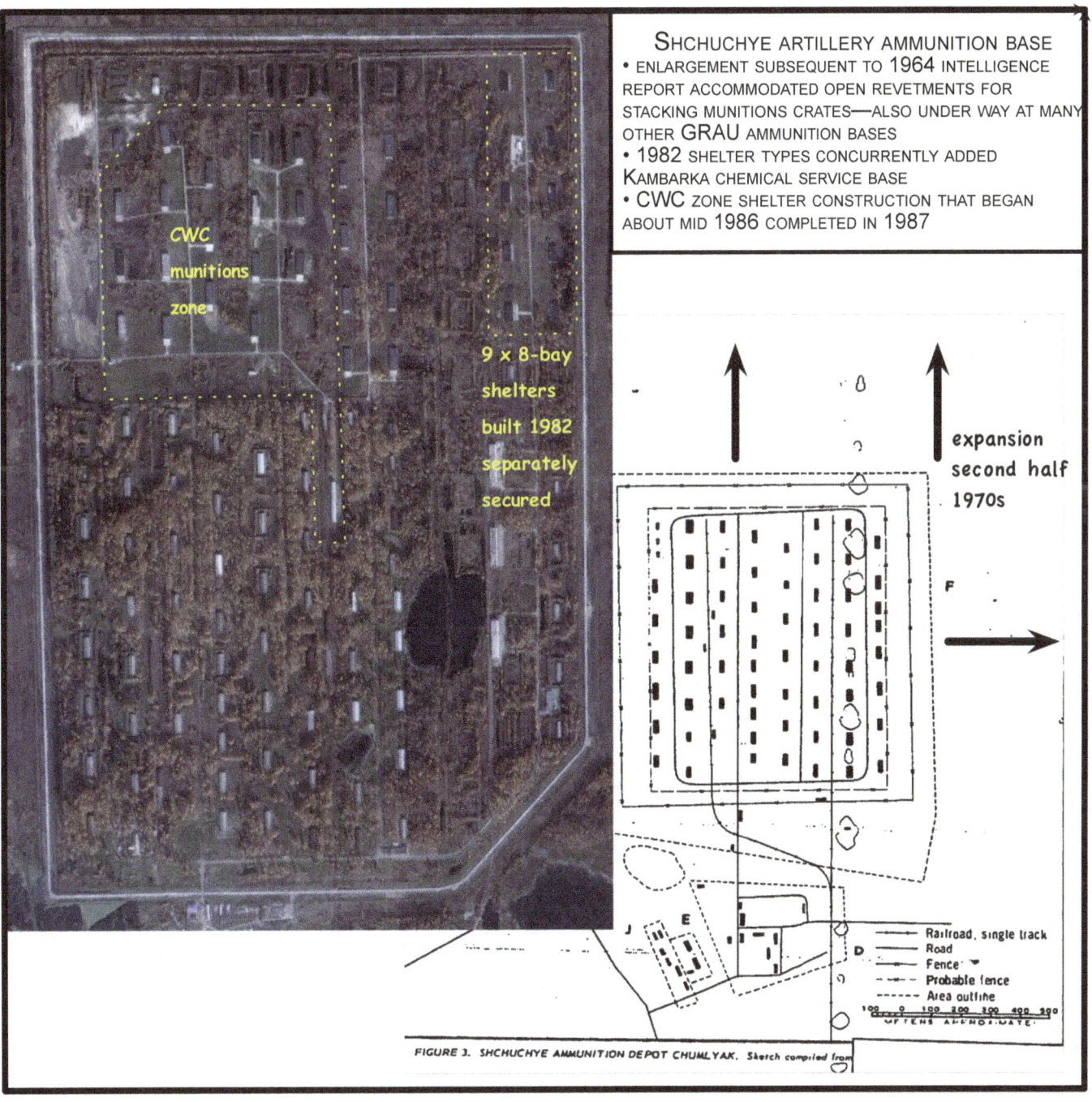

for what may have been other agent and munitions reduction activities.

Russian newspaper articles reported on the early 1960s assembly at the Penza station of about 50 trains, each with 60 wagons, to move chemical bombs for dumping into the Barents Sea.[1182] The bombs must have come from the nearby Leonidovka aviation munitions base (Penza to intelligence). Environmentalists discovered that during this disposal effort a stash of bombs with mixed lewisite-mustard fill, perhaps those in too poor a condition for movement, had been buried near the base. Heavy concentrations of arsenic remained in the soil at the dump with indications of ground water contamination.[1183] The rounded transport numeration permits a gross estimate of the rail loading. The Soviet 20 tonnes single railcar planning factor approximates a 60000 tonnes shipment but this quantity would include agent, explosives, and casings—and likely bomb packing density less than would be the case for non-toxic cargo. The coefficients of agent fill for Soviet bombs varied by size and agent type—four types of Shikhany display bombs ranged from 0.21 to 0.39[1184]—but at roughly a third, the transports would have amounted to some 20000 agent tonnes. In one of those coincidences that bedevil human cognitive attempts to determine reality large storehouses that had been under construction since 1959 had attained completion during 1962 to early 1964 at three alternative repositories; perhaps not all of the trains had been routed to the Barents.

The massive accumulations at a small number, and central USSR locations of all but one (Pochep), of the declared stockpile sites provides immanent evidence of the consolidation uncovered by Fedorov. This geographic positioning could not have constituted an operational deployment, even a retaliatory posture—and is hardly congruent with a Russian semi-official publication depiction that "a modern and rather efficient system of chemical ammunition and stockpiles was established in an amount required for several front operations" in which weapons "on the alert"[1185] had been kept at storage sites. Implied in this statement is an outward positioning in the TVDs to support the delivery means of fronts and armies in a disposition which could meet readiness timelines. No pattern resembling the echeloning of material reserves, including nuclear weapons, specified in the Soviet Manual can be elicited from the CWC locations; that arrangement represented a chemical Potemkin village created and purposed for an international treaty. If the consolidation had taken place during or soon after the 1975 deletion of the chemical variant from the WMD Operation then a higher degree of credibility might be assigned to the realignment.

Throughout the Cold War there had been no definitive, and few solid, indications (Grossenhain moments) pointing toward a substantial chemical out-deployment. Absolutely lacking had been valid evidence collected by any intelligence tool for the presence of filled toxic chemical munitions in the storage locations for Soviet-Warsaw Pact conventional ammunition. The intelligence assertion that bulk toxic agents existed, in massive quantities, in the "chemical depots" had been similarly meritless. Even a detailed calculation by one of their own regarding Soviet Chemical Troops materiel requirements had demonstrated that official "chemical depots" had scarcely any capacity for the storage of offensive chemical substances; on a scale resembling any of the several entirely vaporous quantifications during three decades. The final nails in the coffin of the intelligence chemical estimate came in the CWC declared high proportion of filled munitions, including all modern nerve agents, which directly contradicted the official model. The very lack of incontestable evidence over such a long period might imply that the chemical first echelon had been both limited in extent and highly selective in location especially by or after 1975. Such a restricted realm only amplified the significance of the chemical munitions bases intended to supply operating fronts—wherever and whatever they might be.

Yet there had been a extensive base in evidence for an impressive Soviet offensive chemical warfare scheme, one that would be extended to the countries of the Warsaw Pact. The existence and development of this capability had been promulgated in the body of classified writings, documents, and manuals dating to the 1960s and early 1970s acquired by Western intelligence services. That material has been supplemented and verified by similar period documentation subsequently discovered in the archives of the former allies. All of this data consistently and explicitly manifested wide-ranging preparations to employ chemical weapons in a big way on European battlefields—in conjunction with nuclear means.

The seven Russian CWC locations represented the destinations of a massive reshuffle as well as the subsequent inward collapse of the Soviet Empire and, there are continuing grounds for suspicion that not all chemical armament made the move. A complementary prospect emerges that the perceptual fixations of intelligence chemical connoisseurs, throughout the Cold War, had been mistaken. The substantive difficulties and clashing organizational perspectives that hindered attempts to arrive at a valid, agreed estimate should have alerted those involved that something might be awry with the chosen track, that they might be searching for the verifiably existent capability in the wrong places. The Soviet CW conundrum joined the ever-expanding collection of intelligence issues with an insistent reliance on solutions demonstrably unworkable to an informed investigation; this persistence reinforced by an inability to conceive alternative approaches. Inconclusive evidence should have broadcast to the intelligence chemical cubicles that an implicit question had arisen as to the originating chemical munitions storage sites. Had all or most of the declared stockpile really been at the "chemical depots" and/or conventional ammunition bases. Or did there exist a radically different, unrecognized, solution to this intractable Cold War intelligence problem—a chemical Hypothesis X?

A combination of deficient preparedness, lack of practical planning, and a muddled political consultation process had left NATO vulnerable to the Warsaw Pact chemical variant during the Cold War. One of the primary chemical target sets, US nuclear stores in Europe, had a startling lack of protective measures, even a fatalistic attitude to the prospect of CW attack. All military levels provided inviting subjects for surprise chemical strikes that could achieve the defense breakthroughs so important to the Soviet strategic culture. Warsaw Pact intelligence services deep penetrations into US and NATO military structures afforded insights into vulnerabilities that blazoned the potential winning advantage of the chemical variant. An independent chemical period would have been, logically if not substantiated, an increasingly attractive theater option through at least 1974, after which the WMD collection had been abbreviated. It is historically unfortunate that Soviet intentions for the chemical variant may never be confirmed.

Western political and military leaders had been poorly served by their intelligence services which never solved the problem of the dangerous chemical variant. By comparison nuclear variant intelligence proved relatively solid although here too important analytical shortcomings existed. A strong case could be built for a formidable Soviet offensive chemical capability and, at least during a finite period, planning and preparations for a powerful, concerted, WMD offensive. Considering the details, intelligence persisted largely clueless. But the failure entailed perspective and conceptualization rather than lack of evidence. The insistence of intelligence agencies, the organizational structure, dealing with chemical and nuclear issues as separate realms—which the Soviets approached as unified—ensured perceptual failure. There had been an abundance of doctrinal smoke during a period of fifteen years indicative of a blazing chemical fire.

Providential, ultimately, that the West 'won' a cold war.

Some contemporary observers pointed out that the US insistence on site inspections as part of a prospective chemical arms agreement could be construed as deliberately intended to elicit rejection. But this standpoint also demonstrated a lack of confidence in intelligence assessments. The formal presentment on 18 August 1983 at the Geneva Committee on Disarmament by Ambassador V. L. Israelyan dismissed any verification inspections proposals involving existing chemical arms storage sites (again from the US State Department transcript translation).[1186]

> In particular, it has been suggested that States parties to the future convention, after it enters into force, should declare the locations of declared stocks of chemical weapons, i.e. the storage places where they may be kept. Such a requirement is purely unilateral and unrealistic, since it does not take into account the possible general use* of such places of storage, where chemical weapons are being kept, and might affect the defense interests of States not connected with chemical weapons.
> [*or "universality"]

This pronouncement constituted a categorical rejection of any verification regime that would monitor operational facilities storing chemical armament. The expressed basis for the exemption implied that such a declaration would compromise—something—not subject to the chemical treaty, objects of great importance and evidently in proximity. If anyone in US or other Western intelligence services had been intrigued about the "defense interests" that had such significance as to block provisions of a major international arms control treaty, they did not pursue this obvious hint. Despite their role as professional questioners intelligence types can be a surprisingly incurious lot. The Soviet wording offered systemic testimony, not provided by a Curveball or some other dodgy source, but rather a message direct from the landlord. The Soviets had effectively issued an alert to intelligence (if actually aware of the statement) that there might be an alternative solution to the chemical conundrum. But the curtains of the connoisseurship perceptual window had been tightly drawn regarding this particular evidence of the second kind.

US Intelligence Fabricates Another Model

Through the post-Soviet era, along with uncovered documentation, insiders have conveyed much detail on USSR nuclear weapons development programs, personalities, as well as the centers of the research and production network. Formerly tightly shuttered nuclear facilities became at least partly accessible to outsiders. Several accounts issued by Russians and Westerners since the 1990s have exploited this material to fill in gaps inherent to both open and classified knowledge in the West. Views on the significance and contribution to the Soviet programs of atomic espionage against the US have differed on both sides of the former Iron Curtain.

The destination of weapons after shipment from manufacturing plants—the nuclear stockpile—has been rather less transparent to investigators. Western interest in recent decades has largely been concerned with the vulnerability of the logistics system to terrorist acquisition. But this accumulation is where the shooters obtained their bullets, the overarching reason for the existence of the whole massive nuclear complex. An echeloned and increasingly diversified storage system had been elaborated from the late 1940s in concert with production output and technological advances in both warheads and delivery means. While nuclear technical aspects to a considerable extent presented comparability for US and other Western intelligence services, the why, where, and how of weapons deployment embodied military strategic-operational problems—directly related to the variants of WMD employment. Throughout the Cold War US intelligence nuclear specialists ranked only relatively less inept than those in the chemical cubicles at achieving a perspective that unified both technical and operational aspects.

Delineation of the organization that supplied nuclear ammunition to the delivery means became an early, continuous, and intensive substantive task bringing together the full spectrum of intelligence collection and analysis. Overhead imaging systems comprised the primary means, throughout the Cold War, of storage location discovery, measurement, and activity tracking. Electronic monitors achieved important breaches regarding nuclear structure, planning, and procedures—these successes in marked contrast to the chemical and biological weapons failures. Low level human sources, such as construction workers and truck drivers, provided useful information. Lacking, however, inside sources of any kind or level to explicate the grand plan, the operative concepts, intelligence attempted to discern a regime that did not necessarily replicate US approaches to handling and distributing WMD. Nuclear connoisseurs relied heavily on that most favored intelligence methodology—mirror imaging—deriving their presumptive Soviet stereotype from familiarized US practice. Each generation of analysts passed on the approved nuclear official model to their successors who then force-fit all newly acquired information.

The nuclear weapons complex spawned by the Soviet Union evolved from a few storage installations associated with fabrication plants, and a limited number of delivery aircraft bases, into a massive integrated structure designed to enable global war-fighting with mass destruction weapons. A network of fixed storage facilities and associated mobile technical and transport units provided support to strategic strike systems as well as for TVD strategic operations conducted by ground, aviation, and naval forces. US nuclear intelligence connoisseurs, seconded by their British colleagues, perceived an apparently double-tiered (somehow interlinked) logistics and control system that administered weapons storage bases at national, and at service delivery unit, levels. If this particular intelligence reality had in fact been mistaken, that entirely unfamiliar premises underlay the Soviet strategic-operational concept of mass destruction weapons employment, then intelligence assessments concerning their WMD arsenal must necessarily also be fundamentally distorted.

A Main Directorate (GU) of the Ministry of Defense (MO), numbered 12, managed this WMD empire—at maximum extent supervising Center equities at 27 locations (double counting those at two nuclear plants) within the USSR as well as at least a dozen more specialized external sites. These bases constituted the VGK strategic reserve which would in wartime disgorge and transport mass destruction weapons to delivery units of all the armed forces. Russian sources[1187] have supplemented that (not) known during the Cold War by tracing the evolution of the central administration back to the September 1947 creation of a Special Department in the Soviet General Staff which may also have been numbered 12. Separate nuclear entities originated, evolved, and wandered through the nuclear industrial and military bureaucracy during the 1950s, emerging as the MO Main Directorate for Special Armament in February 1958. In late April of that year the office became 12 GUMO; represented by military unit 31600. Intelligence had identified unit 31600 only in 1960 and later made the connection to 12 GUMO. An independent but closely related organization, designated the sixth and affiliated with the General Staff, worked within the individual armed forces in supervising (ultimately) more than 500 installations in military districts, groups of forces, and fleets, along with strategic missile, air and air defense armies. In February 1959 12 GUMO merged with Directorate Six. The Soviets thus had finally unified several nuclear functions including testing, weapons acceptance, military requirements generation, storage, and employment.

In December 1959 the Soviets implemented a, world-first, decision to create a component of the national armed forces devoted exclusively to nuclear missile attack—unlike ground, air, and naval services entirely bereft of any defensive purpose. Establishment of this strategic strike phalanx instigated the appending of the nuclear Main Directorate to the new RVSN.

After all, this approach thereby fused two key VGK assets, strategic missiles and nuclear warheads for all military arms. The Strategic Rocket Troops hosted the nuclear directorate until a November 1974 reorganization that returned the Directorate to the MO. A directorate six then emerged within the RVSN to supervise nuclear warheads as in the other armed forces.[1188] Intelligence had noted the close relationship between the Main Directorate and the SRF but never quite grasped the organizational details. The 1974 milestone—as well as the subsequent insertion of a sixth directorate—escaped detection by intelligence to include the US Agency and British Headquarters that most closely monitored the relationship.

Retrospective wisdom marks this high level realignment as a potentially significant indication of expanded responsibilities that took place exactly at the juncture of a chemical and biological occultation in WMD strategy. A preceding hierarchical realignment, in the November 1973 MO Decree 99, had implemented the CPSU-Council of Ministers June 1973 Decree 444-138 that transferred responsibility for biological weapons from directorate seven to a, newly formed or revamped, directorate fifteen.[1189] Noted earlier, the seventh directorate had been pinpointed by Oleg Penkovsky as the central entity for both chemical and biological weapons; minimal information concerning this key WMD entity had been subsequently acquired. Both the transfer and existence of the new BW directorate had passed unnoticed by intelligence for as long as the USSR existed.

Adding to the conflicting mix of evidence a 1980 popup regarding 12 GUMO pointed to other stakes held by the Main Directorate. A gathering of sixers from military districts and groups of forces planned for December would address the issue of support to the Soviet Ground Troops and Air Forces with nuclear—and chemical—weapons. This tidbit elicited consternation among the WMD connoisseurs, evidence from a usually credible channel yet incompatible with both nuclear and chemical official models. Ultimately this important clue of the second kind remained unapplied because neither cubicle could accommodate such singularly non-conforming information—an item shelved out of view. At various times and places during the Cold War intelligence suspicions had arisen that there might be a close relationship in the handling of nuclear and chemical weapons but no one would ever generate an alternative, congruent, hypothesis.

Despite the 14 years affiliation with one of the five armed forces both Cold War intelligence and subsequent Russian information attest that the Main Directorate continued to support nuclear-technical activities in the other four services. There had been some evidence that selected 12 GUMO central bases dealt primarily or exclusively with one service. This shared jurisdiction has been confirmed in the post Cold War period during US assistance to Russia under the Cooperative Threat Reduction program for improving the security of WMD facilities. The precise delineation of organizational affiliations is still uncertain. One possibility lies with the distinctive Soviet concept of dual subordination. A particular outfit could be in 'direct' subordination to one entity and simultaneously in 'special' subordination to a different entity. Control schemes had been designed to ensure that the tentacles of the Center reached the subsidiary levels of all hierarchies. Thus the 12 GU could have been part of/subordinate to the strategic missile arm in one form while performing nuclear weapons functions with other services under the MO rubric.

The 12 GUMO tie-in is further complicated by yet another major player in the Soviet military bureaucracy. In 1961 Oleg Penkovsky had been insistent that GRAU Chief General-Colonel N. N. Zhdanov controlled nuclear warhead and bomb stockpiles.[1190] Another key source on warhead-missile organization stated in 1961 that both GRAU and 12 GU participated in deliveries of these components to rear bases of fronts but the author assigned the latter to the MO rather than to the RVSN; possibly reflecting outdated knowledge missing the re-alignment.[1191] Some of us invested much time and effort in achieving an understanding of the role GRAU played in the military hierarchy as well as delineating organization and responsibilities. Front missile-artillery bases, the only echelon in the Ground Troops at that time that had (official) warhead storage, formed constituents of the GRAU armament empire. Significantly, upon dissolution of the USSR control of at least one of the nominal 12 GUMO central bases in Ukraine had initially been assigned to their strategic missile arm, and later to a replicated GRAU,[1192] rather than a nuclear authority. But there may have been another dimension in the GRAU assignments for WMD support until at least the 1974 reshuffle that expanded the missions of 12 GUMO.

**official nuclear model**

During the second half of the 1950s intelligence laid the foundation for a perspective of the Soviet nuclear weapons support system that would endure through the Cold War. Photographs from U-2 aircraft overflights provided the first look at this system upon the inception of a long period of dramatic expansion. Initial observations had been supplemented by satellite imagery, beginning in 1960, to arrive at an ordained, nuclear exclusive, dualism. Intelligence contemplated a echeloned network of strategic reserve complexes augmenting a much larger number of, small-scale, bases affiliated with delivery units of their respective services. Gradually an impermeable perceptual boundary had been established in which, somehow and somewhere, these twain would meet. US nuclear storage in the 1950s had evolved into a system of National Stockpile Sites located within the continental US, and Operational Storage Sites supporting delivery forces at home and overseas.[1193] This strictly bifurcated depiction, and much US terminology, had been embraced by 1960s intelligence in distinguishing a Soviet "national stockpile sites" and "direct support sites" arrangement; persisting unaltered into the 1970s-1980s.[1194] Attempts in the early 1990s to ascertain the redistribution of nuclear weapons during the USSR breakup among constituent republics did not deviate from the official nuclear model.[1195] This model garnered reinforcement from the Western nuclear support structure and military-geographic situation. The Atlantic formed a barrier between the US national WMD stockpile and the storage network supporting our services as well as allies. NATO plans assumed little or no reinforcement of the forward stock during any armed conflict with the Warsaw Pact.

The intelligence model had to be constructed without access to the Soviet organization chart, lacking higher level system information of any sort. Therefore assessors had resorted to the fashionable mirror-imaging approach. The US system became the established point of reference rather than the seeking out (them-thinking) of any potential alternative Soviet blueprint. Unfortunately, a shortcoming of the mirror-image method is that if the other side does not conform, if there is another—even radically differing—conceptual basis, a critical distortion is induced. Even the nature of operations involving the full WMD spectrum might be entirely misconceived.

The USSR, at the epicenter of Eurasia, occupied a unique geographic position that fostered a potentially variant solution keyed to echeloned reserves of mass destruction weapons much of which could be kept well back in the TVDs. By the mid 1970s the US nuclear inventory in Europe amounted to 6951 weapons held at 92 storage sites for air, ground, and naval forces plus 53 sites holding nuclear warheads for the Nike-Hercules air defense missile (more than 700 warheads which the US desired to send home).[1196] Certain stores functioned as custodians for nuclear weapons planned for handover to delivery units of NATO allies. Western intelligence services by 1979 had mapped only 23 permanent forward Soviet aviation and missile (and no confirmed naval or air defense missile) nuclear stores on the territory of Warsaw Pact allies. That the Soviets might not recognize any divide along their radial lines of communication from the Center did not influence the American intelligence perspective.

Also driving the US perspective, one of the signature facets of Soviet strategy, the propensity to shield critical assets within reinforced concrete. Bunkers of widely varied designs and families became Cold War avatars. The Soviets had been motivated primarily by the doctrinal necessity of guarding against potential nuclear surprise attack by adversaries. General-Major P. Ogorodnikov and a couple of fellow Engineer Troops officers, writing in a 1961 issue of the secret edition of VM,[1197] even proposed that fortification should be an independent military-technical discipline, a main component of Soviet military science. They defined principal tasks to be ensuring the stability of the "national fortress" and the armed forces through creation and use of special protective structures; these should be deployed both domestically—no strike-free zones in a nuclear war—and in preparing the TVDs. They noted that fortified structures in the missile troops protected warheads and airframes while enhancing launch readiness. Another colonel, a professor at the Military Engineer Academy, later reiterated the intrinsic value of hardening to enhance combat readiness.[1198]

> Consequently, a fortification structure, or a complex of them, fulfills two fundamental, inseparable functions: maintaining the prescribed combat technology of one or another type of weapon and providing protection against enemy means of mass destruction.

The Soviets had elaborated a scheme that in character, scale, and variety had no Western counterpart.

The Soviets developed a taste for an astonishing collection of designs for most strategic reserve and lower echelon WMD stores markedly dissimilar to US standard igloo-types. We never pinpointed the USSR bunker Bauhaus school, the design bureaus responsible for architectural execution. Hopefully the initalizing architects had been duly awarded for their expressive range of solutions in concrete for protecting weapons, command and communications centers, and other critical systems. No nomenclature schema ever came to light. US intelligence resorted to typology, the classification and description of bunkers by assumed generations. Categorization had been initiated as U-2 reconnaissance aircraft began to snap portraits of key airfields of the USSR basing long range and naval aviation—among the earliest examples of Soviet clusivity analysis.[1199] Intelligence subsequently prodigiously issued detailed imagery bunker and facility reports that continue to be almost entirely classified. Type I applied to facilities identified as nuclear repositories at four airfields apparently completed several years before the first overflights in 1956—these actually structural sets rather than individual bunkers; indicative of the early nuclear technology of massive-sized bombs arriving at delivery units with 'some assembly required' instructions.

Russian accounts now available fill in background detail that had not been, fully, revealed by intelligence sources. This information can be correlated with the imagery baseline and considered with the output of other intelligence sources. Following the first Soviet atomic detonation on 29 August 1949 at the newly created Semipalatinsk test area (later named State Central Scientific Research Test Site 2), parts for fifteen bombs designated RDS-1 had been accumulated by 1 March 1951. Production had been assigned to plants at Sverdlovsk-45 (Nizhnyaya Tura to intelligence) and Arzamas-16 at Sarov (Sarova); also the home of (design bureau) KB-11, the originator of the first Soviet nuclear devices. Atomic bomb components resided in underground vaults of the Sarov complex.[1200] According to a Russian breakdown separable items of a generic nuclear weapon include the capsule containing fissile material and high explosives; an initiation system to generate electric pulses to detonate the explosives; a trigger timing system preset for the desired burst effect; and any safety system to prevent detonation due to impact or unauthorized access.[1201]

While intelligence became aware of both the existence and role of Sarov even in the pre-imagery period of the early 1950s, this location had never joined the official list of nuclear storage sites. Suspicion had been aroused that assembled weapons remained stored prior to the building of dedicated facilities.[1202] The expanding stockpile, and operational requirements that departments in the Soviet General Staff developed, impelled the creation of installations customized to support the delivery means of the armed forces.

The USSR Council of Ministers had created a First Main Directorate on 5 May 1951 to oversee nuclear weapons storage as well as the industrial complex. In 1953 a Ministry of Medium Machine Building or MSM (a commonly used cover ploy using innocuous labels) superseded this directorate, assuming all functions.[1203] The Council issued Resolution No. 3200-1513 on 29 August 1951 ordering the creation of bomb stores at airfields–the four Type I sites—Stryy, Soltsy, Machulische, and Veseloye (intelligence name as Russian accounts vary as to the fourth location place-name). According to the Russians these installations had been completed in 1954, confirmed by the 1956 U-2 aircraft photo reconnaissance. The same decree directed the formation of a bomber aviation regiment equipped with 22 TU-4 (Bull, the plagiarized US B-29) to study nuclear bomb storage procedures and employment. Two teams formed at KB-11 accomplished the complex work required by the early technology to assemble a nuclear bomb;[1204] necessitating several stages denoted by technical readiness conditions. VK-1 marked the normal arrangement of separated components, and VK-2, VK-3, and VK-4 the sequential assemblage. KB-11 initiated readiness VK-4 work but this stage apparently culminated at the airfield.[1205] There may have been at least a VK-5 (not specified by the Russians) readiness to be attained before actual loading of the delivery aircraft.

Russian accounts state that (again for the purpose of concealment) each of these first airfield nuclear weapons permanent storage sites received the designation repair technical base (ремонтно-техническая база remontno-tekhnicheskaya baza) or RTB (ртб).[1206] As missiles arrived in the second half of the 1950s raketnaya- substituted for remontno- in new RTB. Intelligence sources would later transmit these terms but the Soviet cover objective immediately failed. Military personnel staffed these RTBs but in the earliest dispersals the KB-11 assembly teams did all the work because only factory personnel had the requisite technical knowledge and skills to accomplish the myriad tasks of preparing a working nuclear weapon. The first distribution, of sixteen atomic bombs equally among the four RTBs, took place in February 1955[1207] at (presumably) technical readiness stage VK-4. Concurrent effort had been devoted to developing a medium bomber (TU-16 Badger) and heavy bomber (TU-95 Bear and M-4 Bison) delivery force. By 1954 weapons had been sufficiently downsized that a 30-kt bomb based on the RDS-4 design had been developed that could be mounted on the Il-28 (Beagle) light bomber.[1208]

The Soviet military strategic culture, as in all proceedings, prioritized reserves at the Center. A Council of Ministers 1950 decision, prior to creation of airfield RTBs, had directed the establishment of four central stores for nuclear weapons designated numeric *objekt* С. The Soviet designation "S Objects" would only be understood by intelligence at the end of the Cold War. The 'S' may have been derived from the bomb RDS index series which had also been a cover as in "jet engines S" the letter denoting Stalin[1209]—a meaning no doubt later conveniently forgotten. The first US bomb designs had been similarly designated MK-series. Construction then started at two *objekt*, 711 or Ivano-Frankivsk-16 (intelligence Delyatin) run by military unit 51989 in western Ukraine; and 712, possibly Feodosia-13 (Sudak), military unit 62047 in the southern Crimea. Subsequent formation proceeded on 713 *objekt* С, Novgorod-18 (Valday), military unit 71373; and 714, Mozhaysk-10 (intelligence also Mozhaysk), military unit 52025. As these neared completion the assembly teams at KB-11, which had formed two additional teams from military personnel (civilian experts made up the first two), had been transferred.[1210] Now the central objects would handle, and complete assembly, of "products" accepted from the atomic factories.

During a brief Soviet bloc active flying career the U-2 had visited all but one of these first four central bases in the western USSR. Delyatin first showed up on June 1961 (cloud-free) imagery dropped off by the satellite replacement but functional recognition did not immediately ensue. Both Mozhaysk and Valday would soon be identified as important installations[1211] and assessment as "national nuclear weapons stockpile sites" followed. Sudak had been caught on 1957 U-2 oblique imagery but would not be assigned to the NNWSS category until the later 1960s.

Storage at the central objects initially came in the shape of underground, adit or tunnel, construction, a time-consuming, geologically restricted, and expensive approach. The limited utility of subsurface chambering became apparent as the inventory of nuclear weapons rapidly increased and delivery means diversified. An alternative solution emerged in the form of individual bunkers—or "surface (banked, unbanked) structures" per a Russian description[1212]—which had the advantages of more rapid completion with flexibility in siting and functional design. Thus 711 and 712 *objekt* С exploited the mountain ridges of the eastern Carpathians and Crimea, respectively, with underground chamber storage. But the

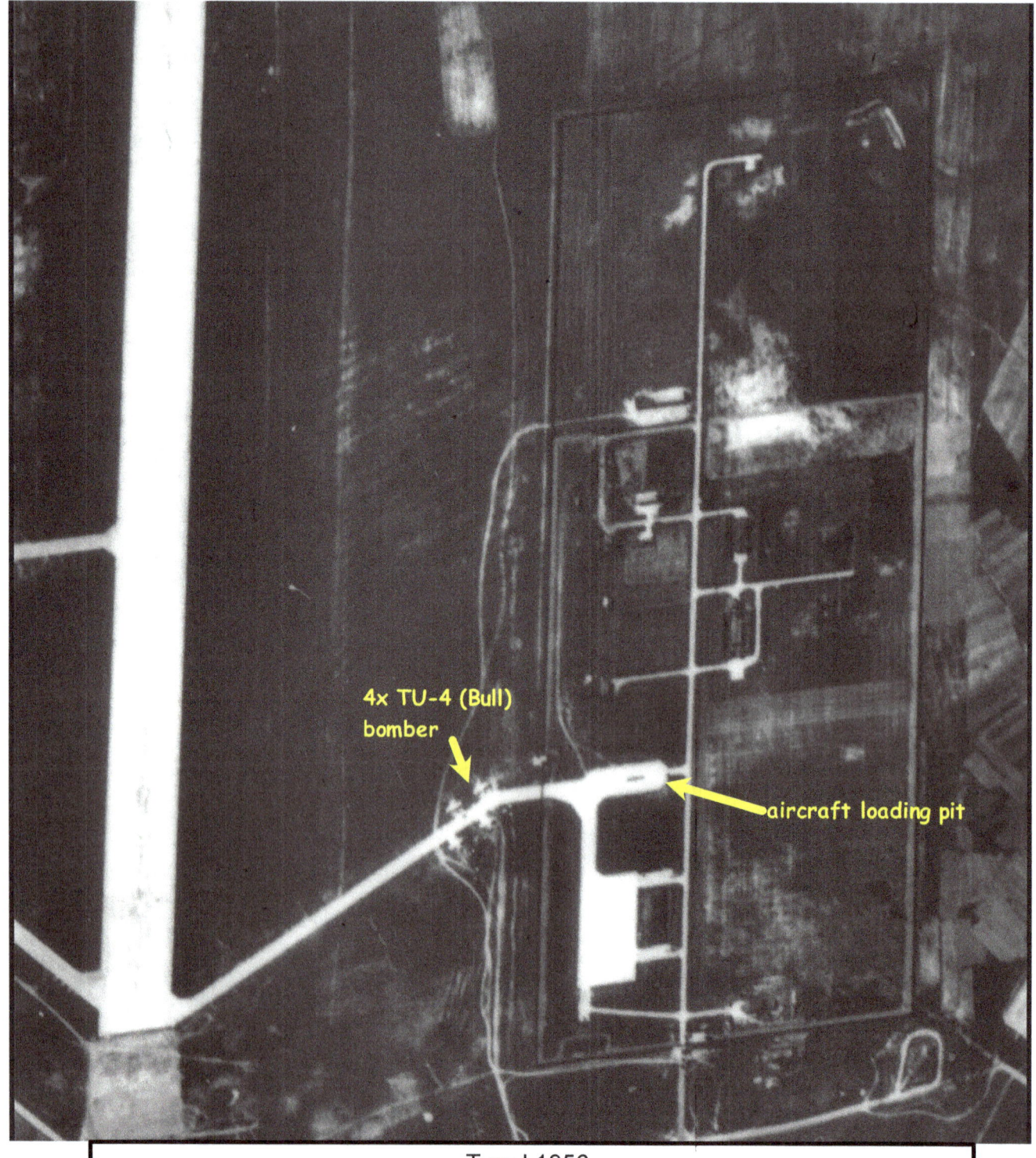

Type I 1956
RTB adjacent to Machulische Airfield near Minsk Belorussian SSR courtesy of U-2 spyplane

slightly later 713 and 714 bases, located on plains northwest and southwest of Moscow, exclusively centered on bunkers. The US system in this case evolved along similar lines from underground to surface bunker storage as nuclear weapons had been reduced in size and improved in safety aspects. But the Soviets would take their bunkers in quite different directions. The Soviet Navy would retain a preference for tunneling and two smaller bases of the Center would still be placed underground in the early 1960s.

Underground facilities then—and continue to this day—to be among the most difficult, opaque intelligence problems. These nuisances first arose when the Germans resorted to the subsurface expedient in order to protect factories and other installations from relentless Allied air attacks during the Second World War. No specific data had ever been acquired regarding the dimensions and configuration of the storage chambers making up the first generation central facilities. Only in the age of the Internet, with posting of internal photos of deactivated sites, can useful details be discerned. The first generation of bunkers achieved somewhat better comprehension thanks to the U-2. One un-earth-mounded exterior suitable for measurement had appeared on imagery of Mozhaysk in July 1956 as construction of this central *objekt* neared completion. A bunker interior configuration shot, however, could only be obtained in March 1958, relatively poor oblique coverage, of the central *objekt* Svobodnyy-21 (intelligence Malaya Sazanka) in the eastern USSR. Construction of this *objekt* may have started in 1954.

The Mozhaysk installation manifestation on two photographic frames returned by mission A2014 on 5 July 1956 had been commented in reporting but lacking particular significance. Not until the issuance of a Photo Intelligence Alert dated 7 September 1956 on possible nuclear reactors at Mozhaysk that priority ranking as a unique facility had been assigned; by the following January "Mozhaysk was the biggest thing in the world" and "first major unidentified Russian installation" according to a history of the contemporary exploitation organization.[1213] Purpose became an issue of intense discussion and consultation—even German missile expert Werner von Braun contributed—with competing functional theories. Non-photographic evidence not available included the increasingly important pairing with SIGINT to identify imaged objects. The US Air Force chimed in with a missile launch complex determination. The whole affair has an eerie resemblance and parallel, an intelligence pathology, to a controversy that would erupt a decade later concerning a new group of Mozhaysk cousins. Only by 1959 would the three installations, along with two others that had been detected, be linked with a common nuclear stockpile theme.[1214]

The 1956 U-2 coverage of Mozhaysk had revealed two unusual mounded edifices, one nearly finished; the completed dome mensuration gave a diameter of 58 meters and height 25-m; a vertical shaft evident at the structure under construction.[1215] Nothing resembling these items would ever be identified at other official nuclear installations. No validated function for these apparitions would be determined by intelligence. One possibility relates to the contemporary Soviet fascination with BRV—combat radioactive substances—the byproducts of nuclear reactors. Among other sources a 1954 MoD handbook[1216] and a 1958 dictionary[1217] cited BRV employment in liquid, powder, or smoke form and both noted the utility of spicing with toxic chemical agents.

Preceding the downsizing of nuclear warheads to fit missiles the Soviet experimented with BRV dissemination. A 2006 Russian book on the strategic missile troops provided some, conflicting, details.[1218] According to a participant a test series in 1955 (1953 in another account) involving the R-2 (SS-2 Sibling) at the Kapustin Yar range examined variant air burst dispersal methods. A massive fill version used a hollowed cone with an axial explosive charge to generate a deadly aerial rainfall of droplets; plus a sub-munitions warhead with a hundred or so individually detonated spheres each containing one or two liters of radioactive liquid. Consequent ground cover eventuated widespread but at a low concentration. The participant attributed the cancer death a few decades later of a colleague to be due to his mistaken sleeping out on the contaminated field. Another test series in 1957 at Kapustin Yar used the R-5, later superseded by the R-5M system (SS-3 Shyster) which had been selected for the 2 February 1956 first-ever missile firing with a live nuclear warhead. The Soviets tried out a bulk filling system using a large stainless steel tank mounted on a multi-axle rail carriage ("a real monster") weighing several hundred tonnes) to transfer the radioactive liquid by hose to an erected missile; the participant noted that thankfully this system did not enter service.

The potential use of 'dirty bombs' by terrorists is a recent revival of interest in such materials. The US had also investigated the value of radioactive munitions but abandoned the project initiated by the Army in 1948 (carried out by the Chemical Corps) by 1954 on concluding that such weapons had no realistic military value.[1219] Soviet efforts had been more persistent. BRV warheads would be developed for both the R-2[1220] battlefield, and the first deployed theater range (1200-km) R-5M, missiles.[1221] Oleg Penkovsky in the early 1960s stated that BRV artillery projectiles and bombs had also been stockpiled although both had been considered ineffective.[1222] Even into the 1980s BRV continued to be a subject of discussion in Eastern military writings.[1223]

The geographic distribution of this initial nuclear support system had at least one correspondence…of the third kind—with four theaters of military actions in the Western Theater of War. The Northwestern TVD received the central *objekt* Novgorod-18 situated 160-km from the Type I at Soltsy Airfield; in the Western TVD Mozhaysk-10 and Machulische

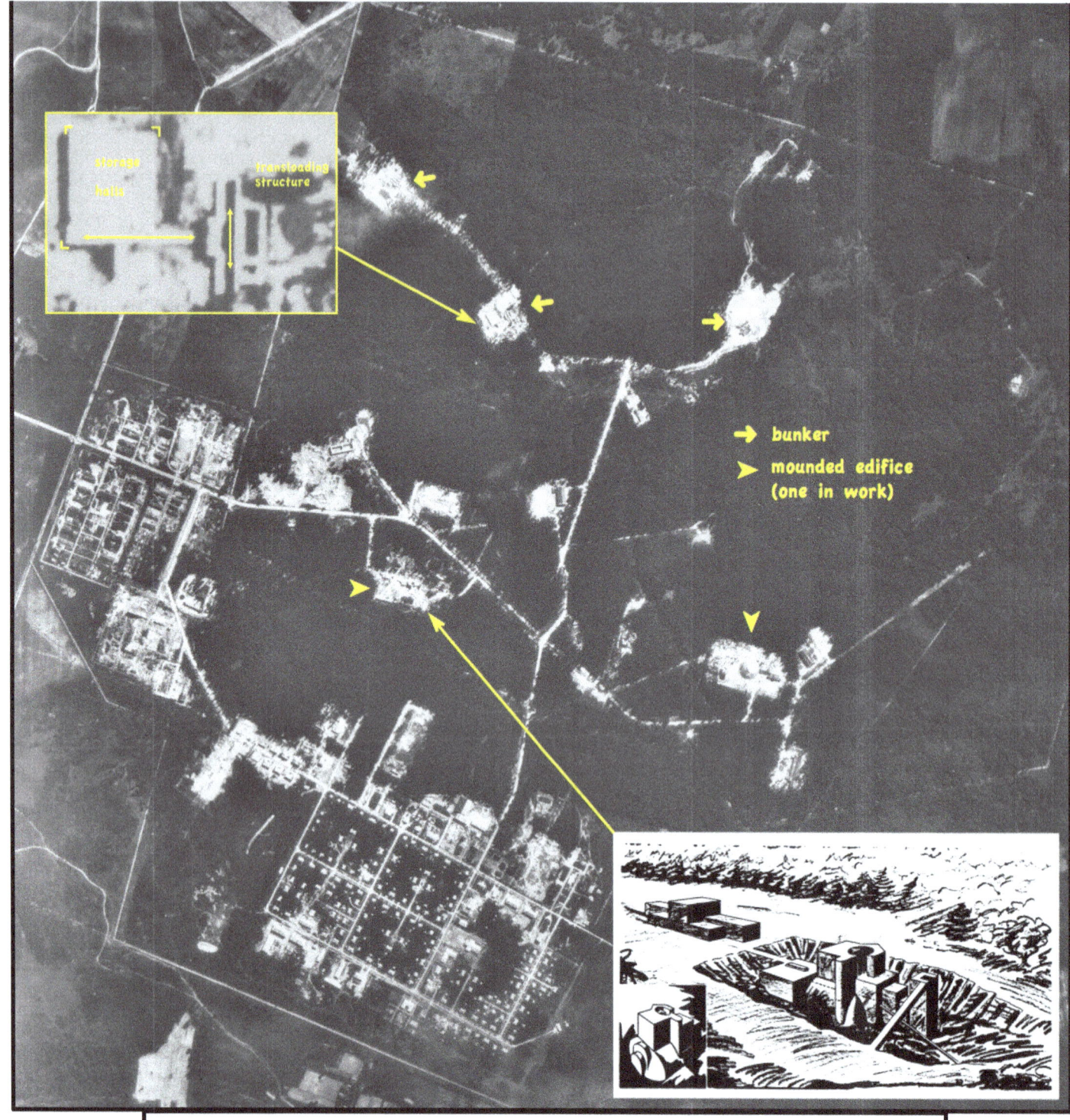

MOZHAYSK-10 1956
FINISHING TOUCHES BEING APPLIED WHEN IMAGED BY THE U-2 BUT THERE WOULD BE LATER ADDITIONS

Airfield, 560-km apart; Ivano-Frankivsk-16 and Stryy Airfield in the Southwestern TVD; and Feodosia-13 with the Veseloye air base in the (later redefined) Near East TVD. The last two pairs each positioned within 100-km. The potential TVD relationship had been unremarked in intelligence reporting throughout the Cold War. Attaining a theater-based perception might have clued intelligence that the mirrored US nuclear organization offered a poor fit for this particular Soviet reality. Thereby a misapprehension had been set that had direct consequences for the ability of intelligence to comprehend the significant innovation accomplished by the Soviets in the following decade. Intelligence connoisseurs could hardly arrive at an accurate assessment if they could not even fathom, much less start at, the first chapter.

Installation of the next iteration of RTBs transpired in the mid 1950s. Nine airfields, including the first non-western at Engels on the River Volga, received a singular bunker designated Type II. As with the Type I, subordinate to the Air Forces long range or to naval aviation, these bases hosted medium and heavy bomber aviation units. The unitary bunker design features indicated advances in nuclear bomb technology that had furthered a reduction in the number of separated components and more simplified assembly tasks that RTB crews could now carry out. All but one Type II had been earth-mounded by the time the U-2 got around to them. The 1956 coverage of Orsha Airfield revealed a finished massive concrete structure with overall dimensions of about 40-m by 20.5-m. Two thick walls that protruded above the storage section indicated three partitioned storage cells within. The characteristic mounded shape led the musically inclined to dub this design a 'guitar' bunker. Interior photos uploaded to the Internet in recent years confirm that arrangement and show the massive plug-type doors of each cell. The cells opened to a transverse elevated section, indicative of the presence of overhead hoist equipment suitable for maintaining the bomb inventory. At opposite ends of this section low passageways lead to portals. This elevated section signified an integrated workshop but all Type II sites also had a separate assembly-service building. Bomb preparation thus still required the accomplishment of extensive measures to attain the highest technical readiness stage.

Russian overviews of developments in the nuclear weapons complex fade out at this point, not addressing the Type II RTBs nor the subsequent expansion of Center reserves. Thereafter Russian accounts are more selective, dealing with specific RTBs or central objects. The increasing reticence may reflect the transfer of control implemented in the second half of the 1950s. Resolution 350-222 of the Central Committee CPSU and Council of Ministers dated 12 March 1956 ordered the MSM to hand over all nuclear storage sites and operational employment functions to the MoD; MSM-MO implementation proposals to be submitted, possibly during or at the end of 1956. But transfer fulfillment proved more complicated than anticipated. MO commissions created to review conditions found troubling deficiencies. In particular the weapon generation capability at central objects amounted to a daily one percent of site total inventory; this outloading rate deemed insufficient to meet operational calculations of the General Staff. Protection of "main entrances" appeared to be inadequate. US U-2 and later satellite imagery confirmed that unhardened transloading structures fronted both tunnel and bunker storage. The number of railcars and special vehicles at the sites could not meet transport requirements. Upgrades conducted during 1959-1960 would increase the daily generation rate by a factor of four or five, with incorporation in the design of future central objects.[1224]

Another Resolution of the CC CPSU-Council of Ministers dated 9 January 1958 had been necessary to finalize the transfer of nine central objects to the MO by 1 June 1958. A previous 23 September 1957 Resolution had ordered the transfer of two central objects by 1 February 1958[1225] accounting for a total of eleven central objects unless the later Resolution cumulated. The intelligence census of "national nuclear weapons stockpile sites" coincided with the uppermost. In addition to the original four those available at the end of the 1950s included later installations in arctic regions, the Urals, Siberia, and the Far East. Urals sites included pairs at the Sverdlovsk-45 weapons plant (one using unique 'pit' storage probably built in the late 1940s) and at the Trekhgorny or Zlatoust-36 (intelligence Yuryuzan) plant that came on line in August 1955.[1226] The Urals also hosted the standalone Chelyabinsk-115 (Karabash). The intelligence count would match the eleven of the Resolutions only if the seconds at the two plants had a post-dated development. The Trekhgorny plant had been built to fulfill a rapidly increasing demand in numbers and types of nuclear weapons. The Urals complexes also had to accomplish developing technical requirements for ensuring weapons reliability. Soviet nuclear weapons, upon formal acceptance by the MO, came with a ten-year warranty that could be renewed only after return to a plant for rebuilding.

The government-to-military transfer of the nuclear weapons complex represented at least one US-comparable organizational development. More details are, not surprisingly, available than for Soviet developments.[1227] A serpentine road to full DoD control had been marked by bureaucratic infighting as much as defense priorities. Whether the actual Soviet transfer to military control went more smoothly or the details are just hidden, completion took place years before the US managed the jurisdictional adjustment. The 1946 Atomic Energy Act assigned the Atomic Energy Commission full oversight of nuclear weapons design, manufacture, custody, military applications and the AEC absorbed the Manhattan Project. An Armed Forces Special Weapons Project created early in the next year connected via a liaison element to the AEC. Only in 1950 did the DoD gain access to weapons but restricted to the non-nuclear components while the 'nuclear capsules' remained in AEC hands; this decision applied to overseas locations and permitted in order to accelerate weapons technical readiness. Service-dedicated Operational Storage Sites appeared subsequent to six National Stockpile Sites established from 1947 to 1955. These shared jurisdiction, with a gradual phaseout of the AEC presence. In the mid 1950s the divide again altered, from components to yield, with the AEC retaining all weapons greater than 600-kt. On 3 January 1959 President Eisenhower approved the transfer of all "dispersed" nuclear weapons to the DoD (nearly three years following the initial Soviet decision), including the high yields, but this allocation left about eighteen percent of the total stockpile still under AEC control. Only in the 10 March 1967 Stockpile Agreement did the AEC surrender all nuclear weapons to military control.

A memoir by retired general V. A. Anastasiev provides some interesting tidbits that include peacetime activities of the central objects.[1228] His account outlined a 32 year career in the Soviet nuclear archipelago which began in July 1955 with courses on 'special products' held at KB-11. He then received an assignment to one of the two new assembly teams. Upon the transfer of all the teams to central objects he, by the end of that year, entered duty in the Crimea at 712 *objekt* C. Anastasiev participated in the transfer of a nuclear bomb to the airfield near Kerch-Bagerovo (the development center for aircraft nuclear delivery techniques) which had been mounted on an unspecified aircraft; flown to Engels Airfield; and then to the Semipalatinsk State Test Site 2; there dropped on 10 September 1956 set to air burst at 340-m. A later weapons transfer, date not given, involved the rail movement of 'products' in covered gondola cars; a change of railcar bogie sets to European gauge at Brest; across Poland; and into the northern GDR to an unspecified base near Fürstenberg. Similar deliveries had been made earlier to Pervomaysk, Balta, and Uman—all strategic missile deployment areas. Problems encountered with the chief of the recipient RTB resulted in his replacement. I have described the context of this event in a prior publication.[1229]

In early September 1962 Anastasiev had been tasked to transport six article 407N bombs—which could be delivered by the IL-28 light bomber—from the 712 *objekt* inventory for the official purpose of testing at the northern Novaya Zemlya range. An ideally remote arctic site had been established to test high yield thermonuclear devices not suitable to Semipalatinsk conditions. Soviet practice often removed selected nuclear weapons, missiles, and other armament from operational inventory to determine viability. At the northern port of Severomorsk 'products' loading took place on the cargo vessel *Indigirka*. Only when issued summer uniforms did awareness dawn on Anastasiev and his colleagues that their deployment would be to a tropical rather than arctic direction and that Operation Anadyr targeted Cuba. Nuclear support operated as an *objekt* C headed by Colonel N. K. Beloborodov (the commander of 713 *objekt* C whose own memoir lists Anastasiev among officers assigned to an Operations Group of the Center as well as involved in the aviation RTB in the Mariel region).[1230] Anastasiev describes the peregrination of the bombs, initially offloaded at the Mariel port into a nearby brick building, to a former ammunition storage tunnel in the mountains, and finally to an unspecified location closer to the IL-28 delivery aircraft base. The 407N bombs departed Cuba on the morning of 1 December aboard the vessel *Arkhangelsk* voyaging back to Severomorsk. Thus a full month after the 'official' ending of the missile crisis six weapons of up to 12-kt for platforms capable of striking the southeastern US remained on hand. The bombs eventually routed back to the Crimea.

By 1966 Anastasiev had been reassigned to another central storehouse complex at a location not specified. But from his description of the, greater variety than at the Crimean *objekt*, the signature facilities can only have been at one of the Urals factory pairs. This likelihood is reinforced by his next assignment on 8 March 1973 to the command of a "twin brother" which had the same arrangement of support structures to include identical building numbers. A final appointment on 28 April 1975 returned Anastasiev to the western USSR to command 711 *objekt* C—he does not specify this location but some of the incidentals related affirm.

U-2 imagery had revealed the pre-mounted exterior forms of some bunkers, and external features of underground structures, at the central complexes. Interiors of a few other bunkers had been observed under construction. However sampling had been insufficient to establish any typing schedule. A varied set of unhardened buildings for weapons assembly, components processing, and servicing accompanied bunkered storage at the central sites. This array of support structures represented the early nuclear weapons design and build technology in which the military users retained substantial assembly tasks after distribution by industry. These complexes broadly typified the Soviet munitions system in which military customers had responsibility for final assembly of components acquired from manufacturing plants. The basic outline of facilities and structures for what constituted a "national nuclear weapons stockpile site" (a.k.a central *objekt*) had been established during the 1950s.

At the end of the 1950s the Soviets set in motion a massive expansion that would dwarf in scale and intricacy what had already been accomplished. New RTBs established introduced a revised bunker, the intelligence Type III. Transition had been demarcated by two new airfield sites that had obviously been laid out as Type II but then fitted with the Type III bunker. This new design essentially modified the Type II in two major aspects for storage and environmental control; with a mirrored, three-cell wing placed opposite the original; while an intervening hall, roof elevated to fit an overhead traveling hoist, provided a servicing area to process and maintain the nuclear inventory. Soviet personnel reported observing nuclear-technical officers at work stations in this hall. Early intelligence reporting described the resultant shape, sacrilegiously, as cruciform, with overall dimensions of about 58-m by 52-m. There had also been an obvious utilities (HVAC in civil parlance) augmentation evidenced by a new annex and multiple vents. Rooms accommodated a substantial air filtration system and standby diesel generators, also described by servicemen, and now open to visitation. Such annexes and vents had not been observed at either the Type II or the bunkers at central sites built in the 1950s. Debut of the Type III coincided with the introduction of a new variety of center *objekt*, complexes which featured radically altered bunker designs and similar environmental control emphasis—all promulgating a revolution in Soviet military strategy.

Some 62 Type III bunkers appeared from 1959 into the early 1960s. Construction of several others had been aborted, not earth-mounded, or modified for other uses. The Soviet cookie cutter stamped out slightly more than half in, satellite imagery-friendly, standard layouts with two Type III bunkers at opposite ends of a narrow rectangular secured facility. A large, separate and standard, service building located roughly in a central position indicated that Soviet weapons technology still required continuous intercession. The Soviets installed this common layout near airfields and even typeset one at central *objekt* 714. Individual Type III bunkers also backfilled all of the existing Type I and II airfield RTBs and one even showed up at 713 *objekt* C. Unlike the previous Types, however, deployment extended beyond the Soviet Air Forces.

The Type III also became the first official nuclear bunker at new RTBs established in support of the Ground Troops missile arm. Four Type III appeared, individually, at front missile-artillery bases. Several of the airfield standard Type III RTBs would later be modified as ground army-level RTBs when this support level debuted. The new form of Soviet missile troops, those of strategic designation, also received Type III. As nuclear weapons introduction proceeded into all the Soviet armed forces, and the RVSN organized, the Type schedule began to break down. The Soviets fielded bunker designs in greater variety than the basic US intelligence classification system could accommodate. Service requirements, particularly for the increasingly complex payloads of intercontinental missiles, resulted in divergent design paths. Cross-fertilization continued between ground, aviation, and air defense forces. New bunker genera subsequently identified encompassed not only airfields, but also central bases, strategic missile and national air defense positions, and ground missile, RTBs. Even the Engineer Troops eventually erected their edition for, at least nuclear, demolition devices. Separate intelligence schedules then devised basically trailed services but deviant configurations would continue to appear that the nuclear specialists could not neatly fit into the categories of accepted Types. Meanwhile the Navy continued tunneling.

Anomalous to the evolving pattern the Type III, despite the accelerating divergence of bunker designs, appeared at RVSN RTBs. Seven of the cookie-cut Type III layout had been added to as many strategic missile arsenals. All of these RTBs remained under construction through 1963, at least one started in 1959. Some of these arsenals had been built for the initial Soviet accumulation of airframe reserves. According to Russian sources the 19 September 1951 USSR Council of Ministers resolution 3540-1647 ordered the establishment of four missile stores as well as the organization of four new RVGK special purpose brigades (two such missile brigades already existed). Each arsenal sizing would accommodate 250 of the first native missile design, the R-1 (SS-1a Scunner), actually a modified German V-2—located near Minsk (at Kolosovo, intelligence Novaya Mezinovka); Staraya Toropa (Toropets); Mikhaylenki (Berdichev); and Karia-Stroganovo (Tambov), apparently already under construction.[1231] All but one of these installations had been covered by the U-2 with varying degrees of completeness. However not until the early 1960s did their missile purposing dawn on intelligence. Eventually the seven missile arsenals transferred to the RVSN. Single Type III also had been built at four ICBM complexes and at least one test center, Plesetsk.

Intelligence evinced no particular interest regarding this odd admixture of service designs, basically general purpose and strategic. Of course no one had been aware that at least one strategic missile system, the widely deployed SS-4, had a chemical warhead option that had been fielded coincidently in the early 1960s with that of shorter range missile systems—and those Type III bunkers. Perhaps had this strategic missile capability been known that rare intelligence breed, the inquisitive, might have raised questions as to what support echelon held a potentially large number of strategic chemical warheads; as well as how and where these might be stored. The infrastructure of strategic missile installations, whether support or delivery unit bases, did not exactly exhibit a profusion of alternative candidates.

Construction of these varied, yet service- and weapon-affiliated, bunker designs, provided the US with a useful identification tool enhancing evaluation of military forces. Ironically, if the Soviets had adopted the American across-the-board approach using plain-jane igloos, much of the intelligence value would have been buried. The US and allied intelligence services had been attempting to penetrate one of the most opaque, difficult targets in modern history using the methods available, and acceptable, to Western democracies. Incredibly the ultimate security State actively provided the designated main enemy with an abundance of evidence that could be used to delineate their military capabilities and plans. The Soviets with their discriminative approach to strategic

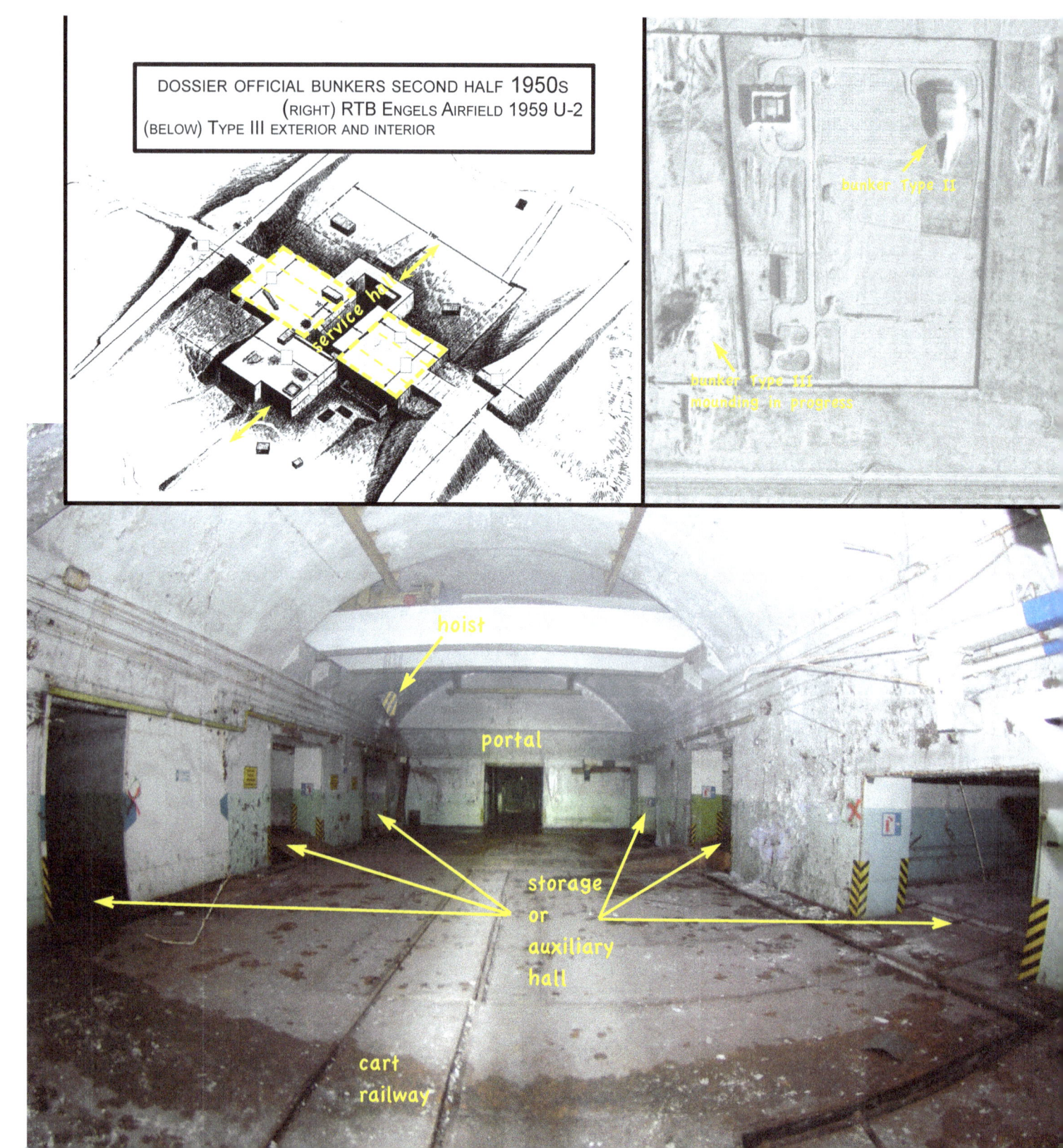

protection directly assisted in the definition of their mass destruction weapons, the most significant element, by openly advertising to one of the great strengths of US intelligence—satellite imagery. The arcane practice of bunkerology during three decades afforded intelligence unique insights not obtainable from other sources.

These signature bunker designs may have been a Soviet gift to US intelligence but also presented an, inadvertent, Trojan offering. As the observers became comfortable with, and self-conditioned to, reliance on such indicators, an Official Bunker Model-Nuclear Edition took hold. This trend had been accentuated when the meandering paths of illogic followed in the US intelligence maze had bestowed ultimate authority for deciding nuclear support questions upon the science-technology directorates in the CIA and the DIA—just as in the case of chemical. However worthy the skills of specialists in these offices regarding technical aspects of mass destruction weapons this issue ownership guaranteed a perspective shorn of wider organizational-operational considerations. CIA-DIA nuclear connoisseurs viewed their Soviet bunkers as if sacred objects, and as the high-priests of a bunker cult in which only they qualified as interpreters of meaning. Nuclear weapons could be stored only in categorized bunkers, representing an exclusive franchise—with a perceptual corollary—the bounds of conceptualization did not sanction the presence of other brands of WMD. Disregarding the consistent and persistent coupling of at least nuclear and chemical weapons evident in Soviet classified documents from 1959 to 1974—a massive trove of evidence of the second kind—nuclear connoisseurs embraced the fetish methodology as readily as did their colleagues in the chemical cubicles. A rigid perspective developed that would pose a fine analytic trap.

Bunkers had starring roles in many Cold War feature films. Among the multitude of data points which US intelligence attempted to discriminate the convoluted tale of the "Arys-type chemical warhead storage bunker"[1232] is worth recovering—and emblematic of the intell aggregation process. Arys is a town in what is now an independent Kazakhstan but in the Soviet era composed an important military logistics complex in the Turkestan MD. During reworking of the military structure opposite the erstwhile Marxist-Leninist colleagues in China this area split off in 1969 as part of a new Central Asian district. During the 1950s US intelligence desperate search for any information regarding an impenetrable USSR, German records captured in 1945 had been plumbed for useful tidbits. An interrogation of a Soviet general taken prisoner in 1941, found and disseminated in 1954 as an intelligence report,[1233] provided a detailed description of installations in the Arys vicinity—including a segregated depot for artillery chemical rounds stored in three brick buildings.

When this area had been imaged by U-2 aircraft missions in 1957, the general's description of facilities eventuated to be quite accurate to include the pinpointing of the chemical shells depot. Of additional interest these photos disclosed two separate rows of cylinders potentially capable of holding bulk chemical agent at this depot. In a prewar listing of chemical stores by a Russian environmentalist this is likely the Arys depot 415 or 42;[1234] a witness reported that from 1946 to 1948 Arys had been the site of disposal in pits of "great quantities" of mustard agent from tanks and bombs including stocks shipped in from at least one chemical service base and a plant.[1235]

Testimony from this general had been the starting point for one of the inputs on a map in the NIE 11-10-63 *Soviet Capabilities and Intentions with Respect to Chemical Warfare*[1236] identifying Arys among only ten "probable storage sites" within the USSR (none westward and some of which would become official "chemical depots"). Text concerning "one suspect tactical guided missile depot" with "especially designed buildings" refers. In 1963-1964 the new satellite imaging constellation had revealed that opposite ends of this rectangular depot had sprouted (what would later be designated) the Type IX Official Nuclear Bunker. As one of the earliest identifications of the bunker and, in the clear desert air, best looks, led to initial dubbing as the Arys bunker. In an application of the popular intelligence guilt-by-association methodology the view arose that, because twin bunkers had been constructed at a location with prior credible evidence of chemical weapons storage, one bunker held chemical and the other nuclear warheads. Another observable at Arys considered chemically indicative derived from the absence of a separate unhardened building, found at earlier-constructed bases, supposed to function as nuclear warhead servicing. For several years this pairing had been promoted by some to be a chemical indicator for missile warheads.

Unfortunately for the model, when the Soviets began inserting many more of this type during the 1960s, most appeared at missile support bases with only one warhead bunker—thus breaking the pairing—while none of these had separate service buildings. This later construction program had in reality marked the introduction of ground army-level RTBs. A 1969 imagery study debunked the non-presence of the service building as a valid chemical indicator by plotting the chronology of bases construction and pointing out that this separate structure had been a characteristic of the earliest built, disappearing after a certain date. Thus, the study concluded, the Soviets had eliminated the requirement for a separate structure to conduct nuclear weapons maintenance; and, therefore, lack of the service building did not necessarily indicate the storage of chemical warheads. That the features in dispute, and the chronological break point, alternatively distinguished front-level bases from the new breed introduced to support individual ground armies constituted...evidence of the second kind—all of which already had been conveniently laid out in the classified documents that had been provided by Oleg Penkovsky. The lack of the service building might rather

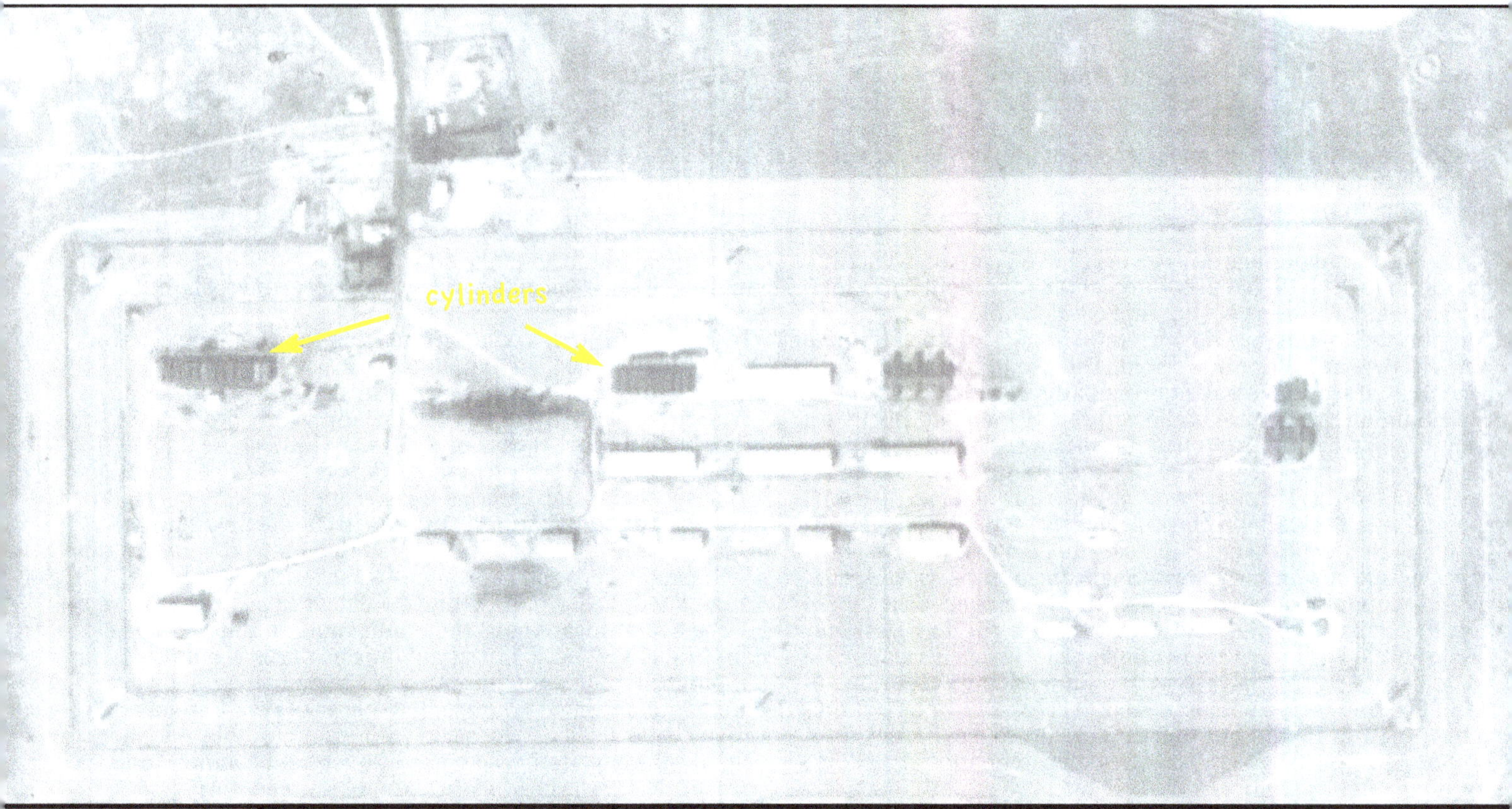

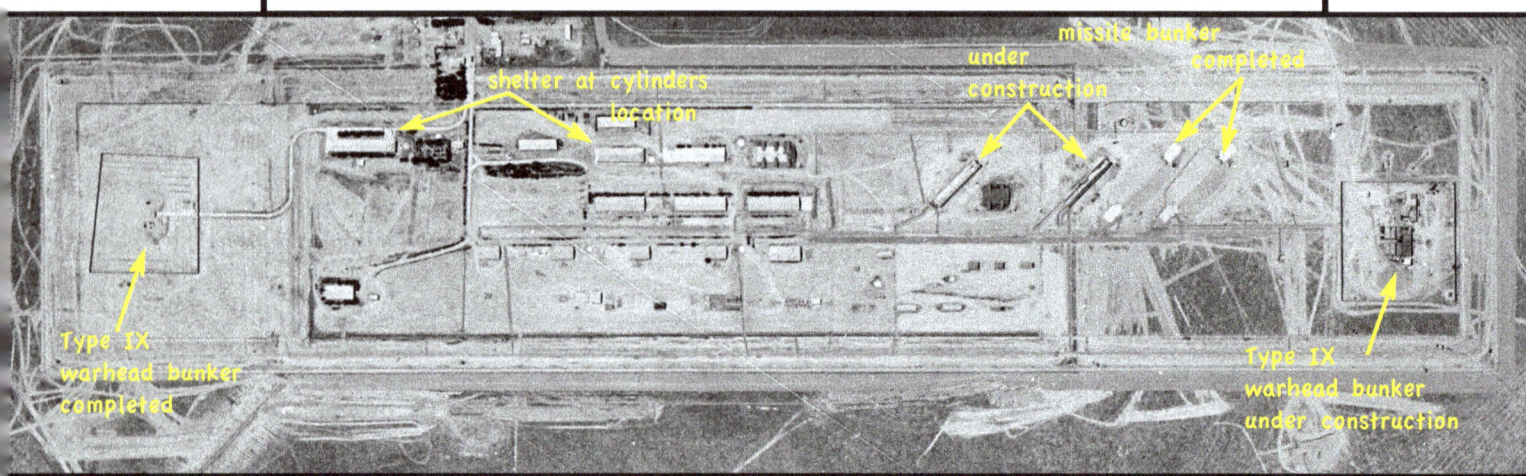

ARYS CHEMICAL DEPOT
ALTERATIONS BETWEEN 1957 (TOP) AND 1965 TRANSFORMING INTO FRONT MISSILE-ARTILLERY BASE

have been related to echeloned military district/front versus army maintenance capabilities. But Soviet writings had not been consulted by the participants involved in the muddle and the missile support hierarchy had not yet been delineated. Nor did anybody notice that the Type IX design already incorporated an elevated central section that would permit the fitting of an overhead hoist for servicing work just as in Types II and III.

So at the end of the 1960s this particular bunker had been discredited as a chemical indicator. Type IXs became one of the most common official warhead bunkers (34 completions) supporting missile systems of the Ground Troops within the USSR. Oddly, despite such a widespread deployment, none of this Type would ever be identified in support of the self-same Soviet missile troops in Central Europe. Any model that might thenceforth be proposed entailing the storage of chemical weapons at official nuclear sites or in their bunkers became untenable. The Arys depot that had been transformed into a support base for missiles with a known CW delivery mission had an historical association with chemical munitions as fully credible as the lineage of the "chemical depots" of the official chemical model. But this heritage did not prevent Arys from being erased from the list of chemical suspects.

## bunkers rebus

In the 1960s occurred a significant amplification of the bunker network. In particular from 1959 to 1961 construction began, in two distinct waves separated by about two years, on ten complexes in the Western Theater. Deployed in an arc from the northwestern USSR to Ukraine SSR, these bases formed a geographic headsman's axe—aimed at the body of Europe. Upon insertion in 1965 of an additional Ukrainian central base, 53 massive bunkers of varied but unique designs would be built at the eleven bases. Individual bunkers required up to three years to complete. These places would soon instigate an intelligence flap, a duel of incompatible models reading from the same evidence. Intelligence conceptualization of the purpose of this wide-ranging scheme would be constrained by the solidifying official nuclear bunker model and the double-tiered nuclear organizational perspective. An eventuating perspective edited out any consideration of evolving concepts of Soviet military doctrine, theater operation variants and, even, the scale and nature of envisioned mass destruction weapons employment.

Reconnaissance missions from 1956 into 1960—U-2 overflights, aircraft peripheral look-sees, the ill-fated Genetrix balloon project—had imaged, with varying degrees of completeness and quality, nine (one each of two factory pairs) Main Directorate central bases. These exhibited common, largely standardized, elements. Loss of the relatively high resolution capability of the U-2 as a result of the Powers debacle in May 1960 engendered a 'collection gap' that would be only partially remedied when the Corona low resolution satellite, the first of the KH-series, began returning usable photographs in the early 1960s. The new bases had been detected and eventually tagged as national nuclear weapons stockpiles. One identified actually turned out to be an addition to the bunker menagerie—a national command complex. In the fall of 1963 five installations had come under suspicion as new nuclear weapons stockpiles but including the Chaadayevka reserve command post;[1237] by early 1964 eight installations had been identified on the basis of common features but this group still included Chaadayevka;[1238] de-listed more than two years later.[1239] Co-identification of the bases derived from installation layout features that appeared to be similar to those at the accepted nuclear stockpiles as far as could be discerned from the limited resolution of Corona photography. That confident appraisal shattered, however, when a new generation of high resolution imaging satellites inaugurated with the KH-7 Gambit in mid 1963. These optical tools permitted examination of structural details of the bunkers while under construction as well as other aspects of the bases.

Boosted imagery acuity by the mid 1960s revealed strange, elaborate structures with layouts that differed radically from those of the bunkers seen at national stockpile sites built in the 1950s. Eight configurations would eventually be identified, necessitating a new classification schedule, with design variants designated by letters from the Greek alphabet. Each base always had two of the bunker designs, in similar numbers, and seemingly in fixed ratios; as well as identical pairing of Alpha and Beta, Delta-Gamma, Eta-Theta, and Delta II-Iota. Their labyrinthine architecture appeared so startling and unprecedented that by 1966 the DIA and certain other intelligence agencies began to challenge the assumed nuclear weapons stockpile function. These offices noted that, when completed, total storage capacity at national sites would exceed by a factor of three or more that deemed necessary even for the intelligence community projected deployment of Soviet nuclear delivery systems. Nevertheless the CIA led the way in insisting on adhering to the national nuclear weapons storage flavor. In typical intelligence fudging mode the sites in dispute segregated as SOCs—sensitive operations complexes. Disagreement focused on the singular question—what is the purpose of the SOCs? The differing perspectives clashed through the second half of the 1960s, escalating into one of the most significant intelligence controversies of the Cold War. But argumentation became entangled by the politics of US defense which emerged during late 1950s 'missile gap' posturing.

The winged component of the Armed Forces assisted DIA connoisseurs in persistently attempting to pin a missile label on these enigmas. Their model, of course, represented a forthright alternative proposition in the finest tradition of intelligence dissent, unrelated to that service's concurrent programmatic drive to expand US strategic missile deployment. More skeptical observers might have pondered

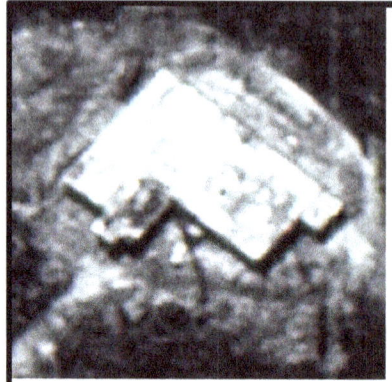 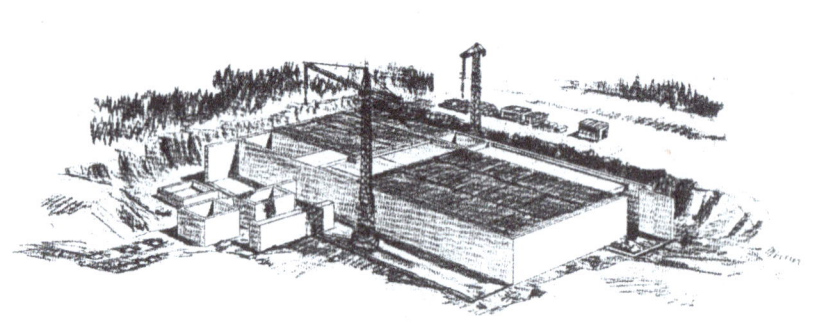

**SOC Gamma bunker under construction**
**Intelligence artist drawing**
18 of this most prevalent design would be completed

## IV. STORAGE AND CONTROL OF SOVIET NUCLEAR WEAPONS

### Storage

34. Soviet nuclear weapons storage includes two general classes of storage sites: national reserve stockpile facilities, and operational storage sites at military bases in direct support of military operations. National reserve stockpile sites are characterized by isolation, extreme security, hardened bunkers, and self-sufficiency in housing and service support. The operational military storage sites associated with military bases are usually located apart from other base facilities and are characterized by stringent physical security measures. Their design has been different in each stage of the stockpile program; most of the earlier sites have been modified by the addition of a bunker of more recent design. In the event of war, the initial needs of Soviet forces for nuclear weapons would be met by the operational storage sites. The national reserve stockpile installations are intended to provide strategic reserve and direct support to the operational sites. Some national sites are located near the borders and could provide direct support to Soviet forces in the area. In addition to the weapons stored at these locations, we believe that sizable numbers of nuclear weapons are deployed with certain operational forces, including the Strategic Rocket Forces, missile-equipped surface ships, and missile submarines.

35. *Sensitive Operations Complexes.* There are 10 large, self-contained, highly secured, military installations located throughout the European USSR which we call Sensitive Operations Complexes (SOCs). Each complex has extensive railroad and motor transport facilities and extensive operations and support areas. They have been under construction since the late 1950's; the first probably became operational in the mid-1960's. The rail and rail-to-road transfer facilities and high degree of security at the SOCs lead us to believe that one function of the SOCs may be nuclear weapons storage. On the other hand, the extensive operations and support areas at the SOCs indicate that they perform operations in addition to nuclear weapons storage, and that these additional activities may, in fact, be an important purpose of the SOCs; some of these activities may be missile associated.

36. The functions of these complexes remain unclear. We believe that one explanation of the purpose of the SOCs is that they are rear area storage and maintenance bases for the support of operational forces. In this role they could support a number of Soviet nuclear missile delivery systems, providing storage, checkout, retrofit, and repair of nuclear weapons and other critical items. Their location and spacing is such that they could give support to Soviet fronts defending the main approaches to the European USSR from the West.

**NIE 11-2-67 *Soviet Atomic Energy Programs* 15 June 1967**
US intelligence perspective on the SOCs would never be rectified

whether this dissenting perspective represented yet another case of intelligence assessment embroiled with a dissociated weapons advocacy that exploited every opportunity to amplify military threat. In the first half of the 1960s a rapidly expanding US deployment of ICBMs had been under way, originally conceived as a response to the prior intelligence 'missile gap' mis-assessment. In the 1960 presidential campaign candidate John Kennedy and his associates had pilloried opponent Richard Nixon for dereliction in regard to a US missile deployment supposedly lagging that of the USSR.[1240] The dispute had adhered to the American political ritual of believers pursuing self-serving agendas lacking any basis in reality.

The new defense secretary, wunderkind Robert McNamara, has stated that following his 20 January 1961 arrival half of the topical business during the first three weeks regarded the 'missile gap' priority.[1241] Examination of the actual evidence, mainly from the new imaging reconnaissance satellites, confirmed a yawning gap—the US had 28 operational Atlas ICBMs by early 1961 (on the way to 78 by the end of 1962 when augmented by the Titan ICBM)[1242] while the Soviets had…four confirmed ICBMs.[1243] An August 1960 NIE had given widely varying Soviet ICBM numbers, with mid 1960 estimates by the CIA (30) and US Air Force (35) nearly in agreement but diverging mid 1961 projections of 150 and 200 respectively. Other intelligence associates came in with significantly fewer operational launchers.[1244] The solidity of the evidence behind this work initially approximated that of the Soviet chemical estimate except that the missile census, unlike CW, eventually achieved a high level of credibility.

Questions regarding the scale of the envisioned US missile deployment began to be raised by the Secretary and his number crunchers. In December 1964 McNamara imposed a cap that cut to nearly a third the land-based ICBM force that had been requested by the Air Force.[1245] Thereupon USAF chiefs and their political allies pummeled this decision. The ceiling for the authorized number of installed missiles would be hit circa 1967—and along came the SOCs. Any intelligence 'finding' that these specters represented a bold new Soviet move in the missile arena would have been welcomed by US proponents of resuming the momentum of the strategic deployment. A 1967 NIE framed the intelligence perceptual waffling.[1246] The field had been opened to alternative solutions and the NIE had ventured about as closely as intelligence would ever get to an inclusive answer.

More than three contentious years would elapse before the CIA had accumulated sufficient analytic cudgels to beat back other scenarios and re-impose the official nuclear-bunker model. The Office of Scientific Intelligence examined the contending hypotheses in the seminal early 1970 assessment *The Major Function of the Soviet Sensitive Operations Complexes*.[1247] In the record of intelligence diligence during the next three decades this report would be the only foundational investigation of the SOCs and consideration of alternative models. By then a twelfth SOC had been identified under construction facing the fraternal Chinese comrades. Propositions accumulated briefly examined and dismissed involved command-control, civil defense, and manufacturing or storage of military materiel. But most discussion concerned the missile model that had been "considered…at some length" by intelligence agencies, not only as bases for missile storage but also for rail-mobile ICBMs. Virtually all the evidence cited had been obtained from satellite imagery; unusually for a declassified publication details of the little available COMINT is not redacted. Nuclear links proffered included the most telling—the Soviets had assisted by adding a single Delta at three of the 1950s bases previously accepted as national nuclear weapons stockpiles thereby confirming related functioning.

The CIA report, however, had failed to explore another potential model. The apparently significant "definite numerical ratio" of two differing bunker designs evident at each and every SOC suggested two rationales. One type might be used for storage and the second for maintenance; that this solution is effectively negated by the independent construction of Delta bunkers at three non-SOC bases, thereby breaking the pairing, did not get a mention. The Summary put forward another solution, that the ratio "could also indicate collocated storage of other weapons" reiterated in the Discussion "The possibility that other weapons are collocated with nuclear weapons also cannot be ruled out at this time." What these other weapons might be is not given the status of an alternative hypothesis, indeed is not even addressed. After all the title of the report, *Major Function*, implies that the new official model might be incomplete. Even as late as 1971, despite having assigned a nuclear role to the SOCs, there remained lingering uncertainty concerning the possibility of other missions as indicated by a puzzled statement in an updated *Soviet Nuclear Programs* NIE.[1248]

> The storage of nuclear weapons is probably only one of the functions of the 12 so-called "sensitive operations complexes". They differ from the national reserve stockpile sites in several respects. We are not able to determine what other functions these complexes may have.

Already ventured had been an observation that scale and complexity might indicate the bunkers did not hold only nuclear weapons, in particular in the wording of one 1968 report "the need for two dissimilar bunker types is difficult to rationalize for only nuclear weapons."

But the SOC account would be closed and filed away by the early 1970s. A conceptual model of nuclear exclusivity remained in effect for the duration of the Cold War. The progenitor of contention—the why of the bunker design elaboration and differentiation—had not been resolved. That question would never again be confronted. The 1960s disputation, a collision of incompatible models, would only be dimly remembered by gradually exiting nuclear veterans who passed on only the official conclusion to those who followed. When I took introductory intelligence courses in early 1973 (spoon-fed the official intelligence view on WMD and other subjects) the SOCs received treatment as co-equal nuclear partners of the preceding national stockpile sites. What appeared to an earlier generation to be a radical innovation had now become perceptually merged. Institutional memory had expunged the SOC controversy. Within a few years I developed a particular interest in WMD—in a unified perception—only when delving into the archives of nuclear intelligence reporting and pinging the memory of those participants still around that the earlier dispute could be reconstructed. Drilling down the buried, forgotten, layers of intelligence reporting and evidence while studying WMD issues raised questions that led me to reopen that SOC dossier.

CONFIDENTIAL

PAGE 01    GENEVA  07785  01 OF 04  231713Z
ACTION ACDA-12

INFO   OCT-00
       AF-10     COPY-01 ADS-00
       ARA-16    CIAE-00 EA-10
       OES-09    NSAE-00        INR-10
                 USIE-00 L-03   H-01    EUR-12   SS-10
                         SP-02  PM-08   IO-15    NEA-06   OIC-02
                                SNP-01  PA-01    PRS-01   NSC-01
                         ----------114754  231720Z /44   TFC-01   SAL-01
                                                         /133 W

P 231704Z AUG 83
FM USMISSION GENEVA
TO SECSTATE WASHDC PRIORITY
INFO JCS WASHDC
SECDEF WASHDC
DOE WASHDC
USCINCEUR VAIHINGEN
USNMR SHAPE
CINCUSAFE RAMSTEIN
AMEMBASSY BONN
AMEMBASSY LONDON
AMEMBASSY MOSCOW
AMEMBASSY PARIS
USMISSION USNATO
USMISSION USUN NEW YORK

C O N F I D E N T I A L  SEC

JCS- FOR J-5/DDIN; SECDEF F

E.O. 12356: DECL: OADR
TAGS: PARM, UNGA, CDG, UR
SUBJECT: COMMITTEE ON DISARMAMENT (CD): SOVIET
PLENARY STATEMENT ON CHEMICAL WEAPONS (CW)
AUGUST 18, 1983

1.  THIS IS CD-261.  (C-ALL COMMENT SECTIONS).

1.  SUMMARY.  IN A PLENARY STATEMENT ON AUGUST 18, SOVIET
CD REP (AMB. ISSRAELYAN) ATTACKED THE U.S. BINARY
CONFIDENTIAL

CONFIDENTIAL

PAGE 02    GENEVA  07785  01 OF 04  231713Z
CHEMICAL WEAPONS PROGRAM, QUESTIONED SERIOUSNESS
OF U.S. INTEREST IN A CW BAN, PRESSED FOR DRAFTING
OF TREATY TEXT, AND DISCUSSED SEVERAL SUBSTANTIVE
ISSUES.  WITH RESPECT TO CW STOCKPILES, HE INDICATED

STOCKPILES AND COMPOSITION OF THE STOCKS AT EACH
LOCATION.
-
C.  STOCKPILE MONITORING.  PROPOSALS FOR DECLARATION
OF STOCKPILE LOCATIONS ARE "PURELY UNILATERAL AND
UNREALISTIC," DO NOT TAKE INTO ACCOUNT "POSSIBLE
UNIVERSITY OF THE STORAGES WHERE CHEMICAL WEAPONS
ARE KEPT, AND MAY AFFECT THE DEFENSE INTERESTS" NOT
RELATED TO CW.  (COMMENT:  IN PRIVATE CONVERSATION
SOVIET OFFICIAL POINTED TO THE "POSSIBILITY" THAT
CHEMICAL WEAPONS COULD BE STORED AT THE SAME LOCATION
AS NUCLEAR WEAPONS.  END COMMENT) THE SOVIET UNION
"PROPOSES" THAT, TO PROVIDE RELIABLE VERIFICATION,
STOCKPILE VERIFICATION STORAGE SITES COULD BE CREATED
AT STOCKPILE DESTRUCTION SITES.  THE LOCATIONS OF THESE
SPECIAL STORAGE SITES AND THE DESTRUCTION FACILITIES
WOULD BOTH BE DECLARED AT THE SAME TIME.  FURTHERMORE,
"AT SUCH STORAGE INTERNATIONAL VERIFICATION ON THE
BASIS OF QUOTA WOULD BE PERMITTED DURING THE ENTIRE
PERIOD OF THE DESTRUCTION OF THE DECLARED STOCKS."

# Hypothesis X

The structural features of the SOCs, bunker arrangements and variegated designs as exhibited in satellite imagery, constituted the only available source for determining purpose. The SOC system exhibited evidence—the third kind—of itself. Information obtained from other intelligence tools as perceived by the nuclear connoisseurs did not elucidate an (unabridged) answer to the crucial question of mission(s). Consideration of imagery indications such as multifarious bunker designs, numbers, and ratios, as well as officially related signals and human intelligence information endured perceptually constrained. The system blueprint remained inaccessible to US intelligence. But unrecognized had been clues of both the second and third kinds, all literally in full view, and consequently potential connections had not been explored. The nuclear cubicles conjured these specters (along with other classes of Soviet bunkers) as if meteorites, objects fallen to earth, devoid of encircling and interconnected relationships.

Someone in the US delegation at the 1983 Geneva session on chemical weapons had demonstrated an initiative concerning Ambassador Israelyan's universality statement entirely absent from the intelligence sector. That person followed up during the informal contacts that accompany such negotiations, and reported the results in a US Mission Geneva cable to Washington dated 23 August 1983.[1249]

> COMMENT: In private conversation Soviet official pointed to the "possibility" that chemical weapons could be stored at the same location as nuclear weapons.

This cable had a listed dissemination to more than 30 offices and entities that included major players such as the National Security Council, the CIA and NSA, INR, the Department of Energy (also in the intell game), and military, headed by the Defense Secretary and Joint Chiefs of Staff. The intelligence reaction to this deafening statement both at the time and thereafter right up to the 1997 US formal ratification of the Chemical Weapons Convention had been an inexplicable silence. The unidentified official might well have been Israelyan who had conducted Soviet chemical arms negotiations for several years. In a 1979 bilateral discussion he attributed lack of progress to issue complexity "inextricably linked to other activities of state"[1250]—no one took this hint either.

The intensive and extensive imagery surveillance that has been conducted over the globe furnishes what is currently one of the few practical time machines (archaeological stratigraphy and various dating techniques along with genetic testing also work if over rather longer periods). The pictorial record of the USSR compiled during more than three decades fostered cross-referencing of interesting objects with potentially related strategic developments; a capability of significant importance during phases involving adjustments and innovations. Eluding analytical sight lines had been the possibility that SOC bunkers both as to design as well as installed genera might represent, rather than merely static repositories, an implementation of particular operational solutions. This situation, involving the inability to incorporate, or even recognize, remote indications persisted an all-to-frequent intelligence cognitive failure; yet another analytic floundering revolving about evidence of the third kind.

Among the, seemingly obvious, transferences for installations built in a concerted program that began in 1959 and extended through the 1960s might be the parallel development of the WMD Operation. A scheme that coupled at least nuclear and chemical weapons on the battlefield during a "nuclear period" had been composed during exactly the same timeframe. This is not a relating of one or the other endeavor to the Bolshoi Ballet. Each synchronous innovation centered on mass destruction weapons thereby instantly constraining the range of possible connections. Most of the modern chemical armament for that operation became available only with the beginning of sarin production in 1959. SOCs, the concept of joint WMD operations, agent technology developments, and other nuclear-chemical coincidences did not represent an apples and oranges and tomatoes and blueberries comparison but could have been inextricably linked. Such an integrated mechanism for applying mass destruction weapon variants in theater operations provided a demonstrable basis for a Soviet official to state "chemical weapons could be stored at the same location as nuclear weapons" in 1983. But somehow perception did not dawn, during three decades, to the connoisseurs of intelligence that a thoroughgoing exploration of possible linkages might be opportune. They proved incapable of achieving the unities essential to good answers—concept, evidence, time, and place.

The official nuclear model acted as an obscurant of indicative evidence of the third kind that had been a proximate visual corroboration of purpose. Three SOC imagery observables in addition to those identified by intelligence—inscribed in space and time—can be discerned as well as indicative bunker architectural manifestations. These indications when cross-referenced to broader considerations of Soviet doctrine, precepts, theater planning, and the nature of the WMD Operation directed attention toward a radically different model—an hypothesis entirely removed from the official universe. If any one or more of these observables had been noticed by specialists during the SOC controversy, no significance had been then attributed, and their successors no longer curious about the details. To solve the SOC problem required meticulous consideration of a wide spectrum of evidence from the architectural details of bunkers to the architecture of Soviet military strategy and everything between, including military organization and relationships as well as WMD technical aspects. This wide range of potentially related variables and their subsets exceeded the capacity of the intelligence analytic culture to break through perceptual bounds and to unify disparate evidence.

The three observables evinced a Soviet regard for the collection of bunkers at each base not just as one unit but as separable, independent, sets. Thus the five bases with the most numerous of the bunker types had sets that each comprised one Delta and two Gamma bunkers. Intelligence nuclear specialists had commented on the two types of bunkers always present at each base which seemingly resolving to a standard ratio such as the 2:1 Gamma-Delta. Bunker sets could be distinguished not only by physical siting but also by a phased, set-concurrent construction chronology. A graphic representation—and a remarkable display of evidence of the third kind—appears in the 1970 CIA report timeline of bunker construction; the bunker numbers (assigned as first identified on satellite photography) correspond exactly to their ground positioning as sets as well as a precise or approximate phased buildout.

- The six-bunker complements of four Gamma-Delta bases had been sited in roughly parallel rows; staggered and rotated for nuclear blast protection; three bunkers each with a minimum ground distance between the bunkers of any one set ranged about 1.3 to 2.8 times the maximum distance between the bunkers within either set. These measurements often appeared in reports, some declassified,[1251] and can be readily approximated in Google Earth imagery as well as that of released intelligence systems. Seven of the eight parallel sets had been sited on the ground as Gamma-Delta-Gamma and one arranged Delta-Gamma-Gamma (someone may have misread the plan but more likely one Gamma had originally been left out). Comparable but less obvious siting distances evidenced for at least two other bases that had been started in the same time frame, but these had only two bunkers (Eta-Theta) in each set.

- A second observable inhered to another elemental factor—time. Exploiting the imagery time machine revealed that, when plotting the construction chronology of all SOC bunkers, an obvious pattern pops out. All but one of the Western bases could be reduced to ten paired sets. At least four of these had been precisely coterminously set-twinned in a phased construction program—bunkers of one set built concurrently with the second set started up to two years later, again concurrently. A close set phasing exhibited at the other bases as well but construction of some bunkers deviated from the strict chronological pattern exhibited at the four bases. Again, this duality had gone unnoticed.

- The arrangement of the smallest of all the SOCs at Kargopol-2 (Nyandoma to intelligence) displayed a third observable. This base had only three bunkers; arranged in one staggered formation of Gamma-Delta-Gamma as other bases; construction initiated concurrently—that is, configured as **one set** rather than the **two sets** of the other bases. The observation of nuclear specialists regarding this base had been a Gamma-Delta ratio of 2:1 as the other four bases with these designs, but with half their number of bunkers. While the bunker physical siting and set-phased construction of the other bases manifested separateness, Kargopol-2 demonstrated that each set actually constituted, in some paramount structured aspect, an independent grouping.

Thus SOC bunker construction featured three aspects consistent across multiple bases. These imaged observables point to a common theme, a unifying conceptualization, in the Soviet blueprint. But US (and British and NATO) intelligence did not access this grand plan during the Cold War and neither has any explanatory information subsequently emerged. Cold War SIGINT had provided important but less comprehensive information regarding the SOCs while human witnesses came from only lower military levels such as truck drivers and construction workers. Nowhere in this body of evidence had there been even a hint as to the overall scheme or any explanation for the observables. To resolve the imaged characteristics entailed a systematic search for connections among all encircling, potentially related, elements; which in turn required a deep and extensive knowledge of the Soviet strategic culture involving more than just a peek at the precepts catalog. Many self-important military forces specialists laid claim to the required cultural familiarity but their knowledge often turned out to not only have substantial gaps but also a shallow grasp of those Soviet precepts. Misconceptions had been further distorted by the tendency to overlay domestic cultural patterns as in the second translation—a transposition of US-think and them-think. Intelligence community nuclear connoisseurs lacked even the most basic acquaintance with the Soviet strategic culture.

I systematically investigated potential sets correlations, upward in scale, among organizational and operational aspects of the military services; WMD delivery forces; the geography and hierarchies of military districts, TVDs; and other potential relationships; all within the perceptual framework of Soviet military strategy—after all, the employment plan for WMD is the most significant expression of a national strategy. The sets resolution, indeed the fundamental operational basis of the SOCs, could be found in…*napravleniya*. A map plot revealed that the SOC locations, and these sets, corresponded exactly to the Soviet alignment of strategic and operational directions in the four TVDs encompassing NATO countries. Examine the cover of this work.

As early as 1961, Oleg Penkovsky had tossed evidence of the second kind to US and British intelligence. He insisted that General-Colonel Zhdanov at the head of GRAU—incorporating a dedicated warhead directorate—controlled both nuclear warheads and bombs.[1252]

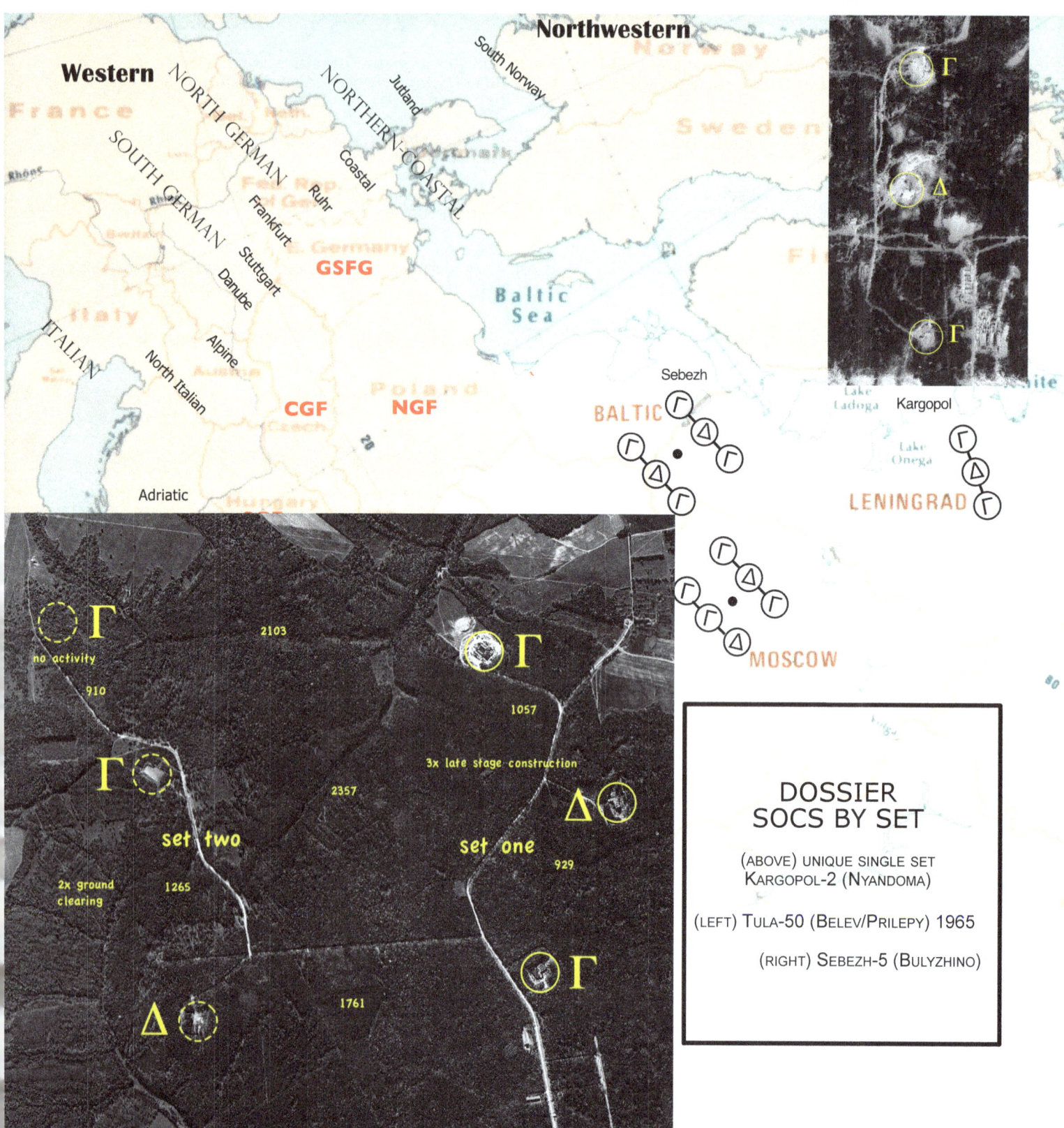

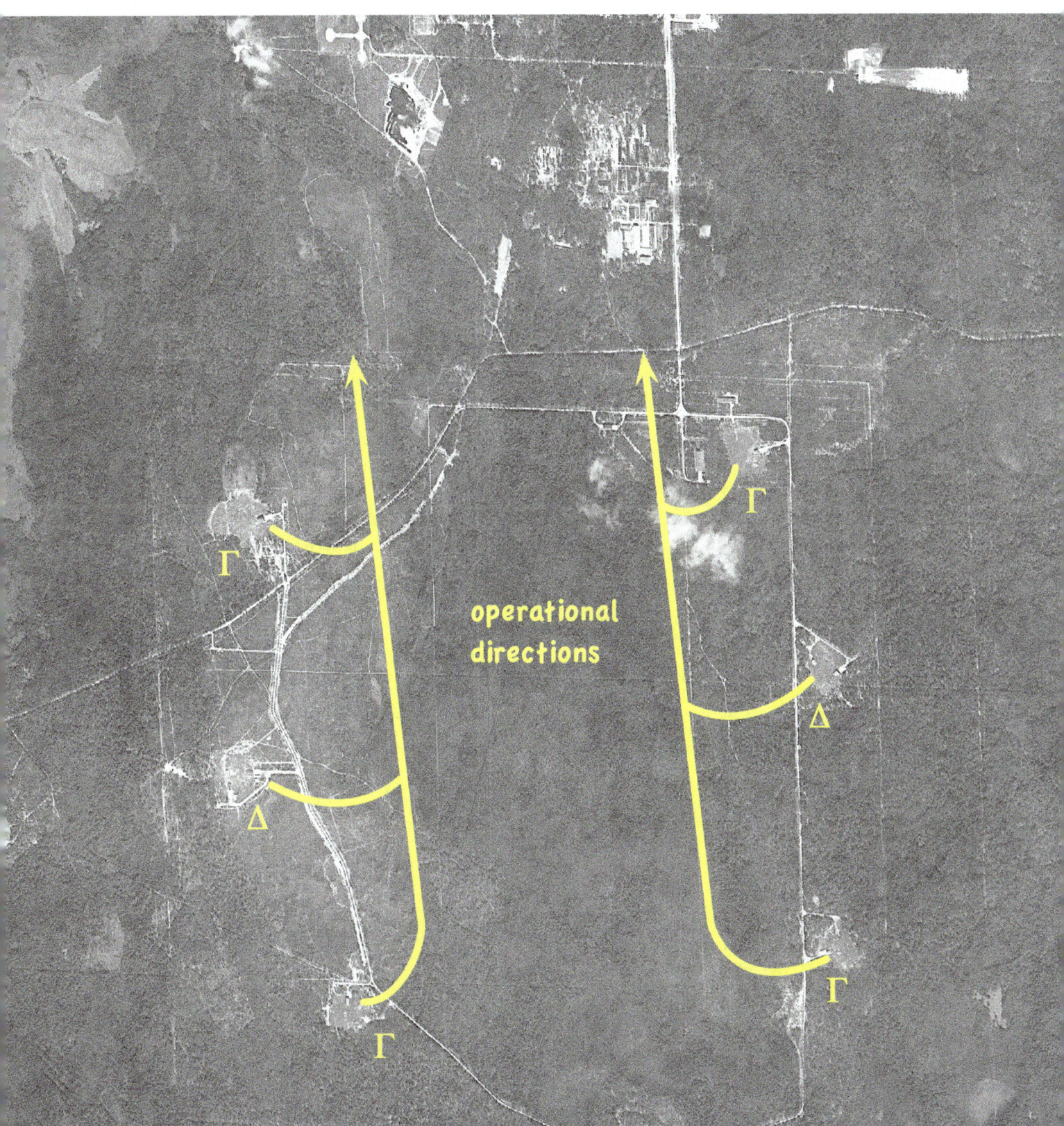

> Zhdanov gets everything. It is Zhdanov's responsibility to conceal everything according to strategic directions. I know definitely. Varentsov personally confirmed this. I will swear to this.

Chief Marshal of Artillery S. S. Varentsov had then been the Commander of the Rocket Troops and Artillery of the Ground Troops, who would presumably have been knowledgeable concerning such topics. This and much other information had been transmitted during meetings in the West with his handlers. Reports officers of the CIA Directorate of Operations then thematically bundled his comments as IRs—information reports—under the rubric Chickadee. Indicative of a dysfunctional CIA, operative to this day, the Penkovsky statement did not feature in any IR. DO assemblers had no clue as to what he meant…so they just 'redacted' this crucial evidence which appears only in the transcript of London meeting twelve. Many Chickadee IRs, including references to the role of Zhdanov, have been declassified. This is not the only example of useful Penkovsky information failing to make the second translation.

The first wave of SOC construction in 1959 had produced three bases using the Alpha-Beta designs. Initial indications had been acquired in December 1959 coverage by the U-2 which revealed bunker excavations in a ravine at an installation named Berezovka by intelligence[1253] (later Krasnoarmeyskoye, the Soviet Saratov-63, 1050 Object S). Much later a Soviet who had served in the military construction troops provided to intelligence useful details regarding the base and bunker layout. He had been conscripted in the late 1958 callup and eventually assigned to work on one bunker; the building of project supporting structures may have been started by late 1957 conscripts; the base had been swarming with officers of the Soviet Air Forces. The three bases are in Russia so his description of building an Alpha is the main source aside from imagery on interiors of this bunker series; in 1998 the head of the US Strategic Air Command had been afforded the opportunity to enter into a storage hall of one bunker at this base.[1254]

Work progression at the two other Alpha-Beta bases as imaged in the early 1960s indicated comparable schedules. Given the timings of likely initial construction as well as prior necessary site and bunker design preliminaries, the military concept and decisions regarding these bases must have been accomplished subsequent, and likely attendant, to the Marshal Zhukov February 1956 doctrinal pronouncement regarding the WMD nature of modern war. The first generation SOCs, in point of fact, represented the implementation of the Soviet provisional conceptualization of the WMD Operation. Due to the staccato overhead imagery resulting from the demise of the U-2 and the debut of satellite exploitation, coverage of the three bases had been too uneven and spotty to develop a precise sequence of bunker construction. But at least one base had obviously been, and one possibly, bunker set-phased constructed. The deeper positioning in the western TVDs of this trio as well as the more limited deployment relative to the second wave suggests an initial concept aligned to strategic directions—only.

The next wave paralleled another pivot, the 1960 Khrushchev pronouncement that sparked the Revolution in Military Affairs. These seven SOCs had been positioned in more advanced locations in the same TVDs and strategic directions. But constituent bunker sets now aligned to the operational directions of each strategic direction. The first three SOCs supported an earlier, provisional, concept; the new wave culminated the Soviet implementation of the envisioned theater WMD Operation that would exploit the availability of a more abundant and diversified assortment of nuclear (and chemical) weapons. Selection and numbers of bunker types seems to have been TVD-customized; five bases with Gamma-Delta-Gamma sets deployed in the Northwestern and Western TVDs; with the two Eta-Theta set bases in the Southwestern and the contemporary Near Eastern TVD. Along came the Makarov-1 (Radomyshl/Malin) Delta II-Iota base in 1965—aligned to the newly reconfigured frontal lineup in the Italian Strategic Direction. At least two of the three Deltas that had been added to the first 12 GUMO bases appear to be aligned to different operational directions than the purpose-built SOCs; while the location of one of the 1950s fab four, 713 Object S, suited another operational direction. The resultant mechanism in the Western Theater is depicted on the cover of this work.

Bunkers arranged in sets had not been the only legible characters of the book of SOCs. Architectural rendering of the bunker types also provided functional clues; but presented in a unique hieroglyphic system that required decipherment. In the great irony of the Soviet bunker mania each distinctive design, examined with consideration of the operational and WMD variants, afforded blueprint insights. Paired designs could be cross-compared, and back-compared to variant pairs, to elicit points of convergence and divergence; each of these points constituted evidence of…something—functional evidence otherwise lacking in the intelligence matrix. The very indications that could be discerned in the ubiquitous US imaging satellite constellation could be used to resolve this Soviet enigma. Other intelligence tools and sources provided no comparable evidence. Unfortunately the intelligence nuclear connoisseurs during the SOC controversy did not pursue these bunker design clues any deeper than the sets arrangement because all these aspects went unperceived, i.e., evidence of the third kind. Upon the official establishment of this particular model of nuclear singularity their successors had moved on without a backward glimpse.

Potentially other paths might be followed in determining the role of the SOCs in the WMD Operation. The Soviet bunker *modus operandi* had no Western counterpart thereby limiting analogies that might reveal the factors behind configuration decisions. Some of these factors could be discerned from bunker structure and additional insights upon design alteration or modification. I systematically parsed the intelligence take in an attempt, with little success, to identify the responsible design bureaus in order to obtain additional viewpoints. Much Soviet and Western information existed on analogous structures such as civil defense shelters and hardened control posts. Another dimension has been added in the age of the Internet. Visitors to abandoned official nuclear bunkers in several countries, that can be difficult for outsiders to access, have been posting their photographs of the Types, including SOC bunkers, to a number of web sites. These photos offer interesting details that could not be acquired even by the Cold War intelligence tools. And now there is commercial space imagery which, when knowledgeably applied, can in some respects be as useful as the product of the US classified satellites.

Two distinctive features of SOC bunker architecture had been evident in the intelligence imagery platforms. Nuclear specialists had sliced and diced these bunkers, in particular, to derive floorspace sizing that provided the starting point for quantifying the Soviet nuclear weapons stockpile. But these two elements had somehow been overlooked. Certain of the designs incorporated a servicing hall that could accommodate one of the technical requirements unique to nuclear weapons. Another salient change introduced in the SOC bunkers, and in the force-level Type III as well—conspicuously absent at the bunkers at both echelons prior to 1959—exhibited a new concern with environmental control. Only external bunker indications had been visible in Cold War intelligence satellite photos; but subsequent personal tours of junior versions built in Central European countries, along with web tourist postings of central bases, have revealed complex, sophisticated machinery for air movement and filtration in certain Types. This obvious concern with internal conditions in selected bunker designs should have, but never did, raise suspicions.

One of the characteristics of SOC bunkers that differentiated these bases from the preceding generation of nuclear storage complexes had been a pronounced downsizing of the infrastructure of processing and assembly buildings. This simplification reflected advances in weapons technology as well as handling procedures. A nuclear weapon is not a store-and-forget device. Custodial units must conduct regular checks and periodic technical maintenance on the condition of batteries, tritium gas, fissile material, and detonators. US terminology designates these as 'limited life components' which require replacement on a scheduled basis even if there are no failures.[1255] As weapons age, more frequent condition assessment is essential. This periodic, intensive, service requirement aids the distinguishing of nuclear from other kinds of weapons. Chemical munitions, in comparison, are relatively simple designs requiring much less attention with the notable exception of a tendency to leak nasties during storage due to the corrosive effects of chemical fills. CW storage regimes entail regular close inspection of agent containers and filled munitions, removing leakers, decontaminating enclosing structures, and spot checking of agent condition, while minimizing destabilizing movement.

The more complex nuclear weapons servicing is also facilitated, and is a trifle safer considering encased explosive components, if accomplished in a dedicated chamber that is separated from storage spaces. Equipment is required for removing container lids, weapons casings and parts. US nuclear ordnance facilities stored weapons in standard igloos and had a separate maintenance building equipped with hoist mechanisms to facilitate movement, disassembly, and component handling. The Soviets also used dedicated buildings in some situations but servicing workspace could also be integrated into the structure of selected official bunker flat-roofed designs including those at nuclear bases directly supporting firing units. Structure visible in US satellite images taken to monitor bunker construction included certain bunkers with maintenance areas indicated by a section raised to permit the use of the hoisting equipment. This service elevation is inherent to arch-sectional Types. Soviet nuclear protocol appeared more open than the US counterpart to technical work within structures that had co-located storage. US and British intelligence presumed the maintenance purposing of this elevated section due to the common technical issues as well as confirmation by some human sources. The work area function can now be verified by inspection of bunkers vacated by the Russians. Heavy-duty doors used to partition maintenance and storage compartments, not visible in the overhead views, can be examined up close. Some useful information on Soviet nuclear weapons bunker servicing procedures had also been obtained from personnel who had served in custodial units as well as from signals intelligence.

The nuclear weapons volume of *Russia's Arms And Technologies*[1256] helpfully expands on the other sources regarding the military tasks involved in the storage of nuclear munitions received from manufacturing plants. This outline can be applied as an overlay to the bunkers and buildings at central and operational bases. A cycle of commissioning > storage > maintenance > transportation > combat preparation > decommissioning is described with details that can be correlated with structural and processing indications. The commissioning stage involves inspections and any required maintenance prior to placement of munitions within "special structures" assigned spaces. The "special structures" are supposed to enable, among other activities, "convenient examination" of weapons, with dedicated rooms for certain functions. Systems in the "special structures" for nuclear weapons include "hoisting and handling machinery." Preparation of the weapons for combat use while still at the "special structures" requires a "service stage" of technical measures. The *Encyclopedia* does not provide any information on the nuclear weapons Special Readiness (SG—*sostoyaniye gotovnosti*—numeric levels) schedule that informed intelligence from classified documents, emigres, and SIGINT. This progression of technical readiness measures would be initiated from the lowest level of technical readiness at the most rearward storage bases. Thus the purpose of the elevated and dedicated service space within Soviet bunkers can be substantiated from both Soviet and Western practice.

The first eight SOC bunker designs evolved from 1959 into the 1970s as two paired but differentiated lineages which might be described, say, as Line A and Line C; that is, characterized by obviously discrete architectural paths. The four Line A bunkers featured an elevated or multistory open hall—indicative of the fitted hoisting apparatus—which provided a workshop for the essential nuclear weapons maintenance regime. Bunkers at national sites in the 1950s lacked this integrated service area; there had been several varieties of standard buildings to assemble and to maintain stored nuclear weapons on delivery from industry. The SOC Beta that debuted in 1959 represented a Line A transitional design, basically a first generation bunker in two levels with an attached elevated hall for nuclear weapons servicing. This modification to the preceding stockpile bunkers had somehow escaped the notice of the anti-nuclear faction during the SOC controversy but the opposing nuclear devotees had been equally inattentive —the presence of the hall not among the evidence adduced for a nuclear weapons storage function. The most important, and conspicuous (except to nuclear intelligence), alteration to the design of the Line A Eta and Delta series that followed in 1961, and the later Delta II, had been the merging, as an open hall spanning two floors within the main structure, of a previously attached section. This service hall provided each Line A bunker with an integrated processing flow for particular inventoried weapons including initial reception, scheduled checks, and shipment technical readiness preparations.

Thus bunker configurations self-constituted evidence of a nuclear handling regime.
- incoming weapons would be moved by railway carts into the service hall to be inspected prior to forwarding to the storage halls and some might have certain components detached to be placed in auxiliary storage compartments;
- stored inventory would be periodically extracted in accordance with the mandatory schedule for inspections and maintenance that could only be performed with the hoists and specialized equipment available in the service hall;
- weapon generation, whether limited shipments to other locations including rotation of stock at delivery units—or full *dislokatsiya* on war threat alert—provided for a dichotomous movement in which warheads requiring assembly actions and preparations to elevate technical readiness levels could be processed outward along the railway in the service hall with any echelon of the inventory already at the established SG-level removed via the secondary portal.

The four Line C bunkers entirely lacked any structural provision for this elevated space. Two single-story designs (Gamma and Iota) had no elevated roof sections and thus could not possibly accommodate any overhead lift apparatus. Two double-story Line C bunkers (Alpha-Theta) lacked any apparent internal service halls. The paired Alpha-Beta bunkers had identical two-level storage halls and lower level appendages—but, crucially, the Alpha did not have the attached service hall and second entrance structure. A generic observation regarding this series is that, whatever might be stored, the Beta design allowed for an integrated servicing regime characteristic of nuclear weapons—absence from the Alpha indicative of contents not requiring such actions. In satellite imagery the upper level of the Theta evidently continued floored throughout thereby precluding the service hall of the Line A bunkers. The functional inference would seem to be that whatever might be stored in Line A had the more complex processing and maintenance regime inherent to nuclear weapons; while the contents of Line C bunkers had no such integrated service requirement. US (and British) intelligence had no answer for this consistent structural opposition because…no one had been sufficiently curious as to ask the why of this evidence of the third kind.

Strangely Line C disappeared after 1974. Construction of a lone, final, Line C Iota had been started in 1974 at a base within the Semipalatinsk nuclear proving grounds. But the Soviet builders seemed to be in no hurry, requiring some five years to finish the job, an unusual prolongation for a SOC bunker. The SOC network in the west had been completed by the late 1960s but then expanded during the 1980s into the southeastern and eastern USSR against the emergent Chinese hostiles. Construction of a new complete SOC began in 1979 in the Far East. But for the first time in the SOC program all four of the bunkers built at this base comprised the same design—a further modified Delta series. No second type of bunker continued the Line C architectural path. Furthermore in the mid 1980s work started on another new base (the thirtieth separate central and SOC number 15) and bunker (all soon abandoned) as well as one bunker each (also aborted) at two existing SOCs in the Chinese directions. But these bunkers also conformed to the modified Delta design. All SOC bunker construction initiated after 1974 exclusively followed one design—the one with nuclear weapons service capability—which in this further modified Delta III (now floored throughout two levels) had been shifted to an external workshop; configured quite like a structure which had mysteriously appeared earlier at an unofficial setting in East Germany.

Thus post 1974 Line C had become extinct. The solution proposed by intelligence nuclear experts to the vanished second design—well, again no one raised a hand to ask any such question. Yet another coincidence had been added to the SOC saga. The duo bunker act had been initiated simultaneously with the appearance of the nuclear-chemical diarchy in Soviet military writings and manuals; and had become a solo performance concurrent with the disappearance of the chemical emphasis in classified documents that marked the deletion of the chemical variant.

Another peculiarity of SOC bunker design resided in the apparent high level of concern for internal air handling. I took advantage of an opportunity in 1986 to consult with a Soviet emigre. He had been an industrial ventilation engineer and, on arrival in the US, continued in the trade. Intelligence reports had cited his remarks on the correspondence of Soviet and American standards. Presenting basic sketches for a sampling of bunkers I asked him to 'design' a ventilation system. His schematics bore no resemblance to the actual Soviet versions. He indicated that the sizing of intake and exhaust vents constituted a direct measure of system capacity. With actual external vent setups provided, quick calculations revealed that some designs had air purging capabilities that exceeded by orders of magnitude what he considered necessary for a storage structure even with a modicum of internal personnel activity. The Iota (the final development of the SOC Line C design) figure amounted to a combined in-out flow exceeding 7500 cubic meters per minute; much of this capacity derived from an adjoining massive triple-pipe blower feeding through a filtration and scrubbing box presumably capable of reversible flow. At this rate the entire bunker atmospheric volume could be exchanged in less than two minutes at the maximum rate although the overall capacity might also be attributed to redundant systems.

Some of these Soviet bunker designs represented not just storage structures but also air control boxes. The Type III, which debuted in 1959 concurrently with the first SOC bunkers, had about 209 square meters of roof ventilators—the preceding Type II had no discernible vents. Similarly any venting on 1950s central base bunkers had been insubstantial although many of these had been obscured by earth cover and vegetation. An obvious trend in successive designs after 1959 beefed up environmental controls. Line A bunkers also had substantial ventilation systems. But a crucial disparity is that these incorporated the semi-industrial nuclear workshop—not present in Line C—entailing a high level of personnel activity and equipment heat generation as well as a requirement for a 'clean' environment for nuclear weapons breakdown. A classified 1976 Polish document[1257] acquired by the CIA that provided the air flow rate standards for manned control post bunkers would have permitted up to 2500 occupants, albeit SRO, at the combined maximum rate of an Iota bunker. The high exchange rates evident in Line C bunkers approached those of documented specifications for air scavenging in closed decontamination stations.[1258] When in 1990 the US moved all chemical munitions from Germany to Johnston Atoll, the two container ships used for the transoceanic passage had been upgraded with decontamination stations as well as special air filtration systems in crew and work areas—for the eventuality of any agent release accident.[1259]

Bunker venting arrangements with such high flow rates could be indicative of toxic materials handling—useful for clearing leakers. The externally visible ventilators provided a standby surge capacity augmenting normal air circulation. Under any warning of nuclear attack these systems would be sealed and air control switched to internal recirculation equipment; so the in-out ventilators must clearly be intended for some peacetime incident. While the extent of environmental utilities alone could not be considered conclusive in regard to bunker content these systems presented a red flag ignored by nuclear connoisseurs—more evidence of the second kind. Despite detailed intelligence bunker studies and measuring over many years no questions had been raised concerning this impressive capability. Even had the expansive bunker ventilation been noticed purpose would have become an issue, per usual in intelligence work, of hot disputation among opposing perspectives.

### coinciding coincidences

SOC construction had been initiated, and proceeded concurrently, with the advent and development of the integrated "nuclear and chemical" battle against NATO discussed since 1959 in Soviet military manuals, exercise documents, and classified journals. But no one had ever recognized the importance of the 1959 strategic pivot and only in 1984 did a lone CIA analyst take note of suspension. US intelligence failed to grasp the ramifications of the US bio-chemical armament buildup for Soviet meditation and that the SOCs might represent a formalized and sweeping response—a manifestation incomprehensible to those with such a shallow grasp of their strategic culture. In another coincidence elimination of one of the paired bunker design lines took place precisely with the disappearance of the chemical variant from Soviet writings on the WMD Operation which had only belatedly been recognized. In 1980, in a rare solid hit on Soviet offensive CW, one of the intelligence tools had acquired information that tied chemical weapons to 12 GUMO. At this time there is no specific evidence linking as related—on the eve of chemical deletion—the November 1974 re-subordination of the Directorate from the RVSN to the MoD. But this promotion at least implied an expansion of responsibilities.

At Geneva three years after the 12 GUMO popup a Soviet diplomat publicly hinted, and an official privately specified,

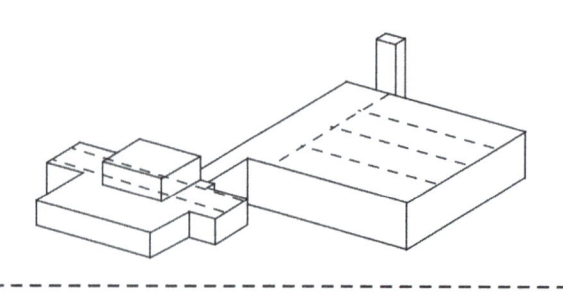

19

---

## Line A

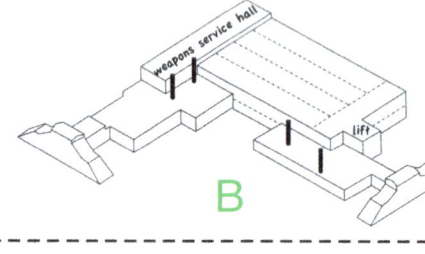

B

19

---

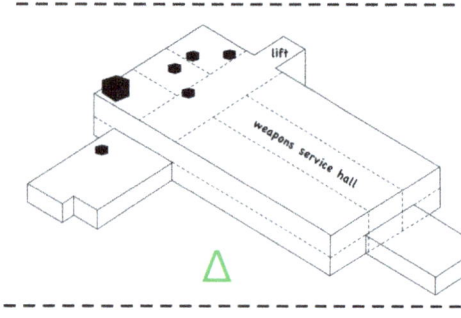

Δ

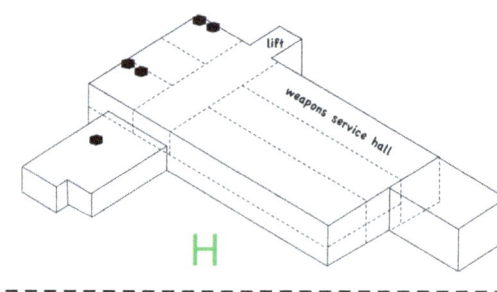

H

19

---

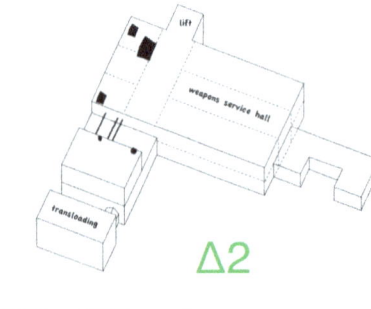

Δ2

19

---

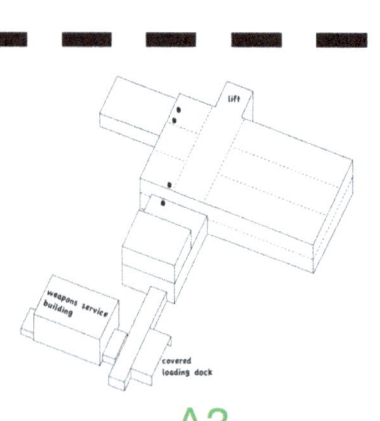

Δ3

50s

Line C

59

A

61

Γ　　　　　　　　　Θ

65

I

75

|  | hypothesis<br>**chemical singularity**<br>"chemical depots"<br><1985 = bulk agent + filled munitions<br>1985> = bulk agent—remote filling | hypothesis<br>**nuclear singularity**<br>official bunkers = NW | hypothesis X<br>**WMD Operation**<br>official bunkers = NW + CW |
|---|---|---|---|
| **first kind evidence** | | | |
| *chemical service* | | | |
| Chemical Troops = offensive CW | bunk | N/A | N/A |
| decon vehicles = offensive CW | not credible | N/A | N/A |
| *chemical service arsenals and bases* | | | |
| historical bulk agent storage | consistent | N/A | N/A |
| stockpile predominate bulk agent | no evidence—<br>CWC declaration contraindicative | N/A | N/A |
| all bulk agent "chemical depots" | no evidence—<br>CWC declaration contraindicative | N/A | N/A |
| bulk agent carrier railcars | possibly consistent BUT<br>legacy ? decontaminants | N/A | N/A |
| bulk agent containers | possibly consistent BUT<br>massive decontaminants | N/A | N/A |
| *ammunition stores* | | | |
| primary locations filled munitions | uncertain evidence—<br>CWC declaration indicative | N/A | not consistent |
| Russian CWC 81% filled munitions | 1985> possibly consistent | N/A | consistent |
| 1963 Arys depot Type IX | possibly not consistent | possibly not consistent | possibly consistent |
| 1975 Grossenhain chemical bombs | possibly not consistent | possibly not consistent | possibly consistent |
| **second kind evidence** | | | |
| 1950s US BW-CW buildup | consistent | N/A | consistent |
| 1959>1974 military lit NW + CW | not consistent | not consistent | consistent |
| 1980 CW interest 12 GUMO | not consistent | not consistent | consistent |
| 1982 buildings Kambarka-Shchuchye | not consistent | N/A | consistent |
| 1983 statement storage CW + NW | contraindicative | contraindicative | strong evidence |
| 1987 CW stores consolidation | possibly consistent | N/A | consistent |
| 1987 Nyandoma SOC closure | possibly not consistent | N/A | consistent |
| SOC bunker air exchange | N/A | possibly not consistent | possible evidence |
| **third kind evidence** | | | |
| 1959 SOC innovation | possibly not consistent | possibly consistent | evidence of purpose |
| SOC Lines A + C | not consistent | not consistent | evidence of purpose |
| SOC Line C disappearance | N/A | possibly not consistent | evidence of purpose |

that chemical weapons might well be stored alongside nuclear. There could hardly have been more authoritative sources for US intelligence. But nobody seems to have been aware of, much less grasped the significance, of these tips. Amidst the mass of dubious and ambiguous information acquired during the Cold War, the 1980 and 1983 tidbits had been the rarest of indications—systemic—placing Soviet chemical weapons in a particular organizational slot. These items ranked at the top of the, short, list of valid evidence concerning Soviet CW available in the West during the Cold War. Deactivation of Nyandoma SOC in 1987 presented another coincidence suggestive of chemical stockpile consolidation; with two Line C bunkers and only one Line A bunker this base would have lost preponderant inventory in the 1987 reshuffle discovered by Lev Fedorov—a substantial downgrade for a central object.

Bedeviling many intelligence (as well as other endeavors) assessments is the problem of coinciding coincidences. Coincidences are, of course, not proof of direct linkage or causation. There is always a risk of ascribing connection to parallel events that actually have independent and unrelated causes. But at some point recurring developments of a comparable nature that point in the same direction can be suspected to be related. The dilemma is that coincidences that are unrelated can appear exactly as do those that are directly linked. Hypothesis X collects a wide array of disparate evidence from multiple sources that closely fit within the same WMD envelope.

• the chemical estimate

The US and NATO intelligence allies had misfired on all counts in evaluating the character of Soviet offensive chemical measures throughout the Cold War. The only innovations lay in finding new elements to misjudge. The CIA chemical assessment, insofar as elaborated, had been the more realistic among the intelligence agencies despite a loyal adherence to the official chemical and nuclear models. The CIA institutional position had consistently bundled chemical with nuclear weapons, i. e., that the Soviets would be unlikely to initiate chemical warfare prior to any nuclear phase; that assessment rooted in the classified Soviet military literature much of which is now available for review. But CIA connoisseurs did not advance the logic of their own conclusion. Such a doctrinal presumption might well have an operational implementation; there might be other points of intersection between Soviet chemical and nuclear weapons. Collectively the CIA, in an egregious example of forest-and-trees perception, never fully explored the possibility that the Soviet WMD support systems might be correspondingly amalgamated. Such suspicions had occurred but the path had been blocked by the lack of any hypotheses (conceptualizations) that could have sustained any investigation of an alternative solution. Instead all defaulted to the intelligence official chemical model.

The official nuclear-bunker model had been fabricated by intelligence analysts according to ingrained US terms of reference, and modal thinking; hindering conceptualization of alternative propositions or even perception of crucial evidence. An essentially technical, and static, interpretation developed of a bifurcated 'stockpile' with weapons repositories revolving in random orbits that might cross at some unknown points. Little sense existed of any relationship to Soviet military doctrine, particularly the manner in which a theater war with mass destruction weapons would actually be conducted. The radical innovation represented by the SOCs had eventually been assimilated into the existent construct. US, and British, intelligence had fixated on the nuclear blade in assessing the function of the new central bases. Both nuclear and chemical connoisseurs persisted unaware of the implications of the WMD Operation, that the SOCs might be the machinery for implementation, a wellspring for echeloned WMD reserves. Chemical weapons assessment wandered off into a separate, ultimately futile, avenue. Nuclear and chemical weapons analyses transpired as independent, technical, issues, entirely divorced from actual developments in Soviet operational prescriptions. Ironically, during the second half of the 1960s, when minds had been open to alternative solutions, US intelligence had little success acquiring Soviet documentation. Only in the 1970s did the CIA develop methods for running inside agents who produced a steady flow of classified material that detailed aspects of the Soviet theater WMD Operation. But by then the SOC books had been closed.

Then there is the alternative chemical solution, a radically different perspective, an Unofficial WMD Model. At the outset of the 1960s the Soviets had conceived, and begun the erection of, an integrated mechanism responsive to, and supportive of, all variants involving mass destruction weapons. This structure formed a multi-layered VGK reserve for strategic and theater forces. The arrangement of the bases of the Center and those of the strike forces not only implemented the precepts of military doctrine but also provided the actualized framework of execution in the form of strategic strikes and theater strategic operations. These bases performed as nodes of a preplanned strategic deployment of armed forces inextricably connected to the concept of operations. The SOCs held reserves echeloned and aligned by the strategic and operational directions that emanated from the Center as in the spokes of a wheel; bunkers functioning as the injectors of the WMD Operation. SOCs constituted a WMD reservoir from which the Soviet political-military leadership could select theater variants, determine the scale of employment, and control allocations to delivery forces. Thus about 48 hours by rail from NATO territory (inclusive of railcar loading and border transload or gauge change) the Soviets had established the world-largest accumulation of ready chemical munitions—with an unknown echelon maintained at an advanced tech readiness level to permit immediate shipment.

A useful summarization can be presented using the competing hypotheses model adopted by intelligence. This method has come under some academic criticism for deficiencies and limited accomplishment. Here we have further modified the model to incorporate other shortcomings—hypothesis X and the three kinds of evidence.

• the nuclear estimate

That SOC bunkers, as well as the official bunkers supplying individual delivery units, may have harbored chemical munitions also had implications for another important intelligence issue—the nuclear weapons numeration. In the fall of 1989 the JAEIC (Joint Atomic Energy Intelligence Committee) assembled the nuclear savants of US intelligence to conduct a stockpile census; one of the more concerted attempts during the Cold War to arrive at an agreed total. The resulting estimate would guide intelligence monitoring of Soviet nuclear weapons redistribution during the breakup that soon followed; into the 1990s; subsequent dismantlement programs; and may still be the gauge for the remaining Russian inventory. The JAEIC estimate remains classified; but a 1991 National Intelligence Council overview of nuclear weapons disposition in the about-to-disappear USSR proffered "about 30,000" a third of these mated to deployed strategic land- and sea-based missiles.[1260] This quantification had also been repeated in open testimony by US officials. During the 1991 nomination hearings for his prospects as Director of Central Intelligence, Robert Gates referred to "30,000 or so nuclear weapons" under Soviet control.[1261] In a May 1992 House appropriations hearing the National Intelligence Officer for Strategic Programs tendered a range of 25000 to 35000 (stated as 30000 +/- 5000) as the coordinated estimate.[1262] The relative error factor of +/- 17 percent demonstrated intelligence uncertainty regarding both the solidity of the evidence and the validity of methodologies used. An intelligence nuclear estimate current a decade earlier fell within the same range; the Soviet stockpile had then been considered to be a third larger than that of the US.

An accepted, precise, number for strategic land-based missiles and aviation plus sea-based missiles in September 1990 amounted to 10271 nuclear warheads courtesy of START I arms control data.[1263] In the aftermath of the Soviet WMD empire dissolution estimates have been forthcoming from Russian sources. A Russian nuclear complex official in the early 1990s claimed that in 1986 the stockpile attained a maximum of 45000[1264] but this high figure has not been further supported—representing the cumulative factory output or capacity rather than a period inventory—the official's own ministry issued a statement disavowing his numeration.[1265] Alexei Arbatov, a Russian defense specialist, provided a breakdown (excluding strategic), cited in some Western studies, that totaled 21700; others attempting a nuclear weapons census have questioned the Arbatov numbers, in particular, that his distribution among general purpose services cannot be reconciled with weapons dismantlement progress.[1266] Russian officials have reported only percentage or proportional figures. None of the public estimates account for more than 3000 warheads (reentry vehicles) for missiles eliminated under the INF Treaty, which controlled airframes but not warheads, at the turn of the 1990s. There have been no attempts at a detailed numeration by the launcher and refire echelons method, the last of which might include warheads at the center for maintenance rotation and other purposes. One calculation suggested that a third of deployed nuclear warheads would have been replaced each year for refurbishment, necessitating that much larger a total stockpile.[1267]

Other Russian sources attribute significantly fewer warheads to 'tactical' or nonstrategic systems.

• David Hoffman, in his 2009 book *The Dead Hand*, cites a March 1991 chart saved by CPSU Central Committee official Vitaly Katayev. The chart displayed a nuclear weapons inventory breakdown that totaled 25355 with a slightly higher strategic number plus an approximated 15000 'tactical' weapons.[1268]

• *The Soviet Army During the Cold War Years* 2004 book, without specifying source, provides a detailed breakdown by systems for the total of 24271 nuclear weapons said to have been in the Soviet inventory in the fall of 1990, with a START-identical figure for strategic plus a rounded 14000 for 'tactical' systems.[1269]

• A Moscow TV station broadcast in early 1992 concerning a meeting of foreign ministers from the "nuclear republics" deciding the future of their nuclear weapons offered an unattributed 24200 count (strategic and not varieties) of which 9200 remained in three other, newly independent, countries.[1270]

• Several statements in the Russian media during 1991-1992 as the breakup of the USSR proceeded, again without attribution (and possibly reflecting Western estimates), tossed out an identical 27000 total nuclear stockpile.

That the Arbatov count exceeded two estimates by 7700 (14000) and 6700 (15000) is indicative of the uncertainty regarding the Soviet/Russian 'tactical' nuke stockpile that persists to this day. Similar higher intelligence numbers have been given to the 'sub/nonstrategic' nuclear stockpile for the early 1990s; in particular the SAC chief in 1998 stated that he had been given figures for 'tactical' weapons by different intell agencies that varied from 17000 to 22000.[1271] However an authoritative intell statement, "The Soviet inventory is assessed to contain some 7,500 to 15,000 tactical nuclear warheads" in 1991[1272] while contributing an uncertainty factor that doubled the minimum, assumed a lower range scaling. If correct, the Arbatov numbers Soviet total, added to the START data, would have fallen within the presumed JAEIC range of about the same timeframe. But if the other informants had been the righter US intelligence had found room for some 3000 to as many as 10000 or more, depending on the Russian source, 'tactical' nuclear weapons that the Soviets did not possess—the wide discrepancies in the JAEIC range and agency numbers demonstrating the indeterminate evidential basis of the estimates.

Another useful lead provided in 2000 by the chief of 12 GUMO telling US officials that a six-square-meter norm, to accommodate fissile material restrictions, governed the footprint for storage of a nuclear weapon.[1273] This statement came in the context of finding room for all the weapons returning to Russia from Central Europe and newly independent states. Floorspace allocation had also been the start point for the methodology employed in US calculations for establishing the size of this stockpile. That is, the architecture of the varied Types as studied and measured; dedicated storage sections distinguished from utility and other functions; and the weapons capacity assessed in accordance with different assumptions. Imputed fragmentary information from intelligence sources along with fissile material factors added to the stew. A multiplication totting ensued based on the identified official bunker population guided by the other factors and evidence. This Soviet nuclear six-square-meter norm can be pertinently applied to the storage halls of 66 completed SOC bunkers at seventeen bases (fourteen SOC plus those at three 1950s installations).

Interior photos of some of these bunkers show an, apparently typical, configuration of longitudinal storage shelves bisected by a cart railway. Positioning weapons axes either perpendicular to the walls, with two meters spacing, or parallel with three meters, derives a capacity of at least 14500, or more than 9600, respectively. Differing lengths, especially for 'tactical' weapons, would permit mixed orientations that places the practical capacity somewhere between the extremities; with an even higher range for weapons such as warheads and artillery rounds stored in a vertical attitude. This total range assumes no stacking. US storage practice may have permitted stacking of certain types. Russian descriptions, especially of early generation nuclear technology, indicate that rack storage of at least some components of each weapon had been a standard practice. A diligent team of Hungarians has managed unique access to documents, along with interviews of senior officers who served in nuclear support units, to produce quite detailed weapons data including storage regimes.[1274]

Stressing the Soviet practice of nuclear device container storage, they identify as stackable eight yield types for 2K6 *Luna* and 9K52 *Luna M* (FROG) warheads; five types 9K79 *Tochka* (SS-21 Scarab); two types 9K72 *Oka* (SS-23 Spider); and at least the container for the 152-mm artillery projectile. Containers for larger 9K72 8K14 (SS-1c Scud B) and some tactical aviation bombs did not qualify for stacking; no information available for other nuclear artillery and mortar rounds, mines, nor regarding strategic and naval warheads. Any use of racks for storing the modern 'tactical' weapons, in particular those at the lower end of the yield spectrum and in smaller packages, would require applying a multiplier greater than 1.0 to the capacity range. Potential storage of separated components complicates the calculation although also facilitating stacking. The Hungarians detail four generations of nuclear weapons technology development and the Soviet five-stage technical readiness system that evolved weight reductions and components integration. Depending on SG-level and factory vs. central object storage, elements such as trigger mechanisms, neutron sources and batteries might be kept apart. Soviet echeloned readiness practice may have also dictated that a proportion of the contents of some or all bunkers at a particular site be held at a higher degree of completeness and technical readiness—alert status—even the SG-4 level preceding launch.

To the SOC design capacity should be added that of the varied storage bunkers and chambers at the fifteen other 12 GUMO central stores; plus the several hundred official bunkers and chambers at strategic and general purpose forces; plus the warheads affixed to silo-based missiles, submarine and other naval vessel patrols, and mobile strategic missiles; plus weapons at factories for periodic major service, refurbishment, and dismantling; and a substantial set of unofficial storage locations should not be omitted. A back-of-the-envelope calculation suggests that this reserve storage-deployed capacity would exceed by an order of magnitude the US intell estimate, that of the Russian informants, and might well bust the 45000 claim. Any imputed excess could, however, be substantially ameliorated by backing out the 38 line C SOC bunkers (most in NATO directions), eliminating some 6000 to 9000 (single level) nuclear placeholders, again depending on package orientation. The Gamma design alone accounted for a bit more than one in four completed SOC bunkers and nearly a third of SOC bunkers west of the Urals. By the early 1990s any chemical inventory had been transferred to the declared CWC sites thus freeing the vacant slots to accommodate the nuclear weapons withdrawn from Central and Eastern Europe as well as now independent Soviet republics.

That a substantial chunk of the calculated usable storage floorspace had not been assigned to nuclear munitions, as assumed by the working groups that evaluated national and force holdings, might tend to seriously exaggerate the maximum—by many thousands of weapons. Thus not only did the US chemical accounting reach an entirely specious upper limit but also the derived nuclear quantification had a dubious foundation. A hellacious misjudgment in one of the columns directly impacted the accuracy of the correspondent.

The 1989 nuclear stockpile symposium could, however, boast of another major accomplishment—the initial acceptance into the official nuclear model of an entire class of storage sites located in Central Europe. That this recognition had been awarded exactly 30 years after the first known representative became operational might not have been particularly timely but did bear witness that US intelligence could/eventually/sometimes solve even the toughest of problems.

The Case Of The Hidden Nukes

Twenty-five of the central WMD bases had been sited in relatively remote areas of the USSR. Each establishment comprised a self-contained multiplex with administrative buildings; military personnel accommodations; rail and motor transport centers; heliport; security and engineer-technical detachments; as well as co-located dependents housing. In the Soviet armaments industry scheme the complexes functioned as the military acceptance authorities and final assembly points for weapons disgorged from the manufacturing plants. These WMD enterprises served in peacetime as weapons warehouses and distributors to lower echelons of the armed forces; with the technical capability for intermediate nuclear weapons maintenance and modification; while tasked to rotate these weapons through delivery unit stores while overseeing stockpile assurance. Four other bases in the Urals had been twinned to closely coordinate with nearby plants in a nuclear cycle of production, refurbishment, and dismantlement while holding a final reserve of active and obsolete weapons. As the system collapsed inward during the 1990s, like some dwarf star, the assembly task reportedly devolved to the nuclear production plants.[1275]

Strike forces storage installations, in contradistinction, operated on a much smaller scale. These RTBs—their nuclear bunkers translated by intelligence into Type parlance—afforded permanent weapons repositories to the WMD first echelon. Logically, missile RTBs at this level of organization jointly stored warheads with their delivery means. RTBs held at least the nuclear weapons of each of the armed services, down organizational levels to strategic missile, aviation, and air defense regiment or ground army or naval base. The presence of a chemical weapons first echelon during the Cold War is less certain but may have been selective rather than widespread; actual deployment extent is further complicated by the potential removal of part or all echeloned chemical munitions to the Center during or after the mid 1970s. Even the few instances of valid information pinpointing CW at the strike forces echelon—as at Grossenhain Airfield which accommodated a RTB—associated storage locations could not be confirmed. The architecture of certain of the several official bunker types had the potential to accommodate co-storage with nuclear weapons while others appear unitary in design. Whether down-echeloning of chemical stocks in any significant quantity took place as the US began binary CW production and tried to establish a European inventory is an even more equivocal issue with only slight evidence.

Although hardened against a surprise enemy nuclear assault the Soviets apparently by the 1970s had reached the conclusion that these bases could not be expected to ride out an all-out nuclear war. An increasingly likely variant encompassed a period of threat with warning indicators. Additional preparation time became available, even if only for an uncertain interval, after the beginning of a war waged with conventional means. Measures taken to enhance *dislokatsiya*, as at soft targets, featured removal of weapons to remote dispersal sites. Beginning in the mid 1970s 12 GUMO implemented an improvements program at the central bases to accelerate stock outloading. Previously the contents of bunkers had been transferred to ground transporters by fixed or mobile cranes positioned near access points. Supplementing this method construction began on a widespread basis of, what we called, loading docks permitting direct roll-in to vehicles backed into pre-configured parking slots.

The Anastasiev memoir[1276] provides some background to the measures observed by intelligence. The Soviets had come to the realization that the enemy had pinpointed the central objects; impelling a solution expediting the removal of 'products' from storage 'rooms' by loading truck and rail transports for regional dispersal. The main bottleneck had been the cycle of loading and unloading bunker portals—to "issue a building"—at an unacceptable rate of one product at a time that required several days. An exercise at a, unnamed, base under the command of V. K. Gapanov developed alternative methods. The emplacement of 'roller tables' at loading docks had been determined to magnify performance by a factor of five to six times. Anastasiev also describes the consequent problem that arose regarding ensuring the safeguarding of weapons held at dispersal areas from "subversive groups" that resulted in certain unspecified engineering actions as well as the eventual creation of dedicated military security units.

Ramps set up at base railyards accelerated vehicle-to-railcar transfers. Both vehicular and rail measures must have been implemented in the context of altered dispersal planning brought about by the new Military Threat combat readiness stage. Similar truck loading docks had already been constructed, sporadically, at the official nuclear bunkers of armed forces RTBs and these now also became a characteristic feature at that level. Regular exercises soon detected practiced weapons removal not only dispersing to preplanned reserve areas but also long distance resupply of combat units down to ground army level. Alert events became more frequent. Parallel General Staff and 12 GUMO command nets disseminated signals to elevate war readiness stages and release weapons in response to VGK orders.

Information from Russian sources now indicates a larger scale, concerted, reorientation under way evident only in outline to US intelligence. Basically this reshaping involved closer integration of strategic assets with the field-deployed fronts by an earlier advance of the forward echelon of the Center. In particular a memoir by General-Major A. Melnikov[1277] provides interesting, if selective, details. Melnikov had commanded the Kirovograd-25 (Aleksandrovka), 12 GUMO subordinate, 341 Object S (SOC) from activation of the parent military unit 14427 in May 1960 until his retirement in 1985. He highlighted aspects of base construction, organization, affiliations, and activities including the delivery of "special articles" to all Soviet forces (except naval) even though he particularizes base subordination to the RVSN command until the 1974 reorganization. Melnikov stated that, beginning in 1974, the Soviets began to experiment with Special Tactical Groups (специальная тактическая группа—СТГ) with enhanced mobility and trained to perform missile launch preparation as well as aircraft bomb loading tasks previously accomplished only by front units. These STGs seem to have evolved from the dispersal area military units described by Anastasiev.

Melnikov discussed a June 1980 exercise in which his base attached an operations group to the headquarters of a front generated by the Odessa MD. An OG accomplished the standard Soviet method of effecting liaison down, and across, commands by teams equipped with their own communications means. Two STGs deployed to the front departure area on alert declaration. The front commander requested and Melnikov, stationed in the base hardened command post then obtained 12 GUMO authorization, that the STGs mate the warheads of two front-level missile brigades as well as for three rocket battalions of front reserve divisions. The STGs thus substituted for the front-level missile-technical units that would normally have performed this prelaunch work for delivery units directly under front control. Transport of at least nuclear warheads and artillery rounds to front rear areas by central 'special operations groups' had been detected in some 1980s exercises by US intelligence monitors but no one understood the overall plan outlined by Melnikov.

Among the motivations for the revised scheme may have been the increasing importance of missiles for delivering mass strikes in the conventional variant. The re-echeloning of nuclear warheads and mating responsibilities would permit missile units to focus on conventional fire missions with a standby nuclear echelon. The 1991 Chief of the ground Rocket-Artillery Troops referenced the mandated dialing of a code on both launcher and "special warhead" in order to replace a missile conventional warhead.[1278] The Soviets may have been grooming the central STGs to participate in the nuclear echelon as a bolster to, or even a replacement for, the front and army missile-technical units that had previously monopolized immediate nuclear support. Cold War intelligence information had been inadequate to establish the exact nature of these developments.

Schematic revisions may also have been related to another action that puzzled intelligence specialists. A GRAU officer informed US intelligence that 12 GUMO in 1979 ordered the removal to central bases of all nuclear warheads from fifteen (named) locations. Moysey Rabinovich later published a monograph on GRAU and activities that repeated this statement.[1279] Twelve equated in my model to front missile-artillery bases. But only missile-type official bunkers existed at two; in the model these had been assigned to a group of six central bases holding the strategic reserve of Ground Troops missiles; his Staraya Toropa location, which also lacked any official nuclear bunker, represents one of the original four 1950s missile arsenals and had been repurposed as a surface-air missile store. A 2011 article in a Belorussian military journal[1280] provides independent confirmation of the removals in regard to the front base given by Rabinovich as Dobrush (intelligence Vyshkov). All nuclear warheads had been shipped out in the early 1980s while retaining the missile storage function. The article noted the "cover" mission of the artillery ammunition store for "the other side" 388 RTB, military unit 11806. During the Cold War RTB activities had been conducted at night, and masked during the day, for the impairment of roaming celestial spies. The elimination of front-level nuclear storage may have indicated that the Soviets by then had sufficiently advanced their STG concept to bypass this echelon in favor of delivering "special articles" from the bases of the Center. A forward central echelon no longer waited rearward of, but had replaced, the front echelon. Soviet logistics principles emphasized a continuous, uninterrupted forward push-flow of replenishment echelons.

Displacement of nuclear warheads from the front bases may have been linked to another event. During 1981 the Soviets systematically, on a one-for-one basis, replaced a certain type of warhead railcar in the base train sets that had been in use for as far back as they could be discerned in satellite imagery with, what appeared to be, standard four-axle boxcars. These boxcars could not be nuclear transporters since those warheads had been removed. But for a preceding development, the switch might be presumed to have been intended for the movement of the conventional warheads of increasing significance in Soviet front missile strikes planning. An identical exchange of the same railcar types had taken place by the mid 1970s at what the intelligence model considered nuclear weapons stockpile sites such as the SOCs. Seemingly unlikely that such high level repositories would be involved in the supply of conventional warheads—certainly no suggestion of such a mission had been offered by any interested intelligence office—and evidence lacking. Soviet *Instructions* on warhead railcar loading have emerged that profile boxcars as well as standard 24-m cars.[1281] Shipment exercises at central bases occasionally detected on satellite imagery involved formation of trains made up solely of boxcars and door-positioned at siding loading ramps. Boxcar transport would conveniently mask weapons movements beyond USSR borders; but could also represent the mode for rapid forward deployment of a substantial chemical armament. This anomaly continues to be a loose end with alternative solutions.

Coverage by the KH-9 system (amplified by still classified high resolution satellites) revealed an unusual convocation during 1980-1981 of ready trains at central base Gomel-30 (Rechitsa) about 430-km direct from the Polish border. Two sets of 24-m V-60 series railcars had been assembled for rapid loading and

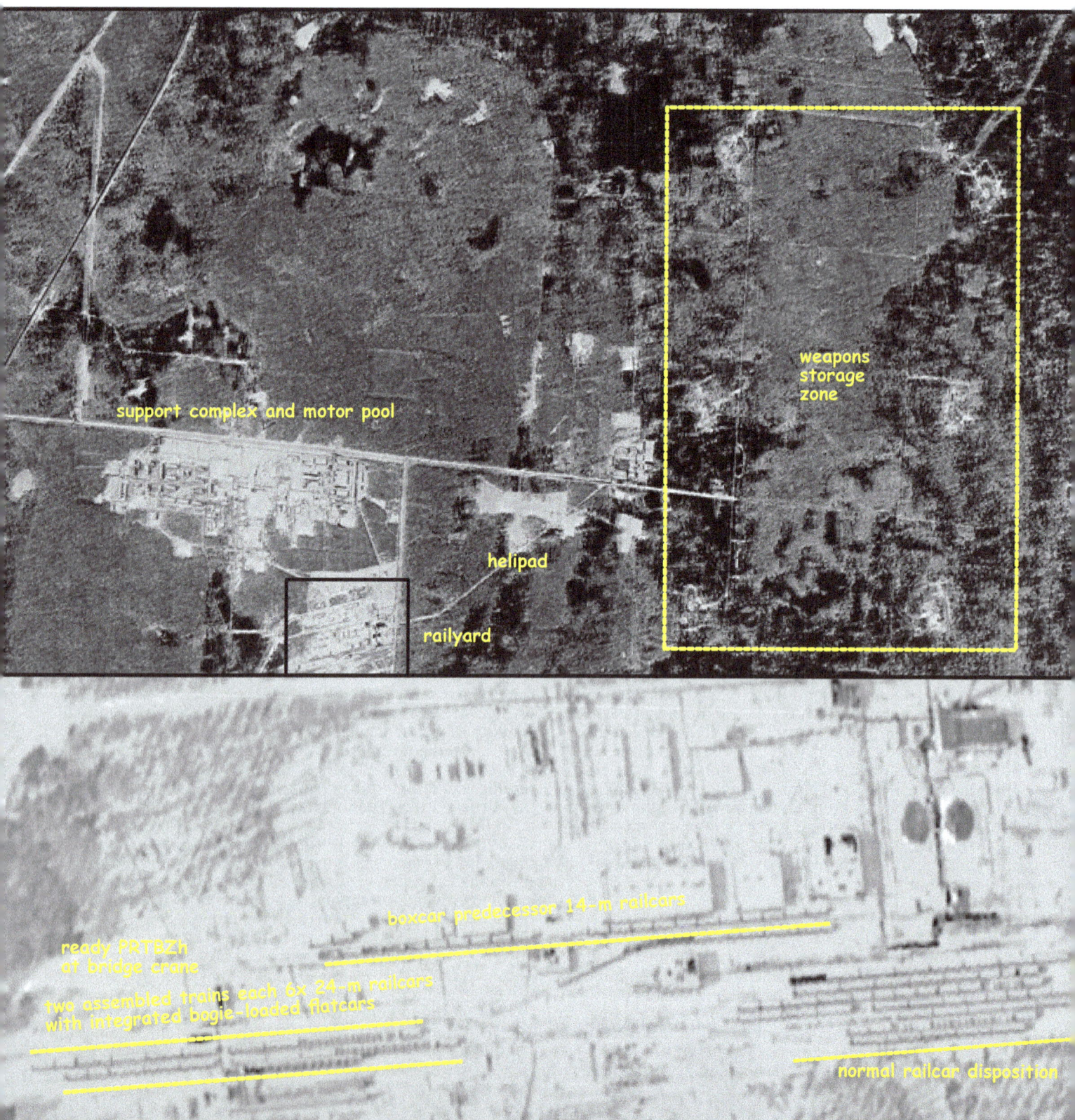

## MoD Instructions 1986
BOXCAR LOADING AND TIEDOWN OF NUCLEAR WARHEAD STORAGE CANISTERS 8F14 [R-300 SS-1c Scud B] AND 9Ya218 [R-900 SS-12 Scaleboard] VARIANTS FIVE OR THREE WHEN ATTACHED TO 9T114 CARTS—LAYOUTS ALSO PROVIDED FOR STORAGE OF THESE CANISTERS ABOARD THREE OTHER TYPES OF LARGER 24-METER RAILCARS

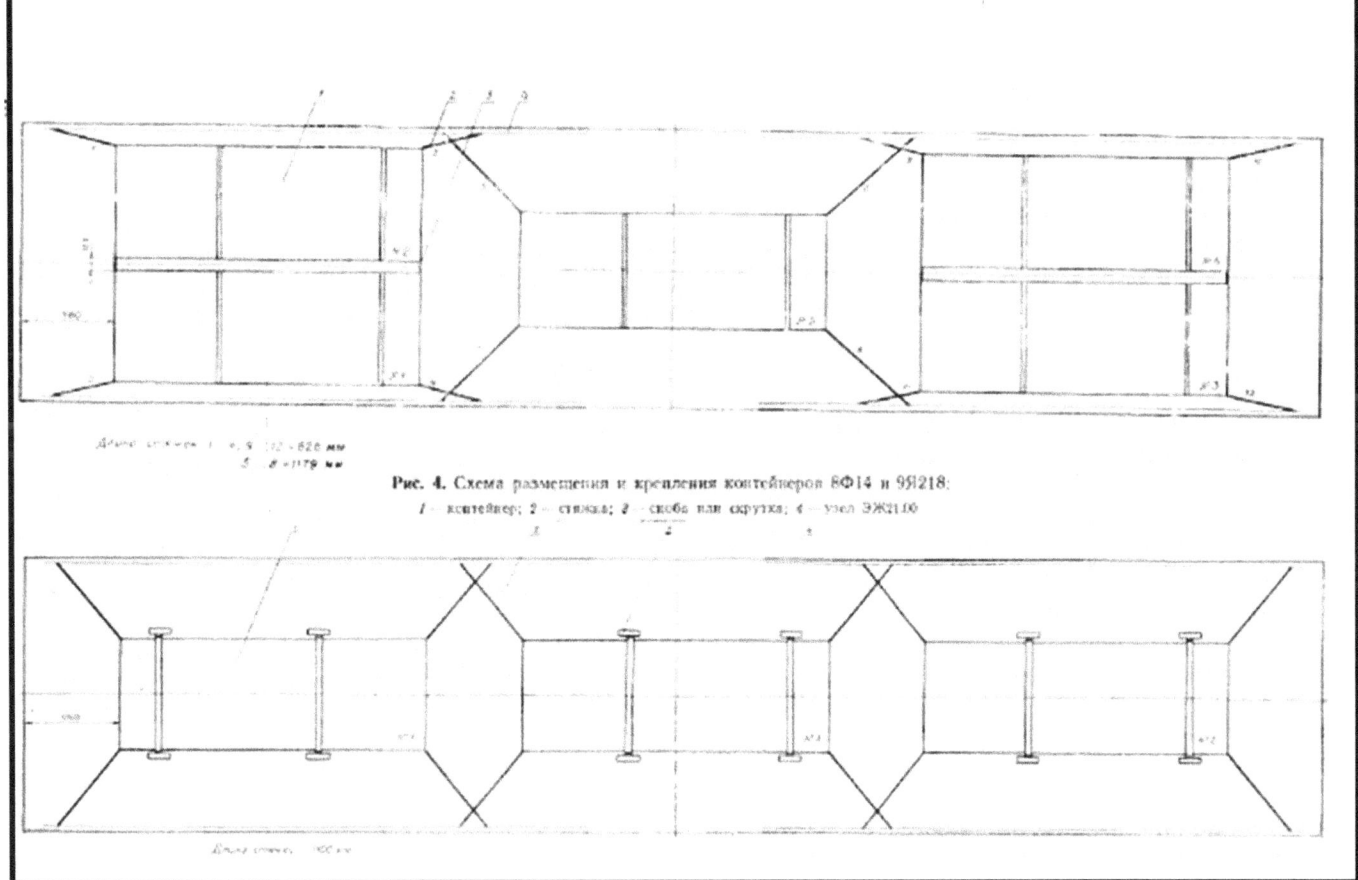

Рис. 4. Схема размещения и крепления контейнеров 8Ф14 и 9Я218:
1 — контейнер; 2 — стяжка; 3 — скоба или скрутка; 4 — узел ЭЖ21.00

Central WMD base Gomel-30 (Rechitsa) February 1981

movement—attached flatcars holding railcar bogies for border gauge transfer, indicative of a planned crossing. Also revealed the startling resurrection of 14-m railcars of the type replaced by boxcars in the mid 1970s (during a crucial WMD transmutation); circa twenty along the same track; absence of bogie flatcars signifying no border crossing intent. Assembly had begun nearly a year earlier and altered late in 1981 thus bookending Soviet concerns regarding the Polish internal crisis. The 14-m railcars again vanished. Note to 'war scare' enthusiasts; despite such close monitoring of central WMD bases no comparable train movement assemblies had been observed during 1983 despite the supposed Soviet apprehension of an imminent Western nuclear surprise.

The linchpin of control, dispersal, and supply throughout the Soviet armed forces, the field equivalent of the permanent base, organizationally centered on mobile (*podvizhnaya* подвижная —ПРТБ) RTB. As combat support units, PRTBs deployed equipped with the requisite transportation means to move nuclear bombs, warheads and artillery rounds as well as, substantiated at least in the Ground Troops, chemical warheads. Missile PRTBs had organic transport batteries for the type of projectile to be supplied to a particular front (army) brigade and/or battalions. The PRTB apparently originated in the first half of the 1950s as an entity for non-organic support to missile launch units, initially to relieve the heavy burden represented by liquid propellant. Two missile warhead teams had been formed at the Kapustin Yar range in 1956 to handle the first nuclear warheads delivered for testing the R-5M; the following year an exercise "under military conditions" would be conducted.[1282] Warhead and propellant functions merged and structurally evolved into the PRTB. Post Cold War information confirmed the intelligence basic observation that a missile PRTB might sustain one system—'special' to the Soviets or 'mixed'—for multiple types. PRTBs composed the foremost of missile-technical units referenced in varied sources, **the vital cog in the Soviet WMD apparatus.**

PRTB activities often featured in exercises as well as occurrences in other SIGINT. There had been, over many years, a limited amount of serviceman reporting. The unique equipping with both warhead and missile transporters assisted identification on satellite imagery; sporadically, over time and locations, instances of complete PRTB outfitting had been acquired—but only within the USSR. Classified writings, lectures, and manuals provided abundant and highly illuminating details of roles and usage. PRTBs functioned concurrently as the control means and the custodial intermediary with the delivery vehicles. Central 12 GUMO bases had both road (PRTBA—*avtomobilnaya*) and rail (PRTBZh—*zheleznodorozhnaya*) counterparts to carry out an orchestrated dispersal of "special articles" during a preplanned strategic deployment. Establishing a mobile forward supply echelon—as in the initial strike echelons—center PRTBs constituted the agents of WMD *dislokatsiya* and the underpinning of the STGs described by Melnikov. Seen in the context of Soviet logistics practice 12 GUMO PRTBs operated as *filial* or branches of the central bases.

Unlike the Center complexes, service RTBs harbored small military caserns sufficient for only mobile detachments; a direct one-to-one relationship, a mirror image, an alter ego the PRTB operated the RTB, maintained stored weapons, and removed all contents on declaration of Military Threat combat readiness. My comprehensive investigation of Soviet missile systems included a study[1283] determining PRTB co-location or garrisoning at most 20-km distant. This PRTB-RTB nexus represented the crucial element of WMD preparedness—an ineluctable bond unperceived by certain dimwitted intelligence nuclear and chemical personalities during most of the Cold War. CW connoisseurs in particular, despite explicit evidence assigning chemical warhead responsibility to missile PRTBs never addressed the obvious followup issue of the contents of RTBs and their official bunkers. PRTB transporters functioned as field depots during combat operations, a roving version of the permanent base, at the onset of war establishing the first WMD supply echelon for delivery units. In the missile chain PRTBs controlled warheads for the initial salvo to be mated on missiles held by firing units as well as complete rounds for up to one full successive launch. Recent Russian material on missile forces has echoed this intelligence appraisal of the echeloning scheme as did the 1977 General Staff Academy lecture outline.[1284]

> The capabilities of the front rocket technical units to maintain, transport, supply, and prepare R-300 and R-70 missiles fully meet the requirements of the rocket troops of the front. Warheads are kept in the rocket technical bases. The warheads slated for the initial nuclear strike it is advantageous to maintain in readiness SG-5. The delivery missiles are kept both in rocket technical bases and in the missile units (usually one per launcher with the appropriate reserve of missile propellant). Keeping and maintaining the warheads and delivery missiles this way ensures their quick preparation for accomplishing the tasks of an initial nuclear strike.

PRTBs had dedicated command channels independent of the military units supported—at Soviet airfields personnel labeled "deaf and dumb" because of the lack of interaction—overseen by the Sixth organization and the front-army missile-artillery armament service. As far as could be determined from our side the Soviets, unlike their opponents, imposed a rigid boundary between these custodians and their customers. End-users manned some categories of US nuclear weapons storage sites in the west of Europe. We never obtained evidence of any Soviet firing unit having peacetime direct, possessive, control of WMD, although the supporting PRTB or a detachment might be nearby. Strictly regulated procedures and steps dictated PRTB hand over—*peredat*—to a delivery unit, detailed

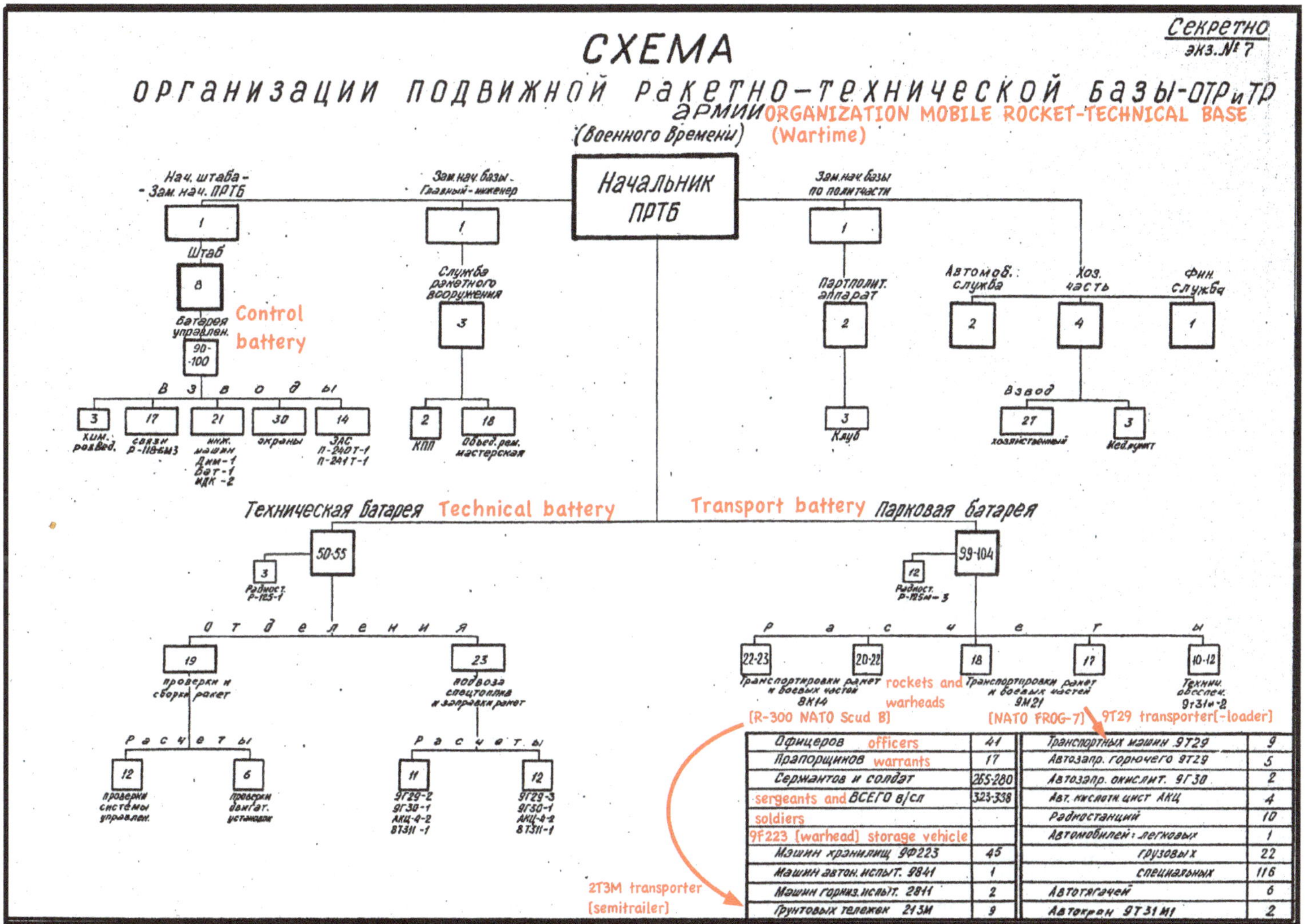

# СХЕМА
## организации подвижной ракетно-технической базы-ОТРиТР армии
### (Военного времени)

**ORGANIZATION MOBILE ROCKET-TECHNICAL BASE (Wartime)**

Секретно
экз.№ 7

Начальник ПРТБ

- Нач. штаба - Зам. нач. ПРТБ — 1
  - Штаб — 8
  - Батарея управлен. (Control battery) 90-100
    - Взводы
      - 3 Хим. развед.
      - 17 Связи Р-118БМ3
      - 21 Инж. машин ДИМ-1, БАТ-1, МДК-2
      - 30 экраны
      - 14 ЗАС П-240Т-1, П-241Т-1
- Зам. нач. базы - Главный-инженер — 1
  - Служба ракетного вооружения — 3
    - 2 КПП
    - 18 Объед. рем. мастерская
- Зам. нач. базы по политчасти — 1
  - Партполит. аппарат — 2
    - 3 Клуб
- Автомоб. служба — 2
- Хоз. часть — 4
  - Взвод
    - 27 хозяйственный
    - 3 мед. пункт
- Фин. служба — 1

### Техническая Батарея (Technical battery) 50-55
- 3 Радиост. Р-125-1
  - Отделения
    - 19 проверки и сборки ракет
      - Расчеты: 12 проверки системы управлен., 6 проверки двигат. установок
    - 23 подвоза спецтоплива и заправки ракет
      - Расчеты: 11 (9Г29-2, 9Г30-2, АКЦ-4-2, 8Т311-1), 12 (9Г29-3, 9Г30-1, АКЦ-4-2, 8Т311-1)

### Парковая Батарея (Transport battery) 99-104
- 12 Радиост. Р-105М-3
  - Расчеты
    - 22-23 Транспортировки ракет и боевых частей 8К14 (R-300 NATO Scud B) — rockets and warheads
    - 20-22 Транспортировки ракет и боевых частей 9М21 (NATO FROG-7)
    - 18
    - 17 9Т31М-2
    - 10-12 Технич. обслуж. 9Т29 transporter(-loader)

| | | | |
|---|---|---|---|
| Офицеров (officers) | 41 | Транспортных машин 9Т29 | 9 |
| Прапорщиков (warrants) | 17 | Автозапр. горючего 9Г29 | 5 |
| Сержантов и солдат (sergeants and soldiers) | 265-280 | Автозапр. окислит. 9Г30 | 2 |
| ВСЕГО в/сп | 323-338 | Авт. кислотн. цист. АКЦ | 4 |
| | | Радиостанций | 10 |
| Машин хранилищ 9Ф223 (9F223 (warhead) storage vehicle) | 45 | Автомобилей легковых | 1 |
| Машин автон. испыт. 9В41 | 1 | грузовых | 22 |
| Машин гориз. испыт. 2В11 | 2 | специальных | 116 |
| Грунтовых тележек 2Т3М (2T3M transporter (semitrailer)) | 9 | Автотягачей | 6 |
| | | Автокран 9Т31М1 | 2 |

PRTB 'MODEL' PROVIDED BY SOVIETS TO WARSAW PACT ALLIES CIRCA 1980 AND ACQUIRED SHORTLY THEREAFTER (ALONG WITH OTHER MISSILE ORGANIZATION CHARTS) BY THE CIA

(LEFT) 9F223 TRANSPORTER—EACH OF THE 45 HAD THE CAPACITY FOR ONE MISSILE WARHEAD

examples having been acquired by intelligence. The General Staff Academy 1974 front operations textbook[1285] ordained that...

> Rocket large units and units can be issued warheads from a mobile rocket technical base only when special permission has been received. When increasing the combat readiness of the troops, and in anticipation of receiving such permission, it is advisable to have transports with ready missiles (warheads) in the disposition areas of rocket brigades (battalions) and to keep them under the protection of representatives of mobile rocket technical units. Upon receipt of the signal to issue warheads to the troops, the preparation of front rocket troops for the initial nuclear strike can in this case be carried out in two to three hours for a separate tactical rocket battalion, and in three to four hours for a rocket brigade.

Not only PRTB but also BRTB (East German), PTBR (Polish), PRTZ (Czech) counterparts supported Warsaw Pact shooters. Beginning in the early 1960s contemporaneous with the formation of national missile units a logistics organization had been created on the Soviet model to perform the same functions. These included warhead handling but with a crucial difference; throughout the Cold War no specific evidence emerged of, at least, nuclear weapons under the direct control of any non-Soviet member. Some grounds, however, for suspicion concerned the possessive status of that most faithful ally, the Bulgarians. Warsaw Pact missile-technical units deployed equipped with warhead, missile, and propellant transporters, and a full range of ancillary technical gear. Soviet-branded warhead vehicles had been described for intelligence by unit personnel who made their way West. Exercise support for missile launch units regularly transpired per the Soviet playbook. While Soviet 'intent' to provide WMD to their allies could not be demonstrated all the necessary pieces had been arranged. Tasking of the national PRTBs in the technical preparation of nuclear warheads is less definitive. Documents from the Polish-directed September 1976 *Tarcza/Shchit* exercise specified that national front and army "field technical rocket bases will receive teams which prepare and assemble the warheads who will bring with them the following numbers of nuclear yield warheads..." which implies Soviet postmen; the warheads to be handed over at the highest level SG-5.[1286]

While extensive information regarding missile PRTBs had been acquired, then and now, evidence is wholly lacking for Warsaw Pact national counterparts to Soviet aviation PRTBs. Neither in the Cold War intelligence take, including exercises, classified documents, and HUMINT, as well as material since found in national archives is there even a hint of the existence of national aviation PRTBs. The 1973 Polish front mobilization listing had no air army nuclear support units.[1287] During the 1976 *Tarcza/Shchit* exercise "warhead maintenance and storage teams" conveyed an unspecified part of the front allocation of 96 nuclear bombs to designated airfields within a, slightly later than missile warheads, four to six hours interval following the Full combat readiness signal (implemented prior to war outbreak).[1288] This absence and indirect indications suggest that the Soviet postmen alone had the responsibility for not only delivering air nuclear munitions but also, remaining under their control, carrying out technical preparation and loading of strike aircraft. The differing situations reflect the disparity in scale between the planned massive missile and limited air nuclear strikes to be conducted by national formations.

In the 1980s the US DoD had awakened to the significance of PRTBs in Warsaw Pact nuclear strike preparations. Technical solutions under development pinpointed and targeted these units on the battlefield. I assisted DARPA (Defense Advanced Research Projects Agency) in their work on one such system by clarifying their understanding of missile troops components and procedures. US recognition ran well behind that of the opposition. As early as 1962 two senior officers lamented the "quite unfortunate" tendency of the Soviet military press to ignore "ordnance companies for supplying special weapons" when considering ways to neutralize enemy nuclear systems.[1289] But in 1967 Colonel A. Khorenkov, also writing in VM (S)[1290] regarding these top priority targets, still had to point out the relative futility of pinpointing the elusive shooters when the "special weapons supply companies" that held US ground nuclear weapons for both US and NATO forces constituted a more critical link for degrading Western nuclear capability. This form of targeting would be especially significant during the non-nuclear period when the NATO nuclear response option could be degraded or even eliminated.

PRTBs functioned as the key implementers of WMD employment plans and actual weapons handover a defining moment of a military campaign. By the 1980s these units also had been assigned the task of delivering the new generation of conventional warheads being developed and fielded. Massed conventional missile firings often featured in Soviet exercises. But missile support routines constituted a dangerous tripwire that in war could precipitate a theater nuclear exchange—the first stage of escalation. No indications emerged of Soviet appreciation of the likely NATO reaction to any detection of missile salvo preparations following a PRTB supply run. The US and NATO intelligence services might consider PRTB transfer of warheads to missile launch units as a signal of nuclear strike intent and could trigger a nuclear release to respective delivery units. Lacking any definitive method for immediately distinguishing which variety of warhead would be incoming, NATO intelligence personnel would have little time to identify an imminent Warsaw Pact nuclear first strike that must be preempted. The other side, in turn, would find NATO weapons release on their list of nuclear strike indicators—and could also invoke the operational imperative to preempt. There would have been a great peril that a European nuclear war could be precipitated by mutual misreading of prescribed indications of intent regardless of the political-military decisions of either side.

One early stipulation on the nuclear role of frontal forces had been the 1963 General Staff *Manual On The Conduct Of Operations*.[1291]

> A front (army) offensive operation can begin with massed nuclear strikes by operational-tactical rocket troops and front aviation coordinated with nuclear strikes by the strategic rocket forces and long range aviation.

The Professor in 1967 considered "essential" the launch of front missiles no more than five to eight minutes subsequent to the firings of USSR-based strategic missiles (with their longer ballistic times) to achieve a concatenated impact against enemy targets; as well as careful timing of delivery aircraft takeoffs and flights. A 1970 Polish summary of variant nuclear strike scheduling, drawn from material of the USSR General Staff Academy, included a full schematic depicting a strategic missile attack from P (*pusk*) to P+30 minutes and front missile strikes underway by at least P+45.[1292] Senior officers expressed concern to limit any lag between strategic and frontal nuclear strikes due to differential readiness, the 1974 General Staff Academy textbook had been emphatic regarding the conjunction.[1293]

> Reducing to a minimum the interval between the time of strike delivery by the strategic rocket forces and the front means (which is of enormous importance) is possible through timely notification of the front about readiness for the initial strike, reduction of the time to bring the rocket troops, atomic artillery, and aviation of the front into combat readiness, and through timely implementation of measures for rocket technical support and deployment of the rocket troops in the departure area.

Similar urgency to minimize any gap between strategic and front missile launches during the initial mass nuclear strike had been expressed in a 1977 lecture at the General Staff Academy; reiterating among key factors "timely implementation of rocket technical support measures" to compensate for the initially lower readiness of front rocket troops.[1294]

Oleg Penkovsky had provided the transcript of an address in late 1961 by his sponsor Chief Marshal of Artillery S. S. Varentsov, then Ground Commander of Rocket-Artillery Troops, to senior MoD officers.[1295] Varentsov's poor choice of a protégé would terminate his career. A special report on nuclear-missile supply dealt with launch preparation problems during exercises held that year—including the Soviet groups in East Germany and Hungary—involving PRTBs working with launch units. Varentsov repeatedly stressed close coordination between PRTBs and firing units in quickly preparing the initial nuclear strike. He stated that preparation of the first salvo "completely dependent" on PRTBs, following a combat alert, required about 31.5 hours for operational-tactical systems (then the R-170) deemed unacceptable. He detailed proposed measures that would reduce this time by nine hours, and even by 18 hours for tactical rockets that had required 35 hours to prepare for a mass firing. The R-300 system pending introduction had an even quicker response time. One of these measures, to be carried out both in the groups and MDs in peacetime, entailed a preferred "common location or a short distance between the PRTB and the brigade with which it coordinates."

The situation of the group in Hungary had been further expounded by General-Major F. Marushchak and a colleague in a 1966 VM (S) article that cited the experience of SGF exercises in 1964-1965.[1296] Concerned with the offensive variant of unit deployments directly from permanent garrisons they stressed the readiness of missile troops and PRTBs; advocating the dispersal of all missile troops "under the guise of exercises" prior to that of other front units. PRTBs, in their view, should have a minimum number of nuclear warheads on hand for not only the front initial strike but also sufficient to fulfill the front immediate task. The warheads in storage should advance to level SG-3 without a check cycle. The preceding technical readiness SG-2 would correspond to a surprisingly low level for a nuclear warhead in a deployed peacetime storage location; levels SG-2 and SG-1 more likely at bases of the Center or even in factory condition. A number of Soviet authors advocated spurring nuclear warhead technical upgrading in the interest of expediting delivery. The clear implication of the 1966 article inhered that one or more PRTBs resided in Hungary prior to the mid 1960s—with a stock of nuclear warheads.

Missile troops officers often proposed schemes for reducing strike time-to-launch through technical and organizational improvements. These writings, and practice in exercises, assumed a quick response necessitating a high degree of missile launcher readiness and a concomitant expectation of readily available nuclear-armed missiles. Only a few of these, among many on the same theme, can be considered in detail. Several articles during 1966-1967 in VM (S) seem to have reflected an ongoing concerted effort to enhance strike readiness. In the first 1967 issue[1297] General-Major L. Sapkov—the First Deputy Commander of the Rocket Troops and Artillery arm and thus a key decision maker—reviewed proposals in these articles with the intent to differentiate between those which "have been applied in practice" and those not yet resolved. He emphasized the critical importance of missile troops readiness to preempt the enemy "it logically follows that a massed nuclear strike by a front should be delivered using the greatest possible amount of nuclear means simultaneously with the first strike by strategic means."

A proposal that missile units should be given pretested airframes at one per launcher had been implemented and this echeloning had reduced strike preparation time by four to six hours. But a continued "weak spot" lay with the two or three hours required to prepare each nuclear warhead. Sapkov noted that "the problem of the prolonged storage of warheads in Special Readiness 5 [SG-5] had been solved technically" and apparently favorably viewed a proposal by General-Colonel G. Kariofilli (RVA chief of staff) in a 1966 article.[1298] Essentially Kariofilli argued that a proportion of nuclear warheads could thus be held by PRTBs which had already been tested "without a monitoring cycle" for transition to SG-5. These could be delivered to firing units during a threat period or when on combat alert for immediate mating to those on-hand missiles. A 1978 Soviet document[1299] issued to a Polish front exercise confirmed that nuclear warheads would be handed over to missile delivery units at the SG-5 level. Sapkov also highlighted a proposal that certain systems carry out initial strikes from siting areas close to their permanent garrisons. The effectiveness of this method in substantially reducing the time for strike preparations had been demonstrated in an early 1966 research war game. To accomplish this of course would necessitate stationing PRTBs, with the minimum required nuclear warheads, in such proximity that the strikes could be carried out in the short time period demanded.

The Soviets ran separate technical readiness schedules for nuclear warheads and missiles. For undiscovered reasons the warhead numeric levels ascended while that of their carriers descended; thus at stage G-1 a launcher would be at the firing point, missile erect, guidance system activated, and mated warhead at SG-5. Further muddling the calculations of the front-army missile-artillery armament service different G-schedules applied to the R-300 (Scud B) and R-65 (FROG-7); operational for much of the Cold War the first a guided, liquid propellant missile and the latter unguided, solid propellant. Into the 1980s procedures would have merged as the intended replacements for both systems became guided as well as solid propellant. Information abounded regarding preparation and launch procedures, discussed in classified documents; from serving officers and crew; along with practice in many exercises. An example of the prescribed arrangements for an initial mass nuclear strike is available in the General Staff Academy 1977 bloc on front operations.[1300]

Lesson 7a outlined a nuclear-missile delivery scheme in three echelons. The first echelon comprised front and army PRTB holdings of R-300 nuclear warheads at level SG-5 which on the transfer signal would be mated in the missile battalions to airframes already on hand; with R-65 held by the PRTBs maintained at G-4 which meant that warheads had already been pre-mated for delivery to tactical rocket battalions.

Notably these deliveries would be accomplished prior to the front attaining the Full combat readiness stage—Military Threat not yet introduced—"kept under the supervision of mobile missile technical base representatives." These missiles made up the first salvo of the initial strike. Subsequent firings during this mass strike, the second echelon, would be immediately prepared either by the launch unit organic technical batteries and platoons or "more typical" by the PRTBs; warheads at level SG-4 shifted to SG-5 without carrying out the normal test cycle; overall time required to transition second salvo warheads and missiles to level G-4 had been calculated at 15 hours for six R-300 and five R-65 within 5:35; the refires would then be moved by ground transporters to the shooters. Third echelon reloads of the front first operation allocation had to be provided by arsenals and bases of the Center.

The ORPDn (independent rocket transport battalion) functioned as the agent for central resupply; this missile-technical unit had the dual responsibility of transshipping missiles of both surface-surface and surface-air types; with a subunit assigned to SSM warheads. Setups positioned OPRDn at rail unloading stations and/or materiel support airfields to receive deliveries from the Center by either transport mode. SAM refires would be transported therefrom to the front-army equivalents to PRTBs, the ZRTB (*zenitnaya*—air defense). All of the Warsaw Pact nationals had OPRDn equivalents such as the German based at Brück. Exercise *Tarcza* 1976 depicted two such units in the multinational Northern Front at different rail stations with each picking up 30 missiles as well as nuclear warheads at SG-4.[1301] The Academy lesson also specified that arriving nuclear warheads would be at level SG-4 but required that the test cycle be carried out to attain SG-5. The ORPDn role would necessarily be altered in the 1980s by the new 12 GUMO STGs which essentially co-opted nuclear warhead delivery. Evidence then and now is lacking as to the measures involved in this segment of re-echeloning. Potentially, the ORPDn had been assigned the primary mission of providing the substantial reloads of conventional warheads entailed in the mass firings becoming a major feature of the non-nuclear period.

A 1998 Russian newspaper interview quoted an officer identified as 12 GUMO-affiliated describing this echeloning as a "three-strike system" with first and follow-on waves, a continuous augmentation with no resemblance to the rigidly bifurcated US intelligence model. His delineation confirmed the lineup depicted by the Academy course and other sources with the first two 'strikes' already held by the PRTBs of the front. The third strike arrived by "motorized and railroad formations" which is to say PRTBA and PRTBZh controlled by 12 GUMO. The officer also pinpointed SG-5 as the most advanced level of nuclear warhead readiness.[1302] Thus the Soviet scheme essentially provided for three nuclear missile reloads, at least in Western directions, much of which would have to be forward positioned to meet the timelines specified in classified documents.

A number of articles had dealt with the alert and dispersal of missile strike units from their permanent garrisons, setting up siting areas, and joining the initial strategic strike. Obviously, given the front systems involved, this applied primarily to those shooters actually within range—in the Soviet Central European groups. Kariofilli in 1966 had focused on the role of PRTBs in preparing the initial strike following a combat alert, which he accounted for as much as 80 percent of the total time expenditure. Kariofilli had been particularly concerned with the variant of an offensive launched from permanent locations in which too much time elapsed dispersing the firing units and PRTB deliveries. He proposed setting up combat duty launch sites for operational-tactical systems within 10- to 15-km of garrisons and pre-assigning targets so that their launchers would be ready to fire within 20 to 30 minutes. Intelligence had identified the out-deployment of at least one battalion of all army-level R-300 brigades in the GSFG; such dispersed basing might have been intended to facilitate this combat duty scheme. Thus the nuclear warheads destined for on-duty missile elements would not only have to be near at hand but even, under PRTB control, at siting areas and perhaps already mated. Kariofilli noted that a larger number of launchers would be available for the initial mass strike if supplied with nuclear warheads at SG-5 on declaration of a threat period.

Colonel V. Aleksandrov, responding to Kariofilli in a 1967 VM (S) article,[1303] went even further in proposing the establishment of permanent alert siting similar to strategic missiles for some front launchers. He advised that dispersing firing units only after a combat alert would provide warning to the enemy. Missiles could be kept at the alert sites in condition G-3 [R-300 fueled and warhead mated, on launcher] or even G-2 [launcher at firing point] for up to several months; nuclear warheads could be "kept in a combat-ready status for a specific time period" but would then require rechecking at the supporting PRTB. Aleksandrov suggested two paths to readying missiles that had not been placed on alert.
- locating PRTB "assembly brigades" in the launch units with initial strike nuclear warheads at SG-5
- storing these first salvo warheads at SG-5 in selected missile battalions, which would necessitate the construction of suitable structures, where scheduled technical work could be carried out

As a result of these measures, in his proposed initial mass nuclear strike schedule the front delivery means at alert sites would be enabled to fire within 20 minutes of the launching of strategic missiles.

Colonel A. Rodin in a 1969 article,[1304] which dealt with missile-technical support in the non-nuclear variant of a front offensive, came to a similar conclusion. He cited operational command-staff and research exercises regarding the non-nuclear period in proposing that ready missiles with nuclear—and chemical—warheads sufficient to fulfill a front immediate task should be held within subordinate missile units. But the 1974 General Staff Academy textbook on front operations cited only Aleksandrov's first path—PRTB controllers in the "disposition areas" of missile units—which would permit an initial mass nuclear strike by missile brigades within three or four hours or an hour less for tactical rocket battalions.[1305] Preparations for the first offensive operation by the Coastal Front, in both nuclear and non-nuclear variants, according to the scenario of the 1977 Academy lessons included placing one battalion of each missile brigade on alert status during the opening deployment of missile troops "following receipt of permission to issue nuclear warheads"—alert launchers could then deliver a strike within ten to twelve minutes.[1306]

So far as known to US intelligence none of Aleksandrov's proposals for maintaining a high level of front missile readiness had been put in effect by the Soviets until 1984 when SS-12 Scaleboard (R-900) brigades redeployed from the USSR to East Germany and Czechoslovakia. Whether or not by intention one brigade had been aligned by each of the three strategic directions of the Western-Northwestern TVDs. This movement had been implemented as a counterpoise to the introduction of US INF missiles. Distinctive nine-pad permanent firing positions had been constructed at the beginning of deployment of this system in late 1967—in fact the sites had been identified on imagery in Western MDs and along the Chinese border long before the missile units and equipment—but the R-900 at that time answered to the strategic missile service.[1307] The brigades in Central Europe established individual battalion fixed alert sites with either four or six concrete pads. Protective shelters erected provided for not only each launcher but also one shelter at each battalion site for warheads. This alert setup constituted the only occurrence known to intelligence during the Cold War of the Aleksandrov second path for storing warheads at SRBM firing units. Unfortunately recent information has revealed that, undetected, Soviet missile troops in Hungary had implemented the Aleksandrov alert mode, perhaps soon after the proposal (to be continued).

The other side already had an established European system of delivery means available for a quick nuclear attack in the 1970s. Alert aircraft had been positioned with their nuclear payloads already fitted while missiles with mated nuclear warheads could launch within 20 minutes.[1308]

But 1960s proposals to enhance launch readiness of front missiles, both in peace and in combat, maintaining nuclear warheads at the highest level SG-5 near or in the delivery units, immediately raised the issue of positive control. Among the measures cited by a General Staff Academy lecture on employment of front-army missile troops in early 1969 (actually prepared the previous year) to ensure readiness for the initial nuclear strike had been "steps to prevent unsanctioned missile launches."[1309] Colonel A. Postovalov expressed particular concern regarding potential unauthorized nuclear launches during the non-nuclear period of operations in VM (S). In a 1967 article[1310] he highlighted the risk of nuclear action without VGK permission by commanders in a "difficult situation" or "spontaneously" during intense combat especially if communications to higher authorities had been disrupted; suggested preventive measures included development of reliable authentication signals as well as "technical" solutions to preclude unauthorized actions by missile crews. Postovalov again addressed the non-nuclear period in a late 1970 article[1311] in which he repeated the situation in much the same words and that "it clearly is also necessary to have a technical solution to the problem by creating a device which would make it impossible for a nuclear missile to be launched" without higher level permission.

Thus nearly two decades into the era of the nuclear variant the Soviets still had no equivalent to the US PAL (permissive action link) system intended to preclude an unplanned nuclear detonation. PAL mechanisms of successive designs had been deployed since the early 1960s[1312] but even the US took many years to fully outfit the nuclear weapons inventory. Postovalov's recommendation had been implemented by at least 1973 when the KBU (*kodoblokirovochnoye ustroystvo*) or 'interlock' came to notice. Automated "electronic code-activated interlocking devices"[1313] required additive code strings to pass strike execution orders from the VGK through the military hierarchy to individual launchers (still requiring 15 to 20 minutes); replacing a telephone call to the responsible commander to open an envelope that had the launch order cipher—but during the time frame of this procedure there had been no block fitted to warheads or missiles.[1314] Strategic missiles also had "a reliable system of NSP" from at least 1975 requiring an unblocking signal and key insertion.[1315] Weapon activation required a code entry; in conformance with orders or a signal from as low as brigade level (a retransmission from higher authorities); entered by only knowledgeable individuals of the Special Service (probably part of the Sixth organization). Unlocking became one of the actions necessary to achieve missile G-1 and could be delayed on aircraft until aloft. At least by the end of the 1970s increasing indications of missile/warhead self-destruct features added an extra layer of assurance in the event of KBU failure.

Abounding evidence, in particular classified writings and manuals, had been acquired by intelligence to trace the development of nuclear-technical support to front missiles onward from the early 1960s. Soviet prescriptions for both weapons and operational procedures had been prioritized to minimizing the interval between strategic and frontal strikes—in the first half of the 1960s conducted on a massive scale marking the outset of a European war. The paramount components of front missile readiness situated with the PRTBs of a front and subordinate armies. These units held most or all of the first two of three envisioned salvos of the nuclear period; which might occur at the outset of the front first offensive operation; necessarily held in peacetime at a RTB to ensure required periodic servicing; a certain proportion of the warheads maintained at the highest level of the technical conditions scale, SG-5, with those at SG-4 to be rapidly upgraded; both the PRTB and nuclear-missile inventory must be within a close distance for carriage to operational-tactical missile brigades and tactical rocket battalions in order to meet a launch requirement measured in a few hours; and in any threat period prior to achievement of Full combat readiness would be expected to be immediately positioned with an alert missile detachment. The final nuclear warhead technical stage SG-5 by Soviet definition pertained only to those quickly available, launch-ready, in contradistinction to those held at lower stages at central bases in the USSR. The disposition of Soviet forces facing NATO dictated that these measures be most urgently implemented for the delivery means in proximate range—those in Central Europe.

## leaning forward

Ace agent Oleg Penkovsky had provided clues regarding deployments of the nuclear missile first echelon during several 1961 meetings with US and British intelligence. Citing as his source Colonel I. A. Gryzlov (deputy chief of the GSFG rocket-artillery armament service)[1316] who had been directly involved setting up.[1317]

> …I have heard that there are two hidden storage areas in the DDR where atomic warheads are stored…I know this "exactly", like 2x2 4—two stockpiles, two locations…I don't know where these depots are, but it should be very simple for you to find out.

This touching confidence in the capabilities of his hosts would, unfortunately, prove to be sadly misplaced. Penkovsky also stated that modifications had been made at existing artillery supply dumps in the GSFG to shelter missiles, and that the first missile brigade assigned to this group may have arrived in 1959. Transcripts of the meetings, along with the extracted summaries of intelligence information reports, have been largely declassified. A 6 September 1961 CIA memo on the status of Warsaw Pact forces presumably alludes to his information in that "there is some evidence that nuclear warheads are presently stocked in East Germany for Soviet ground forces, although storage sites have not been identified."[1318]

Western intelligence services efforts to verify evidence from Penkovsky and other sources ensued both intensely and futile. Signals intelligence supplied much of the data concerning Soviet forces in Central Europe including missiles. Overhead imagery—satellite and aircraft—exploitation hindered initially by poor quality and infrequency improved but effective Warsaw Pact denial measures, frequently assisted by prevalent regional cloudy weather, often degraded surveillance. Within the USSR the relative value of these collection tools reversed; satellite imagery more fruitful in monitoring the full extent of military capability and activities; a circumstance of access. Despite a growing body of evidence concerning Soviet and Warsaw Pact nuclear delivery forces acquired through electronic monitoring, however, there continued to be a gaping hole concerning one aspect of Soviet mass destruction weapons—location. The capabilities and collection intensity of both technical means improved exponentially through the 1960s and into the 1970s but still provided no discernible answers to the WMD problem. Classified Soviet and Warsaw Pact documents acquired, while of great value concerning organization and operations, lacked specificity regarding actual presence. A steady stream of human source reporting, including defectors and emigres, provided little reliable information concerning nuclear (or chemical) weapons deployment.

For NATO the question of the peacetime presence in Central Europe of nuclear and other mass destruction weapons betokened a crucial and disturbing unknown. Their national intelligence services persisted unable to answer the question of location for nukes (and chems) as well as the requisite delivery missiles. Warsaw Pact planners would have to provide a substantial logistics base for their envisioned mass employment by forward-based strike assets of missile- and air-delivered nuclear weapons. If forward warhead stocks did not exist, transportation of hundreds of nuclear weapons during a period of European tension would be a prominent, likely detectable, telegraphing of intentions. The essence of the problem had been stated in the NIE *Capabilities of Soviet General Purpose Forces* edition dated 21 October 1965—with a prescient conclusion.[1319]

> 40. We have been able to identify nuclear weapons storage sites only inside the USSR. If the Soviets do not already have nuclear weapons stored in Eastern Europe, a substantial logistical effort would be required to supply a reasonable quantity for the delivery systems currently in the area. For example, a large number of sorties by transport aircraft would be required to move warheads and bombs forward from storage sites inside the USSR. We estimate that the Soviets could launch nuclear-armed aircraft from East Germany bases within a few hours after the transports had landed at the bases. In the case of Frogs and tactical missiles, we estimate that it would take longer to move the warheads to the delivery units because reshipment by land transport or helicopter would be required. Movement of nuclear weapons from the Soviet Union by rail would, of course, take considerably longer than by air. In view of the above, we think that there is a good chance that nuclear weapons are stored in some GSFG depots, although we have no firm evidence.

This NIE series reiterated the negative finding in November 1966;[1320] and "as yet we have firmly identified nuclear storage sites only in the USSR" in November 1967;[1321] while even the December 1969 edition, having now noticed something at a few airfields, would still assert "We believe that nuclear weapons are not normally stored in the forward area."[1322] But as the 1965 estimate underwent distribution Soviet work had been progressing on the first official nuclear bunkers—designated Type IV—in Central Europe at five airfields in East Germany, Poland, and Hungary; these had been completed far in advance of the 1967 NIE. Construction of the bunkers had actually begun in late 1964 but some had been first identified on imagery only in 1968 and the rest in the early 1970s; even in early 1971 two forward Type IVs had not yet been identified.[1323] The bunker cult scripture seemed thereby to have been verified. But according to one Soviet retrospective exercises as early as 1956 had allocated 20 nuclear bombs to the aviation of a front.[1324] Another seeming anomaly had been that the ten airfields within the USSR where Type IVs appeared, when tenanted, mainly based medium bombers of Long Range and Naval Aviation—and aircraft of this class periodically conducted flight exercises rebasing to Central Europe. The Professor had indicated in 1964 that the TU-16 (Badger) might be included in the complement of front aviation,[1325] an affiliation repeated by others in the later 1960s pages of VM (S); a 1971 CIA report concurred.[1326]

Nuclear-capable IL-28 delivery aircraft had been based in the Soviet groups during the 1950s. But intelligence had no better success identifying aviation nuclear storage prior to the appearance of the Type IV than in finding missile nuclear warheads. Some early speculators hypothesized that the airfield Type IV RTBs might also supply warheads to missile units. But this model would be discounted, judging that insufficient storage space existed even for the number of nuclear bombs in exercise allocations. Another problem concerned the Soviet Air Forces-subordinate KR-180 (FKR-1) nuclear-capable cruise missile that had been identified in the early 1960s circa Ludwigslust. The garrison location in the northern GDR may indicate planned targeting against NATO naval and amphibious operations on the Baltic Sea coast. No source for any KR-180 nuclear warheads, which considering the Cuban deployment may have been plentiful, would ever be (and has not yet been) pinpointed. This system departed service in the later 1960s.

Another wave of Soviet Air Forces RTB construction followed in the early 1970s, centered on the new Type VIII double. Five RTBs augmented IVs in the same countries (identified only after 1975) plus the first Czechoslovak placement. The Soviets apparently called this type *Granit*. In addition a dozen of yet another variant, basically half of the official Type VIII, came out immediately after the doubles; these, after much disputation generally accepted (at least by air analysts) to be "temporary" shelters, that is, for dispersal of aviation nuclear

(Above) Type VIII double with loading dock positioned to left interior of one tube

Dossier Official Nuclear Storage Bunkers

Type IV the first official nuclear bunker identified outside of the USSR
(Above) storage hall
(Left) service bay ceiling elevated for traveling overhead hoist—massive hall entry door
(Below) characteristic loading dock that augmented original gantry crane

weapons during a threat period. Some nuclear specialists remained ambivalent about the breed—your intelligence connoisseurs become highly uncomfortable when confronted with variations on what they think is a reliable known. The largely complete airfield RTB network in Central Europe may have been celebrated by the 1973 GSFG exercise that featured an unusually high front aviation nuclear allocation. The aviation official nuclear bunker network would be rounded out in the 1980s by a Type VI RTB with two bunkers at Nobitz (Altenburg), the only one of this design in the Soviet groups. Choice of a Type VI occasioned surprise since, although 42 of these bunkers had been built from as early as 1964, all remained native to the central and eastern USSR; most had been added in the early 1970s. Geo-locations indicated a strong Chinese flavoring to their WMD. Most Type VI RTBs, evenly divided between front aviation and missiles, had three bunkers.

The airfield official nuclear bunkers in Central Europe had all been identified years after completion. Photo interpreters in aviation cubicles focused on aircraft modernization, eager to spot the latest fuselage protuberances signifying upgrades, rather than the routine details of air bases. Many of the nuclear storage sites and their seemingly distinctive bunkers, all at or in the immediate vicinity of the airfields, had been recognized only after deliberate search by nuclear specialists. Their suspicions had been aroused concerning the lack of forward aviation nuclear storage after identifying such facilities at many airfields within the Soviet Union. In later years the air experts would become more attuned to infrastructure clues to weapons development. Manifest now that the two successive generations of aviation nuclear official bunkers had been built concurrently within the USSR and among the Soviet groups deployed in Central Europe. East German bunkers in fact dated among the first Type IVs and VIIIs to be constructed. The eventual success would not be matched in the identification of missile nuclear warhead stores.

The question of the availability of nuclear warheads for the missiles that had been deployed forward to carry out the Soviet WMD schema presented another matter altogether. Construction of nuclear official bunkers for warheads at USSR Ground Troops RTBs proceeded by 1960 at the front missile-artillery bases. Ground army-level RTBs began to appear in 1962 coincident with the Soviet creation of army PRTBs in a revamping of the missile-technical organization. By the mid 1960s those bases in the western military districts had been largely completed. No RTBs, with official nuclear bunkers, replicating the MD structure had appeared anywhere in Central Europe during this period. This aberrant situation despite the manifestly coincident USSR-forward construction of airfield nuclear official bunkers. Failure to identify any nuclear—and refire missile—storage in the Soviet groups of forces became, an increasingly aggravated, intelligence festering wound.

Soviet ground nuclear capability in Central Europe had steadily improved and expanded across two decades. The preeminent Ground Troops missile strike asset, the Scud series, had been upgraded from the R-170 to the R-300 beginning in 1961, nearly doubling range. A third firing battalion augmented these missile brigades in order to increase first salvo capability while enabling a more flexible displacement by battalion during anticipated rapid offensives. The number of launchers in R-300 missile brigades subordinate to fronts and armies uniformly amplified, led by the front units, from six (in two battalions) per brigade at the outset of deployment; to nine (three battalions) by the mid 1960s; twelve by the early 1970s; and eighteen in front-level brigades in the late 1970s. By 1979 the eleven identified forward Soviet R-300 brigades had at least 150 launchers or more than 2.5 times the original complement. As explained in the 1969 General Staff Academy Rocket Troops and Artillery lecture "The number of missile launchers in a front has a direct bearing on the number of targets to be destroyed simultaneously" during the first salvo of the initial mass nuclear strike.[1327]

In 1981 one of the front-level brigades in the GSFG disappeared and 18 launchers had apparently been distributed among the remaining two front brigades. These brigades subsequently handled the same 54 launchers previously controlled by three brigades; their 27-launcher complements a unique missile organization during the Cold War—each of the six firing battalions had launcher numbers that a decade and a half earlier equated to a full brigade. By the second half of the 1970s the guided *Tochka* missile entered service, replacing the divisional battalion unguided R-65/R-70 (in the following decade a modified version increased maximum range from 70- to 120-km). These battalions in turn had launcher complements increased from two to four during the period. Nuclear artillery made an appearance, at least in exercises, in 1976.

While a rough estimate of the number of Soviet missiles could be obtained from production data, on some systems, US intelligence lacked specific evidence for any precise breakdown by armed service, weapon system, or deployment location which could be used to determine the Central European allotment. The Soviets developed their stockpile requirements in terms of weapons accounting units, e. g., conventional ammunition in combat units or BK (*boevyy komplekt*). A BK norm would be established for each type of weapon; a military unit allotment equalled the number of organic weapons multiplied by the individual weapon BK. General-Colonel (Retired) I. Volkotrubenko discussed the basis for an ammunition stockpile formula in a 1970 VM (S) article,[1328] given as $P_s = (N_z K_0 + (N_v K_0))$ where $P_s$ represented the total requirement for the peacetime stockpile, $N_z$ the Western Theater single gun norm, $N_v$ the Eastern Theater norm, and $K_0$ the number of pieces of a particular caliber. His norms had been set at that particular time on the basis of the pre GPW calculation for a peacetime reserve accumulation of two months expenditure for the West, and three months in the East, plus mobile reserves held by individual ground divisions. Ammunition needs would subsequently be met by industry production upon the conversion to wartime rates initiated during the Special Period.

An early model of nuclear-missile allocation (only partly known by the US during the event) is the Soviet 1962 expedition to Cuba. Given the geographic situation nuclear delivery units had few prospects for any resupply. Intelligence assessed that the Soviets had shipped 36 missiles for the three R-12 (SS-4 Sandal) regiments on the island, each of which built eight launch pads. The reload factor thus amounted to 1.5, identical to launchers of the two R-14 (SS-5 Skean) regiments which never arrived. A 1.5 ratio for both warheads and missiles had been specified in a 24 May 1962 planning document for Operation Anadyr.[1329] But frontal systems had also been shipped with lower yield nuclear warheads considered to be "a kind of extra-powerful artillery shell" by one participant.[1330] The Anadyr planner A. I. Gribkov memoir also provided the battle order of the regrouped contingent including composite motorized rifle regiments with three *Luna* (FROG-3/5) units (normally subordinate to ground divisions) of two launchers each. The regiments had actually been pulled from a different military district than the *Luna*. The 12 *Luna* nuclear warheads delivered amounted to a 2.0 reload factor. Intelligence had identified FROGs, which also sported conventional warheads, during the crisis but remained blissfully unaware of their nuclear ammunition. In startling contrast the two KR-180 (FKR-1) cruise missile regiments, each with eight combat launchers, could draw from a pool of 80 nuclear warheads or a 5.0 reload factor. Intelligence not only failed to identify the regiment genus but also remained unaware of this nuclear machine gun prepared to greet any US landings by sea or air. The reason for the much larger cruise missile allocation has not been revealed by Russian testimony but may have been due to anticipated losses inflicted by enemy air defenses.

Missile reserves available for follow-on strikes, especially strategic systems, had long been a point of contention among intelligence agencies. One prominent example had been the short but intense dispute between the CIA and the DIA regarding the Soviet enumeration of the SS-20 in the 18 November 1987 transmittal of systems data required by the INF Treaty. Late 1975 information on the SS-20 program had indicated that force planning provided for the manufacture of five airframes per launcher and that ratio may have excluded a training stock; but the projected deployment of 28 missile regiments[1331] rather undercounted the 48-regiment force that eventuated. INF Treaty data[1332] for all declared SS-20 locations amounted to a smidgen over 1.2 combat missiles for each launcher (650 missiles and 523 launchers) inclusive of 36 missiles still being assembled at the production plant. Expenditures during testing and troop training (closely monitored by intelligence) could not account for the large discrepancy with the preceding reload plan—Russian sources put that number at 190 including the 72 INF elimination launches.[1333] Even adding these system firings ups the ratio to just 1.6—a 1985 NIE had imputed a 2.0 SS-20 missile inventory.[1334]

The only other fully deployed INF missile, the Scaleboard "OTR-22" (R-900 *Temp*), had a declared total stockpile amounting to 5.6 combat missiles per launcher. One Russian source reported that 427 of the 9K76 variant had been expended during system lifetime[1335] attaining nearly 8.9 missiles for each of the 130 launchers declared under the INF Treaty. From initial deployment in 1965 until about 1969 this system had been controlled by the strategic missile service— the only true mobile missile fully deployed with the RVSN until the introduction of the SS-20. All other INF missiles had been in process of phase out, or in, so other Treaty stockpile declarations could not be definitive for these systems. Three R-900 brigades moved to Central Europe from the end of 1983 into spring 1984 established a ready strike force comparable to deployed SS-20 regiments. The full number of declared "OTR-22" launchers and combat missiles in their two East German siting areas equated to a 1.5 reload factor in the north and 1.7 in the south with a Czech 1.6 ratio. Muddling this calculation the INF data indicated that each brigade had from four to six more launchers than assessed by intelligence. Information eking out from Russian sources indicates that the excess had been purposed to conduct training at the lowest, battery, command element. If training batteries are excluded, the reload factor becomes more than two combat missiles for each launcher.

While the INF Treaty negotiations had been in progress I prepared and gave personalized briefings regarding the Scaleboard system on two occasions to the head of the ACDA (Arms Control and Disarmament Agency) that had been requested by Kenneth Adelman. I also had been tapped to prepare and present an intelligence backgrounder on our capability to monitor the Treaty to the staff of the Senate Select Committee on Intelligence on 27 July 1987—following extensive vetting by the CIA arms control staff. Tasking earlier in 1987 entailed investigation of the SS-20 refire question.

I conducted an exhaustive review, integrating our extensive satellite imagery coverage and SIGINT reporting, that encompassed organization and operations at all 48 bases supporting deployed SS-20 missile regiments as well as ten parent division complexes. There had been a dearth of human sources, including SS-20 crewmen, in marked contrast to the many Soviets who had served in, what the West designated intermediate- and medium range, sedentary missile units. Of course the Soviets had developed mobile missile operational and support procedures on the basis of the preceding regime and intelligence could follow the same path in achieving insights regarding the descendants.

The only plausible conclusion affirmed the lack of any true refire capability at the division-regiment levels. Sufficient time did not remain before Treaty agreement to examine the superior levels, missile armies and the, all-important, arsenals and bases of the Center. Indications suggested that the missile divisions held, tenth, launchers for each subordinate regiment as specified in the preliminary arrangement; the 1985 General Staff Academy lecture on the strategic missile force disclosed that missile regiments, type not identified, comprised ten launchers.[1336] Spares could be used for routine training as with Scaleboard units but also provide a launcher reserve. Soviet INF data had listed one, two, or three launchers and ten transporters (two per regiment)—vehicles that could be used for missile downloading and rotation as well as reloading—at the complexes of the six western divisions, each of which had five subordinate missile regiments. But the Soviets had somehow collected 68 launchers, or more than one for each deployed missile regiment, from somewhere, at their declared elimination base.

Provenance of at least 27 of the 68 launchers could have been nine western missile regiments abruptly reduced from a prior complement of nine launchers to six (also declared in the INF Treaty data). The discounted missile regiments conveniently accorded with the October 1985 Gorbachev proposal during a visit to Paris to freeze at 243 the number of SS-20 launchers targeting Europe.[1337] That level coincided with both the June 1984 deployment preceding the Soviet SS-20 surged response to US INF missiles basing in Europe as well as a claimed equation to the size of the French and British independent strategic nuclear forces. The USSR General Staff Chief clarified the Gorbachev promise to mean the excess would be "withdrawn from combat alert" a nuance that escaped Western public and media comprehension, some second-translating as launcher dismantling or removal eastward.[1338] Marshal Akhromeyev's actual Russian wording likely had been the designation 'combat duty' which is altogether different from 'combat alert' in Soviet terminology. Oddly during exercises conducted by some of the reduced-strength missile regiments the number of launchers had rebounded to nine. The declared pool of non-deployed launchers provided a reserve that could quickly be tapped during any East-West crisis, rendering the Gorbachev initiative essentially meaningless.

A reload factor of 1.5 for longer range missiles so frequently appeared in both exercises and classified writings dealing with allocations for initial operations that this ratio seems to have been a planning norm. Vitaly Katayev had stated that submarines carried a strategic missile BK (term specified) of about 0.7 out of a total 4 to 5 missile BK available for most systems; he thought 1.5 BK would have been an adequate national stockpile.[1339] A combat missile reserve for the SS-20 would thereby require a substantially higher number than declared in the INF Treaty. Most discrepant had been the numbers declared for the "non-deployed" category of combat missiles. A January 1988 briefing text asserted a quantity of declared non-deployed SS-20 missiles "well below the DIA estimate"[1340] while two months later the US Senate Select Committee on Intelligence report on Treaty monitoring and verification found an "unresolved controversy" persisting among intelligence agencies.[1341] The CIA accepted the missile returns, finding harmony in the available evidence for SS-20 manufacturing rates at Votkinsk. Ultimately Reagan administration foreign policy priorities overrode any departmental intelligence skepticism and treaty ratification proceeded.

Cold War evidence pointed to the application of the BK accounting method for both nuclear warheads and missiles in theater forces. Colonel Wardak's notes from the Military Academy of the General Staff indicated that the circa 1973 norm for the initial offensive operation of a front amounted to two nuclear warheads for each R-300 launcher and three for each R-65.[1342] These allocations generally agreed with the "three-strike system" and could be expressed as reload factors of 2.0 and 3.0 respectively. Ratios did not necessarily equate to weapon or delivery unit BK; allocations usually given as a fraction or multiple BK. Intelligence had little information on actual nuclear and missile BK in contrast to an abundance of data on conventional armament. Evidence indicated that one BK for a Soviet R-65 battalion with four launchers amounted to eight rockets or a reload factor of 2.0; a Soviet fire order specifying a battalion expenditure of 0.75 BK would equate to a 1.5 reload or a full salvo followed by a second partial salvo by two launchers. As echeloned, prescribed portions held by the missile delivery unit and respective PRTB would be supplemented during the operation by a delivery from Center stocks. A muddling consideration is that the quantity of resupply warheads and missiles would be magnified by the Soviet logistics requirement that deliveries fulfill the allocation not only for the front first operation but, in the Western TVD, that at achievement reserves meet the norms for the succeeding front operation—i.e. during the first operation central deliveries for two front operations would be ongoing. Lacking are indications in classified writings or exercises for the dimensions of any nuclear warhead reserve allotted for operations deep in the Western TVD including that disposed at the Tula-50 (Belev/Prilepy) SOC and Mozhaysk-10.

Soviet classified writings provided some clues although these came in the form of author proposals rather than established norms. Colonel A. Sulim in 1968[1343] laid out a detailed missile supply calculation that considered operational factors such as the strike-on-vacated-slot problem, degree of damage requirement, launch reliability, and pre-strike losses—but his model encompassed both nuclear and chemical warheads. He presumed that in peacetime an incipient front would store some 60 percent of a warhead-missile allocation with the remainder to be supplied during offensive D+2 to D+7; a derived "coefficient" of 1.6 to 1.9 for operational-tactical missiles and 1.5 to 1.8 for tactical rockets would meet the requirement of the front first operation. In the next year Colonel A. Rodin contemplated[1344] fulfilling the front initial mass strike during the non-nuclear variant, however, his calculations for missile-technical support again included chemical as well as nuclear warheads; the "rough calculation" for a type front reserve for this missile onslaught amounted to 2.0 nuclear and 1.0 chemical each for five operational-tactical missile brigades (nine-launcher complements) and up to thirteen tactical rocket battalions of divisions in the front first echelon; he also allotted both warhead types for a cruise missile regiment (possibly KR-500 as did Sulim). A new problem for the missile support structure, with minimal accumulated experience, had emerged in the increasing prospect of large-scale conventional strikes; a burden eased somewhat because, unlike nuclear, these technologically advanced warheads would come "in ready form" to the front—he recommended additional ORPDn as a conveyance solution. Rodin also stressed reduction of mass strike preparation times which in exercises had been determined to not exceed 24 hours in the peacetime scheme, i.e. the first two of the "three-strike system" echelonment. In 1970 Colonel A. Postovalov[1345] considered only nuclear warheads, again in the non-nuclear period, in proposing echeloning operational-tactical missiles at 1.0 in army brigades (still nine launchers) and at 1.1 in the army PRTB. Divisional tactical rocket battalions (three launchers) would be maxed out at 3.0 on organic transporter-loader vehicles with yet another 2.0 or so at the supporting PRTB; this would permit a double-launch initial mass nuclear strike, the second within two hours by OTR and in an hour or less by TR.

Data acquired from Soviet and Warsaw Pact exercises also provided a basis for estimating nuclear warhead-airframe stocks however these figures, as in classified documents, persisted fragmentary and confined entirely to the first offensive operations of fronts and their subordinate armies, divisions, and aviation-missile delivery units. Extrapolation to USSR district, group of forces, national or TVD level is problematic. Sample data on front allocations as an official school exercise is more comprehensive. The 1977 General Staff Academy course[1346] provided a complete front offensive plan for both the conventional and the nuclear variants. The nuclear-missile allocation for the first operation amounted to launcher reload factors of 1.6 R-300 and 1.8 for the R-65 complement. Quantities for each system available to the front at operation initiation amounted to 80 percent or 1.3 and 1.4 respectively; the tactical rocket allotment far less than that suggested by Postovalov, not concerned with financial aspects. Missile-wise the Academy gave no attention to conventional fires which within a few years attained significant expenditure levels. Thus the June 1980 exercise of the Soviet-Hungarian Balaton Front depicted availability of 1.9 nuclear warheads but 3.7 missiles for each 9K72 (R-300) launcher; 2.0 and 3.7 respectively for 9K52 (R-65/70); with warhead resupply from the Center during ten days of combat amounting to 0.4 and 0.5 of each system.[1347]

Other indications of the actual warhead-missile first echelon had been provided in 1987 by the Soviets in their official data for the INF Treaty. The SS-12 Scaleboard had both nuclear and conventional (and of course chemical) warheads, so the relatively low 2.0 or less ratios for the delivery units in Central Europe points to an interchangeable approach for warhead selection rather than a dedicated missile allotment for each type of warhead. Similar INF data for the R-400 in East Germany amounted to a higher reload factor of 3.3. But this system in the midst of an ongoing deployment throughout the Ground Troops cannot be taken as a valid indication of the full scale of the planned Soviet stockpile of R-400 missiles particularly when a likely significant conventional role is considered.

Factoring the available evidence on Soviet warhead-airframe allocation procedures an informed calculation would assign a minimum 1.5 reload factor for the nuclear warheads actually present in Central Europe; sustaining an immediate massed nuclear strike of one complete salvo and a partial second salvo. Applied to the Soviet missile structure at the end of the 1970s this would amount to 411 nuclear warheads (at least 225 R-300 plus 186 R-65 and R-100); imputing two full salvos, accumulation would reach 548 nuclear warheads. Perhaps 70 percent of the complete allocation for the first front operation might be on hand, considering the data from exercises and classified documents of the 1960s-1970s, in the Soviet forward groups of forces.

However data recently accumulated regarding the Soviet Southern Group nuclear delivery means presents a substantial deviation.[1348] Nuclear warhead inventories at two RTBs supporting operational-tactical missile brigades and tactical rocket battalions of divisions from 1965 to the late 1980s consistently leveled at 1.0—the first strike. Geography suggests a differential equation applicable to the Soviet groups—the distance from missile deployment areas to the strategic reserve at the central objects—which for the GSFG doubled that of the SGF bordering the USSR; and required extended rail-road transit of a potentially troublesome Poland. Only in 1989 is a 2.0 reload factor applied to the recently formed 9M79 *Tochka* (SS-21 Scarab) tactical 459 Missile Brigade (Baj) at the supporting RTB. The Hungarians during the 1980s enjoyed a surfeit OTR nuclear reload varying 1.5 to 2.0 at 1542 RTB Úrkút while their TR barely made 1.2 in 1980; but by 1986 bombs for an incipient national aviation nuclear mission had risen from none in 1982 to 60 available. The Hungarian authors report a doubling of 152-mm 2S3 nuclear artillery rounds for both Soviet and national systems; from 2.0 to 4.0

each designated piece; 44 to 176 at the two Soviet RTBs; and 36 to 72 at 1542 RTB.

Further complicating the situation is the testimony of a Russian officer serving at one RTB in the 1980s, late in the period no longer storing tactical warheads, holding 22 nuclear warheads for an expanded 18-launcher 9K72 brigade still amounting 1.2. He identifies a re-echeloning of all stored nuclear weapons from the "first wave" to the subsequent, i.e. second rather than first strike, no explanation offered. One implication highlights the role of the new central STGs in the first mass nuclear strike; suggesting a penetration down to the level of army attack systems for at least missiles and artillery.

To arrive at the total Warsaw Pact missile nuclear allotment would require the application of at least the 1.5 multiplier to the national missile complements; 1981 Polish missile inventory data[1349] specified 3.0 for 28 R-17 (Scud B) and 4.0 *Luna M* (FROG-7) for 43 launchers but does not discriminate nuclear vs. conventional missions. An upward adjustment in the nuclear numeration for the 1980s would have to be made to account for nuclear artillery rounds and a reorganization of the tactical missile structure that would be implemented. In addition exercise indications of a trend to full second salvos, in the enlarged initial mass nuclear strike, might preference stocking for a minimum 2.0 reload factor as for Hungarian R-17.

Soviet ground and air delivery capabilities had been enhanced as operational priority shifted to conventional variants, posing the potential assignment of the nuclear initial strike to forward-based systems. Front missile and aircraft nuclear armaments became capable of demolishing Western Europe without any strategic assistance. Decoupling represented the more immediate nuclear threat to NATO and a likely first stage of escalation. Pinpointing the nuclear missile support structure in Central Europe posed an ever amplifying critical issue—and a major intelligence gap.

A remedial solution for the missile warhead component of this gap—admissible in the contemporary US intelligence perceptual window —would not be identified until 1971.[1350] Again belatedly, recognition dawned that the Soviets had already inserted a new variety of official nuclear bunker at twelve somewhat remote locations in East Germany, Poland, Czechoslovakia, Hungary, and Bulgaria. The essentially identical bases eventually picked out on satellite imagery had been built from 1966 through 1969. There had been no information from other sources regarding the construction or purpose of these RTBs. Each had two official nuclear bunkers as the centerpieces of dedicated garrisons with co-located housing and vehicle storage. The moniker Type VII had shortly thereafter been applied to this particular design. A collective sigh of relief rose among those connoisseurs following the nuclear warhead question. They now had an opportune answer to a nearly decade long problem.

As is always the case with intelligence issues, this apparent rejoinder to one set of questions only instigated another set. One salient consideration regarded how to fit all the missile nuclear warheads allocated to first echelon fronts—the presumption adopted of both Soviet and Warsaw Pact national warheads—into 24 official nuclear bunkers. A long-running numbers game ensued controlled by varying data in classified documents and exercises. Hindering any precise estimate, uncertainty regarded the portion of the bunker interior arrangement dedicated to storage versus other functions, such as utilities, as well as unknown warhead type mixing and Soviet atomic materials technical norms. Proposed capacity tended to be expressed in terms of high/medium/low based on differing suppositions. The numbers trended lower over several years. A mid 1970s estimate thus, assuming maximum use of interior compartments, posited a range from 172 to 372 warheads per bunker; an early 1979 Warsaw Pact forces NIE revised the individual bunker capacity sharply downward 70 to 120.[1351]

A widespread perceptual 'iron curtain' at the USSR border rendered methodologies applied more problematic. No comprehension of materiel echeloning existed, that these sites composed part of a forward-pushing WMD system extending back to the bases of the Center. After all, that's not the way the US stockpiled nuclear weapons in Europe. Plans for US, and NATO distribution, of nuclear weapons did not envision resupply from US continental stocks. Movement of weapons would have to be accomplished by airlift, which would delay and adversely strain the already heavy, and increasingly significant, demand for aircraft movement of vital troop reinforcements. In addition Europe lacked acceptable storage facilities for early resupply. The estimates might actually have been more realistic had the nuclear and theater forces maestros run the formula as requirement = initial strike + reserve. Or, they could have reversed perspective 180 degrees and applied the Soviet munitions planning formula based on BK allotment by weapon and firing unit. But prevailing contemporary ignorance of the actual structure of Soviet nuclear- and missile-technical support would have negated achievement of any hypothetical reality.

Actually a few other, unquestioned and perceptually disregarded, anomalies inhered within this official model as evolved by the late 1970s.

Construction of Type VII sites had not begun until 1966 and the bases completed, successively, during 1968-1969. Operational status had been achieved as much as a decade following the introduction into the groups of forces of missile systems central to nuclear warfare plans—the spearheads of the WMD Operation. Until the mid-1960s all Soviet theater operation variants assumed mass nuclear exchanges (integrated with chemical strikes) immediately upon the outbreak of a European war. Soviet classified as well as open press writings on nuclear warfare stressed the imperatives of forestalling NATO nuclear strikes and the absolute priority of destroying enemy nuclear means. In their discussions concerning nuclear targeting, as has been pointed out, Soviet officers emphasized the urgency to accelerate the response times of front missiles in order to augment strategic strikes. They specified technical and organizational measures—all of which both assumed and required proximate availability of nuclear warheads.

AND

While cramming hundreds of nuclear warheads into these bunkers a corresponding minor technicality involved delivery. Type VII sites lacked missile storage; no missile facilities nearby; intelligence had not identified storage places for missile reserves anywhere in Central Europe, whether for the Soviets or for their allies. There had been evidence that the launch units themselves held a prescribed complement, the initial salvo, of missiles for which a portion of forward warheads had been allotted. But there would also be a considerable second salvo and in the most likely variant of war outbreak increasingly large numbers of missiles would be assigned to conventional strikes. Intelligence could not account for the substantial stock of refire missiles required, and the expenditure rates depicted, in Soviet military exercises and writings. No such mystery existed within the USSR. Conjoined storage of warheads and missiles characterized some 48 Ground Troops missile RTBs; PRTBs invariably co-located, or nearby, structured and equipped for joint warhead-missile transport.

AND

The critical role of PRTBs in nuclear-missile support had been glaringly evident in the Soviet classified writings acquired in the 1960s-1970s. Exercises through the 1970s, conducted by the Soviet group in East Germany in particular, consistently portrayed PRTB activities to such an extent that, in the context of front and army operations, their presence could hardly have been fictional. But (except for one ignored, second kind, indication) intelligence had no evidence of disposition, and remained blissfully unaware of the significance of these units in the overall scheme.

AND

A striking discrepancy existed between the number of Type VII sited on each allied territory and the actual disposition of the forward-deployed Soviet missile armada. Two bases in the GDR supported some 70 percent of the, steadily increasing, number of Soviet launchers, presumed also to support East German missiles. Three other Warsaw Pact allies each hosted three bases. Proposals had the three in Poland in some way supporting the Soviet group in Germany but these also held the full ground nuclear warhead allocation of a Polish front; two Type VII in northern Poland, moreover, had been poorly positioned to support the GSFG and had all been spotted by Polish MD/army. The observed USSR missile logistics network manifested more complex and diversified; active armies demonstrably each had an affiliated RTB-PRTB, so the GSFG quota would be, a minimum, one base for each of five armies. But exercises conducted in the GSFG since the mid 1970s consistently indicated that ground army support came from two PRTBs: one assigned to the army missile brigade while the other PRTB resupplied the rocket battalions then subordinate to divisions—thus already at the wartime *shtat*. Changes to PRTB organization could be tracked in the classified documents acquired during the 1970s.

AND

Three Type VII each had been built in Bulgaria and in Czechoslovakia. The percentage of forward Soviet missile launchers in the former amounted to zero—no Soviet forces ever stationed in Bulgaria. Construction of the Czech sites had been initiated long before the, uninvited, arrival of Soviet forces during the 1968 Warsaw Pact invasion that terminated the Prague Spring. In both countries work started on the Type VII sites in 1966, the year before initiation in East Germany, Poland, and Hungary. The sole official aviation nuclear storage site in Czechoslovakia had been built after the establishment of the Soviet Central Group—and none identified in Bulgaria. These RTBs, even dispersal bunkers, had been built only at Soviet-controlled airfields in countries with groups of forces.

AND

While Soviet Air Forces RTBs had been built concurrently within the USSR and in the forward groups of forces, construction of the Type VIIs did not even begin until after completion of nearly all Ground Troops missile RTBs in the west of the homeland. Unlike the airfield sites, no installations comparable to the Type VII had been built within the Soviet Union at any time. No exact domestic counterpart to this bunker design materialized, although a version resembling the VII built, or started and never completed, at a limited number of missile RTBs.

AND

Despite the intelligence propensity to apply that favored analytical method, mirror-imaging, one reflection went unnoticed. Soviet storage bases containing only warheads looked rather like those US sites in Europe that retained custody of nuclear weapons for wartime release to NATO delivery units; including warheads for missiles already in national inventories. Planning for such an arrangement, and concurrence at a government leaders meeting in Paris, had taken place in 1957. The subsequent NATO Stockpile Plan had basing countries provide external security but with specific measures to ensure US control even when national alert delivery units took possession of nuclear means. One guidance required that national units be maintained in the same readiness conditions as those of the US.[1352]

AND

…yet more quibbles, all immediately evident reasons why the Type VII solution did not quite work.

Overall the configuration and placement of the Type VII bases demonstrated a glaring inconsistency with the scale and deployment pattern of Soviet missiles yet strangely harmonious with the troop dispositions of their allies. If correct, this official model disposed the Soviets to quite helpfully simplify NATO targeting of the entire nuclear warhead inventory intended for Warsaw Pact missiles by compression into a relatively small number of locations.

The Type VII solution had gaping holes that should have been evident to anyone knowledgeable of Soviet missile troops organization and operations. Inhabitants of the intelligence otherworld, however, are masters of the art of fitting square pegs into round holes. In the ever-recurring theme of Cold War intelligence, the official nuclear bunker model prevailed despite multiple indications of something fundamentally amiss with the perceived WMD structure in Central Europe.

Into this cozy analytical scene in 1979 marched the *praporshchik* from Torgau.

**paradigm bounce**

The Soviet defector informed his CIA interrogators that he had been serving in a communications platoon, under the headquarters battery, of 45 *Podvizhnaya raketno-tekhnicheskaya baza*. In accordance with the intelligence preference to anonymize sources he would be known only as DS-339. The PRTB stationed at the munitions depot near Torgau; with a conventional ammunition storage section but his handlers controlled segregated areas of the same installation. Designated "technical territories" in the PRTB portion separately stored warheads (he had heard nuclear), missiles, and unit vehicles. Bunkers inherited from the original German *Heeres-munitionsanstalt* (Army munitions establishment, *Heeres-muna* or *Hma*) held the warheads, subject to periodic checks. He had observed a "technical" building in the warhead area that somehow related to those items. The PRTB worked with a missile unit in the vicinity of Oschatz.

Ammunition depots in the GSFG had been examined over the previous two decades for evidence of nuclear activity—after all Penkovsky had said to have a look—but nothing of interest had been detected. A late 1970s CIA imagery study of the Soviet missile force in East Germany suggested that some of the depots, including Torgau, exhibited missile indications. Totally unexpected however, a classic bolt-from-the-blue, broke the implication that the familiar USSR arrangements for nuclear missile support had been replicated in Central Europe in a entirely different form. No Western intelligence service had ever fancied such a full-scale deployment. The "technical territories" at Torgau could be immediately confirmed from satellite imagery. These areas exhibited discrete security enclosures and the utilization of original German bunkers and buildings. The Soviets had carefully inserted a nuclear missile logistics base into the preexistent installation, maximizing use of structures that often dated back to the 1940s or earlier, and minimizing distinctive additions. They had accomplished a masterful work of deception, a classic case study in Soviet operational *maskirovka*.

One of many Soviet definitions of *maskirovka*, from the General Staff Academy as presented in volume one of *The Voroshilov Lectures*,[1353] defined

> a collection of measures conducted in terms of aim, time, and space to deceive the enemy about the location, ability, and composition of the troops and targets (especially nuclear rockets), the status of preparation and combat actions of the troops, and the plans and intentions of the troops. It is a type of combat support measure which ensures surprise action and protection of the combat capability of the troops.

*Maskirovka* could be implemented at any level, conducted against all forms of intelligence and reconnaissance. The protective aspect thus offered a viable alternative to conspicuous hardening of installations and, unfortunately for the connoisseurs of intelligence, avoidance of the convenient bunker cult objects.

Ironically, despite the radical departure from the structural ground plan that intelligence observers had been self-conditioned to expect, the Soviets had created a new pattern quickly uncovered—another useful application of imagery clusivity. The bludgeon administered by the Torgau source redirected attention to an alternative, previously unperceived, indications set. Within a short period CIA imagery analysts began to identify installations with features similar to those observed at Torgau. Twelve additional East German suspects would be picked out, and eventually, five in Poland and Hungary. Eleven of these had been plunked within conventional ammunition depots and six partitioned at Ground Troops garrisons; all segregated installations under Soviet control.

Shared characteristics included separate territories for warheads, missiles, vehicles, and at some, Scud fuel (bipropellants) storage—all structural components known to constitute an RTB within the Soviet Union. In East Germany and Poland warhead enclosures at the ammunition depots incorporated groupings of standard German *Hma* bunkers that predated Soviet occupation. Similar bunkers at the garrisons likely had been constructed by the Soviets. Adjacent secured sections contained a variety of elongated shelters with dimensions capable of holding missile airframes. The installations had been hidden in plain sight, not just one or a few places, but a complete frontal nuclear missile logistics system. These substituted RTBs had elements in common but each also represented a local adaptation executed with varying degrees of success.

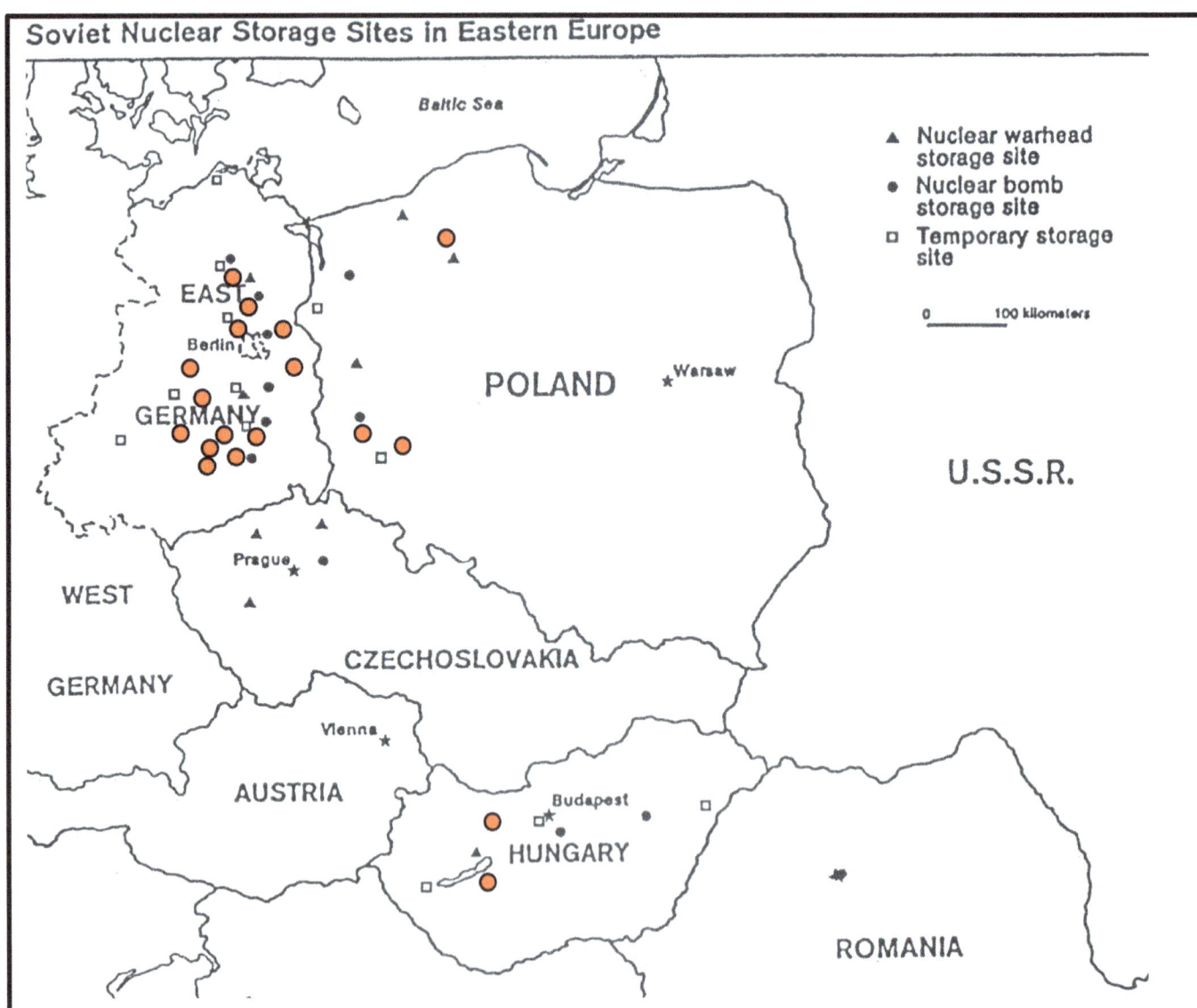

### Soviet Nuclear Storage Sites in Eastern Europe

- ▲ Nuclear warhead storage site
- ● Nuclear bomb storage site
- □ Temporary storage site

PRE-VIEWS

NATIONAL INTELLIGENCE ESTIMATE 11-14-79 *WARSAW PACT FORCES OPPOSITE NATO* DATED 31 JANUARY 1979 MARKED ALL KNOWN OFFICIAL BUNKERS IN THE SOVIET GROUPS OF FORCES—NINE TYPE VII ("WARHEAD") ELEVEN AVIATION TYPE IV AND VIII DOUBLES ("BOMB") AND TWELVE DISPERSAL TYPE VIII SINGLES ("TEMPORARY")—RED DOTS ADD THE 18 MISSING NUCLEAR MISSILE RTBs

A recall of some prior intelligence evidence, of the second kind, enlightened that these bases did not represent a recent deployment.

- In 1974 a KGB officer (DS-317) defected who had been assigned to a line unit of 20 Guards Army near Bad Freienwalde northeast of Berlin. He stated that a PRTB occupied the same garrison and that this unit controlled a nearby facility. His observations had attracted only limited intelligence attention—merely a new order of battle entry—the implications unrecognized.
Bad Freienwalde made the list.

- Extensive information on the deployment and operational procedures of missile-technical units such as PRTBs acquired from signals intelligence monitoring of field training and command-staff exercises throughout the 1970s. This data attested unequivocally to the actual presence of PRTBs, not just notional representation, in the Soviet groups. Ignorance of even a basic outline of the nuclear warhead support structure again ensured inattention.

- Multiple authoritative indications as early as 1961 and into the 1970s from Penkovsky, Varentsov, and others in Soviet classified writings that associated PRTBs, Central Europe, and nuclear warheads. Varentsov in the 1961 briefing had presumed a norm for PRTB delivery of two nuclear salvos at the outset of combat—which meant that each and every Scud and FROG launcher in the groups of forces would require more than one nuclear warhead closely available.

- In a rare instance of tracking, assessed to be the first GSFG exercises involving the actual practice of nuclear/missile weapons handling in 1960 included activity back-traced to ammunition depots Altenhain and Hohenleipisch. Both list entries—and may have been those alluded to by Penkovsky although the connection cannot be affirmed.

US, British, and other NATO intelligence services had failed to track down these PRTBs despite the wide array of clues indicating actuality, from an early date, in the groups of forces. PRTBs functioned as the most significant players, **the** critical interface, in the Soviet WMD game-plan. Absence of intelligence urgency and prioritization directly reflected a widespread superficial understanding of the Soviet military structure in general and missile logistics in particular. Not until the early 1980s would the significance of the PRTB-RTB relationship be fully explicated.

Review of 1960s imagery from intelligence systems revealed that modifications had been made at several suspect bases prior to 1965—simultaneous with missile RTB construction within the USSR. This parallel work of course would then match the aviation deployment pattern of concurrency. Timing can now be moved even further back by Soviet and East German aerial photographs of some of the bases that have become available as well as information from post Cold War Russian sources. *Hma* Altenhain had been altered by August 1959 with a secured bunker grouping and a light railway through missile storage buildings. Hohenleipisch in a photo of May 1959 has no indications in the future warhead and missile storage areas while the eventual PRTB motor pool persisted vegetated. Russian accounts[1354] of the initial deployment of missiles into Central Europe include GSFG brigades during 1958-59; 233 Engineer Brigade in September 1958 to separate garrisons in the area Dessau to Leipzig; and 77 Engineer Brigade by early 1959 to at least one Weissenfels installation—thus confirming Penkovsky. Each, redesignated a Rocket Brigade in 1959, had been equipped with the R-11 (8A61) version of the SS-1b Scud A which could only deliver conventional, high explosive, warheads. In the pivotal year 1959 both had been rearmed with the nuclear-capable R-11M (8K11). A PRTB accompanied the first brigade which subsequently relocated to rail station Kapen (Oranienbaum)—only much later entered on the RTB list. Geographic locations of these units indicate Altenhain likely supported 77 Rocket Brigade. During the progressive introduction of army-level brigades in the early 1960s 233 Rocket Brigade had been subordinated to 18 Guards Army; upon dissolution of that army in 1964 to 1 Guards Tank Army; then retrograded to Slobudka in the Belorussian MD supporting 28 Combined-Arms Army; and in 1985 rearmed as the first 9M714 *Oka* (SS-23 Spider) brigade.

In the mid 1950s the Soviets and their allies had issued varying plans to ban nuclear weapons from certain geographic areas; forestalling US deployments would have important ramifications for Warsaw Pact theater operations. A proposal for a Central European 'nuclear weapons-free zone' had been tabled in 1956 to the United Nations General Assembly.[1355] This campaign had similarities to that of the 1980s failed attempt to stymie the introduction of US INF missiles which, as did the earlier nuclear means, presented a significant danger to Soviet forces—and in both periods the lack of a favorable Western response impelled direct counteractions. The aborted career of the U-2 likely contributed to US intelligence taking the wrong track on Central European nuclear logistics installation. The earliest missions in 1956 had provided extensive coverage that included East Germany and Poland. But President Eisenhower, who personally authorized each sortie, became increasingly skittish concerning overflights of Communist countries. The limited number he permitted had to be prioritized to cover the USSR. Wider imagery coverage had been unavailable during the critical 1956 to 1960 period when construction of a Soviet forward nuclear support complex had likely initiated. If early bases had been noticed there would have been a, minuscule, chance that the ensuing official nuclear bunker model might have been stillborn.

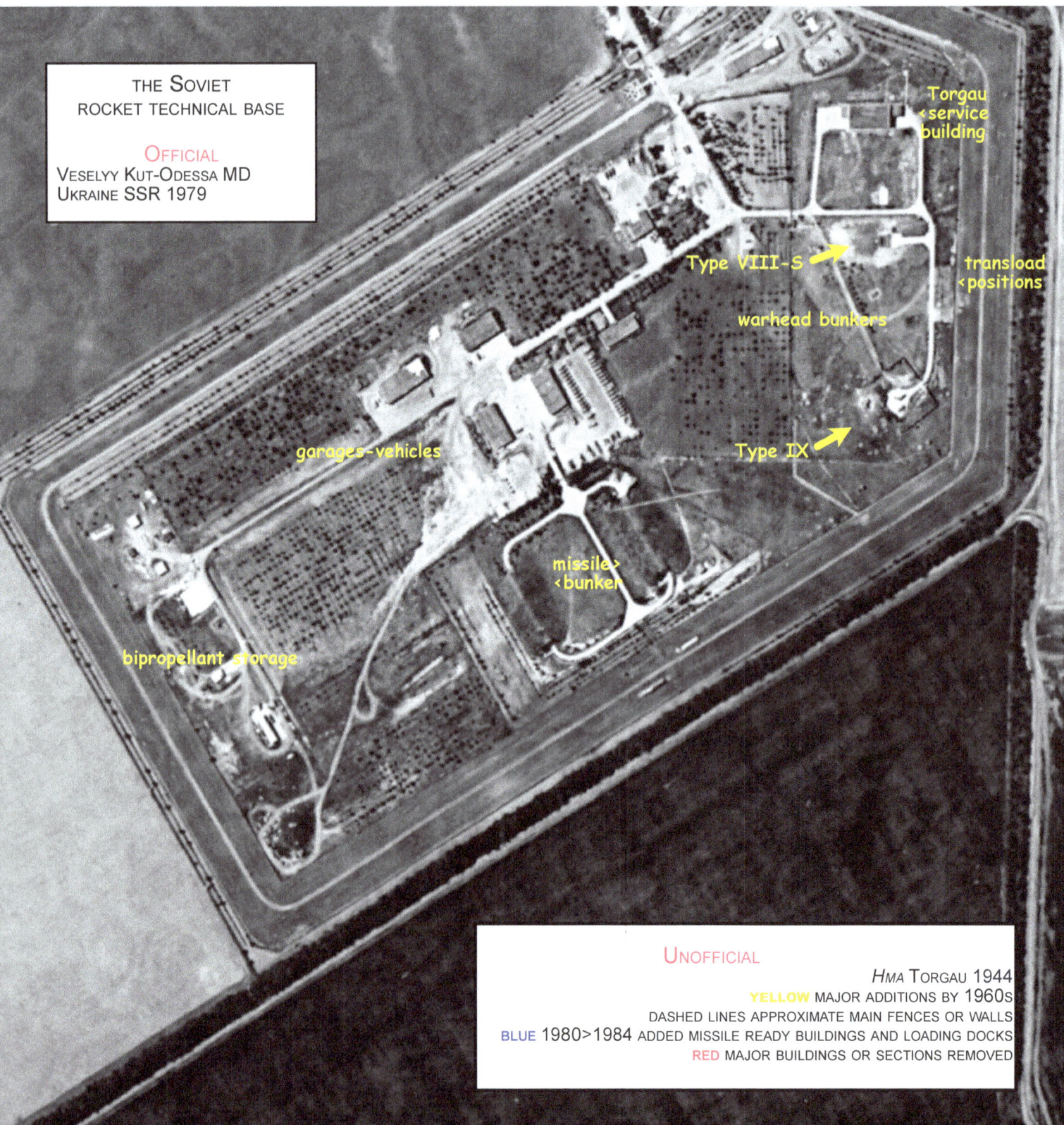

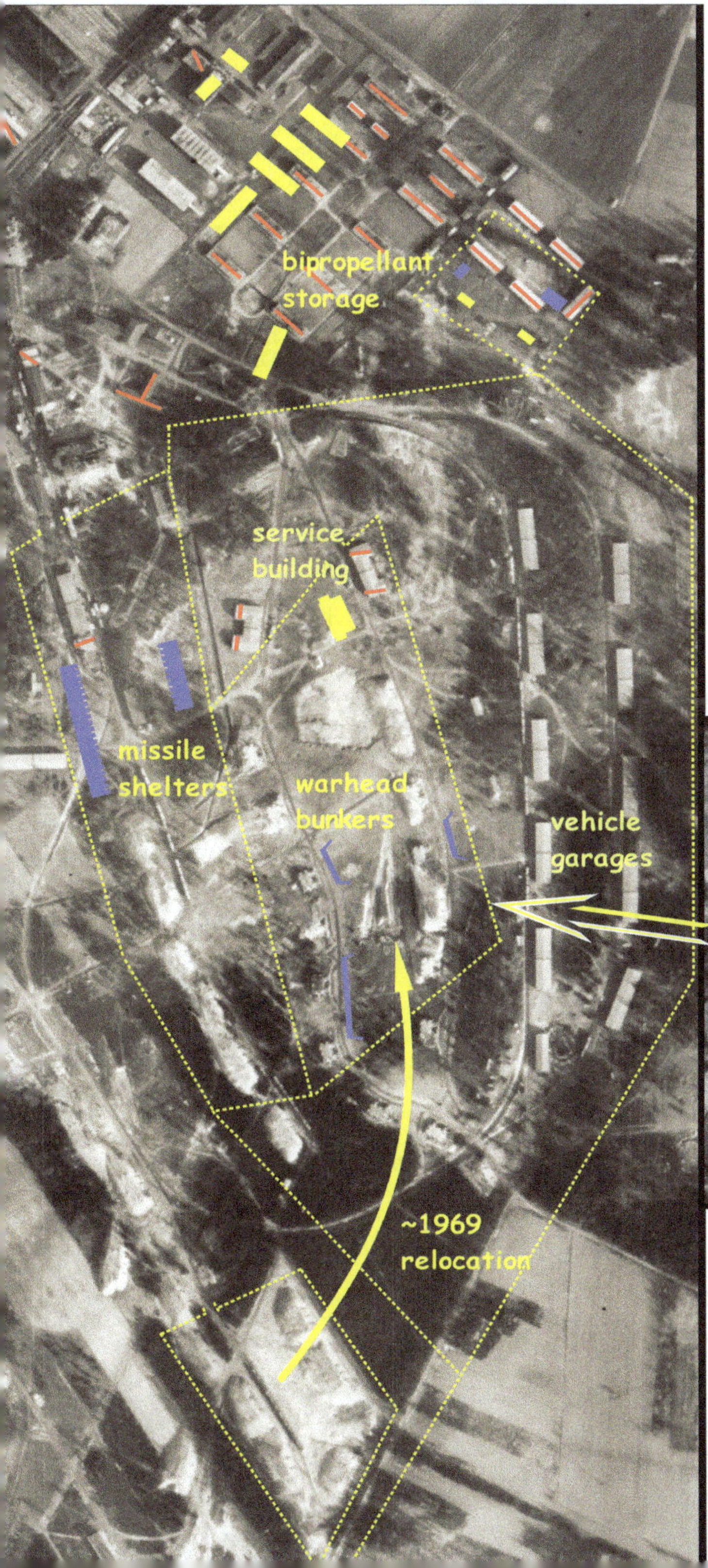

During the turmoil of Russian dissolution of the, redesignated, Western Group of Forces a missile-artillery officer who decided to remain in the West provided intelligence a, confirming, list of ground missile support units; one ORPDn garrisoned in the Fürstenwalde area had not been identified. Additional evidence has been forthcoming from sources in Russia and former members of the Soviet Empire. The Internet has been a popular place to post retrospectives and memoirs. In particular the Russian edition of Wikipedia has a page on 12 GUMO[1356] that attempted to compile a comprehensive profile of the nuclear support structure—but service PRTB listings had been unaccountably expurgated during 2012. The Wiki original page inclusions of unofficial PRTBs of the Ground Troops in the Soviet groups of forces largely coincided with those which we arrived at in the early 1980s. The notation for Torgau, however reliable the source, had 45 PRTB present in the GSFG from 1962 to 1991.

More than a few instances occurred during the Cold War of US intelligence failure to detect nonconforming practice. An even earlier exposition of the official nuclear bunker model transpired during the October 1962 Cuban missile crisis. The discovery of the introduction of strategic missiles had not been

complemented by identification of the whereabouts of the essential nuclear warheads. US intelligence assumed that the warheads must be present but no storage sites could be confirmed. This oversight had no serious consequences as events actually played out. The Soviets did not deploy these missiles to Cuba in order to set up a caviar delivery service for the American market. Where the consequence of intelligence malfunction potentially could have been disastrous entailed the planned invasion option if implemented.

The Soviets had concentrated all nuclear weapons on the island in a few storage locations due to local security concerns. But this action blatantly violated their own operational principle of protective dispersal. A golden targeting opportunity had been presented to the US—if the location of the nuclear sites had been known—to at least interdict transport to the delivery units, if not capture or destroy the nuclear stores. Thirty-six nuclear warheads for the three R-12 (SS-4 Sandal) missile regiments had arrived on 4 October and then transported by road convoys to a storage site near Bejucal.[1357] Of the 134 nuclear weapons debarked from their transport vessels in Cuba (24 warheads for not-deployed R-14, SS-5 Skean, remained aboard) all but 46 had been collected in the Bejucal area including all tactical *Luna* (FROG) and half of the cruise missile warheads.[1358] According to the commander of 51 Rocket Division this "group storage facility" put the warheads at distances varying 110- to 480-km from the three regiments requiring a minimum of 14 hours, and 24 hours for the remotest, to achieve launch readiness. Concern with the threat of US air strikes motivated the subsequent dispersal of the warheads, to unspecified locations, on 27 October, reducing all delivery-mating times to 10 hours. Delayed construction of "structure No. 20"—an official bunker identified by intelligence—complicated the situation.[1359]

The American invasion plan had allocated a substantial proportion of aircraft sorties to destroying the missiles. But without warheads these merely constituted, entirely threatless, scrap metal. The aviation strike diversion would have greatly reduced air support to the amphibious landings, which would have faced a stronger Soviet contingent than expected by US intelligence, ensuring a bloodier outcome if not defeat. An even greater danger, unknown until years later, had been the abundant supply of cruise missile and FROG nuclear warheads intended to greet sea landings. Providential how the US 'won' the Cuban missile crisis.

Only subsequent to the missile retreat had van-bodied trucks, the standard transporters for warheads, been spotted on low level aircraft imagery acquired during the crisis period. The warhead storage sites never retrospectively had been pinpointed and have been revealed only in Russian accounts. American author Michael Dobbs, during research for his 2008 book on the Cuban crisis,[1360] managed to succeed where US intelligence failed and, using the Russian information, identified a Bejucal warhead storage location on crisis aircraft imagery. He also found intelligence reporting on this site that had dismissed importance due to lack of nuclear markers—after all, no evident official nuclear bunker. US intelligence of course did not have Russian testimonials to aid in finding the storage locations. But the imagery found by Dobbs clearly shows a group of van trucks parked at the Bejucal site. Picking out warhead transporters presented a tricky proposition during the Cold War even though some unique features could be discerned on overhead and ground imagery. The Soviets and their allies fielded a wide variety of van bodies on trucks for communications, maintenance, and other specialized functions that often confused identification; while the standard warhead carriers might be van trucks, most van trucks did not transport nuclear warheads. The failure of US intelligence to lock on vans at a Cuban site that had been categorized as munitions related, however, is inexcusable—in this context these vehicles constituted a red flag that should have instigated closer scrutiny.

For two decades, on a much larger scale, an eerily similar fiasco had unfolded in Central Europe. Only one of the 18 suspect installations in East Germany, Poland, and Hungary had official nuclear bunkers. The Vogelsang base north of Berlin had originally been built for an early strategic ballistic missile deployment. This event had somehow gone unnoticed by Western intelligence services. Even in 1979 two bunkers at Vogelsang persisted being misidentified as the type used for missile storage. The tale of this incident has been related in my 2006 monograph *Making the (Right) Connections*.[1361] There had even been a Cuban angle to this particular instance of an egregious intelligence lapse involving strategic missiles deployed to the GDR.

Soviet use of preexisting conventional munitions depots and shelters for nuclear weapons storage, while meeting the concealment objective, did have some drawbacks. On 14 August 1977 a Soviet ammunition train that had pulled into the Dannenwalde depot, 66-km north of the Brandenburg Gate in Berlin, apparently sustained a lightning strike. The apocalyptic results immediately became evident to the townsfolk. Rockets ignited and hurled throughout the depot environs, detonations propagating among storage buildings and revetments jammed with ammunition crates.[1362] Currently available post event overhead photography is nine months subsequent. While this cover reveals extensive ongoing earth movement in the depot northern zone establishing standard ammunition revetments (two immediately south of the secured warhead area and several further away north) there is no obvious explosion damage in this or other zones. German high resolution infrared imagery acquired in 1992 also reveals no apparent residual effects. Three *Hma* bunkers may have been holding circa 24 nuclear warheads—estimating a 1.5 reload allocation to the four-division 2 Guards Tank Army; while also considering individual bunker floorspace and the lift capacity of 3397 APRTB. Warheads for these 16 FROG-7 tactical rocket launchers then had yields varying from 10-kt up to 300-kt. Westward in 1977 no one had been aware of the contents of certain bunkers. To this day little notice outside Germany has been directed at this potential nuclear catastrophe. Chernobyl met with a decidedly more dramatic treatment.

The proposition that there might be an alternative to established dogma on Soviet nuclear weapons procedure immediately encountered an outraged response from the

(TOP) RTB Kapen

Dossier *Hma* bunker (East) Germany

(RIGHT) RTB Wulkow entry triple-layer door arrangement with electrical boxes and water sump

(BELOW) RTB Wulkow interior tie-rod grid for securing and grounding warhead carts

guardians of the official nuclear bunker model. Mainly high-priests of the bunker cult ensconced in the science-technology directorates of the CIA and the DIA; and representative of residents in both organizations with blinkered perspectives of their respective insular topics. Two senior nuclear weapons connoisseurs, in particular, from cubicles in each of the S&T Directorates led an assault on the new paradigm. They not only disputed evidence and conclusions other analysts reached but also exploited their key positions to actively obstruct, through the 1980s, the coordination of any revised intelligence estimate. The CIA connoisseur soon became uncomfortable with his office environment and transferred to the DIA, joining his colleague in an extended campaign throughout the WMD bureaucracy. This dynamic duo accused the CIA interviewers of the Torgau source with 'seeding' to guide his responses. Rejecting storage of nuclear weapons in the old German bunkers on the grounds of technical impossibility, they proclaimed official Types the only visible truth. The bunker cult delimited all perceptual scrutiny of Soviet nuclear weapons storage.

I entered the fray by 1980 having devoted several years investigating the three types of mass destruction weapons and their delivery means within the USSR. Although analytically indoctrinated with the official nuclear bunker model, thoroughly imbibing all postulations, my approach to research had been more broadly systemic. I had conducted an integrated evaluation of all intelligence evidence, historic and contemporary, in order to construct a comprehensive model from launcher to the Center of Soviet missile organization, support, and operations.[1363] Overlaying this model on existing intelligence views of nuclear support to the forward-based missile structure revealed an absolute lack of convergence. No aspects of the official model corresponded to the organization evident within the USSR. Thus unlike the DIA connoisseurs I had no difficulty adjusting to the emerging alternative model. This newly recognized reality worked; a consistent fit with the USSR short-range missile force structure at all identifiable points—except veneer.

The bunker menagerie would continue to be a valuable analytic tool but now a viable alternative path had emerged. Self-education as an analyst involved immersion in Soviet military doctrine, organization and operations of all military services, and had recently focused on the very missile nuclear logistics structure at issue. The Soviet groups conundrum presented a direct extension of ongoing projects facilitating transfer of an exhaustive plumbing into system workings. I then pursued an investigation of the Central European situation independent of the original CIA team. We would differ on some details but operated on the same analytic track while the DIA connoisseurs chugged along…a dead end siding.

The steadfast duo did have the nerve to be the first to make that most risky gesture—they put their views on paper in early 1980. Any documentation of conclusions exposes intelligence operatives to potential future finger pointing by associates in the fraternity. Fortunately for the error-prone the record of past work is usually forgotten by, not only the next generation of analysts, but also by those who run the hierarchy. Who said what, when, soon drops out of the corporate memory. Even if recalled there is a conspiracy of silence among analysts since no one strives to highlight the whoppers of others when one day the situation might be reversed. Only a few oddballs (like me) sought to recover the complete substantive record of both assessments and evidence. Accountability is not among the standards highly valued by US intelligence organizations.

The DIA report[1364] dealt with the preliminary findings of CIA analysts as well as the results of their own investigation. The credibility of the Torgau source came under assault on several points, depicted as vague and contradictory. An imagery count of the number of *Hma* bunkers in the secured section pointed out by the *praporshchik* differed somewhat from his statement. The source supposedly changed his mind regarding the number of access points to each bunker while the given entrance widths—at least as defined by the connoisseurs—appeared restrictive and narrower than stated. They ignored some practicalities including similar restricted access in US storage structures that hampered use of forklifts for standard palletized loads. Environmental utilities, considered essential, could not be discerned. They belittled the "technical" building as insignificant and inconveniently placed for processing nuclear warheads. The DIA duo and their co-authors had particularly scathing comments regarding the section at Torgau stated to be for missile storage—there appeared to be nothing to distinguish the structures from those in the adjoining conventional ammunition area. Their conclusion should an item for every intelligence analyst methodological collection, a "confident judgment" that "The Soviets probably are not storing nuclear weapons in the World War II munitions bunkers at Soviet ammunition depots in East Germany" whether Torgau or in any of the then suspected bases.

To a certain extent the expressed wariness regarding the Torgau source could be justified. To credit the stream of human sources, both Soviet and Central European national, emerging from the communist bloc countries during the decades of the Cold War, a great many Warsaw Pact military installations seemed to be stocked with nuclear, chemical, and biological weapons. A Soviet PRTB at an unrecognized facility—the DIA people did not challenge the *praporshchik* identification of his unit—represented an altogether different matter. We had substantial information from classified documents, signals monitoring, and unit personnel regarding the missions of these special units; the designated WMD custodians across the Soviet armed forces. If a Soviet PRTB resided at Torgau, or at any other simulacrum of a USSR nuclear missile base, then all intelligence analytical assumptions instantly became subject to revisit. In their fixation on the supposed technical requirements for nuclear weapons storage the DIA assessment had willfully disregarded the military organizational and operational aspects of WMD employment. The Soviets might succeed in hiding the visible manifestations of their nuclear missile support bases but the handler entourages, and other telltales, could be traced.

All too often intelligence connoisseurs are quite capable of misapprehending details of even their narrowly defined spheres. Another of the practical aspects to an operational deployment of nuclear weapons which the DIA report had ignored is the essential servicing routine. Alternate RTB features noted in the separately-secured *Hma* bunker zones often included a building that might conduct the necessary maintenance function—the "technical" building reported by the Torgau source. But a lack of such buildings within the secured areas at other bases presented an uncertainty that limited the valuation of this evidence—an ambiguity such as that which often de-clarifies intelligence perspectives. The solution to this particular puzzle became apparent only after the Russian departure from Germany, when by direct observation determination could be finalized that at the RTB warhead territories that lacked dedicated service buildings the Soviets had actually adapted a preexistent German munitions bunker. These had been internally fitted with a service bay, hoists, and adjoining rooms for technical work. No external indications of the warhead maintenance function could be discerned.

By one of those pesky coincidences Torgau again prominently demonstrated the service function. A review of historical imagery had revealed that the warhead territory pointed out by the Soviet *praporshchik* had been located, prior to 1968, at the south border of the depot. Subsequent relocation inward provided a more numerous set of bunkers to supply the increased number of warheads of an expanding missile force within a more protected site. The move had been accompanied by the construction of the distinctive "technical" building. The Soviet builders had been so proud of their work that the completion date "1969" had been incorporated in the brick facade (no—US imaging satellites could not resolve the date—this is a later ground observation). Torgau had the most sophisticated purpose-built workshop for servicing nuclear weapons at any Soviet RTB in Central Europe. Interestingly, after completion of the Torgau job construction of a virtually identical structure began at a Ukrainian missile RTB near official nuclear bunkers. Perhaps a nuclear-technical officer had taken the plan from Torgau to his new station. However service buildings of similar design eventually had been added to selected newly built SOC bunkers; the progenitor slightly wider, and about 5-6 meters longer, than those at three SOC bases. Rather than a one-off the Torgau service building may have been originated by a higher authority for wider application.

Evidential tidbits concerning the suspect nuclear bases began to accumulate. One source unique to East Germany derived from the peculiar leftover of the military alliance that won the Second World War. Postwar agreements permitted the operation of US, British, and French Military Liaison Missions out of Potsdam, officially accredited to the GSFG command.[1365] The missions fielded teams permitted, within restrictions imposed by the Soviets, to roam through the GDR from 1946 to 1990. This security risk acceptable to the Soviets since the privileges had to be reciprocated in West Germany. These MLM teams of courageous, wily Western military personnel acted as front line scouts of the Cold War. In March 1985 a Soviet sentry wielding an AK-47 fatally wounded one of the US contingent, Major Arthur Nicholson, when a two-man team probed a tank regiment garrison near Ludwigslust.[1366] One team had been poking around Torgau in the fall of 1981 when they alertly spotted and recovered a placard that may have fallen from a vehicle, relating to an index 9F21MA, already known from multiple sources to be the Soviet designator for a nuclear weapons transporter van. A diagram specified the placement options for listed container designators—for a missile nuclear warhead and nuclear artillery round.

These teams had developed a novel, if odiferous, technique under the evocative designation Sanddune for scrounging documents as they toured the Soviet zone.[1367] The wretched lifestyle of the Soviet military, devoid of the conveniences afforded to Western armed forces, had unforeseen security consequences. The GSFG did not issue Soviet soldiers some basic necessities such as toilet paper. To satisfy this inescapable need personnel grabbed whatever paperwork lay in their neighborhood which could encompass loose administrative documents as well as tearing up publications—many classified. MLM teams would visit field exercise areas after the departure of military units and somehow manage to hold their noses with one hand while bagging pages with the other. When cleaned after returning to base these papers often proved quite revealing. Through the 1980s Soviet documents occasionally recovered identified and linked PRTBs to at least five of the suspect bases, including Torgau, that had already been pinpointed on imagery. This material betrayed interesting details of unit staffing, organization, and equipment. Sanddune documents also helped settle an intelligence disputation, confirming which viewpoint had been correct, regarding the type of missile-technical units at the bases. MLM teams would eventually surpass the signals crowd in pinpointing the nuclear support units. The latter, with a nudge from 'collateral' evidence, attempted to zero in on the PRTBs at specific bases.

The number of coinciding coincidences involving PRTBs, RTB lookalikes, nuclear weapons data and procedures began to pile up. This accumulating evidence did not deter the DIA connoisseurs or alter their mental lockout. In the spring of 1982 the principal attempted to use his authority to obstruct a briefing (actually with a different focus) I had prepared for the

## Dossier
### NUCLEAR WARHEAD SERVICING SOLUTIONS

**RTB Dannenwalde (East) Germany**
*Hma* bunker adapted with service bay and overhead I-beam for now absent traveling hoist

(OPPOSITE)

**RTB Császár Hungary**
(TOP-MIDDLE) standard warehouse modified with airlock-type entry and interior workshop

**RTB Torgau (East) Germany**
(BOTTOM) purpose built facility with airlock entrance

(FAR RIGHT) interior view of one of two wall-separated service bays equipped with traveling hoist

annual conference we held with the British, that year in London, on nuclear weapons issues under the joint Project Gazebo. Conferences held in the UK had particular value because of the rare opportunity for the military intelligence elements in Europe to tap into Washington currents to obtain insights, influence collection planning, as well as directly present their own work. A parallel joint Project Martello dealt with chemical weapons. Some individuals participated in both groups, however, despite the opportunity presented for cross-fertilization the intelligence twain never converged. That the Soviet reality might not align with the intelligence arrangement of segregated cubicles thereby escaped notice. The DIA connoisseur's ploy failed only because British MoD analysts, wise to the shenanigans, arranged for their co-chair to extend a formal invitation.

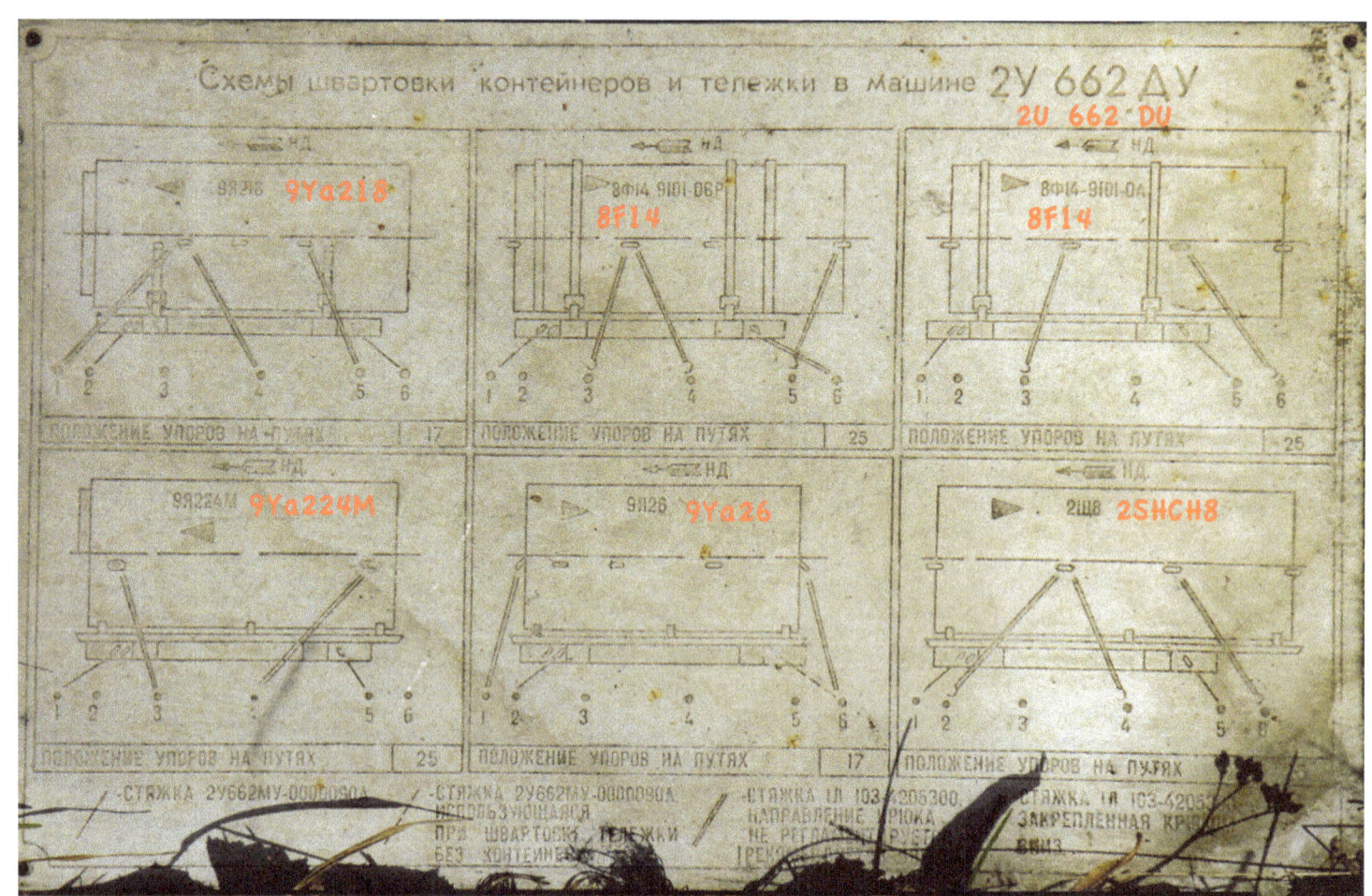

FALLING PLACARDS

First generation 2U662 series warhead transporter had been placed in service during 1961 container 8F14 for article 269A 10-kt yield the first nuclear warhead designed for a battlefield missile indications of an early date for RTB Zeithain (East) Germany—plate found in the motor pool

## remembrance of things past

Prevailing cultural traits within US intelligence organizations have long abetted a temporal abyss. Only the rare analyst peers over the substantive edge to establish his or her bearings. There is a widespread, congenital, amnesiac streak that severely constrains perspective. Few realize that, unlike groceries, evidence do not arrive stamped with expiration dates. Historical antecedents can potentially illuminate the seemingly inexplicable and provide the basis for alternative notional constructs. The protagonists of the official nuclear bunker model abided mired in a perceptual straitjacket that spurned precedent as well as contextual linkages.

The official perspective encompassed not only nuclear weapons but had also developed a complementing missile dogma. Beginning about 1960 the Soviets widely erected hardened shelters to store missile bodies. These bunkers could vary somewhat in size but came in similar configurations in all the delivery forces whether 'tactical' or strategic. Some 270+ bunkers had been added at USSR Ground Troops central-front-army RTBs, storing both surface-surface and surface-air missiles, as well as at some missile brigade garrisons. With customary agility US intelligence added a Missile Edition to the Official Bunker Model. This missile model became for those dealing with the Soviet military scene yet another fixed reference point and an immutable as well as restrictive identifier. Succeeding intelligence generations absorbed this 'known' indicator without question. No instances of missile bunkers had ever been (correctly) distinguished anywhere in Central Europe. This failure had compounded the difficulty experienced by intelligence connoisseurs in fully delineating the forward missile force—or to explain the nuclear warhead surplus they had created at Type VII sites. The only bunker identification as the missile storage type, presumed for nearly two decades, occurred in East Germany; but these three had actually been installed, as indicated earlier, to hold the nuclear warheads of a strategic missile unit.

During my study of missile force structure within the USSR an early, seemingly obvious, reckoning had been that the Soviets acquired missiles for nearly 15 years before they built missile bunkers. Several types of short- and medium-range systems had been fielded in the 1950s and airframes must necessarily have been stocked in large quantities, probably amounting to many hundreds. Recent information confirms that in July 1959 the Soviet accumulation, among other systems, included 1249 missiles for R-1 (SS-1a Scunner) and R-2 (SS-2 Sibling) no longer in service.[1368] All four of the dedicated missile arsenals constructed in accordance with the September 1951 Council of Ministers resolution featured one, essentially identical, type of unhardened storage shelter for each of the two missile categories deployed in the second half of the 1950s. A 70-m building—two of these built in 1959 to support the GDR strategic missile deployment as well as at early medium-range bases within the USSR—basically an up-scaled and modified version of the other type. The 50-m type also appeared at some artillery ammunition bases and arsenals of the Ground Troops—notably at several, when hardened, marked as front missile-artillery bases. Suspected RTBs in Central Europe often had structures remarkably similar to the small type. Unknown until my research re-focused on the suspects, the missile shelter design did not originate with the Soviets.

Those few of us who preferred reading the Soviet play-book rather than US intelligence secondary translations had noticed that, whatever they effectuated, had often been done in some form in the past. One of my contributions to the issue explored the notion that, if the Soviets adapted old German munitions depots as missile support bases, might there be any connection with old German missiles? Germans, after all, had developed world-first combat missiles, the ballistic V-2 (A-4) and cruise V-1 (FZG-76). Perusal of the bounteous collection of published material concerning V-weapons that had appeared since World War II uncovered only a few hints that there had been a logistical system extending from the West European firing sites back into Greater Germany. Only after many hours investigating archival documents did I discover a selection of period intelligence reports to substantiate that retro styling.

The initial German plan for the V-2 campaign provided for establishment of a 1200 missiles accumulation at extensions purpose-built at *Heeres-muna* centered around three factories. Heavy Allied bombing of these factories impelled a decision to concentrate production of all V-weapons at the *Mittelwerk* underground plant near Nordhausen. Manufactured V-2 missiles shipped to *Heeres-muna*, along with warheads from a separate factory, then would be conveyed by special train sets onward to the firing unit rear areas. The German missile crews, however, in the month following September 1944 initiation of V-2 launchings experienced a high failure rate; soon attributed to deterioration of certain components while in storage. In an early example of just-in-time production, the logistics system underwent re-wiring to ship completed V-2 from *Mittelwerk* directly to the firing units.[1369] Minutes of an October production meeting in Berlin indicated that the program managers had been informed that 515 V-2 airframes in the *Heeres-muna* qualified only for parts salvage with 300 still in firing condition.[1370]

By late 1944 Allied intelligence had caught on to the logistics scheme and subsequently realized that the *Heeres-muna* somehow no longer fully participated in the delivery loop.[1371] Aerial photographs had provided the main clues that a large scale support system existed. The British had pioneered a three-phased approach to exploiting the massive volume of photographic cover returned by reconnaissance aircraft. An initial quick scan sought out high priority developments followed by a more systematic examination by a larger proportion of photographic intelligence personnel. Special

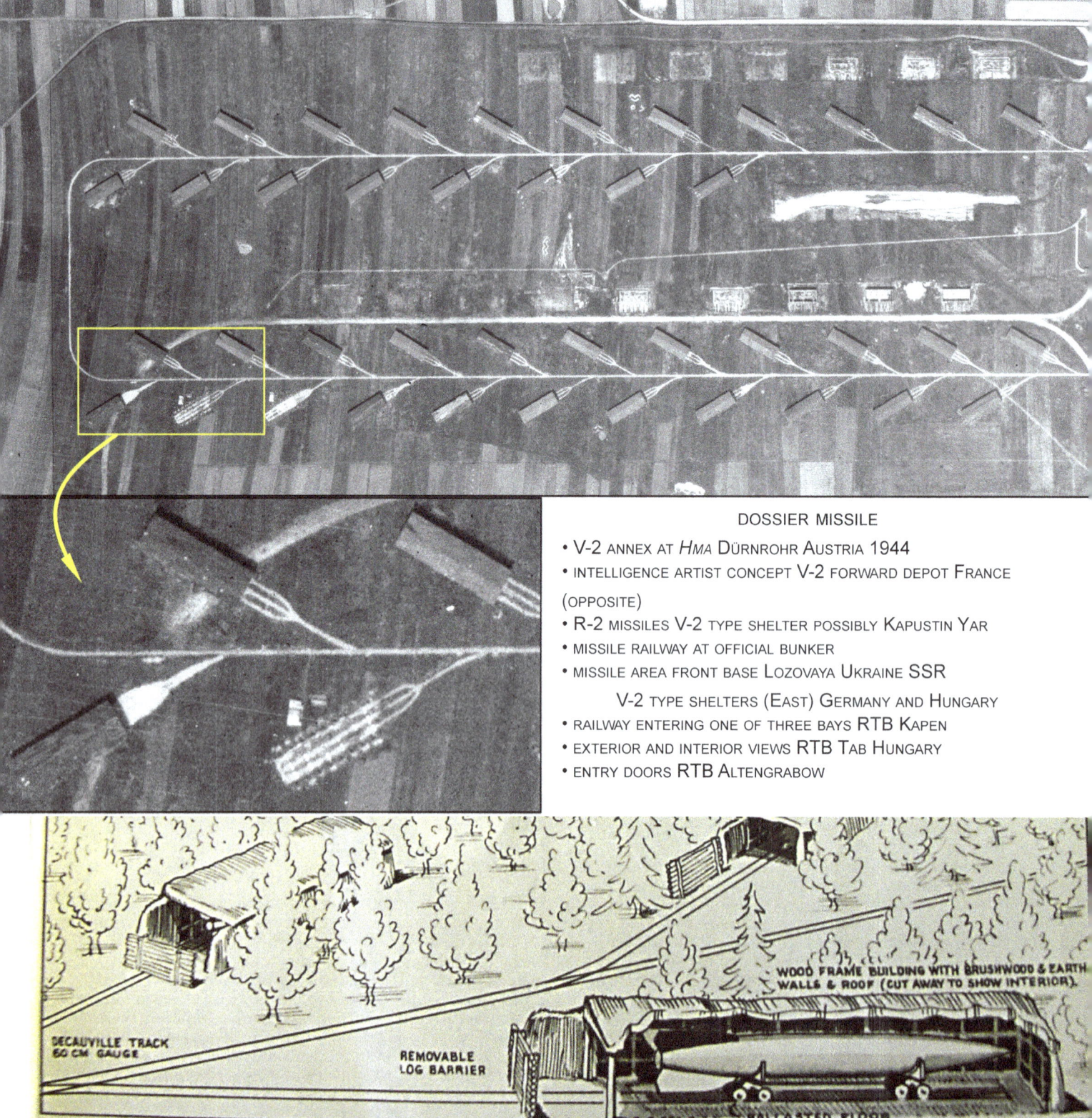

studies teams then examined selected aspects in greater detail. Interpretation reports issued (most still extant) on *Heeres-muna* during the first two phases clearly indicate a failure to recognize the significance of the additions. Only when photographic clusivity analysis had been melded with certain indicative HUMINT reporting that attention focused on the munitions depots.

SIGINT of the celebrated Ultra variety had produced copious material on the A-4 including firing data from test shots at the Peenemünde range; but there had been only oblique references to logistics aspects. During my extensive German predecessor investigation, with the aid of contacts at GCHQ, the British obligingly lent for review the original bound volumes of V-2 Ultra. I also obtained assistance from JARIC (Joint Air Reconnaissance Intelligence Centre) to rectify gaps in the US archive of World War II photographic coverage.

Air recce sorties and inspections of forward missile depots and test centers had led to the identification of distinctive structures with some common features. The relating of similar or nearly similar elements the basic method of imagery studies then as now, understanding always furthered by the availability of material from other sources. Photo interpreters during the summer of 1944 noticed that structures at two depots in France (completed but never occupied due to the D-Day invasion disruption of V-2 preparations) seemed comparable to suspected missile storage areas observed at the Peenemünde, and relocated, Blizna test centers. Although the structures varied by location as to size and configuration, common elements included elongated end-served shelters, with access via individual "Décauville" light railways; recognizing that the function of the characteristic railway facilitated movement of missiles placed on customized cars.[1372] This scheme had then been confirmed by a joint UK-US-Soviet ground tour of Blizna in September 1944 right after the capture of this part of Poland by Soviet forces.[1373] Identification of the depot technique for storing V-2 instigated a systematic photographic investigation of installations within Germany for similar arrangements.

Reconnaissance aircraft brought back photos of distinctive facilities that led to the correct identification of six of the seven *Heeres-muna* V-2 depots originally built by the Germans. These dubbed "herring-bone" sites by the British (doubtless reflecting national culinary habit) because of the arrangement of missile storage shelters along a network of rail sidings and intermediate narrow gauge railways that fanned out into the shelters. Limited historical photography and postwar German information indicates that the V-2 storage structures had been built during the second half of 1943. The first Allied photographic cover of a characteristic depot had been acquired on 1 November 1943 but only a full year later did the deliberate search for V-2 activity at depots in Germany focus on four *Heeres-muna* that had already been imaged. By early 1945 two additional depots had been identified. The tally of shelters at five depots had reached 176 through establishment of a common imagery 'signature'—according to a 12 March 1945 British evidence summarization "...in all cases rectangular sheds, having an entrance at one end.... The entrances are served...by light railway tracks...three such tracks entering each shed..."[1374] A separate German Air Force logistics system for the V-1 also delineated (although mainly from captured personnel and documents rather than photography) stretched back to *Luft-muna* which used a different shelter design joining component storage with an assembly shop.

A traceable lineage for these shelters led into the USSR and right back to the Central Europe RTBs. The Soviets, in exploiting the V-2 as the basis of their own early missile development, had adopted German depot storage techniques. Intelligence interrogations during the early 1950s of a key German recruit, Helmut Gröttrup, to the Soviet program who had eventually been permitted to return home had elicited the statement that the German instructions for V-2 storage had been provided in 1946-1947.[1375] Photo recon missions late in the war revealed that one Austrian *Heeres-muna* V-2 annex had been razed prior to capture. But postwar documents and eyewitnesses indicate that at least *Hma* Slate had been captured intact by the Soviets, the missile shelters dismantled as "reparations" and constituent materials shipped to the USSR.[1376] The Soviets could also directly access one other depot in Poland and possibly the two others in Austria during postwar occupation if these survived. Two stores had been built in what emerged as the FRG.

Shelters, many extended in length, that had been configured almost identically to those built by the Germans to house V-2 rockets had been constructed widely in the 1950s at the missile armament arsenals—which would be assigned to the strategic missile arm created in 1959—and at selected Ground Troops conventional ammunition bases. Western intelligence entirely failed to distinguish and recognize the purpose of these first generation accommodations. Since all residue of World War II knowledge of V-2 procedure had vanished, developments within or without the USSR proceeded invisibly in plain sight, objects of the third kind. At the outset of the 1960s the hardened missile bunkers began to supplement and replace these earlier shelters throughout the Soviet missile forces. V-2 type twins existed at four of the Central Europe RTBs—two, so disparaged by the DIA connoisseurs, at Torgau in the missile territory described by the Soviet defector—with truncated or kindred V-2 analogs at three, and a variety of structures at other, bases. None of the original German V-2 depots had been favored by the Soviets who, for the most part, carefully adapted buildings that usually dated back to the World War II era. Possibly the Germans may have built a limited number of V-2 shelters at other depots, including those selected by the Soviets, but cannot be documented.

The failure to recognize nonofficial missile storage modes would not be limited to the Soviets. Intelligence never verified locations for the missile stocks of the Warsaw Pact members—except in one instance courtesy of Colonel Ryszard Kuklinski. He provided Ministry of National Defense inventory manifests for Polish armament depots and bases. One 1980 document[1377] summarized items held by 20 Regional Technical Base, Mosty (Goleniow to intelligence)—including 195 "operational-tactical and tactical missiles" (a manifest gave systems breakdown). Intelligence had previously been clueless as to the significance of this installation which likely functioned as the Polish equivalent to a Soviet front missile-artillery base. Goleniow had been relegated to the general logistics installations satchel. No priority had been assigned to collection including high resolution satellite imagery despite some HUMINT reporting that pointed a missile finger at Mosty. Occasional coverage by the KH-11 system had been of quality insufficient to reveal features in detail. I did a backwards check of older, better, KH-8 imagery. Photos as early as 1968 exposed in one section of the base a network of narrow gauge rail lines extending between a group of buildings—a conspicuous indicator of the original version of missile storage. The importance of base Mosty is magnified by Polish planning documents regarding their forces in the early 1980s.[1378] A total 256 airframes available for these front missile launchers left only 61 outside of Mosty in the firing and missile-technical units for 71 deployed launchers. Thus some 76 percent of the stockpile of Polish combat missiles intended to deliver mass destruction warheads had been concentrated at a location that US intelligence had not identified as a missile-related target.

A potentially included chapter of the story would be discovered in the late 1980s courtesy of the INF Treaty. Installations declared to be holding treaty objects, subject to onsite inspection, included the Ladushkin Missile Storage Facility near Kaliningrad a.k.a. Königsberg—formally a restricted set of structures within the missile-artillery munitions base of a Soviet coastal front. A startled member of an inspection team observed *Hma* bunkers arranged like those in the forward RTBs. Moreover nearby, although not in the INF-declared inspection zone, a set of V-2 lookalikes closely resembled the GDR variety of missile shelters; all within a short walk of a collection of official bunkers—warhead and missile editions—of the front RTB. This semblance, as the Soviets would often assert, may have been no accident. Ladushkin could have been a deployment prototype and/or familiarization and training base for technical personnel on the way west exploiting the German *muna* patrimony. The V-2 type shelters existed at least by the early 1960s; uncertain in 1956 cover; any earlier presence might relate to unverified reports of German V-2 firings on Leningrad during the great siege.

Despite their cleverness in hiding the forward RTBs the Soviets had made a crucial error by using shelters for missiles essentially identical to both those of the German V-2 and their own version of this design. Salvation derived from the ignorance of their somnolent adversaries. Despite decades of photographic observation no one in US or British—they received all of this coverage—intelligence had even noticed the similarity of early USSR missile storage practice with that of RTBs in the groups of forces. A whopping trove of missile historical origins had been discarded. The essential foundation for any subject, not restricted to missile technology and deployment, is the acquisition of a comprehensive understanding of antecedents encompassing all varieties.

Intelligence analysts and photo interpreters in 1944-1945, although confronted with a military-technological innovation—ballistic missiles—had correctly identified the entire V-2 support organization, the installations, and even the specific mode of storage. They recognized as related variegated missile structures at the experimental stations, as well as main German and forward French depots. They thereby trumped their Cold War colleagues who had totally failed to detect the V-2 origin as well as direct relationship of legacy structures at USSR and Central European missile storage installations. Each intelligence era employed the same tools: overhead imagery, signals intercepts, and human source reporting. But the temporal blindness of the later generation ordained failure. The British no longer recalled their earlier achievements; Germans unaware of their own heritage; and the Americans, as usual, just disregarded all the old stuff.

Historical precursors afforded not only additional evidence to support the proposition that munitions depots in at least three Soviet groups of forces functioned as nuclear missile support bases, but perhaps more importantly, reinforced context. Soviet procedures at these depots had not been radical departures from established practice but rather derived from precedent and military systemic evolution. Incredibly, although the Soviets had not converted V-weapons *Heeresmuna*, someone else did. The US in the postwar period had adapted one of the two depots in, what became, West Germany. *Hma* Siegelsbach had been modified as a nuclear weapons custodial installation with storage bunkers plopped amidst the, now vanished, V-2 shelter grouping. But knowledge of this connection had disappeared from the intelligence corporate memory along with the shelters.

### clashing perspectives

In 1981 revamping fervor swept the Soviet ground missile force throughout Central Europe. Although we never determined the precise motivation the new workings indicated that at least one likely reason entailed Soviet concern with survivability in the face of US-NATO technology developments. NATO military commanders since late 1979 had been enunciating the FOFA strategy of conventional deep strikes employing a new generation of precision long-range weapons.[1379] This approach thereby essentially adopted the Soviet precept, that had been

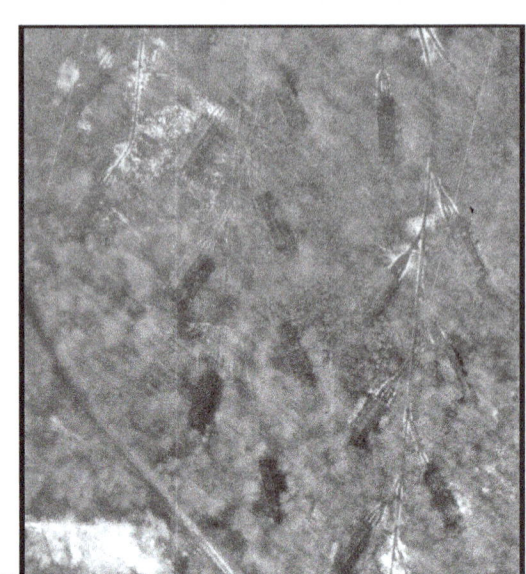

**HMA SIEGELSBACH (NOT EAST) GERMANY**

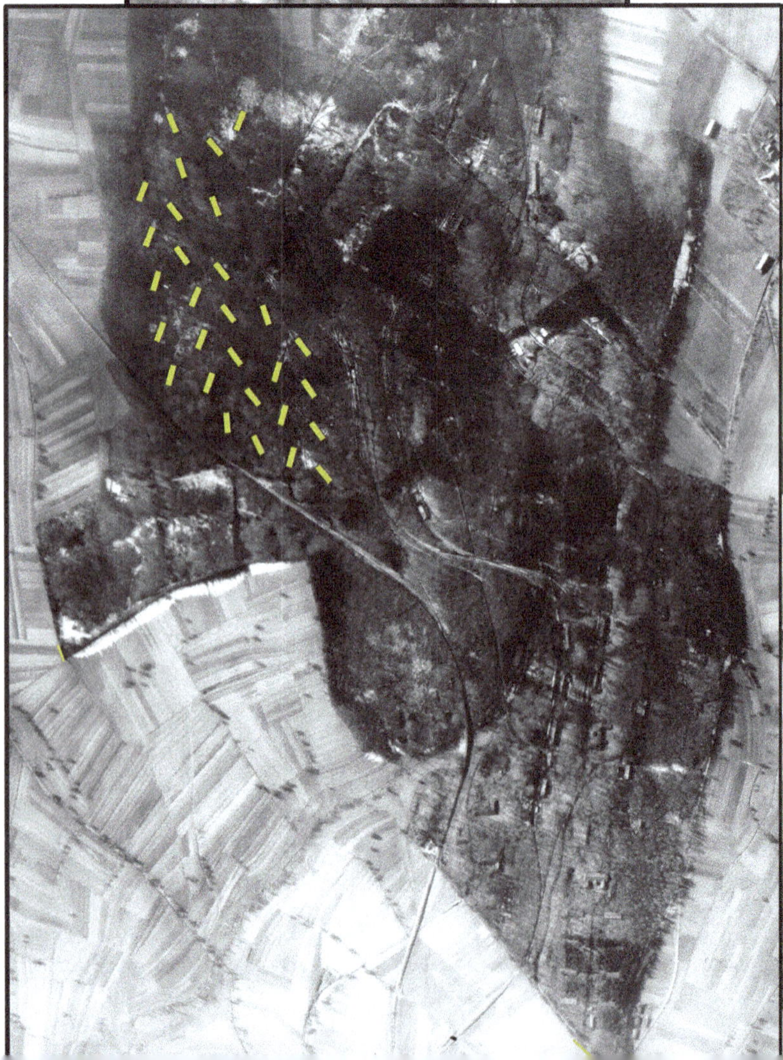

1945 V-2 DEPOT (LEFT) AND RE-PURPOSED FORMER US NUCLEAR WEAPONS SITE—STORAGE IGLOOS ADJACENT TO ROCKET AREA

integral to their operational planning for decades, of striking throughout the entire depth of a theater. Formal approval of the FOFA concept had been granted by NATO in December 1982.[1380] Given the openly stated objective of targeting the rear zones of Warsaw Pact forces in order to destroy key installations the Soviets may have concluded that NATO innovations threatened the critical missile troops.

A newbuilding program[1381] that continued through 1983 at garrisons in East Germany equated to accelerated *dislokatsiya*; exhibiting the common theme of removing the missile troops from the (opponent known) permanent areas as quickly as possible. Concrete earth-mounded buildings outwardly similar in appearance to standard vehicle garages appeared within all missile brigade and battalion caserns at front, army, and division level. Semi-hardened construction afforded limited protection against conventional strikes for missiles stored in the buildings while allowing the airframes to be preloaded on their transporters for quick exit. Uniform variations in the number of bays in these missile ready buildings at each garrison corresponded to reload factors, launcher and transporter complements, even the number of battalions present from each missile brigade. Thus all GSFG divisional missile battalions erected four-bay ready buildings, with a slot for one transporter-loader vehicle, each of which could carry up to two or three (for remaining FROG-7 units) missiles, a reload factor of 2.0 or 3.0. A second phase of missile ready building construction, augmenting those at selected garrisons, later took place upon the formation of consolidated army tactical missile brigades.

Internal detonation protection may also have been a consideration in the design of these missile ready buildings since increasing indications pointed to Soviet planned initiation of combat actions with pre-mated conventional warheads. Further structures added only at R-300 (Scud) garrisons involved oxidizer and fuel liquid propellants that had previously been stored in-ground. Tankers which had normally parked separately from the propellant stores transferred to new unhardened vehicle ready garages usually built within the secured propellants territory; either pre-filled or ready for a quick fill from cylinders or ground tanks. Again the definition centered on rapid egress.

This creative upsurge extended beyond launch unit garrisons. Concurrently at all 13 of the GSFG candidate RTB missile storage areas—concrete ready buildings identical to those of the delivery brethren arose; those RTBs supporting R-300 brigades—sprouted the two propellant buildings. An additional element, however, manifested exclusively at the RTBs. At every one of the secured bunker zones the distinctive loading docks of USSR official nuclear bunkers appeared. In one of those coinciding coincidences these loading docks turned up during the same timeframe at all four of the Type VII bunkers in the GDR. More than suspicious, the earliest indication of any element of the readiness construction program came in late 1980 when loading docks had been built at the Torgau *Hma* bunkers. This seemed to indicate Soviet awareness of the damage inflicted by the defector and/or feedback from their sources regarding the ongoing intelligence mixup. The jig was up.

Regardless of motivation the Soviets had eliminated any lingering uncertainty concerning the validity of individual RTB identification—they had effectively pinpointed all locations. Obviously force protection had superseded concealment as an operational priority. One of the NGF (Pstraze), and both SGF, RTBs took even further measures. During the same period warhead storages at these bases in Poland and Hungary augmented with Type VIII variants—all with loading docks. The intelligence official Type VIII bunker had two side-by-side tubes but in actuality each constituted the cardinal element. The Soviets erected the Type VIII in a building block approach; up to four bunkers observed at RTBs in the USSR. Dispersal airfields in the groups and Soviet military districts used Type VIII singles. A Type VIII single had been built at the Type VII sites in Poland during the late 1970s. The NGF and SGF missile RTBs featured Type VIII triples. These variations, falling between the Type cracks, unhinged the intelligence connoisseurs whose perspective could not accommodate such deviations to nuclear dogma.

The recent detailed history of Soviet nuclear weapons in Hungary[1382] reveals a far more grievous intelligence failure than previously determined. Prior to Type VIII construction at one NGF (1980-1981) and two SGF (1980>1983) RTBs there had been no bunkers of any sort discernible on satellite imagery. While these installations had been identified as Soviet-occupied no particular interest had been aroused or priority assigned—until the bunkers suddenly popped up and focused intelligence minds; attention had been directed pre-building to the Császár ammunition depot when truncated V-2 type buildings had been noticed. Evidently at least nuclear warheads had long been kept at inconspicuous unhardened buildings; a practice affirmed by post Cold War ground inspections. Standard German *Hma* bunkers existed at the two other NGF RTBs and loading docks appeared at these as well. Someone did have a change of mind at the Borne Sulinowo RTB where Type VIII pre-cast concrete sections had been collected but never erected.

RTB Tab would have been constructed sometime after the arrival of 692 PRTB in September 1961 coincident with deployment of the 8K11M 107 Rocket Brigade at Dombóvár—replicating 1959 GSFG. RTB Szákszend (Császár) followed in November 1961, 3105 PRTB likely among many forming in a concerted insertion of new army-level PRTBs (indicated by a common four-digit unit number). Compounding the failure we never detected the colocated presence at each RTB of one

> **DOSSIER**
> **READINESS PROGRAM (EAST) GERMANY**
>
> (UPPER) WARHEAD LOADING DOCKS
> - RTB ALTENGRABOW—
>   12-SLOT POSITIONS BETWEEN *HMA* BUNKERS
> - SOVIET ROAD TRANSPORT *INSTRUCTIONS* FOR CONTAINER LOADING
> - TYPE VII BUNKER RTB HIMMELPFORT—PATH TO PORTAL
>
> (LOWER) MISSILE READY BUILDINGS
> - RTB WILMERSDORF
> - RTB TORGAU—OLD AND NEW MISSILE STYLE

launch battalion out-deployed in an alert stance from each of two Soviet Scud brigades; even worse Szákszend accommodated the battalion of 99 RBr which had been organized in 1967 at Baj which somehow never made the intelligence order-of-battle for Soviet forces in Hungary; up to replacement in 1987 by one of the new Soviet army-level tactical missile brigades. The garage at RTB Tab holding launchers positioned close to warhead storage, a Russian officer has described alert measures involving the *Granit* bunkers. Upon readiness level increase (not specified but likely combat readiness Increased) the twelve stored 9K72 (Scud B) nuclear warheads would be mated to missiles and propellant filled; four of these transloaded to the launchers of 381 Rocket Battalion and the remainder stored on trolleys in one bunker. Concurrently the eight 9K52 (FROG-7) nuclear warheads on hand would also be mated and kept on trolleys in a second bunker. These measures would certainly have been approved by Colonel Aleksandrov. Assembled missiles then awaited a dispersal order (i.e. Military Threat combat readiness). The description not only confirmed a 1.0 load factor for Soviet missiles in Hungary but also that a "second wave" warhead delivery would emanate from a USSR central object.

Potentially there had been additional missile RTBs not identified by Cold War intelligence and for which there has been no subsequent firm information. In particular the army structure of the Soviet CGF, including two missile brigades, indicated that there could be one or two RTBs in western Czechoslovakia. If so, we never found any candidates. Support for the Czech deployment might have been provided by the two RTBs in southwestern Poland which constituted an army twosome as in the GSFG but otherwise had no obvious affiliation. Both of these, however, had been established prior to the 1968 invasion. The pair may have originally supported, variously, the NGF army variant or regrouping of an army of the second/third operational echelon from the USSR.

The early 1980s construction should have been the icing-on-the-cake for the alternative nuclear missile support model. By 1985 I had completed research into all aspects, including the V-weapons connection, and published a comprehensive review of the evidence.[1383] Later that year appeared another report from the CIA analysts who had originally pursued the Torgau story. These two studies, and that of the DIA office in 1980, would be the only intelligence community projects to directly address the contentious issue of forward missile nuclear weapons deployment. Our conclusions percolated through to other agencies in the US and Europe, as well as to NATO allies, but did not penetrate the bunker cult head. The DIA anointed expert stood up before us in May 1986 at the Gazebo joint nuclear weapons conference in London to reiterate—having just inspected similar bunkers in West Germany—his categorical rejection of any possibility of nuclear storage at nonofficial bunkers in the East. I never would hear directly or from witnesses that this high-priest ever amended his views or retracted the 1980 report.

But even the DIA connoisseurs may have been impressed by the truck driver from Kopitnari who came our way in 1988. He had served with a segregated unit in the early 1970s at an airfield near this village in the Georgian SSR. Like many low-level sources he proved to be surprisingly knowledgeable despite stringent Soviet security measures. Although he did not understand the unit overall nature and mission observations concerning activities left no doubt that all represented a Soviet Air Forces PRTB. Comments on details of nuclear bomb handling and dispersal exercises included new material. His description, of particular interest, entailed Soviet use of a certain feature that had long been found helpful in identifying the presence of nuclear weapons but concerning which little direct information had been acquired. In all, worthwhile additions to our knowledge of Soviet nuclear weapons procedures.

However a troubling aspect to his account emerged. Nowhere on or near the grounds of Kopitnari Airfield did there exist an official nuclear bunker. An undistinguished compound identified by the source, incorporating a soft building dedicated to nuclear bomb storage, lacked nuclear indications—except for the one pinpointing element. So unremarkable in fact he related joining comrades to exploit breaks in the security fencing to pursue nightly drinking bouts in the neighborhood. But the nuclear connoisseurs learned with relief of his assignment to a work party later during service engaged in building a new storage structure for nuclear bombs. At the specified location, with construction dates and configuration accurately described, appeared an Official Type VIII Nuclear Weapons Bunker of the double variety. Intriguingly more than a dozen years earlier an imagery study of the first group of seven airfield Type VIII-D to be identified

had observed that all but one had been constructed at or near compounds with preexistent nuclear indicators.

Use of nondescript (perceptually hidden) unhardened buildings to hold nuclear bombs replicated warhead storage practice at the missile support bases in Poland and Hungary prior to 1980. Not only USSR but also forward aviation nuclear support may also have been established on the Kopitnari model early in the Cold War. As early as 1959 a NIE presumed that nuclear stores existed at tactical aviation airfields.[1384] A Soviet aviation ranker pinpointed the 1953 to 1959 period in which newly introduced frontal aircraft provided nuclear capability.[1385] Tantalizing hints acquired during Operation Regal, the celebrated Berlin tunnel communications tap, in 1955-1956 suggest that the Soviet Air Forces may have actually preceded the missile troops in the forward lean. The official CIA history,[1386] summarizing key information obtained—even those who had donned badges had difficulty later accessing Regal data—cited "Development of an improved nuclear delivery capability in the Soviet Air Army in East Germany" among the venture accomplishments; this some nine years prior to completion of the official Type IVs that intelligence considered the first evidence of air delivered nuclear weapons in Central Europe.

As the Cold War entered into a stunning denouement, neglected human source—second kind—information resurrected and examined in conjunction with imagery suggested that the Official Nuclear Bunker Model had been no more valid for air- than in regard to missile-delivery. Such evidence indicated that construction of many Type VIII-D bunkers represented not the introduction of nuclear weapons storage at frontal aviation airfields but rather, at least initially, a hardening program for existing RTBs.

Now those Type VII sites, the intelligence-designated official repository for all nuclear warheads in Central and Eastern Europe. My 1985 report laid out evidence that the (seemingly obvious) discrepancy with Soviet missile troops deployment, and congruency with that of their allies, could be resolved if the network primarily supplied the nuclear weapons allocated to national forces. Amid the groaning archival shelves of intelligence paperwork this report explicated the only argument ever made for the dedicated Warsaw Pact transfer model. In the 1980s some evidence had been acquired that 12 GUMO-subordinated units resided in Central Europe and that the directorate had been addressing at least some Type VIIs. Remarkably two emigres who had served during the early 1970s in the same unit near the Podborsko (Bialogard) Polish Type VII site—descriptively a PRTB—provided evidence on warhead operations and relationships. One had claimed that the unit abetted the RVSN—as did the nuclear directorate at the time of his service—with the primary mission of delivering warheads to Polish units. The other source mentioned close contact with the Soviet Air Forces; already noted that, lacking national aviation PRTBs, responsibility for provisioning and even loading air weapons lay with Soviet teams. Russian veterans of Type VII tours have now confirmed, in online forums which have since disappeared or been shuttered, the 12 GUMO relationship. Likely PRTBA subordinate to 12 GUMO had been collocated, or garrisoned nearby, at all of the sites to deliver and ensure positive control during warhead distribution to Warsaw Pact allies.

The change of regimes in Europe has now released documents, and witnesses, that also confirm the Warsaw Pact national model. Particularly important is the revelation of the February 1965 nuclear delivery test. A series of bilateral legal documents executed in basing countries have been found in national military archives. These agreements provided for national construction of the facilities and hand over to the Soviets upon completion in at least East Germany, Poland, and Czechoslovakia. Soviet-Czech protocols in 1961-1962 provided for supply of nuclear weapons to their front from the USSR. An in-country storage construction agreement had been signed 15 December 1965;[1387] actual building of these bases considerably delayed for unknown reasons. The Soviet-Polish version affirmation dated to 25 February 1967. Polish archive documents indicate that their engineer troops began construction of objects designated 3001, 3002, and 3003—the Type VII RTBs—in 1967, aimed at a mid 1969 completion; however sites and bunkers officially attained certification by a Soviet acceptance inspection on 30 January 1970.[1388] This date is considerably later than the intelligence imagery-based assessment (and Soviet schedule). Another Polish document regarding a 1980 coordination visit with the Soviets confirmed delivery of nuclear warheads from these "Wisla installations" to the Poles.[1389] I have inspected the plans for one of the GDR Type VII sites and bunkers—the original German edition.

German sources[1390] have reported varying individual Type VII bunker maximum capacity at 60 to 80 nuclear weapons or less than the low range in several intelligence estimates—the 1979 NIE max figure for each **bunker** (120) equaled the quantity for an entire two-bunker **site** at the testimonial minimum. The 1967 bilateral covering the three Polish bases imposed a capacity requirement for 178 nuclear weapons[1391] or about 30 in each of their six bunkers. Online Russian veterans discussions indicated that at least some of the Czech and Polish sites stored nuclear bombs and air-launched missile warheads for national aircraft as well as warheads for ground systems. When the Type VII sites had been first discovered some surmised that aviation nuclear weapons might stored along with missile warheads. But this notion soon dropped out as the official bunkers that had been built at Central European airfields had been, tardily, identified. Consideration of aviation weapons storage had not been factored into US and British intelligence estimates of Type VII bunker capacity—inwardly hardly possible to cram into these bunkers the quantity of

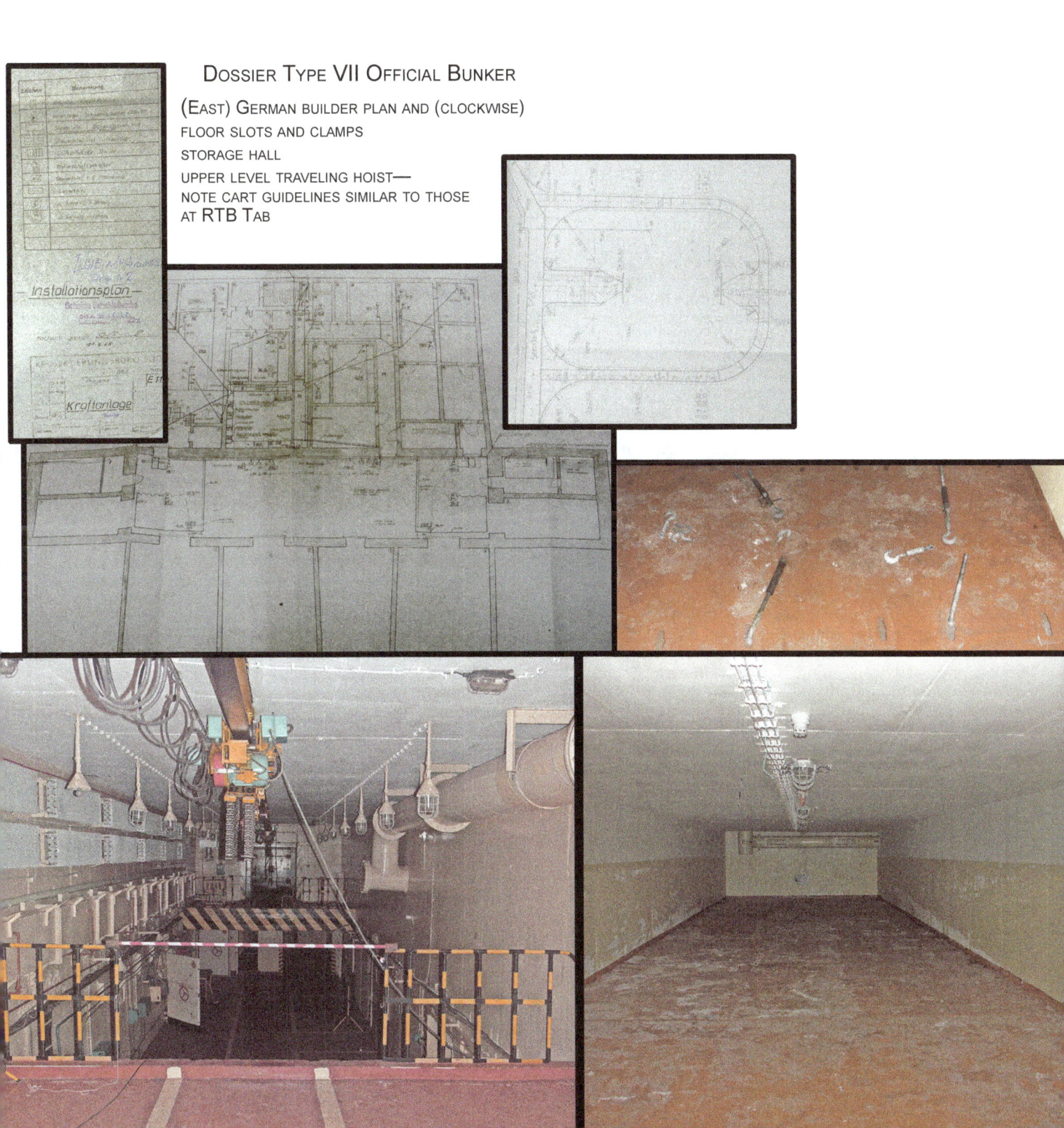

missile warheads for both Soviet and national ground forces that intelligence assumed must be on hand.

Period documents have revealed the actual mid 1980s accumulation for three Polish Type VII installations.[1392] The nuclear weapons inventory of 1 January 1986 amounted to 179 (discrepant with article distribution by site of 178)—36 aircraft bombs and air-launched missile warheads (0.5-, 15-, and 200-kt) plus 143 surface-launched missile warheads (10-, 50-, 200-, and 500-kt). One site had 16 additional rounds for the 2S7 203-mm *Pion* (these 5-kt); eight guns acquired in 1985 by 5 Gun Artillery Brigade. Other site wartime Polish transfer "authorizations" circa 1986 totaled 176 plus the artillery rounds. Air-missile totals are somewhat more than the allocation data contained in a 1978 exercise document[1393] accounting of nuclear weapons "available" in RTBs for Polish forces of 90 missile warheads—yields breakdown absent the 50-kt in 1986—while the aviation total coincided exactly at 36 (adding 5-kt to the otherwise corresponding yields). The number of missile nuclear warheads thereby amounted to 2.0 for each of the 71 Scud B and FROG-7 launchers planned for the Polish Army in the early 1980s[1394] (higher launcher totals given in the 2017 article reduce the reload factor to 1.7); no indication of nuclear-capable artillery appears in those document listings. The 1979 NIE method would have assigned a minimum 426 to as many as 726 warheads to the three bases—notably at variance with the later actual inventory—and no intelligence estimate made any provision for air-delivered nuclear weapons.

Conditional inventory can now be judged by strolling through the four storage halls of a Type VII bunker and examine the layout of floor slots for clamps that secured the weapon carts. These clamps had been intended to prevent carts straying during ground motion induced by nuclear detonations; but could also enhance security (no evidence of seat belts for the handlers). The Muzeum Zimnej Wojny Podborsko 3001 helpfully positioned a secured cart in the hall of one Polish Type VII bunker demonstrating the likely arrangement of three longitudinal rows; four-point clamping would permit at least six carts (with upraised tow bars) in each row or 18 per storage hall, thus 72 in each bunker. Likely differing cart sizes (some in containers with integrated wheels) by weapon model might permit the storage of 20 carts per hall thereby confirming the German 80 weapons per bunker capacity information.

There remains the issue of the brand(s) of WMD held. The Type VII sites had been constructed during the heyday of the chemical variant. Documents from even the early 1960s clearly indicate that the Soviets planned for the allies to receive a share of CW as well as nuclear. Allocation of chemical warheads persisted a constant during period Warsaw Pact exercises (i. e., those for which documents have been acquired). The uniform presence of two bunkers at every Type VII site afforded the opportunity for separately stocking both of the mass destruction weapons then planned for operations in Europe. A unique feature of the Type VII design is that while the portals, secured with blast doors, are at surface-level the bunker internal storage vaults are below-grade. This means that the fitted hoist mechanisms in the usual elevated section performed dual tasks for weapons transfer between levels as well as for nuclear servicing. Nuclear stocks would require fulfillment of both tasks but any other types of weapons held still required a lift between storage and exits; potentially multi-purposing Type VII bunkers.

The Polish 1980s documentation for three sites allowed for an average of 30 items per Type VII bunker—seven in each storage hall—despite an evidential capacity for up to 80. This would have amounted to about 17 square meters for each of 179 weapons or nearly three times the Soviet norm. Further expansion of available floorspace at the each of the Polish bases took place in 1978-1979 when one Type VIII-S bunker added a total of some 500 square meters. The reason for this enlargement is not yet apparent—potentially related to a scheduled deployment of nuclear rounds to Polish ground artillery—identical addition of singles took place at some USSR missile RTBs. Nuclear artillery of the high power variety appeared during exercise Soyuz 1983 in Polish forces along with Czech indications. But no bunker augmentation took place at any of the Type VII bases of other Pact allies. The Polish documented total amounts to 37 percent of the maximum Type VII design capacity indicated by German builders, a surprising under-utilization—unless of course a substantial amount of another type of WMD the Soviets planned to allot during the 1960s had been removed. Put another way, if the Polish total of 179 nuclear weapons had been stored at only one bunker at each site, this quantity would represent a 75 percent capacity utilization at the German maximum or 14 weapons per storage hall—each with almost nine square meters, still substantially in excess of the Soviet norm.

Recent information presented by the Hungarian researchers spotlights the single Type VII double-bunker in Hungary, 1542 RTB Úrkút (intell Veszprém).[1395] Access to documents and interviews with seven Russian officers stationed at the RTB from 1966 to 1990—including the last commander and two nuclear-technical engineers—enabled postulated accounting of not only the two bunkers but also individual storage halls for the years 1969-70, 1980, 1982, 1986, and 1989. Total RTB inventories varied from a low 34 missile warheads in 1980 to a 1989 180 inclusive of 60 bombs in four halls and 72 152-mm artillery rounds in only one hall; the number of warheads or bombs in any one storage hall ranged from 4 weapons to 18 2K6/9K52 (R-30/65 FROG). An inventory document found in USSR Ministry of Defense archives dated 16 October 1982 broke down nuclear missile warheads and artillery projectiles (no bombs) by index and yield; apparently an RTB total 184 authorized/wartime including 72 152-mm but

70 (36 artillery) actually stocked. The 4 November 1967 Soviet-Hungarian agreement regarding this RTB allowed a maximum 220 nuclear weapons...and "special ammunition." However valid their sources, the 1969-70 inventory of 161 missile warheads and artillery rounds assigns 32 chemical warheads for 8K11 (SS-1b Scud A) and 2K6 in two halls—destined for Hungarians. Lack of 1980s CW not only bolsters termination of the chemical variant but also points to inventory retrograde. So far as I am aware, this is the only direct link of an official nuclear bunker to chemical munitions storage.

A generous 2.0 reload for the active missile deployment of the four central Warsaw Pact countries comprising ten operational-tactical brigades (92 launchers) and 37 independent tactical battalions (148 launchers) would have provided about 480 nuclear warheads; the actual 1980s Polish ratio had been 2.0 later reduced to 1.7 by increased launcher complements. At the maximum capacity up to 1440 nuclear weapons could be accommodated in their 18 Type VII bunkers; or applying the six square meter norm at least 1500 weapons—seemingly highly unlikely that about a thousand aviation nuclear weapons had been destined for the remaining spaces.

The actual number of Soviet nuclear missile warheads and artillery rounds stored in both official and unofficial bunkers in Central Europe during the Cold War remains uncertain. Whether either bunker category had a CW allotment before or after deletion of the chemical variant had never been determined by Western intelligence services; nor by anyone subsequently. The only evidence bearing on forward storage of chemical weapons had been the substantial and varied sources assigning supply responsibility to at least missile PRTBs. There are several methods and bounds available to arrive at a forward nuclear estimate including Soviet withdrawal and overall inventory statements; launcher-unit reload factors; PRTB lift capability; exercise and documentary evidence on front-army initial strike and phase allocations; and bunker floorspace. Another consideration is the substantially increased proportion of operation allocations to initial mass strikes in the 1980s that may have enlarged the forward echelon.

Soviet public announcements of withdrawals established a minimum figure totaling 2000 missile, artillery, and aviation nuclear weapons in 1989 (500) and 1990 (1500).[1396] This stock would have presumably been drawn from both Soviet and national allotments. At a uniform 2.0 reload factor there would have been 1050 nuclear warheads (576 Soviet and 474 national) for Warsaw Pact (excluding Bulgaria) missile launchers deployed with the first operational echelon; only the 1989 statement provided a breakdown, 284 for warheads. Artillery nuclear BK evidence not available but a front allocation in exercises, usually fully expended in the initial mass strike, could range up to 170+ shells; 50 to be withdrawn in 1989. Methodological and Soviet totals exclude the four-year deployment of R-900 brigades in East Germany and Czechoslovakia which ended in early 1988. At 2.0 the 13 Soviet unofficial missile RTBs in East Germany may have held 408 nuclear warheads, each 24 to 36 (averaging 32); plus artillery rounds for which evidence is uncertain as to distribution among front- and army-level bases. Types and dimensions of standard German *Hma* bunkers in the warhead storage areas varied but the most common double-entrance type had interiors of about 252 square meters. The six square meter norm would have permitted 42 nuclear devices to be stored in each bunker. But physical factors of internal pillars along with arrangements for individual weapon access and positioning of dollies for movement would have reduced the nominal capacity. These calculations do not account for the potential re-echeloning brought about by interjection of central Special Tactical Groups and mass supply of conventional warheads.

The Hungarian researchers have elicited a foundational accounting of the Soviet nuclear inventory in one Warsaw Pact country. Positing totals for several years between 1965 and 1989 the final count of 548 weapons (108 missile warheads, 248 artillery rounds, and 192 bombs) provides a benchmark on the eve of retrograde. Quantities confirm the 2.0 reload available to the 18 launchers of the operational-tactical (Scud B) missile brigade—with the interesting detail that the second "wave" had been moved forward only during the 1980s—while the newly formed tactical missile brigade amounted to just 1.3; similar differential reload factors applied to Hungarian missile units. Acknowledging the unique and direct sourcing of their information, nevertheless several anomalies occur. Depiction of missile nuclear warheads is consistent with other information but there is a complete absence of treatment, even existence, of the conventional warheads of expanding significance in 1980s missile operations. Not only does the 152-mm artillery count exceed the largest nuclear allocation to a front observed in exercises (which could include 2-kt high power artillery) even when generated from the GSFG; but also stockage attributed as early as 1970 conflicts with other information. As previously noted, the *Encyclopedia* has the 152-mm in service five years later; and actual 152-mm artillery unit field training had not been detected until 1982 in the prioritized GSFG. Placement of 88 shells at each of the two missile RTBs poses the difficult task of extrapolating to the other groups and unofficial RTBs; if the Soviet army norm amounted to 88 then the six armies of the GSFG and CGF would have held 528 nuclear 152-mm rounds—without accounting front-level PRTB inventory. Valuable data is presented on Soviet total and annual nuclear artillery shell production.

Quantification of nuclear bombs in Hungary is also unique as well as anomalous. The authors suppose maximum stowage plans for each of the types of aviation official nuclear bunkers. But the 1989 accounting consigns 132 bombs to not only the single Type IV and one Type VIII-D but also to the three Type

VIII-S; thus disrupting the intelligence view of the latter as wartime dispersal sites lacking the supporting infrastructure characteristic of the former. The other 60 bombs are attributed to both Type VII bunkers at RTB Úrkút; a startling loading for thirty to sixty aircraft considering the minuscule Hungarian nuclear aviation which did not receive aircraft attachment sets until 1985 with bombs first available 1986 at the RTB; and an inexplicable disparity with the 36 air-delivered nuclear weapons held for the larger and earlier established Polish nuclear-capable aviation. If accurate, the number may represent a Soviet air reserve stash. Direct support to Hungarian nuclear aviation by Soviet elements at the Type VII installation is confirmed. Applying their plans at 36 bombs per bunker would amount to a maximum 380 nuclear weapons at ten aviation Type RTBs in the three other groups of forces; but no available evidence would indicate which, if any, of their nine Type VIII-S dispersal sites held a peacetime nuclear inventory.

Forward megatonnage had been aimed at urban as well as military targets in the neighboring NATO member countries. Political and military leaders never received a full, accurate tally of the most immediate menace—the likely first stage of nuclear escalation. For Europeans the strategic nuclear balance represented only a peripheral issue. In this exemplar of WMD threat mis-assessment, how then to adjudge the bigger fools, either the DIA nuclear connoisseurs or their superiors who retained failed analysts in such crucial intelligence positions as those dealing with nuclear weapons. The DIA never held accountable those responsible for an egregious misjudgment concerning nuclear weapons in Europe, who persisted in error despite ever-mounting evidence that pointed toward an alternative reality. The nuclear career of the principal continued long past the end of the Cold War, retiring with the usual round of bureaucratic accolades. All will no doubt be reassured to learn that his apprentices remained on the job, well-placed to fail again.

The decisive intelligence community resolution of a decade of infighting...default. The lead agencies, CIA and DIA, never arrived at any coordinated assessment of the nuclear threat to NATO posed by the hidden nukes for submission to US and allied military commanders. The primary interagency body responsible for appraising nuclear issues, the JAEIC, did not even address the Central Europe missile nuclear weapons issue until 1989. Our findings never would be incorporated in any Warsaw Pact forces or nuclear capability NIE. The issue remained largely an office-level intelligence analytical intramural battle. The withdrawal of Soviet nuclear weapons from Central European countries from 1989 to 1991, a critical intelligence issue at the end of Cold War, underwent scrutiny minus any formally agreed dossier of locations and content. Systematic coverage of the missile RTBs via technical 'INTs occurred but mainly at the initiative of working level analysts.

The prolonged hidden nukes controversy exemplifies the danger of successful deception by an opponent in that, even if the effort ultimately failed, a self-inflicted intelligence paralysis effectively fulfilled much of the original objective. But concealment embodied only the proximate cause of this epic intelligence failure. The fundamental reasons lay with the shallow comprehension and fragmented knowledge of supposed topical experts regarding the dynamics of an alien culture adept at unconceivable solutions. This despite an abundance of complementary evidence from varied sources. A collective tunnel vision that fixed on the Type bunkers for warheads, as well as those for missiles, locked out alternatives. The solipsistic perspective on supposed technical requirements for maintaining WMD constituted a fallacy that missed overriding operational considerations. No matter how meticulous and clever, regardless of the extent of preparations, a deceiver will always commit mistakes that can be detected by an agile, vigilant, knowledgeable intelligence operation—if such an organization exists.

Surviving, now accessible, bases constitute a splendid case study in concealment of a nuclear missile force, a handbook of proliferation indications. Both the mode and scale of the Soviet deployment in Central Europe are quite comparable to that likely to be adopted for other prospective WMD and missile programs. I conducted thorough ground surveys of most of these places to confirm, expand—and correct where necessary—our Cold War perspective on this particular reality. One might suppose, just an errant consideration, that some of these bases might even be preserved as part of a practical training scheme for US and allied personnel involved in all phases of WMD intelligence collection and analysis—perhaps even for international agencies conducting WMD monitoring and inspection. While format should never be rigidly transferred, the bases offer indicative clues that an alert and flexible intelligence can adapt to other situations. Their existence assists the refreshment of institutional memories and lessons learned the hard way.

No indications evidenced during base inspections of national and local government, or private, interest in preserving any of the survivors. Germany, in particular, has been engaged in systematic vandalism against history by razing most or all of the structures at key installations—erasing the Bad Freienwalde RTB shortly after my last visit—in accordance with customary German practice to eliminate undesirable elements. The few remaining examples steadily deteriorate. Not least of considerations is the cultural heritage represented by these objects, *schloss* of the Cold War akin to any of those lining the Rhine.

# Post Mortem

At this writing the Russian Wikipedia page devoted to 12 GUMO has an overview of the development of the Soviet nuclear storage system and a compilation of mainly central locations. Prior to expurgation there had also been listings of PRTBs of the strategic, ground, air, navy, and air defense services. These lists serve as a yardstick for the success of US and other Western intelligence services in finding sources of nuclear ammunition. The final intell grade is impressive, missing some individual places—but with one substantial omission noted below—while identifying many more not in the Wikipedia accounting. The extent of National Air Defense (*PVO Strany*) nuclear support had been a persistent intelligence uncertainty if only due to the limited number of warheads at firing units. Ludwigslust, the early FKR-1 deployment in the GSFG, made the Wikipedia list but not that of intelligence. None of the front missile-artillery bases show up perhaps reflecting the post 1979 withdrawal of at least their nuclear inventory. Other RTBs are also missing e.g. for Hungary the unofficial Császár while listing Tab; and two of the three Bulgarian Type VII.

The major surprise in the Wikipedia order-of-battle, unsuspected by intelligence, is that Soviet Engineer Troops handlers for portable and emplaced nuclear devices had been co-located with 25 central bases ("S" sites). While there had been some evidence of Soviet interest in these 'ADM' (atomic demolition munitions) from a limited number of exercises as well some human and other sources, nothing substantial had ever been obtained concerning deployment in the Western TVD. The hazy intelligence knowledge had been especially troubling in regard to the potential use of nuclear miniatures by Soviet special operations (*spetsnaz*) penetration teams. Only uncertain hints appeared in some sources. A 1985 General Staff Academy lecture on *spetsnaz* tells of a "minelaying company" created to support "reconnaissance groups equipped with special means which are employed only by order of the Party Central Committee" deployed up to 1000 or more kilometers in the enemy rear with a "detonation system [that] can be activated on our territory" via a new radio technology.[1397] Most information obtained had dealt with Soviet and Warsaw Pact national countermeasures, their detection instruments and procedures, for defeating the US versions.

One noteworthy piece of this particular puzzle had been provided by General-Major (Engineer Troops) V. Bystrov in a 1968 VM (S) article.[1398] The text of this article, which seems to have been promotive, has been, mainly, declassified by the CIA. Bystrov laid out a case for the creation of special engineer units to employ "nuclear mines" along with procedural considerations; his discussion of these units implied that they did not yet exist. Bystrov expressed a concern with "sectors of the national border that are under the threat of the initiation of a new front of armed combat"—the Chinese comrades had become increasingly contrarious. A detailed engineer tasking in the 1963 General Staff operations manual did not include any nuclear role.[1399] Little evidence on these special engineer units had been acquired in regard to the Soviet groups of forces or elsewhere in the Western or Southwestern TVDs during the Cold War; the 1985 General Staff Academy lecture on front missile troops did specify that "nuclear landmines" would be used during the first nuclear strike;[1400] while the front Defensive Operation lecture covered "nuclear obstacles" preparation.[1401] Within a year of the publication of the Bystrov advocacy initiation of the construction of the first of several distinctive engineer RTBs had been imaged in two other TVDs. More than a decade would transpire, however, for US intelligence to work out their purpose, i.e., when I published the first comprehensive intelligence study of engineer WMD in 1981.[1402]

The first deployment of these bases had been in the Northwestern TVD, two RTB on the border with Finland. Six others followed along the PRC frontier, pairs in each of the three districts, along with a working model provided for students at the Higher Military Engineer Command School in Tyumen. All could be distinguished via the official bunker method (engineers among the first to use the Type VIII form). A quite unfortunate real estate decision had been made to site one engineer RTB, 12-km southeast of Svobodnyy in the Far East MD, within the confines of an army artillery ammunition depot. In 1982 (possibly on 9 July when a rail traveler observed a sizable flash) this depot provided what must have been a spectacular pyrotechnic exhibition when thousands of tonnes of munitions ignited in a fratricidal cataclysm that obliterated most structures. When rebuilt, more secure bunkers replaced most of the previous soft storage shelters. The event must have both rattled the nerves of the engineers, if still present, and undermined their confidence in the missile-artillery armament service; imagery indicated that the RTB may have actually been deactivated years earlier; then dismantled so thoroughly that few traces are still visible. Fifteen kilometers due west of the ammunition depot situated the vaults and bunkers of the 12 GUMO central object Svobodnyy-21 (Malaya Sazanka to intelligence) with airfield RTB at 25- and 30-km from the opposite side. Perhaps the central base had already become a, more hospitable, host for the engineers; Svobodnyy-21 deactivated in 1996 according to Russian sources.

The nature of intelligence work is such that analysts do not consistently realize, affirmative, wholly correct, resolutions. The chance that any conclusion is 100 percent correct is zero. Unfortunately an entirely erroneous solution is all too possible. Official customers including those in elected bodies, media, and public exhibit an intolerance of uncertainty and ambiguity that reflects the limited understanding of intelligence assessments that are based on contradictory and fragmentary information—and results in answers that must always be considered tentative. There is an evidential juggling act that

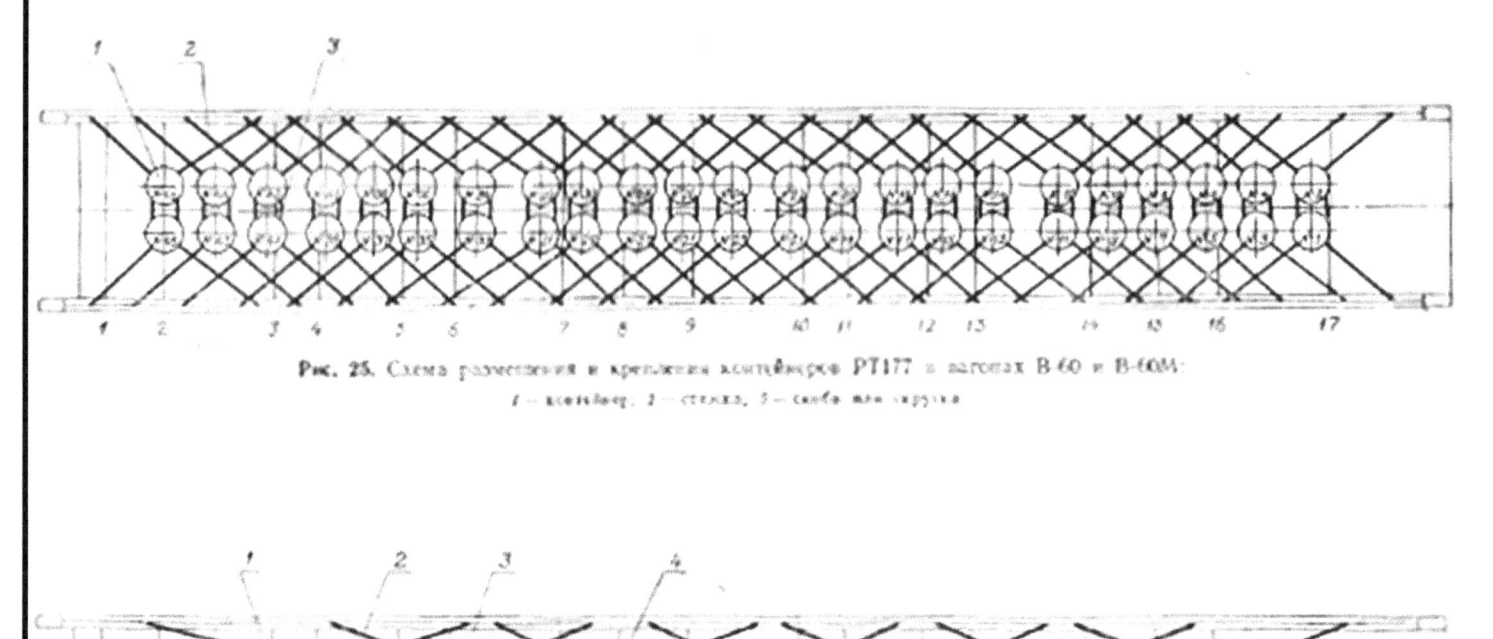

**MoD INSTRUCTIONS 1986**

LOADING AND TIE DOWN ABOARD 24-METER RAILCARS V-60 OR V-60M OF NUCLEAR MINE CANISTERS—46 LOW YIELD RT-177 AND 14 HIGHER YIELD RT-195
OTHER PLANS ALLOWED FOR TRANSPORTS USING BOXCARS

intelligence professionals themselves can mishandle. The successful analyst is not someone who does not make mistakes—such paragons do not exist—but one who is constantly on the alert for non-conforming information, can alter or abandon findings when contrary evidence accumulates, and does not repeat the same mistakes. Failed analysts don't.

# Appendix

## Soviet Missile and Aviation WMD RTB in Warsaw Pact Countries

Compiled from intelligence and post Cold War information; (intelligence name or tentative identification).
pp *polevaya pochta*    number military unit deployed out of USSR
BSP    combat launch position          IAD    fighter aviation division
RBr    rocket brigade                  IBAD  fighter-bomber aviation division
IBr     engineer brigade               BAD   bomber aviation division

My Cold War listing of USSR Ground Troops RTBs, logistics installations, and missile units can be found in declassified period reports.[1403] Limited evidence and investigation precludes identification of the unhardened aviation RTBs that certainly preceded Type versions in the groups of forces.

Central 12 GUMO *Monolit* (Type VII)

Bulgaria
(Karlovo)                       42.6639 | 24.9918                             ui RTB
(Samokov)                      42.3823 | 23.6541                             ui RTB pp 74771
(Vezenkovo)                  42.8316 | 26.6208                             ui RTB

Czechoslovakia
Bela (Mimon)                50.5335 | 14.8031        Object 52       ui RTB pp 85856
Bilin (Most)                  50.4971 | 13.8354        Object 50       ui RTB pp 01806
Mishov-Borovno (Rokycany)  49.6256 | 13.7076        Object 51       ui RTB pp 80990

German Democratic Republic
Himmelpfort/Lychen-2       53.1759 | 13.2806        Object 4001     400 RTB pp 73259
Stolzenhain                  51.8669 | 13.1644        Object 5001     409 RTB pp 73274

Hungary
Úrkút (Veszprém)            47.0477 | 17.7210        Object Duna    1542 RTB pp 16205

Poland
Brzeznica-Kolonia (Borne)   53.4340 | 16.5748        Object 3002     ui RTB pp 85918
Podborsko (Bialogard)       53.9567 | 16.1219        Object 3001     ui RTB pp 01959
Templewo (Sulecin)          52.4246 | 15.3211        Object 3003     ui RTB pp 87648

Czechoslovakia—Central Group of Forces CGF
Theater Missiles
122 RBr R-900           1984 > 1988
*Granit*
(Type VIII-S)
Hranice                       49.5618 | 17.7457                                                1984-1985
(Type VIII-T)
Kozlov                        49.6114 | 17.5445                        1857 PRTB pp 84205    1985 > 1988
Type VIII-S also at three BSP

131 Composite Aviation Division
(Type VIII-D)
Boží Dar (Milovice)          50.2313 | 14.9144                             ui RTB pp 22012

German Democratic Republic—Group of Soviet Forces Germany GSFG
Theater Missiles
Class A/B

| | | | |
|---|---|---|---|
| Neuthyman (Fürstenberg) | 53.2099 \| 13.1975 | 320 PRTB<br>ui PRTB pp 74165 | 1959 72 IBr R-5M<br>1959 > 1966<br>ui RBr R-12 pp 18300 |
| Vogelsang (Templin) | 53.0402 \| 13.366353 | 432 PRTB<br>ui PRTB pp 74165 | 1959 72 IBr R-5M<br>1959 > 1966<br>ui RBr R-12 pp 18300 |

52 RBr R-900        1984 > 1988
*Granit* (Type VIII-D)

| | | |
|---|---|---|
| Waren | 53.5428 \| 12.6312 | ui PRTB pp 80512 |

Class A/B
Neuthyman (Fürstenberg)    53.2099 | 13.1975
Type VIII-S also at launch battalion garrison Alt Strelitz and BSP
119 RBr R-900[1404]        1984 > 1988
*Granit* (Type VIII-S)

| | | |
|---|---|---|
| Königsbrück | 51.2811 \| 13.8774 | 2454 PRTB pp 82431 |

Type VIII-S also at launch battalion garrison Bischofswerda and BSP

USSR Ground Troops Rocket Troops and Artillery
**Heeres-muna**

| | | | |
|---|---|---|---|
| Altengrabow | 52.1884 \| 12.1638 | 1648 APRTB pp 57851 | 3 Shock Army<br>448 RBr R-100/120 |
| Altenhain | 51.3028 \| 12.7015 | 11 PRTB pp 11817 | 8 Guards Army<br>11 RBr R-300 R-400 |
| Dannenwalde | 53.1002 \| 13.1552 | 3397 APRTB pp 57842 | 2 Guards Tank Army<br>458 RBr R-100/120 |
| Hohenleipisch | 51.5201 \| 13.5677 | 2620 PRTB pp 47982 | GSFG<br>164 RBr R-300 |
| Kapen (Oranienbaum) | 51.8043 \| 12.3398 | 52 PRTB pp 92846 | 1 Guards Tank Army<br>181 RBr R-300 |
| Torgau | 51.5491 \| 12.9425 | *45 PRTB pp 11649 | GSFG<br>175 RBr R-300 |
| Lamitsch (Wilmersdorf) | 52.2731 \| 14.1253 | 2618 PRTB pp 78559 | 20 Guards Army<br>27 RBr R-300 |
| Wulkow (Neuruppin) | 52.9435 \| 12.9171 | 3274 PRTB pp 73654 | 3 Shock Army<br>36 RBr R-300 |
| Zeithain/Röderau | 51.3488 \| 13.3240 | 1699 PRTB pp 57845 | GSFG<br>23 RBr Königsbrück (until 1981) |

*Numeric 45 attested multiple sources but a Soviet document has 261 PRTB pp 11649 at Torgau 1959 through at least 1982, an unresolvable discrepancy.
Some information has re-subordinations 1988 Kapen PRTB to 3 SA and Zeithain PRTB to 1 GTA; 1970 Wulkow PRTB from 3 SA to 2 GTA.

**garrison**

| | | | |
|---|---|---|---|
| Bad Freienwalde | 52.7706 \| 14.0087 | 1694 APRTB pp 45291 | 20 Guards Army<br>464 RBr R-100/120 |
| RTB | 52.7575 \| 13.999 | | |
| Halle | 51.4927 \| 11.9157 | 1655 APRTB pp 38673 | 8 Guards Army<br>449 RBr R-100/120 |
| Vogelsang (Templin) | 53.0402 \| 13.3664 | 3272 PRTB pp 55543 | 2 Guards Tank Army<br>112 RBr R-300 |
| Wurzen | 51.3835 \| 12.7212 | 1677 APRTB pp 38690 | 1 Guards Tank Army<br>432 RBr R-100/120 |

Some information has resubordinations 1982 Wurzen APRTB from 8 GA possibly on formation 432 RBr at Wurzen and Halle APRTB from 1 GTA; 1970 Vogelsang PRTB 2 GTA to 3 SA.

16 Air Army
*Basalt* (Type IV)
| | | | |
|---|---|---|---|
| Brand | 52.0115 \| 13.7822 | 1092 RTB pp 66683 | 105 IBAD |
| Finsterwalde | 51.5948 \| 13.7535 | 2952 RTB pp 66698 | 105 IBAD |
| Lärz | 53.2949 \| 12.7671 | 634 RTB pp 53510 | 125 IBAD |

(Type VI)
| | | | |
|---|---|---|---|
| Altenburg | 50.9717 \| 12.537 | 1652 RTB pp 23298 | 6 IAD |

*Granit* (Type VIII-D)
| | | | |
|---|---|---|---|
| Gross Dölln (Templin) | 53.0263 \| 13.5530 | (1658) RTB pp 23318 | 125 IBAD |
| Grossenhain | 51.3052 \| 13.549383 | 1587 RTB pp 21149 | 105 IBAD |
| Werneuchen | 52.6278 \| 13.7715 | 451 RTB pp 26095 | |

Also seven airfield Type VIII-S; nuclear exercises and post Cold War rumormongering indicate a Finow Airfield RTB, if so hardening not accomplished.

Hungary—Southern Group of Forces SGF[1405]
USSR Ground Troops Rocket Troops and Artillery
*Granit* (Type VIII-T)
| | | | |
|---|---|---|---|
| Szákszend (Császár) | 47.4915 \| 18.1921 | 3105 PRTB pp 13355 | (ui army) (1961) R-30 R-70 |
| | | | (1967) 99 RBr R-300 |
| | | | (1987) 459 RBr R-100/120 |
| Tab | 46.7309 \| 18.0755 | 692 PRTB pp 38214 | (1961) 107 RBr R-170 |
| | | | (1967) 22 RBr R-300 |

36 Air Army
*Basalt* (Type IV)
| | | | |
|---|---|---|---|
| Kunmadaras | 47.4028 \| 20.7625 | 2476 RTB pp 27577 | 11 IAD |

*Granit*
(Type VIII-D)
| | | | |
|---|---|---|---|
| Kiskunlacháza | 47.1703 \| 19.0681 | 3345 RTB pp 21674 | 11 IAD |

(Type VIII-S)
| | | | |
|---|---|---|---|
| Debrecen | 47.5015 \| 21.6200 | 2912 RTB | |
| Sármellék | 46.6784 \| 17.1664 | | |
| Tököl | 47.3544 \| 18.9673 | | |

Poland—Northern Group of Forces NGF
**Heeres-muna**
| | | | |
|---|---|---|---|
| Borne Sulinowo | 53.5829 \| 16.5159 | ui PRTB pp 28473 | 114 RBr R-300 |
| Duninuv (Chocianow) | 51.3783 \| 15.8667 | ui PRTB pp 83267 | (CGF ui army) |
| | | | (185 RBr R-300) |

**garrison**
| | | | |
|---|---|---|---|
| Pstraze | 51.4489 \| 15.5600 | ui PRTB | (CGF ui army) |
| | | | (442 RBr R-100/120) |

4 Operational Air Army VGK
*Basalt* (Type IV)
| | | | |
|---|---|---|---|
| Szprotawa | 51.5502 \| 15.6130 | 2843 RTB pp 66593 | 149 BAD |

*Granit* (Type VIII-D)
| | | | |
|---|---|---|---|
| Kluczewo (Stargard) | 53.2611 \| 14.9468 | ui RTB pp 21150 | 239 IAD |

also Type VIII-S at Chojna and Krzywa (Osla) Airfields

# Illustrations

GRAPHIC Puzzled Intelligence — 6
The earth-centric system had been the celestial official model for some 1500 years despite ever-increasing divergences from observed reality.
Andreas Cellarius *Harmonia Macrocosmica* circa 1660 — Wikimedia Commons

PHOTO The View from Torgau — 10-11
American, German, and Russian participants commemorate the meeting on the Elbe.
author photo 25 April 2005

PHOTO Assessing the Soviet WMD Game-Plan — 14
Three nuclear reentry vehicles at the head of an SS-20 theater missile.
*Russia's Arms and Technologies*, *The XXI Century Encyclopedia* V.1 *Strategic Nuclear Forces* p83

PAGE FACSIMILE *Directive*[1406] Precepts — 24

DIAGRAM Directions — 32

PHOTO Front RTB — 42
declassified satellite imagery KH-7 Gambit; 23 September 1966; mission 4032; pass 106; frame 017

PAGEs FACSIMILE Versioned reality — 54-55
CIA report[1407] and *Warning* NIE[1408] identical maps; German Military History Research Office[1409]

DIAGRAM Multi-Level Echelonment — 62

PHOTO Mobilization Center Chegdomyn Far East MD — 77
declassified satellite imagery
KH-9 Hexagon; 26 September 1980; mission 1216-3; pass 787; camera forward; frame 05; index 1

MAP Western Theater — 78

MAP Soviet Front Regrouping Zones[1410] — 92

MAP Southwestern TVD[1411] — 101

PHOTO Nuclear Interlude — 106-107
operational-tactical missile row Artillery Museum St. Petersburg—author photo July 2017

CHART 1977 General Staff Academy Nuclear Strike Plan — 120
Data compiled from several Lessons.

PAGE FACSIMILE 1980 Nuclear War Time Periods[1412] — 128

EMBLEM Elusive Chemical Echelons — 140
Insignia of Soviet Chemical Troops which bedazzled intelligence connoisseurs—expunging alternative solutions.

PHOTO Falkenhagen (East) Germany Sarin Production Plant — 145
author photo March 2006

PHOTO Mal'ta Bio-Weapons Loading Complex                150
declassified satellite imagery KH-9 Hexagon; 1 October 1982; mission 1217-4; pass 1502; camera forward; frame 08

PHOTO Grossenhain Airfield (East) Germany 1975          168
declassified satellite imagery KH-9 Hexagon; 12 June 1975; mission 1210-1; pass 053; camera forward; frame 35

PAGEs FACSIMILE 1985 DIA report[1413]                   176-177

PHOTO Kambarka                                          178
declassified satellite imagery KH-7 Gambit; 28 May 1967; mission 4037; pass 089; frame 005

PHOTO-PLAN[1414] Schuchye Google Earth image            187

EMBLEM 12 GUMO                                          190

PHOTO Machulische Airfield                              196
declassified aircraft imagery U-2; 5 July 1956; mission A2014; camera 6R; frame 298

PHOTO Mozhaysk-10                                       198
declassified aircraft imagery U-2; 5 July 1956; mission A2014; camera 7; frame 467
intelligence artist drawing[1415]

PHOTOs                                                  202
b Engels Airfield
declassified aircraft imagery U-2; 6 December 1959; mission B8005; camera 9L; frame 1674
c Type III under construction intelligence artist drawing Figure 4[1416]
d Type III interior Air Forces RTB Siauliai, Lithuania (SSR) author photo May 2007

PHOTOs Arys                                             204
declassified aircraft imagery U-2; 28 August 1957; mission B4058; camera 7; frame 220
declassified satellite imagery KH-7 Gambit; 29 May 1965; mission 4018; pass 24; frame 11

Gamma bunker                                            206
PHOTO  declassified satellite imagery KH-7 Gambit; 24 April 1966; mission 4027; pass 075; frame 007; index 14
DRAWING[1417]

PAGE FACSIMILE                                          210
State cable 1983 evidence of the second kind indicative of a chemical alternative reality addressed to a bevy of agencies and offices—even the Department of Energy which had a nuclear intell element[1418]

PHOTOs SOC—sets                                         214-215
declassified satellite imagery KH-7 Gambit
Tula-50; 4 October 1965; mission 4022; pass 058; frame 011
Kargopol-2; 24 April 1966; mission 4027; pass 078; frame 004
Sebezh-5; 17 July 1966; mission 4030; pass 091; frame 014

DIAGRAM        SOC—Line A + C                           220-221

PHOTO Hidden Nukes                                                                 228-229
Loading dock fronting *Hma* bunker RTB Dannenwalde (East) Germany
author photo April 2005

PHOTOS          Gomel-30 (Rechitsa)                                                232
declassified satellite imagery KH-9 Hexagon; 27 February 1981; mission 1216-4; pass 1384; camera forward; frame 60; camera aft; frame 61; index 5

PAGE FACSIMILE MoD 1986 [1419]                                                     233

DIAGRAM PRTB Organization                                                          235
PHOTO  <http://www.rwd-mb3.de/pages/9f223.htm>

PHOTOs airfield official nuclear storage bunkers                                   242
Type IV RTB Finsterwalde (East) Germany     author photos April 2005
Type VIII-D RTB Kiskunlacháza Hungary       author photos December 2007

PAGE FACSIMILE 1979 NIE[1420]                                                      250

PHOTOs
Veselyy Kut                                                                        252
declassified satellite imagery KH-9 Hexagon; 24 May 1979; mission 1215-2; pass 603; camera forward; frame 14; index 2

Torgau (East) Germany                                                              253
reconnaissance aircraft; 23 December 1944; 106 Group; sortie 3844; frames 3032 + 3033 merged

PHOTOs *Hma* Bunker (East) Germany                    255
RTB Kapen (Oranienbaum)              author photo mosaic  March 2006
RTB Wulkow (Neuruppin)               author photos—interior mosaic  November 2004

PHOTOs nuclear warhead service                        258-259
RTB Dannenwalde (East) Germany       author photos  April 2005
RTB Császár Hungary                  author photos  December 2007
RTB Torgau (East) Germany            author photos  April 2005

PHOTO                                                 260
RTB Zeithain (East) Germany warhead transporter tie down schematic   contributed by Matthias Karthe

DOSSIER missile                                                                    262-263
*Hma* Dürnrohr    reconnaissance aircraft photo; 16 August 1944; 60 PR; sortie 0670; frame 4116
France forward depot; facsimile 25 August 1944; UK National Archives AIR 40/1219
R-2 storage shelter
RTB Kedainiai Lithuania SSR          author photo April 2005    official missile bunker railway
RTB Kapen (East) Germany             author photo November 2004
RTB Tab Hungary                      author photos December 2007
RTB Altengrabow (East) Germany       author photo November 2004

PHOTOs *Hma* Siegelsbach (West) Germany                                            266
reconnaissance aircraft photo; 9 February 1945; US 7 Group; sortie 67A; frame 3055
Google Earth base image

DOSSIER 268
readiness program (East) Germany early 1980s
Soviet drawing 1988 loading warhead container to open bed truck[1421]
RTB Altengrabow author photo November 2004
RTB Himmelpfort author photo November 2004
RTB Wilmersdorf author photo April 2005
RTB Torgau author photo April 2005

PHOTOs RTB Tab Hungary 270-271
declassified satellite imagery KH-9 Hexagon; 1 August 1984; mission 1219-1; pass 335; camera aft; frame 03; index 3
author photos December 2007

DOSSIER Type VII (East) Germany 273
RTB Stolzenhain author photos original blueprint
RTB Himmelpfort author photos November 2004

PAGE FACSIMILE MoD 1986[1422] 280

# Endnotes

Abbreviations

Declassification
FOIA (case number)    Freedom of Information Act
ISCAP (case number)   Interagency Security Classification Appeals Panel
MDR (case number)     mandatory declassification review (Executive Order 13526)

US sources
NIC     National Intelligence Council
NI(E)   National Intelligence (Estimate)
    IIM     Interagency Intelligence Memorandum
    NIO     National Intelligence Officer
CIA     Central Intelligence Agency
    CREST   CIA Records Search Tool <https://www.cia.gov/library/readingroom/collection/crest-25-year-program-archive>
    DCI     Director of Central Intelligence
    DI      Directorate of Intelligence
    DO      Directorate of Operations
    DST     Directorate of Science and Technology
    FBIS    Foreign Broadcast Information Service
    FDD     Foreign Documents Division
    FPD     Foreign Press Digest
    HCD     Historical Collection Division
    DVD documents collection HR70-14 07-18-2012 catalog [no links]
    <https://www.cia.gov/library/publications/cold-war/the-warsaw-pact-forces/warsaw-pact-catalogue.pdf>
    IAS     Imagery Analysis Service
    IIR     Intelligence Information Report
    IISR    Intelligence Information Special Report
    NFAC    National Foreign Assessment Center
    JPRS    Joint Publications Research Service
    OIA     Office of Imagery Analysis
        IAM     Imagery Analysis Memorandum
    ORR     Office of Research and Reports
    OSI     Office of Scientific Intelligence
    OSR     Office of Strategic Research
    SOVA    Office of Soviet Analysis
DIA     Defense Intelligence Agency
DoD     Department of Defense
    OSD     Office of the Secretary of Defense
DoS     Department of State
    FRUS    Foreign Relations of the United States
NPIC    National Photographic Interpretation Center
    BB      Briefing Board
    BIIR    Basic Imagery Interpretation Report
    IAR     Imagery Analysis Report
    PIR     Photographic Interpretation Report
NRO     National Reconnaissance Office

| | | |
|---|---|---|
| NSA | National Security Agency | |
| USAF | United States Air Force | |
| | FTD | Foreign Technology Division |
| USNA | United States National Archives and Records Administration | |

| | | |
|---|---|---|
| USSR | Union of Soviet Socialist Republics | |
| GS | General Staff of the Armed Forces of the USSR | |
| | GSA | Orders of Lenin and Suvorov Military Academy of the General Staff of the Armed Forces of the USSR i/n K Ye Voroshilov |
| | GRU | Main Intelligence Directorate |
| | VM | Military Thought (journal) |
| IC(R)A | Information Collection Of (Missile Units and) Artillery | |
| MO | Ministry of Defense | |
| VIZ | Military Historical Journal | |

Warsaw Pact

| | |
|---|---|
| WPCAF | Combined Armed Forces of the Member States of the Warsaw Pact |
| WPCAF-HQIC | Information Collection of the Headquarters and the Technical Committee of the Combined Armed Forces |

military rank

| | | |
|---|---|---|
| ADM | *admiral* | |
| MAR | *marshal* | |
| MSU | marshal Soviet Union | |
| GEN | *general* | |
| COL | *polkovnik* | colonel |
| MAJ | *mayor* | major |
| CPT | *kapitan* | captain |
| LT | *leytenant* | lieutenant |

Other Sources

| | |
|---|---|
| FAS | Federation of American Scientists |
| GWU | National Security Archive—George Washington University |
| PHP | Parallel History Project on NATO and Warsaw Pact; Center for Security Studies ETH Zurich |
| SIPRI | Stockholm International Peace Research Institute |
| UKNA | United Kingdom National Archives |

Wilson Center

| | | |
|---|---|---|
| | CWIHP | Cold War International History Project |
| | CWIHP-B | Bulletin |
| | CWIHP-DA | Digital Archive |

| | | |
|---|---|---|
| security classification | TS | top secret |
| | S | secret |
| | R | restricted |
| | U | unclassified (public access) |

## Assessing The Soviet WMD Game-Plan

1 Vojtech Mastny; *How Able Was "Able Archer" Nuclear Trigger And Intelligence In Perspective;* Journal of Cold War Studies 11(1) 2009; 110

2 Graham T Allison; *Questions About The Arms Race And Implications For Strategic Arms Limitation: A Bureaucratic Perspective*; 1973/10/15; UKNA; DEFE 24/790

3 James Farquhar Cant; *The Development Of The SS-20—A Case Study Of Soviet Defence Decisionmaking During The Brezhnev Era*; 1998/05; University of Glasgow/Department of Politics; <http://theses.gla.ac.uk/4814/1/1998CantPhD.pdf> in particular p2 and p35 onward

4 *Net Assessments In National Intelligence*; Memorandum; SP-135/81; DCI NIC; 1981/06/04; CREST RDP83B00140R000200110036-3; 2007/03/20; traces net assessment issue since early 1950s

5 *Prospects For Accelerated Soviet Defense Effort*; SR 81-10096; CIA OSR; 1981/08; S; <https://www.cia.gov/library/readingroom/docs/19810801.pdf>

6 *Disarmament: Who's Against?*; 1983; Progress Publishers translation (Military Publishing House); CWIHP-DA; <https://digitalarchive.wilsoncenter.org/document/110897.pdf?v=48f39fcf2a7a1050235cd5c347368441>; 14

7 James B Bruce; "The Missing Link: The Analyst-Collector Relationship" *Analyzing Intelligence: Origins, Obstacles, And Innovations;* 2008; Georgetown University Press; ISBN 978-1-58901-201-1; 198

8 MSU M V Zakharov; *The Tasks Of Military Science At Its Present Stage And The Main Directions Of Work Of The Journal Military Thought*; VM S (2-90) 1970; CIA IISR; 1973/10/18; <https://www.cia.gov/library/readingroom/docs/1973-10-18.pdf>; also CIA HCD HR70-14 07-18-2012 DVD VII-076

9 Thomas R Robinson; *American Cryptology During The Cold War, 1945-1989; Book II: Centralization Wins, 1960-1972* CCH-E32-95-03 1995; 473; *Book III: Retrenchment And Reform, 1972-1980* CCH-S54-98-01 1998; 81-82; United States Cryptologic History; NSA Center for Cryptologic History; ISCAP 2008-021

10 *Armaments Planning Within The Framework Of The Warsaw Pact*; 1986; CIA IIR FIRDB-312-00537-86; 1986/07/02; <https://www.cia.gov/library/readingroom/docs/1983_06_10_BACKGROUND_INFORMATION.pdf>; 49

11 Jan Hoffenaar and Christopher Findlay ED; *Military Planning For European Theatre Conflict During The Cold War*: An Oral History Roundtable: Stockholm, 24-25 April 2006; Zur Sicherheitspolitik Nr. 79; 2007; Zürcher Beiträge/ETH Zürich Center for Security Studies; ISBN 3-905696-17-7; <http://www.php.isn.ethz.ch/documents/ZB79_000.pdf> 53

12 GEN-MAJ A Slobodenko; *Views Of Our Probable Enemies Concerning Modern Defense*; VM S (1-89) 1970; CIA IISR; 1973/10/26; <https://www.cia.gov/library/readingroom/docs/1973-10-26b.pdf>

13 GEN-MAJ N Smirnov; *Meeting Engagements In Modern Operations*; VM S (3-88) 1969; CIA IISR; 1976/04/21; <https://www.cia.gov/library/readingroom/docs/1976-04-21-A.pdf>; also CREST RDP10-00105R000201810001-4; 2012/04/12

14 Vojtech Mastny and Malcolm Byrne ED; *A Cardboard Castle? An Inside History Of The Warsaw Pact 1955-1991*; 2005; Central European University; ISBN 963-7326-08-1; ISBN 963-7326-07-3; document 80

15 *Warning Of War In Europe*; Memorandum; 1984/06/27; <https://www.cia.gov/library/readingroom/docs/DOC_0001486834.pdf>; 23

16 COL R Simonyan; *Some Problems Of Reconnaissance In The Preparation Of A Front's First Offensive Operation*; VM S (1-62) 1962; CIA IISR FIRDB-312-01150-78; 1978/05/22; <https://www.cia.gov/library/readingroom/docs/1978-05-22a.pdf>

17 *Treaty Between The United States Of America And The Union Of Soviet Socialist Republics On The Elimination Of Their Intermediate-Range And Shorter-Range Missiles*; Treaty Series; 1657(28521) ; Secretariat of the United Nations; 1991/12/13

18 Maritime Museum Of The Atlantic; Nova Scotia Museum; <https://maritimemuseum.novascotia.ca/what-see-do/halifax-explosion/halifax-explosion-infosheet>; exhibit data cited

19 Matthew G McKinzie et al; *The U.S. Nuclear War Plan: A Time For Change*; 2001/06; Natural Resources Defense Council; <http://www.nrdc.org/nuclear/warplan/index.asp>; 126

20 *Russia's Arms And Technologies: Nuclear Weapons Complex: The XXI Century Encyclopedia;* 2007; Arms and Technologies; ISBN 978-5-93799-035-8; XIV; 250-254

21 *The Nuclear Matters Handbook Expanded Edition*; [2011]; Office of Assistant Secretary of Defense for Nuclear, Chemical, and Biological Defense Programs; <http://www.acq.osd.mil/ncbdp/nm>; AP-E 195

22 GEN-COL I Glebov and GEN-MAJ V Yemelin; *Offensive Operations Of A Front To The Entire Depth Of A Theater Of Military Operations*; VM S; (2-72) 1964; CIA IISR; 1975/11/14; <https://www.cia.gov/library/readingroom/docs/1975-11-14b.pdf>; also CREST RDP10-00105R000201480001-1 2012/10/16; 7

23 COL G Luzgin; *Actions By Troops In Zones Of Radioactive Contamination In A Battle And Operation*; VM S (3-64) 1962; CIA IISR; 1978/06/02; <https://www.cia.gov/library/readingroom/docs/1978-06-02a.pdf>

24 Amy F Woolf; *Nonstrategic Nuclear Weapons*; Report for Congress; 2019/09/06; Congressional Research Service; RL32572; <http://fas.org/sgp/crs/nuke/RL32572.pdf>; 14 and 26>28

# Precepts

## Center rules
25  GEN-MAJ N Komkov and COL P Shemanskiy; *Certain Historic Trends In The Development Of Troop Control*; VM R (10) 1964; FDD 914 (20 May 1965); also CREST RDP85T00875R000300090004-2; 2000/08/09; 13

## semicircular authorities
26 Ghulam Dastagir Wardak; *The Voroshilov Lectures: Materials From The Soviet General Staff Academy*; V.I *Issues Of Soviet Military Strategy*; 1989; National Defense University; CH-3

27 S A Tyushkevich; *The Soviet Armed Forces: The History Of Their Organizational Development*; 1978; *Voyenizdat*; JPRS 73655 Military Affairs 1445; USAF Soviet Military Thought 19; 387

28 GEN-COL M Tereshchenko; *Dedicated Service To The Fatherland Was His Ideal (80th Birth Anniversary Of N. Ogarkov, Marshal Of The Soviet Union)*; VM U; 6 (5) 1997;  East View Publications; 95-96

29 *Central Group of Forces*; 2010; web page no longer accessible; see Internet Archive Wayback Machine <https://web.archive.org/web/20080512094220/http://rk72.jino-net.ru:80/page.php?55>

30 Thomas R Robinson; *American Cryptology During The Cold War, 1945-1989; Book II: Centralization Wins, 1960-1972* CCH-E32-95-03 1995; 457; United States Cryptologic History; NSA Center for Cryptologic History; ISCAP 2008-021

31 GEN-COL A Kh Babadzhanyan; *Some Questions In The Preparation And Conduct Of Initial Offensive Operations*; VM TS (Third) 1961; CIA; 1962/03/23; <https://www.cia.gov/library/readingroom/docs/1962-03-23.pdf>

32 *Theory And Practice Of Warsaw Pact Operations; Part II: Organization And Operational Intent In The West European Theater Of War*; CIA IIR; 1972/06/27; CIA HCD HR70-14 07-18-2012 DVD VI-049; 4

33 *1. Polish Peacetime And Wartime Troop Strengths 2. Deployment Of Polish Forces In Wartime*; 1975; CIA HCD HR70-14 07-18-2012 DVD VII-034; 4

34 Wojciech Jaruzelski; *Warsaw Pact Generals In Polish Uniforms*; 2002/09; PHP; <http://www.php.isn.ethz.ch/lory1.ethz.ch/collections/colltopicfo4d.html?lng=en&id=20636&navinfo=15708>

35 COL I Vyrodov; *Strategy And Operational Art: On The Leadership Of Military Operations Of Strategic Troop Groupings In World War II*; VIZ (4) 1979; JPRS 073677 (13 June 1979)

36 GEN-MAJ V Gurkin; *Certain Questions From The Experience Of Establishing And Operating Troop High Commands Of The Sectors In The First Period Of The Great Patriotic War*; VIZ (7) 1984/07; JPRS-UMA-84-073 (28 November 1984); <http://www.dtic.mil/cgi-bin/GetTRDoc?AD=ADA355977>

37 MSU V G Kulikov; *The Status And Development Of The Military Cooperation Of The Combined Armed Forces Of The Warsaw Pact Member States*; 1978/11; CIA IISR FIRDB-312-00867-79; 1979/05/11; <https://www.cia.gov/library/readingroom/docs/1979_05_11_REPORT_ON_THE_WARSAW_PACT_COOPERATION.pdf>; 6

38 *Warsaw Pact Air Power: Forces For Use In Central Europe*; Intelligence Report; SR IR 73-22; CIA DI OSR; 1973/12; CIA HCD HR70-14 07-18-2012 DVD VII-140; 31

39 F F Gayvoronsky et al; *Front Offensive Operations*; GSA; 1974; CIA IISR FIRDB-312-01997-79; 1979/09/27; CIA HCD HR70-14 07-18-2012 DVD VII-223

40 I Y Shavrov; *The Front Offensive Operation*; GSA 1977/05; CIA IISR FIRDB-312-00013-79; 1979/06/15; CIA MDR EOM-2009-0157; also CIA HCD HR70-14 07-18-2012 DVD VII-222

41 *USSR General Staff Academy Lessons; The Front Offensive Operation*; Lesson 5; *Study and Critique of the Decision of the Commander of the Combined Baltic Fleet on the Combat Actions of the Fleet's Forces in the Front Offensive Operation*; 1977; GSA;  CIA IISR FIRDB-312/02033-80; 1980/08/07; CIA HCD HR70-14 07-18-2012 DVD VII-236; 6

42 *Warsaw Pact Exercise "Center"*; 1978/11; CIA IISR TS-798165; 1979/06/08; CIA HCD HR70-14 07-18-2012 DVD VII-320; 5

43 *Materials Of The Critique Of The Operational-Strategic Command-Staff Exercise Zapad-77*; CIA IISR TS-788301; 1978/10/13; CIA HCD HR70-14 07-18-2012 DVD VII-045; 10

44 *The Unified Wartime Command System For The Combined Armed Forces Of The Warsaw Pact*; 1981; CIA IIR FIRDB-312-01928-82; <https://www.cia.gov/library/readingroom/docs/1982_01_01_THE_UNIFIED_WARTIME_COMMAND.pdf>

45 *The Warsaw Pact Soyuz-78 Exercise*; 1978/05/31; CIA IISR FIRDB-312-02313-78; 1978/09/22; CIA HCD HR70-14 07-18-2012 DVD VII-315; 4

46 *Warsaw Pact Exercise "Center"*; 1978/11; CIA IISR TS-798165; 1979/06/08; CIA HCD HR70-14 07-18-2012 DVD VII-320; 5

47 *Operational Mission—Situation As Of 1700 Hours 4 April*; CIA IISR TS-788328; 1978/11/17; CIA HCD HR70-14 07-18-2012 DVD VII-103; 8

48 Vojtech Mastny and Malcolm Byrne ED; *A Cardboard Castle? An Inside History Of The Warsaw Pact 1955-1991*; 2005; Central European University; ISBN 963-7326-08-1; ISBN 963-7326-07-3; document 86

49 MSU V G Kulikov; *Statute On The Combined Armed Forces Of The Warsaw Pact Member States And Their Command Organs For Wartime*; CIA IISR FIRDB-312-00725-80; 1980/04/11; CIA HCD HR70-14 07-18-2012 DVD VII-188; also <https://www.cia.gov/library/readingroom/docs/1980_04_11_FROM_THE_12TH_SESSION.pdf>

50 Wojciech Jaruzelski; *Warsaw Pact Generals In Polish Uniforms*; 2002/09; PHP; <http://www.php.isn.ethz.ch/lory1.ethz.ch/collections/colltopicfo4d.html?lng=en&id=20636&navinfo=15708>

51 *Background Information On The Development Of The Unified Wartime Command System For The Combined Armed Forces Of The Warsaw Pact*; CIA IIR FIRDB-312-01197-83; 1983/06/10; <https://www.cia.gov/library/readingroom/docs/1983_06_10_THE_ORGANIZATION_OF_THE_WARSAW_PACT>

52 *Soviet Plans For Warsaw Pact Theater Commands Opposite NATO*; Intelligence Assessment; SR 79-10033JX; CIA NFAC OSR; 1979/04; TS; CIA HCD HR70-14 07-18-2012 DVD VII-181

53 *The Soviet Union's Control Of The Warsaw Pact Forces*; SOV 83-10175CX; 1983/10; TS; <https://www.cia.gov/library/readingroom/docs/1983_10_01_THE_SOVIET_UNIONS_CONTROL_OF_THE_WARSAW_PACT_FORCES.pdf>; also CIA HCD HR70-14 07-18-2012 DVD VII-206

54 *Agent Reconnaissance In Front Offensive Operations;* 1985; GSA; CIA IISR TS-888283; 10; ISCAP 2012-026 (CIA MDR EOM-2009-00158)

55 MSU V G Kulikov; *Statute On The Combined Armed Forces Of The Warsaw Pact Member States And Their Command Organs For Wartime*; CIA IISR FIRDB-312-01995-80; 1980/07/25; <https://www.cia.gov/library/readingroom/docs/1980_07_25_RATIFICATION_OF_THE_WARTIME_STATUTE_ON_THE_WARSAW_PACT.pdf>; section III

56 [*Statute On The Combined Armed Forces And The Combined Command Of The Warsaw Pact Member States*]; CIA IIR FIRDB-312-01928-82; <https://www.cia.gov/library/readingroom/docs/1982_01_01_THE_UNIFIED_WARTIME_COMMAND.pdf>

57 *Soviet Planning For Front Nuclear Operations In Central Europe*; Intelligence Assessment; SOV 83-10099JX; CIA DI SOVA; 1983/06; TS; CIA HCD HR70-14 07-18-2012 VII-61; 1

58 *Warsaw Pact Tactical Forces: Capabilities And Readiness For Nuclear War*; Research Paper; SOV 85-10107CX; CIA DI SOVA; 1985/06; TS; CIA HCD HR70-14 07-18-2012 DVD VII-119; 2

## finding the way without directions

59 GEN-MAJ V Kruchinin; *Contemporary Strategic Theory On The Goals And Missions Of Armed Combat*; VM R (10) 1963; FDD 965 20 July 1966; CREST RDP85T00875R000300090022-2; 2000/08/09

60 MSU V D Sokolovskiy; *Military Strategy*; 1962; *Voyenizdat*; RAND R-416-PR; <http://www.rand.org/pubs/reports/2005/R416.pdf>; 214

61 GEN-MAJ V Kruchinin; *Contemporary Strategic Theory On The Goals And Missions Of Armed Combat*; VM R (10) 1963; FDD 965 20 July 1966; CREST RDP85T00875R000300090022-2; 2000/08/09

62 MSU Andrei A Grechko; *The Armed Forces Of The Soviet State*; USAF Soviet Military Thought 12; 1975; 280-281

63 GEN-ARM V Ivanov; *The Development Of Soviet Operational Art*; VM R (3) 1967; FPD 1224-67 (26 December 1967)

64 GEN-ARM I Pavlovskiy; *The Ground Troops Of The Soviet Armed Forces*; VM R (11) 1967; FPD 0157-68 (18 November 1968)

65 COL L I Voloshin; *Theory Of The Operation In Depth And Trends In Its Development*; VM R (8) 1978/08; FPD 0079-019 (10 July 1979); CREST RDP05S00365R000200210001-0; 2012/06/14

66 GEN-MAJ Tibor Toth; *Characteristics Of Organizing And Conducting An Offensive Operation Of The Coalition Front And Combined Arms Army*; *Honvedelem* (6) 1980; S; CIA IIR C05798348; 1985/09/06; CIA MDR EOM-2011-0881

67 *Warsaw Pact Forces Opposite NATO*; NIE 11-14-79; 1979/01/31; TS; CIA HCD HR70-14 07-18-2012 DVD VII-4 (V.1) *Summary Estimate* VII-5 (V.2) *The Estimate*

68 *Employment Of Warsaw Pact Forces Against NATO*; NI IIM 83-10002; 1983/07; TS; CIA HCD HR70-14 07-18-2012 DVD VII-062

69 *War In The Western TVD*; DDB-2600-3858-84-SAO; DIA Directorate for Research; 1984/08; S; <http://www.dia.mil/FOIA/FOIA-Electronic-Reading-Room/FOIA-Reading-Room-Russia/FileId/121078/ >

70 *Warsaw Pact Air Forces: Support Of Strategic Operations In Central Europe*; Intelligence Assessment; CIA DI SOVA; SOV 85-10001CX; 1985/01; TS; CIA HCD HR70-14 07-18-2012 DVD VII-159

71 *Statement Of The Director, Office Of Soviet Analysis To The Chairman Of The House Armed Services Committee*; 1988/09/08; <https://www.cia.gov/library/readingroom/docs//1988-09-08.pdf>

72 COL Yu A Martsenyuk and COL S G Chekinov; *Command And Control Problems In Strategic Sectors*; VM U 14 (1) 2005; 90-96; East View Publications

73 GEN ARM Yury Baluyevsky; *Krasnaya Zvezda* 2006/01/25; quoted *Novosti* 2006/01/27

74 Jacob W Kipp; *Russia Nuclear Posture and Threat*; in Stephen J Blank *Russian Nuclear Weapons: Past, Present, And Future*; 463; 2011/11; US Army War College Strategic Studies Institute; ISBN 1-58487-504-6 pdf; <http://www.strategicstudiesinstitute.army.mil/pubs/display.cfm?PubID=1087>

75 *Reconnaissance In Support Of Strategic Operations*; 1985; GSA; CIA IISR C01197777; 1989/09/15; 16; CIA MDR EOM-2015-01160

## more than one way to skin...NATO

76 *Warsaw Pact Forces Opposite NATO*; NIE 11-14-75; DCI; 1975/09/04; TS; Discussion; 8; CREST RDP09T00367R000500130001-9; 2011/08/17

77 *Theory And Practice Of Warsaw Pact Operations; Part II: Organization And Operational Intent In The West European Theater Of War*; CIA IIR; 1972/06/27; CIA HCD HR70-14 07-18-2012 DVD VI-049

78 *Plan Of Actions Of The Czechoslovak People's Army For War Period*; 1964/10/14; CWIHP-B (12/13); 289>298

79 *Central Group of Forces*; 2010; web page no longer accessible; see Internet Archive Wayback Machine <https://web.archive.org/web/20080512094220/http://rk72.jino-net.ru:80/page.php?55>

80 GEN-ARM P I Ivashutin; *Principles Of The Organization And Conduct Of Operational Reconnaissance In A Front Offensive Operation*; 1974; GS GRU; CIA IISR FIRDB-312-00311-78; 1978/05/19; CIA HCD HR70-14 07-18-2012 DVD VII-101; 34

81 COL A Krasnov; *Reconnaissance To Prevent A Surprise Attack*; VM S (5-66) 1962; CIA IISR; 1977/06/02; <https://www.cia.gov/library/readingroom/docs/1977-06-02b.pdf>

82 COL S Sokolov; *The Preparation And Conduct Of An Operation By The Armed Forces In A Theater Of Military Operations In The Initial Period Of War (According To The Views Of The NATO Command)*; VM S (2-78) 1966; CIA IISR; 1976/05/10; CREST RDP10-00105R000201870001-8; 4

83 GEN-COL A Radziyevskiy; *Surprise In Starting A War*; VM S (1-83) 1968; CIA IISR; 1974/06/27; CREST RDP10-00105R000100710001-7; 5

84 Nate Jones and Lauren Harper; *The 1983 War Scare: "The Last Paroxysm" Of The Cold War*; GWU <http://nsarchive.gwu.edu/nukevault/ablearcher/>; links to Electronic Briefing Book 426 427 428; 2013/05;
PT I <http://www2.gwu.edu/~nsarchiv/NSAEBB/NSAEBB426/>;
PT II <http://www2.gwu.edu/~nsarchiv/NSAEBB/NSAEBB427/>;
PT III <http://www2.gwu.edu/~nsarchiv/NSAEBB/NSAEBB428/>

85 *Reconnaissance In Support Of Strategic Operations*; 1985; GSA; CIA IISR C01197777; 1989/09/15; CIA MDR EOM-2015-01160

86 James Farquhar Cant; *The Development Of The SS-20—A Case Study Of Soviet Defence Decisionmaking During The Brezhnev Era*; 1998/05; University of Glasgow/Department of Politics; <http://theses.gla.ac.uk/4814/1/1998CantPhD.pdf>

87 Sergey F Akhromeyev; *The Current State Of Soviet Military Doctrine*; 1988/04/14; CWHIP; trans Polish Institute for National Remembrance archive document; <http://www.wilsoncenter.org/index.cfm?topic_id=1409&fuseaction=va2.document&identifier=6EAB90C7-0525-CB15-5A544CE676AE8D1D&sort=Collection&item=~New%20Documents>; 12

88 Vojtech Mastny and Malcolm Byrne ED; *A Cardboard Castle? An Inside History Of The Warsaw Pact 1955-1991*; 2005; Central European University; ISBN 963-7326-08-1; ISBN 963-7326-07-3; document 143

89 *Military Planning Of The Warsaw Pact In Central Europe: A Study*; CWIHP-B (2); Fall 1992; translation German Defense Ministry publication

90 *National And Multinational Polish Strategic, Operational, Tactical, Combined Division-Level, Specialist And Transit Exercises, War Games, Staff And Training Drills*; CIA IIR FIRDB-312-00934-83; 1983/06/30; CIA HCD HR70-14 07-18-2012 DVD VII-204

91 *Guide On The Organization And Conduct Of Combined Exercises In The Combined Armed Forces Of The Member States Of The Warsaw Pact*; 1975; WPCAF Staff; CIA IISR; 1977/06/14; CIA HCD HR70-14 07-18-2012 DVD VII-302

92 *1. Relationship Of Military Exercises To War Plans 2. Wiosna-69 Exercise*; CIA IIR; 1982/07/30; CIA HCD HR70-14 07-18-2012 DVD VII-324

## ready to roll

93 *Study of the Special Features of a Surprise Outbreak of War*; 1966/02; PHP; <http://www.php.isn.ethz.ch/lory1.ethz.ch/collections/colltopicbc89.html?lng=en&id=19985&navinfo=15697>; Vojtech Mastny and Malcolm Byrne ED; *A Cardboard Castle? An Inside History Of The Warsaw Pact 1955-1991*; 2005; Central European University; ISBN 963-7326-08-1; ISBN 963-7326-07-3; document 38

94 Vojtech Mastny and Malcolm Byrne ED; *A Cardboard Castle? An Inside History Of The Warsaw Pact 1955-1991*; 2005; Central European University; ISBN 963-7326-08-1; ISBN 963-7326-07-3; document 99

95 *Manual On The Conduct Of Operations—Part Two—Ground Forces Operations (Front-Army-Corps)*; 1963; GS; CIA IISR TS-778264; 1977/09/29; CIA HCD HR70-14 07-18-2012 DVD VII-99; 14

96 S P Ivanov *The Initial Period Of War*; Moscow 1974; USAF Soviet Military Thought #20; 14

97 GEN-LT S A Bogdanov; *The Initial Period Of War: Past And Present*; VM U 13 (4) 2004; 46-56; East View Publications

98 S P Ivanov *The Initial Period Of War*; Moscow 1974; USAF Soviet Military Thought #20; 62

99 *The Stages Of Soviet Military Readiness*; CIA OSR; SR M 77-10031J; 1977/03/14; TS; CIA HCD HR70-14 07-18-2012 DVD VII-038; 4

100 Ken Alibek and Stephen Handelman; *Biohazard: The Chilling True Story Of The Largest Covert Biological Weapons Program In The World-Told From The Inside By The Man Who Ran It*; 1998; Random House; ISBN 0-375-50231-9; 5

101 COL-LT S Krylov; *Enemy Agent Reconnaissance In A Theater Of Military Operations In A Modern War*; VM S (2-75) 1965; CIA IISR; 1978/11/30; <https://www.cia.gov/library/readingroom/docs/1978-11-30c.pdf>; 7

102 *Statute On The Combined Fleet Of The Combined Armed Forces Of The Warsaw Pact Member States In A Naval Theater*; WPCAF; 1978/06/27; CIA IISR FIRDB-312-01431-78; <https://www.cia.gov/library/readingroom/docs/1978_06_27_STATUTE_ON_THE_COMBINED_FLEET.pdf>; 4

103 *The Stages Of Soviet Military Readiness*; CIA OSR; SR M 77-10031J; 1977/03/14; TS; CIA HCD HR70-14 07-18-2012 DVD VII-038; 4

104 [Letter of MAR KULIKOV to Polish Minister of National Defense Commenting on Exercise "ZAPAD [WEST]-77."]; CIA IISR FIRDB-312-00080-78 1978/01/23; CIA HCD HR70-14 07-18-2012 DVD VII-047; 8

105 *Memorandum On Marshal Kulikov's Report Regarding Exercise "Zachod-77"*; 1977; CIA IISR 1979/05/07; CIA HCD HR70-14 07-18-2012 DVD VII-319; 5-6

106 MSU I Yakubovskiy and GEN-ARM S Shtemenko; *Directive Of The Commander-In-Chief Of The Combined Armed Forces On The Combat Readiness Of The Troops And Naval Forces Allocated To The Combined Armed Forces No. 001*; WPCAF Staff; 1971/12/27; CIA IISR 1978/03/17; <https://www.cia.gov/library/readingroom/docs/DOC_0005479503.pdf>; also ISCAP 2012-040

107 MSU N Ogarkov; *Warsaw Pact Combined Staff Training Exercise April 1978*; 1978/03; CIA IISR; 1978/08/08; CIA HCD HR70-14 07-18-2012 DVD VII-313

108 [The Warsaw Pact *Soyuz*-78 Exercise]; 1978/05/31; CIA IISR; 1978/09/22; CIA HCD HR70-14 07-18-2012 DVD VII-315; 7

109 *Background Information on the Development of the Unified Wartime Command System for the Combined Armed Forces of the Warsaw Pact*; CIA IIR FIRDB-312-01197-83; 1983/06/10; 11; <https://www.cia.gov/library/readingroom/docs/1983_06_10_THE_ORGANIZATION_OF_THE_WARSAW_PACT.pdf>

110 *Wartime Statute, Combat Readiness, Mobilization, Front Command, etc.*; CIA IISR FIRDB-312-00224-80; 1980/02/07; <https://www.cia.gov/library/readingroom/docs/1980_02_07_WARTIME_STATUTE.pdf>

111 MSU V Kulikov and GEN-ARM A Gribkov; *Directive Of The Commander-In-Chief Of The Combined Armed Forces Of The Warsaw Pact Member States On The Combat Readiness Of The Troops And Naval Forces Allocated To The Combined Armed Forces*; WPCAF Staff; CIA IISR C05508940; 1979/03/30; <https://www.cia.gov/library/readingroom/docs/DOC_0005508940.pdf>; also CIA MDR EOM-2015-01161

112 *The Soviet "War Scare"*; Foreign Intelligence Advisory Board; 1990/02/15; TS Umbra Gamma; GWU; <https://assets.documentcloud.org/documents/2484214/read-the-u-s-assessment-that-concluded-the.pdf>; 64

113 *Combat And Mobilization Readiness Of Armed Forces Of The USSR And Strategic Agent Intelligence*; 1985; GSA; CIA IISR C01197776; 1989/09/11; 7; CIA MDR EOM-2015-01160

114 *Readiness Of Soviet Forces In Central Europe: Implications For A Rapid Transition To War*; Intelligence Assessment; CIA DI SOVA; SOV87-10053CX; 1987/09; TS; CIA HCD HR70-14 07-18-2012 DVD VII-120; 21

115 *NATO-Warsaw Pact Force Mobilization*; The National Defense University; 1988; 291; reorganization 1977 to 1979

116 *Materials Of The Critique Of The Operational-Strategic Command-Staff Exercise Zapad-77*; CIA IISR TS-788301; 1978/10/13; 60; CIA HCD HR70-14 07-18-2012 DVD VII-045

117 *Warsaw Pact Perceptions Of NATO Strengths And Weaknesses*; CIA DO IIR; 1981; 5; CIA HCD HR70-14 07-18-2012 DVD VII-060

118 *NATO-Warsaw Pact Force Mobilization*; The National Defense University; 1988; 41

119 *Theory And Practice Of Warsaw Pact Operations; Part II: Organization And Operational Intent In The West European Theater Of War*; CIA IIR; 1972/06/27; 6; CIA HCD HR70-14 07-18-2012 DVD VI-049

**leading the charge**

120 *Warsaw Pact Concepts And Capabilities For Going To War In Europe: Implications For NATO Warning Of War*; NIE 4-1-78; 1978/04/10; TS; CIA HCD HR70-14 07-18-2012 DVD VII-053; also CREST RDP05T00644R000601570001-5; 2010/04/13 but more redactions; 27

121 *Voyennyy Entsiklopedichesky Slovar'* [*Military Encyclopedic Dictionary*]; *Voyenizdat*; 1983

122 *Manual On The Conduct Of Operations—Part Two—Ground Forces Operations (Front-Army-Corps)*; 1963; GS; CIA IISR TS-778264; 1977/09/29; CIA HCD HR70-14 07-18-2012 DVD VII-99; 153

123 GEN-MAJ (Engineer-Technical Service) I Anureyev and COL B Khabarov; *Principles Of The Automation And Mechanization Of Troop Control*; 1969/10; GSA lecture; CIA IISR FIRDB-312-02296-76; CIA HCD HR70-14 07-18-2012 DVD VII-211; 21-22

124 GEN ARM Sergei Mateevich Shtemenko; *The Soviet General Staff At War 1941-1945*; 1970; Progress Publishers; 32

125 Viktor Suvorov; *Inside The Soviet Army*; 1982; MacMillan; New York; 41>43 high commands—strategic directions; 147-148 fronts—military districts

126 *Protecting Satellite Reconnaissance Photographs*; CIA Studies In Intelligence; nd; 16; <https://www.cia.gov/library/readingroom/docs/DOC_0005812083.pdf>

127 *Military Use Of Space*; 1985; GSA; CIA IISR TS-879255; 1987/12/11; 12; ISCAP 2012-026 (CIA MDR EOM-2009-00158)

128 *KH-11 Exploitation Reference Guide*; 1977/01; S079491; CREST RDP78B07179A000200030001-4; 2010/04/16; 1502

129 Robert A McDonald and Patrick Widlake; *Looking Closer And Looking Broader: Gambit And Hexagon—The Peak Of Film-Return Reconnaissance After Corona*; National Reconnaissance; 2012/01; NRO Center for the Study of National Reconnaissance; 34

130 COL-LT A Andronov and Senior LT R Shevrov; [*U.S. Imaging Reconnaissance Space Systems*]; *Zarubezhnoye Voyennoye Obozreniye* (2) 1995/02; JPRS UMA-95-020 (2 May 1995) Central Eurasia Military Affairs; 85

131 Robert A McDonald and Patrick Widlake *Looking Closer And Looking Broader: Gambit And Hexagon—The Peak Of Film-Return Reconnaissance After Corona*; National Reconnaissance; 2012/01; NRO Center for the Study of National Reconnaissance; 10

132 Charles Tuten; *Rear Services Support Of Soviet Frontal Rocket Troops*; S103999 IAR-061-83; NPIC; 1983/12; CREST RDP85T00840R000200120001-3-9; 1117

133 GEN-LT M Novikov; *Rear Services Support Of Missile Troops In An Offensive Operation Of A Front*; VM TS (Third) 1960; CIA C00012332; <https://www.cia.gov/library/readingroom/docs/1962-02-28.pdf>

134 GEN-COL (Artillery) G. F. Odintsov; *Rear Area Support Of Missile Troops In Front Offensive Operations*; VM TS (Second) 1961; CIA C00012285; <https://www.cia.gov/library/readingroom/docs/1961-08-25-B.pdf>; also CIA HCD HR70-14 07-18-2012 DVD 1961

135 GEN-COL F Malykhin; *Some Problems In The Preparation Of The Rear Area For Support Of The Armed Forces In The Initial Period Of A War*; VM TS (Second) 1960; CIA C00012326; 1962/02/13; <https://www.cia.gov/library/readingroom/docs/1962-02-13.pdf>; also CIA HCD HR70-14 07-18-2012 DVD V-003

136 I Y Shavrov *The Front Offensive Operation*; GSA 1977/05; CIA IISR FIRDB-312-00013-79; 1979/06/15; CIA MDR EOM-2009-0157; also CIA HCD HR70-14 07-18-2012 DVD VII-222; 294; 315

137 S K Kurkotkin ED; *Soviet Armed Forces Rear Services In The Great Patriotic War Of 1941-1945*; Moscow; 1977

138 GEN-MAJ A S Skovoroda; *Organization Of Rear Services Support Of Troops Of An Army And A Front In An Offensive Operation*; 1969/02; GSA lecture; CIA IISR FIRDB-312-00635-77; 1977/03/04; CIA HCD HR70-14 07-18-2012 DVD VII-214; 19

139 I Y Shavrov *The Front Offensive Operation*; GSA 1977/05; CIA IISR FIRDB-312-00013-79; 1979/06/15; CIA MDR EOM-2009-0157; also CIA HCD HR70-14 07-18-2012 DVD VII-222; 294; 311

140 *Soviet Concepts For Initial Military Operations Against NATO In Central Europe*; Intelligence Report; SR 77-10002CX; CIA OSR Theater Forces Division; 1977/02; TS; CIA MDR EOM-2011-01084; also CIA HCD HR70-14 07-18-2012 DVD VII-037; 38

141 Vojtech Mastny and Malcolm Byrne ED; *A Cardboard Castle? An Inside History Of The Warsaw Pact 1955-1991*; 2005; Central European University; ISBN 963-7326-08-1; ISBN 963-7326-07-3; document 95

142 *Warsaw Pact Exercise "Center"*; 1978/11; CIA IISR TS-798165; 1979/06/08; CIA HCD HR70-14 07-18-2012 DVD VII-320

143 GEN-MAJ V V Gurkin and GEN-LT (Retired) M I Golovnin; *On The Question Of Strategic Operations In The Great Patriotic War*; VIZ (10) 1985/10; JPRS-UMA-86-014 (27 February 1986); <https://apps.dtic.mil/dtic/tr/fulltext/u2/a359713.pdf>

144 GEN-LT M I Golovnin; *From The Experience Of The Formation And Abolition Of Front Formations During The Great Patriotic War*; VM R (6) 1979/06

145 MSU M Zakharov; *The Campaign Of The Soviet Armed Forces In The Far East, 9 August-2 September 1945*; VIZ (9) 1980; JPRS 76444 (18 September 1980) Military Affairs 1534

146 S A Tyushkevich; *The Soviet Armed Forces: The History Of Their Organizational Development*; Moscow; *Voyenizdat*; 1978; USAF Soviet Military Thought 19; Chapter 10

147 COL A Bratus et al; *Transportation In The Great Patriotic War*; VM S (1-68) 1963; CIA IISR; 1978/08/10; <https://www.cia.gov/library/readingroom/docs/1978-08-10c.pdf>

148 *Capabilities Of The Warsaw Pact Against NATO*; SNIE 11-17-68; 1968/10/08; S; <https://www.cia.gov/library/readingroom/docs/DOC_0000278484.pdf>; 1>3

149 *Central Group of Forces*; 2010; web page no longer accessible; see Internet Archive Wayback Machine <https://web.archive.org/web/20080512094220/http://rk72.jino-net.ru:80/page.php?55>

150 GEN-ARM V V Kurasov; *The Influence Of Nuclear Weapons On The Principles Of The Offensive Operations Of A Front*; VM TS (Third) 1960; CIA C00012334; 1962/03/09; <https://www.cia.gov/library/readingroom/docs/1962-03-08-A.pdf>; also CIA HCD HR70-14 07-18-2012 DVD III-021; 22

151 GEN-COL I S Glebov; *The Preparation And Conduct Of Front And Army Offensive Operations*; 1969/03; GSA lecture; CIA FIRDB-312-01545-78; 1978/07/28; CIA HCD HR70-14 07-18-2012 DVD VII-221; 9

152 I Y Shavrov *The Front Offensive Operation*; GSA 1977/05; CIA IISR FIRDB-312-00013-79; 1979/06/15; CIA MDR EOM-2009-0157; also CIA HCD HR70-14 07-18-2012 DVD VII-222; 11

153 GEN-ARM V V Kurasov; *The Influence Of Nuclear Weapons On The Principles Of The Offensive Operations Of A Front*; VM TS (Third) 1960; CIA C00012334; 1962/03/09; <https://www.cia.gov/library/readingroom/docs/1962-03-08-A.pdf>; also CIA HCD HR70-14 07-18-2012 DVD III-021; 22

154 I Y Shavrov *The Front Offensive Operation*; GSA 1977/05; CIA IISR FIRDB-312-00013-79; 1979/06/15; CIA MDR EOM-2009-0157; also CIA HCD HR70-14 07-18-2012 DVD VII-222; 12

155 *Ground Forces*; 1985; GSA; CIA IISR TS-878769; 1987/10/23; 8-9; ISCAP 2012-026 (CIA MDR EOM-2009-00158)

156 GEN-LT K Kolganov et al; *Certain Questions Of The Development Of Soviet Military Art From 1953-1960*; VM S (1-77) 1966; <https://www.cia.gov/library/readingroom/docs/1977-04-11c.pdf>; 14
157 COL S Sokolov; *The Preparation And Conduct Of An Operation By The Armed Forces In A Theater Of Military Operations In The Initial Period Of War (According To The Views Of The NATO Command)*; VM S (2-78) 1966; CIA IISR FIRDB-312-00622-76; 1976/05/10; CREST RDP10-00105R000201870001-8; 5
158 Vojtech Mastny and Malcolm Byrne ED; *A Cardboard Castle? An Inside History Of The Warsaw Pact 1955-1991*; 2005; Central European University; ISBN 963-7326-08-1; ISBN 963-7326-07-3; document 66
159 Anthony H Cordesman *The NATO Central Region And The Balance Of Uncertainty*; Armed Forces Journal International 1983/07; CREST RDP90T00155R000500030029-5

**marshaling the troops**
160 COL-LT Ye Pavlov; *The Massed Use Of Missile Troops In Operations*; VM S (6-61) 1961; CIA Ironbark; 1962/06/22; <https://www.cia.gov/library/readingroom/docs/1962-06-22.pdf>
161 COL S Begunov and COL V Glazov; *A Massed Nuclear Strike During A Front Offensive Operation*; VM S (1-68) 1963; CIA IISR; 1978/04/13; <https://www.cia.gov/library/readingroom/docs/1978-04-13b.pdf>
162 COL V Larionov; *The Struggle For The Strategic Initiative In Modern Warfare*; VM S (3-64) 1962; CIA Ironbark; <https://www.cia.gov/library/readingroom/docs/1963-01-25a.pdf>; 21
163 COL V V Larionov; *New Means Of Fighting And Strategy*; Krasnaya Zvezda 1964/04; in William Kintner ED *The Nuclear Revolution In Soviet Military Affairs*; University of Oklahoma; 1968; 40
164 MSU I Yakubovskiy and GEN-ARM S Shtemenko; *Material Of The Critique Of The Operational War Game On Maps Conducted On The Southwestern Axis*; HQ WPCAF Moscow; 1970/07; CIA IIR TS-205587; 1975/06/13; CIA HCD HR70-14 07-18-2012 DVD VII-031; 17
165 GEN-MAJ Kh Dzhelaukhov; *Problems Of The Strategic Deployment Of Armed Forces In Modern Warfare*; VM TS (First) 1962; CIA Ironbark C00012370; (date illegible); <https://www.cia.gov/library/readingroom/docs/1962-10-16-A.pdf>; 7
166 V D Sokolovskiy et al; *Military Strategy*; Voyenizdat; Moscow; 1962; RAND; 1963; <http://www.rand.org/pubs/reports/2005/R416.pdf>; 434
167 GEN-ARM Sergei Mateevich Shtemenko; *The Soviet General Staff At War 1941-1945*; 1970; Progress Publishers; 241
168 MSU M V Zakharov; *Certain Questions Of Soviet Military Art*; VM S (1-68) 1963; CIA IISR; 1977/04/15; <https://www.cia.gov/library/readingroom/docs/1977-04-15b.pdf>; 13
169 COL A Volkov; *Problems Of Armed Combat In The Non-Nuclear Period Of War*; VM S (2-81) 1967; CIA IISR FIRDB-312-00012-77; 1977/02/23; <https://www.cia.gov/library/readingroom/docs/DOC_0001199101.pdf>; 7
170 S P Ivanov *The Initial Period Of War*; Moscow; 1974; USAF Soviet Military Thought #20; 62, 70
171 GEN-MAJ (Technical Troops) Ya Shchepennikov; *Support Of The Strategic Concentration And Deployment Of The Armed Forces In Respect To Transport*; VM TS (Third) 1961; CIA; 1962/04/20; <https://www.cia.gov/library/readingroom/docs/1962-04-18b.pdf>; also CIA HCD HR70-14 07-18-2012 DVD III-038; 3
172 GEN-MAJ (Aviation) V Zinovyev; *Air Support*; VM S (3-70) 1963; CIA IISR; 1975/10/14; <https://www.cia.gov/library/readingroom/docs/1975-10-14.pdf>; also CREST RDP10-00105R000201370001-3 2012/10/16; 9
173 *Manual On The Conduct Of Operations—Part Two—Ground Forces Operations (Front-Army-Corps)*; 1963; GS; CIA IISR TS-778264; 1977/09/29; CIA HCD HR70-14 07-18-2012 DVD VII-99; 72
174 F F Gayvoronsky et al; *Front Offensive Operations*; GSA; 1974; CIA IISR FIRDB-312-01997-79; 1979/09/27; CIA HCD HR70-14 07-18-2012 DVD VII-223; 36
175 *Lectures And Exercises Of The General Staff Academy Of The Armed Forces Of The USSR*; 1975-1976; GSA; CIA IISR FIRDB-312-03018-77; 1977/10/28; CIA HCD HR70-14 07-18-2012 DVD VII-218; 9
176 I Y Shavrov *The Front Offensive Operation*; GSA 1977/05; CIA IISR FIRDB-312-00013-79; 1979/06/15; CIA MDR EOM-2009-0157; also CIA HCD HR70-14 07-18-2012 DVD VII-222; 12
177 *Employment Of Warsaw Pact Forces Against NATO: A Four Front Attack*; NI IIM 83-10002; SC 01700-88; 1988/03; TS; 1988/03; 5; CIA MDR EOM-2010-00681
178 *Rocket Troops And Artillery In A Front Offensive Operation*; 1985; GSA; CIA IISR TS-888443; 1988/05/24; 11; ISCAP 2012-026 (CIA MDR EOM-2009-00158)
179 *Trends And Developments In Warsaw Pact Theater Forces, 1985-2000*; NIE 11-14-85-D; 1985/09; S; CREST RDP87T00495R000600560011-2; 2010/07/20; 19
180 GEN-MAJ V Yuryev; *Materiel Support Of Front Troops In An Offensive Operation In The Initial Period Of War Under Conditions Of The Stoppage Of Rail Deliveries*; VM S (2-78) 1966; CIA IISR FIRDB-312-03277-75; 1975/10/30; <https://www.cia.gov/library/readingroom/docs/1975-10-30.pdf>; also CREST RDP10-00105R000201430001-6; 2012/10/16; 5
181 I Y Shavrov; *The Front Offensive Operation*; GSA 1977/05; CIA IISR FIRDB-312-00013-79; 1979/06/15; CIA MDR EOM-2009-0157; also CIA HCD HR70-14 07-18-2012 DVD VII-222; 29

182 *Manual On The Conduct Of Operations—Part Two—Ground Forces Operations (Front-Army-Corps);* 1963; GS; CIA IISR TS-778264; 1977/09/29; CIA HCD HR70-14 07-18-2012 DVD VII-99; CH-7

183 Ghulam Dastagir Wardak; *The Voroshilov Lectures: Materials From The Soviet General Staff Academy*; V.I *Issues Of Soviet Military Strategy*; 1989; National Defense University; 45

184 *Materials Of The Critique Of The Operational-Strategic Command-Staff Exercise Zapad-77*; CIA IISR TS 788301; 1978/10/13; CIA HCD HR70-14 07-18-2012 DVD VII-045; 64

185 COL N Kalayev and COL-LT A Tarasov; *The Commitment Of A Front's Second Echelon To An Engagement*; VM S (6-67) 1962; CIA IISR; 1977/05/16;<https://www.cia.gov/library/readingroom/docs/1977-05-16-A.pdf>; CIA HCD HR70-14 07-18-2012 DVD II-052; 4-5

186 *Capabilities Of Soviet General Purpose Forces 1964-1970;* NIE 11-14-64; 1964/12/10; S; CIA HCD HR70-14 07-18-2012 DVD V-017; 24

187 *War In The Western TVD*; DDB-2600-3858-84-SAO; DIA Directorate for Research; 1984/08; S; <http://www.dia.mil/FOIA/FOIA-Electronic-Reading-Room/FOIA-Reading-Room-Russia/FileId/121078/>; 24

188 *Soviet Readiness In The Western Theater And Its Impact On Operations*; DDB-1100-476-85; DIA; 1985/02; S; <http://www.dia.mil/FOIA/FOIA-Electronic-Reading-Room/FOIA-Reading-Room-Russia/FileId/121077/>; 23

189 *Warning Of War In Europe: Changing Warsaw Pact Planning And Forces*; NIE 4-1-84; 1989/09; S; CREST RDP94T00754R000200160012-0 2006/03/10; iv map

190 *A Soviet View Of The Balance Of Theater Forces In Central Europe And Of The Ground Campaign Against The NATO Center Region*; Memorandum; CIA DI OSR TS-204684; 1973/08/08; TS; CIA HCD HR70-14 07-18-2012 DVD VII-020; 5

191 Harald Nielsen; *Die DDR Und Die Kernwaffen-Die Nukleare Rolle Der Nationalen Volksarmee Im Warschauer Pakt*; Nuclear History Program 6; 1998; Nomos; ISBN 3-7890-5510-7; 141

192 Viktor Suvorov; *Inside The Soviet Army*; 1982; MacMillan; New York; 43

193 GEN-COL P Koshevoy; *Utilization Of The Missile Troops Of A Front (Army) In An Offensive Operation*; VM TS (Third) 1961; CIA C00012337; 1962/03/22; <https://www.cia.gov/library/readingroom/docs/1962-03-22.pdf>; 2

194 GEN-COL I Glebov and GEN-MAJ V Yemelin; *Offensive Operations Of A Front To The Entire Depth Of A Theater Of Military Operations*; VM S (2-72) 1964; CIA IISR; 1975/11/14; <https://www.cia.gov/library/readingroom/docs/1975-11-14b.pdf>; also CREST RDP10-00105R000201480001-1 2012/10/16; 8

195 *Lectures And Exercises Of The General Staff Academy Of The Armed Forces Of The USSR*; 1975-1976; GSA; CIA IISR FIRDB-312-03018-77; 1977/10/28; CIA HCD HR70-14 07-18-2012 DVD VII-218; 9

196 I Y Shavrov *The Front Offensive Operation*; GSA 1977/05; CIA IISR FIRDB-312-00013-79; 1979/06/15; CIA MDR EOM-2009-0157; also CIA HCD HR70-14 07-18-2012 DVD VII-222; 12

197 GEN-MAJ (Tank) A Shevchenko; *The Strike Groupings Of A Front*; VM TS (Third) 1960; CIA C00012317; 1962/01/19; <https://www.cia.gov/library/readingroom/docs/1962-01-19b.pdf>; also CIA HCD HR70-14 07-18-2012 DVD YEAR 1962

198 MAR (Tank) P A Rotmistrov; *The Paths Of Further Development Of The Tank Troops Of The Soviet Army*; VM TS (First) 1961; CIA C00012293; 1961/10/02; <https://www.cia.gov/library/readingroom/docs//1961-10-02.pdf>; also CIA HCD HR70-14 07-18-2012 DVD III-037; 2

199 GEN-ARM A Zhadov; *Trends In The Development Of The Tank Troops Of The Soviet Army*; VM TS (Second) 1961; CIA C00012288; 1961/09/12; <https://www.cia.gov/library/readingroom/docs//1961-09-12.pdf>; also CIA HCD HR70-14 07-18-2012 DVD III-042; 3

200 *Soviet Operational Art*; 1985; GSA; CIA IISR TS-888644; 1988/07/29; 7; ISCAP 2012-026 (CIA MDR EOM-2009-00158)

201 *Ground Forces*; 1985; GSA; CIA IISR TS-878769; 1987/10/23; 9; ISCAP 2012-026 (CIA MDR EOM-2009-00158)

202 COL G Yefimov; *Planning Modern Operations*; VM S (2-87) 1969; CIA IISR FIRDB-312-03848-74; 1974/11/18; <https://www.cia.gov/library/readingroom/docs/DOC_0001199094.pdf>; also CREST RDP10-00105R000100910001-5; 7

203 *Capabilities Of Soviet General Purpose Forces 1964-1970;* NIE 11-14-64; 1964/12/10; S; CIA HCD HR70-14 07-18-2012 DVD V-017; 24; and NIE 11-14-66; 1966/11/03; S; <https://www.cia.gov/library/readingroom/docs/DOC_0000278472.pdf>; 9

204 *Unit Relocation Confirmed, Borne, Poland;* BB; 1985/10/03; NPIC; CREST RDP87T00076R000102130001-8-13; 2012/07/02

205 *Reorganization Of Soviet Ground Forces In East Germany*; CIA DI SOVA; Intelligence Assessment; SOV 83-10126; 1983/08; S; CIA HCD HR70-14 07-18-2012 DVD VII-112; 3

206 *Employment Of Warsaw Pact Forces Against NATO: A Four Front Attack*; NI IIM 83-10002; SC 01700-88; 1988/03; TS; 1988/03; 10 map; CIA MDR EOM-2010-00681

207 *Materials Of The Critique Of The Operational-Strategic Command-Staff Exercise Zapad-77*; CIA IISR TS-788301; 1978/10/13; CIA HCD HR70-14 07-18-2012 DVD VII-045

208 *Soviet Military Rear Services In East Germany*; CIA DI SOVA OIA; Research Paper; SOV 84-10006JX; IA 84-10012JX; 1984/02; TS; CREST RDP84T00926R000200090002-2; 2010/07/14; also CIA HCD HR70-14 07-18-2012 DVD VII-115; iii, 55

209 GEN-MAJ Tibor Toth; *Characteristics Of Organizing And Conducting An Offensive Operation Of The Coalition Front And Combined Arms Army; Honvedelem* (6) 1980; S; CIA IIR C05798348; 1985/09/06; 7; CIA MDR EOM-2011-0881

210 Vitaly I Feskov et al; *Sovetskaya Armiya v gody «kholodnaya voyna» (1945-1991)* [*The Soviet Army During The 'Cold War'*]; Tomsk State University; 2004; ISBN 5-7511-1819-7; <http://militera.lib.ru/h/0/pdf/feskov_vi02.pdf>; 27-28

211 *Managing And Monitoring Readiness In The Warsaw Pact Ground Forces*; CIA DI SOVA Theater Forces Division; Research Paper; SOV 82-10204CX; 1982/12; TS; CREST RDP83T00853R000200170002-5; 2007/03/15; 4-5

212 *Trends And Developments In Warsaw Pact Theater Forces, 1985-2000*; NIE 11-14-85-D; 1985/09 ; S; <https://www.cia.gov/library/readingroom/docs/DOC_0000802732.pdf>; also CREST RDP87T00495R000600560011-2; 2010/07/20; 20-21

213 *The Readiness Of Soviet Ground Forces*; NI IIM 82-10012; DCI; 1982/11; S; CIA HCD HR70-14 07-18-2012 DVD VII-108-108a; also CREST RDP85T00176R001600060007-7; 2008/04/04; 1, tables 11

214 *Soviet Ground Forces Trends*; CIA-DIA-Army Assessment; CIA DI SOVA; SOV 84-10177; 1984/10; S; <https://www.cia.gov/library/readingroom/document/0000498132>; also CIA HCD HR70-14 07-18-2012 DVD VII-118; also CREST RDP85T00313R000300040006-1; 2010/08/09; 2

215 *Manning Practices And Patterns In Soviet Ground Force Units*; Research Paper; CIA DI SOVA; SOV 83-10143JX; 1983/08; TS; CIA HCD HR70-14 07-18-2012 DVD VII-111; 1-3

216 *Trends And Developments In Warsaw Pact Theater Forces, 1985-2000*; NIE 11-14-85-D; 1985/09 ; S; <https://www.cia.gov/library/readingroom/docs/DOC_0000802732.pdf>; also CREST RDP87T00495R000600560011-2; 2010/07/20; 19

217 *Soviet Ground Forces Trends*; CIA-DIA-Army Assessment; CIA DI SOVA; SOV 84-10177; 1984/10; S; <https://www.cia.gov/library/readingroom/document/0000498132>; also CIA HCD HR70-14 07-18-2012 DVD VII-118; also CREST RDP85T00313R000300040006-1; 2010/08/09; 10

218 Vitaly I Feskov et al; *Sovetskaya Armiya v gody «kholodnaya voyna» (1945-1991)* [*The Soviet Army During The 'Cold War'*]; Tomsk State University; 2004; ISBN 5-7511-1819-7; <http://militera.lib.ru/h/0/pdf/feskov_vi02.pdf>; 128 AP-2.10

219 *Soviet Force Generation Methods*; NPIC Imagery Exploitation Group/Tactical Forces Division; IAR; 1987/06; TS; CREST RDP87T00758R000206120001-7; 2012/07/26

220 *Probable Relocated Motorized Rifle Division Petrozavosk USSR*; BB; S102088  Z-12701-83; 1983/06/09; NPIC; CREST RDP84T00171R000200100001-9; 2012/03/19; 121

221 *Soviet Armor Storage Bases: Maintaining A Reserve Of Combat-Ready Vehicles*; CIA; S111326 IAM-10026-86; 1986/05; CREST RDP87T00076R000101640001-3; 2011/03/25; 81

222 S P Ivanov; *The Initial Period Of War*; Moscow; 1974; USAF Soviet Military Thought #20; 241

223 COL B M Zhukov; *Some Aspects Of Training Reserves And Of The Combat Teamwork Training Of Troops (Based On The Experience Of The Great Patriotic War)*; VM R (11) 1983

224 S A Tyushkevich; *The Soviet Armed Forces: The History Of Their Organizational Development*; Moscow *Voyenizdat*; 1978; USAF Soviet Military Thought 19; 277

225 Vitaly I Feskov et al; *Sovetskaya Armiya v gody «kholodnaya voyna» (1945-1991)* [*The Soviet Army During The 'Cold War'*]; Tomsk State University; 2004; ISBN 5-7511-1819-7; <http://militera.lib.ru/h/0/pdf/feskov_vi02.pdf>; 5, 22

226 Vitaly I Feskov et al; *Sovetskaya Armiya v gody «kholodnaya voyna» (1945-1991)* [*The Soviet Army During The 'Cold War'*]; Tomsk State University; 2004; ISBN 5-7511-1819-7; <http://militera.lib.ru/h/0/pdf/feskov_vi02.pdf>; 28

227 *The Readiness Of Soviet Ground Forces*; NI IIM 82-10012; DCI; 1982/11; S; CIA HCD HR70-14 07-18-2012 DVD VII-108-108a; also CREST RDP85T00176R001600060007-7; 2008/04/04; 1, VI-1

228 F F Gayvoronsky et al; *Front Offensive Operations*; GSA; 1974; CIA IISR FIRDB-312-01997-79; 1979/09/27; CIA HCD HR70-14 07-18-2012 DVD VII-223; 36

229 *Warsaw Pact Concepts And Capabilities For Going To War In Europe: Implications For NATO Warning Of War*; NIE 4-1-78; 1978/04/10; TS; CIA HCD HR70-14 07-18-2012 DVD VII-053; also CREST RDP05T00644R000601570001-5; 2010/04/13; 27

230 *The Readiness Of Soviet Ground Forces*; NI IIM 82-10012; DCI; 1982/11; S; CIA HCD HR70-14 07-18-2012 DVD VII-108-108a; also CREST RDP85T00176R001600060007-7; 2008/04/04; 3

231 *Trends And Developments In Warsaw Pact Theater Forces, 1985-2000*; NIE 11-14-85-D; 1985/09; CREST RDP87T00495R000600560011-2; 2010/07/20; 84 Table D-2

232 *Problems For Discussion Of The Chief Of The General Staff Of The Polish Armed Forces With The Chief Of Staff Of The Combined Armed Forces Of The Warsaw Pact Countries*; 1979; CIA IISR FIRDB-312-00224-80; CIA HCD HR70-14 07-18-2012 DVD VII-186; 9

233 I Y Shavrov; *The Front Offensive Operation*; GSA 1977/05; CIA IISR FIRDB-312-00013-79; 1979/06/15; CIA MDR EOM-2009-0157; also CIA HCD HR70-14 07-18-2012 DVD VII-222; 131

234 *Capabilities Of Soviet General Purpose Forces 1964-1970*; CIA; ORR Contribution NIE 11-14-64; 1964/10/06; TS; CIA HCD HR70-14 07-18-2012 DVD V-016; 26

235 *Tactical Air Command And Control Study*; DST-1370S-279-76; DIA FTD; 1976/12/23; TS; CREST RDP78B07179A000200030001-4; 1381-1382

236 *Spetsnaz Forces And Means In A Front Offensive Operation*; 1985; GSA; CIA IISR TS-878433; 1987/06/12; 4; ISCAP 2012-026 (CIA MDR EOM-2009-00158)

237 Vitaly I Feskov et al; *Sovetskaya Armiya v gody «kholodnaya voyna» (1945-1991)* [*The Soviet Army During The 'Cold War'*]; Tomsk State University; 2004; ISBN 5-7511-1819-7; <http://militera.lib.ru/h/0/pdf/feskov_vi02.pdf>; 172 CH-6

238 *Soviet Readiness In The Western Theater And Its Impact On Operations*; DIA DDB-1100-476-85; 1985/02; S; <http://www.dia.mil/FOIA/FOIA-Electronic-Reading-Room/FOIA-Reading-Room-Russia/FileId/121077/>; 9

239 *Warsaw Pact Nonnuclear Threat To NATO Airbases In Central Europe*; NIE 11-20-6-84; 1984/10/25; TS; CIA HCD HR70-14 07-18-2012 DVD VII-157; 34-35

240 *Materials Of The Critique Of The Operational-Strategic Command-Staff Exercise Zapad-77*; CIA IISR TS-788301; 1978/10/13; CIA HCD HR70-14 07-18-2012 DVD VII-045; 61, 63

241 GEN-LT M I Golovnin; *From The Experience Of The Formation And Abolition Of Front Formations During The Great Patriotic War*; VM R (6) 1979/06

242 GEN-ARM Sergei Mateevich Shtemenko; *The Soviet General Staff At War 1941-1945*; 1970; Progress Publishers; 234>238, 255-256

243 GEN-COL I Glebov; *Certain Problems Of Planning And Conducting Offensive Operations Of Fronts (Based On The Experience Of Research War Games)*; VM S (3-82) 1967; CIA IISR FIRDB-312-02966-74; 1974/08/20; CIA HCD HR70-14 07-18-2012 DVD VII-030; also CREST RDP10-00105R000100820001-5; 2012/09/28; 4

244 I Y Shavrov *The Front Offensive Operation*; GSA 1977/05; CIA IISR FIRDB-312-00013-79; 1979/06/15; CIA MDR EOM-2009-0157; also CIA HCD HR70-14 07-18-2012 DVD VII-222; 294; 7

245 *Letter of Marshal KULIKOV to Polish Minister of National Defense Commenting on Exercise "Zapad [West]-77"*; CIA IISR FIRDB-312-00080-78; 1978/01/23; CIA HCD HR70-14 07-18-2012 DVD VII-047; 5

246 *War In The Western TVD*; DDB-2600-3858-84-SAO; DIA Directorate for Research; 1984/08; S; <http://www.dia.mil/FOIA/FOIA-Electronic-Reading-Room/FOIA-Reading-Room-Russia/FileId/121078/>; 24

247 *Sovetskaya Voyennaya Entsiklopediya*; 1979; V.VII

248 *Manning Practices And Patterns In Soviet Ground Force Units*; Research Paper; CIA DI SOVA; SOV 83-10143JX; 1983/08; TS; CIA HCD HR70-14 07-18-2012 DVD VII-111; iv, 1

249 John G Hines et al; *Soviet Intentions 1965-1985* V.II *Soviet Post-Cold War Testimonial Evidence*; Contract MDA903-92-C-0147 OSD-Net Assessment; BDM Federal; 1995/09/22; 48; GWU; <https://nsarchive2.gwu.edu/nukevault/ebb285/index.htm>; section links

250 S A Tyushkevich; *The Soviet Armed Forces: The History Of Their Organizational Development*; Moscow *Voyenizdat*; 1978; USAF Soviet Military Thought 19; 371

251 COL N Krivopustov; *Reconnaissance During The Advance Of A Combined-Arms (Tank) Army From The Depth And Its Commitment To An Engagement*; VM S (1-86) 1969; <https://www.cia.gov/library/readingroom/docs/1975-08-25-A.pdf>; also CREST RDP10-00105R000201210001-0; 2012/04/11; 4

252 GEN ARM A Gribkov and ADM V Mikhaylin; *Conclusions On Results Of An Inspection Of The 9th Coastal Defense Flotilla Of The PPR Navy*; 1980/07/31; CIA IISR TS-828127; 1982/09/20; <https://www.cia.gov/library/readingroom/document/0005508934>

253 I Y Shavrov; *The Front Offensive Operation*; GSA 1977/05; CIA IISR FIRDB-312-00013-79; 1979/06/15; CIA MDR EOM-2009-0157; also CIA HCD HR70-14 07-18-2012 DVD VII-222; 38

254 *Soviet And East European General Purpose Forces*; NIE 11-14-68; *Contribution*; CIA DI OSR; SR-SP-68-9; 1968/10; TS; CIA HCD HR70-14 07-18-2012 DVD V-058; also <https://www.cia.gov/library/readingroom/docs/1968-10-01a.pdf>; 25

255 COL V Lyadov and COL G Zubarev; *Basic Problems Of Troop Control And Possible Ways Of Resolving Them*; VM S (6-67) 1962; CIA IISR; 1975/12/22; <https://www.cia.gov/library/readingroom/docs/1962-11-06b.pdf> also CREST RDP10-00105R000201560001-2; 2012/09/27
COL P Lyadov; *Certain Problems In Moving A Combined-Arms Army Forward From The Interior Of The Country In The Initial Period Of War*; VM S (4-65) 1962; CIA IISR; 1978/10/12; <https://www.cia.gov/library/readingroom/docs/1978-10-12.pdf>
GEN-LT Yu Naumenko; *Movement Of A Combined Arms Army Over A Sizable Distance (According To The Experience Of Exercises)*; VM S (1-89) 1970; CIA IISR; 1974/03/20; <https://www.cia.gov/library/readingroom/docs/1974-03-20.pdf>

256 COL I Yakovlenko and COL N Aksenov; *Control Of Troops When Dispatching Them On Assignment From An Interior Military District*; VM S (2-84) 1968; CIA IISR; 1975/12/29; <https://www.cia.gov/library/readingroom/docs/1975-12-29a.pdf>; also CREST RDP10-00105R000201590001-9; 2012/10/16
GEN-MAJ I Yakovlenko and COL N Aksenov; *Features Of The Organization Of The Commitment Of An Army Into An Engagement Under Conditions In Which Conventional Means Of Destruction Are Employed (From The Experience Of A Command-Staff Exercise Of The Ural Military District)*; VM S (3-88) 1969; CIA IISR; 1974/02/04; <https://www.cia.gov/library/readingroom/docs/1974-02-04.pdf>; also CIA HCD HR70-14 07-18-2012 DVD VII-025

257 COL V Zemskov; *On Military-Scientific Work In The Ground Forces (From The Experience Of 1961)*; VM S (3-64) 1962; CIA Ironbark; 1963/01/09; <https://www.cia.gov/library/readingroom/docs/1963-01-09c.pdf>; also CIA HCD HR70-14 07-18-2012 DVD III-041

258 GEN-MAJ P Stepshin; *On Regrouping A Combined-Arms Army From The Depth Of The Country In The Initial Period Of A War*; VM S (6-61) 1961; CIA Ironbark; 1962/06/13; <https://www.cia.gov/library/readingroom/docs/1962-06-13.pdf>; also CIA HCD HR70-14 07-18-2012 DVD III-024

259 COL L Sapozhnikov; *Regrouping Of Troops In The Initial Period Of A War (Based On Materials Of A Military Science Conference)*; VM S (1-62) 1962; CIA IISR; 1978/11/17; <https://www.cia.gov/library/readingroom/docs/1978-11-17b.pdf>

260 *Organizational Structure Of The Soviet Armed Forces*; 1985; GSA; CIA IISR TS-888643; 1988/07/29; 10; ISCAP 2012-026 (CIA MDR EOM-2009-00158)

261 *Warsaw Pact Forces Opposite NATO*; NIE 11-14-75; 1975/09/04; DCI; S; CREST RDP09T00367R000500130001-9; 2011/08/17; 16

262 *Soviet Tank Programs*; NI IIM 84-10016; DCI NIO General Purpose Forces; 1984/12; TS; CREST RDP00-01872R001001550001-3; 2012/01/06; 44

263 COL A Grylev; *The Preparation And Use Of Strategic Reserves In The Second World War*; VM S (6-61) 1961; CIA Ironbark; 1962/07/02; <https://www.cia.gov/library/readingroom/docs/1962-07-02.pdf>

264 COL A Grylev; *The Preparation And Use Of Strategic Reserves In The Second World War*; VM S (6-61) 1961; CIA Ironbark; 1962/07/02; <https://www.cia.gov/library/readingroom/docs/1962-07-02.pdf>; 5

265 S P Ivanov *The Initial Period Of War*; Moscow 1974; USAF Soviet Military Thought #20; 240

266 Viktor Suvorov; *Inside The Soviet Army*; 1982; MacMillan; New York; 148

267 *Soviet Concepts For Initial Military Operations Against NATO In Central Europe*; Intelligence Report; SR 77-10002CX; CIA OSR Theater Forces Division; 1977/02; TS; CIA MDR EOM-2011-01084; also CIA HCD HR70-14 07-18-2012 DVD VII-037; 38

268 *Polish Defense Ministry Document Concerning Experiences And Conclusions From The "Narew" Maneuvers*; 1967/01/20; CIA IISR [TS-]195344; 1967/01/20; CIA HCD HR70-14 07-18-2012 DVD VI-014; 3, 7

269 GEN-MAJ (Artillery) P Zherdev et al; *Some Problems In The Control Of The Rocket Troops Of A Reserve Front During Its Movement Forward For Commitment To An Engagement*; VM S (2-75) 1965; CIA IISR 1976/11/15; <https://www.cia.gov/library/readingroom/docs/1976-11-15b.pdf>; also CREST RDP10-00105R000302580001-8; 2012/10/16

270 *Materials Of The Critique Of The Operational-Strategic Command-Staff Exercise Zapad-77*; CIA IISR TS-788301; 1978/10/13; CIA HCD HR70-14 07-18-2012 DVD VII-045; 63

271 F F Gayvoronsky et al; *Front Offensive Operations*; GSA; 1974; CIA IISR FIRDB-312-01997-79; 1979/09/27; CIA HCD HR70-14 07-18-2012 DVD VII-223; 21

272 *Theory And Practice Of Warsaw Pact Operations; Part III: Variant Of The Warsaw Pact"s Operational Intent For The Southwestern Front, August 1968*; CIA IIR; 1972/07/18; CIA HCD HR70-14 07-18-2012 DVD VI-050; 7, 15-16

273 *Warsaw Pact Forces Opposite NATO*; NIE 11-14-75; 1975/09/04; DCI; S; CREST RDP09T00367R000500130001-9; 2011/08/17; 4, 26

274 *Soviet Concepts For Initial Military Operations Against NATO In Central Europe*; Intelligence Report; SR 77-10002CX; CIA OSR Theater Forces Division; 1977/02; TS; CIA MDR EOM-2011-01084; also CIA HCD HR70-14 07-18-2012 DVD VII-037; 38

275 *Capabilities Of The Soviet Theater Forces*; NIE 11-14-62; DCI; 1962/12/05; S; CIA HCD HR70-14 07-18-2012 DVD V-008a; 5

276 *Soviet And East European General Purpose Forces;* NIE 11-14-68; 1968/12/12; S; CIA HCD HR70-14 07-18-2012 DVD V-059; also <https://www.cia.gov/library/readingroom/docs/1968-12-12.pdf>; 4-5

277 *Capabilities Of Soviet General Purpose Forces*; NIE 11-14-66; 1966/11/03; S; <https://www.cia.gov/library/readingroom/docs/DOC_0000278472.pdf>; 26

278 *Soviet Capabilities To Reinforce In Central Europe;* Joint Study—Initial Report; DIA; CIA OSR; SR SP 68-7; 1968/01; TS; CREST RDP80B01554R003300310056-5 2005-04-21; also CIA HCD HR70-14 07-18-2012 DVD V-056-057; 4, 15

279 *The Warsaw Pact Threat To NATO*; Interagency Working Group—Final Report; SR JS 70-3; 1970/05; S; CREST RDP7B00939A000600020002-9; 2002-05-20; also CIA HCD HR70-14 07-18-2012 DVD VII-002; 28

280 *Warsaw Pact Concepts And Capabilities For Going To War In Europe: Implications For NATO Warning Of War*; NIE 4-1-78; 1978/04/10; TS; CIA HCD HR70-14 07-18-2012 DVD VII-053; also CREST RDP05T00644R000601570001-5; 2010/04/13

281 *Warning Of War In Europe: Changing Warsaw Pact Planning And Forces*; NIE 4-1-84; 1989/09; S; CREST RDP94T00754R000200160012-0; 2006/03/10; iii, v

282 *Statement Of The Director, Office Of Soviet Analysis To The Chairman Of The House Armed Services Committee*; 1988/09/08; S; <https://www.cia.gov/library/readingroom/docs/1988-09-08.pdf> and Memorandum For The Record; 1988/09/08 <https://www.cia.gov/library/readingroom/docs/DOC_0000659267.pdf>

- **multi-level echelonment**

283 *Warsaw Pact Forces For Operations In Eurasia*; NIE 11-14-71; DCI; 1971/09/09; 1972/08/10; S; CIA HCD HR70-14 07-18-2012 DVD VII-014

284 *Warsaw Pact Forces Opposite NATO*; NIE 11-14-79; 1979/01/31; TS; CIA HCD HR70-14 07-18-2012 VII-4 V.I, VII-5 V.II

285 *Employment Of Warsaw Pact Forces Against NATO*; NI IIM 83-10002; 1983/07; TS; CIA HCD HR70-14 07-18-2012 DVD VII-062

286 *Trends And Developments In Warsaw Pact Theater Forces, 1985-2000*; NIE 11-14-85-D; 1985/09; S; CREST RDP87T00495R000600560011-2; 2010/07/20

287 *Employment Of Warsaw Pact Forces Against NATO: A Four Front Attack*; NI IIM 83-10002; 1988/03; TS; 11; CIA MDR EOM-2010-00681

288 *Warsaw Pact Ground Forces Facing NATO*; Intelligence Report; CIA DI OSR; SR IR 69-17; 1969/09; TS; CIA HCD HR70-14 07-18-2012 DVD V-61 and VI-43 same; 53

289 *The Readiness Of Soviet Ground Forces*; NI IIM 82-10012; DCI; 1982/11; S; CIA HCD HR70-14 07-18-2012 DVD VII-108 Memorandum VII-108a Executive Summary; also CREST RDP85T00176R001600060007-7; 2008/04/04; quote 23
290 *Soviet Readiness In The Western Theater And Its Impact On Operations*; DIA DDB-1100-476-85; 1985/02; S; <http://www.dia.mil/FOIA/FOIA-Electronic-Reading-Room/FOIA-Reading-Room-Russia/FileId/121077/>; 9

• **trading-off**
291 *Capabilities Of The Soviet Theater Forces*; NIE 11-14-62; 1962/12/05; S; CIA HCD HR70-14 07-18-2012 DVD V-008a; 5, 8, 27
292 *Soviet Capabilities To Reinforce In Central Europe;* Joint Study—Initial Report; DIA; CIA OSR; SR SP 68-7; 1968/01; TS; CREST RDP80B01554R003300310056-5; 2005-04-21; also CIA HCD HR70-14 07-18-2012 DVD V-056-057; 15
293 *Warsaw Pact Mobilization Plans And The Transition To A War Footing*; Intelligence Report; CIA OSR; SR IR 74-2; 1974/03; CIA HCD HR70-14 07-18-2012 DVD VII-026; 21
294 *The Readiness Of Soviet Ground Forces*; NI IIM 82-10012; DCI; 1982/11; S; CIA HCD HR70-14 07-18-2012 DVD VII-108a Executive Summary; also CREST RDP85T00176R001600060007-7; 2008/04/04; 2
295 *Warsaw Pact Concepts And Capabilities For Going To War In Europe: Implications For NATO Warning Of War*; NIE 4-1-78; 1978/04/10; TS; CIA HCD HR70-14 07-18-2012 DVD VII-053; also CREST RDP05T00644R000601570001-5; 2010/04/13; 7, 13-14, 26
296 *Warning Of War In Europe*; NIE 4-1-84; 1984/06/27; TS; GWU; <https://nsarchive2.gwu.edu//dc.html?doc=5028377-Document-21-Warning-of-War-In-Europe-National>; 10
297 *Warning Of War In Europe: Changing Warsaw Pact Planning And Forces*; NIE 4-1-84; 1989/09; S; CREST RDP94T00754R000200160012-0; 2006/03/10; iii
298 *Readiness Of Soviet Forces In Central Europe: Implications For A Rapid Transition To War*; Intelligence Assessment; CIA DI SOVA; SOV87-10053CX; 1987/09; TS; CIA HCD HR70-14 07-18-2012 DVD VII-120; 27
299 *Warsaw Pact Perceptions Of NATO Strengths And Weaknesses*; CIA DO IIR; 1982/08/19; CIA HCD HR70-14 07-18-2012 DVD VII-060
300 *Reconnaissance In Support Of Strategic Operations*; 1985; GSA; CIA IISR C01197777; 1989/09/15; 7-8; CIA MDR EOM-2015-01160
301 *Readiness Of Soviet Forces In Central Europe: Implications For A Rapid Transition To War;* Intelligence Assessment; CIA DI SOVA; SOV87-10053CX; 1987/09; TS; CIA HCD HR70-14 07-18-2012 DVD VII-120; 22
302 *The Front Offensive Operation;* 1977; GSA; CIA HCD HR70-14 07-18-2012
Lesson 01 *Supplementary Material*; CIA IISR FIRDB-312-00106-82; 1982/02/05; DVD VII-274; 5
Lesson 01a; CIA IISR FIRDB-312-02605-80; 1980/10/24; DVD VII-247; 30

• **getting sneaky**
303 *A Study Of The Soviet Ground Forces*; Interim Report; CIA DIA Panel for a Special Study of the Soviet Ground Forces for Secretary McNamara; 1963/08/21; CIA HCD HR70-14 07-18-2012 DVD V-013; 24
304 *Capabilities Of Soviet General Purpose Forces;* NIE 11-14-66; 1966/11/03; S; <https://www.cia.gov/library/readingroom/docs/DOC_0000278472.pdf>; 27
305 *Soviet And East European General Purpose Forces*; NIE 11-14-68; 1968/12/12; S; CIA HCD HR70-14 07-18-2012 DVD V-059; also <https://www.cia.gov/library/readingroom/docs/1968-12-12.pdf>; 29
306 *Warsaw Pact Forces Opposite NATO*; NIE 11-14-75; 1975/09/04; DCI; S; CREST RDP09T00367R000500130001-9; 2011/08/17; 4, 21
307 *Warsaw Pact Forces Opposite NATO*; NIE 11-14-79; 1979/01/31; TS; CIA HCD HR70-14 07-18-2012 VII-4 V.I, VII-5 V.II
308 *Warsaw Pact Forces Opposite NATO*; NIE 11-14-81; 1981/07/07; TS; <https://www.cia.gov/library/readingroom/docs/DOC_0000281660.pdf>
309 *Soviet Concepts For Initial Military Operations Against NATO In Central Europe*; Intelligence Report; SR 77-10002CX; CIA OSR Theater Forces Division; 1977/02; TS; CIA MDR EOM-2011-01084; also CIA HCD HR70-14 07-18-2012 DVD VII-037; 10, 12, 30
310 *War In The Western TVD*; DDB-2600-3858-84-SAO; DIA Directorate for Research; 1984/08; S; <http://www.dia.mil/FOIA/FOIA-Electronic-Reading-Room/FOIA-Reading-Room-Russia/FileId/121078/>
311 *Soviet Readiness In The Western Theater And Its Impact On Operations*; DIA DDB-1100-476-85; 1985/02; S; <http://www.dia.mil/FOIA/FOIA-Electronic-Reading-Room/FOIA-Reading-Room-Russia/FileId/121077/>; vii
312 *Warsaw Pact Concepts And Capabilities For Going To War In Europe: Implications For NATO Warning Of War*; NIE 4-1-78; 1978/04/10; TS; CIA HCD HR70-14 07-18-2012 DVD VII-053; also CREST RDP05T00644R000601570001-5; 2010/04/13; 7, 32
313 *Warning Of War In Europe*; NIE 4-1-84; 1984/06/27; TS; GWU; <https://nsarchive2.gwu.edu//dc.html?doc=5028377-Document-21-Warning-of-War-In-Europe-National>; 68>70; 75
314 *Warning Of War In Europe: Changing Warsaw Pact Planning And Forces*; NIE 4-1-84; 1989/09; S; CREST RDP94T00754R000200160012-0; 2006/03/10
315 *Readiness Of Soviet Forces In Central Europe: Implications For A Rapid Transition To War*; Intelligence Assessment; CIA DI SOVA; SOV87-10053CX; 1987/09; TS; CIA HCD HR70-14 07-18-2012 DVD VII-120; vii, 36

316 *Mutual And Balanced Force Reductions Between NATO And The Warsaw Pact*; National Security Council; 1970/08/26; CIA HCD HR70-14 07-18-2012 DVD DOC VII-003; 9, 17

317 *Military Planning For European Theatre Conflict During The Cold War—An Oral History Roundtable—Stockholm, 24-25 April 2006*; Zur Sicherheitspolitik Nr. 79; 2007; Zürcher Beiträge; ETH Zürich Center for Security Studies; ISBN 3-905696-17-7 pdf; <https://css.ethz.ch/content/dam/ethz/special-interest/gess/cis/center-for-securities-studies/pdfs/ZB-79.pdf>; 53

318 MSU I Yakubovskiy and GEN ARM S Shtemenko; *Directive Of The Commander-In-Chief Of The Combined Armed Forces On The Combat Readiness Of The Troops And Naval Forces Allocated To The Combined Armed Forces No. 001*; WPCAF Staff; 1971/12/27; CIA IISR 1978/03/17; <https://www.cia.gov/library/readingroom/docs/DOC_0005479503.pdf>; also ISCAP 2012-040; 5

319 MSU V Kulikov and GEN ARM A Gribkov; *Directive Of The Commander-In-Chief Of The Combined Armed Forces Of The Warsaw Pact Member States On The Combat Readiness Of The Troops And Naval Forces Allocated To The Combined Armed Forces*; WPCAF Staff; CIA IISR C05508940; 1979/03/30; <https://www.cia.gov/library/readingroom/docs/DOC_0005508940.pdf>; 8; also CIA MDR EOM-2015-01161

320 Vojtech Mastny and Malcolm Byrne ED; *A Cardboard Castle? An Inside History Of The Warsaw Pact 1955-1991*; 2005; Central European University; ISBN 963-7326-08-1; ISBN 963-7326-07-3; document 99

321 *Theory And Practice Of Warsaw Pact Operations; Part II: Organization And Operational Intent In The West European Theater Of War*; CIA IIR; 1972/06/27; CIA HCD HR70-14 07-18-2012 DVD VI-049; 7

322 COL B Zheleznov; *The Going Over Of Front Troops To The Offensive During The Initial Period Of A War With Only A Partial Concentration Of Forces And Means Under Conditions Of Strong Action Against Them From Enemy Missile/Nuclear Weapons (Based On Materials From A Military Science Conference Of The Southern Group Of Forces)*; VM S (2-63) 1962; CIA IISR; 1977/04/14; <https://www.cia.gov/library/readingroom/docs/1977-04-14-A.pdf>

323 GEN-MAJ F Marushchak and COL K Arsenyev; *A Troop Offensive From Permanent Deployment Areas*; VM S (2-78); 1966; CIA IISR; 1977/05/10; <https://www.cia.gov/library/readingroom/docs/1977-05-10a.pdf>

324 MSU V D Sokolovskiy; *Military Strategy*; 1962; *Voyenizdat*; RAND R-416-PR; <http://www.rand.org/pubs/reports/2005/R416.pdf>; 434

325 *Polish Defense Ministry Document Concerning Experiences And Conclusions From The "Narew" Maneuvers*; 1967/01/20; CIA IISR [TS-]195344; 1967/01/20; CIA HCD HR70-14 07-18-2012 DVD VI-014; 6

326 MSU I Yakubovskiy and GEN-ARM S Shtemenko; *Material Of The Critique Of The Operational War Game On Maps Conducted On The Southwestern Axis*; HQ WPCAF Moscow; 1970/07; CIA IIR TS-205587; 1975/06/13; CIA HCD HR70-14 07-18-2012 DVD VII-031; 19

327 *Critique of Exercise "Lato-74"*; 1974/07; CIA IISR TS-788138; 1978/10/20; CIA HCD HR70-14 07-18-2012 DVD VII-151; 16

328 *Material on Exercise "Shield-76"*; CIA IISR TS-210271; 1976/06/30; CIA HCD HR70-14 07-18-2012 DVD VII-293; 11

329 *Materials Of The Critique Of The Operational-Strategic Command-Staff Exercise Zapad-77*; CIA IISR TS-788301; 1978/10/13; CIA HCD HR70-14 07-18-2012 DVD VII-045; 12

330 *Warning Of War In Europe*; NIE 4-1-84; 1984/06/27; TS; GWU; <https://nsarchive2.gwu.edu//dc.html?doc=5028377-Document-21-Warning-of-War-In-Europe-National>; 74

331 MSU V Kulikov and GEN ARM A Gribkov; *Directive Of The Commander-In-Chief Of The Combined Armed Forces Of The Warsaw Pact Member States On The Combat Readiness Of The Troops And Naval Forces Allocated To The Combined Armed Forces*; WPCAF Staff; CIA IISR C05508940; 1979/03/30; <https://www.cia.gov/library/readingroom/docs/DOC_0005508940.pdf>; 29; also CIA MDR EOM-2015-01161

332 [Military Exercise *Tarcza-88*]; CWIHP-DA; *Operational Summary 1*; <https://digitalarchive.wilsoncenter.org/document/114267>; 2

333 Penkovsky Meeting 31 Paris; 1961/09/20; <https://www.cia.gov/library/readingroom/docs/DOC_0000012412.pdf>; items 19-20, 24 quote, 29, 37, 58, 73

334 GEN-MAJ Kh Dzhelaukhov; *Problems Of The Strategic Deployment Of Armed Forces In Modern Warfare*; VM TS (First) 1962; CIA Ironbark C00012370 (date illegible); <https://www.cia.gov/library/readingroom/docs/1962-10-16-A.pdf>; 4

335 Pavel Podvig et al; *Russian Strategic Nuclear Forces*; The MIT Press; Cambridge, Massachusetts; 2001; Table 8.1 493

336 *Warsaw Pact Buildup Capabilities: A Review Of Work In Progress And Analysis To Date*; CIA DI OSR; SR SP 72-3; 1972/10; TS; CIA HCD HR70-14 07-18-2012 DVD VII-018; 13

337 *The President's Intelligence Checklist*; 1961/10/07; TS; CREST RDP79T00936A000300050001-8; 2015/05/04; item 1

338 Aleksandr Dolinin; *The Order That Never Came*; Krasnaya Zvezda (222); 1999/10/16; 2

339 *Warning Of War In Europe*; NIE 4-1-84; 1984/06/27; TS; GWU; <https://nsarchive2.gwu.edu//dc.html?doc=5028377-Document-21-Warning-of-War-In-Europe-National>; 6, 24

340 *Combat And Mobilization Readiness Of Armed Forces Of The USSR And Strategic Agent Intelligence*; 1985; GSA; CIA IISR C01197776; 1989/09/15; 5; CIA MDR EOM-2015-01160

341 *Manning Practices And Patterns In Soviet Ground Force Units*; Research Paper; CIA DI SOVA; SOV 83-10143JX; 1983/08; TS; CIA HCD HR70-14 07-18-2012 DVD VII-111; iv

- **obsoleteness**

342 *Readiness Of Soviet Forces In Central Europe: Implications For A Rapid Transition To War*; Intelligence Assessment; CIA DI SOVA; SOV87-10053CX; 1987/09; TS; CIA HCD HR70-14 07-18-2012 DVD VII-120; 10

343 *Soviet Readiness In The Western Theater And Its Impact On Operations*; DIA DDB-1100-476-85; 1985/02; S; <http://www.dia.mil/FOIA/FOIA-Electronic-Reading-Room/FOIA-Reading-Room-Russia/FileId/121077/>; 4

344 *Eastern Europe And The Warsaw Pact*; NIE 12-65; DCI; 1965/08/26; S; 13

345 *Soviet Ground Forces Trends*; CIA-DIA-Army Assessment; CIA DI SOVA; SOV 84-10177; 1984/10; S; <https://www.cia.gov/library/readingroom/document/0000498132>; also CIA HCD HR70-14 07-18-2012 DVD VII-118; also CREST RDP85T00313R000300040006-1; 2010/08/09; 10

346 Christopher Donnelly; *Red Banner: The Soviet Military System In Peace And War*; 1988; Jane's Information Group; ISBN 0-7106-0488-2; 84

347 COL A Grylev; *The Preparation And Use Of Strategic Reserves In The Second World War*; VM S (6-61) 1961; CIA Ironbark; 1962/07/02; <https://www.cia.gov/library/readingroom/docs/1962-07-02.pdf>; 6

348 Viktor Suvorov; *Inside The Soviet Army*; 1982; MacMillan; New York; 143-144

- **the war in the air**

349 *Warsaw Pact Air Forces: Support Of Strategic Operations In Central Europe*; Intelligence Assessment; CIA DI SOVA; SOV 85-10001CX; 1985/01; TS; CIA HCD HR70-14 07-18-2012 DVD VII-159

350 *Reconnaissance In Support Of Strategic Operations*; 1985; GSA; CIA IISR C01197777; 1989/09/15; 9; CIA MDR EOM-2015-01160

351 MAR (Aviation) P Kutakhov; *The Air Force In The Past And Present*; VM R (10); 1973; FPD 0063 (21 November 1974); 24

- **conning the system**

352 Viktor Suvorov; *Inside The Soviet Army*; 1982; MacMillan; New York; 251>253

353 *Observations On Exercise Danube-83*; *Honvedelem* (4) 1983; S; CIA IIR C05798378; 7; CIA MDR EOM-2011-0881

354 *Managing And Monitoring Readiness In The Warsaw Pact Ground Forces*; Research Paper; CIA DI SOVA Theater Forces Division; SOV 82-10204CX; 1982/12; TS; CREST RDP83T00853R000200170002-5; 2007/03/15

355 *The Readiness Of Soviet Ground Forces*; NI IIM 82-10012; DCI; 1982/11; S; CIA HCD HR70-14 07-18-2012 DVD VII-108; III, IV-3

- **sustainability**

356 *Trends And Developments In Warsaw Pact Theater Forces And Doctrine Through The 1990s*; NIE 11-14-89 Key Judgments; 1989/02; S; <https://www.cia.gov/library/readingroom/docs/CIA-RDP94T00766R000100070003-1.pdf>; 5

357 GEN-COL F Malykhin; *Some Problems In The Preparation Of The Rear Area For Support Of The Armed Forces In The Initial Period Of A War*; VM TS (Second) 1960; CIA C00012326; 1962/02/13; <https://www.cia.gov/library/readingroom/docs/1962-02-13.pdf>; also CIA HCD HR70-14 07-18-2012 DVD V-003; 8

358 1978—*Warsaw Pact Concepts And Capabilities For Going To War In Europe: Implications For NATO Warning Of War*; NIE 4-1-78; 1978/04/10; TS; CIA HCD HR70-14 07-18-2012 DVD VII-053; also CREST RDP05T00644R000601570001-5; 2010/04/13 but more redactions; 7 to 12

1984—*Warning Of War In Europe*; Memorandum; 1984/06/27; <https://www.cia.gov/library/readingroom/docs/DOC_0001486834.pdf>; 11 to 16

1988—*Statement Of The Director, Office Of Soviet Analysis To The Chairman Of The House Armed Services Committee*; 1988/09/08; S; <https://www.cia.gov/library/readingroom/docs/1988-09-08.pdf> and Memorandum For The Record; 1988/09/08 <https://www.cia.gov/library/readingroom/docs/DOC_0000659267.pdf>

1989—*Warning Of War In Europe: Changing Warsaw Pact Planning And Forces*; NIE 4-1-84; 1989/09; S; CREST RDP94T00754R000200160012-0; 2006/03/10; map iv, 5

**going all the way**

359 GEN-ARM Ivan Yegorovich Shavrov; *Fundamentals Of A Strategic Operation In A Continental Theater Of Military Operations*; 1976; GSA; CIA IISR C05995313; 1977/09/30; <https://www.cia.gov/library/readingroom/docs/DOC_0005995313.pdf> 4

360 *Front Offensive Operations*; 1985; GSA; CIA IISR C01197778; 1990/03/02; 4; CIA MDR EOM-2015-01160

361 GEN-LT V Reznichenko and COL I Suddenok; *The System Of Combined Arms And Joint Operations*; VIZ (4) 1981/04; JPRS 78984 (16 September 1981) Military Affairs 1618

362 *Front Offensive Operations*; 1985; GSA; CIA IISR C01197778; 1990/03/02; 7-8; CIA MDR EOM-2015-01160

363 GEN-LT K Kolganov et al; *Certain Questions Of The Development Of Soviet Military Art From 1953-1960*; VM S (1-77) 1966; CIA IISR; 1977/04/11; <https://www.cia.gov/library/readingroom/docs/1977-04-11c.pdf>

364 F F Gayvoronsky et al; *Front Offensive Operations*; GSA; 1974; CIA IISR FIRDB-312-01997-79; 1979/09/27; CIA HCD HR70-14 07-18-2012 DVD VII-223; 26

365 I Y Shavrov; *The Front Offensive Operation*; GSA 1977/05; CIA IISR FIRDB-312-00013-79; 1979/06/15; CIA MDR EOM-2009-0157; also CIA HCD HR70-14 07-18-2012 DVD VII-222; 11

366 *A Warsaw Pact Approach To War In Europe*; 1970; CIA IIR CSDB-312-01857-70; 1970/07/22; 2

367 GEN-COL G I Khetagurov; *Preparation And Conduct Of A Front Offensive Operation On A Maritime Axis In The Initial Period Of A War*; VM TS (Fourth) 1961; CIA Ironbark C00304576; <https://www.cia.gov/library/readingroom/docs/1962-05-28.pdf>; 8

368 Wilson Center Digital Archive—Cold War History; <https://digitalarchive.wilsoncenter.org/theme/cold-war-history>
Parallel History Project <https://www.php.isn.ethz.ch/lory1.ethz.ch/collections/>
Vojtech Mastny and Malcolm Byrne ED *A Cardboard Castle? An Inside History Of The Warsaw Pact 1955-1991*; 2005; Central European University; ISBN 963-7326-08-1; ISBN 963-7326-07-3

369 *Danmark under den kolde krig: Den sikkerhedspolitiske situation 1945-1991*; Dansk Institut For Internationale Studier; Copenhagen; 2005; V.II ISBN 87-7605-093-9; <https://www.diis.dk/publikationer/danmark-kolde-krig>
Christoph Bluth; *The Warsaw Pact And Military Security In Central Europe During The Cold War*; The Journal of Slavic Military Studies; 17 (2); 299>331 2004/04; Taylor & Francis
Beatrice Heuser; *Warsaw Pact Military Doctrines In The 1970s And 1980s: Findings In The East German Archives*; Comparative Strategy; 12 (4); 437>457; 1993; Taylor & Francis
*Military Planning Of The Warsaw Pact In Central Europe: A Study*; Cold War International History Project Bulletin; 2; 1, 13>19; 1992/Fall; Woodrow Wilson International Center for Scholars; Washington DC
*Soviet Concepts For Employment Of Nuclear Weapons In A Conflict With NATO—Evidence From Warsaw Pact Military Exercises*; Memorandum; 1978/03/24; CIA; CIA HCD HR70-14 07-18-2012 DVD VII-052
*Soviet Concepts For Initial Military Operations Against NATO In Central Europe*; Intelligence Report; SR 77-10002CX; CIA OSR Theater Forces Division; 1977/02; TS; CIA MDR EOM-2011-01084; also CIA HCD HR70-14 07-18-2012 DVD VII-037

## • Western Theater of Military Actions

370 *War In The Western TVD*; DDB-2600-3858-84-SAO; DIA Directorate for Research; 1984/08; S; <http://www.dia.mil/FOIA/FOIA-Electronic-Reading-Room/FOIA-Reading-Room-Russia/FileId/121078/>

371 Matthias Uhl; *Storming on to Paris*; in Vojtech Mastny et al ED; *War Plans And Alliances In The Cold War: Threat Perceptions In The East And West*; 2006; Routledge; ISBN 978-0-415-39061-3; ISBN 0-415-39061-3; Part I-2

372 Vojtech Mastny and Malcolm Byrne ED; *A Cardboard Castle? An Inside History Of The Warsaw Pact 1955-1991*; 2005; Central European University; ISBN 963-7326-08-1; ISBN 963-7326-07-3; document 20

373 COL A Bulatov; *Troop Marches Over Great Distances*; VM S (5-66) 1962; CIA IISR 1978/11/30; <https://www.cia.gov/library/readingroom/docs/1978-11-30i.pdf>; 4

374 Vojtech Mastny and Malcolm Byrne ED; *A Cardboard Castle? An Inside History Of The Warsaw Pact 1955-1991*; 2005; Central European University; ISBN 963-7326-08-1; ISBN 963-7326-07-3; document 66

375 *A Soviet View Of The Balance Of Theater Forces In Central Europe And Of The Ground Campaign Against The NATO Center Region*; Memorandum; CIA DI OSR; 1973/08/08; CIA HCD HR70-14 07-18-2012 DVD VII-020

376 *Materials Of The Critique Of The Operational-Strategic Command-Staff Exercise Zapad-77*; CIA IISR TS-788301; 1978/10/13; CIA HCD HR70-14 07-18-2012 DVD VII-045; 9

377 Vojtech Mastny and Malcolm Byrne ED; *A Cardboard Castle? An Inside History Of The Warsaw Pact 1955-1991*; 2005; Central European University; ISBN 963-7326-08-1; ISBN 963-7326-07-3; document 81

378 *Warsaw Pact Command Staff Exercise WEST-77*; CIA IISR TS-778543; 1977/09/21; CIA HCD HR70-14 07-18-2012 DVD VII-044; 4

379 MSU N Ogarkov; *Results Of Operational Training In 1977-1978 And Tasks For 1979-1980*; GS; CIA IISR FIRDB-312-02337-79; 1979/10/25;; CIA HCD HR70-14 07-18-2012 DVD VII-057; 4

380 *Warsaw Pact Exercise "Center"*; 1978/11; CIA IISR TS-798165; 1979/06/08; CIA HCD HR70-14 07-18-2012 DVD VII-320

381 *NATO-Warsaw Pact Force Mobilization*; The National Defense University; 1988; 269; 291 reorganization 1977

382 Vojtech Mastny and Malcolm Byrne ED; *A Cardboard Castle? An Inside History Of The Warsaw Pact 1955-1991*; 2005; Central European University; ISBN 963-7326-08-1; ISBN 963-7326-07-3; document 95

383 *Employment Of Warsaw Pact Forces Against NATO: A Four Front Attack*; NI IIM 83-10002; SC 01700-88; 1988/03; TS; 1988/03; 6; CIA MDR EOM-2010-00681

384 *Military Planning Of The Warsaw Pact In Central Europe: A Study*; CWIHP-B (2) Fall 1992; translation German Defense Ministry publication; 14

385 Vojtech Mastny and Malcolm Byrne ED; *A Cardboard Castle? An Inside History Of The Warsaw Pact 1955-1991*; 2005; Central European University; ISBN 963-7326-08-1; ISBN 963-7326-07-3; document 99

386 *Soviet Readiness In The Western Theater And Its Impact On Operations*; DDB-1100-476-85; DIA; 1985/02; S; <http://www.dia.mil/FOIA/FOIA-Electronic-Reading-Room/FOIA-Reading-Room-Russia/FileId/121077/>; 23

387 *National And Multinational Polish Strategic, Operational, Tactical, Combined Division-Level, Specialist And Transit Exercises, War Games, Staff And Training Drills*; CIA IIR FIRDB-312-00934-83; 1983/06/30; CIA HCD HR70-14 07-18-2012 DVD VII-204; 7

- **Northwestern Theater of Military Actions**

388 Ghulam Dastagir Wardak; *The Voroshilov Lectures: Materials From The Soviet General Staff Academy*; V.I *Issues Of Soviet Military Strategy*; 1989; National Defense University; 116

389 GEN-COL M Tereshchenko; *Dedicated Service To The Fatherland Was His Ideal (80th Birth Anniversary Of N. Ogarkov, Marshal Of The Soviet Union)*; VM U; 6 (5) 1997; East View Publications; 96

390 Vitaly I Feskov et al; *Sovetskaya Armiya v gody «kholodnaya voyna» (1945-1991) [The Soviet Army During The 'Cold War']*; Tomsk State University; 2004; ISBN 5-7511-1819-7; <http://militera.lib.ru/h/0/pdf/feskov_vi02.pdf>; 59

391 Daniel L Galley *The Right Stuff And The Fast Track: A Look At Soviet Military Districts And Their Commanders, 1945-1981*; US Army Russian Institute; 1981/04; <https://apps.dtic.mil/dtic/tr/fulltext/u2/a114659.pdf> 13, 71

392 *Warsaw Pact Exercise "Center"*; 1978/11; CIA IISR TS-798165; 1979/06/08; CIA HCD HR70-14 07-18-2012 DVD VII-320; 4

393 GEN-ARM Sergei Mateevich Shtemenko; *The Soviet General Staff At War 1941-1945*; 1970; Progress Publishers; 113

394 *Warning Of War In Europe*; Memorandum; 1984/06/27; S; <https://www.cia.gov/library/readingroom/docs/DOC_0001486834.pdf>; 27

395 *Warning Of War In Europe*; Memorandum; 1984/06/27; S; <https://www.cia.gov/library/readingroom/docs/DOC_0001486834.pdf>; 27

396 *Conversation with Jaruzelski*; PHP; 2002/09/26; <http://www.php.isn.ethz.ch/kms2.isn.ethz.ch/serviceengine/Files/PHP/20661/ipublicationdocument_singledocument/1b8b0699-b8a3-43e4-890b-34ae46d392d2/en/180902_Jaruzelski_Conversation.pdf>; 3

397 *Agent Reconnaissance In Front Offensive Operations;* 1985; GSA; CIA IISR TS-888283; 1988/03/25; 10; ISCAP 2012-026 (CIA MDR EOM-2009-00158)

- **Southwestern Theater of Military Actions**

398 Ghulam Dastagir Wardak; *The Voroshilov Lectures: Materials From The Soviet General Staff Academy*; V.I *Issues Of Soviet Military Strategy*; 1989; National Defense University; 114, 140

399 *Combat Capabilities And Probable Plans For The Use Of NATO Armed Forces In The Central European Theater Of Operations*; 1966/11; CIA IISR CSDB-312-00300-67; 1967/02/24; CIA HCD HR70-14 07-18-2012 DVD VI-016; 26

400 GEN-MAJ Tibor Toth; *Characteristics Of Organizing And Conducting An Offensive Operation Of The Coalition Front And Combined Arms Army*; Honvedelem (6) 1980; S; CIA IIR C05798348; 1985/09/06; 15, 24 map AT-4; CIA MDR EOM-2011-0881

401 MAJ Jozsef Dobi; *Potential For Underwater Tank Crossing Operations On The Mur River*; Honvedelem (3) 1984; S; CIA IIR C05798396; 1987/12/31; 3; CIA MDR EOM-2011-0881

402 MSU I Yakubovskiy and GEN-ARM S Shtemenko; *Material Of The Critique Of The Operational War Game On Maps Conducted On The Southwestern Axis*; HQ WPCAF Moscow; 1970/07; CIA IIR TS-205587; 1975/06/13; CIA HCD HR70-14 07-18-2012 DVD VII-031; 28

- **Southern Theater of Military Actions**

403 *Soviet Forces And Capabilities In The Southern Theater Of Military Operations*; DCI; NIE 11/39-83 D; 1983/12; S; <https://www.cia.gov/library/readingroom/docs/DOC_0000278543.pdf>

404 GEN-LT L Baukov; *Conducting A Front Offensive Operation Without Nuclear Weapons*; VM S (3-76) 1965; CIA IISR; 1977/02/23; <https://www.cia.gov/library/readingroom/docs/1977-02-23.pdf>; 5

405 *Warsaw Pact Forces Opposite NATO*; NIE 11-14-79; V.II *The Estimate*; 1979/01/31; TS; CIA HCD HR70-14 07-18-2012 VII-5; IV-26-27

406 *Soviet Military Posture Opposite Southwest Asia*; CIA DI; USSR Monthly Review; SOV UR 82-008X; 1982/09; S; CREST RDP83T00853R000300020002-0; 2008/10/15; 7

407 *Readiness Of Soviet Forces In Central Europe: Implications For A Rapid Transition To War*; Intelligence Assessment; CIA DI SOVA; SOV87-10053CX; 1987/09; TS; CIA HCD HR70-14 07-18-2012 DVD VII-120; 6

- **Far Eastern Theater of Military Actions**

408 *Soviet Military Forces In The Far East*; DCI; NIE 11-14/40-81S; V.I *Key Judgments*; NIE 11-14/40-81X; CREST RDP83R00184R001100010012-6; V.II *Supporting Analysis*; CREST RDP83R00184R001100010013-5; 1981/09/01; TS

409 *Soviet Eastern Theater Headquarters And C3 Assets*; NPIC BIIR; Z-14093/84 RCA-03/0003/84; 1984/12; S; CREST RDP85T00060R000300680001-7; 2010/08/02

410 *Soviet Strategy And Capabilities For Multitheater War*; NIE 11-19-85-L; DCI NIO GEN Purpose Forces; 1985/04; TS; CREST RDP87T00495R000700760002-9; 2010/07/14; 5

411 *Soviet Military Forces In The Far East*; DCI; NIE 11-14/40-81; *Memorandum to Holders*; 1985/10; <https://www.cia.gov/library/readingroom/docs/DOC_0000261289.pdf>; NIE 11-14/40-81S; V.I *Key Judgments*; NIE 11-14/40-81X; CREST RDP83R00184R001100010012-6; V.II *Supporting Analysis*; CREST RDP83R00184R001100010013-5; 1981/09/01; TS

412 MSU M Zakharov; *The Campaign Of The Soviet Armed Forces In The Far East, 9 August-2 September 1945*; VIZ (9) 1980; JPRS 76444 (18 September 1980) Military Affairs 1534

- **Heartland**

413 COL V Zemskov; *On Military-Scientific Work In The Ground Forces (From The Experience Of 1961);* VM S (3-64) 1962; CIA Ironbark; 1963/01/09; <https://www.cia.gov/library/readingroom/docs/1963-01-09c.pdf>; also CIA HCD HR70-14 07-18-2012 DVD III-041; 11, 22

414 *Organizational Structure Of The Soviet Armed Forces*; 1985; GSA; CIA IISR TS-888643; 1988/07/29; 10; ISCAP 2012-026 (CIA MDR EOM-2009-00158)

415 *Soviet Forces And Capabilities In The Southern Theater Of Military Operations*; DCI; NIE 11/39-83 D; 1983/12; S; <https://www.cia.gov/library/readingroom/docs/DOC_0000278543.pdf> 16

# Operational Evolutions

## WMD propulsion

416 M A Garelov; From Whence The Threat Derived; Operational Plan Of Actions For Group Of Soviet Occupation Troops In Germany 5 November 1946; VIZ (2) 1989/02; 16>31; JPRS-UMJ-89-008 (25 July 1989); 1>12

417 Zhukov Address To GSFG Senior Troop Commanders; 1957/03; CIA IR TDCSDB-3,631,293; 1957/03/29; correction and additions; CIA HCD HR70-14 07-18-2012 DVD I-039-a-b-c

418 A Study Of The Soviet Ground Forces; Second Report; CIA DIA Panel for a Special Study of the Soviet Ground Forces for Secretary McNamara; 1965/05/06; TS; CIA HCD HR70-14 07-18-2012 DVD V-018; 23

419 GEN-LT K Kolganov et al; Certain Questions Of The Development Of Soviet Military Art From 1953-1960; VM S (1-77) 1966; CIA IISR; 1977/04/11; <https://www.cia.gov/library/readingroom/docs/1977-04-11c.pdf>; 11

420 COL P Grabovskiy; Problems Of Controlling Allied Troop Groupings; VM S (1-62) 1962; CIA IISR; 1976/11/24; <https://www.cia.gov/library/readingroom/docs/1976-11-24.pdf>; also CREST RDP10-00105R000302620001-3; 9

421 *An Exercise To Be Carried Out By An Independent Engineer Battalion In An Offensive Operation By An Army In The Initial Stage Of A War*; ICA (49) 1959; TS; CIA 1961/12/08; <https://www.cia.gov/library/readingroom/docs/1961-12-08.pdf>; also CIA HCD HR70-14 07-18-2012 DVD YEAR 1961

422 GEN-LT S Andryushchenko; *The Deployment And Forward Movement Of A Combined Arms Army Of A Border Military District In The Initial Period Of A War*; VM TS (Second) 1961; CIA C00304550; <https://www.cia.gov/library/readingroom/docs/1961-12-21b.pdf>; also CIA HCD HR70-14 07-18-2012 DVD V-001 and YEAR 1961

423 GEN-MAJ P Stepshin; *On Regrouping A Combined-Arms Army From The Depth Of The Country In The Initial Period Of A War*; VM S (6-61) 1961; CIA Ironbark; 1962/06/13; <https://www.cia.gov/library/readingroom/docs/1962-06-13.pdf>; also CIA HCD HR70-14 07-18-2012 DVD III-024

424 *History Of The Custody And Deployment Of Nuclear Weapons: July 1945 Through September 1977*; Office of the Assistant To The Secretary of Defense (Atomic Energy); 1978/02; TS; DoD FOIA; 232-233

425 COL Theodore C Mataxis and LTC Seymour L. Goldberg; *Nuclear Tactics, Weapons, And Firepower In The Pentomic Division, Battle Group, And Company*; 1958; Military Service Publishing; Harrisburg PA

426 COL-LT N Reshetnikov; *On The Development Of The Theory Of The Combat Employment Of Front Aviation In The Postwar Period*; VM S (5-60) 1961; CIA; <https://www.cia.gov/library/readingroom/docs/1962-03-01b.pdf>

427 GEN-LT K Kolganov et al; *Certain Questions Of The Development Of Soviet Military Art From 1953-1960*; VM S (1-77) 1966; CIA IISR; 1977/04/11; <https://www.cia.gov/library/readingroom/docs/1977-04-11c.pdf>

428 F F Gayvoronsky et al; *Front Offensive Operations*; GSA; 1974; CIA IISR FIRDB-312-01997-79; 1979/09/27; CIA HCD HR70-14 07-18-2012 DVD VII-223; 30 table

429 S P Ivanov *The Initial Period Of War*; Moscow 1974; USAF Soviet Military Thought #20; 250

## wmd blowout

430 MSU M V Zakharov; *Certain Questions Of Soviet Military Art*; VM S (1-68) 1963; CIA IISR 1977/04/15; <https://www.cia.gov/library/readingroom/docs/1977-04-15b.pdf>; 44

431 GEN-LT V Baskakov; *New Developments In Operational Art And Tactics*; VM TS (First) 1960; CIA C00012323; 1962/01/31; <https://www.cia.gov/library/readingroom/docs/1962-01-31-A.pdf>; also CIA HCD HR70-14 07-18-2012 DVD III-017; 5

432 John G Hines et al; *Soviet Intentions 1965-1985* V.I *An Analytical Comparison Of U.S.-Soviet Assessments During The Cold War*; Contract MDA903-92-C-0147 OSD-Net Assessment; BDM Federal; 1995/09/22; 48; GWU <https://nsarchive2.gwu.edu/nukevault/ebb285/index.htm>; section links; 72 AP A

433 GEN-COL A Kh Babadzhanyan; *Some Questions In The Preparation And Conduct Of Initial Offensive Operations*; VM TS (Third) 1961; CIA; 1962/03/23; <https://www.cia.gov/library/readingroom/docs/1962-03-23.pdf>; 11

434 MSU R Malinovskiy; *Some Thoughts On The Development Of The Soviet Army Tank Troops*; VM TS (First) 1962; CIA Ironbark; 1962/10/18; <https://www.cia.gov/library/readingroom/docs/1961-12-29-B.pdf>; also CIA HCD HR70-14 07-18-2012 DVD III-035 + YEAR 1961; 40-41

435 GEN-COL A I Gastilovich; *The Theory Of Military Art Needs Review*; VM TS (First) 1960; CIA; 1961/12/18; <https://www.cia.gov/library/readingroom/docs/1961-12-18.pdf>; also CIA HCD HR70-14 07-18-2012 DVD III-018; 8

436 GEN-COL G I Khetagurov; *A Front Offensive Operation Conducted Under The Conditions Of The Initial Period Of A Nuclear-Missile War*; VM TS (Second) 1960; CIA C00012312; 1962/01/05; <https://www.cia.gov/library/readingroom/docs/1962-01-05.pdf>; also CIA HCD HR70-14 07-18-2012 DVD YEAR 1961; 6

437 F F Gayvoronsky et al; *Front Offensive Operations*; GSA; 1974; CIA IISR FIRDB-312-01997-79; 1979/09/27; CIA HCD HR70-14 07-18-2012 DVD VII-223; 30

438 GEN-COL A Kh Babadzhanyan; *Some Questions In The Preparation And Conduct Of Initial Offensive Operations*; VM TS (Third) 1961; CIA; 1962/03/23; <https://www.cia.gov/library/readingroom/docs/1962-03-23.pdf>; 13

439 GEN-LT (Tank Troops) M Lugovtsev; *Some Problems Of Military Science Work Among The Troops*; VM S (3-64) 1962; CIA IISR; 1978/10/05; <https://www.cia.gov/library/readingroom/docs/1978-10-05d.pdf>; 5

440 COL I Milevskiy; *Some Conclusions Concerning NATO Armed Forces Maneuvers*; VM S (5-60) 1961; CIA Ironbark; 1962/08/27; <https://www.cia.gov/library/readingroom/docs/1962-08-22.pdf>; 12

441 COL-LT L Semeyko and COL-LT (Engineer) L Sokolov-Sokolenok; *Some Problems In The Development And Combat Employment Of Military Transport Aviation*; VM S (5-66) 1962; CIA IISR; 1978/09/07; <https://www.cia.gov/library/readingroom/docs/1978-09-07b.pdf>; 5

442 GEN-MAJ P Stepshin; *On Regrouping A Combined-Arms Army From The Depth Of The Country In The Initial Period Of A War*; VM S (6-61) 1961; CIA Ironbark; 1962/06/13; <https://www.cia.gov/library/readingroom/docs/1962-06-13.pdf>; also CIA HCD HR70-14 07-18-2012 DVD III-024; 3-4

443 COL P Lyadov; *Certain Problems In Moving A Combined-Arms Army Forward From The Interior Of The Country In The Initial Period Of War*; VM S (4-65) 1962; CIA IISR; 1978/10/12; <https://www.cia.gov/library/readingroom/docs/1978-10-12.pdf>; 5

444 *Capabilities Of Soviet General Purpose Forces 1964-1970;* NIE 11-14-64; 1964/12/10; S; CIA HCD HR70-14 07-18-2012 DVD V-017; 37

445 *Capabilities Of Soviet General Purpose Forces*; NIE 11-14-65; 1965/10/21; S; CIA HCD HR70-14 07-18-2012 DVD V-020; 20-21

446 *Capabilities Of Soviet General Purpose Forces*; NIE 11-14-66; 1966/11/03; <https://www.cia.gov/library/readingroom/docs/DOC_0000278472.pdf>; 9

447 *Eastern Europe And The Warsaw Pact*; NIE 12-65; DCI; 1965/08/26; S; <https://www.cia.gov/library/readingroom/docs/DOC_0000273191.pdf>; 9

448 *New Look In The Satellite Armies*; Special Report; CIA DI Office of Current Intelligence; 1964/10/30; TS; CIA HCD HR70-14 07-18-2012 DVD VI-04; 9

449 *Capabilities Of Soviet General Purpose Forces*; NIE 11-14-66; 1966/11/03; S; <https://www.cia.gov/library/readingroom/docs/DOC_0000278472.pdf>; 22

450 *Warsaw Pact Military Strategy: A Compromise In Soviet Strategic Thinking*; Intelligence Study; DDI RSS 0007-65; CIA DI Research Staff; 1965/06/07; CIA HCD HR70-14 07-18-2012 DVD VI-007

451 *Soviet Capabilities To Reinforce In Central Europe;* Joint Study—Initial Report; DIA; CIA OSR; SR SP 68-7; 1968/01; TS; CREST RDP80B01554R003300310056-5; 2005-04-21; also CIA HCD HR70-14 07-18-2012 DVD V-056-057; 153

452 *Warsaw Pact War Plan For Central Region Of Europe*; Intelligence Memorandum; CIA DI OSR; 1968/06/18; TS; CIA HCD HR70-14 07-18-2012 DVD VI-029; 3

453 *Plan Of Actions Of The Czechoslovak People's Army For War Period*; 1964/10/14*;* CWIHP-B (12/13); 289>298

454 Paweł Piotrowski; *A Landing Operation in Denmark: The Polish Military's Losses in the First Phase of a Warsaw Pact Offensive Were to Reach 50 Percent*; Wprost Warsaw; 2002/06/23; translated PHP <http://www.php.isn.ethz.ch/lory1.ethz.ch/collections/coll_polex/piotrowski.html>

455 Vojtech Mastny and Malcolm Byrne ED; *A Cardboard Castle? An Inside History Of The Warsaw Pact 1955-1991*; 2005; Central European University; ISBN 963-7326-08-1; ISBN 963-7326-07-3; document 20, 135

## deferring inevitability

456 V D Sokolovskiy et al; *Military Strategy*; *Voyenizdat*; Moscow; 1962; RAND; 1963; <http://www.rand.org/pubs/reports/2005/R416.pdf>; 152>157

457 GEN-MAJ V Zemskov; *Wars Of The Modern Era*; VM R (5) 1969; FPD 0116-69 (18 December 1969); 59

458 *Statement Made On Saturday 5 May By Secretary McNamera At The NATO Ministerial Meeting In Athens*; North Atlantic Council; C-M(62)55; 1962/05/05; Cosmic TS; GWU; <https://nsarchive2.gwu.edu/NSAEBB/NSAEBB159/>; document 16C; 2

459 *Overall Strategic Concept For The Defense Of The North Atlantic Treaty Organization Area*; 1968/01/16; <https://www.nato.int/archives/strategy.htm>

460 GEN-MAJ (Aviation) G Yarotskiy; *The Defeat Of Enemy Aviation Groupings In A Theater Of Military Operations During A Non-Nuclear Period*; VM S (3-85) 1968; CIA IISR; 1973/10/12; <https://www.cia.gov/library/readingroom/docs/1973-10-12-A.pdf>; also CIA HCD HR70-14 07-18-2012 DVD VII-137; also CREST RDP10-00105R000100300001-2

461 GEN-MAJ (Artillery) I Konoplev and GEN-MAJ (Artillery) V Kuznetsov; *Rocket Troops And Artillery In Offensive Operations Conducted Without The Use Of Nuclear Weapons By Either Side*; VM S (2-75) 1965; CIA IISR; 1973/11/09; <https://www.cia.gov/library/readingroom/docs/1973-11-09-A.pdf>

462 MSU M V Zakharov; *The Development Of The Means Of Armed Combat In The Postwar Period*; VM S (1-86) 1969; CIA IISR FIRDB-312-00679-74; 1974/02/26; <https://www.cia.gov/library/readingroom/docs/1974-02-26.pdf>; also CIA HCD HR70-14 07-18-2012 DVD VII-080; 7

463 *The Development Of Soviet Military Power: Trends Since 1965 And Prospects For The 1980s*; Intelligence Assessment; SR 81-10035X; CIA-OSR; 1981/04; S; CIA HCD HR70-14 07-18-2012 DVD VII-107; 16

464 GEN-MAJ P T Kunitsky; *Massing Of Forces On Sector Of Main Thrust*; VIZ (4) 1987/04; JPRS-UMJ-87-003 (9 September 1987); 9

465 *Operations Of A Group Of Fronts As The Basic Form Of Accomplishing Strategic Tasks In A Theater Of Military Operations*; VIZ (8) 1981/08; JPRS 79427 (12 November 1981)

466 GEN-COL N O Pavlovskiy; *The Initial Period Of A Future War And The Special Features Of The Conduct Of Military Operations During This Period*; VM TS (First) 1961; CIA; 1962/01/10; <https://www.cia.gov/library/readingroom/docs/1962-01-10.pdf>; also CIA HCD HR70-14 07-18-2012 DVD V-002

467 GEN-COL A Kh Babadzhanyan; *Some Questions In The Preparation And Conduct Of Initial Offensive Operations*; VM TS (Third) 1961; CIA; 1962/03/23; <https://www.cia.gov/library/readingroom/docs/1962-03-23.pdf>; 13

468 *Manual On The Conduct Of Operations—Part Two—Ground Forces Operations (Front-Army-Corps)*; 1963; GS; CIA IISR TS-778264; 1977/09/29; CIA HCD HR70-14 07-18-2012 DVD VII-99; CH-3 60

469 MSU M V Zakharov; *The Status And Tasks Of Military Science At The Present Stage Of The Development Of The Armed Forces*; VM S (1-77) 1966; CIA IISR FIRDB-312-00137-76; 1976/03/10; <https://www.cia.gov/library/readingroom/docs/1976-03-10.pdf>; also CREST RDP10-00105R000201680001-9; 8

470 Vojtech Mastny and Malcolm Byrne ED; *A Cardboard Castle? An Inside History Of The Warsaw Pact 1955-1991*; 2005; Central European University; ISBN 963-7326-08-1; ISBN 963-7326-07-3; document 83 416

471 GEN-COL I Glebov and GEN-MAJ V Yemelin; *Offensive Operations Of A Front To The Entire Depth Of A Theater Of Military Operations*; VM S (2-72) 1964; CIA IISR; 1975/11/14; <https://www.cia.gov/library/readingroom/docs/1975-11-14b.pdf>; also CREST RDP10-00105R000201480001-1 2012/10/16

472 COL A Volkov; *The Question Of Offensive Operations Of Fronts Throughout The Entire Depth Of A Theater Of Military Operations*; VM S (1-77) 1966; CIA IISR; 1975/05/28; <https://www.cia.gov/library/readingroom/docs/1975-05-28-B.pdf>; also CREST RDP10-00105R000201070001-6 2012/04/11

473 GEN-COL I Glebov; *Certain Problems Of Planning And Conducting Offensive Operations Of Fronts (Based On The Experience Of Research War Games)*; VM S (3-82) 1967; CIA IISR FIRDB-312-02966-74; 1974/08/20; CIA HCD HR70-14 07-18-2012 DVD VII-030; also CREST RDP10-00105R000100820001-5; 2012/09/28; 4

474 *Materials Of The Critique Of The Operational-Strategic Command-Staff Exercise Zapad-77*; CIA IISR TS-788301; 1978/10/13; CIA HCD HR70-14 07-18-2012 DVD VII-045; 15

475 *Agent Reconnaissance In Front Offensive Operations*; 1985; GSA; CIA IISR TS-888283 C01197689; 1988/03/25; 10; ISCAP 2012-026 (CIA MDR EOM-2009-00158)

476 MSU Nikolay V Ogarkov; *History Teaches Vigilance*; 1985; *Voyenizdat*; JPRS UMA-85-021-L-Corrected (13 November 1985); CREST RDP93T01468R000100110005-2; 2005/06/08; 32

477 *The Warsaw Pact Threat To NATO*; Interagency Working Group—Final Report; SR JS 70-3; 1970/05; S; CREST RDP7B00939A000600020002-9; 2002-05-20; also CIA HCD HR70-14 07-18-2012 DVD VII-002; 15

478 *The Readiness Of Soviet Ground Forces*; NI IIM 82-10012; DCI; Memorandum; 1982/11; S; CIA HCD HR70-14 07-18-2012 DVD VII-108; VI-8

479 *Readiness Of Soviet Forces In Central Europe: Implications For A Rapid Transition To War*; Intelligence Assessment; CIA DI SOVA; SOV87-10053CX; 1987/09; TS; CIA HCD HR70-14 07-18-2012 DVD VII-120; 3

480 *Employment Of Warsaw Pact Forces Against NATO: A Four Front Attack*; NI IIM 83-10002; 1988/03; TS; 5; CIA MDR EOM-2010-00681

481 Rüdiger Wenzke; *Die Streitkräfte der DDR und Polens in der Operationsplanung des Warschauer Paktes*; 2010; Military History Research Office; ISBN 978-3-941571-09-9

## cruising the coast

482 Rear ADM A Kruchenykh; *Seizure Of Straits Under Present Conditions*; VM S (3-82) 1967; CIA IISR; 1977/04/26; <https://www.cia.gov/library/readingroom/docs/1977-04-26a.pdf>; 6

483 *Polish Critique Of The Warsaw Pact "Lato-67" Command Post Exercise*; CIA IISR CSDB-312-01470-68; CIA HCD HR70-14 07-18-2012 DVD VI-034; 14, 16

484 Siegfried Lautsch; in Rüdiger Wenzke *Die Streitkräfte der DDR und Polens in der Operationsplanung des Warschauer Paktes*; 2010; Military History Research Office; ISBN 978-3-941571-09-9; 39

485 GEN-ARM G Khetagurov; *Anti-Landing Defense During A Front Offensive Operation (Based On Experience In Baltic Military District Exercises)*; VM S (2-90) 1970; CIA IISR; 1974/03/12; <https://www.cia.gov/library/readingroom/docs/1974-03-12.pdf>; 17

486 *Material on Exercise "Shield-76"*; CIA IISR TS-210271; 1976/06/30; CIA HCD HR70-14 07-18-2012 DVD VII-293; 13

487 *Combat Instruction Nº 1 Of The Maritime Front*; CWHIP-DA; <https://digitalarchive.wilsoncenter.org/document/114464>; item 3

488 GEN-ARM Sergei Mateevich Shtemenko; *The Soviet General Staff At War 1941-1945*; 1970; Progress Publishers; 204

489 Jan Drzewiecki; *Warsaw Pact Generals In Polish Uniforms*; 2002/09; PHP <http://www.php.isn.ethz.ch/kms2.isn.ethz.ch/serviceengine/Files/PHP/20636/ipublicationdocument_singledocument/9c4b905d-9c95-41ce-80ff-7182ab66e72a/en/excerpts_english.pdf>; II; Stalin and His Legacy

490 Zbigniew Moszumanski; in Rüdiger Wenzke *Die Streitkräfte der DDR und Polens in der Operationsplanung des Warschauer Paktes*; 2010; Military History Research Office; ISBN 978-3-941571-09-9; 71, 73

491 *Polish Defense Ministry Document Concerning Experiences And Conclusions From The "Narew" Maneuvers*; 1967/01/20; CIA IISR [TS-]195344; 1967/01/20; CIA HCD HR70-14 07-18-2012 DVD VI-014; 3

492 *Polish Critique Of The Warsaw Pact "Lato-67" Command Post Exercise*; CIA IISR CSDB-312-01470-68; CIA HCD HR70-14 07-18-2012 DVD VI-034; 6-7

493 *The Development Of Soviet Military Power: Trends Since 1965 And Prospects For The 1980s*; Intelligence Assessment; SR 81-10035X; CIA-OSR; 1981/04; S; CIA HCD HR70-14 07-18-2012 DVD VII-107; 20

494 *Warning Of War In Europe: Changing Warsaw Pact Planning And Forces*; NIE 4-1-84; 1989/09; S; CREST RDP94T00754R000200160012-0; 2006/03/10; iv map

495 Vojtech Mastny and Malcolm Byrne ED; *A Cardboard Castle? An Inside History Of The Warsaw Pact 1955-1991*; 2005; Central European University; ISBN 963-7326-08-1; ISBN 963-7326-07-3; 524 document 112

496 Rüdiger Wenzke *Die Streitkräfte der DDR und Polens in der Operationsplanung des Warschauer Paktes*; 2010; Military History Research Office; ISBN 978-3-941571-09-9

497 *Concept Of Operation For The Polish Front*; CIA IIR; 1984/03/14; CIA HCD HR70-14 07-18-2012 DVD VII-063

498 *Protocol On Assignment Of PPR Army And Navy Forces To The Combined Armed Forces And Their Development In 1981-1985*; 1981/01; CIA IISR TS-828045; 1982/04/19; <https://www.cia.gov/library/readingroom/docs/DOC_0005508933.pdf>

499 *1. Relationship Of Military Exercises To War Plans 2. Wiosna-69 Exercise*; CIA IIR; 1982/07/30; CIA HCD HR70-14 07-18-2012 DVD VII-324

500 *Critique of Exercise "Lato-74"*; 1974/07; CIA IISR TS-788138; 1978/10/20; CIA HCD HR70-14 07-18-2012 DVD VII-151; 14 quote

501 *Draft Of The Discussion Of Exercise "Shield-76"- By The Chief Of The General Staff Of The Polish Armed Forces*; CIA IISR TS-778045; 1977/02/15; CIA HCD HR70-14 07-18-2012 DVD VII-297; TS-778117; 1977/04/11; DVD VII-298; 9 quote

502 *Report On Visit Of Polish Armed Forces General Staff Delegation To The USSR Armed Forces General Staff And To The Combined Command Of The Combined Armed Forces*; CIA IISR FIRDB-312-02329-80; 1980/10/08; <https://www.cia.gov/library/readingroom/docs/1980_10_08_MISCELLANEOUS.pdf>; also CIA HCD HR70-14 07-18-2012 DVD VII-288

503 *Conclusions And Experiences From The "Jesien" (Autumn) Integrated Maneuvers*; CIA IISR CSDB-312-01611-68; 1968/08/08; CIA HCD HR70-14 07-18-2012 DVD VI-035; 8

504 *Conversation with Gen. Wojciech Jaruzelski*; 2002/09/26; PHP; <http://www.php.isn.ethz.ch/lory1.ethz.ch/collections/colltopicf9b3.html?lng=en&id=20661&navinfo=15708>

505 *Warsaw Pact Fronts Within The Western Theater Of Military Operations*; CIA IIR; CIA HCD HR70-14 07-18-2012 DVD VII-326

506 *Polish Maps of Exercise "WEST-77"*; CIA IISR TS-778291; 1977/06/16; CIA HCD HR70-14 07-18-2012 DVD VII-039

507 GEN-MAJ Florian Siwicki; *Discussion Of "Jesien II-73"*; 1973/09/29; CIA IISR TS-206325; 1975/05/21; CIA HCD HR70-14 07-18-2012 DVD VII-282; 9

508 *Warsaw Pact Command Staff Exercise WEST-77*; CIA IISR TS-778543; 1977/09/21; CIA HCD HR70-14 07-18-2012 DVD VII-044; 6-7

509 *Conclusions Drawn from Exercise "ZACHOD [WEST] - 77" and "FALA [WAVE]- 77"*; CIA IISR TS-778572; 1977/11/08; CIA HCD HR70-14 07-18-2012 DVD VII-046; 5-6

510 *Warsaw Pact Fronts Within The Western Theater Of Military Operations*; CIA IIR; CIA HCD HR70-14 07-18-2012 DVD VII-326; 5

511 *Memorandum On Marshal Kulikov's Report Regarding Exercise "Zachod-77"*; CIA IISR TS-798081; 1979/06/07; CIA HCD HR70-14 07-18-2012 DVD VII-319; 10

512 Rüdiger Wenzke; *Die Streitkräfte der DDR und Polens in der Operationsplanung des Warschauer Paktes*; 2010; Military History Research Office; ISBN 978-3-941571-09-9; 10

513 *Soviet Capabilities To Reinforce In Central Europe;* Joint Study—Initial Report; DIA; CIA OSR; SR SP 68-7; 1968/01; TS; CREST RDP80B01554R003300310056-5 2005-04-21; also CIA HCD HR70-14 07-18-2012 DVD V-056; 4

514 *Polish Defense Ministry Document Concerning Experiences And Conclusions From The "Narew" Maneuvers*; 1967/01/20; CIA IISR [TS-]195344; 1967/01/20; CIA HCD HR70-14 07-18-2012 DVD VI-014; 3

515 *USSR General Staff Academy Lessons*; *The Front Offensive Operation*; Table of Contents 1-19*;* 1977; GSA; CIA IISR FIRDB-312-00680-80; 1980/04/18; <https://www.cia.gov/library/readingroom/docs/DOC_0001197532.pdf>; also CIA HCD HR70-14 07-18-2012 DVD VII-224

516 Torsten Diedrich; in Rüdiger Wenzke *Die Streitkräfte der DDR und Polens in der Operationsplanung des Warschauer Paktes*; 2010; Military History Research Office; ISBN 978-3-941571-09-9; 22>24

517 *National And Multinational Polish Strategic, Operational, Tactical, Combined Division-Level, Specialist And Transit Exercises, War Games, Staff And Training Drills*; CIA IIR FIRDB-312-00934-83; 1983/06/30; CIA HCD HR70-14 07-18-2012 DVD VII-204; 3

518 *Warsaw Pact Concepts And Capabilities For Going To War In Europe: Implications For NATO Warning Of War*; NIE 4-1-78; 1978/04/10; TS; CIA HCD HR70-14 07-18-2012 DVD VII-053; also CREST RDP05T00644R000601570001-5; 2010/04/13; 8

519 GEN-COL G I Khetagurov; *A Front Offensive Operation Conducted Under The Conditions Of The Initial Period Of A Nuclear-Missile War*; VM TS (Second) 1960; CIA C00012312; 1962/01/05; <https://www.cia.gov/library/readingroom/docs/1962-01-05.pdf>; also CIA HCD HR70-14 07-18-2012 DVD YEAR 1961; 16-17

520 GEN-COL G I Khetagurov; *Preparation And Conduct Of A Front Offensive Operation On A Maritime Axis In The Initial Period Of A War*; VM TS (Fourth) 1961; CIA Ironbark C00304576; <https://www.cia.gov/library/readingroom/docs/1962-05-28.pdf>; 19

521 Jan Drzewiecki; *Warsaw Pact Generals In Polish Uniforms*; 2002/09; PHP <http://www.php.isn.ethz.ch/kms2.isn.ethz.ch/serviceengine/Files/PHP/20636/ipublicationdocument_singledocument/9c4b905d-9c95-41ce-80ff-7182ab66e72a/en/excerpts_english.pdf>; II; Stalin and His Legacy

522 GEN-MAJ (Artillery) I Dzhordzhadze; *Troop Control During A Front Operation*; VM S (2-75) 1965; CIA IISR; 1978/11/02; <https://www.cia.gov/library/readingroom/docs/1978-11-02b.pdf>

523 GEN-COL G I Khetagurov; *Preparation And Conduct Of A Front Offensive Operation On A Maritime Axis In The Initial Period Of A War*; VM TS (Fourth) 1961; CIA Ironbark C00304576; <https://www.cia.gov/library/readingroom/docs/1962-05-28.pdf>; 19

524 Matthias Uhl; *Storming on to Paris*; in Vojtech Mastny et al ED; *War Plans And Alliances In The Cold War: Threat Perceptions In The East And West*; 2006; Routledge; ISBN 978-0-415-39061-3; ISBN 0-415-39061-3; PT-I-2 56-57

525 GEN-ARM G Khetagurov; *Anti-Landing Defense During A Front Offensive Operation (Based On Experience In Baltic Military District Exercises)*; VM S (2-90) 1970; CIA IISR; 1974/03/12; <https://www.cia.gov/library/readingroom/docs/1974-03-12.pdf>

526 GEN-ARM G Khetagurov; *The Buildup Of Efforts During A Front Offensive Operation*; VM S (1-86) 1969; CIA IISR; 1975/06/09; <https://www.cia.gov/library/readingroom/docs/1975-06-09.pdf>; also CREST RDP10-00105R000201090001-4 2012/04/19; 9

527 GEN-COL G Khetagurov; *Raising The Level Of The Field Training Of Operational Staffs*; VM S (2-81) 1967; CIA IISR; 1976/11/16; <https://www.cia.gov/library/readingroom/docs/1976-11-29a.pdf>; also CREST RDP10-00105R000302640001-1

528 GEN-LT M Ivanov; *The Capabilities Of The Reconnaissance Forces And Means Of A Front And Their Employment*; VM S (2-81) 1967; CIA IISR; 1976/12/23; <https://www.cia.gov/library/readingroom/docs/1976-12-23-A.pdf>; also CREST RDP10-00105R000302770001-7

529 GEN-LT M Ivanov; *Methodology For Conducting Operational Command-Staff War Games On Maps*; VM S (3-85) 1968; CIA IISR; 1976/10/01; <https://www.cia.gov/library/readingroom/docs/1976-10-01.pdf>; also CREST RDP10-00105R000302400001-7

530 GEN-LT M Ivanov; *Radio Camouflage On The Territory Of A Border Military District In Peacetime*; VM S (3-82) 1967; CIA IISR; 1975/10/28; <https://www.cia.gov/library/readingroom/docs/1975-10-28.pdf>; 10

531 GEN-LT M Ivanov; *Ways Of Reducing The Times For Bringing Troops To Full Combat Readiness (Based On The Experience Of The Baltic Military District)*; VM S (3-79) 1966; CIA IISR; 1976/08/25; <https://www.cia.gov/library/readingroom/docs/1976-08-25.pdf>; also CREST RDP10-00105R000302270001-2; 5

532 I Y Shavrov; *The Front Offensive Operation*; GSA 1977/05; CIA IISR FIRDB-312-00013-79; 1979/06/15; CIA MDR EOM-2009-0157; also CIA HCD HR70-14 07-18-2012 DVD VII-222

533 F F Gayvoronsky et al; *Front Offensive Operations*; GSA; 1974; CIA IISR FIRDB-312-01997-79; 1979/09/27; CIA HCD HR70-14 07-18-2012 DVD VII-223

534 *Soviet Plans For Warsaw Pact Theater Commands Opposite NATO*; Intelligence Assessment; SR 79-10033JX; CIA NFAC OSR; 1979/04; TS; CIA HCD HR70-14 07-18-2012 DVD VII-181

535 *Warsaw Pact Forces Opposite NATO*; NIE 11-14-79; 1979/01/31; TS; CIA HCD HR70-14 07-18-2012 DVD VII-4 (V.1) *Summary Estimate*; 50; VII-5 (V.2) *The Estimate*; IV-10

536 *Soviet Concepts For Initial Military Operations Against NATO In Central Europe*; Intelligence Report; SR 77-10002CX; CIA OSR Theater Forces Division; 1977/02; TS; CIA MDR EOM-2011-01084; also CIA HCD HR70-14 07-18-2012 DVD VII-037

537 *Warsaw Pact Command Staff Exercise WEST-77*; CIA IISR TS-778543; 1977/09/21; CIA HCD HR70-14 07-18-2012 DVD VII-044; 4, 6

538 *Central Group of Forces*; 2010; web page no longer accessible; see Internet Archive Wayback Machine <https://web.archive.org/web/20080512094220/http://rk72.jino-net.ru:80/page.php?55>

539 *Warsaw Pact Forces Opposite NATO*; NIE 11-14-75; 1975/09/04; DCI; S; CREST RDP09T00367R000500130001-9; 2011/08/17; 4, table 12

540 *The Readiness Of Soviet Ground Forces*; NI IIM 82-10012; DCI; 1982/11; S; CIA HCD HR70-14 07-18-2012 DVD VII-108; table II-3

541 *Combat And Mobilization Readiness Of Armed Forces Of The USSR And Strategic Agent Intelligence*; 1985; GSA; CIA IISR C01197776; 1989/09/11; 8; CIA MDR EOM-2015-01160

542 *3. Comments On Exercise "Zapad-81"*; CIA FIRDB-312-02950-81; 1981/09/18; <https://www.cia.gov/library/readingroom/docs/1981-09-18.pdf>

543 Rüdiger Wenzke; *Die Streitkräfte der DDR und Polens in der Operationsplanung des Warschauer Paktes*; 2010; Military History Research Office; ISBN 978-3-941571-09-9; 124

544 Vojtech Mastny and Malcolm Byrne ED; *A Cardboard Castle? An Inside History Of The Warsaw Pact 1955-1991*; 2005; Central European University; ISBN 963-7326-08-1; ISBN 963-7326-07.3; document 95 462

545 *Materials Of The Critique Of The Operational-Strategic Command-Staff Exercise Zapad-77*; CIA IISR TS-788301; 1978/10/13; CIA HCD HR70-14 07-18-2012 DVD VII-045; 19

546 Harald Nielsen; *Die DDR Und Die Kernwaffen-Die Nukleare Rolle Der Nationalen Volksarmee Im Warschauer Pakt*; Nuclear History Program 6; 1998; Nomos; ISBN 3-7890-5510-7; 31

547 I Y Shavrov; *The Front Offensive Operation*; GSA 1977/05; CIA IISR FIRDB-312-00013-79; 1979/06/15; CIA MDR EOM-2009-0157; also CIA HCD HR70-14 07-18-2012 DVD VII-222; 347

548 Jerzy Skalski; *Oral History Interviews with Polish Generals*; 2002/09; PHP; <http://www.php.isn.ethz.ch/kms2.isn.ethz.ch/serviceengine/Files/PHP/20636/ipublicationdocument_singledocument/9c4b905d-9c95-41ce-80ff-7182ab66e72a/en/excerpts_english.pdf>; V. *The Elusive Master Plan*

## armageddon on the Rhine

549 *Front Offensive Operations*; 1985; GSA; CIA IISR C01197778; 1990/03/02; 4, 7; CIA MDR EOM-2015-01160

550 I Y Shavrov; *The Front Offensive Operation*; GSA 1977/05; CIA IISR FIRDB-312-00013-79; 1979/06/15; CIA MDR EOM-2009-0157; also CIA HCD HR70-14 07-18-2012 DVD VII-222; 8

551 *USSR General Staff Academy Lessons*; *The Front Offensive Operation*; Lesson 24a; *The Transition of Front Troops to the Conduct of Combat Actions Under Conditions of the Employment of Nuclear Weapons by the Sides;* 1977; GSA; CIA IISR FIRDB-312-00036-81; 1981/01/23; CIA HCD HR70-14 07-18-2012 DVD VII-257; 12

552 GEN-MAJ N I Reut; *Planning The Initial Front Offensive Operation*; VM S (1-89) 1970 CIA IISR CSDB-312-00527-73; 1973/02/01; CIA HCD HR70-14 07-18-2012 DVD VII-019; also RDP10-00105R000100310001-1 2012/05/02; 11

553 GEN-MAJ P Pavlenko and COL V Bulatnikov; *Organization Of Control Of Operational Airborne Landing Forces In The Initial Period Of A War*; VM S (2-63) 1962; CIA IISR; 1976/10/27; <https://www.cia.gov/library/readingroom/docs/CIA-RDP10-00105R000302490001-8.pdf>; also CREST RDP10-00105R000302490001-8

554 *Capabilities Of The Soviet Theater Forces*; NIE 11-14-62; 1962/12/05; S; CIA HCD HR70-14 07-18-2012 DVD V-008a; 19-20

555 *Soviet Strategy And Capabilities For Multitheater War*; NIE 11-19-85-D; 1985/06; S; CIA HCD HR70-14 07-18-2012 DVD VII-064; also CREST RDP09T00367R000300120001-2 2011/03/29; 25

556 GEN-LT A Yakovlev et al; *Methods Of Conducting A Front Offensive Operation Using Means Of Mass Destruction*; VM S (3-70) 1963; CIA IISR; 1978/08/31; <https://www.cia.gov/library/readingroom/docs/1978-08-31bA.pdf>; 7

557 COL N Reshetnikov; *Overcoming Enemy Air Defense Countermeasures By Military-Transport Aviation*; VM S (1-89) 1970; CIA IISR; 1973/07/03; <https://www.cia.gov/library/readingroom/docs/1973-07-06b.pdf>

558 I Y Shavrov; *The Front Offensive Operation*; GSA 1977/05; CIA IISR FIRDB-312-00013-79; 1979/06/15; CIA MDR EOM-2009-0157; also CIA HCD HR70-14 07-18-2012 DVD VII-222; 247 CH-9

559 *USSR General Staff Academy Lessons*; *The Front Offensive Operation*; Supplementary Material for Lesson No. 1; 1977; GSA; CIA IISR FIRDB-312-00106-82; 1982/02/05; CIA HCD HR70-14 07-18-2012 DVD VII-273; 13

560 *Front Offensive Operations*; 1985; GSA; CIA IISR C01197778; 1990/03/02; 4; CIA MDR EOM-2015-01160

561 *Employment Of Warsaw Pact Forces Against NATO: A Four Front Attack*; NI IIM 83-10002; SC 01700-88; 1988/03; TS; 4-5; CIA MDR EOM-2010-00681

562 *Employment Of Warsaw Pact Forces Against NATO*; NI IIM 83-10002; 1983/07; TS; CIA HCD HR70-14 07-18-2012 DVD VII-062

563 *Warning Of War In Europe*; NIE 4-1-84; 1984/06/27; TS; GWU; <https://nsarchive2.gwu.edu//dc.html?doc=5028377-Document-21-Warning-of-War-In-Europe-National>

## alpine rambling

564 Paul Gorman; *Measuring The Military Balance In Central Europe*; CIA Studies In Intelligence 23 (4); Winter 1979; S; TR-SINT 79-004; CREST RDP80-00630A000100090001-0; 2007/01/18; 18, 23

565 *Employment Of Warsaw Pact Forces Against NATO: A Four Front Attack*; NI IIM 83-10002; SC 01700-88; 1988/03; TS; 1988/03; 6; CIA MDR EOM-2010-00681

566 *Plan Of Actions Of The Czechoslovak People's Army For War Period*; 1964/10/14; CWIHP-B (12/13); 289>298

567 *Principles Of The Operational Group Directorate For Execution Of The Staff Exercise Of May And June 1963, 5 June 1963*; PHP; 2001/11; <http://www.php.isn.ethz.ch/kms2.isn.ethz.ch/serviceengine/Files/PHP/19959/ipublicationdocument_singledocument/f3c7f853-3ca3-4924-8a4f-874b89657ec2/en/630605_E_Translation.pdf>

568 COL B Zheleznov; *The Going Over Of Front Troops To The Offensive During The Initial Period Of A War With Only A Partial Concentration Of Forces And Means Under Conditions Of Strong Action Against Them From Enemy Missile/Nuclear Weapons (Based On Materials From A Military Science Conference Of The Southern Group Of Forces)*; VM S (2-63) 1962; CIA IISR; 1977/04/14; <https://www.cia.gov/library/readingroom/docs/1977-04-14-A.pdf>

569 *1965 War Game Exercise*; PHP; document index-links <http://www.php.isn.ethz.ch/lory1.ethz.ch/collections/colltopic13cd.html?lng=en&id=16606&nav1=1&nav2=2&nav3=2>; also Vojtech Mastny and Malcolm Byrne ED *A Cardboard Castle? An Inside History Of The Warsaw Pact 1955-1991*; 2005; Central European University; ISBN 963-7326-08-1; ISBN 963-7326-07-3; document 31

570 *Capabilities Of Soviet General Purpose Forces*; NIE 11-14-65; 1965/10/21; S; CIA HCD HR70-14 07-18-2012 DVD V-020; 9

571 *Employment Of Warsaw Pact Forces Against NATO: A Four Front Attack*; NI IIM 83-10002; SC 01700-88; 1988/03; TS; 8-9; CIA MDR EOM-2010-00681

572 GEN-LT K Arsenyev; *Certain Matters In Preparing And Conducting The Soyuz-77 Combined Operational Command-Staff Exercise*; WPCAF-HQIC S (13) 1977; CIA IISR TS-798048; 1979/03/09; CIA HCD HR70-14 07-18-2012 DVD VII-316

573 GEN-MAJ F Sarychev; *Certain Matters Pertaining To The Organization And Conduct Of Combined Operational Command-Staff Exercises*; WPCAF-HQIC S (14) 1977; CIA IISR TS-798143; 1979/06/21; CIA HCD HR70-14 07-18-2012 DVD VII-321; 5

574 Vojtech Mastny and Malcolm Byrne ED *A Cardboard Castle? An Inside History Of The Warsaw Pact 1955-1991*; 2005; Central European University; ISBN 963-7326-08-1; ISBN 963-7326-07-3; document 79 402

575 *Warsaw Pact Forces Opposite NATO*; NIE 11-14-79; 1979/01/31; TS; CIA HCD HR70-14 07-18-2012 DVD VII-4 (V.1) *Summary Estimate*; 65 map; VII-5 (V.2) *The Estimate*

576 Laszlo Becz et al; *OKSNAR - Fully Assembled State—Soviet Nuclear Weapons In Hungary 1961-1991*; Veszprém; 2019; 204-205; exercise designation given as Ocean but other information nominates *Eroed* (Fortress)

577 COL L Shapovalov; *Reconnaissance In A Combined Arms Army During Its Commitment Into An Engagement From The March (Based On Training Exercises)*; VM S (1-89) 1970; CIA IISR; 1974/02/07; <https://www.cia.gov/library/readingroom/docs//1974-02-07.pdf>

578 GEN-MAJ Tibor Toth; *Characteristics Of Organizing And Conducting An Offensive Operation Of The Coalition Front And Combined Arms Army*; Honvedelem (6) 1980; S; CIA IIR C05798348; 1985/09/06; CIA MDR EOM-2011-0881

579 *Central Group of Forces*; 2010; web page no longer accessible; see Internet Archive Wayback Machine <https://web.archive.org/web/20080512094220/http://rk72.jino-net.ru:80/page.php?55>

## nonnuclear variant

580 *Soviet Concepts Of War In Europe: Transition From Conventional To Nuclear Conflict*; Intelligence Memorandum; SR IM 71-9; CIA DI OSR; 1971/05; TS; CIA HCD HR70-14 07-18-2012 VII-11; 5

581 *Polish Defense Ministry Document Concerning Experiences And Conclusions From The "Narew" Maneuvers*; CIA IISR [TS-]195344; 1967/01/20; CIA HCD HR70-14 07-18-2012 DVD VI-014

582 Petr Lunák; *Planning for Nuclear War: The Czechoslovak War Plan of 1964*; CWIHP-B (12/13); 291

583 F F Gayvoronsky et al; *Front Offensive Operations*; GSA; 1974; CIA IISR FIRDB-312-01997-79; 1979/09/27; CIA HCD HR70-14 07-18-2012 DVD VII-223; 30

584 *Front Offensive Operations*; 1985; GSA; CIA IISR C01197778; 1990/03/02; 8; CIA MDR EOM-2015-01160

585 GEN Bernard W Rogers; *Follow-On Forces Attack (FOFA): Myths And Realities*; NATO Review 32 (6); 1984/12; <https://www.cia.gov/library/readingroom/docs/CIA-RDP85M00364R000801310018-3.pdf>

586 GEN-LT (Retired) Ye I Malashenko; *Movement To Contact And Commitment To Combat Of Reserve Fronts (Great Patriotic War Experience And Modern Times)*; VM U 13 (2) 2004; East View Publications; 185

587 Vojtech Mastny and Malcolm Byrne ED *A Cardboard Castle? An Inside History Of The Warsaw Pact 1955-1991*; 2005; Central European University; ISBN 963-7326-08-1; ISBN 963-7326-07-3; document 81, 407

588 John G Hines et al; *Soviet Intentions 1965-1985* V.I *An Analytical Comparison Of U.S.-Soviet Assessments During The Cold War*; Contract MDA903-92-C-0147 OSD-Net Assessment; BDM Federal; 1995/09/22; 48; GWU <https://nsarchive2.gwu.edu/nukevault/ebb285/index.htm>; section links; 9, 45-46

589 *Soviet Operational Art*; 1985; GSA; CIA IISR TS-888644; 1988/07/29; 16; ISCAP 2012-026 (CIA MDR EOM-2009-00158)

590 *Front Offensive Operations*; 1985; GSA; CIA IISR C01197778; 1990/03/02; 11-12; CIA MDR EOM-2015-01160

**strategic defense variant**
591 V M Chebrikov; *About Deficiencies In The Staff Of The Military Units Participating In The Chernobyl Nuclear Disaster Elimination*; 1986; USSR Committee for State Security; CWIHP-DA; <http://digitalarchive.wilsoncenter.org/document/121649>
592 *Communique On Conference Of Warsaw Pact States' Political Consultative Committee*; Pravda 1987/05/30; JPRS TAC-87-045 Arms Control; 21
593 Vojtech Mastny and Malcolm Byrne ED *A Cardboard Castle? An Inside History Of The Warsaw Pact 1955-1991*; 2005; Central European University; ISBN 963-7326-08-1; ISBN 963-7326-07-3; document 124, 572
594 MSU M V Zakharov; *Certain Questions Of Soviet Military Art*; VM S (1-68) 1963; CIA IISR 1977/04/15; <https://www.cia.gov/library/readingroom/docs/1977-04-15b.pdf>; 29
595 COL I Rachok; *Defensive Operations Of Ground Forces In A Strategic Operation In A Theater Of Military Operations*; VM S (2-84) 1968; CIA IISR; 1976/10/27; <https://www.cia.gov/library/readingroom/docs/1976-10-27a.pdf>; also CREST RDP10-00105R000302500001-6
596 COL I Lyutov; *Defense Of Troops Without The Use Of Nuclear Weapons*; VM S (3-91) 1970; CIA IISR; 1974/01/22; <https://www.cia.gov/library/readingroom/docs//1974-01-22a.pdf>
597 *Military Planning Of The Warsaw Pact In Central Europe: A Study*; CWIHP-B (2) Fall 1992; translation German Defense Ministry publication; 15
598 Siegfried Lautsch; in Rüdiger Wenzke *Die Streitkräfte der DDR und Polens in der Operationsplanung des Warschauer Paktes*; 2010; Military History Research Office; ISBN 978-3-941571-09-9; 49
599 Rüdiger Wenzke; *Die Streitkräfte der DDR und Polens in der Operationsplanung des Warschauer Paktes*; 2010; Military History Research Office; ISBN 978-3-941571-09-9; 105
600 Karel Sieber and Vojtech Mastny; *Oral History Interviews With Czechoslovak Generals*; 2005/01; PHP; <http://www.php.isn.ethz.ch/lory1.ethz.ch/collections/colltopic7e37.html?lng=en&id=20415&navinfo=15706>; 40
601 *Principles Of Preparation And Conduct Of A Front Defensive Operation*; 1985; GSA; CIA IISR TS-888548; 1988/06/30; 6; ISCAP 2012-026 (CIA MDR EOM-2009-00158)
602 *Military Exercise Shchit-88 Operational Summary No. 1 For The Period 0800 25 May To 0800 2 June 1988*; CWIHP-DA; <https://digitalarchive.wilsoncenter.org/document/114267>; 2
603 GEN-MAJ V Manilov and GEN-MAJ V Kuklev; *The Legend Of The Vanishing Tanks*; Sovetskaya Rossiya 1991/01/05; JPRS TAC-91-003 (30 January 1991) Arms Control; 30
604 *Statement Of The Director, Office Of Soviet Analysis To The Chairman Of The House Armed Services Committee*; 1988/09/08; <https://www.cia.gov/library/readingroom/docs//1988-09-08.pdf>
605 *The Nature Of Soviet Military Doctrine*; Research Paper; CIA DI; SOV 89-10037CX; 1989/04; TS; <https://www.cia.gov/library/readingroom/docs/DOC_0000499601.pdf>; 20
606 *The Readiness Of Soviet General Purpose Forces Through The 1990s*; NIC M 90-10009; 1990/06; S; <https://www.cia.gov/library/readingroom/docs/DOC_0000265645.pdf>
607 Christopher Donnelly; *Red Banner: The Soviet Military System In Peace And War*; 1988; Jane's Information Group; ISBN 0-7106-0488-2; 112
608 Graham H Turbiville Jr. et al; *Soviet Military Doctrine From Lenin To Gorbachev, 1915-1991*; 1992; Greenwood; ISBN 0-313-27713-3; 277

# Nuclear Interlude

609 John G Hines et al; *Soviet Intentions 1965-1985* V.I *An Analytical Comparison Of U.S.-Soviet Assessments During The Cold War*; Contract MDA903-92-C-0147 OSD-Net Assessment; BDM Federal; 1995/09/22; 48; GWU <https://nsarchive2.gwu.edu/nukevault/ebb285/index.htm>; section links; 26, 43-44
610 GEN-MAJ (Engineering-Technical Service) M Goryainov; *Nuclear-Missile Armament And Some Principles Of Military Doctrine*; VM TS (Second) 1960; CIA C00012302; 1961/12/27; <https://www.cia.gov/library/readingroom/docs/1961-12-27.pdf>; also CIA HCD HR70-14 07-18-2012 DVD III-020; 14
611 GEN-MAJ (Artillery) I Dzhordzhadze; *Classical Military Art And Nuclear-Missile Warfare*; VM TS (Fourth) 1961; CIA Ironbark; 1962/05/16; <https://www.cia.gov/library/readingroom/docs/1962-01-22.pdf> attached second article; also CIA HCD HR70-14 07-18-2012 DVD YEAR 1962 second article; 14
612 John G Hines et al; *Soviet Intentions 1965-1985* V.II *Soviet Post-Cold War Testimonial Evidence*; Contract MDA903-92-C-0147 OSD-Net Assessment; BDM Federal; 1995/09/22; 48; GWU <https://nsarchive2.gwu.edu/nukevault/ebb285/index.htm> section links; 7>10
613 Raymond L Garthoff; *Deterrence And The Revolution In Soviet Military Doctrine*; 1990; Brookings Institution; ISBN 0-8157-3056-X; ISBN 0-8157-3055-1; 83-84

614 John G Hines et al; *Soviet Intentions 1965-1985* V.II *Soviet Post-Cold War Testimonial Evidence*; Contract MDA903-92-C-0147 OSD-Net Assessment; BDM Federal; 1995/09/22; 48; GWU <https://nsarchive2.gwu.edu/nukevault/ebb285/index.htm> section links; 136>157 V N Tsygichko

615 COL-LT Ye I Rybkin; *On The Nature Of World Nuclear Rocket War*; *Kommunist Vooruzhennykh Sil* 1965/09; in William Kintner; *The Nuclear Revolution In Soviet Military Affairs*; 1968; University of Oklahoma; 113

616 GEN-MAJ K Bochkarev; *The Question Of The Sociological Aspect Of The Struggle Against The Forces Of Aggression And War*; VM R (9) 1968/09; FPD 0115-69 (16 December 1979)

617 John G Hines et al; *Soviet Intentions 1965-1985* V.II *Soviet Post-Cold War Testimonial Evidence*; Contract MDA903-92-C-0147 OSD-Net Assessment; BDM Federal; 1995/09/22; 48; GWU <https://nsarchive2.gwu.edu/nukevault/ebb285/index.htm> section links; 23 GEN-COL A A Danilevich

618 GEN-MAJ S N Kozlov ED; *The Officer's Handbook*; Moscow 1971; USAF Soviet Military Thought #13; 63

619 P I Ivashutin; *Strategic Operations Of The Nuclear Forces*; 1964/08/28; GS GRU; <http://www.jrnyquist.com/may14/ussr_war_plan.htm>; Defense section

620 *Military Planning Of The Warsaw Pact In Central Europe: A Study*; CWIHP-B (2) Fall 1992; translation German Defense Ministry publication; 15

621 *Manual On The Conduct Of Operations—Part Two—Ground Forces Operations (Front-Army-Corps)*; 1963; GS; CIA IISR TS-778264; 1977/09/29; CIA HCD HR70-14 07-18-2012 DVD VII-99; 58-59

622 GEN-MAJ A S Skovoroda; *Organization Of Rear Services Support Of Troops Of An Army And A Front In An Offensive Operation*; 1969/02; GS; CIA IISR FIRDB-312-00635-77; 1977/03/04; CIA HCD HR70-14 07-18-2012 DVD VII-214

623 F F Gayvoronsky et al; *Front Offensive Operations*; GSA; 1974; CIA IISR FIRDB-312-01997-79; 1979/09/27; CIA HCD HR70-14 07-18-2012 DVD VII-223; 370

624 I Y Shavrov *The Front Offensive Operation*; GSA 1977/05; CIA IISR FIRDB-312-00013-79 1979/06/15; CIA MDR EOM-2009-0157; also CIA HCD HR70-14 07-18-2012 DVD VII-222; 319

625 *Materials Of The Critique Of The Operational-Strategic Command-Staff Exercise Zapad-77*; CIA IISR TS-788301; 1978/10/13; CIA HCD HR70-14 07-18-2012 DVD VII-045; 37

**sharing the load**

626 I Y Shavrov *The Front Offensive Operation*; GSA 1977/05; CIA IISR FIRDB-312-00013-79 1979/06/15; CIA MDR EOM-2009-0157; also CIA HCD HR70-14 07-18-2012 DVD VII-222; 9

627 *Front Offensive Operations*; 1985; GSA; CIA IISR C01197778; 1990/03/02; 17; CIA MDR EOM-2015-01160

628 *Soviet Planning For Front Nuclear Operations In Central Europe*; Intelligence Assessment; SOV 83-10099JX; CIA DI SOVA; 1983/06; TS; CIA HCD HR70-14 07-18-2012 VII-61; 3

629 GEN-MAJ (Artillery) A P Suntsovyy and GEN-MAJ (Artillery) A K Gorlinskiy; *The Combat Employment Of Rocket Troops And Artillery In An Offensive Operation Of A Front And Army*; 1969/02; GSA; CIA IISR FIRDB-312-03096-76; 1976/12/22; CIA HCD HR70-14 07-18-2012 DVD VII-213; 5

630 GEN-COL I S Glebov; *Principles Of A Modern Offensive Operation Of A Front*; 1970; CIA IIR CSDB-312-02313-70; 1970/10/01; CIA HCD HR70-14 07-18-2012 DVD VII-006; 11

631 GEN-COL I Glebov; *Certain Problems Of Planning And Conducting Offensive Operations Of Fronts (Based On The Experience Of Research War Games)*; VM S (3-82) 1967; CIA IISR FIRDB-312-02966-74; 1974/08/20; CIA HCD HR70-14 07-18-2012 DVD VII-030; also CREST RDP10-00105R000100820001-5; 2012/09/28

632 *The Strategic Operation In A Theater Of War*; CIA IIR CSDB-312-01433-70; 1970/11/06; <https://www.cia.gov/library/readingroom/docs/DOC_0001199065.pdf>; 25, 42

633 *Material on Exercise "Shield-76"*; 1976/09; CIA IISR TS-768153; 1976/12/23; CIA HCD HR70-14 07-18-2012 DVD VII-296; 46

634 *USSR General Staff Academy Lessons*; *The Front Offensive Operation*; Lesson 7a; *Preparation and Critique of the Plan of the Combat Employment of the Rocket Troops and Artillery in a Front Offensive Operation*; 1977; GSA; CIA IISR FIRDB-312-01110-80; 1980/06/06; CIA HCD HR70-14 07-18-2012 DVD VII-229; 7

635 GEN-COL Ye Ivanov; *A Turning Point In The Development Of Soviet Military Art*; VM TS (Second) 1961; CIA; <https://www.cia.gov/library/readingroom/docs/1961-01-01.pdf>; also CIA HCD HR70-14 07-18-2012 DVD YEAR 1961

636 GEN-COL A Kh Babadzhanyan; *Some Questions In The Preparation And Conduct Of Initial Offensive Operations*; VM TS (Third) 1961; CIA; 1962/03/23; <https://www.cia.gov/library/readingroom/docs/1962-03-23.pdf>; 10

637 *The Balance Of Nuclear Forces In Central Europe*; Intelligence Assessment; SR 78-10004; CIA NFAC OSR; 1978/01; S; CIA HCD HR70-14 07-18-2012 DVD VII-051; ii

638 *Reconnaissance In Support Of Strategic Operations*; 1985; GSA; CIA IISR C01197777; 1989/09/15; 21; CIA MDR EOM-2015-01160

## selecting the victims

639 *Reconnaissance In Support Of Strategic Operations*; 1985; GSA; CIA IISR C01197777; 1989/09/15; 11; CIA MDR EOM-2015-01160

640 I Y Shavrov; *The Front Offensive Operation*; GSA 1977/05; CIA IISR FIRDB-312-00013-79; 1979/06/15; CIA MDR EOM-2009-0157; also CIA HCD HR70-14 07-18-2012 DVD VII-222; 74

641 GEN-COL P Koshevoy; *Utilization Of The Missile Troops Of A Front (Army) In An Offensive Operation*; VM TS (Third) 1961; CIA C00012337; 1962/03/22; <https://www.cia.gov/library/readingroom/docs/1962-03-22.pdf>; 4-5

642 *Polish Critique Of The Warsaw Pact "Lato-67" Command Post Exercise*; CIA IISR CSDB-312-01470-68; CIA HCD HR70-14 07-18-2012 DVD VI-034; 17

643 MSU I Yakubovskiy and GEN-ARM S Shtemenko; *Material Of The Critique Of The Operational War Game On Maps Conducted On The Southwestern Axis*; HQ WPCAF Moscow; 1970/07; CIA IIR TS-205587; 1975/06/13; CIA HCD HR70-14 07-18-2012 DVD VII-031; 39, 88-89

644 Brigadier GEN Jerzy Skalski; *Employment Of Rocket Troops And Artillery*; 1970; CIA IISR FIRDB-312-00112-84; 1984/01/19; <https://www.cia.gov/library/readingroom/docs/1984-01-19A.pdf>; 6

645 *Material on Exercise "Shield-76"*; CIA IISR TS-768153; 1976/12/23; CIA HCD HR70-14 07-18-2012 DVD VII-296; 67

646 GEN-MAJ P Altukhov; *Operational Calculations For The Use Of Nuclear Weapons*; VM S (1-77) 1966; CIA IISR; 1978/01/19; <https://www.cia.gov/library/readingroom/docs/1978-01-19b.pdf>; 5

647 F F Gayvoronsky et al; *Front Offensive Operations*; GSA; 1974; CIA IISR FIRDB-312-01997-79; 1979/09/27; CIA HCD HR70-14 07-18-2012 DVD VII-223; 46

648 I Y Shavrov; *The Front Offensive Operation*; GSA 1977/05; CIA IISR FIRDB-312-00013-79; 1979/06/15; CIA MDR EOM-2009-0157; also CIA HCD HR70-14 07-18-2012 DVD VII-222; 51

649 *Troop Control In Front Offensive Operations*; 1985; GSA; CIA IISR TS-888527; 1988/06/24; 4; ISCAP 2012-026 (CIA MDR EOM-2009-00158)

650 *Reconnaissance On Behalf Of A Front Offensive Operation*; 1985; GSA; CIA IISR TS-888284; 1988/03/25; 8>11; ISCAP 2012-026 (CIA MDR EOM-2009-00158)

651 *Reconnaissance In Support Of Strategic Operations*; 1985; GSA; CIA IISR C01197777; 1989/09/15; 10-11; CIA MDR EOM-2015-01160

652 *Agent Reconnaissance In Front Offensive Operations*; 1985; GSA; CIA IISR TS-888283 C01197689; 1988/03/25; 5; ISCAP 2012-026 (CIA MDR EOM-2009-00158)

653 *USSR General Staff Academy Lessons*; *The Front Offensive Operation*; 1977; GSA; ; CIA HCD HR70-14 07-18-2012
Lesson 9; *Preparation and Critique of the Plan for Reconnaissance in the Front Offensive Operation*; CIA IISR FIRDB-312-01830-80; 1980/07/18; DVD VII-234; 8-9
Lesson 19; *Preparation and Critique of the Plan for the Front Offensive Operation*; CIA IISR FIRDB-312-01599-80; 1980/07/03; DVD VII-233; 12, target table 21>24

654 *Soviet Planning For Front Nuclear Operations In Central Europe*; Intelligence Assessment; SOV 83-10099JX; CIA DI SOVA; 1983/06; TS; CIA HCD HR70-14 07-18-2012 VII-61; 3, 10

655 *Warsaw Pact Tactical Forces: Capabilities And Readiness For Nuclear War*; Research Paper; SOV 85-10107CX; CIA DI SOVA; 1985/06; CIA HCD HR70-14 07-18-2012 DVD VII-119; 3>5

656 Dennis M Gormley; *Emerging Attack Options in Soviet Theater Strategy*; in *Swords And Shields: NATO, The USSR, And New Choices For Long-Range Offense And Defense*; 1987; Lexington MA; D.C. Heath; ISBN 0-669-14249-2; 106-107

657 *Warsaw Pact Nonnuclear Threat To NATO Airbases In Central Europe*; NIE 11-20-6-84; 1984/10/25; TS; CIA HCD HR70-14 07-18-2012 DVD VII-157; 9, 19

658 *Soviet Short-Range Ballistic Missiles And The Impact Of A Ban On Long-Range INF Missiles*; NI IIA 87-10006JX; DCI; 1987/03; TS; <https://www.cia.gov/library/readingroom/docs/DOC_0000802743.pdf>; 16

659 I Y Shavrov; *The Front Offensive Operation*; GSA 1977/05; CIA IISR FIRDB-312-00013-79; 1979/06/15; CIA MDR EOM-2009-0157; also CIA HCD HR70-14 07-18-2012 DVD VII-222; 51-52

660 F F Gayvoronsky et al; *Front Offensive Operations*; GSA; 1974; CIA IISR FIRDB-312-01997-79; 1979/09/27; CIA HCD HR70-14 07-18-2012 DVD VII-223; 46

661 *Rocket Troops And Artillery In A Front Offensive Operation*; 1985; GSA; CIA IISR TS 888443; 1988/05/24; 11; ISCAP 2012-026 (CIA MDR EOM-2009-00158)

662 *Military Planning Of The Warsaw Pact In Central Europe: A Study*; CWIHP-B (2) Fall 1992; translation German Defense Ministry publication; 15

663 COL V Turchenko and COL (Engineer) N Bazanov; *The Tabular Method Of Making Operational-Tactical Calculations For Estimating The Effectiveness Of Nuclear Strikes*; VM S 3 (88) 1969; CIA IISR FIRDB-312-01292-74; 1974/04/08; CREST RDP10-00105R000100360001-6 2012/04/18; 7-8

664 GEN-LT L S Sapkov; *Improving The Control Of Front Rocket Troop In The Transition From Non-Nuclear Actions To the Use Of Nuclear Weapons*; VM S (2-90) 1970; CIA IISR; 1974/03/05; <https://www.cia.gov/library/readingroom/docs/1974-03-05.pdf>; 7

665 GEN-ARM P I Ivashutin; *Principles Of The Organization And Conduct Of Operational Reconnaissance In A Front Offensive Operation*; 1974; GS GRU; CIA IISR FIRDB-312-00311-78; 1978/05/19; CIA HCD HR70-14 07-18-2012 DVD VII-101; 79

666 *Agent Reconnaissance In Front Offensive Operations; 1985*; GSA; CIA IISR TS-888283; 1988/03/25; 10; ISCAP 2012-026 (CIA MDR EOM-2009-00158)

667 GEN-MAJ G Semenov; *Ways Of Further Increasing The Combat Readiness Of Troops*; VM TS (First) 1961; CIA C00114450; 1962/01/08; <https://www.cia.gov/library/readingroom/docs/1962-01-08.pdf>; also CIA HCD HR70-14 07-18-2012 DVD YEAR 1961; 4

668 *1965 War Game Exercise*; PHP; document index-links <http://www.php.isn.ethz.ch/lory1.ethz.ch/collections/colltopic13cd.html?lng=en&id=16606&nav1=1&nav2=2&nav3=2>; *Plan of the "Easterners" First Massive Nuclear Strike*; <http://www.php.isn.ethz.ch/lory1.ethz.ch/collections/colltopic5b8f.html?lng=en&id=19632&navinfo=16606>; also Vojtech Mastny and Malcolm Byrne ED *A Cardboard Castle? An Inside History Of The Warsaw Pact 1955-1991*; 2005; Central European University; ISBN 963-7326-08-1; ISBN 963-7326-07-3; document 31

669 *Operational Directive No. 2 Of The Maritime Front*; 1967/05/31; PHP; <http://www.php.isn.ethz.ch/lory1.ethz.ch/collections/colltopic374b.html?lng=en&id=20318&navinfo=16446>

670 MSU I Yakubovskiy and GEN-ARM S Shtemenko; *Material Of The Critique Of The Operational War Game On Maps Conducted On The Southwestern Axis*; HQ WPCAF Moscow; 1970/07; CIA IIR TS-205587; 1975/06/13; CIA HCD HR70-14 07-18-2012 DVD VII-031; 24, 53

671 COL L Vinnitskiy et al; *Combat Actions Of Troops Under Special Conditions*; VM S (6-67) 1962; CIA IISR; 1978/12/15; <https://www.cia.gov/library/readingroom/docs/1978-12-15a.pdf>; 14

672 GEN-LT L S Sapkov; *Improving The Control Of Front Rocket Troop In The Transition From Non-Nuclear Actions To the Use Of Nuclear Weapons*; VM S (2-90) 1970; CIA IISR; 1974/03/05; <https://www.cia.gov/library/readingroom/docs/1974-03-05.pdf>; 6

673 F F Gayvoronsky et al; *Front Offensive Operations*; GSA; 1974; CIA IISR FIRDB-312-01997-79; 1979/09/27; CIA HCD HR70-14 07-18-2012 DVD VII-223; 211

674 John G Hines et al; *Soviet Intentions 1965-1985* V.II *Soviet Post-Cold War Testimonial Evidence*; Contract MDA903-92-C-0147 OSD-Net Assessment; BDM Federal; 1995/09/22; 48; GWU; <https://nsarchive2.gwu.edu/nukevault/ebb285/index.htm> section links; 60 GEN-COL A A Danilevich

675 GEN-MAJ (Artillery Professor) A Matveyev and MAJ (Engineer) Yu Orlov; *The Destruction Of Enemy Groupings With Nuclear Warheads Using Surface Bursts*; VM S 1(89) 1970; CIA IISR; 1974/04/04; CREST RDP10-00105R000100350001-7 2012/04/19

676 COL A Drozhzhin; *Negotiation Of Enemy Air Defense Opposition By Aviation*; VM S 2(81) 1967; CIA IISR TS-788299; 1978/11/30; 5; CIA MDR EOM-2015-00545

677 *Operational Mission—Situation As Of 1700 Hours 4 April*; CIA IISR TS-788328; 1978/11/17; CIA HCD HR70-14 07-18-2012 DVD VII-103; AP-7 Table-3

678 *Rocket Troops And Artillery In A Front Offensive Operation*; GSA; 1985; CIA IISR TS-888443; 1988/05/24; 4; ISCAP 2012-026 (CIA MDR EOM-2009-00158)

679 *Warning Of War In Europe*; NIE 4-1-84; 1984/06/27; TS; GWU; <https://nsarchive2.gwu.edu//dc.html?doc=5028377-Document-21-Warning-of-War-In-Europe-National>; 24

680 COL (Engineer) A Ambartsumyan; *Fortification In Modern Warfare*; VM S 1(80) 1967; CIA IISR C05826983; 1975/07/09; CREST RDP10-00105R000201130001-9 2012/10/16; 13

681 GEN-MAJ (Artillery) L Sapkov and COL I Zakharov; *Reconnaissance Data Requirements In Support Of Rocket Troops And Artillery*; VM S (1-77) 1966; CIA IISR; 1978/05/16; <https://www.cia.gov/library/readingroom/docs/1978-05-16.pdf>

682 COL A Sulim; *Operational-Tactical And Tactical Rocket Requirements For A Front Offensive Operation*; VM S (1-83) 1968; CIA IISR; 1974/06/13; <https://www.cia.gov/library/readingroom/docs/1974-06-13.pdf>; 6

683 COL Yu Gordon and COL B Druganov; *Reconnaissance And Final Reconnaissance Of Objectives For The Initial Strike By Front Rocket Troops*; VM S (3-91) 1970; CIA IISR; 1974/06/19; <https://www.cia.gov/library/readingroom/docs/1974-06-19.pdf>; 7

684 *Warsaw Pact Tactical Forces: Capabilities And Readiness For Nuclear War*; Research Paper; SOV 85-10107CX; CIA DI SOVA; 1985/06; TS; CIA HCD HR70-14 07-18-2012 DVD VII-119; 3

685 COL Ervin Polgar; *Some Thoughts On Reconnaissance*; Honvedelem S (1) 1984; CIA IIR C05798403; 1988/[05]/31; 4; CIA MDR EOM-2011-0881

686 *Reconnaissance In Support Of Strategic Operations*; 1985; GSA; CIA IISR C01197777; 1989/09/15; 24; CIA MDR EOM-2015-01160

687 *Agent Reconnaissance In Front Offensive Operations; 1985*; GSA; CIA IISR TS-888283; 1988/03/25; 7; ISCAP 2012-026 (CIA MDR EOM-2009-00158)

688 *A Warsaw Pact Approach To War In Europe*; 1970; CIA IIR CSDB-312-01857-70; 1970/07/22; 3

689 GEN-MAJ (Artillery) F Narkhodzhayev and COL V Daragan; *Methodology Of Training For Combat Against Nuclear Attack Means*; VM S (1-68) 1963; CIA IISR; 1977/07/11; <https://www.cia.gov/library/readingroom/docs/1977-07-11.pdf>; 7

690 COL-LT (Engineer) V Shmakov et al; *Hydrometeorological Support Of Troops*; VM S (1-77) 1966; CIA IISR; 1978/08/30; <https://www.cia.gov/library/readingroom/docs/1978-08-30a.pdf>; 9

691 GEN-ARM P I Ivashutin; *Principles Of The Organization And Conduct Of Operational Reconnaissance In A Front Offensive Operation*; 1974; GS GRU; CIA IISR FIRDB-312-00311-78; 1978/05/19; CIA HCD HR70-14 07-18-2012 DVD VII-101; 118

692 COL Yu Gordon and COL B Druganov; *Reconnaissance And Final Reconnaissance Of Objectives For The Initial Strike By Front Rocket Troops*; VM S (3-91) 1970; CIA IISR; 1974/06/19; <https://www.cia.gov/library/readingroom/docs/1974-06-19.pdf>; 6

693 *Reconnaissance In Support Of Strategic Operations*; 1985; GSA; CIA IISR C01197777; 1989/09/15; 13, 17; CIA MDR EOM-2015-01160

694 Kaylene Hughes; *The Army's Precision "Sunday Punch": The Pershing II And The Intermediate-Range Nuclear Forces Treaty*; Army History 73; Fall 2009; ISSN 1546-5330; <http://www.history.army.mil/armyhistory/AH73%28W%29.pdf>; 9

695 *Mutual And Balanced Force Reductions Between NATO And The Warsaw Pact*; National Security Council; 1970/08/26; S; CIA HCD HR70-14 07-18-2012 DVD VII-003; 19

## divvying out the goods

696 GEN-COL V Chizh; *Planning The Utilization Of Nuclear-Missile Weapons In A Front Offensive Operation*; VM TS (Third) 1961; CIA C00012342; 1962/04/04; <https://www.cia.gov/library/readingroom/docs/1962-04-04b.pdf>; 9

697 MSU I Yakubovskiy and GEN-ARM S Shtemenko; *Material Of The Critique Of The Operational War Game On Maps Conducted On The Southwestern Axis*; HQ WPCAF Moscow; 1970/07; CIA IIR TS-205587; 1975/06/13; CIA HCD HR70-14 07-18-2012 DVD VII-031

698 *Materials Of The Critique Of The Operational-Strategic Command-Staff Exercise Zapad-77*; CIA IISR TS-788301; 1978/10/13; CIA HCD HR70-14 07-18-2012 DVD VII-045; 36

699 *Warsaw Pact Air Forces: Support Of Strategic Operations In Central Europe*; Intelligence Assessment; CIA DI SOVA; SOV 85-10001CX; 1985/01; TS; CIA HCD HR70-14 07-18-2012 DVD VII-159; 43 Table 5

700 GEN-LT K Kolganov et al; *Certain Questions Of The Development Of Soviet Military Art From 1953-1960*; VM S (1-77) 1966; CIA IISR; 1977/04/11; <https://www.cia.gov/library/readingroom/docs/1977-04-11c.pdf>; 12-13

701 GEN-COL A Kh Babadzhanyan; *Some Questions In The Preparation And Conduct Of Initial Offensive Operations*; VM TS (Third) 1961; CIA; 1962/03/23; <https://www.cia.gov/library/readingroom/docs/1962-03-23.pdf>; 2

702 GEN-COL (Artillery) N Fomin; *The Role And Control Of Missile Units In The Ground Forces*; VM S (4-65) 1962; CIA IISR; 1976/11/22; <https://www.cia.gov/library/readingroom/docs/1976-11-22.pdf>; also CREST RDP10-00105R000302570001-9; 17

703 COL A Bulatov; *Some Questions Of The First Front Offensive Operation In The Initial Period Of A War (Based On Materials Of A Military Science Conference Of The Carpathian Military District)*; VM S (2-63) 1962; CIA IISR; 1977/03/11; <https://www.cia.gov/library/readingroom/docs/1977-03-11b.pdf>; 5

704 GEN-COL I Glebov and GEN-MAJ V Yemelin; *Offensive Operations Of A Front To The Entire Depth Of A Theater Of Military Operations*; VM S (2-72) 1964; CIA IISR; 1975/11/14; <https://www.cia.gov/library/readingroom/docs/1975-11-14b.pdf>; also CREST RDP10-00105R000201480001-1 2012/10/16; 16

705 *A Warsaw Pact Approach To War In Europe*; 1970; CIA IIR CSDB-312-01857-70; 1970/07/22; 2

706 *Soviet Operational Art*; 1985; GSA; CIA IISR TS-888644; 1988/07/29; 15; ISCAP 2012-026 (CIA MDR EOM-2009-00158)

707 *The Offensive Operation Of A Combined-Arms Army*; 1973; Academy of Armored Troops; CIA IISR FIRDB-312-03389-77; 1977/12/12; CIA HCD HR70-14 07-18-2012 DVD VII-219; 9

708 *USSR General Staff Academy Lessons*; *The Front Offensive Operation*; Lesson 1a; *The Making and Critique of the Decision of the Front Commander for an Offensive Operation—Report of the Chief of the Front Rocket Troops and Artillery*; 1977; GSA; CIA IISR FIRDB-312-02605-80; 1980/10/24; CIA HCD HR70-14 07-18-2012 DVD VII-247; 37-38

709 F F Gayvoronsky et al; *Front Offensive Operations*; GSA; 1974; CIA IISR FIRDB-312-01997-79; 1979/09/27; CIA HCD HR70-14 07-18-2012 DVD VII-223; 134

710 GEN-MAJ (Aviation) S Shimanskiy and GEN-MAJ (Aviation) V Povarkov; *Actions Of Front Aviation In The First Front Offensive Operation In The Initial Period Of War*; VM S (2-63) 1962; CIA IISR FIRDB-312-03836-74; 1976/10/27; <https://www.cia.gov/library/readingroom/docs/1976-10-27b.pdf>; also CREST RDP10-00105R000302480001-9 2012/10/03

711 *The Strategic Operation In A Theater Of War*; CIA IIR CSDB-312-01433-70; 1970/11/06; <https://www.cia.gov/library/readingroom/docs/DOC_0001199065.pdf>; 42

712 I Y Shavrov; *The Front Offensive Operation*; GSA 1977/05; CIA IISR FIRDB-312-00013-79 1979/06/15; CIA MDR EOM-2009-0157; also CIA HCD HR70-14 07-18-2012 DVD VII-222; 12

713 *USSR General Staff Academy Lessons*; *The Front Offensive Operation*; Supplementary Material for Lesson No. 1—Report of the Chief of the Operations Directorate of the Coastal Front (variant); 1977; GSA; CIA IISR FIRDB-312-00106-82; 1982/02/05; CIA HCD HR70-14 07-18-2012 DVD VII-273; 4

714 *Warsaw Pact Air Forces: Support Of Strategic Operations In Central Europe*; Intelligence Assessment; CIA DI SOVA; SOV 85-10001CX; 1985/01; TS; CIA HCD HR70-14 07-18-2012 DVD VII-159; 43 Table 5

715 GEN-COL I S Glebov; *The Preparation And Conduct Of Front And Army Offensive Operations*; 1969/03; GSA lecture; CIA FIRDB-312-01545-78; 1978/07/28; CIA HCD HR70-14 07-18-2012 DVD VII-221; 26

716 *Military Planning Of The Warsaw Pact In Central Europe: A Study*; CWIHP-B (2) Fall 1992; translation German Defense Ministry publication; 15
717 *The Balance Of Nuclear Forces In Central Europe*; Intelligence Assessment; SR 78-10004; CIA NFAC OSR; 1978/01; S; CIA HCD HR70-14 07-18-2012 DVD VII-051; 7 Table 2
718 Matthew G McKinzie et al *The U.S. Nuclear War Plan: A Time For Change*; 2001/06; Natural Resources Defense Council; <http://www.nrdc.org/nuclear/warplan/index.asp>; 126 Table 5.7
719 GEN-LT K Kolganov et al; *Certain Questions Of The Development Of Soviet Military Art From 1953-1960*; VM S (1-77) 1966; <https://www.cia.gov/library/readingroom/docs/1977-04-11c.pdf>; 5
720 F F Gayvoronsky et al; *Front Offensive Operations*; GSA; 1974; CIA IISR FIRDB-312-01997-79; 1979/09/27; CIA HCD HR70-14 07-18-2012 DVD VII-223; 37
721 *Russia's Arms And Technologies: Nuclear Weapons Complex: The XXI Century Encyclopedia;* 2007; Arms and Technologies; ISBN 978-5-93799-035-8; XIV; 123
722 I Y Shavrov *The Front Offensive Operation*; GSA 1977/05; CIA IISR FIRDB-312-00013-79; 1979/06/15; CIA MDR EOM-2009-0157; also CIA HCD HR70-14 07-18-2012 DVD VII-222
723 *Warsaw Pact Forces Opposite NATO*; NIE 11-14-79; 1979/01/31; TS; CIA HCD HR70-14 07-18-2012 DVD VII-4; V.1 *Summary Estimate*; 45
724 *Russia's Arms And Technologies: Nuclear Weapons Complex: The XXI Century Encyclopedia;* 2007; Arms and Technologies; ISBN 978-5-93799-035-8; XIV; 123
725 *Reorganization Of Soviet Ground Forces In East Germany*; CIA DI SOVA; Intelligence Assessment; SOV 83-10126; 1983/08; S; CIA HCD HR70-14 07-18-2012 DVD VII-112; 27-28
726 Laszlo Becz et al; *OKSNAR - Fully Assembled State—Soviet Nuclear Weapons In Hungary 1961-1991*; Veszprém; 2019; 209
727 Vitaly I Feskov et al; *Sovetskaya Armiya v gody «kholodnaya voyna» (1945-1991)* [*The Soviet Army During The 'Cold War'*]; Tomsk State University; 2004; ISBN 5-7511-1819-7; <http://militera.lib.ru/h/0/pdf/feskov_vi02.pdf>; 131
728 *Rocket Troops And Artillery In A Front Offensive Operation*; 1985; GSA; CIA IISR TS-888443; 1988/05/24; 11; ISCAP 2012-026 (CIA MDR EOM-2009-00158)

**a massing of nukes**

729 *Kapustin Yar*; 2009; web page no longer accessible; see Internet Archive Wayback Machine <https://web.archive.org/web/20081226172040/http://9k72.ru/page.php?14>
730 MSU M V Zakharov; *Certain Questions Of Soviet Military Art*; VM S (1-68) 1963; CIA IISR 1977/04/15; <https://www.cia.gov/library/readingroom/docs/1977-04-15b.pdf>; 8
731 *Rocket Troops And Artillery In A Front Offensive Operation*; 1985; GSA; CIA IISR TS-888443; 1988/05/24; 17; ISCAP 2012-026 (CIA MDR EOM-2009-00158)
732 I Y Shavrov; *The Front Offensive Operation*; GSA 1977/05; CIA IISR FIRDB-312-00013-79; 1979/06/15; CIA MDR EOM-2009-0157; also CIA HCD HR70-14 07-18-2012 DVD VII-222; 8, 13
733 F F Gayvoronsky et al; *Front Offensive Operations*; GSA; 1974; CIA IISR FIRDB-312-01997-79; 1979/09/27; CIA HCD HR70-14 07-18-2012 DVD VII-223; 46
734 *Rocket Troops And Artillery In A Front Offensive Operation*; 1985; GSA; CIA IISR TS-888443; 1988/05/24; 17; ISCAP 2012-026 (CIA MDR EOM-2009-00158)
735 *Warsaw Pact Tactical Forces: Capabilities And Readiness For Nuclear War*; Research Paper; SOV 85-10107CX; CIA DI SOVA; 1985/06; CIA HCD HR70-14 07-18-2012 DVD VII-119; 3
736 I Y Shavrov; *The Front Offensive Operation*; GSA 1977/05; CIA IISR FIRDB-312-00013-79; 1979/06/15; CIA MDR EOM-2009-0157; also CIA HCD HR70-14 07-18-2012 DVD VII-222; 23-24
737 GEN-COL G Kariofilli; *Front Rocket Troops In The Transition To The Offensive From Areas Of Permanent Location*; VM S (2-78) 1966; CIA IISR; 1974/05/20; <https://www.cia.gov/library/readingroom/docs/1974-05-20.pdf>; also CREST RDP10-00105R000101030001-1
738 GEN-MAJ (Artillery) L Sapkov and COL P Shkarubskiy; *Theoretical Recommendations And Their Application By The Troops*; VM S (1-80) 1967; CIA IISR FIRDB-312-00002-78; 1978/01/04; <https://www.cia.gov/library/readingroom/docs/DOC_0001199104.pdf>; 7-8
739 F F Gayvoronsky et al; *Front Offensive Operations*; GSA; 1974; CIA IISR FIRDB-312-01997-79; 1979/09/27; CIA HCD HR70-14 07-18-2012 DVD VII-223; 37, 47
740 *Soviet Planning For Front Nuclear Operations In Central Europe*; Intelligence Assessment; SOV 83-10099JX; CIA DI SOVA; 1983/06; TS; CIA HCD HR70-14 07-18-2012 VII-61; iii, iv
741 *USSR General Staff Academy Lessons*; *The Front Offensive Operation*; Supplementary Material for Lesson No. 1—Report of the Chief of the Operations Directorate of the Coastal Front (variant); 1977; GSA; CIA IISR FIRDB-312-00106-82; 1982/02/05; CIA HCD HR70-14 07-18-2012 DVD VII-273; 4

742 *Military Planning Of The Warsaw Pact In Central Europe: A Study*; CWIHP-B (2) Fall 1992; translation German Defense Ministry publication; 15
743 MSU M V Zakharov; *The Development Of The Means Of Armed Combat In The Postwar Period*; VM S (1-86) 1969; CIA IISR FIRDB-312-00679-74; 1974/02/26; <https://www.cia.gov/library/readingroom/docs/1974-02-26.pdf>; also CIA HCD HR70-14 07-18-2012 DVD VII-080; 25 Table 1
744 *Rocket Troops And Artillery In A Front Offensive Operation*; 1985; GSA; CIA IISR TS-888443; 1988/05/24; 17; ISCAP 2012-026 (CIA MDR EOM-2009-00158)

## up the escalation ladder

745 *The Threat To Europe*; 1981; Progress Publishers
746 *Theory And Practice Of Warsaw Pact Operations; Part II: Organization And Operational Intent In The West European Theater Of War*; CIA IIR; 1972/06/27; CIA HCD HR70-14 07-18-2012 DVD VI-049; 13
747 Vojtech Mastny and Malcolm Byrne ED *A Cardboard Castle? An Inside History Of The Warsaw Pact 1955-1991*; 2005; Central European University; ISBN 963-7326-08-1; ISBN 963-7326-07-3; document 28, 135
748 GEN-LT P Melnikov; *Problems Of Conducting A War In Europe (Based On The Views Of The NATO Command);* VM S (3-79) 1966; CIA IISR FIRDB-312-03146-76; 1976/12/22; <https://www.cia.gov/library/readingroom/docs/1976-12-22b.pdf>
749 *Evolution Of Soviet Concepts And Forces For Nuclear War In Europe*; Intelligence Report; SR IR 74 4-S; CIA DI; 1974/11; TS; CIA HCD HR70-14 07-18-2012 DVD VII-28; CREST RDP80M01133A001100110009-6
750 V D Sokolovskiy et al; *Military Strategy*; *Voyenizdat*; Moscow; 1968; FTD; <https://apps.dtic.mil/dtic/tr/fulltext/u2/a052778.pdf>; CH-2 addition 66>71
751 *Evolution Of Soviet Concepts And Forces For Nuclear War In Europe*; Intelligence Report; SR IR 74 4-S; CIA DI; 1974/11; TS; CIA HCD HR70-14 07-18-2012 DVD VII-28; CREST RDP80M01133A001100110009-6; 7
752 Vojtech Mastny and Malcolm Byrne ED *A Cardboard Castle? An Inside History Of The Warsaw Pact 1955-1991*; 2005; Central European University; ISBN 963-7326-08-1; ISBN 963-7326-07-3; document 28, 173
753 *Polish Defense Ministry Document Concerning Experiences And Conclusions From The "Narew" Maneuvers*; CIA IISR [TS-]195344; 1967/01/20; CIA HCD HR70-14 07-18-2012 DVD VI-014; 20
754 *Conclusions And Experiences From The "Jesien" (Autumn) Integrated Maneuvers*; CIA IISR CSDB-312-01611-68; 1968/08/08; CIA HCD HR70-14 07-18-2012 DVD VI-035; 14, 16
755 *Speeches at the Critique Of Exercise KRAJ-73*; 1973/05/17; CIA IISR TS-205445; 1974/05/23; 14
756 *Draft of the Discussion of Exercise "Shield-76" By the Chief of the General Staff of the Polish Armed Forces*; CIA IISR TS-778045; 1977/02/15; CIA HCD HR70-14 07-18-2012 DVD 007-297; 14>16
757 *History Of The Custody And Deployment Of Nuclear Weapons: July 1945 Through September 1977*; Office of the Assistant To The Secretary of Defense (Atomic Energy); 1978/02; TS; DoD FOIA; 108
758 GEN-LT P Melnikov; *Problems Of Conducting A War In Europe (Based On The Views Of The NATO Command);* VM S (3-79) 1966; CIA IISR FIRDB-312-03146-76; 1976/12/22; <https://www.cia.gov/library/readingroom/docs/1976-12-22b.pdf>; 8
759 COL (Engineer) Yu Dorofeyev; *Negotiating Nuclear Mine Barriers*; VM S 3(85) 1968; CIA IISR C01189555; 1973/10/09; 4; CIA MDR EOM-2015-00545
760 COL Yu Korolev and COL V Shamshurov; *Some Problems Of Engineer Support Of The Negotiation Of Nuclear Minefields*; VM S 2 (81) 1967; CIA IISR TS-788032; 1978/02/14; 4; CIA MDR EOM-2015-00545
761 *Polish Defense Ministry Document Concerning Experiences And Conclusions From The "Narew" Maneuvers*; CIA IISR [TS-]195344; 1967/01/20; CIA HCD HR70-14 07-18-2012 DVD VI-014; 16
762 John G Hines et al; *Soviet Intentions 1965-1985*; Contract MDA903-92-C-0147 OSD-Net Assessment; BDM Federal; 1995/09/22; V.I *An Analytical Comparison Of U.S.-Soviet Assessments During The Cold War*; 37; V.II *Soviet Post-Cold War Testimonial Evidence*; 41 GEN-COL A A Danilevich; 101 V L Kataev; GWU <https://nsarchive2.gwu.edu/nukevault/ebb285/index.htm> section links
763 *Trends And Developments In Warsaw Pact Theater Forces, 1985-2000*; NIE 11-14-85-D; 1985/09; S; CREST RDP87T00495R000600560011-2; 2010/07/20; 16
764 GEN-MAJ M Cherednichenko; *The Combined-Arms Army In A Modern Operation*; VM S (1-71) 1964; CIA IISR; 1977/01/28; <https://www.cia.gov/library/readingroom/docs/1977-01-28-A.pdf>; 7
765 GEN-COL M Povaliy; *On The Question Of The Initial Period Of A Modern War*; VM S (1-80) 1967; CIA IISR FIRDB-312-02424-74; 1974/07/08; CIA HCD HR70-14 07-18-2012 DVD VII-029; also CREST RDP10-00105R000100770001-1
766 COL A Volkov; *Problems Of Armed Combat In The Non-Nuclear Period Of War*; VM S (2-81) 1967; CIA IISR FIRDB-312-00012-77 1977/02/23; <https://www.cia.gov/library/readingroom/docs/DOC_0001199101.pdf>
767 COL P Simonok; *Conducting Offensive Operations Without Employing Nuclear Weapons (Based On The Views Of The NATO Command)*; VM S (1-83) 1968; CIA IISR C01190472; 1977/01/14; <https://www.cia.gov/library/readingroom/docs/1977-01-14c.pdf>; 12

768 CPT (First Rank) N Vyunenko and Rear ADM (Reserve) D Tuz; *The Employment Of Naval Forces At The Beginning Of A War*; VM S (1-83) 1968; CIA IISR FIRDB-312-01562-74; 1974/04/18; CREST RDP10-00105R000100450001-6; 14

769 COL I Rachok; *Defensive Operations Of Ground Forces In A Strategic Operation In A Theater Of Military Operations*; VM S (2-84) 1968; CIA IISR; 1976/10/27; <https://www.cia.gov/library/readingroom/docs/1976-10-27a.pdf>; also CREST RDP10-00105R000302500001-6; 14

770 GEN-ARM G Khetagurov; *The Buildup Of Efforts During A Front Offensive Operation*; VM S (1-86) 1969; CIA IISR; 1975/06/09; <https://www.cia.gov/library/readingroom/docs/1975-06-09.pdf>; also CREST RDP10-00105R000201090001-4 2012/04/19; 5, 17-18

771 GEN-LT F Gayvoronsky; *New Questions Of Operational Art At Its Present Stage Of Development*; VM S (1-89) 1970; CIA IISR FIRDB-312-00903-74; 1974/03/07; <https://www.cia.gov/library/readingroom/docs/DOC_0001199073.pdf>; 4, 17

772 MSU M Zakharov; *The Possible Nature Of Modern Wars And The Tasks Of The Branches Of The Armed Forces*; VM S (2-87) 1969; CIA IISR FIRDB-312-01563-74; 1974/04/26; <https://www.cia.gov/library/readingroom/docs/CIA-RDP10-00105R000100460001-5.pdf>; also CREST RDP10-00105R000100460001-5; 9-10

773 GEN-LT L S Sapkov; *Improving The Control Of Front Rocket Troop In The Transition From Non-Nuclear Actions To the Use Of Nuclear Weapons*; VM S (2-90) 1970; CIA IISR; 1974/03/05; <https://www.cia.gov/library/readingroom/docs/1974-03-05.pdf>; 6

774 *Soviet Concepts Of War In Europe: Transition From Conventional To Nuclear Conflict*; Intelligence Memorandum; SR IM 71-9; CIA DI OSR; 1971/05; TS; CIA HCD HR70-14 07-18-2012 VII-11; 11

775 *Tactical Nuclear Capabilities Of Warsaw Pact Ground Forces In The Reduction Area*; SR SP 72-2; CIA DI OSR; 1972/10; TS; CIA HCD HR70-14 07-18-2012 VII-72; 5

776 *Evolution Of Soviet Concepts And Forces For Nuclear War In Europe*; Intelligence Report; SR IR 74 4-S; CIA DI; 1974/11; TS; CIA HCD HR70-14 07-18-2012 DVD VII-28; CREST RDP80M01133A001100110009-6

777 *Soviet Concepts For Initial Military Operations Against NATO In Central Europe*; Intelligence Report; SR 77-10002CX; CIA OSR Theater Forces Division; 1977/02; TS; CIA MDR EOM-2011-01084; also CIA HCD HR70-14 07-18-2012 DVD VII-037; 19

778 F F Gayvoronsky et al; *Front Offensive Operations*; GSA; 1974; CIA IISR FIRDB-312-01997-79; 1979/09/27; CIA HCD HR70-14 07-18-2012 DVD VII-223; 312

779 MSU N Ogarkov; *Results Of Operational Training In 1977-1978 And Tasks For 1979-1980*; GS; CIA IISR FIRDB-312-02337-79; 1979/10/25;; CIA HCD HR70-14 07-18-2012 DVD VII-057; 12-13

780 *Warsaw Pact Forces Opposite NATO*; NIE 11-14-79; 1979/01/31; TS; CIA HCD HR70-14 07-18-2012 DVD VII-5 (V.2) *The Estimate*; Key Judgments 5 item 3; I-5

781 *Soviet Planning For Front Nuclear Operations In Central Europe*; Intelligence Assessment; SOV 83-10099JX; CIA DI SOVA; 1983/06; TS; CIA HCD HR70-14 07-18-2012 VII-61; 5

782 *Warning Of War In Europe*; Memorandum; 1984/06/27; S; <https://www.cia.gov/library/readingroom/docs/DOC_0001486834.pdf>: 24

783 *Soviet Capabilities For Strategic Nuclear Conflict Through The Mid-1990s*; NIE 11-3/8-84/85; DCI; V.I *Summary*; 1985/04/25; TS; 42>45

784 GEN-MAJ Tibor Toth; *Characteristics Of Organizing And Conducting An Offensive Operation Of The Coalition Front And Combined Arms Army*; *Honvedelem* (6) 1980; S; CIA IIR C05798348; 1985/09/06; 20 Chart; CIA MDR EOM-2011-0881

785 *Comments On The Military Aspects Of The Current Crisis In Poland*; CIA FIRDB-312-00985-81; 1981/03/30; <https://www.cia.gov/library/readingroom/docs/1981-03-30.pdf>

786 John G Hines et al; *Soviet Intentions 1965-1985* V.II *Soviet Post-Cold War Testimonial Evidence*; Contract MDA903-92-C-0147 OSD-Net Assessment; BDM Federal; 1995/09/22; 48; GWU; <https://nsarchive2.gwu.edu/nukevault/ebb285/index.htm> section links; 7>10

787 *Organizational Structure Of The Soviet Armed Forces*; 1985; GSA; CIA IISR TS-888643; 1988/07/29; 5; ISCAP 2012-026 (CIA MDR EOM-2009-00158)

788 John G Hines et al; *Soviet Intentions 1965-1985* V.II *Soviet Post-Cold War Testimonial Evidence*; Contract MDA903-92-C-0147 OSD-Net Assessment; BDM Federal; 1995/09/22; 48; GWU; <https://nsarchive2.gwu.edu/nukevault/ebb285/index.htm> section links; 8 GEN-LT G V Batenin

789 John G Hines et al; *Soviet Intentions 1965-1985* V.II *Soviet Post-Cold War Testimonial Evidence*; Contract MDA903-92-C-0147 OSD-Net Assessment; BDM Federal; 1995/09/22; 48; GWU; <https://nsarchive2.gwu.edu/nukevault/ebb285/index.htm> section links; 64 GEN-COL A A Danilevich

790 *Tactical Nuclear Capabilities Of Warsaw Pact Ground Forces In The Reduction Area*; SR SP 72-2; CIA DI OSR; 1972/10; TS; CIA HCD HR70-14 07-18-2012 VII-72; 5

791 John G Hines et al; *Soviet Intentions 1965-1985* V.II *Soviet Post-Cold War Testimonial Evidence*; Contract MDA903-92-C-0147 OSD-Net Assessment; BDM Federal; 1995/09/22; 48; GWU; <https://nsarchive2.gwu.edu/nukevault/ebb285/index.htm> section links; 62 GEN-COL A A Danilevich

792 I Y Shavrov; *The Front Offensive Operation*; GSA 1977/05; CIA IISR FIRDB-312-00013-79; 1979/06/15; CIA MDR EOM-2009-0157; also CIA HCD HR70-14 07-18-2012 DVD VII-222; 77

793 *Theory And Practice Of Warsaw Pact Operations; Part II: Organization And Operational Intent In The West European Theater Of War*; CIA IIR; 1972/06/27; CIA HCD HR70-14 07-18-2012 DVD VI-049; 8

794 COL V Savkin; *Principles Of Military Art And Their Development*; VM R (5) 1972; FPD 0051-73 (10 December 1973); 67-68

795 F F Gayvoronsky et al; *Front Offensive Operations*; GSA; 1974; CIA IISR FIRDB-312-01997-79; 1979/09/27; CIA HCD HR70-14 07-18-2012 DVD VII-223; 174-175, 315

796 GEN-ARM P I Ivashutin; *Principles Of The Organization And Conduct Of Operational Reconnaissance In A Front Offensive Operation*; 1974; GS GRU; CIA IISR FIRDB-312-00311-78; 1978/05/19; CIA HCD HR70-14 07-18-2012 DVD VII-101; 26>29

797 COL A Postovalov; *Transition To The Use Of Nuclear Weapons In The Course Of An Offensive Operation*; VM S (3-91) 1970; CIA IISR FIRDB-312-02892-73; 1973/06/15; CIA HCD HR70-14 07-18-2012 DVD VII-021; also CREST RDP10-00105R000100170001-7 2012/09/27; 14-15

798 I Y Shavrov; *The Front Offensive Operation*; GSA 1977/05; CIA IISR FIRDB-312-00013-79; 1979/06/15; CIA MDR EOM-2009-0157; also CIA HCD HR70-14 07-18-2012 DVD VII-222; 268

**allies pitch in**

799 *Main Trends In Soviet Capabilities And Policies 1960-1965*; NIE 11-4-60; 1960/12/01; TS; CIA HCD HR70-14 07-18-2012 DVD II-009; 29

800 *Theory And Practice Of Warsaw Pact Operations; Part I: Soviet/Czechoslovak Operational Doctrine, Directives, And Tactics*; CIA IIR; 1972/05/22; CIA HCD HR70-14 07-18-2012 DVD VI-048; 6-7

801 *Plan Of Actions Of The Czechoslovak People's Army For War Period*; 1964/10/14; CWIHP-B (12/13); 293

802 *Polish Critique Of The Warsaw Pact "Lato-67" Command Post Exercise*; CIA IISR CSDB-312-01470-68; CIA HCD HR70-14 07-18-2012 DVD VI-034; 17

803 MSU I Yakubovskiy and GEN-ARM S. Shtemenko; *Material Of The Critique Of The Operational War Game On Maps Conducted On The Southwestern Axis*; HQ WPCAF Moscow; 1970/07; CIA IIR TS-205587; 1975/06/13; CIA HCD HR70-14 07-18-2012 DVD VII-031; 39, 77

804 *Danmark under den kolde krig: Den sikkerhedspolitiske situation 1945-1991*; Dansk Institut For Internationale Studier; Copenhagen; 2005; V.II ISBN 87-7605-093-9; <https://www.diis.dk/publikationer/danmark-kolde-krig>; 636-637

805 *Material on Exercise "Shield-76"*; CIA IISR TS-768153; 1976/12/23; CIA HCD HR70-14 07-18-2012 DVD VII-296; 8

806 GEN-MAJ Tibor Toth; *Characteristics Of Organizing And Conducting An Offensive Operation Of The Coalition Front And Combined Arms Army*; Honvedelem (6) 1980; S; CIA IIR C05798348; 1985/09/06; 9; CIA MDR EOM-2011-0881

807 *Comments On The Military Aspects Of The Current Crisis In Poland*; CIA FIRDB-312-00985-81; 1981/03/30; <https://www.cia.gov/library/readingroom/docs/1981-03-30.pdf>

808 Rüdiger Wenzke; *Die Streitkräfte der DDR und Polens in der Operationsplanung des Warschauer Paktes*; 2010; Military History Research Office; ISBN 978-3-941571-09-9; 51, 81

809 *Report On Visit Of Polish Armed Forces General Staff Delegation To The USSR Armed Forces General Staff And To The Combined Command Of The Combined Armed Forces*; CIA IISR FIRDB-312-02329-80; 1980/10/08; <https://www.cia.gov/library/readingroom/docs/1980_10_08_MISCELLANEOUS.pdf>; also CIA HCD HR70-14 07-18-2012 DVD VII-288; 29

810 *Supply Of Free Rockets And Guided Missiles By The USSR To Members Of The Sino-Soviet Bloc*; CIA Chickadee; 1963/03/05

811 Matthias Uhl; *Nuclear Warhead Delivery Systems For The Warsaw Pact, 1961-65*; Collection *The 1961 Berlin Crisis and Soviet Preparations for War in Europe*; 2003/12/04; PHP; <http://www.php.isn.ethz.ch/lory1.ethz.ch/collections/coll_berlin/intro_uhl78c2.html?navinfo=16161>

812 COL-LT Z Poczatek; *Experiences From The "Rajd" Exercise Conducted By The Warsaw Military District Staff*; Mysl Wojskowa S (2) 1967; CIA IISR CSDB-312-01190-68; 1968/06/18; CIA HCD HR70-14 07-18-2012 DVD VI-030

813 Harald Nielsen; *Die DDR Und Die Kernwaffen-Die Nukleare Rolle Der Nationalen Volksarmee Im Warschauer Pakt*; Nuclear History Program 6; 1998; Nomos; ISBN 3-7890-5510-7; 143, 206 Table 16-2

814 *Military Exercise Shchit-88 Operational Summary No. 1 For The Period 0800 25 May To 0800 2 June 1988*; CWIHP-DA; <https://digitalarchive.wilsoncenter.org/document/114267>; 4

815 *Polish Army Mobilization Periods And Executors*; 1973; CIA IISR TS-204587; 1974/03/11; CIA HCD HR70-14 07-18-2012 DVD VII-027

816 *Operational Mission—Situation As Of 1700 Hours 4 April*; CIA IISR TS-788328; 1978/11/17; CIA HCD HR70-14 07-18-2012 DVD VII-103; 20 AP 3

817 *Polish Army Mobilization Periods And Executors*; 1973; CIA IISR TS-204587; 1974/03/11; CIA HCD HR70-14 07-18-2012 DVD VII-027; 64; however a 1972 document has 21 Tactical Reconnaissance-Artillery Aviation Regiment at Powidz equipped with MIG-21R; *The Material-Technical Plan For The Support Of The Air Force In The Years 1971-75*; CIA IISR TS-204486; 1974/02/12;CIA HCD HR70-14 07-18-2012 DVD VII-142; 7

818 *Plan Of Actions Of The Czechoslovak People's Army For War Period*; 1964/10/14; CWIHP-B (12/13); 294

819 Paul Piotrowski and Thomas Pompowski; *Polska miała arsenał broni nuklearnej [Poland Had An Arsenal Of Nuclear Weapons]*; Dziennik.pl; 2007/01/26; web page no longer accessible; see Internet Archive Wayback Machine <https://web.archive.org/web/20160303212816/http://wiadomosci.dziennik.pl/polityka/artykuly/198972,polska-miala-arsenal-broni-nuklearnej.html>

820 Laszlo Becz et al; *OKSNAR - Fully Assembled State—Soviet Nuclear Weapons In Hungary 1961-1991*; Veszprém; 2019; 102>106; Meteor exercise 6 through 13 March 1966
821 *Material on Exercise "Shield-76"*; CIA IISR TS-768153; 1976/12/23; CIA HCD HR70-14 07-18-2012 DVD VII-296; 57 AT-4 Rocket Troops and Artillery, 120 AT-10 Technical Services
822 *Operational Mission—Situation As Of 1700 Hours 4 April*; CIA IISR TS-788328; 1978/11/17; CIA HCD HR70-14 07-18-2012 DVD VII-103; 25 AP-7 Chart, 27 AP-8

**conventional complexities**
823 *Soviet Operational Art*; 1985; GSA; CIA IISR TS-888644; 1988/07/29; 10; ISCAP 2012-026 (CIA MDR EOM-2009-00158)
824 *Rocket Troops And Artillery In A Front Offensive Operation*; 1985; GSA; CIA IISR TS-888443; 1988/05/24; 14; ISCAP 2012-026 (CIA MDR EOM-2009-00158)
825 *Reconnaissance In Support Of Strategic Operations*; 1985; GSA; CIA IISR C01197777; 1989/09/15; 8; CIA MDR EOM-2015-01160
826 *Front Offensive Operations*; 1985; GSA; CIA IISR C01197778; 1990/03/02; 5; CIA MDR EOM-2015-01160
827 GEN-MAJ P G Yesaulov and COL M P Dukhachev; *Field Service Regulations Of The Armed Forces Of The Union Of SSRs (Division-Regiment)*; 1962; MO Military Publishing House; CIA IR CSDB-3-652,360; 1963/04/30; CIA HCD HR70-14 07-18-2012 DVD III-010 V-010; 8
828 *Manual On The Conduct Of Operations—Part Two—Ground Forces Operations (Front-Army-Corps)*; 1963; GS; CIA IISR TS-778264; 1977/09/29; CIA HCD HR70-14 07-18-2012 DVD VII-99; 10
829 MSU V I Chuykov; *The New Field Service Regulations Of The Armed Forces Of The USSR*; VM S (1-71) 1964; CIA IISR; 1978/12/14; <https://www.cia.gov/library/readingroom/docs/1978-12-14A.pdf>; also CIA HCD HR70-14 07-18-2012 DVD III-011; 9
830 Jenõ Köteles; *Report On The Moscow Conference Of Unified Armed Forces Headquarters*; 1963/10/29; Ministry of Defense Hungarian People's Army; PHP; <http://www.php.isn.ethz.ch/lory1.ethz.ch/collections/colltopicoaa7.html?id=19981&navinfo=16606>
831 MSU M V Zakharov; *The Status And Tasks Of Military Science At The Present Stage Of The Development Of The Armed Forces*; VM S (1-77) 1966; CIA IISR FIRDB-312-00137-76; 1976/03/10; <https://www.cia.gov/library/readingroom/docs/1976-03-10.pdf>; also CREST RDP10-00105R000201680001-9; 7
832 S A Tyushkevich; *The Soviet Armed Forces: The History Of Their Organizational Development*; Moscow *Voyenizdat*; 1978; USAF Soviet Military Thought 19; 471
833 COL Imre Gabor; *With Nuclear Weapons Or Without Them*; VM S (2-72) 1964; CIA IISR; 1978/06/29; <https://www.cia.gov/library/readingroom/docs/1978-06-29b.pdf>; also CIA HCD HR70-14 07-18-2012 DVD VII-054
834 GEN-COL I Glebov; *Certain Problems Of Planning And Conducting Offensive Operations Of Fronts (Based On The Experience Of Research War Games)*; VM S (3-82) 1967; CIA IISR FIRDB-312-02966-74; 1974/08/20; CIA HCD HR70-14 07-18-2012 DVD VII-030; also CREST RDP10-00105R000100820001-5; 2012/09/28
835 GEN-COL F Malykhin; *Features Of The Rear Support Of Troops In An Offensive Operation Of A Front Conducted Without The Use Of Nuclear Weapons*; VM S (3-76) 1965; CIA IISR; 1975/10/01; <https://www.cia.gov/library/readingroom/docs/1975-10-01.pdf>; also CREST RDP10-00105R000201350001-5 2012/10/03
836 GEN-COL F Malykhin; *Some Problems In The Preparation Of The Rear Area For Support Of The Armed Forces In The Initial Period Of A War*; VM TS (Second) 1960; CIA C00012326; 1962/02/13; <https://www.cia.gov/library/readingroom/docs/1962-02-13.pdf>; also CIA HCD HR70-14 07-18-2012 DVD V-003
837 COL A Postovalov et al; *Features Of An Offensive Operation When Neither Side Employs Nuclear Weapons*; VM S (2-75) 1965; CIA IISR; 1978/11/08; <https://www.cia.gov/library/readingroom/docs/1978-11-08.pdf>
838 COL M Skoptsov and COL M Vasilenkov; *Combat Actions Of Troops Without The Employment Of Means Of Mass Destruction*; VM S (3-79) 1966; CIA IISR; 1977/04/27; <https://www.cia.gov/library/readingroom/docs/1977-04-27a.pdf>; 5
839 COL A Postovalov et al; *Features Of An Offensive Operation When Neither Side Employs Nuclear Weapons*; VM S (2-75) 1965; CIA IISR; 1978/11/08; <https://www.cia.gov/library/readingroom/docs/1978-11-08.pdf>; 7-8
840 GEN-COL I Glebov; *Certain Problems Of Planning And Conducting Offensive Operations Of Fronts (Based On The Experience Of Research War Games)*; VM S (3-82) 1967; CIA IISR FIRDB-312-02966-74; 1974/08/20; CIA HCD HR70-14 07-18-2012 DVD VII-030; also CREST RDP10-00105R000100820001-5; 2012/09/28; 6
841 GEN-LT V Petrenko; *Certain Problems In Planning Combat Operations Without Using Nuclear Weapons*; VM S (3-82) 1967; CIA IISR FIRDB-312-01212-75; 1975/06/09; CREST RDP10-00105R000201100001-2 2012/04/18; 13
842 COL G Yefimov; *Planning Modern Operations*; VM S (2-87) 1969; CIA IISR FIRDB-312-03848-74; 1974/11/18; <https://www.cia.gov/library/readingroom/docs/DOC_0001199094.pdf>; also CREST RDP10-00105R000100910001-5; 7
843 GEN-LT F Gayvoronsky; *New Questions Of Operational Art At Its Present Stage Of Development*; VM S (1-89) 1970; CIA IISR FIRDB-312-00903-74; 1974/03/07; <https://www.cia.gov/library/readingroom/docs/DOC_0001199073.pdf>; 6-7
844 *Front Offensive Operations*; 1985; GSA; CIA IISR C01197778; 1990/03/02; 8; CIA MDR EOM-2015-01160
845 *Front Offensive Operations*; 1985; GSA; CIA IISR C01197778; 1990/03/02; 8; CIA MDR EOM-2015-01160

846 *Soviet Operational Art*; 1985; GSA; CIA IISR TS-888644; 1988/07/29; 13; ISCAP 2012-026 (CIA MDR EOM-2009-00158)
847 *Soviet Operational Art*; 1985; GSA; CIA IISR TS-888644; 1988/07/29; 13; ISCAP 2012-026 (CIA MDR EOM-2009-00158)
848 GEN-MAJ A S Milovidov and COL V G Kozlov ED; *The Philosophical Heritage Of V. I. Lenin And The Problems Of Contemporary War*; Moscow; 1972; USAF Soviet Military Thought #5; Chapter VII 127
849 I Y Shavrov *The Front Offensive Operation*; GSA 1977/05; CIA IISR FIRDB-312-00013-79; 1979/06/15; CIA MDR EOM-2009-0157; also CIA HCD HR70-14 07-18-2012 DVD VII-222; 46
850 *Draft Of The Discussion Of Exercise "Shield-76"- By The Chief Of The General Staff Of The Polish Armed Forces*; CIA IISR TS-778045; 1977/02/15; CIA HCD HR70-14 07-18-2012 DVD VII-297; TS-778117; 1977/04/11; DVD VII-298; 20
851 *Warsaw Pact Tactical Forces: Capabilities And Readiness For Nuclear War*; Research Paper; SOV 85-10107CX; CIA DI SOVA; 1985/06; TS; CIA HCD HR70-14 07-18-2012 DVD VII-119; iii
852 COL B Samorukov; *Combat Operations Involving Conventional Means Of Destruction*; VM R (8) 1967; FPD 0125-68 (26 August 1968); 34-35
853 GEN-COL (Retired) I Volkotrubenko; *Determining Norms For The Stockpiling And Expenditure Of Artillery Ammunition*; VM S (1-89) 1970; CIA IISR; 1974/01/02; <https://www.cia.gov/library/readingroom/docs/1974-01-02.pdf>; also CIA HCD HR70-14 07-18-2012 DVD VII-078; 9
854 MAR (Artillery) K Kazakov; *The Artillery Offensive—The Principal Method For The Combat Employment Of Artillery In An Offensive Operation Conducted With Conventional Means Of Destruction*; VM S 2 (84) 1968; CIA IISR C05827032; 1976/02/13; CREST RDP10-00105R0002001610001-6; 2012/04/11
855 I Y Shavrov; *The Front Offensive Operation*; GSA 1977/05; CIA IISR FIRDB-312-00013-79; 1979/06/15; CIA MDR EOM-2009-0157; also CIA HCD HR70-14 07-18-2012 DVD VII-222; 99>101
856 I Y Shavrov; *The Front Offensive Operation*; GSA 1977/05; CIA IISR FIRDB-312-00013-79; 1979/06/15; CIA MDR EOM-2009-0157; also CIA HCD HR70-14 07-18-2012 DVD VII-222; 120
857 GEN-MAJ M Kozhevnikov; *Air Forces Actions At The Beginning Of A War Without The Employment Of Nuclear Weapons*; VM S (2-78) 1966; CIA IISR; 1975/10/29; <https://www.cia.gov/library/readingroom/docs/1975-10-29.pdf>; also CREST RDP10-00105R000201420001-7; 2012/10/16; 5
858 MAR (Aviation) S Krasovskiy; *The Air Forces In Operations With The Employment Of Conventional Means Of Destruction*; VM S (3-76) 1965; CIA IISR; 1976/02/17; <https://www.cia.gov/library/readingroom/docs/1976-02-17.pdf>; also CIA HCD HR70-14 07-18-2012 DVD VII-146; also CREST RDP10-00105R000201620001-5; 2012/04/11; 8
859 *Material on Exercise "Shield-76"*; CIA IISR TS-768153; 1976/12/23; CIA HCD HR70-14 07-18-2012 DVD VII-296; 211, 286
860 *USSR General Staff Academy Lessons*; *The Front Offensive Operation*; Lesson 22b; *Combat Actions of Front and Army Aviation When Developing an Offensive Operation with the Commitment of the Front's Second Echelon to Battle*; 1977; GSA; CIA IISR FIRDB-312-02997-80; 1980/11/14; CIA HCD HR70-14 07-18-2012 DVD VII-253; 8
861 COL A Volkov; *Problems Of Armed Combat In The Non-Nuclear Period Of War*; VM S (2-81) 1967; CIA IISR FIRDB-312-00012-77; 1977/02/23; <https://www.cia.gov/library/readingroom/docs/DOC_0001199101.pdf>; 14
862 COL B Samorukov; *Combat Operations Involving Conventional Means Of Destruction*; VM R (8) 1967; FPD 0125-68 (26 August 1968); 32
863 *Warsaw Pact Tactical Nuclear Forces In Central Europe*; Joint Memorandum; CIA DIA; SR IM 75-1; 1975/03; TS; CREST RDP86T00608R000700070001-8; 2003-09-29; also CIA HCD HR70-14 07-18-2012 DVD VII-085; 12
864 COL A Konstantinov; *New Developments In The Combat Use Of The Air Forces Of A Theater Of Military Operations In The Initial Period Of A War (According To American Views)*; VM S (5-60) 1961; CIA Ironbark C01151496; <https://www.cia.gov/library/readingroom/docs/1963-01-23-A.pdf>; second article; 15
865 *Report On Visit Of Polish Armed Forces General Staff Delegation To The USSR Armed Forces General Staff And To The Combined Command Of The Combined Armed Forces*; CIA IISR FIRDB-312-02329-80; 1980/10/08; <https://www.cia.gov/library/readingroom/docs/1980_10_08_MISCELLANEOUS.pdf>; also CIA HCD HR70-14 07-18-2012 DVD VII-288; 31
866 I Y Shavrov; *The Front Offensive Operation*; GSA 1977/05; CIA IISR FIRDB-312-00013-79; 1979/06/15; CIA MDR EOM-2009-0157; also CIA HCD HR70-14 07-18-2012 DVD VII-222; 69
867 *Warsaw Pact Nonnuclear Threat To NATO Airbases In Central Europe*; NIE 11-20-6-84; 1984/10/25; TS; CIA HCD HR70-14 07-18-2012 DVD VII-157; 15, 16 Table 2
868 COL N Semenov; *Gaining Supremacy In The Air*; VM R (4) 1968; FPD 0052-69
869 COL A Postovalov et al; *Features Of An Offensive Operation When Neither Side Employs Nuclear Weapons*; VM S (2-75) 1965; CIA IISR; 1978/11/08; <https://www.cia.gov/library/readingroom/docs/1978-11-08.pdf>; 6
870 GEN MAJ (Artillery) G Biryukov and COL G Khoroshilov; *Destruction Of Enemy Air Defense Installations In The Flight Zone Of An Airborne Landing Force*; VM S (1-83) 1968; CIA IISR; 1976/11/30; <https://www.cia.gov/library/readingroom/docs/1976-11-30a.pdf>; also CREST RDP10-00105R000302650001-0; 2012/09/27

871 I Y Shavrov *The Front Offensive Operation*; GSA 1977/05; CIA IISR FIRDB-312-00013-79; 1979/06/15; CIA MDR EOM-2009-0157; also CIA HCD HR70-14 07-18-2012 DVD VII-222; 125

872 *Warsaw Pact Nonnuclear Threat To NATO Airbases In Central Europe*; NIE 11-20-6-84; 1984/10/25; TS; CIA HCD HR70-14 07-18-2012 DVD VII-157; 22>32

873 *Military Planning Of The Warsaw Pact In Central Europe: A Study*; CWIHP-B (2) Fall 1992; translation German Defense Ministry publication; 16

## Elusive Chemical Echelons

### origins

874 John Hemsley; *The Soviet Biochemical Threat To NATO*; 1987; St. Martin's/Royal United Services Institute; ISBN 0-312-01589-5; AP-1, 79

875 *Field Regulations Of The RKKA 1929* [Worker-Peasant Red Army]; 1929/06/21; USSR Report Military Affairs; JPRS-UMA-85-019 (13 March 1985)

876 *Provisional Field Regulations Of The RKKA 1936*; 1936/12/30; USSR Report Military Affairs; JPRS-UMA-86-031 (12 June 1986)

877 *Krasnaya Zvezda*; 1995/03/21; quoted in Chemical Weapons Convention Bulletin; Issue No. 28; June 1995; 21; <http://www.sussex.ac.uk/Units/spru/hsp/pdfbulletin.html>

878 Lev A Fedorov; *Chemical Armament: A Country's War Against Its Own People*; 2009; V.I CH-2.2, -2.3; J Med CBR Defense web page-links no longer accessible see Internet Archive Wayback Machine <https://web.archive.org/web/20101101000000*/http://www.jmedcbr.org/issue_0701/Fedorov/Fedorov3_08_09.html>; also limited information in *Chemical Weapons in Russia: History, Ecology, Politics*; 1994; FAS; <https://fas.org/nuke/guide/russia/cbw/jptac008_l94001.htm>

879 quoted in Milton Leitenberg et al; *The Soviet Biological Weapons Program: A History*; 2012; Harvard University Press; ISBN 978-0674047709; 25

880 COL Doctor Walter Hirsch; *Soviet BW And CW Preparations And Capabilities*; Harvard University Widener Library; compiled M Meselson 1996/11

881 *Marshal Zhukov On The Nature Of A Future War*; Radio Propaganda Report; CIA FBIS CD 62; 1957/04/05; <https://www.cia.gov/library/readingroom/docs/1957-04-05-A.pdf>; also CIA HCD HR70-14 07-18-2012 DVD I-040

882 GEN-MAJ G I Pokrovskiy; *Science And Technology In Contemporary War*; 1956; 49-50; *The Role Of Science And Technology In Contemporary War;* 1957; 148; Raymond Garthoff; Praeger; Russian History and World Communism No.74; 1959

883 *Atomic Weapons And Actions Under Conditions Of Their Employment: A Manual For Sergeants*; MO; 1954; S; CIA IR CSDB-35586; 1955/09/27; CIA HCD HR70-14 07-18-2012 DVD I-031-031a

884 GEN-LT S Shatilov; *An Important and Noble Theme*; Literary Gazette; 1955/05/28; in *General Shatilov On Surprise Atomic Attack: "A Double-Edged Weapon"*; Radio Propaganda Report; CIA FBIS CD 30; 1955/06/15; CIA HCD HR70-14 07-18-2012 DVD I-023; 12

885 MSU P A Rotmistrov; *On The Role Of Surprise In Modern War*; VM R (2) 1955/02

886 Joachim Krause and Charles K Mallory; *Chemical Weapons In Soviet Military Doctrine: Military And Historical Experience, 1915-1991*; 1992; Westview; ISBN 0-8133-8406-0; 127

887 *Chemical (Toxic) And Biological Warfare Readiness*; DoD Directive TS-3145.1; II A; 1956/10/06; FAS accessed at<http://www.fas.org/cw/cwc_archive/CW_history/1956_chemicaltoxicandbiologicalwarfarereadiness.pdf>

888 *US Policy On Chemical And Biological Warfare And Agents*; Report to the National Security Council; 1969/11/10; DoS Foreign Relations of the United States 1969-1976

889 David E Hoffman; *The Dead Hand—The Untold Story Of The Cold War Arms Race And Its Dangerous Legacy;* 2009; Doubleday (Random House); ISBN 978-0-385-52437-7; CH-4

890 A R Hylton; *Studies On The Technical Arms Control Aspects Of Chemical And Biological Warfare*; V. IV *The History of Chemical Warfare Plants and Facilities in the United States*; 1972/11/13; Midwest Research Institute; Contract No. ACDA/ST-197; FAS accessed at <http://www.fas.org/cw/cwc_archive/CW_history/1972_Chemical%20arfarePlantsAndFacilitiesUSA.pdf>

891 *Report by the Inspector-General of the Royal Air Force on Visit to No. 31 Maintenance Unit—Llandwrog*; Report No. 538; 1956/05/03; UKNA AIR 20/8727

892 *Chemical Warfare Policy*; Ministry of Defence; Chiefs of Staff Committee; COS 76/72; 1972/07/27; AN A-1; UKNA DEFE 24/791

893 Jonathan B Tucker; *War Of Nerves: Chemical Warfare From World War I To Al-Qaeda*; 2006; Pantheon; ISBN 0-375-42229-3; 107

894 *Negotiations For Storage Rights In USEUCOM*; [1962]; NARA RG-218 CCS-3260 1961/11/27 SEC 2 ; accessed at FAS <http://www.fas.org/cw/cwc_archive/CW_history/1961_NegotiationsforStorageRightsinUSEUCOM.pdf>

895 Chemical Weapons Convention Bulletin; Issue No. 14; December 1989; <http://www.sussex.ac.uk/Units/spru/hsp/pdfbulletin.html>; US declared 29000 tonnes

896 *Response to NSSM 192 United States Chemical Weapons Posture*; National Security Study Memorandum 192 Ad Hoc Group; in DoS Foreign Relations Of The United States 1969-1976; V.35; National Security Policy 1973-1976; 2014; 184 item 39

897 R L Tate et al; *Retaliatory Chemical Warfare—Interim Study Results;* DAS-TR-84-6; Directorate of Aerospace Studies; Air Force Systems Command; 1984/06; S; 54-55; ISCAP 2009-085

898 *Chemical Warfare: DOD's Successful Effort To Remove U.S. Chemical Weapons From Germany*; Report to Congressional Requestors; 1991/02; US GEN Accounting Office; GAO/NSIAD-91-105

899 COL A Kuchin; *Chemical Warfare Weapons Of The USA And The Lines Along Which They Are Being Developed*; VM S (6-61) 1961; CIA Ironbark; <https://www.cia.gov/library/readingroom/docs/1962-09-10-A.pdf>

900 MSU M V Zakharov; *The Development Of The Means Of Armed Combat In The Postwar Period*; VM S (1-86) 1969; CIA IISR FIRDB-312-00679-74; 1974/02/26; <https://www.cia.gov/library/readingroom/docs/1974-02-26.pdf>; also CIA HCD HR70-14 07-18-2012 DVD VII-080; 5

901 V D Sokolovskiy et al; *Military Strategy*; *Voyenizdat*; Moscow; 1962; RAND; 1963/04; <http://www.rand.org/pubs/reports/2005/R416.pdf>; 337

902 COL G Ashin; *More On The Cooperation Of Large Units Of The Soviet Army With Border Guards*; VM (3-70) 1963; CIA IISR; <https://www.cia.gov/library/readingroom/docs/1978-09-13.pdf>; 6

903 GEN MAJ A S Skovoroda; *Organization Of Rear Services Support Of Troops Of An Army And A Front In An Offensive Operation*; GSA; 1969/02; CIA IISR FIRDB-312-00635-77; 1977/03/04; CIA HCD HR70-14 07-18-2012 DVD VII-214; 24

904 COL M Belov; *Modern Means And Methods Of Combat Against Airborne Landing Forces*; VM S (2-69); 1963; CIA IISR; 1978/09/22; <https://www.cia.gov/library/readingroom/docs/1978-09-22bA.pdf>

905 COL-LT I Rodya; *Some Problems Of Combat Against Army Aviation*; VM S (1-86); 1969; CIA IISR; 1974/10/18; <https://www.cia.gov/library/readingroom/docs/1974-10-18a.pdf>; also CREST RDP10-00105R000100880001-9; 4

906 COL I Lyutov; *Defense Of Troops Without The Use Of Nuclear Weapons*; VM S (3-91); 1970; CIA IISR; 1974/01/22; <https://www.cia.gov/library/readingroom/docs//1974-01-22a.pdf>; 6, 9

907 COL P Lyadov; *Certain Problems In Moving A Combined-Arms Army Forward From The Interior Of The Country In The Initial Period Of War*; VM S (4-65) 1962; CIA IISR; 1978/10/12; <https://www.cia.gov/library/readingroom/docs/1978-10-12.pdf>; 5

908 MAJ I Grabovoy; *Protection Of Troops Against Toxic And Radioactive Substances And Bacterial Means*; VM S (1-71); 1964; CIA IISR; 1977/04/26; <https://www.cia.gov/library/readingroom/docs/1977-04-26b.pdf>; 8

909 GEN MAJ (Technical Troops) G Ostapchuk; *The Rapid Elimination Of The Aftereffects Of Enemy Nuclear And Chemical Strikes*; VM S (1-86); 1969; CIA IISR; 1974/06/18; <https://www.cia.gov/library/readingroom/docs/1974-06-18.pdf>; also CREST RDP10-00105R000100670001-2 2012/05/02; 8

910 COL P Simonok; *Conduct Of Meeting Engagements By A Field Army In The Initial Period Of War (According To American Views)*; VM S (2-72); 1964; CIA IISR; 1978/11/30; <https://www.cia.gov/library/readingroom/docs/1978-11-30b.pdf>; 9

911 COL V Chagorov; *Cooperation Between A Front And A Fleet In Protection Against Weapons Of Mass Destruction During An Offensive On A Coastal Axis*; VM S (2-75); 1965; CIA IISR; 1975/11/11; <https://www.cia.gov/library/readingroom/docs/1975-11-11.pdf>; also CREST RDP10-00105R000201450001-4

912 GEN-MAJ (Signal Troops) A Listrovoy; *Organizing Protection Against Weapons Of Mass Destruction Among Special Troops*; VM S (1-77); 1966; CIA IISR; 1978/04/28; <https://www.cia.gov/library/readingroom/docs/1978-04-28.pdf>

913 GEN-MAJ (Technical Troops) N Rumyantsev and COL-LT Yu Vaulin; *The System Of Collecting And Processing Data On The Radiation And Chemical Situation*; VM S (2-81); 1967; CIA IISR; 1974/07/23; <https://www.cia.gov/library/readingroom/docs/1974-07-23.pdf>; also CREST RDP10-00105R000100780001-0 2012/09/25

914 GEN-MAJ A Ovchinnikov et al; *The Protection Of Troops From Weapons Of Mass Destruction*; VM S (1-86); 1969; CIA IISR; 1974/06/17; <https://www.cia.gov/library/readingroom/docs/1974-06-17b.pdf>; also CREST RDP10-00105R000100660001-3

915 GEN-MAJ M Kiryan; *Protection Of Rear Area Troops And Installations From Weapons Of Mass Destruction During An Offensive Operation*; VM S (2-87); 1969; CIA IISR FIRDB-312-02285-74; 1974/07/01; <https://www.cia.gov/library/readingroom/docs/1974-07-01-A.pdf>; also CREST RDP10-00105R000100730001-5; 2012/09/25

916 COL N Krivopustov; *Reconnaissance During The Advance Of A Combined-Arms (Tank) Army From The Depth And Its Commitment To An Engagement*; VM S (1-86) 1969; <https://www.cia.gov/library/readingroom/docs/1975-08-25-A.pdf>; also CREST RDP10-00105R000201210001-0; 2012/04/11; 7-8

917 COL P Dubok et al; *Restoration Of Combat Effectiveness Of Rocket Large Units and Units In Operations*; VM S (1-89); 1970; CIA IISR; 1973/03/22; <https://www.cia.gov/library/readingroom/docs/1973-03-22.pdf>; also CREST RDP10-00105R000100340001-8; 7, 10

918 GEN-MAJ (Aviation) V Kruglov and COL M Yegorov; *The Military Doctrines Of The NATO Countries*; VM R (8); 1966; FPD 0761-67 (7 August 1967); 93

919 G Frank; *Modern War And Certain Biological Problems*; VM S (4-65); 1962; CIA IISR; 1978/05/10; <https://www.cia.gov/library/readingroom/docs/1978-05-10.pdf>

920 COL (Medical Services) A Vorobyev; *The Employment Of Biological Weapons (According To American Information)*; VM S (2-72); 1964; CIA IISR; 1976/04/08; <https://www.cia.gov/library/readingroom/docs/1976-04-08a.pdf>; 4, 15

921 COL S Sokolov; *The Preparation And Conduct Of An Operation By The Armed Forces In A Theater Of Military Operations In The Initial Period Of War (According To The Views Of The NATO Command)*; VM S (2-78); 1966; CIA IISR FIRDB-312-00622-76; 1976/05/10; CREST RDP10-00105R000201870001-8; 14

## Soviet WMD Operation 1959 to 1974

922 *Report Of Colonel-General István Bata, Hungarian Minister Of Defense, To Members Of The HWP Central Committee On The Conduct Of The Staff-Command Exercise Held, 17 July 1956*; 1956/07/17; PHP; <http://www.php.isn.ethz.ch/lory1.ethz.ch/collections/colltopic6938.html?id=19909&navinfo=16606>

923 *Artillery Manual of the Soviet Army*; 1957; MO Military Publishing House; CIA IR C05641016; CIA MDR EOM-2009-0668

924 *Certain Questions In The Combat Utilization Of Artillery In An Offensive Operation Of An Army Being Moved Up From The Depth Of Operational Deployment*; ICA TS (45); 1958; CIA; 1962/01/26; <https://www.cia.gov/library/readingroom/docs/1962-01-26-A.pdf>; also CIA HCD HR70-14 07-18-2012 DVD I-083; *Planning The Combat Use Of The Artillery Of A Motorized Rifle Division In An Offensive Battle With The Use Of Atomic Ammunition*; ICA TS (46); 1958

925 *Artillery Operations During A Divisional Offensive With The Landing Of An Airborne Force In The Tactical Depth Of The Enemy Defense*; ICA TS (46); 1958; CIA; 1962/05/25; <https://www.cia.gov/library/readingroom/docs/1962-05-25.pdf>

926 Lev A Fedorov; *Chemical Armament: A Country's War Against Its Own People*; 2009; V.I CH-4.4; J Med CBR Defense web page-links no longer accessible see Internet Archive Wayback Machine <https://web.archive.org/web/20101101000000*/http://www.jmedcbr.org/issue_0701/Fedorov/Fedorov3_08_09.html>

927 Presentations at 15 June 1999 Moscow International Conference; cited Chemical Weapons Convention Bulletin; Issue No. 45; September 1999; 30; and Lev A Fedorov; *Rossiya*; 1993/12/08; cited Chemical Weapons Convention Bulletin; Issue No. 23; March 1994; 16; <http://www.sussex.ac.uk/Units/spru/hsp/pdfbulletin.html>; also see *Russia's Arms And Technologies: Ordnance and Munitions: The XXI Century Encyclopedia;* 2006; Arms and Technologies; ISBN 5-93799-023-4; XII; part 18 table 440 agents final production year

928 Lev A Fedorov; *Chemical Armament: A Country's War Against Its Own People*; 2009; V.I CH-4.4 V-gas discussion between Tables 4.2 and 4.3; J Med CBR Defense web page-links no longer accessible see Internet Archive Wayback Machine <https://web.archive.org/web/20101101000000*/http://www.jmedcbr.org/issue_0701/Fedorov/Fedorov3_08_09.html>

929 *Soviet Capabilities And Intentions With Respect To Chemical Warfare*; NIE 11-10-63; 1963/12/27; S; <https://www.cia.gov/library/readingroom/docs/DOC_0000242856.pdf>; 3

930 *Soviet Chemical And Biological Warfare Capabilities*; NIE 11-11-69; 1969/02/13; S; <https://www.cia.gov/library/readingroom/docs/DOC_0000283815.pdf>; 4

931 *The Use Of Artillery In Support Of An Army Counterattack*; ICA TS (49); 1959; CIA; 1961/11/28; <https://www.cia.gov/library/readingroom/docs/1961-11-28.pdf>; also CIA HCD HR70-14 07-18-2012 DVD I-085; 5

932 *The Maneuver Of Missile Units In An Offensive Operation*; ICA TS (49); 1959; CIA; 1961/12/15; <https://www.cia.gov/library/readingroom/docs/1961-12-15.pdf>; also CIA HCD HR70-14 07-18-2012 DVD YEAR 1961; 23

933 *Combat Against Enemy Nuclear Artillery, Free Rockets, And Guided Missiles In Offensive And Defensive Operations Of An Army*; 1960/10; TS; Artillery Scientific-Research Institute No. 1; Leningrad; CIA Ironbark; 1962/09/04; <https://www.cia.gov/library/readingroom/docs/1962-09-04a.pdf>; 25 item 26

934 Pavel Felgenhauer; *Perfect Anthrax Application*; Moscow Times; 2001/10/18; web page no longer accessible; see Internet Archive Wayback Machine <https://web.archive.org/web/20011026051746/http://www.cdi.org/russia/176-4.cfm>

935 *Manual On The Conduct Of Operations—Part Two—Ground Forces Operations (Front-Army-Corps);* 1963; GS; CIA IISR TS-778264; 1977/09/29; CIA HCD HR70-14 07-18-2012 DVD VII-99; 11, 66

936 GEN-MAJ P G Yesaulov and COL M P Dukhachev; *Field Service Regulations Of The Armed Forces Of The Union Of SSRs (Division-Regiment)*; 1962; MO Military Publishing House; CIA IR CSDB-3-652,360; 1963/04/30; CIA HCD HR70-14 07-18-2012 DVD III-010 V-010; 66

937 COL (Medical Services) A Vorobyev and A Maslov; *Biological Weapons And Some Problems Of Antibiological Defense;* VM S; CIA IISR; 1976/04/30; CREST RDP10-00105R000201850001-0; 4

938 COL G Yeletskikh; *Aerial Reconnaissance In Support Of The Initial Nuclear Strike Of A Front*; VM S (2-78); 1966; CIA IISR; 1977/01/14; <https://www.cia.gov/library/readingroom/docs/1977-01-14a.pdf>; also CREST RDP10-00105R000100470001-4; 2012/04/13; 5

939 *Warsaw Pact Forces Opposite NATO*; NIE 11-14-79; 1979/01/31; TS; CIA HCD HR70-14 07-18-2012 DVD VII-4 (V.1) *Summary Estimate*; 24; VII-5 (V.2) *The Estimate*; I-8-9

940 Milton Leitenberg et al; *The Soviet Biological Weapons Program: A History*; 2012; Harvard University Press; ISBN 978-0674047709; 135

941 *Solo Voyage*; accessed 2015/06/24; <https://aja-scavesova.livejournal.com/54092.html#cutid1>

942 Nicholas Wade; *24,000-Year-Old Body Shows Kinship To Europeans And American Indians*; New York Times; 2013/11/20; <http://www.nytimes.com/2013/11/21/science/two-surprises-in-dna-of-boy-found-buried-in-siberia.html>

943 *Disarmament: Who's Against?*; 1983; Progress Publishers translation (Military Publishing House; Moscow); 47

944 GEN-MAJ P G Yesaulov and COL B S Zlatoverov (supervisors); *Field Service Regulations Of The Armed Forces Of The Union Of SSRs (Division-Corps)*; Order No. 031; 1959/03/02; S; MO; CIA CSDB-3-648,642; 1961/12/19; CIA CREST 2011-02-07 RDP80T00246A029300140001-1; also CIA HCD HR70-14 07-18-2012 DVD III-003

945 *A Look Back … CIA Asset Pyotr Popov Arrested*; CIA; 2011/01/21; <https://www.cia.gov/news-information/featured-story-archive/2011-featured-story-archive/pyotr-popov.html>

946 GEN-MAJ V A Nebuchinov and COL S G Yefarov (supervisors); *Field Service Regulations Of The Armed Forces Of The USSR (Corps-Division)*; Order No. 0138; 1948/12/28; Ministry of the Armed Forces of the Union SSR; CIA IR CSDB-31680; 1955/05/31; CIA HCD HR70-14 07-18-2012 DVD I-020

947 Abraham S Becker and Edmund D Brunner; *The Evolution Of Soviet Military Forces And Budgets, 1945-1953*; Defense Advanced Research Projects Agency; WN(L)-9248-ARPA; 1975/09; S; access Internet Archive Wayback Machine<https://web.archive.org/web/20120511112402/http://www.dod.mil/pubs/foi/Science_and_Technology/DARPA/553.pdf>; 9

948 *Field Service Regulations Of The Soviet Army (Regiment-Battalion)*; Order No. 065; 1953/04/10; MO; CIA IR; 1955/05/31; CIA HCD HR70-14 07-18-2012 DVD I-21

949 *Field Service Regulations Of The Armed Forces Of The Union Of SSRs (Division-Regiment)*; 1962; MO Military Publishing House; CIA IR CSDB-3-652,360; 1963/04/30; CIA HCD HR70-14 07-18-2012 DVD III-010 and V-010

950 *Manual On The Conduct Of Operations—Part Two—Ground Forces Operations (Front-Army-Corps)*; 1963; GS; CIA IISR TS-778264; 1977/09/29; CIA HCD HR70-14 07-18-2012 DVD VII-99; quote CH-3 66

951 *Principles Of The Employment Of Chemical Missiles*; ICRA TS (54); 1961; CIA; CREST RDP10-00105R000403620001-1; 2012/05/03

952 Presentations at 15 June 1999 Moscow International Conference; cited Chemical Weapons Convention Bulletin; Issue No. 45; September 1999; 30; <http://www.sussex.ac.uk/Units/spru/hsp/pdfbulletin.html>

- **strategic missiles**

953 A Shirokorad and M Pervov; *Ballistic Missiles Of A Great Country*; *Aviatsiya I Kosmonavtika*; 1999; No. 1 38-39 and No. 2 29-30; R-12 section

954 A B Shirokorad; *Atomnyy taran XX veka* [*Atomic Ram Of The XX Century*]; 2005; Veche; Moscow; ISBN 5-9533-0664-4; <http://lib.rus.ec/b/216417/>; PT III, CH-6 system R-12

955 G I Smirnov ED; *Raketnyye Sistemy RVSN Ot R-1 - K «Topolyu-M» 1946-2006* [*Missile Systems Of The RVSN From R-1 To The Topol-M*]; Academy of Military Sciences of the Russian Federation; Council of Veterans of Strategic Missile Troops; Smolensk; 2006; see R-12 section; accessed at <http://www.nauka.x-pdf.ru/17tehnicheskie/213660-5-raketnie-sistemi-rvsn-r-1-topolyu-m-1946-2006-sbornik-materialov-razvitii-raketnogo-oruzhiya-sssr-smolensk-2006-sos.php>; also web site *All about Ruzhany* original page chemical warhead statement see Internet Archive Wayback Machine <https://web.archive.org/web/20090118111539/http://ruzhany.narod.ru/rvsn/SS_4.html>; table R-12U complex specialized versions

956 Lev A Fedorov; *Chemical Armament: A Country's War Against Its Own People*; 2009; V.I CH-4.4 Lethal Chemical Warfare Agents Second Generation; J Med CBR Defense web page-links no longer accessible see Internet Archive Wayback Machine <https://web.archive.org/web/20101101000000*/http://www.jmedcbr.org/issue_0701/Fedorov/Fedorov3_08_09.html>

957 Web site no longer accessible; see Internet Archive Wayback Machine <https://web.archive.org/web/20081226133606/http://9k72.ru/page.php?20>

958 A B Shirokorad; *Atomnyy taran XX veka* [*Atomic Ram Of The XX Century*]; 2005; Veche; Moscow; ISBN 5-9533-0664-4; <http://lib.rus.ec/b/216417/>; PT III, CH-4 system 9K71 *Temp*

- **operational-tactical and cruise missiles**

959 Web site no longer accessible; see Internet Archive Wayback Machine <https://web.archive.org/web/20081226133658/http://9k72.ru/page.php?39>

960 *Soviet Capabilities And Intentions With Respect To Chemical Warfare*; NIE 11-10-63; 1963/12/27; S; <https://www.cia.gov/library/readingroom/docs/DOC_0000242856.pdf>; 8

961 A B Shirokorad; *Atomnyy taran XX veka* [*Atomic Ram Of The XX Century*]; 2005; Veche; Moscow; ISBN 5-9533-0664-4; <http://lib.rus.ec/b/216417/>; PT III, CH-4 system R-17 8K14 9K72

962 *Oka (OTRK)*; Wikipedia RU; <https://ru.wikipedia.org/wiki/%D0%9E%D0%BA%D0%B0_(%D0%9E%D0%A2%D0%A0%D0%9A)>

963 COL P Plyachenko; *The Combat Utilization Of Front Cruise Missiles In A Front Offensive*; VM S (6-61); 1961; CIA Ironbark; 1962/06/15; <https://www.cia.gov/library/readingroom/docs/1962-06-15-A.pdf>; 5

964 A B Shirokorad; *Atomnyy taran XX veka* [*Atomic Ram Of The XX Century*]; 2005; Veche; Moscow; ISBN 5-9533-0664-4; <http://lib.rus.ec/b/216417/>; PT III, CH-5 system S-5 FKR-2 4K95

- **tactical missiles**

965 A B Shirokorad; *Atomnyy taran XX veka* [*Atomic Ram Of The XX Century*]; 2005; Veche; Moscow; ISBN 5-9533-0664-4; <http://lib.rus.ec/b/216417/>; PT III, CH-2 system 9K52 *Luna-M*; CH-3 system 9K79 *Tochka*

966 *Tochka (takticheskiy raketnyy kompleks)*; Wikipedia RU; <https://ru.wikipedia.org/wiki/%D0%A2%D0%BE%D1%87%D0%BA%D0%B0_(%D1%82%D0%B0%D0%BA%D1%82%D0%B8%D1%87%D0%B5%D1%81%D0%BA%D0%B8%D0%B9_%D1%80%D0%B0%D0%BA%D0%B5%D1%82%D0%BD%D1%8B%D0%B9_%D0%BA%D0%BE%D0%BC%D0%BF%D0%BB%D0%B5%D0%BA%D1%81)>

967 *Russia's Arms And Technologies: Ordnance and Munitions: The XXI Century Encyclopedia;* 2006; Arms and Technologies; ISBN 5-93799-023-4; XII; part 18 440>447

968 Chemical Weapons Convention Bulletin; Issue No. 48 Supplement No 2; June 2000; <http://www.sussex.ac.uk/Units/spru/hsp/pdfbulletin.html>; 19

969 Jonathan B Tucker; *War Of Nerves: Chemical Warfare From World War I To Al-Qaeda*; 2006; Pantheon; ISBN 0-375-42229-3; 381

- **tube artillery and rockets**

970 *An Important Confidence Building Step: Foreign Observers Visit The Shikhany Military Area In The Soviet Union*; *Novosti* Press Agency Publishing House; Moscow; 1988; 12, 18 Table 1

971 *Russia's Arms And Technologies: Ordnance and Munitions: The XXI Century Encyclopedia;* 2006; Arms and Technologies; ISBN 5-93799-023-4; XII; part 18 443>447

- **aviation-delivered**

972 *Kratkiy slovar' operativno-takticheskykh i obshchevoyennykh slov (terminov)* [*Short Dictionary Of Operational, Tactical, And General Military Words (Terms)*]; 1958; MO-Military Academy *imeni* M V Frunze; US Department of the Army; Office of the Assistant Chief of Staff for Intelligence; 60-21783; 320 translation chemical aerial bomb; "Bomb used to destroy enemy personnel and contaminate combat equipment and the terrain with poisonous substances of various persistency and toxicity. Chemical aerial bombs may be of impact or time action."

973 *Slovar' osnovnykh voyennykh terminov* [*Dictionary Of Basic Military Terms*]; MO; Moscow; 1965; USAF Soviet Military Thought #20

974 CPT (First Rank) A Zheludev; *Chemical Weapons For Repulsing An Amphibious Landing*; VM S (2-78); 1966; CIA IISR; 1976/02/18; <https://www.cia.gov/library/readingroom/docs/1976-02-18-A.pdf>; also CREST RDP10-00105R000201630001-4

975 COL A Kuchin; *Chemical Warfare Weapons Of The USA And The Lines Along Which They Are Being Developed*; VM S (6-61) 1961; CIA Ironbark; <https://www.cia.gov/library/readingroom/docs/1962-09-10-A.pdf>; 5-6

976 COL A Postovalov et al; *Features Of An Offensive Operation When Neither Side Employs Nuclear Weapons*; VM S (2-75) 1965; CIA IISR; 1978/11/08; <https://www.cia.gov/library/readingroom/docs/1978-11-08.pdf>; 8

977 GEN-LT V Petrenko; *Certain Problems In Planning Combat Operations Without Using Nuclear Weapons*; VM S (3-82) 1967; CIA IISR FIRDB-312-01212-75; 1975/06/09; CREST RDP10-00105R000201100001-2 2012/04/18

978 COL A Postovalov and COL I Pivovar; *The Transition By Troops From Combat Operations With The Exclusive Use Of Conventional Means Of Destruction To The Use Of Nuclear Weapons*; VM S (2-81); 1967; CIA IISR FIRDB-312-01470-74; 1974/04/16; <https://www.cia.gov/library/readingroom/docs/1974-04-16.pdf>; also CREST RDP10-00105R000100410001-0; 2012/04/18

979 GEN-LT F Gayvoronsky; *New Questions Of Operational Art At Its Present Stage Of Development*; VM S (1-89) 1970; CIA IISR FIRDB-312-00903-74; 1974/03/07; <https://www.cia.gov/library/readingroom/docs/DOC_0001199073.pdf>; 7

980 COL A Postovalov and COL I Pivovar; *The Transition By Troops From Combat Operations With The Exclusive Use Of Conventional Means Of Destruction To The Use Of Nuclear Weapons*; VM S (2-81); 1967; CIA IISR FIRDB-312-01470-74; 1974/04/16; <https://www.cia.gov/library/readingroom/docs/1974-04-16.pdf>; also CREST RDP10-00105R000100410001-0; 2012/04/18

981 COL A Kurkov; *Problems Of Conducting Military Operations During A Non-Nuclear Period (Combat Operations Of A Tank Army)*; VM S (1-83); 1968; CIA IISR; 1975/03/12; <https://www.cia.gov/library/readingroom/docs/1975-03-12.pdf>; also CREST RDP10-00105R000100980001-8; 2012/04/11

982 GEN-ARM G Khetagurov; *The Buildup Of Efforts During A Front Offensive Operation*; VM S (1-86) 1969; CIA IISR; 1975/06/09; <https://www.cia.gov/library/readingroom/docs/1975-06-09.pdf>; also CREST RDP10-00105R000201090001-4; 2012/04/19; 6

983 COL A Sulim; *Operational-Tactical And Tactical Rocket Requirements For A Front Offensive Operation*; VM S (1-83) 1968; CIA IISR; 1974/06/13; <https://www.cia.gov/library/readingroom/docs/1974-06-13.pdf>

984 COL V Popov and COL-LT I Apanovich; *Some Results Of The Use Of The PLATFORMA Mobile Computer Post*; VM S (2-81); 1967; CIA IISR; 1976/05/25; <https://www.cia.gov/library/readingroom/docs/1976-05-25.pdf>; also CREST RDP10-00105R000201930001-1; 9>11

985 COL D Shein); *Forewarning And Notifying Troops About Radioactive Contamination*; VM S (3-64); 1962; CIA Ironbark; 1963 illegible date; <https://www.cia.gov/library/readingroom/docs/1963-01-09b.pdf>

986 COL-LT Ye Zhuravlev; *Radiation Situation Or Nuclear Situation?*; VM S (1-80); 1967; CIA IISR; 1975/06/16; <https://www.cia.gov/library/readingroom/docs/1975-06-16.pdf>; also CREST RDP10-00105R000201110001-1; 5-6

987 COL A Novoselov; *Replacement Of Personnel Losses In An Army Offensive Operation*; VM S (2-87); 1969; CIA IISR; 1973/03/26; <https://www.cia.gov/library/readingroom/docs/1973-03-26.pdf>; also CREST RDP10-00105R000100010001-4; 2012/04/13; 6

988 GEN-MAJ P G Yesaulov and COL M P Dukhachev; *Field Service Regulations Of The Armed Forces Of The Union Of SSRs (Division-Regiment)*; 1962; MO Military Publishing House; CIA IR CSDB-3-652,360; 1963/04/30; CIA HCD HR70-14 07-18-2012 DVD III-010 V-010; 10

989 MSU V I Chuikov and GEN-ARM M M Popov; *Critique Of The Front Two-Stage Operational-Rear Exercise Conducted In July 1961*; MO; 1961; CIA CSDB-3-649,129; 1962/03/14; CIA HCD HR70-14 07-18-2012 DVD II-051 V-005; also <https://www.cia.gov/library/readingroom/docs/1962-03-14.pdf>

990 *Plan of the Two-Stage Front-Army War Game for Commanders and Staff Officers to be Conducted on Maps, May 1965*; PHP; <http://www.php.isn.ethz.ch/kms2.isn.ethz.ch/serviceengine/Files/PHP/19635/ipublicationdocument_singledocument/0e169cd9-75ef-493a-8b64-035b470ae241/en/6505_Plan_E.pdf>; table XIII

991 COL A Andryushchenko and COL G Prokopenko; *Some Problems Of Operational Training (According To The Experience Of The Southern Group Of Forces)*; VM S (6-67); 1962; CIA IISR; 1978/11/30; <https://www.cia.gov/library/readingroom/docs/1978-11-30e.pdf>; 12

992 COL A Rodin; *Missile Technical Support In A Front Offensive Operation Beginning Without The Employment Of Nuclear Weapons*; VM S (1-86); 1969; CIA IISR; 1976/07/12; <https://www.cia.gov/library/readingroom/docs/1976-07-12a.pdf>; also CREST RDP10-00105R000302140001-6; 2012/05/02

993 *Operational Plan For An Attack On NATO Forces In Northern Europe By The Missile And Artillery Forces Of The Polish Maritime Front*; CIA IISR CSDB-312-00394-68; 1968/03/11; CIA HCD HR70-14 07-18-2012 DVD VI-022-022a; Tables 5-6

994 *Polish Critique Of The Warsaw Pact "Lato-67" Command Post Exercise*; CIA IISR CSDB-312-01470-68; CIA HCD HR70-14 07-18-2012 DVD VI-034; 17

995 *Danmark under den kolde krig: Den sikkerhedspolitiske situation 1945-1991*; Dansk Institut For Internationale Studier; Copenhagen; 2005; V.II ISBN 87-7605-093-9; <https://www.diis.dk/publikationer/danmark-kolde-krig>; 637

996 Harald Nielsen; *Die DDR Und Die Kernwaffen-Die Nukleare Rolle Der Nationalen Volksarmee Im Warschauer Pakt*; Nuclear History Program 6; 1998; Nomos; ISBN 3-7890-5510-7; 161

997 *Chef Artillerie Des 35. AK*; 1962/10/27; PHP; <http://www.php.isn.ethz.ch/kms2.isn.ethz.ch/serviceengine/Files/PHP/16685/ipublicationdocument_singledocument/64112b63-ef89-46f5-a1fe-d2b49db5c515/de/combat_order.pdf>

998 *Theory And Practice Of Warsaw Pact Operations; Part I: Soviet/Czechoslovak Operational Doctrine, Directives, And Tactics*; CIA IIR; 1972/05/22; CIA HCD HR70-14 07-18-2012 DVD VI-048; 9

999 Dr K Wayne Smith; *Responses to Questions Concerning "Soviet Concepts Of War In Europe"*; TS-202400; CIA DI OSR; 1971/07/01 per catalog; TS; CIA HCD HR70-14 07-18-2012 VII-13; 23

1000 *Overall Strategic Concept For The Defense Of The North Atlantic Treaty Organization Area*; 1968/01/16; <https://www.nato.int/archives/strategy.htm>

1001 GEN-ARM V V Kurasov; *The Influence Of Nuclear Weapons On The Principles Of The Offensive Operations Of A Front*; VM TS (Third) 1960; CIA C00012334 1962/03/09; <https://www.cia.gov/library/readingroom/docs/1962-03-08-A.pdf>; also CIA HCD HR70-14 07-18-2012 DVD III-021; 17

1002 GEN-MAJ S Kuznetsov and GEN-MAJ A Tikhomirov; *Questions Of The Control Of Missile Units In An Offensive Operation*; VM TS (First); 1960; CIA C00012301; 1961/12/20; <https://www.cia.gov/library/readingroom/docs/1961-12-20.pdf>; also CIA HCD HR70-14 07-18-2012 DVD YEAR 1961; 5-6

1003 COL Ye M Nazarov; *Dissertations (For The Candidate's Degree)*; VM S (1-68); 1963; CIA IISR; 1977/08/10; <https://www.cia.gov/library/readingroom/docs/1977-08-10.pdf>; 7 #5

1004 GEN-MAJ S Tarasov; *Special Features Of The Organization And Conduct Of Operations In A Mountainous Theater Of Military Operations*; VM S (6-61); 1961; CIA Ironbark; 1962/07/12; <https://www.cia.gov/library/readingroom/docs/1962-07-12b.pdf>; 2-3

1005 COL G Yefimov; *Coordination Of Adjacent Units During The Use Of Nuclear-Missile Weapons In Operations*; VM S (6-61); 1961; CIA Ironbark; 1962/06/06; <https://www.cia.gov/library/readingroom/docs/1962-07-08.pdf>; also CIA HCD HR70-14 07-18-2012 DVD III-008; 5-6

1006 GEN-LT (Reserve) L. Skvirskiy; *The Meeting Engagement In The Initial Period Of A War*; VM S (5-60); 1961; CIA Ironbark C00304590; <https://www.cia.gov/library/readingroom/docs/1962-07-31.pdf>; 24

1007 MAR (Artillery) S. Varentsov; *The Problem Of Combat With The Nuclear Means Of The Enemy And Its Solution*; VM S (5-60); 1961; CIA Ironbark; 1962/06/01; <https://www.cia.gov/library/readingroom/docs/1962-06-11b.pdf>; 14

1008 GEN-MAJ (Artillery) V Ilinykh and GEN-LT (Signal) P A Kurochkin; *The Question Of Increasing The Stability Of Troop Control*; VM TS (Third); 1961; CIA C00012344; 1962/04/12; <https://www.cia.gov/library/readingroom/docs/1962-04-12.pdf>; 10

1009 COL I Kotov; *Fire Support Of The Landing Operation Of An Airborne Division*; VM S (5-60); 1961; CIA Ironbark; 1962/08/01; <https://www.cia.gov/library/readingroom/docs/CIA-RDP80T00246A029700670001-9.pdf>; 9-10

1010 GEN-MAJ (Artillery) L Sapkov and COL-LT P Pogarskiy; *Methods Of Control Of Rocket Troops In An Offensive Operation Of A Front*; VM S (2-63); 1962; CIA IISR; 1976/12/01; <https://www.cia.gov/library/readingroom/docs/1976-12-01b.pdf>; 4, 10

1011 COL A Lapenin; *Combat Against Enemy Operational Airborne Landing Forces*; VM S (1-62); 1962; CIA IISR; 1978/01/24; <https://www.cia.gov/library/readingroom/docs/1978-01-24-A.pdf>; 8, 18

1012 GEN-MAJ (Aviation) S Shimanskiy and GEN-MAJ (Aviation) V Povarkov; *Actions Of Front Aviation In The First Front Offensive Operation In The Initial Period Of War*; VM S (2-63) 1962; CIA IISR FIRDB-312-03836-74; 1976/10/27; <https://www.cia.gov/library/readingroom/docs/1976-10-27b.pdf>; also CREST RDP10-00105R000302480001-9; 2012/10/03; 15

1013 GEN-MAJ M Bulanov and COL-LT (Engineer) L Potiyenok; *The Planning Of Radioelectronic Countermeasures In Preparing A Front's Offensive Operation*; VM S (5-66); 1962; CIA IISR; 1978/06/01; <https://www.cia.gov/library/readingroom/docs/1978-06-01-A.pdf>; 14

1014 GEN-MAJ (Technical Troops) N Rumyantsev et al; *Work Of A Computation And Analysis Station*; VM S (5-66); 1962; CIA IISR; 1976/11/16; <https://www.cia.gov/library/readingroom/docs/1976-11-16.pdf>; also CREST RDP10-00105R000302600001-5; 5

1015 COL P Shkarubskiy; *Some Matters Of The Employment Of Rocket Troops And Artillery In The Antilanding Defense Of A Seacoast*; VM S (2-69); 1963; CIA IISR; 1977/05/06; <https://www.cia.gov/library/readingroom/docs/1977-05-06b.pdf>; 4-5

1016 MSU M V Zakharov; *Certain Questions Of Soviet Military Art*; VM S (1-68) 1963; CIA IISR 1977/04/15; <https://www.cia.gov/library/readingroom/docs/1977-04-15b.pdf>; 31

1017 COL I Popov and COL I Charikov; *Operations Of A Front Air Army In Support Of A Tank Army*; VM S (3-70); 1963; CIA IISR; 1975/10/17; <https://www.cia.gov/library/readingroom/docs/1975-10-17.pdf>; also CREST RDP10-00105R000201390001-1; 2012/10/16; 6-7

1018 GEN-MAJ (Artillery) A Yanchinskiy; *The Relocation Of Rocket Troops During An Offensive Operation*; VM S (1-71); 1964; CIA IISR; 1975/04/22; <https://www.cia.gov/library/readingroom/docs/1975-04-22.pdf>; also CREST RDP10-00105R000201050001-8; 4-5

1019 GEN-MAJ Yu Abramov et al; *A System Of Collection, Processing, And Transmission Of Information In A Military District*; VM S (2-72); 1964; CIA IISR; 1978/06/20; <https://www.cia.gov/library/readingroom/docs/1978-06-20a.pdf>; 7

1020 GEN-COL I Glebov and GEN-MAJ V Yemelin; *Offensive Operations Of A Front To The Entire Depth Of A Theater Of Military Operations*; VM S (2-72) 1964; CIA IISR; 1975/11/14; <https://www.cia.gov/library/readingroom/docs/1975-11-14b.pdf>; also CREST RDP10-00105R000201480001-1; 2012/10/16; 9

1021 GEN-MAJ N Reut; *Special Operational Exercises*; VM S (2-72); 1964; CIA IISR; 1976/09/13; <https://www.cia.gov/library/readingroom/docs/1976-09-13.pdf>; also CREST RDP10-00105R000302320001-6; 2012/09/27

1022 GEN-MAJ (Artillery) P Zherdev et al; *Some Problems In The Control Of The Rocket Troops Of A Reserve Front During Its Movement Forward For Commitment To An Engagement*; VM S (2-75) 1965; CIA IISR 1976/11/15; <https://www.cia.gov/library/readingroom/docs/1976-11-15b.pdf>; also CREST RDP10-00105R000302580001-8; 2012/10/16; 8

1023 GEN-LT N Ogarkov; *Meeting Engagements In Offensive Operations In The Initial Period Of War*; VM S (3-76); 1965; CIA IISR; 1976/11/30; <https://www.cia.gov/library/readingroom/docs/1976-11-30b.pdf>; also CREST RDP10-00105R000302660001-9; 11

1024 GEN-COL F Malykhin; *Features Of The Rear Support Of Troops In An Offensive Operation Of A Front Conducted Without The Use Of Nuclear Weapons*; VM S (3-76) 1965; CIA IISR; 1975/10/01; <https://www.cia.gov/library/readingroom/docs/1975-10-01.pdf>; also CREST RDP10-00105R000201350001-5 2012/10/03; 7-8, 14

1025 GEN-MAJ S Pogudin et al; *Experience In The Control Of The Rocket Troops*; VM S (2-78); 1966; CIA IISR; 1975/11/14; <https://www.cia.gov/library/readingroom/docs/1975-11-14a.pdf>; also CREST RDP10-00105R000201470001-2; 5

1026 COL M Skoptsov and COL M Vasilenkov; *Combat Actions Of Troops Without The Employment Of Means Of Mass Destruction*; VM S (3-79) 1966; CIA IISR; 1977/04/27; <https://www.cia.gov/library/readingroom/docs/1977-04-27a.pdf>; 9

1027 COL V Yerofeyev; *Repelling An Enemy Tank And Armored Infantry Attack In A Defense*; VM S (1-80); 1967; CIA IISR; 1975/05/27; <https://www.cia.gov/library/readingroom/docs/1975-05-27-A.pdf>; also CREST RDP10-00105R000201060001-7; 2012/05/02; 8

1028 COL A Laptev; *The Use Of Electronic Computers In Military Science Research*; VM S (1-80); 1967; CIA IISR; 1978/07/12; <https://www.cia.gov/library/readingroom/docs/1978-07-12.pdf>; 6, 9-10

1029 COL A Lukash; *The Problem Of Coastal Antilanding Defense*; VM S (3-82); 1967; CIA IISR; 1975/09/29; <https://www.cia.gov/library/readingroom/docs/1975-09-29.pdf>; also CREST RDP10-00105R000201310001-9; 2012/10/04; 5, 8

1030 COL F Trofimov; *Continuous Control Of Army And Front Rocket Troops And Artillery*; VM S (1-80); 1967; CIA IISR; 1973/12/11; originally accessed collection <https://www.cia.gov/library/readingroom/collection/soviet-and-warsaw-pact-military-journals> this article seems to have been wrongly renumbered and effectively lost; see  Internet Archive Wayback Machine <https://web.archive.org/web/20100617050348/http://www.foia.cia.gov/SovietandWarsawPact/1973/1973-12-11b.pdf>; 4, 7

1031 COL A Kurkov; *Problems Of Conducting Military Operations During A Non-Nuclear Period (Combat Operations Of A Tank Army)*; VM S (1-83); 1968; CIA IISR; 1975/03/12; <https://www.cia.gov/library/readingroom/docs/1975-03-12.pdf>; also CREST RDP10-00105R000100980001-8; 2012/04/11; 8

1032 COL Yu Bryukhanov; *The Balance Of Forces Of Opposing Sides In Aviation*; VM S (1-83); 1968; CIA IISR; 1976/10/12; <https://www.cia.gov/library/readingroom/docs/1976-10-12b.pdf>; also CREST RDP10-00105R000302420001-5; 7, 10

1033 COL A Tonkikh; *Overcoming Antitank Defense*; VM S (2-84); 1968; CIA IISR FIRDB-312-04866-73; 1973/11/20; <https://www.cia.gov/library/readingroom/docs/1973-11-20-A.pdf>; 8>10

1034 GEN-MAJ (Artillery) A Prudnikov; *Combat With Enemy Antitank Means In An Offensive Operation*; VM S (2-84); 1968; CIA IISR; 1976/11/15; <https://www.cia.gov/library/readingroom/docs/1976-11-15a.pdf>; 4, 7

1035 GEN MAJ (Artillery) G Biryukov and COL G Khoroshilov; *Destruction Of Enemy Air Defense Installations In The Flight Zone Of An Airborne Landing Force*; VM S (1-83) 1968; CIA IISR; 1976/11/30; <https://www.cia.gov/library/readingroom/docs/1976-11-30a.pdf>; also CREST RDP10-00105R000302650001-0; 2012/09/27; 4

1036 MAR (Tank Troops) A Babadzhanyan; *The Meeting Engagement Of A Tank Army During A Front Offensive Operation*; VM S (3-85); 1968; CIA IISR; 1977/02/10; <https://www.cia.gov/library/readingroom/docs/1977-02-10.pdf>; also CREST RDP10-00105R000100490001-2; 2012/04/18; 11

1037 COL I Rachok; *Defensive Operations Of Ground Forces In A Strategic Operation In A Theater Of Military Operations*; VM S (2-84) 1968; CIA IISR; 1976/10/27; <https://www.cia.gov/library/readingroom/docs/1976-10-27a.pdf>; also CREST RDP10-00105R000302500001-6; 12

1038 GEN-MAJ N Smirnov; *Meeting Engagements In Modern Operations*; VM S (3-88); 1969; CIA IISR; 1976/04/21; <https://www.cia.gov/library/readingroom/docs/1976-04-21-A.pdf>; also CREST RDP10-00105R000201810001-4; 2012/04/12; 13-14

1039 COL N Popov and COL-LT V Krysanov; *Evaluation Of The Effectiveness Of Preemptive Strikes In A Meeting Engagement Of A Tank Army*; VM S (3-88); 1969; CIA IISR; 1974/10/09; <https://www.cia.gov/library/readingroom/docs/1974-10-09.pdf>; also CREST RDP10-00105R000100860001-1; 2012/10/16; 8

1040 COL (Engineer) A Tatarchenko; *The Use Of Mathematical Methods By Staffs In The Process Of Preparing The Decision For An Operation*; VM S (3-88); 1969; CIA IISR; 1976/04/08; <https://www.cia.gov/library/readingroom/docs/1976-04-08b.pdf>; also CREST RDP10-00105R000201760001-0; 2012/04/12; 17

1041 COL V Mozolev et al; *The Development Of Airborne Landing Large Units And The Creation Of Airborne Shock Large Units*; VM S (1-89); 1970; CIA IISR; 1973/07/20; <https://www.cia.gov/library/readingroom/docs/1973-07-20b.pdf>; 7, 10

1042 COL I Magerya; *The Commitment Of A Combined Arms Army To An Engagement From The March (From The Experience Of Command-Staff Exercises And War Games In The Carpathian Military District)*; VM S (3-91); 1970; CIA IISR; 1974/01/08; <https://www.cia.gov/library/readingroom/docs/1974-01-08.pdf>; 5, 9

1043 *The Offensive Operation Of A Combined-Arms Army*; 1973; Academy of Armored Troops; CIA IISR FIRDB-312-03389-77; 1977/12/12; CIA HCD HR70-14 07-18-2012 DVD VII-219. F F Gayvoronsky et al; *Front Offensive Operations*; GSA; 1974; CIA IISR FIRDB-312-01997-79; 1979/09/27; CIA HCD HR70-14 07-18-2012 DVD VII-223

1044 Ghulam Dastagir Wardak; *The Voroshilov Lectures: Materials From The Soviet General Staff Academy*; V.I *Issues Of Soviet Military Strategy*; 1989; National Defense University; 341, 343

1045 *Critique of Exercise "Lato-74"*; 1974/07; CIA IISR TS-788138; 1978/10/20; CIA HCD HR70-14 07-18-2012 DVD VII-151; 51-52

1046 *Soyuz*-1975 only enemy chemical strikes depicted; CWIHP-DA; translations from Polish archive Institute of National Remembrance; *Combat Instruction No 04 of the Maritime Front* <https://digitalarchive.wilsoncenter.org/document/114547>; *Combat Instruction No 17 for Radioelectronic Warfare of the Maritime Front* <https://digitalarchive.wilsoncenter.org/document/114548>

1047 Harald Nielsen; *Die DDR Und Die Kernwaffen-Die Nukleare Rolle Der Nationalen Volksarmee Im Warschauer Pakt*; Nuclear History Program 6; 1998; Nomos; ISBN 3-7890-5510-7; 162-163

1048 *USSR General Staff Academy Lessons*; *The Front Offensive Operation*; Table of Contents 1-19; 1977; GSA; CIA IISR FIRDB-312-00680-80; 1980/04/18; <https://www.cia.gov/library/readingroom/docs/DOC_0001197532.pdf>; also CIA HCD HR70-14 07-18-2012 DVD VII-224

1049 I Y Shavrov *The Front Offensive Operation*; GSA 1977/05; CIA IISR FIRDB-312-00013-79; 1979/06/15; CIA MDR EOM-2009-0157; also CIA HCD HR70-14 07-18-2012 DVD VII-222

1050 GEN-ARM P I Ivashutin; *Principles Of The Organization And Conduct Of Operational Reconnaissance In A Front Offensive Operation*; 1974; GS GRU; CIA IISR FIRDB-312-00311-78; 1978/05/19; CIA HCD HR70-14 07-18-2012 DVD VII-101; 14

1051 COL Ye Rybkin and COL S Dmitriyev; *V I Lenin And The Essence, Character, And Types Of Wars*; VM R (1); 1975/01

1052 Agreement Between The United States of America and The Union of Soviet Socialist Republics on the Prevention of Nuclear War; 1973/06/22; <https://2009-2017.state.gov/t/isn/5186.htm>

1053 MSU N V Ogarkov; *Always In Readiness To Defend The Homeland*; 1982; *Voyenizdat*; Moscow; JPRS L/10412 (25 March 1982); CREST RDP82-00850R000500040058-9; 2007/02/09; 13

1054 Ken Alibek and Stephen Handelman; *Biohazard: The Chilling True Story Of The Largest Covert Biological Weapons Program In The World-Told From The Inside By The Man Who Ran It*; 1999; Random House-Delta; ISBN 0-385-33496-6; mobilization plan 89

1055 Milton Leitenberg et al; *The Soviet Biological Weapons Program: A History*; 2012; Harvard University Press; ISBN 978-0674047709; 38, 60, 64-65

1056 Oleg Penkovskiy and Peter Deriabin; *The Penkovskiy Papers*; 1965; Doubleday; New York; 249

1057 COL Doctor Walter Hirsch; *Soviet BW And CW Preparations And Capabilities*; Harvard University Widener Library; compiled M Meselson 1996/11; War Gas Research in the USSR 74

1058 Vil S Mirzayanov; *State Secrets: An Insider's Chronicle Of The Russian Chemical Weapons Program*; 2009; Outskirts Press; ISBN 978-1-4327-2566-2; ISBN 978-1-4327-1923-4; AN-40 quote 541

1059 Milton Leitenberg et al; *The Soviet Biological Weapons Program: A History*; 2012; Harvard University Press; ISBN 978-0674047709; 508

## begetting the official chemical model

1060 *Warsaw Pact Forces Opposite NATO*; NIE 11-14-79; 1979/01/31; TS; CIA HCD HR70-14 07-18-2012 DVD VII-4 (V.1) *Summary Estimate*; 3; VII-5 (V.2) *The Estimate*; I-7

1061 *The Soviet Offensive Chemical Warfare Threat To NATO*; SNIE 11-17-2-84-L; 1984/11/20; TS; <https://www.cia.gov/library/readingroom/docs/DOC_0000284028.pdf>; 9-10

1062 *Capabilities Of Soviet General Purpose Forces 1964-1970;* NIE 11-14-64; 1964/12/10; S; CIA HCD HR70-14 07-18-2012 DVD V-017; 40

1063 *Slovar' osnovnykh voyennykh terminov* [*Dictionary Of Basic Military Terms*]; MO; Moscow; 1965; USAF Soviet Military Thought #20

1064 COL Ye Yefimov; *The Actual Requirement For And Supplying Of Troops With Conventional Ammunition In Present-Day Operations*; VM S (3-76); 1965; CIA IISR; 1975/09/15; <https://www.cia.gov/library/readingroom/docs/1975-09-15.pdf>; also CREST RDP10-00105R000201280001-3; 2012/10/03

1065 GEN-COL (Artillery) I Volkotrubenko; *Units Of Fire And Norms Of Ammunition Reserves*; VM S (2-78); 1966; CIA IISR; 1977/04/12; <https://www.cia.gov/library/readingroom/docs/1977-04-12.pdf>

1066 GEN-COL (Retired) I Volkotrubenko; *Determining Norms For The Stockpiling And Expenditure Of Artillery Ammunition*; VM S (1-89) 1970; CIA IISR; 1974/01/02; <https://www.cia.gov/library/readingroom/docs/1974-01-02.pdf>; also CIA HCD HR70-14 07-18-2012 DVD VII-078; 9

1067 COL G Yefimov; *Determining Norms For The Stockpiling And Expenditure Of Ammunition By Artillery*; VM S (3-91) 1970; CIA IISR FIRDB-312-00369-74; 1974/04/11; <https://www.cia.gov/library/readingroom/docs/1974-04-11.pdf>; also CIA HCD HR70-14 07-18-2012 DVD VII-082; also CREST RDP10-00105R000100390001-3

1068 *Indications And Warning Of Soviet Intentions To Use Chemical Weapons During A NATO-Warsaw Pact War*; NI IIM 78-10018J; 1978/08; TS; CIA HCD HR70-14 07-18-2012 VII-55; 9

1069 *The Commission On The Intelligence Capabilities Of The United States Regarding Weapons Of Mass Destruction*; Report to the President of the United States; 2005/03/31; FAS; <http://www.fas.org/irp/offdocs/wmd_report.pdf>; 123

1070 *Raketnaya tekhnika* [Rocket Technology]; *Operativno-takticheskiy raketnyy kompleks 9K72 Elbrus* [Operational-tactical missile system 9K72 Elbrus]; <http://rbase.new-factoria.ru/missile/wobb/8k14/8k14.shtml>; section Testing and Operation

1071 *Soviet Chemical Weapons Threat*; DST-1620F-051-85; DIA; 1985; available CREST RDP88B00745R000100140027-5; 2009/10/19

1072 [*U.S. Chemical Arms Pullout From FRG Hailed*]; TASS 1990/07/26 in English; JPRS TAC-90-024 (15 August 1990) Arms Control; 23

1073 [*General Updates Soviet Withdrawal Status*]; Prague CTK 1991/03/25 in English; JPRS TAC-91-008 (8 April 1991) Arms Control; 3

1074 *Soviet Offensive Use Of Chemical Weapons*; Research Report; TCS-5548/83; CIA DI SOVA; 1984/07/31; TS; AP F-1; ISCAP 2012-071 (CIA MDR EOM-2011-00638); also *Warsaw Pact Forces Opposite NATO*; NIE 11-14-75; 1975/09/04; DCI; S; 6; CREST RDP09T00367R000500130001-9; 2011/08/17; and *Indications And Warning Of Soviet Intentions To Use Chemical Weapons During A NATO-Warsaw Pact War*; NI IIM 78-10018J; 1978/08; TS; 10; CIA HCD HR70-14 07-18-2012 DVD VII-55

1075 *An Important Confidence Building Step: Foreign Observers Visit The Shikhany Military Area In The Soviet Union*; *Novosti* Press Agency Publishing House; Moscow; 1988; 18 Table 1

1076 COL A Lapenin; *Combat Against Enemy Operational Airborne Landing Forces*; VM S (1-62); 1962; CIA IISR; 1978/01/24; <https://www.cia.gov/library/readingroom/docs/1978-01-24-A.pdf>; 18

1077 *World Armaments And Disarmament*; Yearbook; 1988; SIPRI; ISBN 0-19-829126-4; <https://www.sipri.org/sites/default/files/SIPRI%20Yearbook%201988.pdf>; Chemical and Biological Warfare 108 quote

1078 Witold Pawlowski; *Bugging Out Is My Specialty*; *Polityka* (15); 1991/04/13; JPRS UMA-91-018 (8 July 1991) Military Affairs; 27

1079 Vojtech Mastny and Malcolm Byrne ED *A Cardboard Castle? An Inside History Of The Warsaw Pact 1955-1991*; 2005; Central European University; ISBN 963-7326-08-1; ISBN 963-7326-07-3; document 112

1080 Karlheinz Lohs; *Postwar Destruction of Chemical Weapons in the Former German Democratic Republic*; in Bernd Appler et al ED; *The Challenge Of Old Chemical Munitions And Toxic Armament Wastes*; 1997; SIPRI/Oxford University; ISBN 0-19-829190-6; 180>183

1081 *NVA Does Not Have Chemical Weapons*; *Berliner Zeitung*; 1990/08/01; JPRS TAC-90-024 (15 August 1990) Arms Control; 14

1082 [*No CWs Reportedly Stored In Hohenleipisch*]; Hamburg DPA; 1990/08/14; JPRS TAC-90-025 (14 August 1990) Arms Control; 3

1083 I Y Shavrov; *The Front Offensive Operation*; GSA 1977/05; CIA IISR FIRDB-312-00013-79; 1979/06/15; CIA MDR EOM-2009-0157; also CIA HCD HR70-14 07-18-2012 DVD VII-222; 23-24

1084 *Soviet Doctrine For Offensive Chemical Warfare Against NATO*; Intelligence Assessment; SOV 84-10105CX; CIA DI SOVA; 1984/06; TS; CIA HCD HR70-14 07-18-2012 DVD VII-116; 3

1085 *Continuing Development Of Chemical Weapons Capabilities In The USSR*; DoD; 1983/10

1086 *Public Affairs Package: Soviet Chemical Threat*; NIC 6097-83; 1983/08/24; C; CREST RDP85T00757R000100200011-7; 2008/01/11

1087 *Soviet Capabilities And Intentions With Respect To Chemical Warfare*; NIE 11-10-63; 1963/12/27; S; 5 stockpile "at least 50,000 tons"; <https://www.cia.gov/library/readingroom/docs/DOC_0000242856.pdf>; Memorandum; 1965/08/19; S; 1 stockpile "at least 200,000 tons and could be considerably larger."; <https://www.cia.gov/library/readingroom/docs/DOC_0000283837.pdf>

1088 *Capabilities Of Soviet General Purpose Forces;* NIE 11-14-65; 1965/10/21; S; CIA HCD HR70-14 07-18-2012 DVD V-020; 13 stockpile "at least 200,000 tons" toxic agent "most are stored in the interior of the USSR."

1089 *Soviet And East European General Purpose Forces;* NIE 11-14-68; 1968/12/12; S; CIA HCD HR70-14 07-18-2012 DVD V-059; also <https://www.cia.gov/library/readingroom/docs/1968-12-12.pdf>; 23

1090 *Soviet Chemical And Biological Warfare Capabilities*; NIE 11-11-69; 1969/02/13; S; <https://www.cia.gov/library/readingroom/docs/DOC_0000283815.pdf>; 5

1091 *Soviet Offensive Chemical Warfare Capabilities: A Preliminary Reassessment*; Working Paper; SR WP 70-3; CIA DI OSR; 1970/06; TS; CIA HCD HR70-14 07-18-2012 DVD VII-66; Introduction, 5

1092 *UK/US Talks on Chemical Warfare: 27/28 July*; 1972/08/11; S; UKNA DEFE 24/791; 3

1093 A G Bohannan; *Soviet Chemical Warfare Offensive Capability*; D/DIS/16/8/1; 1972/09/11; TS UK Eyes Only; UKNA DEFE 24/792

1094 *UK/US Talks on Chemical Warfare: 27/28 July*; 1972/08/11; S; UKNA DEFE 24/791; 3 installations; *Soviet Chemical Warfare Offensive Capability*; D/DIS/16/8/1; 1972/08/03; DEFE 24/791; stockpile; and 1972/09/11; TS UK Eyes Only; DEFE 24/792; 1(d) no forward storage

1095 *Response To NSSM 157: Review Of United States Position On Chemical Weapon Prohibitions*; 1972/08/11; FRUS 1969–1976 V.E–2 Documents on Arms Control and Nonproliferation 1969–1972; <https://history.state.gov/historicaldocuments/frus1969-76ve02/d264>; 2

1096 *Warsaw Pact Forces Opposite NATO*; NIE 11-14-75; 1975/09/04; DCI; S; CREST RDP09T00367R000500130001-9; 2011/08/17; 4, 24

1097 *Warsaw Pact Forces Opposite NATO*; NIE 11-14-79; 1979/01/31; TS; CIA HCD HR70-14 07-18-2012 DVD VII-4 V.I; *Summary Estimate*; 23, 47

1098 *The Development Of Soviet Military Power: Trends Since 1965 And Prospects For The 1980s*; Intelligence Assessment; SR 81-10035X; CIA-OSR; 1981/04; S; CIA HCD HR70-14 07-18-2012 DVD VII-107; 19

1099 *The Soviet Offensive Chemical Warfare Threat To NATO*; SNIE 11-17-2-84-L; 1984/11/20; TS; <https://www.cia.gov/library/readingroom/docs/DOC_0000284028.pdf>; 7

1100 *Trends And Developments In Warsaw Pact Theater Forces, 1985-2000*; NIE 11-14-85-D; 1985/09; S; CREST RDP87T00495R000600560011-2 2010/07/20; 42 sidebar

1101 *Chemicals From Behind Closed Russian Doors*; The Times; 1982/02/24; 4

1102 *Briefing For New Ministers: Brief 4d Arms Control And Disarmament—Chemical Weapons*; D/DS17/8/14; 1983/05/27; S; UKNA CAB 196/123; 15

1103 John Hemsley; *The Soviet Biochemical Threat To NATO*; 1987; St. Martin's/Royal United Services Institute; ISBN 0-312-01589-5; 18

1104 *Review Of Significant Storage Features At Selected Soviet Installations*; Memorandum; Project 250772; 1970/06; TS; NPIC Imagery Exploitation Group; CREST RDP78T04759A009600010014-7; 2002/08/12

1105 *Soviet Capabilities And Intentions With Respect To Chemical Warfare*; NIE 11-10-63; 1963/12/27; S; <https://www.cia.gov/library/readingroom/docs/DOC_0000242856.pdf>; 4

1106 *Warsaw Pact Forces Opposite NATO*; NIE 11-14-79; 1979/01/31; TS; CIA HCD HR70-14 07-18-2012 DVD VII-4 V.I; *Summary Estimate*; 47

1107 S A Tyushkevich; *The Soviet Armed Forces: The History Of Their Organizational Development*; Moscow *Voyenizdat*; 1978; USAF Soviet Military Thought 19; 232

1108 *Soviet Chemical Weapons Threat*; DST-1620F-051-85; DIA; 1985; available CREST RDP88B00745R000100140027-5; 2009/10/19; 15

1109 Jonathan B Tucker; *Biological Weapons In The Former Soviet Union: An Interview With Dr. Kenneth Alibek*; The Nonproliferation Review; Spring-Summer 1999; 7

1110 *Soviet Offensive Chemical Warfare Capabilities: A Preliminary Reassessment*; Working Paper; SR WP 70-3; CIA DI OSR; 1970/06; TS; CIA HCD HR70-14 07-18-2012 DVD VII-66; Introduction, 5

1111 *Trends And Developments In Warsaw Pact Theater Forces, 1985-2000*; NIE 11-14-85-D; 1985/09 ; S; <https://www.cia.gov/library/readingroom/docs/DOC_0000802732.pdf>; also CREST RDP87T00495R000600560011-2; 2010/07/20; 42

1112 *Soviet Chemical And Biological Warfare Program*; NIE 11-17-86; 1986/08; TS; CREST RDP87T00051R000200150001-4; 4, 13, 19 quote

1113 R L Tate et al; *Retaliatory Chemical Warfare—Interim Study Results;* DAS-TR-84-6; Directorate of Aerospace Studies; Air Force Systems Command; 1984/06; S; 20, 26; ISCAP 2009-085

1114 *Memorandum From Jessica Tuchman Mathews and Leslie G. Denend of the National Security Council Staff to the President's Assistant for National Security Affairs (Brzezinski) and the President's Deputy Assistant for National Security Affairs (Aaron)*; 1978/11/30; FRUS 1977–1980 Volume XXVI Arms Control And Nonproliferation; <https://history.state.gov/historicaldocuments/frus1977-80v26>; item 95; 208

1115 *Chemical Warfare Developments-USSR: Soviet Chemical Logistics*; DST-1620S-051-87; DIA/US Army Foreign Science and Technology Center; 1987/06/15; S; <http://www.dia.mil/FOIA/FOIA-Electronic-Reading-Room/FOIA-Reading-Room-Nuclear-Biological-and-Chemical/FileId/39944/>

1116 *Guide On The Organization And Conduct Of Combined Exercises In The Combined Armed Forces Of The Member States Of The Warsaw Pact*; 1975; WPCAF Staff; CIA IISR 1977/06/14; CIA HCD HR70-14 07-18-2012 DVD VII-302; 25-26

1117 Amy E Smithson; *Improving the Security of Russia's Chemical Weapons Stockpile*; 6; and MAJ GEN (Retired) Roland Lajoie; *Cooperative Threat Reduction Support to the Destruction of Russia's Chemical Weapons Stockpile*; 35-36; in *Chemical Weapons Disarmament In Russia: Problems And Prospects*; 1995/10; The Henry L Stimson Center; <https://www.stimson.org/sites/default/files/file-attachments/Report17_1.pdf>

1118 *Russia's Arms And Technologies: Ordnance and Munitions: The XXI Century Encyclopedia;* 2006; Arms and Technologies; ISBN 5-93799-023-4; XII; PT-18 table 440 agents final production year

1119 Sergey Kudryashov; *Vesicant Depot, Chemical Weapons From The Time Of The Great Patriotic War Are Still Posing A Danger To Inhabitants of Udmurtia, Bashkiria, Tataria, And Perm Oblast'*; *Izvestia* Moscow; 1994/07/01; 4; JPRS-TAC-94-007-L (13 July 1994)

1120 Viktor Litovkin; *Russia Lacks The Money To Destroy Its Chemical Weapons*; *Izvestia* Moscow; 1994/09/27; 1, 5; JPRS-TAC-94-014-L (20 October 1994)

1121 *Shikhany Knot*; First Channel Network, Moscow Ostankino TV; 1241 GMT 1994/07/02; JPRS-TAC-94-007-L (13 July 1994)

1122 V. Litovkin; *Chemical Weapons: Steps Toward Zero Level*; *Izvestiya* Moscow; 1990/08/07; 6; JPRS TAC-90-024 (15 August 1990) Arms Control

1123 Lev A Fedorov; *The Soviet Legacy*; CBRNe World; 2009/Summer; subscription required <https://cbrneworld.com/magazine>; 34

1124 Lev A Fedorov; *Chemical Weapons In Russia: History, Ecology, Politics*; 1994; Center of Ecological Policy of Russia; FAS; <https://fas.org/nuke/guide/russia/cbw/jptac008_l94001.htm>

1125 *Trends And Developments In Warsaw Pact Theater Forces, 1985-2000*; NIE 11-14-85-D; 1985/09 ; S; <https://www.cia.gov/library/readingroom/docs/DOC_0000802732.pdf>; also CREST RDP87T00495R000600560011-2; 2010/07/20; 42

1126 *Soviet Chemical And Biological Warfare Program*; NIE 11-17-86; 1986/08; TS; CREST RDP87T00051R000200150001-4; 4, 13

1127 COL Doctor Walter Hirsch; *Soviet BW And CW Preparations And Capabilities*; Harvard University Widener Library; compiled M Meselson 1996/11; PT-I 48

1128 GEN-MAJ A Kuntsevich; *What Lies Behind The Binary Program*; *Mezhdunarodnaya Zhizn* (10); 1986/10; 36>44; JPRS TAC-86-092 (4 December 1986) Arms Control; 86

1129 *Field Regulations Of The RKKA 1929* [Worker-Peasant Red Army]; 1929/06/21; CH-VIII Logistical Support—102 artillery supply; USSR Report Military Affairs; JPRS-UMA-85-019 (13 March 1985); 40

**chemical excision**

1130 *Soviet Doctrine For Offensive Chemical Warfare Against NATO*; Intelligence Assessment; SOV 84-10105CX; CIA DI SOVA; 1984/06; TS; CIA HCD HR70-14 07-18-2012 DVD VII-116

1131 *Hearings Before The Select Committee On Intelligence Of The United States Senate One Hundred Second Congress First Session On Nomination Of Robert M. Gates To Be Director Of Central Intelligence*; US Government Printing Office; 1992; V.II October 2, 1991 273, AP September 25, 1991 707; GWU; <http://nsarchive.gwu.edu/NSAEBB/NSAEBB208/>

1132 *The Soviet Offensive Chemical Warfare Threat To NATO*; SNIE 11-17-2-84-L; 1984/11/20; TS; <https://www.cia.gov/library/readingroom/docs/DOC_0000284028.pdf>; 2, 11-12

1133 *Warsaw Pact Forces Opposite NATO*; NIE 11-14-81; 1981/07/07; TS; <https://www.cia.gov/library/readingroom/docs/DOC_0000281660.pdf>; 6

1134 *Soviet Chemical And Biological Warfare Program*; NIE 11-17-86; 1986/08; TS; CREST RDP87T00051R000200150001-4; 3, 8-9, 37-38 quote

1135 John Hemsley; *The Soviet Biochemical Threat To NATO*; 1987; St. Martin's/Royal United Services Institute; ISBN 0-312-01589-5; 44

1136 GEN-MAJ P P Vechnyy and COL D V Shebalin ED; *Polevoy ustav krasnoy armii* [*Red Army Field Regulations*]; 1944 reprint of 1943; V.1; JPRS-UMA-85-006 (17 January 1985); USSR Report Military Affairs

1137 Amoretta Hoeber and Joseph D Douglass Jr; *The Neglected Threat Of Chemical Warfare*; International Security 3 (1); 1978/Summer; CREST RDP80B01554R003300310056-5; 2005-01-13; 71

1138 *Memorandum from David D. Elliot...;* 1975/01/25; FRUS 1969–1976 V.XXXV; National Security Policy, 1973-1976; item 50 fn #3; <http://history.state.gov/historicaldocuments/frus1969-76v35>; *Telegram From the Department of State to the United States Mission to the*

*North Atlantic Treaty Organization*; 1977/04/20; FRUS 1977–1980 V.XXVI; Arms Control And Nonproliferation; item 65 151; <https://history.state.gov/historicaldocuments/frus1977-80v26>

1139 *The Soviet Offensive Chemical Warfare Threat To NATO*; SNIE 11-17-2-84-L; 1984/11/20; TS; <https://www.cia.gov/library/readingroom/docs/DOC_0000284028.pdf>; 8-9

1140 *Compliance With The Convention On The Prohibition Of The Development, Production, Stockpiling And Use Of Chemical Weapons And On Their Destruction*; Condition (10)(C) Report; 2019/04/15; Russian Federation (Russia); <https://www.state.gov/wp-content/uploads/2019/05/AVC-Condition-10c-2019.pdf>; 12

1141 Douglas P Schultz; *AirLand Battle Doctrine and Its Implications for a Chemical Weapons Convention*; in Joachim Krause ED; *Security Implications Of A Global Chemical Weapons Ban*; 1991; Westview; ISBN 0-8133-8326-9; CH-3 24

1142 Amoretta Hoeber and Joseph D Douglass Jr; *The Neglected Threat Of Chemical Warfare*; International Security 3 (1); 1978/Summer; CREST RDP80B01554R003300310056-5; 2005-01-13; 61-62

1143 Manfred R Hamm; *Deterring Chemical War: The Reagan Formula*; Heritage Foundation; 1983/06/15; Backgrounder Report 272; <http://s3.amazonaws.com/thf_media/1983/pdf/bg272.pdf>

1144 *United States Chemical And Biological Weapons Arms Control Policy*; National Security Decision Directive Number 18; 1982/01/04; S; CREST CIA-RDP85T00176R001000020001-3; 2007/10/19

1145 *World Armaments And Disarmament*; Yearbook; 1988; SIPRI; ISBN 0-19-829126-4; <https://www.sipri.org/sites/default/files/SIPRI%20Yearbook%201988.pdf>; Chemical and Biological Warfare 109

1146 Douglas P Schultz; *AirLand Battle Doctrine and Its Implications for a Chemical Weapons Convention*; in Joachim Krause ED; *Security Implications Of A Global Chemical Weapons Ban*; 1991; Westview; ISBN 0-8133-8326-9; CH-3 25

1147 GEN Bernard W Rogers; *Follow-On Forces Attack (FOFA): Myths And Realities*; NATO Review 32 (6); 1984/12; 7

1148 *The Soviet Offensive Chemical Warfare Threat To NATO*; SNIE 11-17-2-84-L; 1984/11/20; TS; <https://www.cia.gov/library/readingroom/docs/DOC_0000284028.pdf>; 7

1149 *US Policy On Chemical And Biological Warfare And Agents*; FRUS 1969-1976; V.E-2; Documents on Arms Control and Nonproliferation, 1969–1972; 1969/11/10; <https://history.state.gov/historicaldocuments/frus1969-76ve02/d156-06>

1150 *Accuracy Of Russia's Report On Chemical Weapons*; 1994/02/03; <https://www.cia.gov/library/readingroom/docs/DOC_0001239709.pdf>

1151 N Turkatenko; *Building Up The Chemical Weapons Arsenal*; Krasnaya Zvezda 1985/05/04; JPRS TAC-85-014 (21 June 1985) Arms Control; 91; [*U.S. Speeding Up Program*]; TASS Moscow English; 1985/06/01 GMT 1931; JPRS TAC-85-019 (19 July 1985) Arms Control; 143

1152 *An Important Confidence Building Step: Foreign Observers Visit The Shikhany Military Area In The Soviet Union*; Novosti Press Agency Publishing House; Moscow; 1988; 19-20

1153 Oleg Vishnyakov; '*I Was Making Binary Bombs*'—*This Man Is Talking After Five Years Of Silence. He Was Poisoned By Chemical Weapons Made By His Own Hands*; Novoye Vremya (50); 1992/12; 46>49; JPRS-TAC-92-037 (30 December 1992) Arms Control; 58>61

1154 *The Scientist Who Developed "Novichok": "Doses Ranged From 20 Grams To Several Kilos"*; The Bell; 2018/03/20; <https://thebell.io/en/the-scientist-who-developed-novichok-doses-ranged-from-20-grams-to-several-kilos/>; interview Vladimir Uglev

1155 Lev A Fedorov; *Chemical Weapons In Russia: History, Ecology, Politics*; 1994; Center of Ecological Policy of Russia; FAS; <https://fas.org/nuke/guide/russia/cbw/jptac008_l94001.htm>; Third Generation Chemical Weapons

1156 Dr Vil S Mirzayanov; *Dismantling the Soviet/Russian Chemical Weapons Complex: An Insider's View*; in *Chemical Weapons Disarmament In Russia: Problems And Prospects*; 1995/10; The Henry L Stimson Center; <https://www.stimson.org/sites/default/files/file-attachments/Report17_1.pdf>; 21, 25 Table 2

1157 Victor Israelyan; *On The Battlefields Of The Cold War: A Soviet Ambassador's Confession*; 2003; Pennsylvania State University; ISBN 0-271-02297-3; 343

1158 John G Hines et al; *Soviet Intentions 1965-1985* V.II *Soviet Post-Cold War Testimonial Evidence*; Contract MDA903-92-C-0147 OSD-Net Assessment; BDM Federal; 1995/09/22; 48; GWU; <https://nsarchive2.gwu.edu/nukevault/ebb285/index.htm> section links; 25 GEN-COL A A Danilevich

1159 Charles E Arnold; *History Of The Headquarters, 7th Air Division 1 October 1983-31 March 1984;* 1984/09/20; Headquarters 7th Air Division; GWU; <http://www.gwu.edu/~nsarchiv/NSAEBB/NSAEBB427/>; document 11; 181

1160 *WINTEX 83 Senior Level First Impressions Conference, 22 Mar 83*; Memorandum for Record; 1983/03/22; Joint Chiefs of Staff; GWU; <http://www.gwu.edu/~nsarchiv/NSAEBB/NSAEBB427/>; document 2; briefing slide 8-9 March

1161 *US V Corps OPLAN 33001*; 1981/01/01; in Vojtech Mastny ED; *A Cardboard Castle? An Inside History Of The Warsaw Pact 1955-1991*; 2005; Central European University; ISBN 963-7326-08-1; ISBN 963-7326-07-3; document 97

1162 *East German Evaluation of NATO's 1988 Exercises, November 15, 1988*; in Vojtech Mastny ED; *A Cardboard Castle? An Inside History Of The Warsaw Pact 1955-1991*; 2005; Central European University; ISBN 963-7326-08-1; ISBN 963-7326-07-3; document 138

1163 GEN-MAJ V V Larionov; *Problems Of Preventing Conventional War In Europe*; Mirovaya Ekonomika; 1989/07; FBIS-SOV-89-188 (29 September 1989)

1164 GEN-LT V G Reznichenko et al; *Taktika*; 1987; Voyenizdat Moscow; JPRS-UMA-88-008-L-I (29 June 1988); CH-1 6-7, 20

**arms control variant**

1165 *Committee On Disarmament (CD): Delegation Analysis and Recommendations Concerning U.S.-Soviet Chemical Weapons (CW) Consultations*; US Mission Geneva; 1983/08/27; DoS FOIA 200700306

1166 T J Gander; *Soviet Air-launched Chemical Munitions*; Jane's Soviet Intelligence Review; 1989/06; 256-257

1167 *World Armaments And Disarmament*; Yearbook; 1988; SIPRI; ISBN 0-19-829126-4; <https://www.sipri.org/sites/default/files/SIPRI%20Yearbook%201988.pdf>; Chemical and Biological Warfare 109-110

1168 TASS; 1987/12/29

1169 N Bolshakova; *Military Secrecy*; <http://kargopol-2.narod.ru/pressa/pressa36.htm>

1170 Dr Lev A Fedorov; *Pre-Convention Liquidation of Soviet Chemical Weapons*; in Alexander V Kaffka ED; *Sea-Dumped Chemical Weapons: Aspects, Problems And Solutions*; 1996; Kluwer Academic; ISBN 0-7923-4090-6; 20

1171 *Accuracy Of Russia's Report On Chemical Weapons*; 1994/02/03; <https://www.cia.gov/library/readingroom/docs/DOC_0001239709.pdf>

1172 *Treaty Between The United States Of America And The Union Of Soviet Socialist Republics On The Elimination Of Their Intermediate-Range And Shorter-Range Missiles*; Treaty Series V.1657; Secretariat of the United Nations; registered 1991/12/13; No. 28521

1173 *Relocation And Resubordination Of Soviet Ground Equipment: Motives And Significance*; NIC NIO GEN Purpose Forces; 1991/02/07; <https://www.cia.gov/library/readingroom/docs/DOC_0001325076.pdf>

1174 MAJ GEN (Retired) Roland Lajoie; *Cooperative Threat Reduction Support to the Destruction of Russia's Chemical Weapons Stockpile*; 35-36; and Laurie H Boulden; AP Chronology of Events 66 28 July 1988; in *Chemical Weapons Disarmament In Russia: Problems And Prospects*; 1995/10; The Henry L Stimson Center; <https://www.stimson.org/sites/default/files/file-attachments/Report17_1.pdf>

1175 Amy E Smithson; *Improving the Security of Russia's Chemical Weapons Stockpile*; 17 fn #63; in *Chemical Weapons Disarmament In Russia: Problems And Prospects*; 1995/10; The Henry L Stimson Center; <https://www.stimson.org/sites/default/files/file-attachments/Report17_1.pdf>

1176 *Probable Advanced Weapons Storage At Ammunition Depots USSR*; BB; 1983/12/28; NPIC; CREST CIA-RDP91T00712R000100140008-0

1177 John Hart; *The Concept Of 'Order Of Destruction' And Resulting Implications For Destruction Of Chemical Weapons In Russia*; 1996/05; SIPRI; AN-I Table-1

1178 *Committee On Disarmament (CD): Delegation Analysis and Recommendations Concerning U.S.-Soviet Chemical Weapons (CW) Consultations*; US Mission Geneva; 1983/08/27; DoS FOIA 200700306

1179 [*Committee On Disarmament (CD): Soviet Plenary Statement On Chemical Weapons (CW) Issues August 18, 1983*]; DoS untitled document; CD/PV 235; 20; DoS FOIA 200700306

1180 Lev A Fedorov; *The Soviet Legacy*; CBRNe World; 2009/Summer; subscription required <https://cbrneworld.com/magazine>; 34

1181 Judith Perera; *Chemical Munitions in the Commonwealth of Independent States and the Surrounding Seas*; in Bernd Appler et al ED; *The Challenge Of Old Chemical Munitions And Toxic Armament Wastes*; 1997; SIPRI/Oxford University; ISBN 0-19-829190-6; 121

1182 Judith Perera; *Chemical Munitions in the Commonwealth of Independent States and the Surrounding Seas*; in Bernd Appler et al ED; *The Challenge Of Old Chemical Munitions And Toxic Armament Wastes*; 1997; SIPRI/Oxford University; ISBN 0-19-829190-6; 133 sourced to *Izvestia* 1992/12/03 and *Komsomolskaya Pravda* 1991/06/08

1183 David Hoffman; *Russia's Forgotten Chemical Weapons*; Washington Post; 1998/08/16; <http://www.washingtonpost.com/wp-srv/inatl/longterm/coldwar/leonidovkaa.htm>

1184 *An Important Confidence Building Step: Foreign Observers Visit The Shikhany Military Area In The Soviet Union*; Novosti Press Agency Publishing House; Moscow; 1988; 18 Table-1

1185 *Russia's Arms Catalog: Precision Guided Weapons And Ammunition*; 1997; Military Parade Ltd; V.VII; PT-17, 705

1186 [*Committee On Disarmament (CD): Soviet Plenary Statement On Chemical Weapons (CW) Issues August 18, 1983*]; DoS untitled document; CD/PV 235; 20; DoS FOIA 200700306

## US Intelligence Fabricates Another Model

1187 *Russia's Arms And Technologies: Nuclear Weapons Complex: The XXI Century Encyclopedia;* 2007; Arms and Technologies; ISBN 978-5-93799-035-8; XIV; 370-371; and Pavel Podvig et al; *Russian Strategic Nuclear Forces*; 2001; MIT; ISBN 0-262-16202-4; 109>111

1188 G I Smirnov ED; *Raketnyye Sistemy RVSN Ot R-1 - K «Topolyu-M» 1946-2006* [*Missile Systems Of The RVSN From R-1 To The Topol-M*]; Academy of Military Sciences of the Russian Federation; Council of Veterans of Strategic Missile Troops; Smolensk; 2006; see R-5-5M section; accessed at <http://www.nauka.x-pdf.ru/17tehnicheskie/213660-5-raketnie-sistemi-rvsn-r-1-topolyu-m-1946-2006-sbornik-materialov-razvitii-raketnogo-oruzhiya-sssr-smolensk-2006-sos.php>

1189 Milton Leitenberg et al; *The Soviet Biological Weapons Program: A History*; 2012; Harvard University Press; ISBN 978-0674047709; 64

1190 Penkovsky Meetings; 1961; CIA
#2 1961/04/21 [London]; <https://www.cia.gov/library/readingroom/docs/DOC_0000012393.pdf>; para 35
#12 1961/05/01 London; <https://www.cia.gov/library/readingroom/docs/DOC_0000012400.pdf>; para 14-15
1191 GEN-COL (Artillery) G F Odintsov; *Rear Area Support Of Missile Troops In Front Offensive Operations*; VM TS (Second) 1961; CIA C00012285; <https://www.cia.gov/library/readingroom/docs/1961-08-25-B.pdf>; also CIA HCD HR70-14 07-18-2012 DVD YEAR 1961
1192 Kirovograd-25; web page no longer accessible; see Internet Archive Wayback Machine <https://web.archive.org/web/20130916105959/http://kirovograd-25.com/site/history/index.php>

## official nuclear model

1193 Clarke Ketter; *Outline Of A Cold War Mission: The National Stockpile Sites And Operational Storage Sites*; Cold War Times 8 (3); 2008/08
1194 *Soviet Nuclear Weapons Logistics Operations*; DIA Directorate for Scientific and Technical Intelligence—Nuclear Energy Division; 1988/04; S; 15; ISCAP 2010-063 (DIA MDR-0108-2009)
1195 *Soviet Tactical Nuclear Forces And Gorbachev's Nuclear Pledges: Impact, Motivations, And Next Steps*; NI IIM 91-10006; DC ; 1991/11; S; 2; GWU; <http://nsarchive.gwu.edu/NSAEBB/NSAEBB561-1991-nuclear-pullback-sparked-US-Soviet-arms-race-in-reverse/> Document 19
1196 *The DOD Modernization Program for Tactical Nuclear Forces in Europe*; DoS Action Memorandum; 1975/09/11; S; in *The Euromissiles Crisis And The End Of The Cold War, 1977-1987*; PT-II Document Reader; item 1 under 1975; Woodrow Wilson Center; <https://www.wilsoncenter.org/sites/default/files/Euromissles_Reader_PartII_Section%20A.pdf>
1197 GEN-MAJ (Engineer Troops) P Ogorodnikov et al;; *Fortification And Its Tasks In Modern Warfare*; VM S (5-60); 1961; CIA Ironbark; 1962/09/17; <https://www.cia.gov/library/readingroom/docs/1962-09-17.pdf>
1198 COL (Engineer) A Ambartsumyan; *Fortification In Modern Warfare*; VM S 1(80); 1967; CIA IISR; 1975/07/09; CREST RDP10-00105R000201130001-9; 2012/10/16; quote 9
1199 *Comparison Of US And USSR Atomic Energy Programs*; 1962/07; S; <https://www.cia.gov/library/readingroom/docs/DOC_0000873163.pdf>; AN-C IV(D) Stockpile Facilities 20-21
1200 *12-ye Glavnoye upravleniye ministerstva oborony Rossii* [12th Main Directorate of the Ministry of Defense of Russia]; Wikipedia RU; <http://ru.wikipedia.org/wiki/12_%D0%93%D0%A3%D0%9C%D0%9E>
1201 *Russia's Arms And Technologies: Nuclear Weapons Complex: The XXI Century Encyclopedia;* 2007; Arms and Technologies; ISBN 978-5-93799-035-8; XIV; 162-163, 174>177
1202 *The Soviet Atomic Energy Program*; NIE 11-2A-59; 1959/08/18; TS; <https://www.cia.gov/library/readingroom/docs/DOC_0000843185.pdf>; 12, 46
1203 Pavel Podvig et al; *Russian Strategic Nuclear Forces*; 2001; MIT; ISBN 0-262-16202-4; 69, 75
1204 Anton Nikitin; *Iz istorii obrazovaniya 12 GU MO* [History of the formation of 12 GU MO]; <http://frankovsk-16.ru/index.php/articles/7-gumo/2-iz-istorii-obrazovaniya-12-gu-mo.html>
1205 V A Anastasiev; *O moyem uchastii v sozdanii yadernogo shchita Otechestva* [About my participation in the creation of the nuclear shield of the Fatherland]; <http://frankovsk-16.ru/index.php/articles/7-gumo/1-0-moem-uchastii-v-sozdanii-yadernogo-shchita-otechestva.html>
1206 Anton Nikitin; *Iz istorii obrazovaniya 12 GU MO* [History of the formation of 12 GU MO]; <http://frankovsk-16.ru/index.php/articles/7-gumo/2-iz-istorii-obrazovaniya-12-gu-mo.html>
1207 Vladimir Verkhovtsev; *O glavnom yadernom upravlenii*; [About the main nuclear directorate]; <http://frankovsk-16.ru/index.php/articles/7-gumo/3-o-glavnom-yadernom-upravlenii.html>
1208 Pavel Podvig et al; *Russian Strategic Nuclear Forces*; 2001; MIT; ISBN 0-262-16202-4; 69, 73
1209 Jeffrey T Richelson; *Spying On The Bomb—American Nuclear Intelligence From Nazi Germany To Iran And North Korea;* 2006; W W Norton; ISBN 978-0-393-05383-8; 67
1210 *12-ye Glavnoye upravleniye ministerstva oborony Rossii* [12th Main Directorate of the Ministry of Defense of Russia]; Wikipedia RU; <http://ru.wikipedia.org/wiki/12_%D0%93%D0%A3%D0%9C%D0%9E>
1211 *Briefing Paper For The Joint Chiefs Of Staff*; 1957/08/26; CREST RDP61S00750A000600150028-8; 2003-12-18
1212 *Russia's Arms And Technologies: Nuclear Weapons Complex: The XXI Century Encyclopedia;* 2007; Arms and Technologies; ISBN 978-5-93799-035-8; XIV; 387
1213 *National Photographic Interpretation Center: The Years Of Project HTAUTOMAT, 1956-1958*; 1974/12; S; V.I; CIA History Staff; CREST RDP04T00184R000400010001-1; 2010/03/12; 23, 59, 84>94, 90 quote
1214 *National Photographic Interpretation Center: The Years Of Project HTAUTOMAT, 1956-1958*; 1974/12; S; V.III; CIA History Staff; CREST RDP04T00184R000400030001-9; 2012/07/09; 493 fn #163
1215 *National Photographic Interpretation Center: The Years Of Project HTAUTOMAT, 1956-1958*; 1974/12; S; V.IV; CIA History Staff; CREST RDP04T00184R000400040001-8; 2010/07/21; 28 sketch

1216 *Handbook For Soldiers And Sergeants On Defense Against Atomic Weapons*; 1954; MO, CIA IR; 1955/02/25; CREST RDP80-00810A006000260001-9; 2008/02/14; 5, 8-9

1217 *Kratkiy slovar' operativno-takticheskykh i obshchevoyennykh slov (terminov)* [*Short Dictionary Of Operational, Tactical, And GEN Military Words (Terms)*]; 1958; MO-Military Academy *imeni* M V Frunze; US Department of the Army; Office of the Assistant Chief of Staff for Intelligence; 60-21783; 50 *boyevyye radioaktivnyye veshchestva*

1218 G I Smirnov ED; *Raketnyye Sistemy RVSN Ot R-1 - K «Topolyu-M» 1946-2006* [*Missile Systems Of The RVSN From R-1 To The Topol-M*]; Academy of Military Sciences of the Russian Federation; Council of Veterans of Strategic Missile Troops; Smolensk; 2006; Birth of Nuclear Missiles memoir section 3; accessed at <http://www.nauka.x-pdf.ru/17tehnicheskie/213660-5-raketnie-sistemi-rvsn-r-1-topolyu-m-1946-2006-sbornik-materialov-razvitii-raketnogo-oruzhiya-sssr-smolensk-2006-sos.php>;

1219 *U.S. Foresaw Radiological Weapon To Kill Leaders In Cold War*; Associated Press; 2007/10/09

1220 *P-2*; Wikipedia RU; <https://ru.wikipedia.org/wiki/%D0%A0-2>

1221 A Shirokorad and M Pervov; *Ballistic Missiles Of A Great Country*; *Aviatsiya I Kosmonavtika*; 1999; No. 1 38-39 and No. 2 29-30; R-5M section

1222 *Soviet Nuclear Weapons*; CIA IR; 1963/03/11; <https://www.cia.gov/library/readingroom/docs/1963-03-11d.pdf>

1223 COL (Reserve) G Ivanov; *Radiological Weapons (According To The Views Of Foreign Specialists)*; *Zarubezhnoye Voyennoye Obozreniye* (3); 1985/03; JPRS-UMA-85-043 (26JUL85)

1224 Anton Nikitin; *Iz istorii obrazovaniya 12 GU MO* [History of the formation of 12 GU MO]; <http://frankovsk-16.ru/index.php/articles/7-gumo/2-iz-istorii-obrazovaniya-12-gu-mo.html>

1225 *12-ye Glavnoye upravleniye ministerstva oborony Rossii* [12th Main Directorate of the Ministry of Defense of Russia]; Wikipedia RU; <http://ru.wikipedia.org/wiki/12_%D0%93%D0%A3%D0%9C%D0%9E>

1226 *Russia's Arms And Technologies: Nuclear Weapons Complex: The XXI Century Encyclopedia;* 2007; Arms and Technologies; ISBN 978-5-93799-035-8; XIV; 387

1227 *History Of The Custody And Deployment Of Nuclear Weapons: July 1945 Through September 1977*; Office of the Assistant To The Secretary of Defense (Atomic Energy); 1978/02; TS; DoD FOIA; 15 1950 transfers, 53 Eisenhower approval ,113 Stockpile Agreement

1228 V A Anastasiev; *O moyem uchastii v sozdanii yadernogo shchita Otechestva* [About my participation in the creation of the nuclear shield of the Fatherland]; <http://frankovsk-16.ru/index.php/articles/7-gumo/1-o-moem-uchastii-v-sozdanii-yadernogo-shchita-otechestva.html>

1229 Charles Tuten; *Making The (Right) Connections*; 2006; ISBN 978-1-881625-22-3

1230 GEN-LT Nikolai Beloborodov; *The War Was Averted*; in *U kraya yadernoi bezdny* [On the edge of nuclear abyss];1998; Moscow; 204>213; GWU; <http://www2.gwu.edu/~nsarchiv/NSAEBB/NSAEBB449/>; document 2

1231 *P-1*; Wikipedia RU; <https://ru.wikipedia.org/wiki/%D0%A0-1_(%D1%80%D0%B0%D0%BA%D0%B5%D1%82%D0%B0)>

1232 *OAK Mission 4037 UR 23 to 30 May 1967*; 1967/06/03; NPIC; CREST RDP78B03817A000500040044-8; 2009/06/11; Spassk-Dalniy Tactical SSM Support Fac

1233 *Military Depots, Camps, Casernes, Training Centers, Officers' Schools And Artillery "Polygons" Of The Central Asian Military District*; CIA IR; 1954/05/03; CREST RDP82-00047R000400400001-1; 2002/08/07

1234 Lev A Fedorov; *Chemical Armament: A Country's War Against Its Own People*; 2009; V.I CH 1.6; J Med CBR Defense web page-links no longer accessible see Internet Archive Wayback Machine <https://web.archive.org/web/20101101000000*/http://www.jmedcbr.org/issue_0701/Fedorov/Fedorov3_08_09.html>

1235 Lev A Fedorov; *Chemical Weapons In Russia: History, Ecology, Politics*; 1994; Center of Ecological Policy of Russia; FAS; <https://fas.org/nuke/guide/russia/cbw/jptac008_l94001.htm>

1236 *Soviet Capabilities And Intentions With Respect To Chemical Warfare*; NIE 11-10-63; 1963/12/27; S; <https://www.cia.gov/library/readingroom/docs/DOC_0000242856.pdf>; 5, 21 map

## bunkers rebus

1237 *Search Of Five Sites To Determine If They Have Nuclear Weapons Stockpile Function*; Memorandum; NPIC PID/ABCB 218/63; 1963/10/02; TS; CREST CIA-RDP78T04743A000100040001-9; 2004-05-05

1238 *Sensitive Operations Complex Near Bulyzhino, USSR*; PIR; NPIC R-237/64; 1964/04; TS; CREST CIA-RDP78T05439A000300310021-5; 2012/11/08

1239 *Chaadayevka Sensitive Operations Complex, Chaadayevka, USSR*; BB; NPIC; 1966/08/28; TS; CREST CIA-RDP78TO5929A002000040022-1; 2007/03/01

1240 Christopher A Preble; *John F. Kennedy And The Missile Gap*; 2004; Northern Illinois University Press; DeKalb; 151

1241 James G Blight et al; *Cuba On The Brink: Castro, The Cuban Missile Crisis, And The Soviet Collapse*; 1993; Pantheon; IBN 0-679-42149-1; 135

1242 Ernest R May et al; *History Of The Strategic Arms Competition 1945-1972*; OSD Historical Office; 1981/03; TS; PT-II; [576] Table-4

1243 *Wohlstetter, Soviet Strategic Forces, And National Intelligence Estimates*; [1974]; S; CREST CIA-RDP83M00171R001600010001-9; 2005/04/18; 5

1244 *Soviet Capabilities For Long Range Attack Through Mid-1965*; NIE 11-8-60; DCI; 1960/08/01; <https://www.cia.gov/library/readingroom/docs/1960-08-01.pdf>; 3

1245 Ernest R May et al; *History Of The Strategic Arms Competition 1945-1972*; OSD Historical Office; 1981/03; TS; PT-II; [576] Table-4

1246 *Soviet Atomic Energy Programs*; NIE 11-2-67; 1967/06/15; TS; <https://www.cia.gov/library/readingroom/docs/DOC_0001028263.pdf>; 18-19

1247 *The Major Function Of The Soviet Sensitive Operations Complexes*; Scientific and Technical Intelligence Report; CIA DST OSI; 1970/03; TS; ISCAP 2012-033 (CIA EOM-2011-00299)

1248 *Soviet Nuclear Programs*; NIE 11-2-71; 1971/06/10; TS; <https://www.cia.gov/library/readingroom/docs/DOC_0000843192.pdf>; 11

## Hypothesis X

1249 *Committee On Disarmament (CD): Soviet Plenary Statement on Chemical Weapons (CW) Issues, August 18, 1983*; US Mission Geneva; CD-261; 1983/08/23; DoS FOIA 200700306

1250 *Subject: US–USSR Chemical Weapons Negotiations, Round nine: Sixth (Final) Plenary Meeting, April 12, 1979.*; 1979/04/19; FRUS 1977–1980 Volume XXVI Arms Control And Nonproliferation; <https://history.state.gov/historicaldocuments/frus1977-80v26>; item 99; 219

1251 *Sensitive Operations Complex Near Bulyzhino, USSR*; PIR; NPIC R-237/64; 1964/04; TS; CREST CIA-RDP78T05439A000300310021-5; 2012/11/08

1252 Penkovsky Meeting 12 London; 1961/05/01; <https://www.cia.gov/library/readingroom/docs/DOC_0000012400.pdf>; 18

1253 *Sensitive Operations Complex Berezovka, USSR*; Joint PIR; PIC/JR-12/60; 1960/06; TS; CREST RDP78T04751A000400010034-4; 2003-02-27

1254 Oleg Bukharin and Kenneth Luongo; *U.S.-Russian Warhead Dismantlement Transparency: The Status, Problems, And Proposals*; PU/CEES Report No. 314; 1999/04; Princeton University/Center for Energy and Environmental Studies; <http://www.bits.de/NRANEU/NonProliferation/docs/ransac_transparency.html>; fn #30

1255 *The Nuclear Matters Handbook—Expanded Edition*; Office of Assistant Secretary of Defense for Nuclear, Chemical, and Biological Defense Programs; [2011] 11; current edition <https://www.acq.osd.mil/ncbdp/nm//NMHB/index.htm>

1256 *Russia's Arms And Technologies: Nuclear Weapons Complex: The XXI Century Encyclopedia;* 2007; Arms and Technologies; ISBN 978-5-93799-035-8; XIV; 387>391

1257 *General Technical-Utilization Requirements For Preparation Of Hardened Control Post Installations;* National Defense Committee Resolution No. 1/77; AT 1; CIA IISR TS-798315; 1979/11; CIA HCD HR70-14 07-18-2012 DVD VII-185; 17-18

1258 *Protection Against Chemical And Biological Agents And Radiological Fallout*; 1961/01/19; US Army; EM 1110-345-461; 2, 13

1259 *Chemical Warfare: DOD's Successful Effort To Remove U.S. Chemical Weapons From Germany*; Report to Congressional Requestors; 1991/02; US General Accounting Office; GAO/NSIAD-91-105; 16

## coinciding coincidences

### • the nuclear estimate

1260 *Impact Of Republic Sovereignty On Soviet Strategic Forces*; Memorandum; NIC M 91-10007; 1991/09; GWU; <https://nsarchive.gwu.edu/briefing-book/nuclear-vault-nunn-lugar-russia-programs/2016-12-12/nunn-lugar-25th-anniversary-shows>; document 1, 1

1261 *Hearings Before The Select Committee On Intelligence Of The United States Senate One Hundred Second Congress First Session On Nomination Of Robert M. Gates To Be Director Of Central Intelligence*; US Government Printing Office; 1992; ISBN 0-16-039542-9; V.III October 3, 1991; 54; GWU; <http://nsarchive.gwu.edu/NSAEBB/NSAEBB208/>

1262 Oleg Bukharin and Kenneth Luongo; *U.S.-Russian Warhead Dismantlement Transparency: The Status, Problems, And Proposals*; PU/CEES Report No. 314; 1999/04; Princeton University/Center for Energy and Environmental Studies; <http://www.bits.de/NRANEU/NonProliferation/docs/ransac_transparency.html>; fn #1

1263 Jon Brook Wolfsthal et al ED; *Nuclear Status Report—Nuclear Weapons, Fissile Material, And Export Controls In The Former Soviet Union;* Number 6; 2001/06; Monterey Institute of International Studies/Carnegie Endowment for International Peace; 3

1264 Thomas B Cochran et al; *Making The Russian Bomb: From Stalin To Yeltsin*; 1995; Westview/Natural Resources Defense Council; ISBN 0-8133-2328-2; 31-32

1265 *Ministry Refutes Data On Nuclear Potential Of Former USSR*; ITAR-TASS; 1993/10/01; JPRS TND-93-034 (27 October 1993) Proliferation Issues

1266 Andrei Zagorski; *Russia's Tactical Nuclear Weapons: Posture, Politics And Arms Control*; 2011/02; Institut Für Friedensforschung Und Sicherheitspolitik; <https://www.files.ethz.ch/isn/127021/hb156.pdf>; 16

1267 Oleg Bukharin; *A Breakdown Of Breakout: U.S. And Russian Warhead Production Capabilities*; Arms Control Today 32(8); 2002/10; <https://www.armscontrol.org/act/2002-10/features/breakdown-breakout-us-russian-warhead-production-capabilities>

1268 David E Hoffman; *The Dead Hand—The Untold Story Of The Cold War Arms Race And Its Dangerous Legacy;* 2009; Doubleday (Random House); ISBN 978-0-385-52437-7; 400, 542 fn #42

1269 Vitaly I Feskov et al; *Sovetskaya Armiya v gody «kholodnaya voyna» (1945-1991)* [*The Soviet Army During The 'Cold War'*]; Tomsk State University; 2004; ISBN 5-7511-1819-7; <http://militera.lib.ru/h/0/pdf/feskov_vi02.pdf>; CH-3 Strategic Rocket Troops 131

1270 Rina Mishina; *Novosti*; First Channel Network, Moscow Ostankino TV; 1100 GMT 1992/04/11; JPRS TND-92-012 (22 April 1992) Proliferation Issues; 8

1271 Oleg Bukharin and Kenneth Luongo; *U.S.-Russian Warhead Dismantlement Transparency: The Status, Problems, And Proposals*; PU/CEES Report No. 314; 1999/04; Princeton University/Center for Energy and Environmental Studies; <http://www.bits.de/NRANEU/NonProliferation/docs/ransac_transparency.html>; fn #1

1272 *Soviet Tactical Nuclear Forces And Gorbachev's Nuclear Pledges: Impact, Motivations, And Next Steps*; NI IIM 91-10006; DC ; 1991/11; S; 2; GWU; <http://nsarchive.gwu.edu/NSAEBB/NSAEBB561-1991-nuclear-pullback-sparked-US-Soviet-arms-race-in-reverse/> Document 19, 2

1273 Gunnar Arbman and Charles Thornton; *Russia's Tactical Nuclear Weapons Part II: Technical Issues and Policy Recommendations*; 2005/02; Swedish Defence Research Agency—Systems Technology; FOI-R-1588-SE; ISSN 1650-1942; 59 fn #130 source

1274 Laszlo Becz et al; *OKSNAR - Fully Assembled State—Soviet Nuclear Weapons In Hungary 1961-1991*; Veszprém; 2019; 19 nuclear weapons generations; 23 special readiness conditions; 24 table containers stacked

## The Case Of The Hidden Nukes

1275 Aleksey Sinelnikov; *Can A Nuclear Train Be Seized?*; *Komsomolskaya Pravda*; Moscow; 1998/01/16; 2; FBIS-TOT-98-009

1276 V A Anastasiev; *O moyem uchastii v sozdanii yadernogo shchita Otechestva* [About my participation in the creation of the nuclear shield of the Fatherland]; <http://frankovsk-16.ru/index.php/articles/7-gumo/1-o-moem-uchastii-v-sozdanii-yadernogo-shchita-otechestva.html>

1277 GEN-MAJ (Retired) Alexander Melnikov; *Perevernutyye stranitsy* [*Turned Pages*]; web pages no longer accessible; see Internet Archive Wayback Machine <https://web.archive.org/web/20120407115726/http://kirovograd-25.com/site/history/general/index.php?story=vyh> exercise page

1278 V Litovkin; *Who Holds The Keys To The Nuclear Button*; *Izvestiya*; 1991/09/23; JPRS TAC-91-024 (18 October 1991) Arms Control

1279 Moysey Rabinovich; *Soviet Conventional Arms Transfers To The Third World: Main Missile And Artillery Directorate (1966-1990)*; Global Consultants Inc.; 1993; 8 fn, 26-27, 29

1280 *Yadernyye tayny: 43-ho arsenala* [Nuclear Secrets: 43rd Arsenal]; *Armija* (5); 2011/09; 12>15; article no longer accessible; see Internet Archive Wayback Machine <https://web.archive.org/web/20120329095859/http://www.mod.mil.by/armia/pdf/2011n5/4.pdf>

1281 *Instruktsiya po perevozke spetsial'nykh gruzov zheleznodorozhnym transportom* [*Instructions On The Transport Of Special Cargo By Rail Transportation*]; 1986; UN-64dsp-1.Zh2 [УН-64дсп-1.Ж2]; MO Military Publishing House; Moscow

1282 G I Smirnov ED; *Raketnyye Sistemy RVSN Ot R-1 - K «Topolyu-M» 1946-2006* [*Missile Systems Of The RVSN From R-1 To The Topol-M*]; Academy of Military Sciences of the Russian Federation; Council of Veterans of Strategic Missile Troops; Smolensk; 2006; see R-5-5M section; accessed at <http://www.nauka.x-pdf.ru/17tehnicheskie/213660-5-raketnie-sistemi-rvsn-r-1-topolyu-m-1946-2006-sbornik-materialov-razvitii-raketnogo-oruzhiya-sssr-smolensk-2006-sos.php>

1283 Charles Tuten; *Rear Services Support Of Soviet Frontal Rocket Troops*; S103999 IAR-061-83 Z-12114-83; NPIC; 1983/12; CREST CIA-RDP85T00840R000200120001-3-9; 1117-1118

1284 I Y Shavrov; *The Front Offensive Operation*; GSA 1977/05; CIA IISR FIRDB-312-00013-79; 1979/06/15; CIA MDR EOM-2009-0157; also CIA HCD HR70-14 07-18-2012 DVD VII-222; 76

1285 F F Gayvoronsky et al; *Front Offensive Operations*; GSA; 1974; CIA IISR FIRDB-312-01997-79; 1979/09/27; CIA HCD HR70-14 07-18-2012 DVD VII-223; 132

1286 *Material on Exercise "Shield-76"*; 1976/09; CIA IISR TS-768153; 1976/12/23; CIA HCD HR70-14 07-18-2012 DVD VII-296; AT-4 Situation of Rocket Troops and Artillery 68, AT-10 Situation of the Technical Services 122>125

1287 *Polish Army Mobilization Periods And Executors*; 1973; CIA IISR TS-204587; 1974/03/11; CIA HCD HR70-14 07-18-2012 DVD VII-027

1288 *Material on Exercise "Shield-76"*; 1976/09; CIA IISR TS-768153; 1976/12/23; CIA HCD HR70-14 07-18-2012 DVD VII-296; AT-10 Situation of the Technical Services—Tab No. 4 24th Air Army 233

1289 COL A Lasenin and GEN-MAJ (Artillery) F Gorlenko; *Combat Against Enemy Nuclear Weapons In A Front Offensive Operation*; VM S (4-65); 1962; CIA IISR; 1978/06/20; <https://www.cia.gov/library/readingroom/docs/1978-06-20b.pdf>

1290 COL A Khorenkov; *Combat With Enemy Tactical Means Of Nuclear Attack*; VM S (3-82); 1967; CIA IISR; 1975/09/30; <https://www.cia.gov/library/readingroom/docs/1975-09-30a.pdf>

1291 *Manual On The Conduct Of Operations—Part Two—Ground Forces Operations (Front-Army-Corps)*; 1963; GS; CIA IISR TS-778264; 1977/09/29; CIA HCD HR70-14 07-18-2012 DVD VII-99; 95

1292 Brigadier GEN Jerzy Skalski; *Employment Of Rocket Troops And Artillery*; 1970; CIA IISR FIRDB-312-00112-84; 1984/01/19; <https://www.cia.gov/library/readingroom/docs/1984-01-19A.pdf>; 6, AT-1 schematic [18]

1293 F F Gayvoronsky et al; *Front Offensive Operations*; GSA; 1974; CIA IISR FIRDB-312-01997-79; 1979/09/27; CIA HCD HR70-14 07-18-2012 DVD VII-223; 176

1294 I Y Shavrov; *The Front Offensive Operation*; GSA 1977/05; CIA IISR FIRDB-312-00013-79; 1979/06/15; CIA MDR EOM-2009-0157; also CIA HCD HR70-14 07-18-2012 DVD VII-222; 107

1295 MAR (Artillery) S Varentsov; *On The Report Of The Commander Of Missile Troops And Artillery, Chief Marshall Of Artillery Comrade S. S. Varentsov*; CIA IR; 1963/03/13; <https://www.cia.gov/library/readingroom/docs/1963-03-13c.pdf>

1296 GEN-MAJ F Marushchak and COL K Arsenyev; *A Troop Offensive From Permanent Deployment Areas*; VM S (2-78); 1966; CIA IISR; 1977/05/10; <https://www.cia.gov/library/readingroom/docs/1977-05-10a.pdf>

1297 GEN-MAJ (Artillery) L Sapkov and COL P Shkarubskiy; *Theoretical Recommendations And Their Application By The Troops*; VM S (1-80) 1967; CIA IISR FIRDB-312-00002-78; 1978/01/04; <https://www.cia.gov/library/readingroom/docs/DOC_0001199104.pdf>; 4-5 quotes

1298 GEN-COL G Kariofilli; *Front Rocket Troops In The Transition To The Offensive From Areas Of Permanent Location*; VM S (2-78) 1966; CIA IISR; 1974/05/20; <https://www.cia.gov/library/readingroom/docs/1974-05-20.pdf>; also CREST RDP10-00105R000101030001-1; 8

1299 *Operational Mission—Situation As Of 1700 Hours 4 April*; CIA IISR TS-788328; 1978/11/17; CIA HCD HR70-14 07-18-2012 DVD VII-103; 25 AP-7 Table-3 notes

1300 *USSR General Staff Academy Lessons*; *The Front Offensive Operation*; Lesson 7a; *Preparation and Critique of the Plan of the Combat Employment of the Rocket Troops and Artillery in a Front Offensive Operation*; 1977; GSA; CIA IISR FIRDB-312-01110-80; 1980/06/06; CIA HCD HR70-14 07-18-2012 DVD VII-229; 17>20

1301 *Material on Exercise "Shield-76"*; 1976/09; CIA IISR TS-768153; 1976/12/23; CIA HCD HR70-14 07-18-2012 DVD VII-296; AT-10 Situation of the Technical Services 126

1302 Aleksey Sinelnikov; *Can A Nuclear Train Be Seized?*; *Komsomolskaya Pravda*; Moscow; 1998/01/16; 2; FBIS-TOT-98-009

1303 COL V Aleksandrov; *Concerning The Problem Of Increasing The Readiness Of Rocket Troops Of The Front For Delivering An Initial Nuclear Strike*; VM S (3-82); 1967; CIA IISR FIRDB-312-01469-74; 1974/04/12; CREST RDP10-00105R000100400001-1; 2012/04/13

1304 COL A Rodin; *Missile Technical Support In A Front Offensive Operation Beginning Without The Employment Of Nuclear Weapons*; VM S (1-86); 1969; CIA IISR; 1976/07/12; <https://www.cia.gov/library/readingroom/docs/1976-07-12a.pdf>; also CREST RDP10-00105R000302140001-6; 2012/05/02; 6

1305 F F Gayvoronsky et al; *Front Offensive Operations*; GSA; 1974; CIA IISR FIRDB-312-01997-79; 1979/09/27; CIA HCD HR70-14 07-18-2012 DVD VII-223; 132

1306 *USSR General Staff Academy Lessons*; *The Front Offensive Operation*; 1977; GSA; CIA HCD HR70-14 07-18-2012 Supplementary Material for Lesson No. 1—Report of the Chief of the Operations Directorate of the Coastal Front (variant); CIA IISR FIRDB-312-00106-82; 1982/02/05; DVD VII-273; 5 alert rocket troops and aviation strike times
Lesson 1c; *Preparation and Reporting of Proposals of the Chief of Rocket Troops and Artillery on the Combat Employment of Rocket Troops and Artillery in a Front Offensive Operation*; CIA IISR FIRDB-312-0966-80; 1980/04/23; DVD VII-225; 11 permission

1307 *Scaleboard SSM Launch Facilities At Soviet Rocket Forces Installations*; PIR; 1967/11; TS; NPIC; CREST CIA-RDP78T04759A007500010046-5; 2003-08-04 and *Modified MRBM Sites May Be For Scaleboard*; IAS Notes; 1968/11/08; TS; CIA DI IAS; CREST CIA-RDP78T04759A008300010028-6; 2002-05-07

1308 *The Balance Of Nuclear Forces In Central Europe*; Intelligence Assessment; SR 78-10004; CIA NFAC OSR; 1978/01; S; CIA HCD HR70-14 07-18-2012 DVD VII-051; 2

1309 GEN-MAJ (Artillery) A P Suntsovyy and GEN-MAJ (Artillery) A K Gorlinskiy; *The Combat Employment Of Rocket Troops And Artillery In An Offensive Operation Of A Front And Army*; 1969/02; GSA; CIA IISR FIRDB-312-03096-76; 1976/12/22; CIA HCD HR70-14 07-18-2012 DVD VII-213; 10

1310 COL A Postovalov and COL I Pivovar; *The Transition By Troops From Combat Operations With The Exclusive Use Of Conventional Means Of Destruction To The Use Of Nuclear Weapons*; VM S (2-81); 1967; CIA IISR FIRDB-312-01470-74; 1974/04/16; <https://www.cia.gov/library/readingroom/docs/1974-04-16.pdf>; also CREST RDP10-00105R000100410001-0; 2012/04/18; 14

1311 COL A Postovalov; *Transition To The Use Of Nuclear Weapons In The Course Of An Offensive Operation*; VM S (3-91) 1970; CIA IISR FIRDB-312-02892-73; 1973/06/15; CIA HCD HR70-14 07-18-2012 DVD VII-021; also CREST RDP10-00105R000100170001-7; 2012/09/27; 10

1312 Richard Garwin; *The Test Ban And National Security*; 2011/05/10; Arms Control Association; presentation at Thomas J Watson IBM Research Center; <http://www.armscontrol.org/events/2011AnnualMeeting#2>

1313 *Combat Regulations Of The Navy For Division, Brigade, Regiment, And Ship*; 1983; MO Military Publishing House; CIA IISR TS-878129; 1987/03/13; <https://www.cia.gov/library/readingroom/docs/DOC_0001430731.pdf>; 33-34 CH-12
 1314 GEN-LT Yu Kardashevsky; *In Whose Hands Is The "War Button"*; *Argumenty I Fakty* (52); Moscow; 1991/12; 2; JPRS TND-92-002 (31 January 1992) Proliferation Issues; 39
 1315 *Strategic Rocket Forces*; 1985; GSA; CIA IISR TS-878526; 1987/07/24; 13; ISCAP 2012-026 (CIA MDR EOM-2009-00158)

**leaning forward**
 1316 Penkovsky Meetings; 1961; CIA
#1 1961/04/20 London; <https://www.cia.gov/library/readingroom/docs/DOC_0000012392.pdf>; para 101 finding
#4 1961/04/23 Leeds; <https://www.cia.gov/library/readingroom/docs/DOC_0000012394.pdf>; para 36 Gryzlov source—two hidden areas
#12 1961/05/01; London; <https://www.cia.gov/library/readingroom/docs/DOC_0000012400.pdf>; para 19 2x2 4
#18 1961/07/18-19; London; CIA HCD HR70-14 07-18-2012 DVD II-021; para 65 artillery dumps modifications
#38 1961/10/05 Paris; <https://www.cia.gov/library/readingroom/docs/DOC_0000012418.pdf>; para 16 first missile brigade
 1317 *Assignments Of Senior Soviet Military Officials*; CIA Chickadee IR; 1963/03/12; <https://www.cia.gov/library/readingroom/docs/1963-03-12c.pdf>
 1318 *Current Status Of Soviet And Satellite Military Forces And Indications Of Military Intentions*; Memorandum; CIA; 1961/09/06; Annex item 2; GWU collection The Cuban Missile Crisis 1962; microfiche 1398 #21 item 106
 1319 *Capabilities Of Soviet General Purpose Forces;* NIE 11-14-65; 1965/10/21; S; CIA HCD HR70-14 07-18-2012 DVD V-020; 12 para 40
 1320 *Capabilities Of Soviet General Purpose Forces*; NIE 11-14-66; 1966/11/03; S; <https://www.cia.gov/library/readingroom/docs/DOC_0000278472.pdf>; 14 para 39
 1321 The *Soviet And East European General Purpose Forces;* NIE 11-14-67; 1967/11/16; S; CIA HCD HR70-14 07-18-2012 DVD V-055; 18 para 61
 1322 *Soviet And East European General Purpose Forces;* NIE 11-14-69; 1969/12/04; S; CIA HCD HR70-14 07-18-2012 DVD VII-001-001a; 13 para 33
 1323 *Warsaw Pact Mobilization And Reinforcement*; SR JS 71-2; Verification Panel Working Group for Mutual and Balanced Force Reduction—Interagency Team on Mobilization and Reinforcement; 1971/02; TS; CIA HCD HR70-14 07-18-2012 DVD VII-008; 60
 1324 GEN-LT K. Kolganov et al; *Certain Questions Of The Development Of Soviet Military Art From 1953-1960*; VM S (1-77) 1966; CIA IISR; 1977/04/11; <https://www.cia.gov/library/readingroom/docs/1977-04-11c.pdf>; 13
 1325 GEN-COL I Glebov and GEN-MAJ V Yemelin; *Offensive Operations Of A Front To The Entire Depth Of A Theater Of Military Operations*; VM S (2-72) 1964; CIA IISR; 1975/11/14; <https://www.cia.gov/library/readingroom/docs/1975-11-14b.pdf>; also CREST RDP10-00105R000201480001-1; 2012/10/16; 9
 1326 *Soviet Strategic Forces For Peripheral Strike*; Intelligence Report; SR IR 71-5; CIA DI OSR; 1971/05; TS; CIA HCD HR70-14 07-18-2012 DVD VII-010; 13
 1327 GEN-MAJ (Artillery) A P Suntsovyy and GEN-MAJ (Artillery) A K Gorlinskiy; *The Combat Employment Of Rocket Troops And Artillery In An Offensive Operation Of A Front And Army*; 1969/02; GSA; CIA IISR FIRDB-312-03096-76; 1976/12/22; CIA HCD HR70-14 07-18-2012 DVD VII-213; 11
 1328 GEN-COL (Retired) I Volkotrubenko; *Determining Norms For The Stockpiling And Expenditure Of Artillery Ammunition*; VM S (1-89) 1970; CIA IISR; 1974/01/02; <https://www.cia.gov/library/readingroom/docs/1974-01-02.pdf>; also CIA HCD HR70-14 07-18-2012 DVD VII-078; 9-10
 1329 MAR R Malinovskiy and MAR M Zakharov; *To The Chairman Of The Defense Council Comrade N. S. Khrushchev*; 1962/05/24; MO; CIA HCD HR70-14 07-18-2012 DVD IV-013 (from CWIHP)
 1330 GEN Anatoli Gribkov and GEN William Y Smith; *Operation Anadyr: U.S. And Soviet Generals Recount The Cuban Missile Crisis*; 1994; Edition Q; ISBN 0-86715-266-4; 28
 1331 *Warsaw Pact Forces Opposite NATO*; NIE 11-14-79; 1979/01/31; TS; CIA HCD HR70-14 07-18-2012 DVD VII-4 (V.1) *Summary Estimate*; 85; VII-5 (V.2) *The Estimate*; VI-12
 1332 *Treaty Between The United States Of America And The Union Of Soviet Socialist Republics On The Elimination Of Their Intermediate-Range And Shorter-Range Missiles*; Treaty Series V.1657; Secretariat of the United Nations; registered 1991/12/13; No. 28521
 1333 A Shirokorad and M Pervov; *Ballistic Missiles Of A Great Country*; *Aviatsiya I Kosmonavtika*; 2000; No. 1 16>18 and No. 2 35>39; *Pioner* RSD-10 section
 1334 *Soviet Capabilities For Strategic Nuclear Conflict Through The Mid-1990s*; NIE 11-3/8-84/85; DCI; V.I *Summary*; 1985/04/25; TS; 26 para 39, 30 para 42
 1335 *Temp-S*; Wikipedia RU; <https://ru.wikipedia.org/wiki/%D0%A2%D0%B5%D0%BC%D0%BF-%D0%A1>
 1336 *Strategic Rocket Forces*; 1985; GSA; CIA IISR TS-878526; 1987/07/24; 10; ISCAP 2012-026 (CIA MDR EOM-2009-00158)
 1337 James M Markham; *Gorbachev Offensive: Splitting Allies*; The New York Times; 1985/10/04
 1338 James M Markham; *Excerpts From Soviet Official's Response To Arms Questions*; The New York Times; 1985/10/18

1339 John G. Hines et al; *Soviet Intentions 1965-1985*; Contract MDA903-92-C-0147 OSD-Net Assessment; BDM Federal; 1995/09/22; V.I *An Analytical Comparison Of U.S.-Soviet Assessments During The Cold War*; 62; V.II *Soviet Post-Cold War Testimonial Evidence*; 97-98 V L Kataev; GWU; <https://nsarchive2.gwu.edu/nukevault/ebb285/index.htm> section links

1340 *Briefing On INF Monitoring*; 1988/01/18; <https://www.cia.gov/library/readingroom/docs/DOC_0000273323.pdf>; 7

1341 *The INF Treaty Monitoring And Verification* [sic] *Capabilities*; 1988/03/21; <https://www.nti.org/media/pdfs/US_Senate_1988_INF_treaty.pdf?_=1439479996>; 5, 7 quote

1342 Ghulam Dastagir Wardak; *The Voroshilov Lectures: Materials From The Soviet General Staff Academy*; V.III *Issues Of Operational Art*; 1992; National Defense University; 222-223

1343 COL A Sulim; *Operational-Tactical And Tactical Rocket Requirements For A Front Offensive Operation*; VM S (1-83) 1968; CIA IISR; 1974/06/13; <https://www.cia.gov/library/readingroom/docs/1974-06-13.pdf>

1344 COL A Rodin; *Missile Technical Support In A Front Offensive Operation Beginning Without The Employment Of Nuclear Weapons*; VM S (1-86); 1969; CIA IISR; 1976/07/12; <https://www.cia.gov/library/readingroom/docs/1976-07-12a.pdf>; also CREST RDP10-00105R000302140001-6; 2012/05/02

1345 COL A Postovalov; *Transition To The Use Of Nuclear Weapons In The Course Of An Offensive Operation*; VM S (3-91) 1970; CIA IISR FIRDB-312-02892-73; 1973/06/15; CIA HCD HR70-14 07-18-2012 DVD VII-021; also CREST RDP10-00105R000100170001-7; 2012/09/27

1346 *USSR General Staff Academy Lessons*; *The Front Offensive Operation*; 1977; GSA; CIA HCD HR70-14 07-18-2012
Lesson 1a; *The Making and Critique of the Decision of the Front Commander for an Offensive Operation—Report of the Chief of the Front Rocket Troops and Artillery*; CIA IISR FIRDB-312-02605-80; 1980/10/24; DVD VII-247; 37-38
Lesson 1c; *Preparation and Reporting of Proposals of the Chief of Rocket Troops and Artillery on the Combat Employment of Rocket Troops and Artillery in a Front Offensive Operation*; 1977; GSA; CIA IISR FIRDB-312-0966-80; 1980/04/23; DVD VII-225; 8-9
Lesson 01e; *Decision-Making and Critique of the Front Commander's Decision for the Offensive Operation*; CIA IISR FIRDB-312/02229-80 1980/09/19; DVD VII-242; 13>20
Lesson 7a; *Preparation and Critique of the Plan of the Combat Employment of the Rocket Troops and Artillery in a Front Offensive Operation;* CIA IISR FIRDB-312-01110-80; 1980/06/06; DVD VII-229; 8, 16>18

1347 Laszlo Becz et al; *OKSNAR - Fully Assembled State—Soviet Nuclear Weapons In Hungary 1961-1991*; Veszprém; 2019; 204-205; 9K72 27x launchers 51x nuclear warheads and 99x missiles with 12x resupply and 9K52 34x launchers 68x nuclear warheads and 126x rockets with 17x resupply

1348 Laszlo Becz et al; *OKSNAR - Fully Assembled State—Soviet Nuclear Weapons In Hungary 1961-1991*; Veszprém; 2019; 234-235 tables delivery systems and nuclear warheads 1965>1989, 240 doubling, 123 Russian officer

1349 *Protocol On Assignment Of PPR Army And Navy Forces To The Combined Armed Forces And Their Development In 1981-1985*; 1981/01; CIA IISR TS-828045; 1982/04/19; <https://www.cia.gov/library/readingroom/docs/DOC_0005508933.pdf>; AT-4 Materiel Reserves 56 I. Missiles and Ammunition

1350 *Warsaw Pact Forces For Operations In Eurasia*; NIE 11-14-71; DCI; Memorandum to Holders; 1972/08/10; S; <https://www.cia.gov/library/readingroom/docs/DOC_0000278527.pdf>; 2-3 para 9; identification of five warhead storage sites [Type VII] in addition to the seven first noted in the September 1971 base NIE—information that may have been in V.II Annexes not declassified; 1971/09/09; <https://www.cia.gov/library/readingroom/docs/1971-09-09.pdf>; also CIA HCD HR70-14 07-18-2012 DVD VII-014

1351 *Warsaw Pact Forces Opposite NATO*; NIE 11-14-79; 1979/01/31; TS; CIA HCD HR70-14 07-18-2012 DVD VII-5 (V.2) *The Estimate*; II-47

1352 *History Of The Custody And Deployment Of Nuclear Weapons: July 1945 Through September 1977*; Office of the Assistant To The Secretary of Defense (Atomic Energy); 1978/02; TS; DoD FOIA; 61

## paradigm bounce

1353 Ghulam Dastagir Wardak; *The Voroshilov Lectures: Materials From The Soviet General Staff Academy;* V.I *Issues Of Soviet Military Strategy;* 1989; National Defense University; 360 Glossary

1354 A A Bobrikov and V F Ivashchenko; *O raketakh, raketnykh formirovaniyakh i 233-y raketnoy brigade* [*About Missiles, Missile Formations And The 233rd Missile Brigade*]; 2005; <https://web.archive.org/web/20160305004502/http://www.bestin.ru/forum/viewtopic.php?f=1&t=119>

1355 *Nuclear Disarmament Timeline*; Nuclear Threat Initiative; web page no longer accessible; see Internet Archive Wayback Machine <https://web.archive.org/web/20150824212505/http://www.nti.org/analysis/articles/nuclear-disarmament-timeline/>; date 1956; the 1957 'Rapacki Plan' had similar objectives—see Ryan Alexander Musto; *Polish Perspectives On The Rapacki Plan For The Denuclearization Of Central Europe*; Woodrow Wilson International Center; 2019/09/23; <https://www.wilsoncenter.org/blog-post/polish-perspectives-the-rapacki-plan-for-the-denuclearization-central-europe>

1356 *12-ye Glavnoye upravleniye ministerstva oborony Rossii* [12th Main Directorate of the Ministry of Defense of Russia]; Wikipedia RU; <http://ru.wikipedia.org/wiki/12_%D0%93%D0%A3%D0%9C%D0%9E>; pre expurgation version see Internet Archive Wayback Machine <https://web.archive.org/web/20111119091012/http://ru.wikipedia.org/wiki/12_%D0%93%D0%A3%D0%9C%D0%9E>

1357 GEN-LT Nikolai Beloborodov; *The War Was Averted*; in *U kraya yadernoi bezdny* [On the edge of nuclear abyss];1998; Moscow; 204>213; GWU; <http://www2.gwu.edu/~nsarchiv/NSAEBB/NSAEBB449/>; document 2

1358 GEN Anatoli Gribkov and GEN William Y Smith; *Operation Anadyr: U.S. And Soviet Generals Recount The Cuban Missile Crisis*; 1994; Edition Q; ISBN 0-86715-266-4; 45-46

1359 GEN-MAJ I D Statsenko; *Report Of Major-General Igor Demyanovich Statsenko, Commander Of The 51st Missile Division, About The Actions Of The Division From 07.12.62 Through 12.01.1962*; GWU; <http://www2.gwu.edu/~nsarchiv/NSAEBB/NSAEBB449/>; document 1

1360 Michael Dobbs; *One Minute To Midnight—Kennedy, Khrushchev, And Castro On The Brink Of Nuclear War;* 2008; Alfred A Knopf/Borzoi; ISBN 978-1-4000-4358-3; 172>175; also GWU; <https://nsarchive2.gwu.edu//nsa/cuba_mis_cri/dobbs/warheads.htm>

1361 Charles Tuten; *Making The (Right) Connections*; 2006; ISBN 978-1-881625-22-3

1362 Michael Erler; *Das Inferno von Dannenwalde; DDR-Geheim*; 2006/10/05; web page no longer accessible; see Internet Archive Wayback Machine <https://web.archive.org/web/20090502194328/http://www.heimatmuseum-wiefelstede.de/2008%20Das%20Erbe%20der%20Sonnensucher.htm>; program listing

1363 Charles Tuten; *Rear Services Support Of Soviet Frontal Rocket Troops*; S103999 IAR-061-83 Z-12114-83; NPIC; 1983/12; CREST CIA-RDP85T00840R000200120001-3-9; 1117-1118

1364 *Soviet Nuclear Weapons Logistics: The German Depot Problem*; Defense Technical Intelligence Report; DIA; 1980/04/10; TS; ISCAP 2010-060 (DIA MDR-0198-2009)

1365 *MBFR Monitoring Summary*; 1975/09/05; DCI NIO-Conventional Forces; CREST RDP79R01142A000900010001-8; 2006/11/17; AP-C Collection Resources

1366 Web page no longer accessible; see Internet Archive Wayback Machine <https://web.archive.org/web/20120211181838/http://www.usmlm.org/home/nicholson/ludwigslust.htm>

1367 Stephen V Hoyt; *Cold War Pioneers In Combined Intelligence And Analysis*; Intelligence And National Security 23 (4); 2008/08

## remembrance of things past

1368 *Dokladnaya zapiska R.YA. Malinovskogo, K.N. Rudneva, M.I. Nedelina v TSK KPSS o remonte raket R-1 i R-2, khranyashchikhsya v boyevom zapase Ministerstva oborony SSSR*; [*Memorandum of R. Ya. Malinovsky, K.N. Rudnev, M.I. Nedelin in the Central Committee of the CPSU on the repair of the R-1 and R-2 missiles stored in the combat stock of the USSR Ministry of Defense*]; 1959/08/07; TS; <https://rvsn.info/library/docs/doc_1_0298.html>

1369 *The German Long-Range Rocket Programme 1930-1945*; 1945/10/30; and *Supplement: Organisation, Training And Supply*; 1945/12/27; M.I.4/14; [UK] War Office; UKNA; DEFE 40/22

1370 *Aktenvermerk über die Besprechung am 24. Oktober 1944 bei Generallt.d.Waffen-SS Kammler in Berlin* [Note For The Record on the 24 October 1944 conference…]; 1944/10/25; Smithsonian National Air and Space Museum microfiche collection

1371 *"Crossbow": Enemy Long Range Weapons—Intelligence And Counter-Measures*; C.O.S (45) 191 (O); 1945/03/20; [UK] War Cabinet—Chiefs of Staff Committee; Part I para 4; UKNA; AIR 20/8200

1372 *Dispersed Storage Units At Blizna (4177/47-33), Peenemunde (4414/1848), Bois De Baugy (4250/6F/2), And Foret De Nieppe (4040/51)*; Crossbow; Interpretation Report No. B.S. 779; 1944/08/04; A.C.I.U; UKNA; DEFE 40/0123

1373 *Preliminary Report On The Visit Of The Anglo-American Mission To The German Experimental Rocket Station In Poland*; 1944/09/22; UKNA; AIR 40/2517

1374 *"Herring-bone" Sites Suspected Of Rocket Storage*; 1945/03/12; A.I.2.(h)/108/6; USNA RG 319 ID Document 131810

1375 *U.S.S.R.—Guided Weapon Development: Reinterrogation Of Dipl. Ing. Helmut Groettrup*; D.S.I./J.T.I.C. Report No. 15; [UK] Ministry of Defence; 1954/09; UKNA DEFE 44/101; 27 para 174

1376 Rainer Gessert; *Geheime Kommandosache A4—Heimat Lager Slate*; *Der Kanonier* No. 29; 1/2006; Parchim; 2-3; <http://home.snafu.de/veith/Texte/Lager-Slate.pdf>

1377 *Report On The Availability And Location Of Materiel Reserves For Support Of Forces Of The Polish Army And Navy Assigned To The Composition Of The Combined Armed Forces In Wartime (As Of 1 January 1980)*; CIA IISR C05508932; 1980/10/06; <https://www.cia.gov/library/readingroom/docs/DOC_0005508932.pdf>; 7

1378 *Protocol On Assignment Of PPR Army And Navy Forces To The Combined Armed Forces And Their Development In 1981-1985*; 1981/01; CIA IISR TS-828045; 1982/04/19; <https://www.cia.gov/library/readingroom/docs/DOC_0005508933.pdf>; AT-4 *Materiel Reserves* 56 table airframes 84xR-17 [Scud-B] plus 172xLuna M [FROG-7] planned end 1985

## clashing perspectives

1379 GEN Bernard W. Rogers; *Follow-On Forces Attack (FOFA): Myths And Realities*; NATO Review 32 (6); 1984/12; <https://www.cia.gov/library/readingroom/docs/CIA-RDP85M00364R000801310018-3.pdf>

1380 *Trends And Developments In Warsaw Pact Theater Forces, 1985-2000*; NIE 11-14-85-D; 1985/09 ; S; <https://www.cia.gov/library/readingroom/docs/DOC_0000802732.pdf>; also CREST RDP87T00495R000600560011-2; 2010/07/20; 13

1381 Matthias Karthe; *Katalog der Splitterschutzgaragen der GSSD* [GSFG Hardened Garages]; 2018/12; independent publication; comprehensive study of chronology, unit deployment background and subordination, configurations-dimensions, with individual location aerial and ground-level photographs of missile launch garrisons and RTBs

1382 Laszlo Becz et al; *OKSNAR - Fully Assembled State—Soviet Nuclear Weapons In Hungary 1961-1991*; Veszprém; 2019; 67 RTB Tab establishment and out-deployed battalion of 107 RBr Dombóvár; 72-73 RTB Szákszend establishment and out-deployed battalion of 99 RBr Baj; 195, 197, 201 officer alert description

1383 Charles Tuten; *Soviet Short-Range Ballistic Missile Logistics in Eastern Europe*; S108156 IAR-0005-85; NPIC; 1985/04; CREST RDP87T00076R000102120001-9-13; 2011/06/02; 986

1384 *The Soviet Atomic Energy Program*; NIE 11-2A-59; 1959/08/18; TS; <https://www.cia.gov/library/readingroom/docs/DOC_0000843185.pdf>; 46 para 188, 50 para 213

1385 MAR (Aviation) P Kutakhov; *The Air Force In The Past And Present*; VM R (10); 1973; FPD 0063 (21 November 1974); 32

1386 *The Berlin Tunnel Operation 1952-1956*; Clandestine Services History; CIA; 1968/06/24; CREST RDP07X00001R000100010001-9; 2007/10/19; also CIA HCD HR70-14 07-18-2012 DVD I-034; AP-B 3

1387 Mark Kramer; *"Lessons" Of The Cuban Missile Crisis For Warsaw Pact Nuclear Operations*; CWIHP-B (8/9); 1996-1997 Winter; 350

1388 Szulc Tomasz and Nicpon Krzysztof; *Magazyny Broni Jądrowej na Terytorium Polski* [*The Warehouses Of Nuclear Weapons In The Territory Of Poland*]; *Poligon* (3); 2007

1389 *Report On Visit Of Polish Armed Forces General Staff Delegation To The USSR Armed Forces General Staff And To The Combined Command Of The Combined Armed Forces*; CIA IISR FIRDB-312-02329-80; 1980/10/08; <https://www.cia.gov/library/readingroom/docs/1980_10_08_MISCELLANEOUS.pdf>; also CIA HCD HR70-14 07-18-2012 DVD VII-288; 29

1390 Matthias Uhl; *Nuclear Warhead Delivery Systems For The Warsaw Pact, 1961-65*; Collection *The 1961 Berlin Crisis and Soviet Preparations for War in Europe*; 2003/12/04; PHP; <http://www.php.isn.ethz.ch/lory1.ethz.ch/collections/coll_berlin/intro_uhl78c2.html?navinfo=16161>; fn #16 capacity each of two East German installations 120[/2=60] but the historic marker at the Himmelpfort (Lychen-2) RTB assigns 80 per bunker—20 in each of four 5.7x22-m storage halls—which by the 6-m² norm could hold 21 weapons

1391 Szulc Tomasz and Nicpon Krzysztof; *Magazyny Broni Jądrowej na Terytorium Polski* [*The Warehouses Of Nuclear Weapons In The Territory Of Poland*]; *Poligon* (3); 2007

1392 Paweł Piotrowski; *Operacja „Wisła" Broń jądrowa na terytorium Polski* [*Operation "Vistula" Nuclear weapons on Polish territory*]; *Przegląd Historyczno-Wojskowy* [Historical-Military Review] (1); 2017; <https://wbh.wp.mil.pl/c/pages/atts/2023/4/bPawe_Piotrowski_-_Operacja_Wisa._Bron_jadrowa_na_terytorium_Polski.pdf>

1393 *Operational Mission—Situation As Of 1700 Hours 4 April*; 1978; CIA IISR TS-788328; 1978/11/17; CIA HCD HR70-14 07-18-2012 DVD VII-103; AP-7 25 Chart

1394 *Protocol On Assignment Of PPR Army And Navy Forces To The Combined Armed Forces And Their Development In 1981-1985*; 1981/01; CIA IISR TS-828045; 1982/04/19; <https://www.cia.gov/library/readingroom/docs/DOC_0005508933.pdf>; AT-3 I *Ground Forces Weapons and Military Equipment* 42 table 28xR-17 [Scud-B] plus 43x*Luna M* [FROG-7] launchers planned end 1985

1395 Laszlo Becz et al; *OKSNAR - Fully Assembled State—Soviet Nuclear Weapons In Hungary 1961-1991*; Veszprém; 2019; 120 and 235 tables, 136 agreement, 206 document 1982, 251 interview list

1396 Joshua Handler; *Russian Nuclear Warhead Dismantlement Rates And Storage Site Capacity—Implications For The Implementation Of START II And De-alerting Initiatives;* PU/CEES Report No. AC-99-0; 1999; Center for Energy and Environmental Studies, Princeton University; 35-36 fn #95

## Post Mortem

1397 *Spetsnaz Forces And Means In A Front Offensive Operation*; 1985; GSA; CIA IISR TS-878433; 1987/06/12; 6; ISCAP 2012-026 (CIA MDR EOM-2009-00158)

1398 GEN-MAJ (Engineer Troops) V Bystrov; *A Brief Discussion Of An Important Subject: The Use Of Nuclear Means When Constructing Obstacles During An Operation*; VM S (1-83); 1968; CIA IISR; 1974/06/28; <https://www.cia.gov/library/readingroom/docs/1974-06-28.pdf>; also CREST RDP10-00105R000100720001-6

1399 *Manual On The Conduct Of Operations—Part Two—Ground Forces Operations (Front-Army-Corps);* 1963; GS; CIA IISR TS-778264; 1977/09/29; CIA HCD HR70-14 07-18-2012 DVD VII-99; CH-1 39

1400 *Rocket Troops And Artillery In A Front Offensive Operation*; 1985; GSA; CIA IISR TS-888443; 1988/05/24; 17; ISCAP 2012-026 (CIA MDR EOM-2009-00158)

1401 *Principles Of Preparation And Conduct Of A Front Defensive Operation*; 1985; GSA; CIA IISR TS-888548; 1988/06/30; 15; ISCAP 2012-026 (CIA MDR EOM-2009-00158)

1402 Charles Tuten; *Sensitive Demolition Munitions Storage Facilities, USSR*; 1981/04; S93700 IAR-0076-81 Z-20061-81; NPIC; CREST RDP82T00709R000200750001-3; 2010/01/08; 1092-1093

# Appendix

1403 See *Soviet Mobile Missile Activity* series including *Summary Report 26*; BIIR RCA-01/0001/85; NPIC; 1985/02; TS; CREST CIA-RDP85T00840R00001130001-2; 45 Table A5 SS-12 Scaleboard; 45>47 Table A6 SS-1c Scud B; 48 Tables A7 Schools, A8 Central missile and armament; 49>52 Table A9 RTB; 52 Table A10 Group-MD armament. Correction Table A9 Baltic MD Radviliskis should be demoted to army-level, third operational echelon, possibly 18 Guards. Note moronic whiteout applied to Soviet Groups of Forces listings.

1404 Christof Schuster, Matthias Karthe, Thomas Petzold; *Tarnname "Kolybel" Sowjetische Atomraketen in der Oberlausitz*; 2016; Geschichtsverein Truppenübungsplatz Königsbrück e.V.; Königsbrück Germany

1405 Laszlo Becz et al; *OKSNAR - Fully Assembled State—Soviet Nuclear Weapons In Hungary 1961-1991*; Veszprém; 2019; comprehensive order of battle

# Illustrations

1406 MSU V Kulikov and GEN ARM A Gribkov; *Directive Of The Commander-In-Chief Of The Combined Armed Forces Of The Warsaw Pact Member States On The Combat Readiness Of The Troops And Naval Forces Allocated To The Combined Armed Forces*; WPCAF Staff; CIA IISR C05508940; 1979/03/30; <https://www.cia.gov/library/readingroom/docs/DOC_0005508940.pdf>; 29; also CIA MDR EOM-2015-01161

1407 *Warsaw Pact Ammunition Logistics In The Western Theater: Sustainability For Offensive Operations*; Intelligence Assessment; CIA DI Office of Soviet Analysis; 1989/06; CIA HCD HR70-14 07-18-2012 DVD VII-121; 8

1408 *Warning Of War In Europe: Changing Warsaw Pact Planning And Forces*; NIE 4-1-84; 1989/09; S; CREST RDP94T00754R000200160012-0; 2006/03/10; iv map

1409 Rüdiger Wenzke; *Die Streitkräfte der DDR und Polens in der Operationsplanung des Warschauer Paktes*; 2010; Military History Research Office; ISBN 978-3-941571-09-9; 36

1410 *Warsaw Pact Fronts Within The Western Theater Of Military Operations*; CIA IIR; CIA HCD HR70-14 07-18-2012 DVD VII-326; 4-5

1411 *Warsaw Pact Forces Opposite NATO*; NIE 11-14-79; 1979/01/31; TS; CIA HCD HR70-14 07-18-2012 DVD VII-4 (V.1) *Summary Estimate*; 65 Figure 20

1412 GEN-MAJ Tibor Toth; *Characteristics Of Organizing And Conducting An Offensive Operation Of The Coalition Front And Combined Arms Army*; Honvedelem (6) 1980; S; CIA IIR C05798348; 1985/09/06; CIA MDR EOM-2011-0881; 20

1413 *Soviet Chemical Weapons Threat*; DST-1620F-051-85; DIA; 1985; available CREST RDP88B00745R000100140027-5; 2009/10/19; 18-19

1414 *Shchuchye Ammunition Depot Chumlyak, Shchuchye, USSR, Ural MD*; 1964/07; NPIC-R-530-64; TS; CREST RDP78T05439A000400090045-3; 2003-09-02; 5

1415 *National Photographic Interpretation Center: The Years Of Project HTAUTOMAT, 1956-1958*; 1974/12; S; V.IV; CIA History Staff; CREST RDP04T00184R000400040001-8; 2010/07/21; 23 drawing

1416 *Unusual Facilities At Dolon Airfield, USSR*; Joint PIR; NPIC; 1961/06

1417 *Belev Sensitive Operations Complex USSR*; PIR; NPIC; 1965/10; CREST CIA-RDP02T06408R00060010002-2; 2005-08-02; 4 Figure 3

1418 *Committee On Disarmament (CD): Soviet Plenary Statement on Chemical Weapons (CW) Issues, August 18, 1983*; US Mission Geneva; CD-261; 1983/08/23; DoS FOIA 200700306

1419 *Instruktsiya po perevozke spetsial'nykh gruzov zheleznodorozhnym transportom* [*Instructions On The Transport Of Special Cargo By Rail Transportation*]; 1986; UN-64dsp-1.Zh2 [УН-64дсп-1.Ж2]; MO Military Publishing House; Moscow

1420 *Warsaw Pact Forces Opposite NATO*; NIE 11-14-79; 1979/01/31; TS; CIA HCD HR70-14 07-18-2012 DVD VII-4 (V.1) *Summary Estimate*; 56 Figure 14

1421 *Instruktsiya po perevozke spetsial'nykh gruzov avtomobil'nym transportom* [*Instructions On The Transport Of Special Cargo By Road Transportation*]; Part I; 1988; UN-64dsp-1.A [УН-64дсп-I.А]; MO Military Publishing House; Moscow

1422 *Instruktsiya po perevozke spetsial'nykh gruzov zheleznodorozhnym transportom* [*Instructions On The Transport Of Special Cargo By Rail Transportation*]; 1986; UN-64dsp-1.Zh2 [УН-64дсп-1.Ж2]; MO Military Publishing House; Moscow

# Index

## A
Aldrich Ames  19
analysis
    evidence—three kinds  8
    hypothesis X—defined  9
    net assessment  16
    official model  8

## B
Biological
    biological weapons (BW)  17
    Mal'ta plant  149
    US  147
    USSR  149

## C
Chemical
    armament  153
        binary  183
    bump-down 1975  163
    bump-up 1959  151
    Chemical Troops  167
    Chemical Weapons Convention CWC
        Israelyan statement 1983  189
        negotiations  184
        Russian declaration  174
    exercises  157
        1980s US  184
        1980s USSR-Warsaw Pact  184
    intelligence
        chemical excision  180
        CIA report 1970  172
        CIA report 1984  180
        DIA report 1985  167
        FSTC report 1987  173
        Iraq 2003  166
        official model  165
    Military Thought itemization  160
    *Regulations*  142, 151–152, 181
    stockpile
        "chemical depots"  169
            barrel fetish  171
            markers  170
        ammunition  175
            author investigation  179
        Arys  203
        consolidation  185
        CWC sites  185
            Shchuchye  186
        estimates  169
        GRAU  179
        Grossenhain 1975  167
        UK-US  144
            US buildup 1980s  182
Cuba
    Anastasiev memoir  200
    missile crisis  244
Czechoslovakia
    Operation Danube 1968  27

## E
Exercises. See Theater Operations
    Burya 1961  38, 47, 59, 65–66, 70–71, 84–85, 94, 130, 132
    cover  38
    General Staff programs  35
    reporting  19
    series  35
    Soyuz
        1983  72
        1984  74
        1987  72
    Tsentr
        1978  28, 71
        1982  74
        1987  72
    TVD Far Eastern  75
    TVD Northwestern  72
    TVD Southern  74
    TVD Southwestern  73
    TVD Western  70
    war plans  36
    Zapad (West)
        1969  71
        1977  38, 49
        1984  72

## F
Front
    armies  45
    armies, air  52
    armies, national  49
    defined-complement  38
    deployment  43
        exercise May 1973  43
        exercise Tsentr 1978  43
        exercise Tsentr 1982  43
        Great Patriotic War  43
    divisions  50
    divisions, national  51
    index formations  52
    missile-artillery bases  40
        creation  41
        nuclear warhead removal  231
    operations
        zones  43
    strategic echelons  39

## G

General Staff USSR
- Academy 18
- GOU (Main Operations Directorate) 20

Group of Soviet Forces Germany (GSFG)
- Dannenwalde blowup 254
- East Germans 47
- maskirovka 249
- missile readiness program 267
- nuclear stores 240
- reorganization 1964 47
- Sanddune 257
- tank armies 47
- Torgau 13
  - defector 13
  - DIA report 256
  - DS-339 249
  - service building 257

## H

Halifax explosion 21

## I

Imagery
- clusivity analysis 39
- system KH-8 Gambit 40
- system KH-9 Hexagon 40
- system KH-11 Kennen 40

Intermediate-Range Nuclear Forces Treaty (INF) 21

## M

Missiles
- arsenals 201
- Pioner (SS-20 Saber) 21
  - refires 244
- reload factor 244–246, 267, 275
- storage
  - bunker 261
- Temp R-900 (SS-12 Scaleboard) 239
  - refires 244
- V-2 261
  - shelter 264

## N

Nuclear
- armament
  - combat radioactive substances BRV 197
  - engineer munitions 279
  - positive control 239
- artillery 119
- intelligence
  - bunker cult 203
  - official model 192–193
- limitation
  - limited period 126
  - NATO Flexible Response 124
- NRDC simulation 21
- periods
  - nonnuclear 133
  - *periodizatsiya* (periodization) 124
- plan
  - 1977 Academy lessons 120
  - allocation scheme 117
  - allocations front 119
- RTB rocket/repair base
  - designation 195
  - loading docks 230, 267
  - ORPDn 238
  - PRTB 234
  - PRTB national 236
- stockpile
  - 12 GUMO 192
  - bunkers 194
  - bunkers SOC 216. See Also Sensitive Operations Complexes
  - bunkers Type I 194
  - bunkers Type II 199
  - bunkers Type III 200
  - bunkers Type IV 241
  - bunkers Type IX 203
  - bunkers Type VI 243
  - bunkers Type VII 247, 272
    - chemical 274
  - bunkers Type VIII 241
    - Kopitnari 269
  - central bases 195
    - Mozhaysk 197
  - Central Europe 246, 275
  - GRAU 193
- strategic demarcation line 110
- strikes, Belgium 21
- strikes, front initial 121
- strikes, strategic 114
  - front interval 237
- targeting 111
  - accuracy 116
- testing USSR 21
- three-strike system 238, 246
- transition 114
  - conventional 135
- transport, rail 231
- war scare 35, 65, 184, 234
- Warsaw Pact national 130

## P

Poland
- internal crisis 1980-1981 40
  - Gomel-30 trains 231
- Mosty Base 265

## R

Readiness
- Directive 1979  37
- Dislokatsiya  37
- dispersal  38
- gaming  68
- Initial Period  36
- military levels  37
- Military Threat insertion  37
- Special Period  36

## S

Sensitive Operations Complexes
- bunkers
  - architecture  217
  - lines A + C  218
  - service hall  217
  - ventilation  219
- chemical statement  212
- CIA report 1970  207
- directions  213
- dispute  205
- distorted chemical estimate  223
- distorted nuclear estimate  224
- identification  205
- integrated mechanism  17

Sources
- classified documents  18
- Oleg Penkovsky  19
- Ryszard Kuklinski
  - alert system view  37
  - General Staff Poland  27
  - GK  29
- second translation  18
- Voennaya Mysl (Military Thought) Journal  18

Strategic Deployment
- covert  63
  - Burya 1961  65
  - exercise masking  65
- defined  44
- echelons, logistics  68
- echelons, multilevel  56
  - intelligence perspective  61
- echelons, operational  45
  - second  59
  - third  57
  - TVD Western  53
- echelons, strategic  45
  - intelligence perspective  53
  - second
    - interior districts  76
- intelligence timeline  60
- obsolete equipment  67
- regrouping  46
- TVD Far Eastern  75
  - mobilization centers  76

## T

Theater Operations. See Exercises
- aviation  67
  - Air Operation  136
- conventional
  - missiles  137
  - nonnuclear variant  102
- defense
  - strategic defense variant  104
- formulations  34
- strategic operation, concept  69
- surprise  35
- TVD Southwestern
  - Strategic Direction Italian  98

TVD Western
- Strategic Direction North German  97
- Strategic Direction Northern-Coastal  89
- Strategic Direction South German  98
- variants  34

Troops
- Chemical  167
- Ground
  - tank armies  48
- Strategic Missile RVSN  26

TVD (theater of military action)
- defined  27
- GK (high command)
  - 1980 Statute  29
  - defined  27
  - establishment  29
  - organization  29
  - napravleniya (directions)  30
    - Grechko quote  30
    - intelligence  31
    - operational  30
    - strategic  30

## V

VGK (Supreme High Command)  20, 26–30, 34–37, 45, 49, 51–53, 73, 90–91, 95–96, 110, 112, 114, 117–118, 121, 129, 137, 149, 156, 158, 192, 223, 230, 240
- RVGK  26

## W

WMD
- Operation  17
- Warsaw Pact national  16

www.ingramcontent.com/pod-product-compliance
Lightning Source LLC
Chambersburg PA
CBHW080633230426
43663CB00016B/2853